Between Ourselves

Published in the UK by Imprint Academic
PO Box 1, Thorverton EX5 5YX, UK

Published in the USA by Imprint Academic
Philosophy Documentation Center,
PO Box 7147, Charlottesville, VA 22906-7147 , USA

ISBN 0 907845 14 2 (paperback)

ISSN 1355 8250 (*Journal of Consciousness Studies*, **8**, number 5–7, 2001)

British Library Cataloguing in Publication Data
A catalogue record for this book is available from the British Library
Library of Congress Card Number: 2001087835

Front Cover Picture:
Husband and Wife Playing Trick-Track by Jan Sanders Van Hermessen
(Photo: Superstock)

Printed in Exeter UK by Short Run Press Ltd.

Between Ourselves

Second-Person Issues in the Study of Consciousness

edited by
Evan Thompson

For Francisco J. Varela

1946–2001

In memoriam

IMPRINT ACADEMIC

Contents

Ethics and the Co-Emergence of Self and Other

Intersubjectivity and Illness Experience

Interspecies Subjectivity

Editor's Preface

The recent resurgence of interest in consciousness has focused mainly on the relationship between first-person and third-person perspectives on consciousness, often to the neglect of intersubjective and interpersonal dimensions of conscious experience. The aim of this volume is to redress this imbalance by bringing together a number of articles from a wide variety of viewpoints on various facets of intersubjective experience.

The original impetus for the volume came from a three-day meeting in September 1999 on 'The Intersubjectivity of Human Consciousness: Integrating Phenomenology and Cognitive Science', which the Fetzer Institute invited me to convene and chair at 'Seasons', its conference and retreat centre in Kalamazoo, Michigan. Many of the participants at that meeting have contributed to this volume. I wish to express my gratitude to the Fetzer Institute, to Chuck Willis and Arthur Zajonc for making possible the meeting at Seasons, and to Anthony Freeman and Keith Sutherland of the *Journal of Consciousness Studies* for their enthusiasm and help in producing this volume.

At the time this volume was going to press, one of the contributors, Francisco J. Varela, passed away at his home in Paris, as a result of the illness he poignantly describes in his contribution. Francisco was an inspiration for many of the contributors to this volume, and his life and work will continue to inspire many of us in the field of consciousness studies for years to come. His absence will be deeply felt. This volume is dedicated to his memory.

Evan Thompson

Evan Thompson

Empathy and Consciousness[1]

This article makes five main points. (1) Individual human consciousness is formed in the dynamic interrelation of self and other, and therefore is inherently intersubjective. (2) The concrete encounter of self and other fundamentally involves empathy, understood as a unique and irreducible kind of intentionality. (3) Empathy is the precondition (the condition of possibility) of the science of consciousness. (4) Human empathy is inherently developmental: open to it are pathways to non-egocentric or self-transcendent modes of intersubjectivity. (5) Real progress in the understanding of intersubjectivity requires integrating the methods and findings of cognitive science, phenomenology, and contemplative and meditative psychologies of human transformation.

I: Preamble

My aim in this article is to set forth a context for the following essays and a framework for future research on the topic of intersubjectivity in the science of consciousness. To this end, I will present, in broad strokes, an overview of this topic, drawing from three main sources — cognitive science and the philosophy of mind, continental European phenomenology, and the psychology of contemplative or meditative experience. Since my aim is integrative and constructive, I will not offer detailed conceptual and empirical arguments for each step, though I will try to give a taste of some of these arguments along the way.

---

[1] This article draws from two earlier papers, the first a consulting report prepared for the Fetzer Institute (Kalamazoo, MI) that also served as the discussion paper for the meeting I convened at Fetzer on 'The Intersubjectivity of Human Consciousness: Integrating Phenomenology and Cognitive Science' (September 24–27, 1999), and the second my opening address to this meeting. The discussions at this meeting have greatly influenced this article; therefore a special debt of gratitude is here acknowledged to all the participants: Yoko Arisaka, Jonathan Cole, Natalie Depraz, Joel Elkes, Shaun Gallagher, Al Kaszniak, Jim Laukes, Eduard Marbach, Lis Nielsen, Alva Noë, Sue Savage-Rumbaugh, Marilyn Schlitz, Brian Smith, S. Kay Toombs, Francisco J. Varela, Dan Zahavi, and Arthur Zajonc. I also wish to thank Margaret Donaldson for helpful critical comments on an earlier draft. Finally, I gratefully acknowledge the support of the McDonnell Foundation for a grant received through the McDonnell Project in Philosophy and the Neurosciences (Thompson, 1999), as well as helpful discussions with two of the McDonnell Project Advisors, Vittorio Gallese and Ralph Adolphs.

II: Introduction

The theme of this article is that the individual human mind is not confined within the head, but extends throughout the living body and includes the world beyond the biological membrane of the organism, especially the interpersonal, social world of self and other. This theme, long central to the tradition of continental European phenomenology, derived from Edmund Husserl (1859–1938), has lately begun to be heard in cognitive science. Indeed, there is a remarkable convergence between these two traditions, not simply on the topic of intersubjectivity, but on virtually every area of research within cognitive science, as a growing number of scientists and philosophers have discussed (Varela, 1996; Gallagher, 1997; Petitot *et al.*, 1999). In the case of intersubjectivity, much of the convergence centres on the realization that *one's consciousness of oneself as an embodied individual in the world is founded on empathy* — on one's empathic cognition of others, and others' empathic cognition of oneself. Yet despite this convergence, to be explored in this article, many questions remain about how to understand the relationship between the cognitive scientific and the phenomenological treatments of consciousness. In the end, these questions all come back to the question of what kind of science the science of consciousness is or can be. Put another way, *if we are to have a cognitively and ethically satisfying understanding of consciousness, what form should this understanding take?*

To frame my discussion here, let me propose two key points that go to the heart of the matter. I call these points the Core Dyad:

THE CORE DYAD

- **Empathy is the precondition (the condition of possibility) for the science of consciousness.**

- **Empathy is an evolved, biological capacity of the human species, and probably of other mammalian species, such as the apes.**

The first side of the Core Dyad comes from phenomenology. I will explain its meaning more fully later, but the basic idea is that the mind as a scientific object is an abstraction from, and hence presupposes, our empathic cognition of each other. The second side of the Dyad comes from cognitive science and is comparatively straightforward. My aim in putting the two together, side-by-side, is to create a kind of hub or axis for all of the many different issues that can be raised about intersubjectivity and consciousness as seen from the viewpoints of phenomenology and cognitive science. Underlying all these issues is the fundamental question of how to conceptualize or understand the relationship between these two poles. I will come back to this question later in the article.

III: Enactive Cognitive Science and the Embodied Mind

The development of cognitive science over the past two decades or so has seen a movement from the classical, cognitivist view that an inner mind represents an outer world using symbols in a computational language of thought, to the view that mental processes are embodied in the sensorimotor activity of the organism and embedded in the environment (see Clark, 1999, and Beer, 2000, for recent discussions). This viewpoint has come to be known as *enactive* or *embodied* cognitive science (Varela *et al.*,

1991; Clark, 1997). Enactive cognitive science, as Francisco J. Varela and I currently conceive of it (Thompson & Varela, forthcoming), involves the following three theses:

- **Embodiment**. The mind is not located in the head, but is embodied in the whole organism embedded in its environment.
- **Emergence**. Embodied cognition is constituted by emergent and self-organized processes that span and interconnect the brain, the body, and the environment.
- **Self–Other Co-Determination**. In social creatures, embodied cognition emerges from the dynamic co-determination of self and other.

Embodiment

Visual perception serves as a good illustration of the embodiment thesis. The perception of visual space, for instance, does not arise from a unified model of space in the brain, but from numerous spatial maps, many of which are located in cortical areas involved in the control of bodily movements (of the eyes, head, arms, and so on) (Rizzolatti *et al.*, 1994). Perceptual space is not a uniform external container, but rather a medium moulded by our sensing and moving bodies: our movements 'progressively carve out a working space from undifferentiated visual information' and this 'movement-based space . . . becomes then our experiential peripersonal visual space' (Rizzolatti *et al.,* 1997, p. 191).

In general, from the enactive perspective, visual perception — or more simply, seeing — is a way of acting: it is visually guided exploration of the world (Thompson *et al.*, 1992; Thompson, 1995). As Kevin O'Regan and Alva Noë put it in a recent article: 'Activity in internal representations does not generate the experience of seeing. . . . The experience of seeing occurs when the organism masters what we call the governing laws of sensorimotor contingency' (O'Regan & Noë, in press).

Emergence

Emergence pertains to systems in which local elements and rules give rise to global patterns of activity. What enactive cognitive science stresses is that emergence *via* self-organization is a two-way street involving circular causality (Kelso, 1995; Freeman, 1999; Thompson & Varela, in press). In addition to the 'upwards' causation of local interactions giving rise to global patterns, there is the reciprocal 'downwards' causation of global patterns controlling and modulating local interactions (e.g., by setting their context and boundary conditions). Thus, in addition to the 'upwards' causation of personal consciousness by neural and somatic activity, there is the reciprocal 'downwards' causation of neural and somatic activity by the active animal or person as a conscious agent. For example, Francisco J. Varela's group in Paris has shown in epileptic patients that purposeful cognitive activity on the part of the patient changes the neurodynamic patterns of epileptic activity (Le Van Quyen *et al.*, 1997; Thompson & Varela, in press). Similarly, J.A. Scott Kelso has shown that the conscious intention of an agent to move a finger in a certain way is able (within limits) to stabilize one dynamic pattern of neural-somatic activity and destabilize another (Kelso, 1995, pp. 145–53). Thus 'downwards' (global-to-local) causation is no metaphysical will-o'-the-wisp, but a typical feature of complex (nonlinear) dynamical systems, and may occur at multiple levels in the coupled dynamics of brain, body and environment, including that of conscious cognitive acts in relation to local neural activity. In Kelso's words: 'Mind itself is a spatiotemporal pattern that molds the metastable dynamic patterns of the brain' (1995, p. 288).

These two theses — the embodiment thesis and the emergence thesis — although by no means uncontroversial, have been reasonably well explored compared with the third thesis, explored in this article.

Self–other co-determination

According to this thesis, embodied cognition emerges from the dynamic co-determination of self and other.[2] What recent cognitive science has begun to drive home is that the embodied mind is intersubjectively constituted at the most fundamental levels. Our own human self-consciousness, for example, emerges from a primordial and preverbal sense of self, present in newborn infants, that is inseparably coupled to the perceptual recognition of other human beings (Gallagher & Meltzoff, 1996; Meltzoff & Moore, 1999). To what extent this experiential coupling of self and other, operative from birth, is distinctively human or present in other primate or mammalian species remains an open issue for current research.

The thesis of self–other co-determination is linked to the (re)discovery of the importance of affect and emotion in cognition. Classical cognitive science was cognocentric: it conceived of cognition as the manipulation of affectless representations. New developments, especially in affective neuroscience, have shown that affect and emotion lie at the basis of the mind (Damasio, 1994; 1999; Panksepp, 1998a,b), particularly in the domain of social cognition, in which impaired social behaviour can be linked to fundamental deficits in affective cognition (see Adolphs, 1999, for a recent review).

The prominence of affect reinforces the two enactive theses of embodiment and emergence. Douglas F. Watt (1998) describes affect as 'a prototype "whole brain event"', but we could go further and say that affect is a prototypical whole-organism event. Affect has numerous dimensions that bind together virtually every aspect of the organism — the psychosomatic network of the nervous system, immune system, and endocrine system; physiological changes in the autonomic nervous system, the limbic system, and the superior cortex; facial-motor changes and global differential motor readiness for approach or withdrawal; subjective experience along a pleasure–displeasure valence axis; social signalling and coupling; and conscious evaluation and assessment (Watt, 1998). Thus the affective mind isn't in the head, but in the whole body; and affective states are emergent in the reciprocal, co-determination sense: they arise from neural and somatic activity that itself is conditioned by the ongoing embodied awareness and action of the whole animal or person.

Now, having just described affect as a prototypical whole-organism event, I wish to go one step further and say that much of affect is a prototypical *two-organism event*, by which I mean a prototypical *self–other event*. I now turn to review some of the diverse evidence for this point, evidence that gives more substance to the thesis of self–other co-determination and to the second pole of the Core Dyad (that empathy is an evolved, biological capacity).[3]

---

[2] See **Arisaka** (this volume) for the elaboration of a parallel point in the context of twentieth-century Japanese philosophy.

[3] This review is by no means exhaustive. Rather, it is meant as a representative sample of some of the most important relevant lines of research.

IV: Intersubjectivity — Views From Cognitive Science

Affective neuroscience:
basic emotional operating systems of the mammalian brain

Jaak Panksepp (1998a,b) has proposed that the panoply of emotional states we experience can be analysed into certain core affective comportments, probably common to all mammals, that depend on distinct, basic emotional operating systems in the brain, and are tied to an animal's social and biological relationships to conspecifics and members of other species. These core affective comportments are seeking/expectancy, rage/anger, fear, nurturance/sexuality, social bonding/separation distress, and play/joy. (**Cheyne**,[4] this volume, provides a fascinating exploration of the link between fear and the endogenous activation of a hypervigilant state — as in the face of a carnivorous predator — and the sensed presence of the Other during sleep paralysis and hypnagogic hallucinations.) Panksepp hypothesizes that each of these affective comportments is subserved by its own core neural network in the midbrain-diencephalon. Each network has certain key chemical neuromodulators, and all project to an area called the periaquaductal grey (PAG). Panksepp proposes that the PAG serves as the substrate for a primordial sense of self, again probably common to all mammals, because in this area 'there is a massive convergence of a diversity of basic emotional systems (fundamental value schema), various simple sensory abilities (perceptual schema), and primitive but coherent response systems (action schema)' (1998b, p. 568).

Cognitive ethology: empathy in primate life

In primates, especially apes and humans, affective comportment clearly plays a huge role in the interpretation and understanding of mental states, both of others and of oneself (**Savage-Rumbaugh, Fields & Taglialatela**, this volume; **Smuts**, this volume). Higher primates excel at interpreting others as psychological subjects on the basis of their bodily presence — their facial expressions, postures, vocalizations, and so on (Povinelli & Preus, 1995). It is here that we see affective comportment blossoming into empathy, in the sense of a meta-affective cognitive capacity for grasping another's point of view.

The presence and extent of empathy among animals is currently a subject of much debate (Gallup, 1998; Povinelli, 1998). One central thread in this debate concerns the 'mirror test' for self-recognition, which Gordon Gallup introduced in the 1970s. An individual unknowingly received a dot of red dye placed above the eyebrow so that it would be invisible without a mirror. Chimpanzees and orangutans, as well as human children more than 18 months old, guided by their reflection in a mirror, rubbed the spot with their hands and inspected their fingers after touching it, thus apparently recognizing that the dot on the reflected image was on their own face. Other animals, including a variety of primates, failed to connect the reflected image to their own bodies. Thus it seems that chimpanzees and orangutans have a self-concept and a capacity for self-recognition, whereas other animals do not. Gallup went on to argue that self-recognition implies self-awareness and 'that such self-awareness enables these animals to infer the mental states of others. In other words, species that pass the mirror test are also able to sympathize, empathize, and attribute intent and emotions

---

[4] Names in bold type refer to the contributors' articles in this volume.

in others — abilities that some might consider the exclusive domain of humans' (Gallup, 1998, p. 66).

The mirror test is controversial: most agree that the test is evidence for possession of a self-concept and that such a concept appears to be restricted to humans and the great apes, but some argue that such a capacity for self-recognition in a mirror does not imply awareness of one's own psychological states and the understanding that others possess such states (Povinelli, 1998). For this reason, it seems better not to take the mirror test in isolation, and instead to ask the more general question of which elements of human intersubjectivity are recognizable in other animals (de Waal, 1996, p. 79).

The primatologist Frans de Waal, in his landmark book, *Good Natured: The Origins of Right and Wrong in Humans and Other Animals* (de Waal, 1996), makes the important point that empathy is not an all-or-nothing phenomenon:

> Many forms of empathy exist intermediate between the extremes of mere agitation at the distress of another and full understanding of their predicament. At one end of the spectrum, rhesus infants get upset and seek contact with another as soon as one of them screams. At the other end, a chimpanzee recalls a wound he has inflicted, and returns to the victim to inspect it (de Waal, 1996, p. 69).

De Waal shows that the animal kingdom exhibits a wide range of other-involved behaviour of various degrees of complexity and sophistication — parental care-giving, succorant behaviour to endangered individuals other than progeny; emotional contagion (vicarious arousal by the emotions of others), and cognitive empathy and sympathy (see also Sober & Wilson, 1998). Underlying all caring behaviour is mutual attachment and bonding, and therefore the ultimate evolutionary source for this kind of behaviour is parental care. Succorant behaviour — helping or providing care to distressed individuals other than progeny — emerges from parental care-giving, but radiates outward to include the social group. To this can be added emotional contagion, which, at its simplest, takes the form of 'total identification without discrimination between one's feelings and those of the other' (de Waal, 1996, p. 80). Cognitive empathy emerges as a further step, in which there is recognition of the other's experience as belonging to the other, without losing the distinction between self and other in emotional contagion. Cognitive empathy in turn makes possible the moral emotions of sympathy and compassion, in which we feel genuine concern for the other. These emotions require certain cognitive abilities and a well developed sense of self, both of which may not be widespread in the animal world: they seem limited to humans and, to varying extents, our evolutionary cousins, the great apes.

Evolutionary neurobiology: sociability and large brains
We have seen that parental care is the evolutionary source of attachment and bonding, and that the affective comportments involved in these forms of sociality — such as nurturance/sexuality and social bonding/separation distress — depend on basic emotional operating systems of the limbic system in the mammalian brain. According to John Morgan Allman (1999), it was the formation of the extended family as a social support structure for the nurturing of slowly developing offspring that drove the evolution of large brains in apes and humans: 'the development of the brain to the level of

complexity we enjoy — and that makes our lives so rich — depended on the establishment of the human family as a social and reproductive unit' (Allman, 1999, p. 2).

Developmental neuroscience:
care-giving and early environmental regulation of brain development

Evidence is now accumulating that experience-dependent brain activity in particular environmental contexts plays a huge role in the development of the individual brain. Rather than being a collection of pre-specified modules, the brain appears to be an organ that constructs itself in development through spontaneously generated and experience-dependent activity (Quartz & Sejnowski, 1997; Quartz, 1999; Karmiloff-Smith, 1998), a developmental process made possible by robust and flexible developmental mechanisms conserved in animal evolution (Gerhart & Kirschner, 1997). In mammals — especially human beings, who undergo a protracted period of development even in comparison with other primates — much of early experience takes place in the social context of parental care. It has been shown that the care infants receive regulates the synaptic and chemical properties of the brain, including even altering the rates at which certain genes are expressed, with implications for the long-term viability and health of the organism (Meany *et al.*, 1996). Such findings show that the affective interaction of self and other in infancy can modify the very constitution of the living body. (See also **Savage-Rumbaugh** *et al.*, this volume, for related points on brain development in bonobo chimpanzee infants raised in a mixed chimpanzee/human or *Pan/Homo* culture).

Developmental psychology: infant imitation

There is now a large amount of evidence showing that human infants possess, at birth, interpersonal body schemas for emotional contagion and facial imitation, and that these schemas underlie the development of more sophisticated empathic abilities (Meltzoff & Moore, 1999). Studies have shown that newborns (less than an hour old in some cases) can imitate the facial gestures of another person (Meltzoff & Moore, 1994). This kind of imitation is known as 'invisible imitation' because the infant uses parts of his body invisible to himself to imitate the other's movements. For this kind of imitation to be possible, the infant must be able to match a visual display (the facial movements of the other) to his own motor behaviour; therefore, he must have a developed body schema, which organizes his experience of his own body's position and movement, and to which he can relate the visible gestures of the other person. If imitation requires such a body schema, and newborns can imitate, then such a schema must be operative from birth, rather than having to wait upon the infants' acquisition of a visual image of themselves (contrary to what earlier theorists, such as Piaget, proposed).

How would such a schema work? The basic idea is that the infant, faced with novel gestures, uses her proprioceptive awareness of her own unseen facial movements to copy what she sees in the face of the other person. This performance depends upon a 'supramodal' body schema that enables the infant to recognize equivalencies between herself and the other person (Meltzoff & Moore, 1994; 1999; Gallagher & Meltzoff, 1996). The schema links the perceptual modalities of vision and proprioception, both to each other and to the motor processes of action. As a result, the gestures of the other are recognizable to the infant in the terms of her own proprioceptive awareness (*via* the intermodal link between vision and proprioception), and she is able to move so that her proprioceptive awareness of her own body coincides with what she sees (*via* the intermodal link between visuo-proprioception and motor action). There is no need to learn to translate back-and-forth between vision, proprioception, and action, because from the start the senses are linked to each other and to possibilities of action in a supramodal and inter-personal body schema.

These findings about infant imitation call for the revision of earlier conclusions made by Merleau-Ponty (1962) about the phenomenology of infant experience. Merleau-Ponty seems to have believed, on the basis of the psychology available to him at the time, that development unfolds 'from the inside out': the sensorimotor equivalence between vision and proprioception must first be established in one's own case, and only then is transferable to one's perception of the world and others. The research just mentioned, however, implies that the trajectory of the interpersonal dynamic is precisely *not* 'from the inside out'. Although an intracorporeal schema makes possible the interpersonal dynamic, the schema operates *intercorporeally* from the start:

> No . . . transfer [from self to other] is necessary because it is already accomplished, and already intersubjective. A supramodal code already reaches across the child's relations with others. . . . From early infancy . . . the visual experiences of the other person commu-nicate in a code that is related to the self. This communication is organized on the basis of an innate system that does not necessarily give priority to body experience over and against the experience of the other. . . . The body schema, working systematically with proprioceptive awareness, operates as a proprioceptive self that is always already 'cou-pled' with the other (Gallagher & Meltzoff, 1996, pp. 225–6).

Merleau-Ponty also believed, again on the basis of the psychology of his time, that the infant's early experience did not involve a differentiation of self and other, because such a differentiation must wait for the acquisition of a body schema. Yet invisible imitation in newborns clearly shows that such a body schema is operative from birth, and therefore does not have to be acquired in the way Merleau-Ponty envisioned:

> The phenomenon of newborn imitation suggests that much earlier [than self-recognition in a mirror] there is a 'primordial' or 'embryonic' notion of self, what we might call a proprioceptive self — a sense of self that involves a sense of one's motor possibilities, body postures, and body powers, rather than one's visual features. The newborn infant's ability to imitate others, and its ability to correct its movement, which implies a recogni-tion of the difference between its own gesture and the gesture of the other, indicates a rudimentary differentiation between self and non-self. This may be a bare framework of self based on an innate body system, but it serves to introduce a disruptive moment into the supposed indifferentiation of the earliest hours. Furthermore, it suggests that this ear-liest period is not a '*pre*-communication' phase, but is already an experience of pre-verbal communication in the language of gesture and action. And this, we note, would actually support some of Merleau-Ponty's other views about the relation between the infant and language (Gallagher & Meltzoff, 1996, p. 227).

This intersubjective framework of self and other becomes increasingly refined as children grow and develop. Between the ages of two and five, children begin to be able to interpret themselves and others in the human psychological framework of thoughts, feelings, beliefs, desires, and perceptions (Astington, 1993). This interpretive ability reflects a particular type of social intelligence, which, from an evolutionary standpoint, is likely to be a recent innovation, one that probably emerged before the divergence of humans and apes, for it seems to be present among great apes such as chimpanzees (de Waal, 1996; Gallup, 1998; **Savage-Rumbaugh et al.**, this volume; **Smuts**, this volume). Indeed, there are striking similarities in the development of children's and chimpanzees' psychological abilities, although there are crucial differences too, ones which exemplify the cognitive refinements in the evolution of the human interpersonal dynamic of self and other (see Povinelli & Preuss, 1995; Povinelli, 1998).

Cognitive neuroscience: mirror neurons
Giacomo Rizzolatti, Vittorio Gallese, and their colleagues have uncovered in area F5 of the premotor cortex in macaque monkeys a class of neurons they call 'mirror neurons' (see **Gallese**, this volume). These neurons display the same pattern of activity, both when the animal accomplishes certain goal-directed hand movements, and when the animal observes the experimenter performing the same actions. Of particular note is that the activity of the neurons is correlated with specific motor acts (defined by the presence of a goal) and not with the execution of particular movements, such as contractions of particular muscle groups. The neurons can be classified according to the type of action, such as 'grasp with the hand', 'grasp with the hand and mouth', 'reach', and so on. All the neurons of the same type encode actions that meet the same objective. On the basis of these properties, mirror neurons appear to form a cortical system that matches the observation and the performance of motor actions. There is also evidence in humans for such a mirror neuron system for gesture recognition (Gallese & Goldman, 1998).

    These findings are notable for several reasons. First, the neural system for recognizing the intentional meaning of the actions of another agent appears to be primarily of a practical nature, rather than inferential or judgmental, for it involves the direct pairing or matching of the bodies of self and other. There seems to be an immediate pairing between the animal's understanding of its own actions and its understanding of those of another, an understanding whose structure is not that of an initial perception of a non-interpreted bodily movement followed by a judgement that attributes meaning to the movement and thereby interprets it as an action. Rather, the movement of the other is already understood as a goal-directed action because of its match to a self-performed action. It seems that primates recognize actions made by others because the neural pattern of activity in their premotor areas when they observe an action is similar to that internally generated to produce the same type of action. As we will see, this kind of non-inferential bodily pairing of self and other is one of the hallmarks of the phenomenological analysis of empathy. Indeed, the mirror neuron findings support Husserl's position that our empathic experience of another depends on one's 'coupling' or 'pairing' with the other (**Depraz**, this volume), rather than some kind of affective fusion, as some of Husserl's contemporaries held (see Petit, 1999).

    Second, Rizzolatti and Arbib (1998) have proposed that the gesture recognition mirror neuron system may be part of the basis for the development of language (see also Corballis, 1998). The evidence for a mirror neuron system for gesture recognition in humans includes Broca's area, an area that is known to be involved in speech and is probably the homologue of area F5 of the monkey premotor cortex. Rizzolatti and Arbib propose that 'the development of the human lateral speech circuit is a consequence of the fact that the precursor of Broca's area was endowed, before speech appearance, with a mechanism for recognizing actions made by others. This mechanism was the neural prerequisite for the development of interindividual communication and finally of speech' (Rizzolatti & Arbib, 1998, p. 190).

This development, as Rizzolatti and Arbib envision it, comprises two main steps, corresponding to two gaps that have to be bridged on the path from action recognition to speech — first, the gap between recognizing actions made by others and sending and receiving messages with communicative intent; and second, the gap between gestural communication and speech. In general, premotor areas are activated when an individual is about to perform an action or observes another individual performing an action. There are usually mechanisms that inhibit the observer from emitting a motor behaviour that mimics the observed action, and that inhibit the actor from initiating the action prematurely. But the premotor system sometimes will allow a brief prefix of the movement to be exhibited, and this prefix will be recognizable by the other individual:

> This fact will affect both the actor and the observer. The actor will recognize an intention in the observer, and the observer will notice that its involuntary response affects the behavior of the actor. The development of the capacity of the observer to control his or her mirror system is crucial in order to emit (voluntarily) a signal. When this occurs, a primitive dialogue between the observer and actor is established. This dialogue forms the core of language (pp. 190–1).

Thus the first gap between action recognition and communication is bridged in the form of a mimetic dialogue.

Merlin Donald (1991) has proposed that the evolution of the mimetic capacity — a capacity that still figures centrally in human culture — was a necessary precursor to the evolution of language. Rizzolatti and Arbib build on this proposal. They argue that in the case of individual-to-individual communication, the gestures that were most likely to be used first were oro-facial ones, because these are used extensively by monkeys, apes, and humans for communication. It seems unlikely, however, that speech arose from oro-facial gestures alone, because they limit communication to two actors at a time. But if manual gestures (e.g., pointing) are associated with oro-facial ones, then the communicative possibilities increase considerably:

> These considerations suggest that, at a certain stage, a brachio-manual communication evolved complementing the oro-facial one. This development greatly modified the importance of vocalization and its control. Whereas during the closed oro-facial stages, sounds could add very little to the gestural message . . . their association with gestures allowed them to assume the more open, referential character that brachiomanual gestures had already achieved. An object or event described gesturely... could now be accompanied by vocalization. If identical sounds were constantly used to indicate identical elements . . . a primitive vocabulary of meaningful sounds could start to develop (p. 193).

This development bridges the second gap between gestural communication and speech.

Philosophy of mind and psychology: theories of 'mind-reading'

In the philosophy of mind and psychology, intersubjectivity and empathy have been discussed in the context of the debate between the 'theory-theory' and the 'simulation-theory' of 'mind-reading' — our capacity to attribute mental states to ourselves and others, and to understand our behaviour and actions in light of those attributions (Davies & Stone, 1995a,b; Carruthers & Smith, 1996). According to the theory-theory (TT), normal human adults are able to mind-read because they possess a commonsense or folk-psychological 'theory of mind' that they employ to explain and predict human behaviour. Many advocates of the theory-theory (though not all) consider this folk-psychological body of knowledge to be essentially equivalent to a scientific theory: mental states, according to this view, are unobservable entities (like electrons), and our attribution of mental states to each other involves causal-explanatory generalizations (comparable in form to those of physics) that relate mental states to each other and to observable behaviour. According to the simulation-theory (ST), on the other hand, mind-reading depends not on the possession of a tacit psychological theory, but on the ability to mentally 'simulate' another person, that is, on being able to use the resources of one's own mind to create a model of another person and thereby identify with him or her, projecting oneself imaginatively into his or her situation.

Although there are different versions of these two theories, as well as various ways in which they might be reconciled or combined, there remain important differences of emphasis between them. As Gallese and Goldman (1998, p. 497) observe in their discussion of mirror neurons and the simulation theory: 'The core difference between TT and ST, in our view, is that TT depicts mind-reading as a thoroughly "detached" theoretical activity, whereas ST depicts mind-reading as incorporating an attempt to replicate, mimic, or impersonate the mental life of the target agent' (see also **Gallese**, this volume). Similarly, Gordon (1996, p. 11) describes the theory-theory as a '*cold* methodology . . . that chiefly engages our intellectual processes, moving by inference from one set of beliefs to another, and makes no essential use of our own capacities for emotion, motivation, and practical reasoning', and the simulation-theory as a '*hot* methodology, which exploits one's own motivational and emotional resources and one's own capacity for practical reasoning.'

Given this difference, it is not surprising that empathy figures prominently in the simulation-theory account of mind-reading (Goldman, 1993; 1995a,b; Gordon, 1996). According to this account, the simulation heuristic by which we understand the mental states of other subjects has three main elements:

> The initial step . . . is to imagine being 'in the shoes' of the agent. . . . This means pretending to have the same initial desires, beliefs, or other mental states that the attributer's background information suggests the agent has. The next step is to feed these pretend states into some inferential mechanism, or other cognitive mechanism, and allow that mechanism to generate further mental states as outputs by its normal operating procedure. . . . More precisely, the output should be viewed as a pretend or surrogate state, since presumably the simulator doesn't feel the *very same* affect or emotion as a real agent would. Finally, upon noting this output, one ascribes to the agent an occurrence of this output state. Predictions of behavior would proceed similarly. . . . In short, you let your own psychological mechanism serve as a 'model' of his (Goldman, 1995a, p. 189).

Empathy, on this view, is a special case of mental simulation, in which the output states are affective or emotional states: 'empathy consists of a sort of "mimicking" of one person's affective state by that of another' (Goldman, 1995a, p. 198).

Overall, the simulation-theory seems more attractive than the theory-theory, because of the role it gives to affect, emotion, and empathy in the co-determination of self and other. The theory-theory is cognocentric in the manner of classical cognitive science: it emphasizes belief-like representations and has very little to say, if anything, about emotion. The simulation-theory seems more congruent with the message coming from affective neuroscience that affect and emotion are basic to social cognition (Adolphs, 1999).

Nevertheless, I think that the simulation-theory does not provide a satisfactory account of empathy. First, it is not clear whether the hypothetical simulation heuristic is supposed to be a subpersonal mechanism of the 'cognitive unconscious' or a structure of personal consciousness (but see **Gallese,** this volume, for further discussion). Second, in either case, the strategy of the simulation-theory is to begin from the individual self and then try to work outward to other selves through the mechanisms of mimicry and imaginative projection. But these mechanisms on their own cannot account for the openness of the self to the other; on the contrary, the self must already be 'intersubjectively open' in its very structure for these mechanisms to function effectively at all. (This notion of 'intersubjective openness' will be explained more precisely in the next section.) Mimicry and the imaginative transposition of oneself to the place of the other are no doubt elements of empathy, but they are founded on more fundamental pre-reflective couplings of self and other at the level of the lived body: it is the passive (not voluntarily initiated), pre-reflective experience of the other as an embodied being like oneself that sets the stage, as it were, for mimicry and the more elaborate mental act of imaginative self-transposal (see Section VI). As Max Scheler pointed out in his *The Nature of Sympathy:* 'imitation, even as a mere "tendency," already presupposes some kind of acquaintance with the other's experience, and therefore cannot explain what it is supposed to do . . . the impulse to imitate only arises when we have already apprehended the gesture as an expression of fear or joy' (1954, p. 10, as quoted in Hamrick, 2000; this article presents a number of other important criticisms of the simulation-theory from a phenomenological perspective).

Finally, the very terms of the simulation-theory versus theory-theory debate about mind-reading seem problematic. The presupposition both theories share is that mind-reading is primarily a 'spectatorial' process of explanation and prediction (McGeer, 1999). On this way of thinking, self and other stand in relation to each other as observer and observed, and mind-reading is a proto-scientific activity, conceived either as causal-explanatory generalization or as model-building and simulation. This view of intersubjective relations seems distorted, for as phenomenologists have long argued, these relations are primarily embodied, practical, and mutually defining in nature (**Gallagher,** this volume). For this reason, **Victoria McGeer's** 'know-how' or 'regulative' account of folk psychology (this volume; see also McGeer, 1996; 1999) is an important advance beyond the theory-theory versus simulation-theory debate, one that can establish a meeting ground for Anglo-American philosophy of mind and continental European phenomenology:

> There is something right about understanding our folk-psychological abilities in terms of the predictive/explanatory power they buy for us. But this has to be understood in a larger context. I claim that our mindreading skills are part of a more fundamental capacity, or set of capacities, for regulating our own minds in concert with others. That is, we regulate our minds in accord with the intersubjective norms of folk-psychology, becoming in the

process agents that are well predicted and explained from the intentional stance. In becoming well-regulated folk-psychologists, we also develop the capacity for reading the minds of others, especially (normal) human others whose patterns of thought and action are similarly stabilized by the regulative function of folk-psychological norms. A plausible evolutionary account of why this capacity developed in our species concerns its value for us as social beings, to be sure, but, unlike the standard account, it focuses on the prior need to create and maintain stable patterns of behaviour amongst ourselves in order that we can predict and explain one another in a reliably robust way. On this view, a developmental account of the human mind must explain how we develop an active capacity for intentional self-regulation, rather than simply a spectatorial capacity for mindreading (McGeer, 1999).

From the perspective of phenomenology, our active capacity for intentional self-regulation is grounded on the perceptuo-motor capacities of our lived body. The theory-theory and the simulation-theory both take mind-reading to be a matter of how we infer from outward behaviour that others possess unobservable inner mental states (what they disagree about is the nature of the internal representations we use to make these inferences), and thereby they foster a conception of the mental as an inner realm separated from outward behaviour by an epistemic gulf that can be crossed only by inference.[5] In contrast, phenomenologists have long emphasized the importance of affective engagement and perceptuo-motor schemas as the basis of empathy and intersubjective understanding; thus from the start the phenomenological analyses have always been grounded on the idea that self and other recognize each other first and foremost as *persons* (**Kern & Marbach,** this volume), and hence as living bodily subjects or embodied agents, not as inner mental spectators of the outer world. Let us now take a closer look at this perspective.

V: Phenomenology and Intersubjectivity

The topic of intersubjectivity in phenomenology is vast and cannot possibly be reviewed comprehensively here (see **Zahavi**, this volume, for an overview). For this reason, I will concentrate on certain general features of the approach to intersubjectivity taken in Husserlian phenomenology. Many Anglo-American analytic philosophers believe that Husserl's final position on the issue of intersubjectivity is to be found in his *Cartesian Meditations* (Husserl 1960), a position that is arguably solipsistic and hence incapable of accounting for intersubjectivity (though, it must be pointed out, the putative solipsism is transcendental, certainly not empirical). Yet during the last period of his thought Husserl revisited over and over again the issue of intersubjectivity and developed a much richer account, both of intersubjective experience and of phenomenology as an intersubjective endeavour (Husserl, 1973; see also **Marbach and Kern**, this volume; **Depraz**, this volume; **Zahavi**, this volume; as well

---

[5] The same conception plagues most discussions of the 'hard problem' of consciousness. Thus David Chalmers writes: 'It also seems that this is as good a solution to the problem of other minds as we are going to get. We note regularities between experience and physical or functional states in our own case, postulate simple and homogeneous underlying laws to explain them, and use those laws to infer the existence of consciousness in others. This may or may not be the reasoning that we implicitly use in believing that others are conscious, but in any case it seems to provide a reasonable justification for our beliefs' (1996, p. 246). The inadequacies of this type of account had already been detailed by Max Scheler in 1912 (see **Zahavi**, this volume).

as Depraz, 1995; Steinbock, 1995; Zahavi,1999). There are two key features of this richer account that I wish to emphasize here: the first is that consciousness is intrinsically 'intersubjectively open', that is, it is structurally open to the Other in advance of any actual, concrete encounter of self and other (Zahavi, 1996; 1997); the second is that one's awareness of oneself as an embodied individual embedded in the world depends on empathy, in particular on one's empathic grasp of the Other's empathic grasp of oneself (this second point is taken up in Section VI).

Open intersubjectivity

Drawing from Husserl, Dan Zahavi (1997) has presented a phenomenological analysis of perceptual experience that reveals how the first-person perceptual experience of an objective thing is founded on the open intersubjectivity of consciousness. The point of this analysis is to show that the open intersubjectivity of consciousness is fundamental not simply for the encounter between oneself and other persons, but for any experience of the world at all.

When I perceive a thing before me, the thing is given to me (experienced by me) as having sides or profiles that I do not currently see. Indeed, it belongs to the very sense or meaning 'objective thing' — a sense or meaning implicit in my very perception — that, at any given moment, the thing comprises a plurality of co-existing profiles. If this aspect were not implicit in my perception, then my perceptual experience would present to me a two-dimensional image, not a three-dimensional thing. But despite long prejudice to the contrary in the empiricist tradition, our immediate experience is not of two-dimensional sensory patches, on the basis of which we then infer to the presence of things in the world. Rather, we automatically 'appresent' to ourselves the absent sides in and through our perception of the present sides.[6] How exactly are we to understand the structural relationship in perceptual experience between the present profile and the absent profiles? More pointedly, is it the case that this structural relationship can be accounted for entirely in terms that do not imply any reference to another perceiving consciousness besides myself? Husserl's answer is no: the co-intended or appresented profiles must be understood as the correlates of the possible perceptions of another subject.

To retrace the main steps leading to this conclusion, let us suppose, first, that the absent profiles are appresented as profiles given in *my* past perceptions or possible future perceptions. The problem with this interpretation is that it makes the unity of the perceptual object — its 'thingness' for experience — the result of a series of temporally separated profiles, but this does not match our experience: the profile facing me is not experienced as present with respect to a past or future absent profile, but as present with respect to other co-present, absent profiles. Perhaps, then, we should say that the absent profiles are appresented as the correlates of the perceptions that I would have right now if I were over there looking at the thing, rather than here. In other words, perhaps the absent profiles are appresented as the correlates of my fictitious co-present perceptions (fictitious because it is impossible for them to be had simultaneously by me: I cannot see the thing from more than one perspective at once).

---

[6] Husserl uses the term 'appresentation' to refer to one's intending in a mental act the presence of one thing on the basis of the actual presence of another: thus, in perception, we appresent or co-intend the backside of an object, which is not immediately present to us, on the basis of what is present, the front side.

But this interpretation too cannot account for the perceptual unity of the object, because it makes the unity a composite of fictitious slices (the correlates of the fictitious perceptions). What the object looks like from another vantage point is a contingent matter, but that there are other vantage points from which it can be seen is a necessity, and therefore cannot be explicated as a fictitious (non-actual) possibility.

The upshot of these considerations is that the co-intended absent profiles cannot be correlated with *my* possible perceptions, but must be understood as the correlates of the possible perceptions of an *Other*.[7] Yet clearly there need be no actual Other present for me to be able to co-intend the absent profiles, nor need there even be any others present in the world at all (as Husserl says, I might be the last survivor of a universal plague). What must be the case, however, is that the very meaning or sense of my perceptual experience refer to the perceptions of possible others. Thus first-person perceptual experience is essentially *intersubjectively open,* 'and precisely for that reason . . . is incompatible with any solipsism which, in principle, would deny the possibility of a plurality of subjects' (Zahavi, 1997, p. 312).

Open intersubjectivity and concrete intersubjectivity
One of the main contributions of Husserlian phenomenology has been to provide an 'experiential logic' (**Depraz**, this volume) of some of the different kinds of intersubjectivity. In addition to the open intersubjectivity of consciousness just discussed, two other kinds of intersubjectivity can be distinguished in Husserl's analyses — the concrete bodily experience of the Other, and the generative/ generational intersubjectivity of communally handed-down norms, conventions, and historical traditions (Zahavi 1996; 1997; Steinbock 1995). For the moment, I wish to consider only the relation between the open intersubjectivity of consciousness and intersubjectivity as the concrete bodily experience of the Other (here I follow Zahavi, 1997, pp. 313–19).

One might think that the intersubjective openness of consciousness depends on one's concrete perceptual experience of the Other — in other words, that one's concrete perceptual experience of the Other is the basis for the intersubjective openness of consciousness. One could argue, for instance, that when I experience another person as experiencing me, I realize (tacitly or pre-reflectively) that I am an other for the Other, that I am given to the Other as the Other is given to me, and thus that I am only one among many in a context of Others. In this way, my consciousness becomes intersubjectively opened, as it were, from the outside.

The problem with this account, however, is that it gets things backwards: for me to *perceive* the Other, the open intersubjectivity essential to perceptual experience must already be in play. Thus 'the actual experience of another embodied subject is founded upon an *a priori* reference to the Other' (Zahavi, 1997, p. 315). For the same reason, the intersubjective openness of consciousness cannot be reduced to any

---

[7] One might argue that although the co-intended absent profiles cannot be correlated with the correlates of my fictitious *co-present* perceptions, they can nevertheless be correlated with the correlates of my perceptions were I to walk around the thing and look at it from over there. The problem with this interpretation, however, is that it makes the absent profiles the correlates of my possible future perceptions, which has already been shown to be inadequate. Moreover, this interpretation itself involves the open intersubjectivity of consciousness, in the form of the *alterity* or *otherness* built into consciousness, for it requires that one imagine or otherwise mentally grasp oneself as *altered* or *othered* with respect to one's present self.

contingent and factual relation of self and other; it must belong *a priori* to the very
structure of subjectivity (**Zahavi**, this volume). At the same time, there is clearly
much more to our embodied experience of other subjects than its mere dependence on
the open intersubjectivity of consciousness: 'Whereas the contribution of the *open
intersubjectivity* is primarily at play in the formal structure of our intentionality, *concrete intersubjectivity* (which for the first time allows dissension and thus a sharpened
experience of the *alterity* of the Other) is the condition of possibility for the central
change in our categories of validity [from subjective to intersubjectivity validity]'
(Zahavi, 1997, p. 317).

What I propose to do now is to consider one aspect of concrete intersubjectivity in
more depth, namely, the nature of empathy.

VI: Empathy

According to Husserl, and those who have followed his analysis, such as Edith Stein
in her 1916 doctoral dissertation prepared under Husserl's direction, *On the Problem
of Empathy* (Stein, 1964), empathy is a unique and irreducible kind of intentional
experience: although it is based on sense perception and may involve inference (in
difficult or problematic situations), it is not reducible to some additive combination
of the two, after the fashion of the theory that we understand others by perceiving
their bodily behaviour and then inferring or hypothesizing that their behaviour is
caused by particular experiences or inner mental states. Rather, we experience
another person as a unified whole through empathy.

(Let me note parenthetically that **Steinbock**, this volume, provides an important
critical discussion of the assumption that the only manner in which beings who are
persons can be experienced is in the mode or manner of perceptual 'presentation', that
is, in the mode of givenness belonging to perceptual objects and, according to this
assumption, to perceptually empathized subjects. His discussion of 'revelation' as the
mode in which the *person as such* is given, and of 'loving' as the act by which the
person is 'revealed', resonates well with **Pitkin's** contribution, and should be
compared also to **Zahavi's** discussion of intersubjectivity 'beyond empathy'.)

Stein describes empathy as the experience of feeling led by an experience that is
not one's own, and distinguishes in it 'three levels or modalities of accomplishment,
even if in a concrete case people do not always go through all levels but are often satisfied with one of the lower ones' (1964, p. 11). First, the experience of another
emerges before me: 'it arises before me all at once, it faces me as an object (such as
the sadness I "read in another's face")' (p. 10). Second, I can inquire into the content
of the experience and 'its implied tendencies', in which case I become directed
toward the object of the experience, that is, I imaginatively transpose myself to the
place of the other subject to comprehend the object of the subject's experience from
his or her point of view. Third, once this clarification of the other's experience is complete, the experience faces me again, but now in a clarified or explicated way. Stein
refers to these three levels as: '(1) the emergence of the experience, (2) the fulfilling
explication, and (3) the comprehensive objectification of the explained experience'
(p. 11).

It is also possible for these levels of empathy to be 'reiterated' back onto me, such
that I can empathetically grasp the other's empathic experience of me. In other words,

'among the acts of another that I grasp empathetically there can be empathetic acts in which the other grasps another's acts. This "other" can be a third person or me myself. In the second case we have "reflexive sympathy" where my original experience returns to me as an empathized one' (p. 18).

Within the full performance of empathy, then, we can distinguish at least four possible kinds of empathy (**Depraz**, this volume):

(1) The passive association of my lived body with the lived body of the Other
(2) The imaginative transposal of myself to the place of the Other
(3) The interpretation or understanding of myself as an Other for you
(4) Ethical responsibility in the face of the Other

The first sort of empathy is passive (not voluntarily initiated on the part of the ego), pre-reflective, and bodily; it serves as the support for the others. When we see another person, we do not perceive his or her body as a mere physical thing, but rather as a lived body like our own. Thus empathy is not simply the grasping of another person's particular experiences (sadness, joy, and so on), but on a more fundamental level the experience of another as an embodied subject of experience like oneself.

This sort of empathy occurs through the immediate 'pairing' or 'coupling' of the bodies of self and other in action. We find here a clear connection between phenomenology and recent cognitive neuroscience, in particular to the mirror neuron findings discussed earlier (see Petit, 1999; **Gallese** this volume). 'Every time we are looking at someone performing an action, the same motor circuits that are recruited when we ourselves perform that action are concurrently activated' (Gallese & Goldman, 1998, p. 495). It is in part because of this neural-somatic match to a self-performed action that the Other's movement is understood as a goal-directed action. Thus the mirror neuron findings indicate some of the biological depth of empathy at the level of the passive association of the living bodies of self and other in embodied action.

Following Stein, this sort of empathic experience can be explicated further. In experiencing another as an embodied subject, we perceive the Other (1) as animated by his or her own fields of sensation; (2) as animated by general feelings of life or being in one's living body (growth, development, aging, health and sickness, vigour and sluggishness, and so on); (3) as expressive of his or her own subjective experience; (4) as another centre of orientation in space; and (5) as capable of voluntary action (see **Toombs**, this volume, for discussion of these levels in the context of illness experience and clinical practice).

The empathic grasping of another as animated by his or her own fields of sensation Stein calls 'sensual empathy' or 'sensing-in'. To take Stein's example: 'The hand resting on the table does not lie there like the book beside it. It "presses" against the table more or less strongly; it lies there limpid or stretched; and I "see" the sensations of pressure and tension' (p. 54). So far this example includes only the first level of accomplishment in empathy — the emergence of the experience of another. The second level involves delving into the content of the Other's experience. If this happens, then there is a movement from empathy as the passive association of our two lived bodies to empathy as the imaginative transposal of myself to the place of the Other: 'my hand is moved (not in reality but "as if") to the place of the foreign one. It is moved into it and occupies its position and attitude, now feeling its sensations, though not primordially [i.e., not in the original] and not as being its own . . . the foreign hand

is continually perceived as belonging to the foreign physical body so that the empathized sensations are continually brought into relief as foreign in contrast with our
own sensations' (p. 54).

Clearly, for this kind of sensual empathy to be possible, one's own body and the
Other's body must be of a similar type. What the limits of this type might be is an open
and important question. Stein notes that 'empathy is quite successful with men's and
children's hands which are very different from mine' (p. 54), and then raises the crucial point: 'The type "human physical body" does not define the limits of the range of
my empathic objects, more exactly, of what can be given to me as a living body.' For
example: 'Should I perhaps consider a dog's paw in comparison with my hand, I do
not have a mere physical body, either, but a sensitive limb of a living body... I may
sense-in pain when the animal is injured.' Nevertheless, 'the further I deviate from
the type "man," the smaller does the number of possibilities of fulfillment become'
(p. 55) (see also the contributions by **Gallese**, **Savage-Rumbaugh** *et al.*, and **Smuts**).

Interwoven with sensual empathy is the experience of the Other as animated by
general feelings of life (health, vitality, sickness, and so on), and as expressive of subjective experience: 'we "see" shame "in" blushing, irritation in the furrowed brow,
anger in the clenched fist' (p. 70). As blushing shows, the facial expression of feeling
and emotion is a paradigm of these aspects of empathy (see **Cole**, this volume).[8] As
Jonathan Cole has recently written:

> The face involves an injunction not only to express, and to observe expressions, but to
> immerse oneself in what is expressed and to feel something of it oneself. Though comple-
> mentary to body language, in this it may go beyond what is usually considered to be
> expressed through posture. Expressions actually help in constituting what is within. A
> face, therefore, is not only an expression of a self available for others to read, but to some
> extent the self is constituted in the face and developed, and experienced, in the interaction
> between faces (Cole, 1997, p. 482).

Another ingredient of empathy is the experience of the Other as being another
centre of orientation in the space of the world. In general, one's experience of space
and one's sense of self-identity are tied together: we perceive things to be arrayed
around us, while we are 'here', at the centre or 'zero-point' of our orientation in
space. This differentiation between 'here' and 'there' does not belong to space considered as a medium independent of one's body; it belongs to bodily space, to what
philosophers call 'egocentric' space. When we perceive another, we perceive her as
'there' in relation to us 'here', and we grasp her as having her own egocentric space,
defined by her own bodily movements. Furthermore, we perceptually grasp that her
body is capable of voluntary movement (the third aspect in the list from Stein above).
We do not experience another's movements as merely mechanical, but as alive and
spontaneous. Neither sentience (having fields of sensation) nor spatial orientation
(having an egocentric space) can be separated from voluntary movement in our
empathic grasp of another. In empathetically experiencing another person as a sentient being capable of voluntary movement, we experience her as occupying her own
'here', in relation to which we stand 'there'.

---

[8] The 'Face' is one of the central motifs of the phenomenology of Emmanuel Levinas (1969), but to
     discuss the role this notion plays in his thought would take us too far afield (see **Zahavi**, this volume,
     and **Pitkin**, this volume).

Once again, this experience can remain at the first level of accomplishment — the emergence of experience, where it remains tacit and prereflective, a matter of passive association — or it can proceed to the second level — the fulfilling explication, where it unfolds according to the imaginative self-transposal to the place of the Other. This imaginative self-transposal presupposes the open intersubjectivity of consciousness discussed earlier. It enables us to gain a new spatial perspective on the world, that of the Other. At the same time, we continue to have (and must always have) our own centre of spatial orientation. Thus the open intersubjectivity of consciousness and its concrete articulation in empathy make it possible for us to comprehend an intersubjective field in which there is no one single zero-point or bodily centre of orientation. To put the point another way: the intersubjective openness of consciousness and empathy are the preconditions for our experience of inhabiting a common, intersubjective, spatial world. Empathy, as we have just seen, provides a viewpoint in which one's centre of orientation becomes one among others. Clearly, the space correlated to such a viewpoint cannot be one's own egocentric space, for that space is defined by one's own zero-point, whereas the new spatial perspective contains one's zero-point as simply one spatial point among many others.

This experiential grasp of intersubjective space is a condition of possibility for one's ability to experience one's own living body as a physical body like other physical things of the world. If one were confined to one's own first-person point of view, such that one had absolutely no empathic openness to others (an impossibility because of the open intersubjectivity of consciousness), and hence to how one would be experienced by another (empathy as the experience of myself as being an other for you), one would be incapable of grasping that one's own body is a physical object equivalent to the other physical things one perceives. A physical object is something that can stand before one in perception, but the living body, from an exclusively first-person point of view, cannot stand before one in this way. No matter how one turns, one's body is always 'here', at the zero-point, never 'there'; one cannot walk around it to behold it from all sides (see Merleau-Ponty, 1962, pp. 90–7). In general, one's body, as that by which one experiences a world, cannot show up as a fully present object in the world; it is always 'absently available' (Gallagher, 1986; Leder, 1990). Therefore, as long as we consider the living body simply from the first-person singular perspective, it seems like no other physical object, indeed like 'the strangest object' (Stein, 1964, p. 38), something radically 'incomplete' (p. 58). In Husserl's words: 'The same Body [*Leib*] which serves me as means for all my perception obstructs me in the perception of it itself and is a remarkably imperfectly constituted thing' (1989, p. 167). It is through empathy as the experience of oneself as an other for the alter-ego that one gains a viewpoint of one's own embodied being beyond the first-person singular perspective.

Stein elaborates this important point in terms of 'reiterated empathy'. In reiterated empathy, I see myself from your perspective. Stated more precisely, I empathetically grasp your empathic experience of me. As a result, I acquire a view of myself not simply as a physical thing, but as a physical-thing-empathetically-grasped-by-you-as-a-living-being. In other words, I do not merely experience myself as a sentient being 'from within', nor grasp myself as also a physical thing in the world; I experience myself as recognizably sentient 'from without', that is, from your perspective, the perspective of another. In this way, one's sense of self-identity, even at the most fundamental levels of embodied agency, is inseparable from recognition by another, and from the ability to grasp that recognition empathetically.

Let us now explicitly link empathy back to the open intersubjectivity of consciousness discussed earlier. Empathy — like imagination, recollection, and reflection — can be described as a 'self-displacing' or 'self-othering' act (see Zahavi 1999, p. 150). Empathy involves a displacement or fission between my empathizing self and the empathized other; recollection between my present recollecting self and my past recollected self (whom I 'see' from the vantage point of the Other who is me now); imagination between myself imagining and myself imagined (whom I 'see' from the vantage point of the Other who is me imagining); and reflection between my reflecting self and the experiences I reflect upon. What such self-displacing experiences indicate is that, as **Natalie Depraz** puts it (this volume), the ego is structured or inhabited by many 'inner splittings' or 'inner openings,' openings that intrinsically involve otherness or alterity, and thus manifest the open intersubjectivity of consciousness. In Dan Zahavi's words: 'even if consciousness could turn its attention so completely toward itself that everything else were excluded, it would not escape the confrontation with Otherness' (Zahavi 1999, p. 125). (For a moving meditation on the complex and intertwined dimensions of self-displacing experience in the context of illness experience, see **Varela**, this volume).

VII: The Core Dyad Revisited

We have now reached the point where we can return to the Core Dyad, beginning with the phenomenological side.

Empathy as the precondition of the science of consciousness
If the phenomenological analysis of empathy and the open intersubjectivity of consciousness is on the right track, then it follows that the naturalistic perspective of cognitive science presupposes empathy as its condition of possibility, in particular the reciprocal empathy by which self and other are concretely co-determined. By this assertion I do not simply mean that cognitive science is an intersubjective enterprise that depends on the shared, pre-theoretic, lived experience of the scientists themselves. I mean something more radical, namely, that the very object of cognitive science — the embodied mind as a natural entity — is constituted as a scientific object through reciprocal or reiterated empathy in the human life-world.

Husserl himself makes this type of point about the human organism, indeed the whole of the realm of nature as conceived by empirical science. The basic idea is that the living body (or all of nature), understood as an objective entity governed by natural laws, is the intentional correlate of a certain mental attitude, the naturalistic attitude, and that this attitude presupposes (conceptually, epistemologically, and developmentally), the personalistic attitude, in which we relate to each other empathically as living bodily subjects. In Zahavi's words: 'It is through the Other that I learn to carry out an objectifying, ideative, and abstractive apprehension of my own body, which conceives it as a part of nature, as a mere complex of physiological organs embedded within and determined by causal relations in the world' (1999, p. 161).

This point has important implications for the science and philosophy of consciousness. Consider what is often taken to be the central challenge faced by consciousness studies, that of the so-called 'hard problem' of consciousness (Chalmers, 1996; 1997), also known as the problem of the 'explanatory gap' between consciousness and nature. Many philosophers have argued that there seems to be a gap between the objective, naturalistic facts of the world and the subjective facts of conscious experience. The hard problem is the conceptual and metaphysical problem of how to bridge this apparent gap. There are many critical things that can be said about the hard problem (see Thompson & Varela, forthcoming), but what I wish to point out here is that it depends for its very formulation on the premise that the embodied mind as a natural entity exists 'out there' independently of how we configure or constitute it as an object of knowledge through our reciprocal empathic understanding of one other as experiencing subjects. One way of formulating the hard problem is to ask: if we had a complete, canonical, objective, physicalist account of the natural world, including all the physical facts of the brain and the organism, would it conceptually or logically entail the subjective facts of consciousness? If this account would not entail these facts, then consciousness must be an additional, non-natural property of the world. One problem with this whole way of setting up the issue, however, is that it presupposes we can make sense of the very notion of a single, canonical, physicalist description of the world, which is highly doubtful, and that in arriving (or at any rate approaching) such a description, we are attaining a viewpoint that does not in any way presuppose our own cognition and lived experience. In other words, the hard problem seems to depend for its very formulation on the philosophical position known as transcendental or metaphysical realism. From the phenomenological perspective explored here, however — but also from the perspective of pragmatism à la Charles Saunders Peirce, William James, and John Dewey, as well as its contemporary inheritors such as Hilary Putnam (1999) — this transcendental or metaphysical realist position is the paradigm of a nonsensical or incoherent metaphysical viewpoint, for (among other problems) it fails to acknowledge its own reflexive dependence on the intersubjectivity and reciprocal empathy of the human life-world.

Another way to make this point, one which is phenomenological, but also resonates with William James's thought (see Taylor, 1996), is to assert the primacy of the personalistic perspective over the naturalistic perspective. By this I mean that our relating to the world, including when we do science, always takes place within a matrix whose fundamental structure is I-You-It (this is reflected in linguistic communication: I am speaking to You about It) (Patocka, 1998, pp. 9–10). The hard problem gives epistemological and ontological precedence to the impersonal, seeing it as the foundation, but this puts an excessive emphasis on the third-person in the primordial structure of I–You–It in human understanding. What this extreme emphasis fails to take into account is that the mind as a scientific object has to be constituted as such from the personalistic perspective in the empathic co-determination of self and other.

The upshot of this line of thought with respect to the hard problem is that this problem should not be made the foundational problem for consciousness studies. The problem cannot be 'How do we go from mind-independent nature to subjectivity and consciousness?' because, to use the language of yet another philosophical tradition, that of Madhyamika Buddhism (**Wallace**, this volume), natural objects and properties are not intrinsically identifiable (*svalaksana*); they are identifiable only in relation to the 'conceptual imputations' of intersubjective experience.

Empathy as an evolved, biological capacity of the human and other mammalian species

It is important to realize that even though the embodied mind is constituted as a scientific object on the basis of the lived body and reciprocal empathy, it does not follow that the embodied mind and the lived body are two different entities, or belong to two different orders of reality. Rather, they are, we might say, two *aspects* of one single spatiotemporal individual.[9] Husserl himself wrote an intriguing statement to this effect in 1934 near the end of his life: 'The lived body is at one with the physical body, membered thus and so… [it is] precisely organ and system of organs' (1973, Vol. III, p. 643, as quoted by Welton, 1999, p. 51). It is precisely because the lived body is 'at one' with the organism that phenomenology needs to go outside itself to embrace other ways of knowing, natural science in particular. On the one hand, phenomenology is needed to understand the lived body as the primordial subject of lived experience. The lived body is the presupposition of our ability to know anything, in particular of our ability to know anything of the embodied mind as an object of biological and cognitive scientific study. As Merleau-Ponty says, it is not possible to comprehend the lived body without 'abandoning the body as an object . . . and . . . going back to the body which I experience at this moment' (1962, p. 75). On the other hand, without biology and cognitive science we can know nothing of the lived body as an organism in the vast web of life that is always anterior to 'the body which I experience at this moment' and that claims this body as its own. Accordingly, these two forms of understanding, phenomenology and cognitive science, should not be opposed, but must be joined together in a relationship of mutual illumination.

To move forward on this task two steps need to be taken. First, from the phenomenological side, phenomenology needs to give more attention to the development of methods for the careful and sustained examination of lived experience, methods that are intersubjective and open to the objective, empirically based descriptions of biology and cognitive science.[10] The gesture of mindful awareness on which such methods need to be based is a basic human capacity, but one whose exercise needs cultivation and practice (Depraz *et al.*, 2000). To recognize the necessity of cultivating this gesture is, I believe, the first step toward a 'mature' science of consciousness (Varela *et al.*, 1991; Donaldson, 1991; Varela & Shear, 1999).

Second, from the cognitive science side, we need to pursue an understanding of consciousness that is commensurate with phenomenology, and that looks to the phenomenology of the lived body and intersubjectivity as its complement. Among other things, this means incorporating phenomenological methods and data into the research protocols of cognitive science.

---

[9] Robert Hanna and I are currently engaged in a research project supported by the Center for Consciousness Studies at the University of Arizona, Tucson, titled 'The Spontaneity of Consciousness: Neurophenomenology and Dual Aspect Metaphysics.' One aim of this project is to spell out a coherent and defensible dual aspect metaphysics of consciousness using the metaphysical terminology and argumentation of analytic philosophy, but grounded on neurophenomenology (in the sense of Varela, 1996). See Hanna and Thompson (forthcoming).

[10] A common misconception is that phenomenological *reflection* is a form of solipsistic, first-person singular *introspection*. For one thing, phenomenological reflection is fundamentally different in its methods and aims from introspection. For another, as we have seen, phenomenology emphasizes that otherness or alterity, and intersubjective openness, are built into the very structure of consciousness: thus the first-person singular always already inhabits the first-person plural.

A growing number of researchers believe that cognitive science and phenomenology must complement each other in this fashion if there is to be a cognitively and ethically satisfying science of consciousness. Although a full exploration of this ethical dimension is beyond the scope of this article, in the final section I wish to explore in a tentative fashion a few aspects of this important dimension, having to do with the developmental possibilities of empathy as ethical responsiveness to the Other.

VIII: From Intersubjectivity To Interbeing

One of the unique possibilities that human empathy affords is the development of non-egocentric or self-transcendent modes of consciousness. To understand these modes we need to explore the path that leads from intersubjectivity to what we can call, borrowing a term from the Vietnamese Buddhist teacher Thich Naht Hanh (1987), 'interbeing'.

Pathways of self-transcendence, although long familiar to the world's spiritual or wisdom traditions, have barely begun to be acknowledged by cognitive science. What needs to be realized, however, is that cognitive science, as a result of its own internal development, is now beginning to find itself in the position of being able to understand, in concepts commensurate with its own scientific approach to the mind, that there are such pathways and that they exemplify one of the most significant aspects of the human mind — its intersubjective and empathic openness.

Emotion and value feeling

Within Western moral philosophy there is a long tradition, going back to Immanuel Kant, that privileges reason over feeling: to act out of duties legislated by reason is thought to have greater moral worth than acting on the basis of feeling or sentiment. Yet as Frans de Waal observes, echoing David Hume: 'Aid to others in need would never be internalized as a duty without the fellow-feeling [sympathy] that drives people to take an interest in one another. Moral sentiments came first; moral principles second' (de Waal, 1996, p. 87). As discussed earlier, the precondition, both logically and evolutionarily, for moral sentiments such as sympathy and compassion, is cognitive empathy, and cognitive empathy is not a disembodied and affectless comprehension of the Other, but rather the feeling of being led by another's experience, to use Stein's formulation. Feeling, in this context, does not mean simply bodily sensation, but also value feeling or emotion. In Margaret Donaldson's words: 'how do "emotions" differ, if at all, from "feelings"? The crux is that emotions are our value feelings. They mark importance. We experience emotion only in regard *to that which matters*' (Donaldson, 1991, p. 12).

According to this conception, emotions are a subclass of feelings, the value feelings. Emotions enact or constitute the world of values: 'a new object realm is constituted in feeling. This is the world of values. In joy the subject has something joyous facing him, in fright something frightening, in fear something threatening' (Stein 1964, p. 83). We have many feelings that are not emotions, such as hunger, fatigue, or pain. Such feelings are, of course, typically accompanied by emotions, such as anger or fear, which, as value feelings, reflect our evaluation of the situation in which we find ourselves. Emotions mark importance, and therefore involve conceptually structured meaning and the evaluative stance of an intersubjective, personal self (Lazarus, 1991; Lazarus & Lazarus, 1994).

If it is feeling in the sense of bodily affect — especially proprioception and kinaesthesis — that makes one experience one's body as one's own (Sheets-Johnstone, 1999, pp. 41–87), then it is emotion or value feeling that makes one experientially aware of one's personal self. As Stein puts it: 'as it [the subject] feels it not only experiences objects, but it itself. It experiences emotions as coming from the "depths of its 'I'". . . the "I" experienced in emotion has levels of various depths. These are revealed as emotions arise out of them . . . in feelings we experience ourselves not only as present, but also as constituted in such and such a way. They announce personal attributes to us' (1964, pp. 89–90).

Thus emotions, as value feelings, make possible the evaluative experience of oneself and the world, and therefore are the very precondition of moral perception, of being able to 'see' a situation morally before deliberating rationally about it. As Arne Johan Vetlesen (1994, p. 4) has recently argued:

> We experience the objects of moral judgments through emotion. . . . Judgment presupposes perception in the sense that perception 'gives' judgment its object; we pass moral judgment on things that are already given, or disclosed, to us through acts of perception. . . . It is on this level, which logically precedes that of judgment . . . that we locate the emotions. Emotions anchor us to the *particular* moral circumstance, to the aspect of a situation that addresses us immediately, to the *here and now*. To 'see' the circumstance and to see oneself as addressed by it, and thus to be susceptible to the way a situation affects the weal and woe of others, in short, to identify a situation as carrying *moral significance* in the first place — all of this is required in order to enter the domain of the moral, and none of it would come about without the basic emotional faculty of empathy.

The issue that we need to consider now is the range of developmental possibilities open to us in empathy and value feeling, in particular the possibility of cultivating self-transcendent or non-egocentric value feelings.

Modes of mind in human development
The developmental psychologist Margaret Donaldson, in her remarkable book, *Human Minds: An Exploration*, has shown that the human potential for emotional development is as great as that for intellectual development, despite the present imbalance between the two in our culture (Donaldson, 1991). Her argument rests on a developmental map of the human mind, in which there are four main 'modes of mind', each made up of various mental components — perception, action, thought, and emotion — and each defined by its own 'locus of concern':

- The Point Mode
    Locus of concern: here and now
    Components: perception, action, thought, and emotion

- The Line Mode
    Locus of concern: there and then
    Components: thought and emotion

- The Construct Mode
    Locus of concern: somewhere/sometime (no specific place or time)
    Components: thought and emotion

- The Transcendent Mode
    Locus of concern: nowhere (i.e., not in space and time)
    Components: thought and emotion

These modes emerge progressively in human development, without one replacing the other; each is retained along the way and influences the others. Their progressive unfoldment involves a process of 'opening out' or 'disembedding' of the mental context: 'to begin with, the mind functions in the context of its own totality and in the external context of people, things, and happenings. . . . Then step by step the unity breaks up and new ways of doing and experiencing become possible' (1991, p. 17).

The point mode emerges first and is the only one available to the young infant (under eight months). In this mode the locus of concern is always the present moment, the directly apprehensible 'here and now'. (This is not an extensionless point, but rather the kind of short span of duration that William James called the specious present.) Adult experience in the point mode is highly absorbed perception in the moment, in which past and future drop away, as can occur in losing oneself in a piece of music.

The line mode expands the locus of concern to include the personal past and the personal future, a development that apparently begins to occur at eight to ten months: 'it is very likely that the baby, in the first half-year of life at least, while having a sort of "rolling" sense of movement from immediate past to immediate present to immediate future, has no sense of an extended past in which specific events can be located — and likewise no sense of a future filled with events yet to come' (p. 54). The line mode, however, enables one to look forward as well as back, so that one can locate oneself in relation to a remembered past and a possible future.

The step from the line mode to the next mode, the construct mode, consists in a movement away from personal happenings toward the impersonal nature of things: 'Instead of here/now or there/then the mind will next begin to concern itself with a locus conceived as somewhere/sometime or anywhere/anytime. Thus in the third mode we are no longer restricted to a consideration of episodes in our own experience — or even those we have heard about from others. We start to be actively and consciously concerned about the general nature of things' (p. 80). This mode is called the construct mode because its context is not provided by perception, memory, or anticipation, but depends instead on a deliberate constructive act of imagination. It apparently begins to emerge around the age of three.

When thought and emotion occur on an equal footing in the construct mode, then Donaldson speaks of the *core construct mode*. In some construct mode activity, however, the intention is to think unemotionally or dispassionately, and hence thought predominates over emotion. This effort gives rise to what Donaldson calls the *intellectual construct mode*, in which one's concern is with the nature of impersonal phenomena in space and time.

The next development is the movement from the intellectual construct mode to the *intellectual transcendent mode*, which Donaldson believes emerges around the age of nine. Whereas in the former case, the locus of concern is still bound to space and time, in the latter case, a 'disembedding' from this context has been achieved: 'the fourth mode is "spaceless". It needs no local habitation, present, remembered, foreseen or imagined. To speak paradoxically, we may say that the locus of concern is nowhere'

(p. 126). The paradigmatic mental activities of the intellectual transcendent mode are logic and mathematics. One's concern is no longer with spatiotemporal things themselves, but rather with the patterns of relationships into which things can enter.

We now come to the key question Donaldson raises in her book: do there exist, or could there exist, developments of the emotions that parallel those of the intellectual modes? Donaldson shows that such parallels do indeed exist, and she calls them the *value-sensing modes*, 'with the proviso that the values in question must transcend personal concerns' (p. 143).

The value-sensing modes

There are two value-sensing modes — the *value-sensing construct mode* and the *value-sensing transcendent mode:* 'A value-sensing construct mode would be one where the main component of experience was an apprehension of transpersonal importance, powerfully felt, but where the functioning of the mode depended upon the support of the imagination . . . [In] the value-sensing transcendent mode . . . the need for a constructed context is gone, so that self-transcending values can now be experienced and responded to without the props provided by the working of the imagination' (pp. 150–1).

As Donaldson goes on to say, 'once [the] defining features [of these two modes] have been recognized it is not hard to find evidence that they have indeed formed part of the repertoire of at least some human minds' (p. 152). The main body of evidence, some of which Donaldson discusses, comes from the world's contemplative wisdom traditions — Christian mysticism; Jewish Cabala; Sufism; Buddhism (Theravada, Mahayana, and Vajrayana); Advaita Vedanta; and Taoism and Neo-Confucianism.

One of her examples is St John of the Cross who, in explaining 'how to reach divine union quickly,' distinguishes between meditation, which involves focusing on an image, such as beautiful light, and contemplation, which involves emptying oneself of all images so as to attain a heightened, open, and receptive awareness of divine love. Donaldson comments: 'It is clear that meditation in John's sense belongs in the value-sensing construct mode. But in his view this mode, though useful, is strictly limited in its value for us since the divine reality far surpasses anything that we can know through the imagination' (p. 153). Proficiency in contemplation, on the other hand, belongs to the value-sensing transcendent mode: 'The locus of concern is certainly not in space–time. Concern centres rather on something conceived as infinite and eternal — something conceived also as having supreme value. Accordingly, the response evoked is one of deep emotion' (p. 154).

Another example, notable for its precision, can be found in the Tibetan Buddhist practice of *samatha* meditation, which aims at achieving clear and attentive stability of mind (**Wallace**, this volume; see also 1998; 1999). One of the main methods involves focusing the attention upon a mental image, while cultivating mindfulness (attention to the image without forgetfulness) and introspection (repeated checking of the quality of one's attentiveness). There are said to be nine distinct stages in the development of *samatha*, leading to firm and sustained attention upon the meditative object. These stages, given their image-based character, fall within the value-sensing construct mode. On the other hand,

> [w]ith the full achievement of *Samatha*, one disengages the attention from the previous
> meditative object, and the entire continuum of one's attention is focused single-

pointedly, non-conceptually, and internally in the very nature of consciousness. . . . Only the aspects of sheer awareness, clarity, and joy of the mind appear, without the intrusion of any sensory objects (Wallace, 1999, p. 182).

Upon attaining *Samatha*, by focusing attention on the *sheer* clarity and the *sheer* cognizance of experience, one attends to the defining characteristics of consciousness alone, as opposed to the qualities of other *objects* of consciousness (p. 183).

This description clearly suggests a transition from the value-sensing construct mode to the value-sensing transcendent mode. (The point mode is also present, because *samatha* is sustained attention to the here and now.) Indeed, the final aim of *samatha* is 'to realize the ultimate nature of awareness, free of all conceptual mediation and structuring, transcending even the concepts of existence and nonexistence. Such primordial awareness, known in this tradition as "the Buddha nature", is said to be our essential nature, and it is the fathomless well-spring of intuitive wisdom, compassion, and power' (p. 186).

Compassion

The progression of the value-sensing modes amounts to an 'opening out' or 'disembedding' of the egocentric sense of self. Many wisdom traditions testify that the natural and spontaneous expression of this disembedding is compassion (see **Pitkin** and **Wallace**, this volume) or love (see **Steinbock**, this volume). Compassion is the heart of interbeing, and is the superlative expression of the human capacity for empathy.

Compassion is not merely an expression of nonegocentric value-feeling, one that can emerge only as a result of inward meditative disembedding, for it plays a guiding role in moving from one mode to another, in the expansion of the value-sensing repertoire. This is the reason that practices of compassion, benevolence, or love are emphasized so strongly right from the start in the practices of many wisdom traditions. The example most familiar to Westerners is Jesus' injunction to 'love thy neighbour' and the Golden Rule 'Do to others as you would have them do to you'. Another example is the central Confucian virtue of benevolence or human-heartedness (*ren*). When asked to explain benevolence, Confucius replied: 'Do not impose on others what you yourself do not desire' (*Analects* XII: 2); and he explained the method of benevolence as 'the ability to take as analogy what is near at hand' (VI: 30). 'What is near at hand' means oneself; hence the method consists 'in using oneself as a measure to gauge others' (IV: 15), that is, in placing oneself in the position of the Other and asking what one would like or dislike. In the Bodhisattva path of Mahayana Buddhism, as described by the eighth century Indian philosopher Shantideva (1997), the cultivation of *bodhicitta* or awakened mind, whose main attributes are wisdom and compassion, requires the specific contemplative practices of 'meditation on the equality of self and other' and 'meditation on the exchange of self and other'. In the first, one aims to transcend the egocentric opposition of self and other through considering the sufferings of others as one's own; in the second, one puts oneself in the place of others to understand how they feel, and how one appears in their eyes (see **Wallace**, this volume).[11]

[11] In citing these examples, I do not mean to suggest that love as understood by Christians, compassion as understood by Buddhists, and benevolence as understood by Confucians are equivalent or interchangeable. There are, of course, important philosophical, spiritual, and cultural differences among these traditions and their conceptions of human virtues.

Earlier, when discussing the phenomenological conception of empathy, I raised the question of the limits of empathy: how far can empathy radiate beyond the human case? Here the wisdom traditions give different answers. The extension of empathy and compassion to the nonhuman world seems rather foreign to the Judaeo-Christian tradition (at least until recently), but is central to the Buddhist ideal of compassion for all sentient beings, and to the Neo-Confucian ideal of 'forming one body with the universe' (Tu, 1985; see also Leder, 1990, pp. 156–73).

The Neo-Confucian perspective, which arose as a synthesis of Confucianism, Buddhism and Taoism in the eleventh century CE in China, presents us with an example of the great openness that some have found in the human capacity for empathy and compassion. Neo-Confucianism builds on the philosophy of Mencius (371–289 BCE), who held that benevolence was innate to the human 'heart-mind' (*xin*):

> When I say that all men have the mind which cannot bear to see the suffering of others, my meaning may be illustrated thus: Now, when men suddenly see a child about to fall into a well, they all have a feeling of alarm and distress, not to gain friendship with the child's parents, nor to seek the praise of their neighbors and friends, nor because they dislike the reputation [of lack of humanity if they did not rescue the child]. From such a case, we see that a man without the feeling of commiseration is not a man. . . . The feeling of commiseration is the beginning of humanity (Chan, 1963, p. 65).

The Neo-Confucian philosopher, Wang Yang Ming (1472–1529), took this line of thought much further, saying that even when the mind of the 'small man'

> sees a child about to fall into a well, he cannot help a feeling of alarm and commiseration. This shows that his humanity forms one body with the child. It may be objected that the child belongs to the same species. Again, when he observes the pitiful cries and frightened appearance of birds and animals about to be slaughtered, he cannot help feeling an 'inability to bear' their suffering. This shows that his humanity forms one body with birds and animals. It may be objected that birds and animals are sentient beings as he is. But when he sees plants broken and destroyed, he cannot help a feeling of pity. This shows that his humanity forms one body with plants. It may be said that plants are living things as he is. Yet, even when he sees tiles and stones shattered and crushed, he cannot help a feeling of regret. This shows that his humanity forms one body with tiles and stones. This means that even the mind of the small man necessarily has the humanity that forms one body with all (Wang, 1963, p. 272).

Our culture today finds it hard to comprehend such a perspective. Yet the basic premise — that heart–mind and empathy are what distinguish human beings from other animals — is familiar from both cognitive ethology and phenomenology. Whereas cognitive ethology shows us the evolutionary roots of the human heart–mind, and phenomenology shows us the experiential structure of empathy, traditions such as Neo-Confucianism and Mahayana Buddhism challenge us to consider how we as members of a Western scientific culture might conceive the range of empathy in relation to what David Abram (1996) has called the more-than-human-world (see also Tucker & Berthrong, 1998). (In fact, a path to this idea can be found in the recent discussions by biologists and environmentalists of 'biophilia', the idea that humans have a biologically rooted affinity for the natural world. See Wilson, 1984; Kellert, 1997). Whatever we might decide, we cannot know the range of empathy and compassion short of investigating the human heart–mind with the full range of tools available — cognitive science, phenomenology, and the contemplative and meditative psychologies of the wisdom traditions.

IX: The Next Step

It has become commonplace to say that we — contemporary Westerners — are children of the European Enlightenment and its discovery of reason and science. Some believe that we now need to abandon the Enlightenment, but the path followed in this article confirms Margaret Donaldson's suggestion that what we need is a second 'value-sensing enlightenment' to complement the first:

> The very possibility of emotional development that is genuinely on a par with — as high as, level with — the development of reason is only seldom entertained. So long as this possibility is neglected, then if reason by itself is sensed as inadequate where else can one go but back? Thus there arises a regressive tendency, a desire to reject reason and all that was best in the Enlightenment, a yearning for some return to the mythic, the magical, the marvelous in old senses of these terms. This is very dangerous; but it has the advantage that it is altogether easier than trying to move forward into something genuinely new.
>   Now we have clearly seen that the cultivation of the advanced value-sensing modes is not of itself new. It has ancient roots. What *would* be new would be a culture where both kinds of enlightenment were respected and cultivated together. Is there any prospect that a new age of this kind might be dawning? (1991, p. 264).

The path that I have followed in this article leads not so much to a fixed conclusion, but to a clear sense of the next step that needs to be taken for such a second enlightenment: *we need to pursue a 'science of interbeing'* (Varela, in press) *that integrates the methods and findings of cognitive science, phenomenology, and the contemplative and meditative psychologies of the world's wisdom traditions.*

What steps can be taken now in this endeavour? Clearly the first step is to bring together cognitive scientists, phenomenological philosophers and psychologists, and contemplative practitioners to explore more thoroughly the common ground presented in this article. Especially important would be to establish a research programme for the following tasks:

- Clarification of the phenomenological method of investigating experience and exploration of its scope and limits in relation to cognitive science and contemplative practices.

- Development of more refined taxonomies of empathy and value-sensing.

- Development of experimental techniques to explore the neurocognitive dimensions of value sensing.

- Development of experimental techniques to assess the neurocognitive effects of value-sensing training (e.g., the Mahayana Buddhist meditations on equality of self and other, and exchange of self and other).

- Consideration of the implications of this research for biomedicine (e.g., psycho-neuroimmunology), illness experience, and for empathy in the physician-patient relationship.

- Consideration of the implications of this research for our treatment of animals, especially in the context of scientific research on consciousness.

It is my hope that the articles collected in this volume will provide some of the resources for creating the research programs needed to pursue these tasks.

References

Abram, D. (1996), *The Spell of the Sensuous: Perception and Language in a More-Than-Human-World* (New York: Vintage Books).

Adolphs, R. (1999), 'Social cognition and the human brain', *Trends in Cognitive Sciences*, **3**, pp. 469–79.

Allman, J.M. (1999), *Evolving Brains* (New York: Scientific American Library).

Astington, J.W. (1993), *The Child's Discovery of the Mind* (Cambridge, MA: Harvard University Press).

Beer, R.D. (2000), 'Dynamical approaches to cognitive science', *Trends in Cognitive Sciences*, **4**, pp. 91–9.

Carruthers, P. & Smith, P.K. (ed. 1996), *Theories of Theories of Mind* (Cambridge: Cambridge University Press).

Chalmers, D.J. (1996), *The Conscious Mind: In Search of a Fundamental Theory* (New York: Oxford University Press).

Chalmers, D.J. (1997), 'Moving forward on the problem of consciousness', *Journal of Consciousness Studies*, **4** (1), pp. 3–46.

Chan, W-T. (1963), *A Source Book in Chinese Philosophy* (Princeton, NJ: Princeton University Press).

Clark, A. (1997), *Being There: Putting Brain, Body, and World Together Again* (Cambridge, MA: The MIT Press/A Bradford Book).

Clark, A. (1999), 'An embodied cognitive science?', *Trends in Cognitive Sciences*, **3**, pp. 345–51.

Confucius (1979), *The Analects*. trans. D.C. Lau. (Harmondsworth, Middlesex: Penguin Books).

Corballis, M.C. (1998), 'Cerebral asymmetry: motoring on', *Trends in Cognitive Sciences* 2, pp. 152-157.

Cole, J. (1997), 'On being "faceless": Selfhood and facial embodiment', *Journal of Consciousness Studies*, **4** (5–6), pp. 467–84.

Damasio, A.R. (1994), *Descartes' Error. Emotion, Reason, and the Human Brain* (New York: Grosset/Putnam).

Damasio, A.R. (1999), *The Feeling of What Happens: Body and Emotion in the Making of Consciousness* (New York: Harcourt Brace).

Davies, M. & Stone, T. (ed. 1995a), *Folk Psychology. The Theory of Mind Debate* (Oxford: Blackwell).

Davies, M. & Stone, T. (ed. 1995b), *Mental Simulations: Evaluations and Applications* (Oxford: Blackwell).

Depraz, N. (1995), *Transcendence et incarnation: le statut de l'intersubjectivité comme altérité à soi chez Husserl* (Paris: Librarie Philosophique J. Vrin).

Depraz, N., Varela, F.J. & Vermersch, P. (2000), 'The gesture of awareness: an account of its structural dynamics', in *Investigating Phenomenal Consciousness*, ed. Max Velmans (Amsterdam/Philadelphia: John Benjamins Publishing).

Donald, M. (1991), *Origins of the Modern Mind: Three Stages in the Evolution of Culture and Cognition* (Cambridge, MA: Harvard University Press).

Donaldson, M. (1991), *Human Minds: An Exploration* (London: Penguin Books).

Freeman, W. (1999) *How Brains Makes Their Minds* (London: Wiedenfeld & Nicholson).

Gallagher, S. (1986), 'Lived body and environment', *Research in Phenomenology*, **16**, pp. 139–70.

Gallagher, S. (1997), 'Mutual enlightenment: recent phenomenology and cognitive science', *Journal of Consciousness Studies*, 4 (3), pp. 195–214.

Gallagher, S. & Meltzoff, A. (1996), 'The earliest sense of self and others: Merleau-Ponty and recent developmental studies', *Philosophical Psychology*, **9**, pp. 211–33.

Gallese, V. & Goldman, A. (1998), 'Mirror neurons and the simulation theory of mind-reading', *Trends in Cognitive Sciences*, **2**, pp. 493–501.

Gallup, Jr., G. (1998), 'Can animals empathize? Yes', *Scientific American*, **9**, pp. 66–71.

Gerhart, J. & Kirschner, M. (1997), *Cells, Embryos, and Evolution: Toward a Cellular and Developmental Understanding of Phenotypic Variability and Evolutionary Adaptability* (Malden, MA: Blackwell Science Publications).

Goldman, A. (1993), *Philosophical Applications of Cognitive Science* (Boulder, CO: Westview Press).

Goldman, A. (1995a), 'Empathy, mind, and morals', in Davies. & Stone (1995a).

Goldman, A. (1995b), 'In defense of the simulation theory', in Davies & Stone (1995b).

Gordon, R.M. (1996), '"Radical" simulationism', in Carruthers & Smith (1996).

Hamrick, W.S. (2000), 'Empathy, cognitive science, and literary imagination,' *Journal of the British Society for Phenomenology*, **31**, pp. 116–30.

Hanh, T.N. (1987), *Interbeing* (Berkeley, CA: Parallax Press).

Hanna, R. & Thompson, E. (forthcoming), 'The spontaneity of consciousness'.

Husserl, E. (1960), *Cartesian Meditations*, trans. Dorian Cairns (The Hague: Martinus Nijohff).

Husserl, E. (1973), *Zur Phänomenologie der Intersubjektivität I, II, & III. (Husserliana Vols. 13, 14, & 15.)* (The Hague: Martinus Nijhoff).

Husserl, E. (1989), *Ideas Pertaining to A Pure Phenomenology and to a Phenomenological Philosophy, Second Book*, trans. R. Rojcewicz & A. Schuwer (Dordrecht: Kluwer Academic Publishers).

Karmiloff-Smith, A. (1998), 'Development itself is the key to understanding developmental disorders', *Trends in Cognitive Sciences*, **2**, pp. 389–98.

Kellert, S.R. (1997), *Kinship to Mastery: Biophilia in Human Evolution and Development* (Washington, DC: Island Press/Shearwater Books).

Kelso, J.A.S. (1995), *Dynamic Patterns: The Self-Organization of Brain and Behavior* (Cambridge, MA: The MIT Press).

Lazarus, R. (1991), *Emotion and Adaptation* (New York: Oxford University Press).

Lazarus, R. & Lazarus, B.N. (1994), *Passion and Reason: Making Sense of Our Emotions* (New York: Oxford University Press).

Le Van Quyen, M., Adam, C., Lachaux, J-P., Martinerie, J., Baulac, M., Renault, B. & Varela, F.J. (1997), 'Temporal patterns in human epileptic activity are modulated by perceptual discriminations', *NeuroReport*, **8**, pp. 1703–10.

Leder, D. (1990), *The Absent Body* (Chicago: University of Chicago Press).

Levinas, E. (1969) *Totality and Infinity: An Essay on Exteriority,* trans. Alphonso Lingis (Pittsburgh, PA: Dusquesne University Press).

McGeer, V. (1996), 'Is "self-knowledge" an empirical problem? Renegotiating the space of philosophical explanation', *Journal of Philosophy*, **93**, pp. 483–515.

McGeer, V. (1999), 'Rethinking "mindreading": philosophical, psychological, and neurological implications of a regulative account of our "folk-psychological" capacities', Project Description, McDonnell Project in Philosophy and the Neurosciences. http://www.sfu.ca/neurophilosophy.

Meany, M.J., Diorio, J., Francis, D., Widdowson, J., LaPlante, P., Caldji, C., Sharma, S., Seckl, J.R. & Plotsky, P.M. (1996), 'Early environmental regulation of forebrain glucocorticoid receptor gene expression: implications for adrenocortical responses to stress', *Developmental Neuroscience*, **18**, pp. 49–72.

Meltzoff, A. & Moore, M.K. (1994), 'Imitation, memory, and the representation of persons', *Infant Behavior and Development*, **15**, pp. 479–505.

Meltzoff, A. & Moore, M.K. (1999), 'Infant intersubjectivity: broadening the dialogue to include imitation, identity and intention', in *Intersubjective Communication and Emotion in Early Ontogeny*, ed. S. Braten (Cambridge: Cambridge University Press).

Merleau-Ponty, M. (1962), *Phenomenology of Perception*, trans. Colin Smith (London: Routledge).

O'Regan, J.K. & Noë, A. (in press), 'A sensorimotor account of vision and visual consciousness', *Behavioral and Brain Sciences*.

Panksepp, J. (1998a), *Affective Neuroscience. The Foundations of Human and Animal Emotions* (New York: Oxford University Press).

Panksepp, J. (1998b), 'The periconscious substrates of consciousness: Affective states and the evolutionary origins of self', *Journal of Consciousness Studies*, **5** (5–6), pp. 566–82.

Patocka, J. (1998), *Body, Community, Language, World,* trans E. Kohak (Chicago & La Salle, IL: Open Court Publishing).

Petit, J-L. (1999), 'Constitution by movement: Husserl in light of recent neurobiological findings', in Petitot *et al.* (1999).

Petitot, J., Varela, F.J., Pachoud, B. & Roy, J-M. (ed. 1999), *Naturalizing Phenomenology: Issues in Contemporary Phenomenology and Cognitive Science* (Stanford, CA: Stanford University Press).

Povinelli, D.J. (1998), 'Can animals empathize? Maybe not', *Scientific American*, pp. 67–75.

Povinelli, D.J. & Preuss, T.M. (1995), 'Theory of mind: evolutionary history of a cognitive specialization', *Trends in Neurosciences*, **18**, pp. 418–24.

Putnam, H. (1999), *The Threefold Chord: Mind, Body, and World*. New York: Columbia University Press.

Quartz, S. (1999), 'The constructivist brain', *Trends in Cognitive Sciences*, **3**, pp. 48–57.

Quartz, S. & Sejnowski, T.J. (1997), 'The neural basis of cognitive development: a constructivist manifesto', *Behavioral and Brain Sciences*, **20**, pp. 537–96.

Rizzolatti, G. & Arbib, M. (1998), 'Language within our grasp', *Trends in Neurosciences*, **21**, pp. 188–94.

Rizzolatti, G., Riggio, L. & Sheliga, B.M. (1994), 'Space and selective attention', in *Attention and Performance IV. Conscious and Nonconscious Information Processing*, ed. C. Umiltà & M. Moscovitch (Cambridge, MA: The MIT Press).

Rizzolatti, G., Fadiga, L., Fogassi, L. & Gallese, V. (1997), 'The space around us', *Science*, **277**, pp. 190–1.

Shantideva (1997), *The Way of the Bodhisattva*, trans. the Padmakara Translation Group. (Boston, MA: Shambala Press).

Sheets-Johnstone, M. (1991), *The Primacy of Movement* (Amsterdam/Philadelphia: John Benjamins Publishing Company).

Sober, E. & Wilson, S.W. (1998), *Unto Others: The Evolution and Psyvhology of Unselfish Behavior* (Cambridge, MA: Harvard University Press).

Stein, E. (1964), *On the Problem of Empathy*, trans. Waltraut Stein (The Hague: Martinus Nijhoff).

Steinbock, A. (1995), *Home and Beyond: Generative Phenomenology After Husserl* (Evanston, IL: Northwestern University Press).

Taylor, E. (1996), *William James: On Consciousness Beyond the Margin* (Princeton, NJ: Princeton University Press).

Thompson, E. (1995), *Colour Vision: A Study in Cognitive Science and the Philosophy of Perception.* (London: Routledge Press).

Thompson, E. (1999), 'Empathy and the affective mind-brain: the importance of affective neuroscience for understanding everyday mind-reading', Project Description, McDonnell Project in the Philosophy and the Neurosciences. .

Thompson, E. & Varela, F.J. (in press) 'Radical embodiment: neural dynamics and conscious experience', *Trends in Cognitive Sciences.*

Thompson, E. & Varela, F.J. (forthcoming), *Why the Mind Isn't in the Head* (Cambridge, MA: Harvard University Press).

Thompson, E., Palacios, A. & Varela, F.J. (1992) 'Ways of coloring: comparative color vision as a case study for cognitive science', *Behavioral and Brain Sciences*, **15**, pp. 1–26.

Tu, W-M.. (1985), *Confucian Thought: Selfhood as Creative Transformation* (Albany, NY: State University of New York Press).

Tucker, M.E. & Berthrong, J. (ed. 1998), *Confucianism and Ecology: The Interrelation of Heaven, Earth, and Humans* (Cambridge, MA: Harvard University Press).

Varela, F.J. (1996), 'Neurophenomenology: a methodological remedy for the hard problem', *Journal of Consciousness Studies*, **3** (4), pp. 330–50.

Varela, F.J. (in press), 'Steps to a science of interbeing: unfolding the dharma implicit in modern cognitive science', in *The Psychology of Awakening*, ed. S. Batchelor, G. Claxton & G. Watson.

Varela, FJ. & Shear, J. (ed. 1999), *The View from Within: First-Person Approaches to the Study of Consciousness* (Thorverton, UK: Imprint Academic). Also published as *Journal of Consciousness Studies* **6** (2–3), 1999.

Varela, F.J., Thompson, E., & Rosch, E. (1991), *The Embodied Mind: Cognitive Science and Human Experience* (Cambridge, MA: The MIT Press).

Vetlesen, A.J. (1994), *Perception, Empathy, and Judgment: An Inquiry into the Preconditions of Moral Performance* (University Park, PA: Pennsylvania State University Press).

de Waal, F. (1996), *Good Natured: The Origins of Right and Wrong in Humans and Other Animals* (Cambridge, MA: Harvard University Press).

Wallace, B.A. (1998), *The Bridge of Quiescence: Experiencing Tibetan Buddhist Meditation* (Chicago and LaSalle, IL: Open Court).

Wallace, B.A. (1999), 'The Buddhist tradition of *Samatha*: Methods for refining and examining consciousness', in Varela & Shear (1999). Also published in *Journal of Consciousness Studies*, **6** (2–3), pp. 175–87.

Wang, Y-M. (1963), *Instructions for Practical Living and Other Neo-Confucian Writings*, trans. by Wing-Tsit Chan (Princeton: Princeton University Press).

Watt, D.F. (1998), 'Emotion and consciousness: implications of affective neuroscience for extended reticular thalamic activating system theories of consciousness', http://server.philvt.edu/assc/watt/default.htm.

Welton, D. (1999), 'Soft, smooth hands: Husserl's phenomenology of the lived body,' in *The Body*, ed. Donn Welton (Oxford: Basil Blackwell).

Wilson, E.O. (1984), *Biophilia* (Cambridge, MA: Harvard University Press).

Zahavi, D. (1996), 'Husserl's intersubjective transformation of transcendental philosophy', *Journal of the British Society for Phenomenology*, **27**, pp. 228–45.

Zahavi, D. (1997), 'Horizontal intentionality and transcendental intersubjectivity', *Tijdschrift Voor Filosofie*, **59**, pp. 304–21.

Zahavi, D. (1999), *Self-Awareness and Alterity. A Phenomenological Investigation* (Evanston, IL: Northwestern University Press).

Vittorio Gallese

The 'Shared Manifold' Hypothesis

From Mirror Neurons To Empathy

I: Introduction

We are social animals. We share this feature with many other species. A complexity and sophistication that we do not observe among ants, bees or wolves, however, characteristically define the social life of primates. This complexity and sophistication is epitomized at its highest level by the social rules our conduct in everyday life is supposed to comply with. Living in a complex society requires individuals to develop cognitive skills enabling them to cope with other individuals' actions, by recognizing them, understanding them, and reacting appropriately to them. No one doubts that the extant primate ancestors of ours, monkeys and apes, who indeed also live in complex, hierarchically organized societies, are perfectly able to cope with *their own* social rules. Nevertheless, it is commonly argued that to achieve that goal non-human primates simply rely on behaviour observation. Animals do not represent rules in their minds, and they do not engage in any *inference*-based reasoning. Accordingly, what non-human primates are lacking would sharply define what is considered to be uniquely human: *truly* cognitive states, such as intentions, desires and beliefs.

In our daily life we are constantly exposed to the actions of the individuals inhabiting our social world. We are not only able to describe these actions, to understand their content, and predict their consequences, but we can also attribute *intentions* to the agents of the same actions. We can immediately tell whether a given observed act or behaviour is the result of a purposeful attitude or rather the unpredicted consequence of some accidental event, totally unrelated to the agent's will. In other words, we are able to understand the behaviour of others in terms of their mental states. I will designate this ability as *mind-reading*. How do we 'read' intentions in the mind of other individuals? A common view maintains that all normal humans develop the capacity to *represent* mental states in others by means of a conceptual system, commonly designated as 'Theory of Mind' (TOM, see Premack and Woodruff, 1978).

My initial scope will be limited: starting from a neurobiological standpoint, I will analyse how actions[1] are possibly *represented* and *understood*. The main aim of my

---

[1] In this paper I will mostly focus on action understanding. This of course doesn't exhaust the issue of social cognition. The reader can refer to the excellent review by Adolphs (1999) for an appreciation of the role of emotions in social cognition. See Damasio (1994; 1999); Ellis and Newton (2000); Jarvilehto (forthcoming); Panksepp (2000) for a discussion of the relation between emotions and consciousness.

Journal of Consciousness Studies, **8**, No. 5–7, 2001, pp. 33–50

arguments will be to show that, far from being *exclusively* dependent upon mentalistic/linguistic abilities, the capacity for understanding others as intentional agents is deeply grounded in the *relational* nature of action. Action is relational, and the relation holds both between the agent and the object target of the action (see Gallese, 2000b), as between the agent of the action and his/her observer (see below). *Agency* constitutes a key issue for the understanding of intersubjectivity and for explaining how individuals can interpret their social world. This account of intersubjectivity, founded on the empirical findings of neuroscientific investigation, will be discussed and put in relation with a classical tenet of phenomenology: empathy.[2] I will provide an 'enlarged' account of empathy that will be defined by means of a new conceptual tool: the *shared manifold* of intersubjectivity.

II: How Do We Perceive Actions?

To 'navigate' in our social environment we rely basically on vision. It is through vision that we are able to recognize different individuals, to locate them in space, and to record their behaviour. Vision, among the different sensory modalities, is indeed by far the most extensively studied one both by psychology and by neuroscience. About fifty years of neuroscientific investigation have clarified many aspects of vision, from the transduction processes carried out at the interface between light stimuli and receptors in the retina, to the different stages along which visual images are processed and analysed by the brain. In this section I will confine my review to data obtained from monkeys. The problem of how the human brain processes actions will be addressed later on in the paper.

The most widely accepted model of how the brain analyses visual information maintains that visual processing is carried out in a piecemeal fashion, with specialized cortical regions 'dedicated' to the analysis of shape, colour and motion (for a comprehensive neuroscientific account of vision, see Zeki, 1993).

Motion analysis is crucial to discriminate and recognize observed actions performed by other individuals. Area MT, or V5 (Zeki and Shipp, 1988), which in the monkey is located in the caudal part of the ventral bank of the Superior Temporal Sulcus (STS), is one of the most studied among the so-called extrastriate visual areas. Several electrophysiological studies have shown that area MT is specialized for the analysis of visual motion (Dubner and Zeki, 1971; Zeki, 1974; Van Essen *et al.,* 1981; Maunsell and Van Essen, 1983; Desimone and Ungerleider, 1986). Interestingly enough, however, comparatively little effort has been devoted to the investigation of where and how *biological motion* is analysed and processed in the brain.

The seminal studies carried out by David Perrett and co-workers since the mid-eighties (Perrett *et al.,* 1989; 1990; Oram and Perrett, 1994), have filled this gap by clarifying that in a cortical sector buried within the anterior part of the Superior Temporal Sulcus (STSa) of the monkey there are neurons, not tested for the presence of motor properties, selectively activated by the observation of various types of body movements such as walking, turning the head, stretching the arm, bending the torso, etc. (for review, see Carey *et al.*, 1997; Jellema and Perrett, 2001). Particularly interesting

---

[2] The theoretical approach I'll be advocating here is in part related to Simulation Theory (see Gordon, 1986; Harris, 1989; Goldman, 1989; 1992; 1993a,b; 2000).

are cells responsive to *goal-related behaviours*: these neurons do not respond to static presentations of hands or objects, but require, in order to be triggered, the observation of a meaningful, goal-related hand–object interaction (Perrett *et al.*, 1990). Incidentally, it must be noted that no attempt has been made by these authors to test the responsiveness of these neurons during active movements of the monkey. Comparable hand actions without target object or hand movements without physical contact with the object in view do not evoke any response. The responses of these neurons generalize across different viewing conditions including distance, speed and orientation. The responses of some of these neurons have been shown not to be sensitive to form, so that even light dot displays moving with a biologically plausible kinematics are as good as true limbs and hands in evoking the neurons' discharge (Oram and Perrett, 1994; Jellema and Perrett, 2001).[3] Neurons responding to complex biological visual stimuli such as walking or climbing were reported also in the amygdala (Brothers *et al.*, 1990).

Altogether these results provide strong evidence supporting the notion that distinct specific sectors of the visual system are selectively involved in the representation of behaviours of others. *Visual representation*, however, is not *understanding*. A visual representation of a given stimulus doesn't necessarily convey all the information required to assign a meaning to it, and therefore to understand such a stimulus. What a purely visual representation of a behaviour doesn't allow for is to code/represent it as an *intended, mind-driven* behaviour.

In the next section I will briefly present some empirical results that may help in elucidating the neural mechanisms at the basis of a more comprehensive account of action understanding.

III: Mirror Neurons and Action Representation

In a series of single neuron recording experiments we discovered (diPellegrino *et al.*, 1992; Gallese *et al.*, 1996a; Rizzolatti *et al.*, 1996a; Gallese, 1999; 2000a; see also Rizzolatti *et al.*, 2000) in a sector of the monkey ventral premotor cortex, area F5 (Matelli *et al.*, 1985; Rizzolatti *et al.*, 1998), that a particular set of neurons, activated during the execution of purposeful, goal-related hand actions, such as grasping, holding or manipulating objects, discharge also when the monkey observes similar hand actions performed by another individual. We designated these neurons as 'mirror neurons' (Gallese *et al.*, 1996a; Rizzolatti *et al.*, 1996a). Mirror neurons require, in order to be activated by visual stimuli, an interaction between the action's agent (human being or a monkey) and its object. Control experiments showed that neither the sight of the agent alone nor of the object alone were effective in evoking the neuron's response. Similarly, much less effective were mimicking the action without a target object or performing the action by using tools (Gallese *et al.*, 1996a).

---

[3] These results suggest that the triggering feature for neurons responsive to the observation of goal-related behaviours is the embedded motor schema rather than a purely visual representation of the observed behaviour. The results of Cutting and Kozlowski (1977) seem to support this view. When human subjects watch moving light-dot displays they are not only able to recognize a walking person, but also to discriminate whether it is them or someone else that they are watching. Since in normal conditions we never look at ourselves when walking, this recognition process can be much better accounted for by a simulation mechanism in which the observed moving stimuli activate the observer's motor schema for walking, than solely by means of a purely visual process. See also Churchland *et al.* (1994) for a critique of *pure* vision.

Frequently, a strict congruence was observed between the observed action effective in triggering the neuron and the effective executed action. In one third of the recorded neurons the effective observed and executed actions corresponded both in terms of the general action (e.g. grasping) and in terms of the way in which that action was executed (e.g. precision grip). In the other two thirds only a general congruence was found (e.g. any kind of observed and executed grasping elicited the neuron's response). This latter class of mirror neurons is particularly interesting, because they appear to generalize across different ways of achieving the same goal, thus perhaps enabling a more abstract type of action coding.

The lack of responsivity of mirror neurons during the observation of actions performed with tools is reminiscent of a study of Meltzoff (1995) where he studied and described the capacity of 18-month-old children to re-enact observed goal-directed actions displayed by adult demonstrators. In one case the adult demonstrator pulled the end of a toy dumbbell designed to be pulled apart, but actually failed in pulling it apart. Toddlers who observed this intended — but failed — action were nevertheless able to re-enact it successfully, even if they had never been exposed before to a successful version of the same action. This capacity, however, disappeared when they observed the same failed attempt to pull the dumbbell apart demonstrated by a mechanical device.

These results tell us that in order to understand the intended goal of an observed action, and to eventually re-enact it, a *link* must be established between the observed agent and the observer. My proposal is that this link is constituted by the *embodiment* of the intended goal, shared by the agent and the observer. We can speculate on the mechanisms enabling the embodiment of the intended goal to be shared. My suggestion is that the embodiment of the action goal, shared by agent and observer, depends on the motor schema of the action, and not only on a purely visual description of its agent.[4] When the motor schema of the agent is different from that of the observer — as in the case of the mechanical demonstrator, or for mirror neurons, in the case of grasping achieved by using a tool — the observed action cannot be matched on the observer's motor repertoire, and therefore the intended goal cannot be detected and/or attributed to the mechanical agent.

A striking resemblance can be found between mirror neurons and the STSa neurons responsive to biological meaningful visual stimuli, described in the macaque brain by Perrett and coworkers (see above). Mirror neurons differ from these complex visual neurons in that the former discharge also during active movements of the observer. They constitute, therefore, a specific neural system matching action observation and execution. The observed action produces in the observer's premotor cortex an activation pattern resembling that occurring when the observer actively executes the same action.

A problematic issue since the discovery of F5 mirror neurons has been the source of their visual input. At first sight the STSa neurons described by Perrett and coworkers (for a recent review, see Jellema and Perrett, 2001) could provide a particularly

---

[4] It can be objected that a tool or a mechanical device looks *stranger* to a primate observer because of its shape. This is certainly true. However, the action-observation neurons described by Perrett (Oram and Perrett, 1994) that respond to moving light dot-displays seem to suggest that action schemas constitute a major cue for the detection of goal-relatedness (see also note 3).

well suited source of visual input to F5 mirror neurons. However, area F5 does not receive direct projections from the STS region. One of the major inputs to area F5 comes from the inferior parietal lobule (Petrides and Pandya, 1984; Matelli *et al.*, 1986; Cavada and Godman-Rakic, 1989), and in particular from area 7b or PF (see Rizzolatti *et al.*, 1998). The inferior parietal lobule, in turn, is reciprocally connected with the STS region (Seltzer and Pandya, 1984; Cavada and Goldman-Rakic, 1989).

Thus, visual information about actions could be fed to area F5 from the STSa region through an intermediate step in the posterior parietal cortex. In order to verify whether 'mirror properties' could be detected in the posterior parietal cortex, my colleagues and I decided to study the functional properties of area 7b by means of single neuron recording experiments. Neuron properties were examined during active movements of the monkey and in response to somatosensory and visual stimuli, including goal-related hand movements. About one third of the recorded neurons responded both during action execution and action observation (Fogassi *et al.* 1998; Gallese *et al.*, 2001a). These data, although preliminary, indicate that an action observation/execution matching system exists also in the posterior parietal cortex, possibly constituting part of a cortical network for action recognition (see Gallese *et al.*, 2001a).

What may be the function of a neural system matching action observation and execution? Before discussing this issue it is important to stress that the presence of such a system has been demonstrated also in humans. Fadiga *et al.* (1995) tested the excitability of the motor cortex of normal human subjects with the technique of transcranic magnetic stimulation under three different conditions: observation of an experimenter grasping objects; observation of objects; detection of the dimming of a small spot of light. The results showed that during grasping observation the motor-evoked potentials recorded from the hand muscles markedly increased with respect to other conditions, including the attention-demanding dimming-detection task. Furthermore, the increase of excitability was present only in those muscles that were used by the subjects when actively performing the observed movements.

Similar results were obtained also by Cochin *et al.* (1998), who recorded EEG from subjects who observed video movies in which human movements were displayed. As control, objects in movement, and still objects were also presented. The results showed that the observation of human movements, but not that of objects, desynchronizes the EEG pattern of the precentral motor cortex. The same results have been replicated (Hari *et al.*, 1998) by using a different technique, magnetoencephalography (MEG).

All these studies suggested that humans have a 'mirror matching system' similar to that originally discovered in monkeys. Whenever we are looking at someone performing an action, beside the activation of various visual areas, there is a concurrent activation of the motor circuits that are recruited when we ourselves perform that action. Although we do not overtly reproduce the observed action, nevertheless our motor system becomes active *as if*[5] we were executing that very same action that we are observing. To spell it out in different words, action observation implies *action simulation*.[6]

---

[5] *As if* mechanisms have been pinpointed by Damasio (1999) as being part of the system enabling the experience of emotional feelings (see also below).

[6] For a discussion of simulation in relation to representation, see Gallese (2000b).

With the use of brain imaging techniques the localization of cortical areas active during action observation was made possible. Initial studies showed that during the observation of different type of hand grips performed on a variety of objects there is an activation of left STS region, of the inferior parietal lobule and of Broca's area (see Rizzolatti *et al.*, 1996b; Grafton *et al.*, 1996; Decety *et al.*, 1997; for review, see Decety and Grézes, 1999; Allison *et al.*, 2000). This circuit roughly corresponds to that of mirror neurons in the monkey.[7] However, in all these brain imaging experiments the actions that human subjects were required to observe were limited only to hand actions.

More recently, in a fMRI study, subjects were shown object-directed actions made with the mouth (e.g. biting an apple), the hand (e.g. grasping a cup) and the foot (e.g. kicking a ball). The results showed that observation of object-related actions determines, among other activations, a somatotopically-organized activation of the premotor cortex. During mouth actions observation there is a bilateral activation of the ventral premotor cortex (Brodmann's area 6) plus an activation of Broca's area. During hand actions observation a more dorsal part of ventral area 6 plus Broca's area are recruited. Finally, the observation of foot actions elicits an activation of dorsal area 6 (Buccino *et al.*, 2001).

It appears therefore that when we observe goal-related behaviours executed with different effectors, different specific sectors of our pre-motor cortex become active. These cortical sectors are those same sectors that are active when we actually perform the same actions. In other words, when we observe actions performed by other individuals our motor system 'resonates' along with that of the observed agent.

As stated above, action observation both in humans and monkeys seems to imply a concurrent action simulation. This notion is corroborated by evidence coming from neurological patients. Demented patients with 'echopraxia' (Dromard, 1905; Stengel *et al.*, 1947) show an impulsive tendency to imitate other people's movements. Imitation is performed immediately with the speed of a reflex action. Imitation concerns gestures that are commonly executed as well as those that are rare and even bizarre for the observing patient. It can be hypothesized that echopractic behaviour represents a 'release' of a covert action simulation present also in normal subjects, but normally inhibited in its expression by the cortical areas that in these patients are functionally defective. A similar case has been reported of patients that, due to lesion of the orbito-frontal cortex, display what has been defined as 'imitative behaviour' (Lhermitte *et al.*, 1986). Unlike in echopraxia, however, patients with imitation behaviour do not imitate the *movements* of the acting individual, but rather perform an *action* identical to the observed one. It is the goal rather than movement to be imitated in this pathology.[8] A much less dramatic example of 'contagious behaviour' commonly

[7] Broca's area is considered the human homologue of the monkey's area F5 (see Matelli and Luppino, 1997; Rizzolatti *et al.*, 1998). For a discussion of mirror neurons in relation to motor theories of speech perception and the origin of language, see Fadiga and Gallese (1997); Rizzolatti and Arbib (1998); Gallese (1999).

[8] Imitation plays a major role in the cognitive development of humans. Much debated, however, is the relevance of imitative behaviour among non-human primates (see Hayes, 1998; Tomasello *et al.*, 1993; Byrne and Whiten, 1988; Byrne, 1995; Byrne and Russon, 1999; Whiten, 1996; Whiten and Ham, 1992). The reader interested to know more about the possible relation between mirror neurons and imitation can refer to Jeannerod (1994; 1997); Gallese and Goldman (1998); Rizzolatti *et al.* (1999; 2001).

experienced in our daily life, in which the observation of particular actions displayed by others leads to our repetition of them, is represented by yawning and laughter.

In the next section I will try to demonstrate that it is not fortuitous that part of the motor system is involved in *representing* action, by showing that a link can be established between action control and action representation (for a discussion of representation in relation to motor control, see also Gallese, 2000b).

IV: Agency and Intersubjectivity

So far we have seen that both humans' and monkeys' motor systems are active not only during the execution of goal-related movements but also during their observation.

Why do individuals possess a 'mirror matching mechanism'? The capability of individuals to adapt to a particular social environment relies upon the possibility to select a certain type of behaviour also on the basis of the understanding of the behaviour displayed by other individuals. My proposal is that action understanding heavily relies on a neural mechanism that matches, in the same neuronal substrate, the observed behaviour with the one executed (Gallese *et al.*, 1996a; Rizzolatti *et al.*, 1996a; Gallese, 2000a). According to this hypothesis, 'understanding' is achieved by modelling a *behaviour* as an *action* with the help of a motor equivalence between what the others do and what the observer does.[9]

The neuroscientific results here briefly summarized seem to point to a crucial role played by action, in virtue of its *relational nature*, in establishing a meaningful link between agent and observer. Action execution and action observation both impinge upon the same cortical network: why is this so? How come that when we observe someone acting, our motor system starts to covertly simulate the actions of the observed agent? Why shouldn't a purely visual representation of the observed behaviour of others suffice to account for it? I will try to answer this question by providing a non-conventional account of *action representation*.

The fact that the motor system is activated not only when a given action is executed, but also when it is observed, suggests that a relationship may exist between *action control* and *action representation*. As I hope it will become clearer in a while, both achievements are necessarily tied to the necessity of organisms to model themselves (see also Metzinger, 1993; 2000). Furthermore, it must be noted that social cognition also has action control as one of its main purposes, namely controlling the action of others. These statements, nevertheless, need to be qualified and substantiated by empirical data. The neurophysiological study of the functional organization of the ventral premotor cortex of the monkey provides very interesting clues that may help us to provide a new and unconventional account of how actions are represented.

Mirror neurons have been discovered in area F5, which constitutes the most rostral part of the ventral premotor cortex.[10] This area can be functionally parcelled in two sectors: one sector occupies the cortical convexity, and it is in this sector that mirror

---

[9] Unlike introspection, however, this process is automatic, unconscious and non predicative. This is not meant to deny that this particular type of representational content is open to introspective access. My point is that conscious introspective access is not *necessarily required* to detect intentions in the observed behaviour of others (see also Goldman, 2000, on this point).

[10] The majority of F5 neurons code goal-related hand, mouth or hand and mouth actions such as grasping, holding, and tearing objects. Part of these neurons has also visual properties (see below).

neurons are mostly clustered. The second sector is buried within the inferior limb of the arcuate sulcus, of which it constitutes the posterior bank. In this latter sector, a second class of visuomotor grasping-related neurons have been described, 'canonical neurons' (Rizzolatti *et al.*, 1988; Murata *et al.*, 1997; Rizzolatti *et al.*, 2000; Gallese, 2000a). Canonical neurons are activated during the execution of goal-related movements such as grasping, holding, and manipulating objects. Unlike mirror neurons, however, they are not activated by action observation. They discharge during object observation, typically showing congruence between the type of grip they motorically code and the size/shape of the object that visually drives them. Both sectors of F5 are reciprocally connected to the primary motor cortex, area F1 (see Matelli *et al.*, 1986; Rizzolatti *et al.*, 1998).

In a particular sector of the premotor cortex — area F5 — there are therefore two distinct classes of neurons that code goal-related hand movements, and which differ for their visual responsiveness: mirror neurons respond to action observation, while canonical neurons respond to object observation. Why are there two distinct populations of grasping-related premotor neurons? By answering this question we can start to develop a new account of *re-presentation*.

My proposal is to interpret the motor activity of mirror neurons in terms of an *efference copy* of the motor program signal. Once the features of the object to be grasped are specified, and 'translated' by canonical neurons into the most suitable motor program enabling a successful action to be produced (see Jeannerod *et al.*, 1995; Gallese *et al.*, 1996b; Rizzolatti *et al.*, 2000), a copy of this signal is fed to mirror neurons. This signal would act as a sort of 'simulator' of the programmed action. This *simulation* of the action is used to predict its consequences, thus enabling the achievement of a better control strategy.

My hypothesis can be framed within the logic of the so-called *forward models*. Forward models are so defined because they can capture the forward or causal relationship between actions, as signalled by efference copy, and outcomes. By means of forward models the outcomes of motor commands can be estimated (Wolpert *et al.*, 1995; Wolpert, 1997; Kawato, 1997; 1999).

An instantiation of the activity of forward models can be found in the domain of postural control (Cordo and Nashner, 1982). When I am going to stretch my arm to grasp a handle in front of me, the resulting postural perturbation that would follow, causing my body to bend, is cancelled by a forward signal sent to the posterior muscles of my leg, which stabilize my standing posture. The muscles of the leg indeed contract well before my arm is set into motion. The contraction of leg muscles anticipates, *predicts* the outcome of the programmed action of the arm, that is, the forecast postural perturbation, preventing it to occur. Neither overt knowledge nor conscious inference is involved in this process.

I posit that a similar functional architecture might be at work also in the far more complex domain of intersubjective relationships. The same basic functional architecture that proved itself to be so useful in one domain can be exploited also in a different one. When trying to account for the cognitive abilities of human beings we tend to forget that these abilities were not modelled and put in place as such, but they are the result of a long evolutionary process. The hypothetical scenario here briefly sketched has the advantage of being more plausible in evolutionary terms than accounts that emphasize a sharp discontinuity between human cognition and that of all other living creatures (see below; see also Gallese *et al.*, 2001b).

Mirror neurons are active during action execution: if we interpret the *motor activation* of mirror neurons as the result of an *efference copy signal*, it is possible to speculate that this system may have originally developed to achieve a better control of action performance. The coupling of this forward model architecture with the vision of the agent's own hand, and its later generalization to the hands of others, may have allowed this system to be used also for totally different purposes, namely to represent other individuals' actions. Action representation, following my hypothesis, can be envisaged as the emergence of a new skill that developed by exploiting in totally new ways resources that had been previously selected for other purposes, namely for motor control purposes.

I must admit that this is no more than a purely speculative scenario. We don't know whether there is a developmental stage in which mirror neurons respond to the sight of the acting agent's own hand, but not yet to the sight of another observed agent. We don't even know whether mirror neurons in the monkey — or analogous neurons in humans — are already present at birth,[11] or whether they are the developmental result of the exposure of the developing individual to action observation.[12] Whatever the evolutionary history of the mirror matching system may be, at the phylogenetic as well as at the ontogenetic level, it is clear that the discovery of mirror neurons provide a strong neurobiological basis for a subpersonal account of inter-subjective representational content.

When a given action is planned, its expected motor consequences are forecast. This means that when I am going to execute a given action I can predict its consequences. Through a process of 'motor equivalence' I can use this information also to predict the consequences of actions performed by others. This *implicit, automatic,* and *unconscious* process of motor simulation enables the observer to use his/her own resources to penetrate the world of the other without the need for *theorizing* about it (see note 9), without the need to necessarily use *propositional attitudes*. A process of action simulation automatically establishes a direct implicit link between agent and observer. Action is the 'a priori' principle enabling social bonds to be initially established. By an implicit process of *action simulation*, when I observe other acting individuals I can immediately recognize them as goal-directed agents like me, because the very same neural substrate is activated as when I myself am bound to achieve the

---

[11] The capacity of newborn babies to imitate facial gestures, such as opening the mouth or protruding the tongue (Meltzoff and Moore, 1977), suggests that some form of 'mirror-like' mechanisms may be in place already at birth, at least for parts of the body that cannot be directly observed, and therefore likely require an active mirroring into the body of others to be better controlled.

[12] There is evidence that congenitally limb deficient patients develop phantom limb sensations (the so-called *aplasic phantoms*), despite the fact that they never moved these absent parts of their bodies (see Ramachandran, 1993; Melzak *et al.*, 1997; Ramachandran and Rogers-Ramachandran, 1996; Ramachandran and Hirstein, 1998). In a recently published study, Brugger *et al.* (2000) describe one of these cases. fMRI imaging of their patient during phantom limb sensations of hand movements showed no activation of primary sensorimotor areas, but of premotor and posterior parietal cortex. The authors of this study conclude that aplasic phantoms could be explained by postulating the existence of an innate but plastic schema for matching the observation with the execution of motor actions. Phantom limbs could therefore be explained as the phenomenal correlate of planning action with an absent limb.

same goal by acting. In sum, my suggestion is that through a process of 'motor equivalence' a meaningful link between agent and observer can be established.

Mirror neurons are found in cortical regions endowed with motor properties because premotor neurons are able to establish relationships between expectancies and results. Thus, action understanding can be viewed as a *subpersonally instantiated function*. It relies on neural circuits involved in action control. This pushes us to discuss the relationship between the *embodied mechanisms* at the basis of intersubjectivity that I have briefly illustrated here and the *disembodied* accounts of how the mind can represent the world of living creatures heralded by cognitivism.

V: The Social Mind, Its Theories, and Empathy

As anticipated in the Introduction, it is commonly held that all normal humans develop the capacity to *represent* mental states in others by means of a conceptual system, commonly designated as 'Theory of Mind' (TOM, see Premack and Woodruff, 1978). TOM has rapidly become a major topic in the cognitive sciences and in the philosophy of mind (see Carruthers and Smith, 1996, for an excellent survey of the issue). The concept of TOM can be addressed from many different perspectives. We can describe TOM in terms of a domain specific ability, supported by an innate, encapsulated, and specific module, whose function is segregated from the other intellectual capacities of the individual (Leslie, 1987; Baron-Cohen, 1995; Fodor, 1992; 1994). Alternatively, we can conceive TOM as the final stage of a developmental process in which different scientific theories about the world and its inhabitants are tested and eventually discarded to adopt new ones (see the 'child-as-scientist' hypothesis by Gopnik and Meltzoff, 1997). Both accounts of TOM are often referred to as Theory-Theory. Or, finally, we can conceive TOM as the result of a *simulation routine* by means of which we can *pretend* to be in the other's 'mental shoes' and use our own mind as a model for the mind of others (Gordon, 1986; Harris, 1989; Goldman, 1989; 1992; 1993a, b; 2000).

Both theory-theory approaches can be framed within classic cognitivism. The picture of the mind conveyed by classic cognitivism is that of a functional system whose processes can be described in terms of manipulations of informational symbols according to a set of formal syntactic rules (see Fodor, 1981; Pylyshyn, 1984). Thus, following the line of arguments of cognitivism, representations are symbolic in their nature, and thinking can be reduced to computation. It is therefore consequent that the understanding of other minds is conceived solely as a predicative, inferential, theory-like process.

It is out of the scope of this paper to add more to the debate on TOM (for an interdisciplinary discussion of Simulation Theory and its possible neural bases, see Gallese and Goldman, 1998, and Goldman and Gallese, 2000). The empirical data that I briefly reviewed in the first part of the paper suggest that it is possible to considerably deflate the role played by abstract *theorizing* when ascribing mental states (at least *some* mental states) to others. My thesis is that many aspects of our felt capacity to entertain social relationships with other individuals, the ease with which we 'mirror' ourselves in the behaviour of others and recognize them as similar to us, they all have a common root: empathy.

My proposal is to revise the concept of empathy by extending it so to account for all different aspects of behaviour enabling us to establish a meaningful link between others and ourselves. This 'enlarged' account of empathy will open up the possibility to provide a more comprehensive account of intersubjective intercourses, leading to a new conceptual tool that I'll define in the next section. But let us first try to clarify the meaning of the term empathy.

Empathy is a later English translation of the German word Einfühlung, originally introduced by Theodore Lipps (1903a) into the vocabulary of the psychology of aesthetic experience, to denote the relationship between an artwork and the observer, who imaginatively projects herself into the contemplated object. Lipps (1903b) extended the concept of Einfühlung also to the domain of intersubjectivity that he characterized in terms of *inner imitation* of the perceived movements of others. When I am watching an acrobat walking on a suspended wire, Lipps (1903b) notes, *I feel myself inside of him* (Ich Fühle mich so in ihm).

Phenomenology has further developed this concept. In the posthumously published Ideen II (1989, English translation), Husserl emphasizes the role of the acting body in perceiving.[13] To use an updated terminology, we could say that according to Husserl there can be no perception without *awareness of the acting body*. Following the perspective I tried to sketch in the present paper, it could be added that the *awareness* of our acting body cannot be detached from the mechanisms presiding over *action control* (see also Gallese, 2000a, b). By accepting these premises, the bridge to be crossed to get from *acting* to *thinking* narrows considerably.

According to Husserl, what makes the behaviour of other agents intelligible is the fact that their body is experienced not as material object (Körper), but as something alive (Leib), something analogous to our own experienced acting body (for a discussion of the concept of *bodily presence*, or Leibhaftigkeit, see Pacherie, 1999). Empathy is deeply grounded in the experience of our lived-body, and it is this experience that enables us to directly recognize others not as bodies endowed with a mind but as *persons* like us.[14] Persons are rational individuals. What we now discover is how a rationality assumption can be grounded in bodily experience.

This relationship between agency and intersubjectivity becomes even more evident in the works of Edith Stein and Merleau-Ponty. In her book *On the Problem of Empathy* (1912/1964, English translation), Edith Stein clarifies that the concept of empathy is not confined to a simple grasp of the other's feelings or emotions. There is a more basic — and I would add aboriginal — connotation of empathy: the other is experienced as another being like oneself through an appreciation of *similarity*. An important component of this similarity resides in the common experience of action. As Edith Stein points out, if the size of my hand were given at a fixed scale, as something predetermined, it would become very hard to empathize with any other types of hand not matching these predetermined physical specifications. However, we can perfectly recognize children's hands and monkeys' hands as such despite their different visual appearance. It is indisputable that we recognize hands because, basically, they all look the same, they all have five fingers, a thumb, etc. However, we can recognize hands as such even when all these visual details are not available, even despite

---

[13] The relation between Husserl's thought on intersubjectivity and neuroscience has been extensively explored by Jean-Luc Petit (1996; 1997; 1999). See also Sheets-Johnstone (1999).

[14] A similar account can be found in Metzinger (1993; 2000) when he posits that the seen body of the other is modelled as 'Leib' through the phenomenal self-model.

shifts of our point of view, and even when no visual shape specifications are provided
as in the case of the luminous dot-display experiments mentioned above. This seems
to suggest that our 'grasping' of the meaning of the world doesn't *exclusively* rely on
its visual representation, but is strongly influenced by action-related sensorimotor
processes.

Merleau-Ponty in the *Phenomenology of Perception* (1962) writes:

> The sense of the gestures is not given, but understood, that is, recaptured by an act on the
> spectator's part. The whole difficulty is to conceive this act clearly without confusing it
> with a cognitive operation. The communication or comprehension of gestures come
> about through the reciprocity of my intentions and the gestures of others, of my gestures
> and intentions discernible in the conduct of other people. It is as if the other person's
> intention inhabited my body and mine his.

Self and other relate to each other, because they both represent opposite extensions
of the same correlative and reversible system *self/other.* The observer and the
observed are part of a dynamic system governed by reversibility rules.
Merleau-Ponty argues against the Cartesian equivalence between seeing and thinking, emphasizing the 'narcissistic' character of vision.

This line of thought, however, is not a prerogative of 'continental philosophy', but
permeates also the tradition of American Pragmatism. Herbert Mead (1912) writes:

> Any gesture by which the individual can himself be affected as others are affected, and
> which therefore tends to call out in him a response as it would call out in another, will
> serve as a mechanism for the construction of a self.

One important aspect of the *self* is the result of the individual's mirroring in the
social organization of the outer world. According to Mead, the only way to *objectify*
us is to assume the other's perspective, like looking at our reflection in a mirror.
Through the medium of intersubjective communication the consequences produced
by our actions in the observed behaviour of others contribute to build our personal
identity (see Mead, 1934).

VI: The *Shared Manifold* Hypothesis

The main thesis of this paper so far has been that agency plays an important role in
establishing meaningful bonds among individuals, by enabling them with a direct,
automatic, non-predicative, and non-inferential simulation mechanism, by means of
which the observer can recognize and understand the behaviour of others. I submit
that the neural matching mechanism constituted by mirror neurons — or by equivalent neurons in humans — described in the present paper, is crucial to establish an
empathic link between different individuals.

However, action is certainly not the only medium through which we can empathize
with others. When we enter in relation with others there is a multiplicity of states that
we share with them. We share emotions, our body schema,[15] our being subject to pain
as well as to other somatic sensations. At this point we need a conceptual tool to capture the richness of the experiences we share with others.

I will introduce this conceptual tool as the *shared manifold* of intersubjectivity. I
posit that it is by means of this shared manifold that we recognize other human beings

---

[15] See Berlucchi and Aglioti (1997) for a discussion of the neural bases of body awareness.

as similar to us. It is just because of this shared manifold that intersubjective communication and mind-reading become possible.

The shared manifold can be operationalized at three different levels: A phenomenological level; a functional level; and a subpersonal level.

- The *phenomenological level* is the one responsible for the sense of similarity, of being individuals within a larger social community of persons like us, that we experience anytime we confront ourselves with other human beings. It could be defined also as the *empathic* level, provided that empathy is characterized in the 'enlarged' way I was advocating before. Actions, emotions and sensations experienced by others become meaningful to us because we can *share* them with them.
- The *functional level* can be characterized in terms of simulation routines, *as if* processes enabling models of others to be created.
- The *subpersonal level* is instantiated as the result of the activity of a series of mirror matching neural circuits. A dual mode of operation, an *expressive* mode and a *receptive* mode characterizes these circuits. The activity of these neural circuits is, in turn, tightly coupled with multi-level changes within body-states (see below).

So far I have provided evidence supporting the notion that the representation and understanding of the observed behaviour of others is made possible through a simulation mechanism that matches action observation and execution onto the same neural substrate. What about the other elements that compose the *phenomenological level* of the aforementioned *shared manifold*? What about sensations, pains, and emotions? My proposal is that also sensations, pains and emotions displayed by others can be empathized, and therefore understood, through a mirror matching mechanism.

Let us now see how this hypothesis can be supported by empirical data (this is what people expect from neurophysiologists . . .). Preliminary evidence suggests that in humans a 'mirror phenomenon' occurs in pain-related neurons. Hutchison *et al.* (1999) studied pain-related neurons in the human cingulate cortex. Cingulotomy procedures for the treatment of psychiatric disease provided an opportunity to examine prior to excision whether neurons in the anterior cingulate cortex of locally anesthetized awake humans respond to painful stimuli. It was noticed that a neuron that responded to noxious mechanical stimulation applied to the patient's hand also responded when the patient watched pinpricks being applied to the examiner's fingers. Both applied and observed painful stimuli elicited the same response in the same neuron. It is not difficult to characterize the behaviour of this human nervous cell during observation in the functional terms of *simulation, simulation of pain experience*.

A recent study published by Calder *et al.* (2000) shows that a Huntington patient who suffered damage to subcortical structures such as the insula and the putamen, is selectively impaired in detecting disgust in many different modalities, such as facial signals, non-verbal emotional sounds, and emotional prosody. The same patient is also selectively impaired in subjectively experiencing disgust and therefore in reacting appropriately to it. This clinical case, with all cautions required when single cases are involved, seems to suggest that once the subject has lost the capacity to *experience* and *express* a given emotion, the same emotion cannot be easily *represented* and *detected* in others.

As recently underlined by Jarvilehto (forthcoming), emotions are not an unnecessary addition to cognitive processes, but they constitute one of the earliest ways to acquire knowledge about the situation of the living organism, and therefore to reorganize it in the light of its relations with others.

This points to a strong interaction between emotion and action. We dislike things that we seldom touch, look at or smell. We do not 'translate' these things into motor schemas suitable to interact with them, which are likely 'tagged' with positive emotions, but rather into aversive motor schemas, likely 'tagged' with negative emotional connotations. The coordinated activity of sensorimotor and affective neural systems results in the simplification and automatization of the behavioural responses that living organisms are supposed to produce in order to survive.

I posit that the strict coupling between affect and sensorimotor integration can be one of the most powerful drive leading the developing individual to the achievement of progressively more 'distal' and abstract goals.

VII: Conclusions

To summarize, there is preliminary evidence that the same neural structures that are active during sensations and emotions are active also when the same sensations and emotions are to be detected in others. It appears therefore that a whole range of different 'mirror matching mechanisms' may be present in our brain. This subpersonal architecture of simulation, that we originally discovered and described in the domain of actions (diPellegrino *et al.*, 1992; Gallese *et al.*, 1996a; Rizzolatti *et al.*, 1996a), is likely a *basic* organizational feature of our brain. Damasio (1999) has clearly pointed out that one of the mechanisms enabling feelings of emotion to emerge, is the activation of neural '*as if* body loops'. These simulation mechanisms, by-passing the body proper through the *internal* activation of sensory body maps, create a representation of emotion-driven body-related changes. The activation of these '*as if* body loops' can likely be not only internally driven, but also triggered by the observation of other individuals (for a discussion of the relation between empathy and Simulation Theory, see Goldman, 1993b).

The discovery of mirror neurons in the monkey premotor cortex has unveiled a neural matching mechanism that, in the light of more recent findings, appears to be present also in a variety of non motor-related human brain structures. Different *simulation routines* are applied in different domains, being sustained by a dual-mode of operation (*active* and *passive*, *expressive* and *receptive*) of given brain structures.

How can we reconcile this *embodied* account of representation with reason and thought? As already pointed out by Hume (1978, ed. Selby-Bigge), inductive reasoning forms a large part of our explanatory approach to the world in which we live. By inductive reasoning, we can apply the results of our previous experiences to unprecedented events and novel states of affairs. Induction, although not necessarily inferentially sound, determines our pervasive tendency to detect cause–effect relations. I hope that at the end of my paper the reader will be able to appreciate how the inductive aspects or reasoning — considered by many theory-theorists to be at the basis of the human understanding of other minds — could be underpinned by the different embodied simulation routines unveiled by neuroscientific investigation, here briefly summarized.

Complex traits, such as mind-reading abilities, are the result of a long evolutionary process. It is reasonable to hypothesize that this evolutionary process proceeded along a line of continuity (see Gallese and Goldman, 1998; Gallese *et al.*, 2001b). Andrew Whiten (1996) has written:

> mind-reading is not telepathy. So, the recognition of another's state of mind must rest on observation of certain components within the complex of others' behaviour patterns together with their environmental context: that's all we can see. . . . This means that the contrast of mind-reading with behaviour-reading is not so straightforward as it may first appear.

Much of what we ascribe to the mind of others when witnessing their actions depends on the 'resonance mechanisms' that their actions trigger in us. The detection of intentions that we ascribe to observed agents and that we assume to underpin their behaviour is constrained by the necessity for an intersubjective link to be established. The shared manifold I described above determines and constrains this intersubjective link. It could be provocatively added that — quite opposite to what many theory-theorists maintain — explicit theorizing is the only strategy available when the embodied resonance mechanisms of the shared manifold are deficient, as likely occurring in the case of autism.

My conclusion is that the more we'll know about how our brain-body system works, the less remote the nature of thought and reasoning will appear from it.

Acknowledgment

The author wishes to thank Giacomo Rizzolatti, Thomas Metzinger, and Christian Keysers for their most valuable comments on an earlier version of this article. This work was supported by grants from MURST and HFSP to V.G.

References

Adolphs, R. (1999), 'Social cognition and the human brain', *Trends in Cognitive Sciences*, **3**, pp. 469–79.

Allison, T., Puce, A. and McCarthy, G. (2000), 'Social perception from visual cues: Role of the STS region', *Trends in Cognitive Sciences*, **4**, pp. 267–78.

Baron-Cohen, S. (1995), *Mindblindness: An Essay on Autism and Theory of Mind* (Cambridge, MA: MIT Press).

Berlucchi, G. and Aglioti, S. (1997), 'The body in the brain: Neural bases of corporeal awareness', *Trends in Neuroscience*, **20**, pp. 560–4.

Brothers, L., Ring, B. and Kling, A. (1990), 'Response of neurons in the macaque amygdala to complex social stimuli', *Behav. Brain Res.*, **41**, pp. 199–213.

Brugger, P., Kollias, S.S., Muri, R.M., Crelier, G. and Hepp-Reymond, M-C. (2000), 'Beyond re-membering: phantom sensations of congenitally absent limbs', *Proc. Natl. Acad. Sci. USA*, **97**, pp. 6167–72.

Buccino, G., Binkofski, F., Fink, G.R., Fadiga, L., Fogassi, L., Gallese, V., Seitz, R.J., Zilles, K., Rizzolatti, G. and Freund, H-J. (2001), 'Action observation activates premotor and parietal areas in a somatotopic manner: An fMRI study', *European Journal of Neuroscience*, **13**, pp. 400–4.

Byrne, R.W. (1995), *The Thinking Ape: Evolutionary Origins of Intelligence* (Oxford: OUP).

Byrne, R.W. and Russon, A.W. (1998), 'Learning by imitation: A hierarchical approach', *Behavioral and Brain Sciences*, **21**, pp. 667–721.

Byrne, R.W. and Whiten, A. (1988), *Machiavellian Intelligence: Social Expertise and the Evolution of Intellect in Monkeys Apes and Humans* (Oxford: Clarendon Press).

Calder, A.J, Keane, J., Manes, F., Antoun, N. and Young, A.W. (2000), 'Impaired recognition and experience of disgust following brain injury', *Nature Neuroscience*, **3**, pp. 1077–8.

Carey, D.P., Perrett, D.I. and Oram, M.W. (1997), 'Recognizing, understanding and reproducing actions' in *Action and Cognition*, ed. M. Jeannerod and J. Grafman (Elsevier Science BV: *Handbook of Neuropsychology*, vol 11, sect 16).

Carruthers O. and Smith P.K. (ed. 1996), *Theories of Theories of Mind* (Cambridge: CUP).

Cavada, C. and Goldman-Rakic, P.S. (1989), 'Posterior parietal cortex in rhesus monkey: II. Evidence for segregated corticocortical networks linking sensory and limbic areas with the frontal lobe', *Journal of Comparative Neurology*, **287**, pp. 422–45.

Churchland P.S., Ramachandran, V.S. and Sejnowski T.J. (1994), 'A critique of pure vision', in Large-Scale Neuronal Theories of the Brain, ed. C. Koch and J.L. Davis (Cambridge, MA: MIT Press).

Cochin, S., Barthelemy, C., Lejeune, B., Roux, S. and Martineau, J. (1998), 'Perception of motion and qEEG activity in human adults', Electroenc. Clin. Neurophysiol., 107, pp. 287–95.

Cutting, J.E., and Kozlowski, L.T. (1977), 'Recognizing friends by their walk: Gait perception without familiarity cues', Bull. Psychonomic Soc., 9, pp. 353–6.

Damasio, A.R. (1994), Descartes' Error (New York: G.P. Putnam's Sons).

Damasio, A.R. (1999), The Feeling of What Happens: Body and Emotion in the Making of Consciousness (New York: Harcourt Brace).

Decety, J. and Grèzes, J. (1999), 'Neural mechanisms subserving the perception of human actions', Trends in Cognitive Sciences, 3, pp. 172–8.

Decety, J., Grezes, J., Costes, N., Perani, D., Jeannerod, M., Procyk, E., Grassi, F. and Fazio, F. (1997), 'Brain activity during observation of actions: Influence of action content and subject's strategy', Brain, 120, pp. 1763–77.

Desimone, R. and Ungerleider, L. (1986), 'Multiple visual areas in the caudal superior temporal sulcus of the macaque', J. Comp. Neurol., 248, pp. 164–89.

di Pellegrino G., Fadiga L., Fogassi L., Gallese V. and Rizzolatti G. (1992), 'Understanding motor events: A neurophysiological study', Exp. Brain Res., 91, pp. 176–80.

Dromard, G. (1905), 'Etude psychologique et clinique sur l'échopraxie', J. Psychol. (Paris), 2, pp. 385–403.

Dubner, R. And Zeki, S. (1971), 'Response properties and receptive fields of cells in an anatomically defined region of the superior temporal sulcus in the monkey', Brain Res., 35, pp. 528–32.

Ellis, R. and Newton N. (2000), 'Editorial: The interdependence of consciousness and emotion', Consciousness and Emotion, 1, pp. 1–12.

Fadiga, L. and Gallese, V. (1997), 'Action representation and language in the brain', Theoretical Linguistics, 23, pp. 267–80.

Fadiga, L., Fogassi, L., Pavesi, G. and Rizzolatti, G. (1995), 'Motor facilitation during action observation: A magnetic stimulation study', J. Neurophysiol., 73, pp. 2608–11.

Fodor, J. (1981), Representations (Cambridge, MA: MIT Press).

Fodor, J. (1992), 'A theory of the child's theory of mind', Cognition, 44, pp. 283–96.

Fodor, J. (1994), The Elm and the Expert: Mentalese and its Semantics (Cambridge, MA: MIT Press).

Fogassi, L., Gallese, V., Fadiga, L. and Rizzolatti, G. (1998), 'Neurons responding to the sight of goal-directed hand/arm actions in the parietal area PF (7b) of the macaque monkey', Society of Neuroscience Abstracts, 24, p. 257.5.

Gallese, V. (1999), 'From grasping to language: Mirror neurons and the origin of social communication', in Towards a Science of Consciousness, ed. S. Hameroff, A. Kazniak and D. Chalmers (Cambridge, MA: MIT Press).

Gallese, V. (2000a), 'The acting subject: Towards the neural basis of social cognition', in Neural Correlates of Consciousness: Empirical and Conceptual Questions, ed. T. Metzinger (Cambridge, MA: MIT Press).

Gallese, V. (2000b), 'The inner sense of action: Agency and motor representations', Journal of Consciousness Studies, 7 (10), pp. 23–40.

Gallese, V. and Goldman, A. (1998), 'Mirror neurons and the simulation theory of mind-reading', Trends in Cognitive Sciences, 12, pp. 493–501.

Gallese, V., Fadiga, L., Fogassi, L. and Rizzolatti, G. (1996a), 'Action recognition in the premotor cortex', Brain, 119, pp. 593–609.

Gallese, V., Fadiga, L., Fogassi, L., Luppino, G. and Murata, A. (1996b), 'A parietal-frontal circuit for hand grasping movements in the monkey: Evidence from reversible inactivation experiments', in Parietal Lobe Contributions To Orientation In 3D-Space, ed. P. Thier and H.O. Karnath; Exp. Brain Res. Suppl. Series (Berlin-New York: Springer Publ.).

Gallese, V., Fogassi, L., Fadiga, L. and Rizzolatti, G. (2001a), 'Action representation and the inferior parietal lobule', in Attention and Performance XIX, ed. W. Prinz and B. Hommel (Oxford: OUP), in press.

Gallese, V., Ferrari, P.F., Kohler, E. and Fogassi, L. (2001b), 'The eyes, the hand, and the mind: Behavioral and neurophysiological aspects of social cognition', in The Cognitive Animal, ed. M. Bekoff, C. Allen and G. Burghardt (Cambridge, MA: MIT Press), in press.

Goldman, A. (1989), 'Interpretation psychologized', Mind and Language, 4, pp. 161–85.

Goldman, A. (1992), 'In defense of the simulation theory', Mind and Language, 7, pp. 104–19.

Goldman, A. (1993a), 'The psychology of folk psychology', Behavioral and Brain Sciences, 16, pp. 15–28.

Goldman, A. (1993b), Philosophical Applications of Cognitive Science (Boulder, CO: Westview Press).

Goldman, A. (2000), 'The mentalizing folk', in Metarepresentation, ed. D. Sperber (London: OUP).

Goldman, A. and Gallese, V. (2000), 'Reply to Schulkin', Trends in Cognitive Sciences, 4, pp. 255–6.

Gopnik, A. and Meltzoff, A.N. (1997), Words, Thoughts, and Theories (Cambridge, MA: MIT Press).

Gordon, R. (1986), 'Folk psychology as simulation', Mind and Language, 1, pp. 158–71.

Grafton, S. T., Arbib, M.A., Fadiga, L. and Rizzolatti, G. (1996), 'Localization of grasp representations in humans by PET: 2. Observation compared with imagination', Exp. Brain Res., 112, pp. 103–11.

Hari, R., Forss, N., Avikainen, S., Kirveskari, S., Salenius, S. and Rizzolatti, G. (1998), 'Activation of human primary motor cortex during action observation: A neuromagnetic study', *Proc. Natl. Acad. Sci. USA*, **95**, pp. 15061–5.

Harris, P. (1989), *Children and Emotion* (Oxford: Blackwell Publishers).

Hayes C. (1998), 'Theory of mind in nonhuman primates', *Behavioral and Brain Sciences*, **21**, pp. 101–48.

Hume, D. (1978), *A Treatise of Human Understanding*, ed. Selby-Bigge (Oxford: Oxford University Press).

Husserl, E. (1989), *Ideas Pertaining to a Pure Phenomenology and to a Phenomenological Philosophy, Second Book: Studies in the Phenomenology of Constitution* (Dordrecht: Kluwer Academic Publishers; Cited as Ideen II).

Hutchison, W., Davis, K., Lozano, A., Tasker, R. and Dostrovxky, J. (1999), 'Pain related neurons in the human cingulate cortex', *Nature Neuroscience*, **2**, pp. 403–5.

Jarvilehto, T. (forthcoming), 'Feeling as knowing, Part I: Emotion as reorganization of the organism-environment system', *Consciousness and Emotion* (accepted).

Jeannerod, M. (1994), 'The representing brain: neural correlates of motor intention and imagery', *Behavioral and Brain Sciences*, **17**, pp. 187–245.

Jeannerod, M. (1997), *The Cognitive Neuroscience of Action* (Oxford: Blackwell).

Jeannerod M., Arbib M.A., Rizzolatti G. and Sakata H. (1995), 'Grasping objects: The cortical mechanisms of visuomotor transformation', *Trends in Neuroscience*, **18**, pp. 314–20.

Jellema, T. and Perrett, D.I. (2001), 'Coding of visible and hidden actions', in *Attention and Performance XIX*, ed. W. Prinz and B. Hommel (Oxford: Oxford University Press), in press.

Kawato, M. (1997), 'Bidirectional theory approach to consciousness', in *Cognition, Computation and Consciousness*, ed. M. Ito, Y. Myashita and E.T. Rolls (Oxford: Oxford Univerity Press).

Kawato, M. (1999), 'Internal models for motor control and trajectory planning', *Neuroreport*, **9**, pp. 718–27.

Leslie, A.M. (1987), 'Pretence and representation: The origins of "theory of mind"', *Psychol. Rev.*, **94**, pp. 412–26.

Lhermitte, F., Pillon, B. and Serdaru, M. (1986), 'Human autonomy and the frontal lobes: I. Imitation and utilization behavior: A neuropsychological study of 75 patients', *Annals of Neurology*, **19**, 326–34.

Lipps, T. (1903a), *Grundlegung der Aesthetik* (Bamburg und Leipzig: W. Engelmann).

Lipps, T. (1903b), 'Einfulung, innere nachahmung und organenempfindung', *Archiv. F. die Ges. Psy.*, vol I, part 2 (Leipzig: W. Engelmann).

Matelli, M. and Luppino, G. (1997), 'Functional anatomy of human motor cortical areas', in *Handbook of Neuropsychology, vol. 11*, ed. F. Boller and J. Grafman (Elsevier Science B.V.).

Matelli, M., Luppino, G. and Rizzolatti, G. (1985), 'Patterns of cytochrome oxidase activity in the frontal agranular cortex of the macaque monkey', *Behavioral Brain Research*, **18**, pp. 125–37.

Matelli, M., Camarda, R., Glickstein, M. and Rizzolatti, G. (1986), 'Afferent and efferent projections of the inferior area 6 in the Macaque Monkey', *Journal of Comparative Neurology*, **251**, pp. 281–98.

Maunsell, J. and Van Essen, D. (1983), 'Functional properties of neurons in middle temporal visual area of the macaque monkey, 1: Selectivity for stimulus direction, speed, and orientation', *J. Neurophysiol.*, **49**, pp. 1127–47.

Mead, G.H. (1912), 'The mechanism of social consciousness', *Journal of Philosophy, Psychology and Scientific Methods*, **9**, pp. 401–6.

Mead, G.H. (1934), *Mind, Self, and Society* (Chicago: Chicago University Press).

Meltzoff, A.N. and Moore, M.K. (1977), 'Imitation of facial and manual gestures by human neonates', *Science*, **198**, pp. 75–8.

Meltzoff, A. (1995), 'Understanding the intentions of others: Re-enactment of intended acts by 18-month old children', *Developmental Psychology*, **31**, pp. 838–850.

Melzack, R., Israel, R., Lacroix, R. and Schultz, G. (1997), 'Phantom limbs in people with congenital limb deficiency or amputation in early childhood', *Brain*, **120**, pp. 1603–20.

Merleau-Ponty, M. (1962), *Phenomenology of Perception*, trans. C. Smith (London: Routledge).

Metzinger, T. (1993), *Subjekt und Selbstmodell* (Padeborn: Schoeningh).

Metzinger, T. (2000), 'The subjectivity of subjective experience: A representationalist analysis of the first-person perspective', in *Neural Correlates of Consciousness*, ed. T. Metzinger (Cambridge, MA: MIT).

Murata, A., Fadiga, L., Fogassi, L., Gallese, V., Raos, V. and Rizzolatti, G. (1997), 'Object representation in the ventral premotor cortex (Area F5) of the monkey', *J. Neurophysiol.*, **78**, pp. 2226–30.

Oram, M.W. and Perrett, D.I. (1994), 'Responses of anterior superior temporal polysensory (STPa) neurons to 'biological motion' stimuli', *Journal of Cognitive Neurosciences*, **6**, pp. 99–116.

Pacherie, E. (1999), '*Leibhaftigkeit* and representational theories of perception', in Petitot *et al.* (1999).

Panksepp, J. (2000), 'The neuro-evolutionary cusp between emotion and cognition: Implications for understanding consciousness and the emergence of a unified mind science', *Consciousness and Emotion*, **1**, pp. 17–56.

Perrett, D., Harries, M., Bevan, R., Thomas, S., Benson, P., Mistlin, A., Chitty, A., Hietanen, J. and Ortega, J. (1989), 'Frameworks of analysis for the neural representation of animate objects and actions', *J. Exp. Biol.*, **146**, pp. 87–113.

Perrett, D., Mistlin, A., Harries, M., Chitty, A. (1990), 'Understanding the visual appearance and conse-
    quence of hand actions', in *Vision and Action: The Control of Grasping*, ed. M. Goodale (Norwood, NJ:
    Ablex).
Petit, J-L. (1996), *Solipsisme et intersubjectivité: Quinze lecons sur Husserl et Wittgestein* (Paris: Eds. du Cerf).
Petit, J-L. (1997), *Les Neurosciences et la philosophie de l'action* (Paris: J. Vrin).
Petit, J-L. (1999), 'Constitution by movement: Husserl in light of recent neurobiological findings', in
    Petitot *et al.* (1999).
Petitot, J., Varela, F.J., Pachoud, B., and Roy, J-M. (ed. 1999), *Naturalizing Phenomenology* (Stanford,
    CA: Stanford University Press).
Petrides, M. and Pandya, D.N. (1984), 'Projections to the frontal cortex from the posterior parietal region
    in the rhesus monkey', *Journal of Comparative Neurology*, **228**, pp. 105–16.
Premack, D., and Woodruff, G. (1978), 'Does the chimpanzee have a theory of mind?', *Behav. Brain Sci.*,
    4, pp. 515–26.
Pylyshyn, Z.W. (1984), *Computation and Cognition: Toward a Foundation for Cognitive Science* (Cam-
    bridge, MA: MIT Press).
Ramachandran, V.S. (1993), 'Filling in gaps in perception II: Scotomas and phantom limbs', *Curr. Direct.
    Psychol. Sci.*, **2**, pp. 36–65.
Ramachandran, V.S. and Rogers-Ramachandran, D. (1996), 'Synaesthesia in phantom limbs induced
    with mirrors', *Proc. R. Soc. Lond. B. Biol. Sci.*, **263**, pp. 377–86.
Ramachandran, V.S. and Hirstein, W. (1998), 'The perception of phantom limbs', *Brain*, **121**,
    pp. 1603–30.
Rizzolatti, G. and Arbib, M.A. (1998), 'Language within our grasp', *Trends in Neuroscience*, **21**,
    pp. 188–94.
Rizzolatti G., Camarda R., Fogassi M., Gentilucci M., Luppino G. and Matelli M. (1988), 'Functional
    organization of inferior area 6 in the macaque monkey: II. Area F5 and the control of distal move-
    ments', *Exp. Brain Res.*, **71**, pp. 491–507.
Rizzolatti, G., Fadiga, L., Gallese, V. and Fogassi, L. (1996a), 'Premotor cortex and the recognition of
    motor actions', *Cog. Brain Res.*, **3**, pp. 131–41.
Rizzolatti, G., Fadiga, L., Matelli, M., Bettinardi, V., Paulesu, E., Perani, D. and Fazio, G. (1996b), 'Lo-
    calization of grasp representations in humans by PET: 1. Observation versus execution', *Exp. Brain
    Res.*, **111**, pp. 246–52.
Rizzolatti, G., Luppino, G. and Matelli, M. (1998), 'The organization of the cortical motor system: New
    concepts', *Electroencephalography and Clinical Neurophysiology*, **106**, pp. 283–96.
Rizzolatti, G., Fadiga, L., Fogassi, L. and Gallese, V. (1999), 'Resonance behaviors and mirror neurons',
    Arch. It. Biologie, **137**, pp. 83–99.
Rizzolatti, G., Fogassi, L. and Gallese, V. (2000), 'Cortical mechanisms subserving object grasping and
    action recognition: A new view on the cortical motor functions', in *The Cognitive Neurosciences*, Sec-
    ond Edition, ed. M.S. Gazzaniga (Cambridge, MA: MIT Press).
Rizzolatti, G., Fadiga, L., Fogassi, L. and Gallese, V. (2001), 'From mirror neurons to imitation: Facts and
    speculations', in The Imitative Mind: Development, Evolution and Brain Bases, ed. W. Prinz and A.
    Meltzoff (Cambridge: Cambridge University Press), in press.
Seltzer, B. and Pandya, D.N. (1984), 'Further observations on parieto-temporal connections in the rhesus
    monkey', *Experimental Brain Research*, **55**, pp. 301–12.
Sheets-Johnstone, M. (1999), *The Primacy of Movement* (Amsterdam, Philadelphia: John Benjamins).
Stein, E. (1964), *On the Problem of Empathy* (The Hague: Martinus Nijhoff; English translation).
Stengel, E., Vienna, M.D. and Edin, L.C.R.P. (1947), 'A clinical and psychological study of echo-
    reactions', *Journal of Mental Science*, **93**, pp. 598–612.
Tomasello, M., Kruger, A. and Rattner, H. (1993), 'Cultural learning', *Behav. Brain Sci.*, **16**, pp. 495–511.
Van Essen, D., Maunsell, J. and Bixby, J. (1981), The middle temporal visual area in the macaque:
    Myeloarchitecture, connections, functional properties, and topographic organization', *J. Comp.
    Neurol.*, **199**, pp. 293–326.
Whiten, A. (1996), 'When does smart behaviour reading become mindreading?', in *Theories of Theories
    of Mind*, ed. O. Carruthers and P.K. Smith (Cambridge: Cambridge University Press).
Whiten, A. and Ham, R. (1992), 'On the nature and evolution of imitation in the animal kingdom: Reap-
    praisal of a century of research', *Adv. Study Behav.*, **21**, pp. 239–83.
Wolpert, D.M. (1997), 'Computational approaches to motor control', *Trends in in Cognitive Sciences*, **1**,
    pp. 209–16.
Wolpert, D.M., Ghahramani, Z. and Jordan, M.I. (1995), 'An internal model for sensorimotor integra-
    tion', *Science*, **269**, pp. 1880–2.
Zeki, S. (1974), 'Functional organization of a visual area in the posterior bank of the superior temporal
    sulcus of the rhesus monkey', *J. Physiol.* (London), **236**, pp. 549–73.
Zeki, S. (1993), *A Vision of the Brain* (Oxford: Blackwell).
Zeki, S. and Shipp, S. (1988), 'The functional logic of cortical connections', *Nature*, **355**, pp. 311–17.

Jonathan Cole

Empathy Needs a Face

The importance of the face is best understood, it is suggested, from the effects of visible facial difference in people. Their experience reflects the ways in which the face may be necessary for the interpersonal relatedness underlying such 'sharing' mind states as empathy. It is proposed that the face evolved as a result of several evolutionary pressures but that it is well placed to assume the role of an embodied representation of the increasingly refined inner states of mind that developed as primates became more social, and required more complex social intelligence.

The consequences of various forms of facial disfigurement on interpersonal relatedness and intersubjectivity are then discussed. These narratives reveal the importance of the face in the development of the self-esteem that seems a prerequisite of being able to initiate, and enter, relationships between people. Such experiences are beyond normal experience and, as such, require an extended understanding of the other: to understand facial difference requires empathy. But, in addition, it is also suggested that empathy itself is supported by, and requires, the embodied expression and communication of emotion that the face provides.

I: Introduction — Affinity and Understanding

An 'affinity between certain things, by virtue of which they are similarly . . . affected by the same influence'. So sympathy is defined by the *Shorter Oxford English Dictionary* (1983) in its first usage in 1579. Later, in 1662, came the more pertinent use for the present discussion, 'the quality or state of being affected by the condition of another with a feeling similar or corresponding to that of another or others; the fact or capacity of entering into or sharing the feelings of another'. In contrast, empathy, 'the power of projecting one's personality into, and so *fully understanding*, the object of contemplation' [my italics], was not defined, by the *OED*, until 1912, though Sober and Wilson (1998) date it a little earlier, in 1909, from the German, *Einfühlung*.[1]

From these simple definitions, empathy and sympathy are close, and indeed overlap. Sympathy involves an identification and similarity of feeling with another. Empathy, though a closer and more intimate process, does not necessarily involve such an emotional correspondence, though usually it does. A clinical psychologist may try to understand a criminal by an empathetic approach without being

---

[1] It is obviously arrogant in a consideration of the etymology of a word to only consider its English language origins.

Journal of Consciousness Studies, **8**, No. 5–7, 2001, pp. 51–68

sympathetic to him: as a doctor I may sympathize with the plight of a patient without being able, completely, to place myself in their position and empathize with them.

In this brief review I will consider, primarily, the role and importance of the face in the development and sustenance of intersubjectivity and empathy. I will consider two perspectives. First, the parallel strands of evidence on the evolution of the face, the importance of larger social groups and of social intelligence in the evolution of man, and the role of the face in the development of theory of mind. After this theoretical — and largely speculative — melange I will go on to consider some consequences of facial difference on self–other balance that reveals, uniquely, the importance of an embodied self for the social interaction that underlies intersubjectivity. I will argue that the face, as a visible projection of self and of affective mind, is crucial for many social encounters.

II: The Demilitarization of the Face

In my book, *About Face*, I gave an account of the evolution of the face from the front end of fish to the exquisitely mobile, individually unique and expressive representations of self it is in man (Cole, 1998).[2] A single sheet of muscle covering the head of cold-blooded vertebrates acted for respiratory function and to open and close the mouth. This muscle divided so that in mammals the facial muscles allow movement in the face for sucking and chewing (and more recently, in evolutionary terms, for more complex display). Chewing required more mobile jawbones, lips and cheeks and did not require such a large opening mouth. To place manageable amounts of food in the mouth depended on the use of arms and forepaws to present, acquire and parcel such small amounts of food. The face, therefore, followed the development of forelimbs and probably the adoption of an upright posture.

In parallel with this, the senses of smell and touch, so dominant in 'earlier' animals, became less important as a more distant sense, vision, increased in importance. In a more athletically challenging environment, tree dwelling for instance, more frontal-facing eyes, allowing binocular vision, developed. And once smell and touch were no longer dominant, large facial hairs were unnecessary and the muscles controlling them were available for other facial movement and became smaller and more finely controlled. Whilst warm bloodedness may have allowed the softer more malleable skin essential for facial expression, in the primates the skin round the mouth also became more mobile allowing the alterations in facial posture or facial expressions. And to see these movements, a denuded, bare face evolved.

The reduced jawbone and forehead, bare face, forward-facing eyes and use of muscles for expression, are what Daniel McNeill, memorably, has called the demilitarization of the face (McNeill, 1998).

As McNeill also points out, the evolution of the face may have required not only an upright posture to free the forelimbs for manipulation; an upright posture also meant that the animal was slower and had to depend on something other than power and brawn for its survival. The development of the face is linked with the evolution, within a skull freed from the need for a large crushing jaw, of a refined and expanded brain. He suggests that the human face finally arrived around 130,000 years ago. It is of interest, however, that we share some facial expressions, the appeasement and

---

[2]   One wonders what genetic mechanism is used to generate millions of subtly different faces, and for our being attuned to them visually.

genuine enjoyment smiles, for instance, with nonhuman primates from which we parted 4.5 to 6 million years ago.

III: New Faces, Larger Brains?

In parallel with the anatomical evolution of the face came the evolution of an elaborated social structure, which allowed a larger social group and may have been a key for the evolutionary success of man as a species. Nick Humphrey (1986), after studying groups of gorillas in Rwanda in the early 1970s, wondered why, when food was easily and plentifully available, they had developed such large brains (which require a large amount of food to maintain and so which have a large evolutionary cost). He wrote:

> Life in the forest seems to pose so few problems for these apes precisely because the gorilla family, as a social unit, is so well adapted to it. . . . A gorilla infant does not have to discover what is good or bad to eat; his mother teaches him.
>
> The problems of creating and maintaining such a stable group are quite another matter. They know each other intimately, they know their place. Nonetheless, there are endless small disputes about social dominance.
>
> The intelligence required to survive socially is something of a quite different order to that needed to cope with the material world. Social intelligence is clearly the key to the great ape's biological success. . . . Suddenly, I saw the animals with new eyes. I realized that, for them too, their problems were probably primarily social ones.

If one reason for the evolution of primates is the selective advantage a large social group brought (protection, division of labour, pack hunting), then such groups required a constantly reinforced social structure, and, apparently, a social structure entirely different to that of, say, bees and ants. It was based on social intelligence and interrelatedness between its members. The cognitive skill required to remember and service many such relationships must have been large and may have been a reason for the development of larger brains. Robin Dunbar has provided evidence that the relative size of primates increases with the size of their social group (Dunbar, 1990).

The increasingly complex behaviours necessary to develop and maintain these relationships may have required new and subtler ways of communication between individuals and, indeed, the development of more complex cognitive capacities within the larger brains. This seems to have required that social intelligence recognized internal mental states within others, and this, in turn, may have required a recognition that these states are similar to those we have ourselves. In other words, a primitive theory of mind may have been required.

In a beautifully clear account, Simon Baron-Cohen relates the necessary conditions for building a theory of mind (Baron-Cohen, 1995). He suggests a model with four mechanisms; an intentionality detector, an eye detection detector, a shared attention mechanism and, lastly, a theory of mind module.

Innate within us humans, he suggests, there is an 'intentionality detector' which allows us to distinguish the motion of external objects, or animate beings, in terms of volitional mental states. This allows the crucial distinction to be made between whether motion was caused by an animate being or not. Then this motion may be interpreted in terms of the mover's goal or desire.

Whereas the 'intentionality detector' can operate through touch or sound as well as vision, the second, the 'eye direction detector', only works through vision. There are known to be potent neurophysiological mechanisms allowing one animal to detect another's eyes, to know if the eyes are looking at them or away, and then from this to know whether their gaze is mutual or not. The next step is to know that another's eyes are sharing in your view or ideas. The 'shared attention mechanism' allows this by knowledge that the object of attention is shared, say, by a parent. This requires constant feedback that *my* object is *her* object of attention, so that both the object of attention and the mother's eyes must be monitored. Similarly, the three mechanisms must relate to each other, so that shared attention allows information about, for instance, intentionality. The last step for Baron-Cohen is for the development of a 'theory of mind mechanism'; something that allows inference of a full range of mental states to another, so that behaviour can be read in terms of the mental states of volition (desire and goal), and epistemy (pretending, thinking, imagining, etc.).

Gaze direction is stressed as a way into another's mind. Baron-Cohen and others interested in the origin of the theory of mind focus on the eyes but less on the whole face as a gestalt. But, arguably, we do not only look at eyes. Birds and snakes, after all, can do this and react differently towards people according to their gaze direction. We go further than mutual gaze; we interpret others' behaviour in mentalistic ways that nonhuman primates do not. One way this quantum leap of mental development may have arisen is by increasing the amount of subtle mind states that may be seen not just from the eyes but also from the face as a whole in humans. The face, then, may be a necessary part of a development of a theory of mind.

For Peter Hobson, a difficulty for models of the genesis of theory of mind is in their origin; how might cognitive states be inferred in one mind from another, or how might a person conceptualize his own mental state as a precondition of ascribing similar states to others (Hobson, 1993).[3] For Hobson, the solution for this is to avoid a cognitive primacy and, instead, to suggest that an *affective, embodied* origin for others having similar states of feeling to oneself, i.e., for intersubjectivity itself. Difficulties in calibrating a mental state in one as being the same as in another may be avoided if there are observable criteria for some mental states. Anger, for instance, is not only a subjective private inner state but must also be observable in facial, gestural and vocal expression. Before an intellectual, cognitive, understanding of another, there was a more emotional, affective reaching towards through an innate interpersonal relatedness. In the beginning was not the word but the feeling. If this is true then the crucial role of the face in delineating affective mind states of another may be seen. For Hobson, as for Wittgenstein, happiness or grief is not cognitively disencoded from another's posture or gesture, but is shown explicitly and innately on the face.

> We describe a face immediately as sad . . . even when we are unable to give any other description of the features. . . . We see emotion. — As opposed to what? — We do not see facial contortions and make the inference that he is feeling joy, grief, boredom. We describe a face immediately as sad, radiant, bored, even when we are unable to give any

[3] This parallels arguments about the origins of consciousness. For many it may have arisen from precognitive awareness of various states, including internal ones of proprioception (Bermudez, 1998; Damasio, 1999). In contrast, for Edmund Rolls, full reflective consciousness is a unitary, higher-order, thought system. Feelings, for instance, could then only emerge subsequent to consciousness (Rolls, 1999).

other description of the features. Grief, one would like to say, is personified in the face. This is essential to what we call 'emotion'. . . . The content of an emotion — here one imagines something like a picture. The human face might be called such a picture. . . . (Wittgenstein, 1980).[4]

For Hobson, the development of ways into the minds of others was not through the development, initially, of knowledge of another's cognitive states. Instead, as increasingly complex inner states evolved, they were revealed, expressed and, in part, experienced through the body in an affective domain. And with their development came the need for an increasingly eloquent bodily means of communication. Affective states were shown directly to the other in a manner of which increasingly sophisticated facial expression was an important part. Perception of, and understanding of, the other was, and is, *embodied.*

More than this, however, facial expressions evolved not simply to display or communicate but to share. Hobson wrote,

the perception is not a two-stage process of which the first stage is the perception of . . . behavioural or bodily form, and the second is an intellectually based attribution of meaning. Rather, the perception is of the meaning itself. . . . To perceive a smile is to be inclined to feel certain things (Hobson, 1993).

This echoes Wittgenstein once more,

for a child to perceive a smile as a smile is for the child to be drawn into a quality of relatedness to the smiling person, such that the child is inclined to smile. . . . 'Would [a] fixed smile really be a smile? And why not? — I might not be able to react as I do to a smile. Maybe it would not make me smile myself (Wittgenstein, 1980).

The face, then, may have evolved not simply to display complex affective inner states but for those to influence the observer to feel the same. Here in the face, then, theory of mind, affective states, intersubjectivity, sympathy and empathy seem mutually dependent and interweaved. Perhaps, you may think, I have overstated the case. Perhaps. But to some extent my thinking has been influenced by the experience of those with profound problems with their faces and the consequent difficulties they have encountered with interpersonal relatedness and self esteem. From such accounts the importance of the face for the ability to go out into the world and interchange with others is revealed in ways otherwise not available.

IV: Living with Facial Difference

Thus far my arguments have been theoretical and concerned with our past and our origins. My main work, though, has been to explore the consequences of facial loss. It is very difficult to understand how important the face is because our faces are usually given. One way is to consider the experience of those with facial visible difference. From those for whom normal social interaction is not possible because of facial problems is revealed the importance of the face for empathy, intersubjectivity and, indeed, a normal self-esteem. To draw out such accounts I sat and listened to the stories of people with facial disfigurement, neurological disease and congenital problems with expression. Such an approach is subjective and individual, and large numbers of

---

[4] One cannot suggest that emotions are only embodied on the face, obviously bodily posture and gesture are important too. But in humans the face is perhaps the most expressive area of emotional embodiment and the area we attend to in this respect.

subjects cannot be encompassed. Such a narrative approach sits uneasily alongside more objective empirical science. Despite this it seems essential to approach a full understanding of what the face does and is.

In our normal social interaction we have conversations, interchanges of information and of feelings by two-way interactions with a give and take between people. At their best, people do this with a natural effortless flow, as people loop experience feelings and opinions between them. In such exchanges, Merleau-Ponty's suggestion that 'I live in the facial expression of the other, as I feel him living in mine' (Merleau-Ponty, 1964), appears pertinent. In these relationships and situations there is a subjective absence of a sense of self. Any sense of this that we do feel may have its origin in the way other people reflect our social competence in their response to us. In a way, true social competence leads to an attentional absence of oneself, as Leder has suggested (Leder, 1990). Those with facial difference, being aware of their visibility, may never experience such an absence. But they do have other and more distressing absences; absences of confidence and, at times, absences of relatedness and relationship with others.

In my earlier work I adopted a structure based on individual's narrative accounts. I structured the book according to the problem and person focussed on, whether it was someone with late-onset blindness (when faces suddenly vanish after a lifetime of immersion in them), autism (when faces are hardly encompassed at all), or congenital facial problems (when people's whole personality and experience may be overshadowed by that problem). In the present account I will try to show what may underlie alterations in self–other balance that lead to a lack of effortless intersubjectivity.

1. Facial difference and stigma

In my earlier work, concerned to understand the subjective effect of facial difference, I sat with people and listened, trying to put myself in their position (Cole 1998). With John Hull, for instance, who was blinded in his forties, I sat in a small room, straining to get nearer and nearer his face, feeling a little guilty that I was gazing so closely. I knew he could not know I was doing this, and that my own face was absent from him. Talking with Donna Williams, in contrast, with autism, no facial conversation took place and I sat at a table looking at the wall in front of me. She walked round me talking to, but never looking at, me. It was similarly awkward conversing with a woman with a facial disfigurement, so neither of us used much mutual gaze.

I wanted to understand their situation and position as a person, and I hope we sat as two equals. As such, stigma about our difference was absent from our conversation. As a consequence I think I may have failed to give the effect of stigma on people with facial difference sufficient weight. Stigma associated with illness and disease is well researched and understood. But having a visible facial difference can be more shocking and upsetting than a problem elsewhere on the body, partly because the face is always visible, but also because the face seems more a part of our self than, say, a leg, or even a hand. Not surprisingly, prejudice against people with the largest differences, say after burns to the face, or cancer surgery (as James Partridge [1990] has written), was also greatest when meeting new people, so that for some actually going out may be a continual trial. (Partridge suffered severe burns to the face and body as a young man and described his recovery and social rehabilitation in the book cited. He has gone on to help many with facial difference through an organization, also called Changing Faces, that he helped start.) One man with a disfigurement told him,

> I avoid public transport, I avoid going to parties, I avoid going anywhere where I don't know people. I avoid going anywhere I will be stared at, I cannot cope, I just turn my face away. I find myself so unattractive that I feel I should not be mixing with others, I feel as if I am letting the side down. I get nervous, and that makes the other person nervous — I give out bad vibes. [All subsequent quotes are taken from Cole, 1998, unless otherwise stated.]

Problems with facial difference vary with age. I recently went to a conference for those born with Moebius Syndrome, a congenital absence of the ability to move the muscles of the face. The early problems were in feeding (without the ability to close or purse the lips or suck), swallowing and choking. As the children grew so problems with speech had to be addressed, since labial sounds like 'b', and 'p' were difficult. But for young children in small loving family groups, there were no problems with stigma. First school can lead to the beginnings of being considered different, but young children are very accepting. Often, it seemed, problems with stigma arose later when the social groups one normally belong to widen and enlarge. Then these difficulties mount with adolescence and the awful problems of the first kiss and romance. For those with Moebius, adolescence can be a great trial: their difference becomes more significant and the distance between them and their peers widens. One man with Moebius told me,

> The lack of the smile is a scourge in the teenage years and is more of a problem than anything else, more than the eating in public. Being misunderstood, not being able to register recognition or salutation, particularly with girls.

Unwittingly, parents can reinforce this; one person with Moebius relating the pain she felt when her mother made an assumption that her daughter would not marry.[5] We normally learn a certain social confidence and competence. This may be beyond some, though of course not all, of those with facial problems. It may even disappear once formed. At the Moebius conference it was clear that the adults with Moebius and the (unaffected) parents of children with Moebius were two completely different groups. The latter talked of their young kids doing well socially and being happy, once the practical problems of feeding and speech, etc. had been addressed. The adults with Moebius were far more circumspect and aware of their continuing, and at times apparently, insuperable difficulties in creating and maintaining a social life. A group of researchers following a cohort of people with Moebius over some years discussed how anxiety in young people might be related to the increased incidence of depression in adults. A challenge is to maintain the confidence as children grow and enter the wider world.

At the meeting I spent much of my time with a group of a dozen or so adult people with Moebius. Relaxed with themselves they were able to laugh and joke, enjoying a few days when they were not different and not looked at by strangers. For the problems associated with stigma are not inherently problems of those with the facial difference, but problems projected onto them by others; the responses of others gnawed at the self-confidence of those with the disfigurement.

James Partridge (personal communication) has suggested that the stigma for those with facial disfigurement may have become worse over the last century or so. As

---

[5] In the UK Moebius Support Group they have several women who are married but only know of one man.

health care improves, and also as the influence of the visual media widens, so the standards for acceptable faces may have narrowed. A hundred years ago we might have seen far more disease around and so have been more accepting of it. But also the social groups we lived in were smaller and we were more likely to know those we met well. As we get to know someone, what they are like as a whole person becomes more important and their more superficial visible self less so. In a world in which we increasingly meet more new people, and know them less well, first impressions and appearance, the immediate visible self, may count for more and place an additional burden on those with facial and other physical differences.

2. Altered ability to communicate emotion on the face (or to read it in others?)

An unusual face may lead to a puzzlement or prejudice more connected with self than, say, a broken leg, as we have discussed. Not simply because of the unusual and, to some, unsightly appearance but because the problem with the face prevents easy expression of some emotions. This may be most easily understood from those with Moebius. These individuals are unable to move the muscles of their face at all and so cannot register amusement, sadness, happiness or anything facially. James,[6] a man in his fifties who has Moebius, told me

> I have sometimes thought, when I have felt low, if only other people knew what I am thinking. Other people may not want to have thoughts that they're feeling portrayed to others. I know that none of my thoughts will ever be seen by others on my face.

Note that James talked of thoughts on the face, not feelings. This will be taken up later. One family with an adolescent son with the condition has taken to verbalizing all their emotions to try and make him do the same. Many of those with Moebius have had to cope with the problems of not being able to register emotion on the face and the distancing effect this has on their ability to relate with others. The way out is to communicate through intonation of voice, through the words themselves and through gesture. But my impression is that these channels are interrelated and that without facial expression feelings themselves may take on a more intellectual aspect (see section below about Parkinson's Disease). Skilful though many — most — with Moebius are at displaying emotion through laughter and gesture, the absence of facial movement remains a most profound difference. They also have to cope with difficulties with eye gaze that means that they cannot glance at another quickly from the corner of their eye. To look at another requires movement of the head, which is slower and always invites the other to look back.

For those blind as mature adults the situation is very different. They have built up relationships before their loss of sight. They are left, however, not being able to see their loved ones and bereft of others' facial expressions. For John Hull the loss of visual representation of his wife and family was a terrible loss. He swore to himself that he would never lose a photographic memory of them, but over months and years this did occur. It was this loss, rather than his loss of sight itself, which precipitated his most depressed period. Then, slowly, he realized just how much affective communication was in the voice and found ranges of emotion in speech he had previously hardly needed to be aware of. It was not just mood or emotion that was the problem. He had to find ways of building up pictures of others using sound alone and worked

---

[6]   James is a pseudonym. Subjects' anonymity has been preserved where appropriate.

on this for several years. But, even then, he was still aware of the losses his blindness had imposed and the distance it had introduced between him and his family:

> Anger, impatience; such emotions are more easily expressed in the voice than thought-fulness or sadness. It is very difficult to detect sadness. The emotional range *is* narrowed. This is something I feel most acutely when I'm telling stories to my children and an even worse time is when I want to listen to music with them. That is an acute frustration. I'm not getting the feedback that allows that refreshment and rejuvenation. I would love my son Tom, say, to come and listen to a Beethoven violin concerto but he would be sitting there next to me and I have no way of knowing what it means to him. When it's finished I'd say at the end, 'Well what's it like?' and he'd say 'Great' and walk off and I still wouldn't know.

> Not knowing about tears is worse than not knowing about smiling. Tears are silent. Its perhaps more important to know about tears than about smiles. Tears take longer; laugh-ter is so ephemeral. I think there's no doubt that the loss of the [ability to see the] face is a profound loss. A deeply dehumanising loss.

3. *Altered perception of character and selfhood associated with facial difference*

Physiognomy has enjoyed a long and disreputable history. The fallacy of facial fea-tures telling of the personality of character is deeply ingrained in us, despite having no truth scientifically. Close-set eyes are no more likely to convey untrustworthiness than blue eyes or blond hair, except that occasionally we can create reality socially, and if we all treat someone as being untrustworthy then he may eventually see himself as that.[7] To some extent altered perception by others of a person with a facial disfig-urement is what underlies stigma, though, as Sander Gilman has pointed out, at vari-ous times in history facial scars from duelling were not a handicap but a distinct advantage (Gilman, 1999). My concern here, however, is to consider the effects that changes in facial expression, with no disfigurement, may have on the perception of oneself by others.

In some cases of Parkinson's Disease, a neurological disease associated with tremor, stiffness and difficulty in initiating movement, the person comes to have reduced facial expression, giving him or her a rather fixed disinterested expression. This, coupled with the reduced bodily movements associated with the syndrome, leads some with the condition to be seen as dull and boring. Iona Lister, a speech ther-apist, was working with a lady with Parkinson's disease.

> Chatting with her, I must confess, was stodgy and heavy going — just like the disease. Towards the end of the session she mentioned her interest in art and she described some of the pictures she painted. She also mentioned that she used to be involved in belly danc-ing! Once I had left her I realized how surprised I was that she had such an interesting set of hobbies — as though in my mind I had decided that she was a rather dull, colourless person. I then realised why my impressions had been formed and was so amazed and ashamed. I was judging her by her inability to be animated facially, and I should have known better. I went onto a case conference about this lady and all my colleagues described her as being drab and uninterested.

> Her whole persona, which had been projected through a lack of facial animation, for her speech was normal — not even monotonous as some people with Parkinson's become

---

[7] See Hacking (1995) for a consideration of one aspect of this 'looping'. There are several reports of peo-ple asking for plastic surgery to correct facial features simply because other people view them as being, say, aggressive, when they are not. Such surgery can have excellent results.

— had led to various assumptions about her lifestyle. It was only because I had listened that I learnt about the richness of her life and then realized, not without some shame, how and why I had judged her. She was unaware of the way she was perceived. I managed to introduce it in what I hoped was a sensitive manner and she was interested in my observations. She came back a couple of weeks later saying that she had decided it was a problem. We decided to work on her facial expression, consciously, together.

Iona became involved with the local Parkinson's Disease Society, which met once a month for a social, and immediately saw the social dynamics of the meeting.

I didn't set out to observe this, but it came to me with a thundering clarity, and I saw the same on many subsequent occasions. It was that if, in the group of 40 attendees and people with Parkinson's, there might be five with facial problems, and people tended not to gravitate towards those. Not only that, but often their partner rather than them would be asked how they were. People would ask these facially impoverished people questions that demanded 'yes, no' answers rather than more expansive ones, so avoiding an engaged conversation. There was a definite movement away from these people at the meetings. Perhaps people did not get any feedback from the patients and so did not feel engaged and encouraged.

People with Parkinson's have a social isolation on two levels. One a static unattractiveness, in that they are just sitting there, and the human face, when not putting on quirky unusual expressions as it does when there are people around, tends to become set and to look rather petulant and glum. That is what people actually see in a resting face in these patients. Then when the face does start to move it is elaborating all sorts of things about what we are saying. For example, as I sit here talking you are reading my movements. That adds to the attractiveness. The face complements the subtlety of communication: wrong clues can actually alter meaning. If you say, 'Nice to see you', with no facial movement or with the wrong movement, it can actually appear sarcastic or whatever. These patients are patronized, isolated and lose acknowledgement of themselves.

Iona subsequently produced a video seeking to help those with Parkinson's reconnect with faces to use them again emotionally. In it she shows how to focus attention on the face; for example, by stroking and touching it, and by using mirrors to practice facial expression. In some cases this has led to re-establishment of an enjoyment in, and relish of, life as people are re-awakened. Their problem was not terminal and not related to a facial disfigurement *per se*, but to a loss of facial expression which led to profound alterations in the way a person is perceived by others and in a subsequent interpersonal distancing and loss of relatedness.

This may not always have been understood or realized by the person actually involved. One man with Parkinson's who had been through Iona's treatment discussed his feelings after eight years or so of Parkinson's.

I had, by this time, found myself less able to join in conversations. I had never had that before and I had no idea why. I still did not know my face was affected at all. Seeing Iona's video was very dramatic, I immediately recognised myself as being like the woman in the video. I immediately understood that the face could have explained some of the problems. I did the exercises on my face in front of a mirror. I had always thought that I was quite mobile with the face, but quickly realized this was no longer the case. I freed up my face and then it moved again automatically. Then, when I went back to talking with people, I noticed that I was moving my face more. Since the exercises I have been a bit more confident, more aware of where my face is than before. I realize now that I was I looking a little vacant and that is why people were not involving me in conversation.

We may be aware of the stigma associated with facial visible difference, but it is clear that there are also effects of a loss of expression that may have consequences just as profound, and may also be compounded by their not being perceived. Most of us pride ourselves on our abilities to 'read' people. Here, what we read, facial responsiveness or expressivity, had altered leading to wild erroneous conclusions about a person's whole self.

4. Being less available to others

In his moving account of his 'descent' into quadriplegia, Robert Murphy described how he wanted to retreat from others and from a social existence (Murphy, 1987). Acquired problems do make one turn inward and become more self-concerned. When the problem is facial this can lead to a complete turning from others, as was seen in the person with a facial disfigurement who spoke with James Partridge. Others with facial problems have also described the way they have found it almost impossible to engage in conversation with others at all. If one has a disfigurement and cannot bear to look at another, because of the way they look at you, then one loses an important way to discern how another is viewing and approaching you, and can, in turn, lose the ability to take the initiative. People with facial disfigurement often become passive, only ever reacting to others and never daring to control conversations and interactions themselves. One person with Moebius told me,

> It's much more difficult to go out to people. Some days I could go out and see four or five people, some days I'd sit at home, not able to do it. I interpreted that as my being not very good at the job. I was judgmental on myself about this.

They may also be unaware of the facial origin of these problems. This was apparent in the story of the person with Parkinson's, when a slow deterioration in facial mobility had occurred. But it was also the case with some of those with Moebius, a far more obvious facial difference and even in some with facial disfigurement. James told me on several occasions that he felt that he had put his poor social skills down to his own inadequacy and that he had not related them to his facial problems until this was pointed out.

> I now realize that some things which may have been due to the condition I felt were just down to me. Rather than saying that the condition has made life difficult, I have been saying I have made life difficult. It was *my* fault. I have failed.

One may suggest that the cause of the problem was repressed. It says much about the state of mind of people with such visible differences that they can withdraw so far from them and from their embodied selves.

5. Reduced ability to experience emotions?

Talking with some people with Moebius it is apparent that, without the reinforcement of a full range of both positive and negative, subtle and less subtle, emotions we receive from others via facial conversations, or, possibly, from the elaboration within the body of those emotions,[8] the experience of those emotions themselves may be

---

[8] Here, I am not suggesting that an emotion has to be expressed and experienced in the body to be experienced at all, as William James and, to some extent, Damasio have argued (James, 1950; Damasio, 1994). But those with Moebius do lead me to suspect that without expression on the body, and the communication with others and the feedback inherent in this, emotional experience itself may be different. It seems difficult to imagine emotional looping between people without some embodiment of emotions. During telephone talking, emotional expression continues in the visual absence of the

reduced. One mother told me that her young son with Moebius was never excited, even at Christmas or his own birthday party. When upset he would bottle it up and perhaps get back at his brothers hours or days later, rather than immediately. James again

> I have been told I am a very placid person. My sister said, 'You never cried, you were a very good child in that sense'. I had all these things, operations, manipulations, splints, but I can't know now how much was a placidness of nature and how much was a suppression of feeling.

Without the ability to communicate emotion, facially and fully, it was as though the experience of the emotions might be diluted and reduced. James certainly felt this, describing an almost disconnection from his emotions and from others. And with, maybe, a reduced capacity for sympathy or empathy

> I have a notion which has stayed with me over much of my life — that it is possible to live in your head, entirely in my head. I think I get trapped in my mind or my head. I sort of *think* happy or I *think* sad, not really saying or recognizing actually feeling happy or feeling sad. Perhaps I have had a difficulty in recognizing that which I'm putting a name to is not a thought at all but it is a feeling, maybe I have to intellectualize mood. I have to say this thought is a happy thought and therefore I am happy. When there are things that are sad I tell the person that I feel very sorry for you but I'm *thinking* that rather than *feeling* it.
>
> Of course, since I have never been able to move my face, I've never associated movement of the face with feeling of an emotion. If I have expressed any emotion I must have spoken it or I might put my arm around someone, of course. Coming back to my job, [as a priest], however, I am not required to feel what I am trying to express.

If the subjective experience of emotion may differ with congenital facial immobility, this might, to some extent, be because such facial interaction and reinforcement from others has never been experienced. One person with an acquired and temporary bilateral facial paralysis (Bell's palsy) told me that his condition had led to him actually feeling less

> I suppose I don't feel constantly happy, but then I don't feel sad. . . . I feel almost as if I am in a limbo between feelings — just non-emotional. . . . I don't know . . . it is within myself, an emotional limbo. I still feel happy to see or hear something I like, but I don't think that I feel it as much because I am not actually smiling. I have started to write a diary. . . . Writing it out helps a lot. Such and such has happened and I *feel* this. Writing allows me to express.

If emotional feeling may alter with facial problems, this may not simply be a lessening or reduction. Talking with some people with Moebius Syndrome, it appears that the ability to express emotions, both positive and negative, is a necessary part of learning to control them, and express them, with the correct force and duration. As children, during tantrums and heightened episodes of emotion, we may be learning, from others, how to express and to experience feelings. A calm, quiescent, 'good' childhood may not prepare us for our subsequent experience. One person with Moebius Syndrome has been hospitalized on several occasions because of episodic dyscontrol. She had no way of expressing or controlling her emotions until they erupted; no way of telling people of frustration or anger until they took her over completely.

---

other. Perhaps email conversations and mobile phone text messages allow this more. It may be pertinent, however, that email is used by people with autism: it allows communication without a sense of the other.

6. Self–other balance

Normally in relationships and conversations there is give and take, with turn taking and a balance between what people say and not say, reveal or not reveal, in words and looks. In mutual gaze we experience another person in a more extensive and intimate way than most other animals. In agreeing to enter such relationships, and so frequently in revealing and thoughts and feelings, we expose our emotions and ourselves. Levinas has discussed how, in such face-to-face relationships, we must always see the other face as being foreign and, whilst we can gain much reinforcement from it, there is also the possibility of the reverse (Levinas, 1993). The other may ignore us or fail to return positive feeling to us, so undermining our interpersonal skills and even placing our selves into question.

This self–other balance is clearly seen in those with facial disfigurement. Some cannot look another in the face for fear of what the other will reflect back. One person with Moebius described the daily horror of walking down the street, not knowing if people would say hello to him or not, and not knowing how to respond. 'For the face of the other requires me to respond and enter into a relationship, but a relationship I cannot fully control.' It involves a risk so evident for many of those with facial problems that they avoid it. For some with facial difference, the presence of others in normal social interaction and relatedness may threaten, and jeopardize, their fragile senses of self.

7. Congenital versus acquired problems and individuality

In Hollywood films of disability, which traditionally and predictably follow a 'triumph over adversity' plot, the hero's self confidence is rarely altered by his or her misfortune, and is indeed used to conjure triumph. In reality, those with physical misfortune often have a profound loss of confidence and may regain it, in part and to varying extents, only through a long period of soul searching. Their sense of loss of an 'intact' embodied self can be an enormous problem. Hollywood often uses examples of cases in which a problem arises during adult life or later childhood. But it may be much more difficult to find that confidence when the problem is congenital, for people in this situation must seek what they have never known. In those with congenital problems the early period of family life, when those problems are not stigmatized, must therefore assume more importance. We all seek to bolster our children's self-confidence in the home, but for those with facial and other problems this may be even more important, for when they grow up and leave the family, their confidence will be tested far more than most people's.

This contrasts with the experience of those with congenital blindness; they have fewer problems than those who lose their sight because they have learnt as children to take every thing they can from the voice. One person with congenital blindness told me that he effortlessly constructs character and personality in others from their voice. He 'resides in voice', he told me, as I might in visible representation of others. Someone who had lost sight as an adult thought, in his blackest periods, that the lucky ones were those who had never seen, for they could not miss what they had not had. They were also able from an early age to learn to compensate, and to do so during early 'critical' periods for this.

In addition to the origin of the problem (congenital or acquired), it is also obvious, from talking to people with various facial problems, that individual's responses to

similar problems are very different. Some people are naturally outgoing, and therefore more able to overcome their problem; some more hesitant or introspective. One
the first things that Changing Faces, a charity helping those with facial disfigurement,
noted when it opened its doors was how the extent of the problem with an individual's
face bore little relation to the objective degree of difference. Some with large scars
made light of them, and were well adjusted socially, while some with apparently triv-
ial marks were socially isolated.

V: Facial Difference — A Way Back

Thus far, the picture of living with facial difference has largely been negative, showing how it can reduce the ability to socialize and negate the exploration of interrelatedness upon which a normal seamless intersubjectivity relies. But this is not always
the case. Many people with various forms of facial difference manage their lives and
manage to overcome — or go beyond — their faces to project themselves through
their remaining channels of expression; through voice, gesture, clothes, etc. One man
who has had major surgery to the face and lost one eye started back to work with a
black eyepatch. People asked him about the problem. Then his wife made him a series
of patches in the same flamboyant patterns as his loud bow ties. People so enjoyed
this that they no longer focussed on the absent eye behind the patch. A woman with
Moebius who is married with three young children uses gesture and intonation of
voice to communicate what her face cannot.

Some with disfigurement stumble on solutions, but some have to be helped. And in
this is the crucial recognition that, for many, the problem is not within themselves but
in the response of others.

In the UK, James Partridge, a man whose face and body were badly burnt in a car
accident, received excellent plastic surgery over several years to reconstruct his face.
However, no one told him how to go back into the world with this new face. In his
own words he spent seven years of trial and error learning the social skills to order a
drink in a bar, or a bus ticket, or succeed at a job interview (Partridge, 1990). There
was a gap in his rehabilitation in the psychosocial support to re-establish ways to meet
people and to put them at ease with his new look.

In collaboration with Nichola Rumsey, a health psychologist, he set up Changing
Faces, a charity to help people with facial disfigurement become assimilated into a
real social world. Their approach was to view disfigurement as being initially a sort of
bereavement, followed by a tremendous, almost overpowering, sense of inadequacy
and isolation. Their aim was somehow to enable people to recover their feelings of
self-worth, building on their talents and giving them a confidence to go out into the
world and to manage the way in which other people responded to them. They did this
by setting up a series of workshops, interviews, and one-to-one sessions with clients
with facial disfigurement.

They found that people with facial disability often became passive and retiring,
reacting only to other people, never initiating and controlling conversations or decisions. They had to be given help to actually manage the social relationships in their
own way and to their own advantage. James arranged workshops for clients. He soon
realised that the first thing was to ask clients to do something most found extraordinarily difficult: to look each other straight in the face and describe their problems.

Through this he sought a shared experience of disability and loss. Each person had to realize they were not unique, and to realize that to regain a social currency and recover self-esteem they needed to do the most difficult thing imaginable; they had reach out to others.

He suggested ways in which this might be done, at work, at school and in restaurants. They played games. They discussed how not all groups of people are the same. One's loved ones, one's family and one's immediate friends may be relied on. Nurses and professionals, who are trained to react in certain ways and to be aware of certain problems, may be another group not too difficult to approach. But unknown people may react in a different and distressing way. Clients had to be made aware of these differences in order to cope.

Disfigured people needed reassurance that they did not have to be purely passive. They also needed to reassure others. If people with facial disabilities don't feel they can look someone in the eye then the end of their nose may do (it is very difficult for someone to realize that the gaze is actually directed at the nose). If they can't move the skin around the eyes, for whatever reason, then use the forehead or the mouth. If they don't feel they can move their face then they were taught to use the body and arms, or their voice. Use what is left, but use it. They received reassurance from the group and, more importantly, were taught to give it to those they meet, for people are awkward when faced with a disfigured person.

As James had found, all people with disabilities, of whatever sort, have to try harder to function socially. They have to learn that they will live at higher energy states, whether it's in their posture or in their desire to reach out to people. They don't have to be passive recipients; they need to be able to reach the right level of self-projection both to engage with others and to cope with adverse comments or to prevent them occurring in the first place.

Programmes like those of Changing Faces have grown up in many places. Theirs have expanded and the charity has enlarged to teach health care professionals, to lobby parliament and the media, and to acquire hard data on effectiveness. Its ultimate aim is for such support methods to be assimilated into mainstream healthcare. Its success has shown that the confidence and social skills of those with facial problems can be improved. It can alter the self–other balance and allow people with facial disfigurement to gain, or regain, sufficient confidence to explore human relationships.

VI: Conclusions — 'The Ultimate Barrier to Empathy'

One could not seek to argue that intersubjectivity depends exclusively on the face, that would be preposterous. But I hope I have shown how the face does play an important role in interpersonal relatedness. From the narratives and experiences of those with unusual features, those forced to explore the seam between face and self which otherwise is scarcely revealed, the importance of the face is revealed. Without easy, almost unconscious, facial communication profound problems with self-esteem and relatedness may occur.

As I have suggested, the face may have evolved as a result of several pressures to do with altered environment and feeding habits. But at some time after this anatomical evolution the face was available to develop in another way, in the expression of inner mind states, and to become part of them. This may have facilitated the social development that was one reason for our evolutionary success. And to communicate inner states led to an emotional contagion whereby the observer entered into the states of the other, and hence to sympathy and to empathy.[9]

The evolutionary pressures that led to the development of these mind states are unclear. In a social environment it obviously has advantages to any one individual to be adept at relationships and at obtaining the approval of others. For neo-Darwinians, for whom the gene is selfish, this behavioural adaptation may simply be a consequence of genes that program, within the brain, for adaptations in action according to situation without specifying what those are (see Dawkins, 1976; 1989; Rolls, 1999; Pinker, 1997). Then sympathy becomes a device for earning gratitude from others and altruism a way of extending this to others for our own ultimate advantage. For some more interested in higher primate social evolution such models may be too limited and mechanistic (see Sober and Wilson, 1998). My concern is less with the fascinating tensions between these two groups debating how far Darwinian principles can be applied to the behaviour of culturally rich species like man. My interests are rather how the face reveals our dependence on social referencing for our self-esteem, and how the face — by its emotional expressivity — reveals the importance of our affective, embodied self. In discussing how one person can know the mind of another, Steven Pinker wrote that

> The body is the ultimate barrier to empathy. Your toothache does not hurt me the same way as it hurts you. But genes are not imprisoned. . . . Love, compassion, and empathy are invisible fibres that connect genes in different bodies. When a parent wants to take the place of a child having surgery it is not her species or body that wants to have that unselfish emotion, it is her selfish genes (Pinker, 1997).

It is an extraordinary thing that this ultimate barrier to accessing the feelings of others has been broken down. I may not be able to feel your pain, that most private of feelings, but I can share your suffering. It is through behaviour that this is possible, through the embodiment of inner states in a way which leads to them being available for others to see and then more, for by taking them into themselves they can then be felt and are used to motivate another.[10] And if one feels as another then can one but share, whether it be happiness or sadness? In this process, facial expression, as much as gesture and posture, has a key role. And before the development of language it may have been a key in the development and communication of these states themselves.[11]

---

[9] My wife keeps animals, (horses, dogs and sheep), and can tell their moods and feelings far better than I. When one has an injury that in you or I would cause severe pain, their pain related behaviour is minimal. Not surprisingly if other animals have no sympathy and no way of improving the pain, expression and communication of this inner state is pointless. Contrast this with our small children. They may fall down unobserved and just get up and carry on. If observed when falling by one of us and seeing the opportunity for sympathy and fuss their pain related behaviour is operatic.

[10] I would suggest that the evolution of emotional refinement began with the means of expressing it, which may have been through face, as well as posture and vocalization. More recently, however, emotional experience continued to be refined and facial expressions are not able to communicate all of them. An obvious example is jealousy, which does not have a distinctive expression. Munch, for instance, was reduced to painting a rather sad yet frustrated figure in the foreground with an embracing couple behind. Despite this use of context and facial expression he felt it necessary to entitle the picture 'Jealousy', to avoid ambiguity.

[11] I am not suggesting that language was not a huge advance for cognition and for emotional development. But language seems far better at communication of facts than feelings. Much communication remains non-verbal.

I hope that I have shown the importance of the face and how it reveals the embodiment of some emotions. But more, for I had never thought of how the face defines us as individuals and how, by its expressions, it is the 'visible affective mind', until I saw a woman who had lost facial expression as an elderly woman. When presented to a group of neurologists, some thought her demented, simply because she could not respond facially. Puzzled and yet intrigued, I talked with her on several occasions. For to understand and sympathize with her, and with the other people with facial problems, it was insufficient for me to look. Our abilities to sympathize and to empathize, like our imaginations, are bounded to some extent by our experience. For a fuller understanding I had to listen to their experiences as they told me, in their own way and in their own time. I required what Kay Toombs has called a form of extended empathy or imaginative self-transposal (see Toombs, 1993). She describes the process as being that of seeing the world through the eyes of another and grasping something of another's suffering, even though that other's experience is never fully shared. As she suggests, this entering into another's feelings is, to an extent, a creative act. This echoes what I wrote in *About Face* concerning our inquisitiveness about others and interpretation of others' moods and feelings;

> Looking into other's minds — feeling towards others —, then, is not a precise science but requires imagination and creativity. It is perhaps the most creative thing we do each day, as we seek to match faces to characters to personal experiences. . . .

This is as necessary for a neurologist as for a psychiatrist or even for an actor trying to understand a new character.[12] I would suggest that in order to understand what the face really does and means in relation to selfhood and to intersubjectivity, we must extend the range of our empathy to enter the experiences of those with facial difference. Just as the face may have been necessary for the evolution of complex inner states (of which empathy is one), so we need an enriched and full sense of empathy for an understanding of those with facial difference. This, in turn, allows us a fuller comprehension of what the face means in all of us.

References

Baron-Cohen, S. (1995), *Mindblindness: An Essay on Autism and Theory of Mind* (Cambridge, MA and London: MIT Press).

Bermudez, J. (1998), *The Paradox of Self-Consciousness* (Cambridge, MA: MIT Press).

Cole, J.D. (1998), *About Face* (Cambridge, MA: MIT Press).

Damasio, A.R. (1994), *Descartes' Error* (New York: Grosset/Putnam).

Damasio, A.R. (1999), *The Feeling of What Happens* (London: Heinemann).

Dawkins, R. (1976, 1989), *The Selfish Gene* (Oxford: Oxford University Press).

Dunbar, R.I.M. (1990), 'Ecological modelling in an evolutionary context', *Folia Primatologica*, [Basel], **53**, pp. 235–46 (Quoted from Donald, D. 1993, *Origins of the Modern Mind* (Cambridge, MA: Harvard University Press)).

Gilman, S. (1999), *Making the Body Beautiful* (Princeton: Princeton University Press).

---

[12] Peter Brook (during an interview for Grove TV) once described how an actor studies character, say the jealousy of Macbeth, learning how to take his own slight emotions and to magnify them in order to understand Macbeth's character in the light of his own experience. But when playing people with neurological problems for the play 'L'Homme Qui' such an 'inside-out' approach, depending on an empathetic understanding was not possible, since the actors had no experience of, say, movement and position sense, to fall back on. They had to approach their acting 'outside-in', exploring the phenomenology of a neurological problem and only then, once it was encompassed technically, could they begin to explore its consequences for the individual; only then could they empathize.

Hacking, I. (1995), *Rewriting the Soul* (Princeton: Princeton University Press).

Hobson, R.P. (1993), *Autism and the Development of Mind* (Hillsdale, NJ: Erlbaum).

Humphrey, N. (1986), *The Inner Eye* (London: Faber and Faber).

James, W. (1950), *The Principles of Psychology*, 2 Volumes (New York: Dover).

Leder, D. (1990), *The Absent Body* (Chicago: University of Chicago Press).

Levinas, E. (1993), *Collected Philosophical Papers* (Dordrecht, Boston, London: Kluwer).

McNeill, D. (1998), *The Face* (New York: Little, Brown).

Merleau-Ponty, M. (1964), *The Primacy of Perception* (Evanston, IL: Northwestern University Press).

Murphy, R.L. (1987), *The Body Silent* (New York: Henry Holt).

Partridge, J. (1990), *Changing Faces* (London: Penguin Books).

Pinker, S. (1997), *How the Mind Works* (New York: W.W. Norton, London: Allen Lane The Penguin Press).

Rolls, E.T. (1999), *The Brain and Emotion* (Oxford: Oxford University Press).

Shorter Oxford English Dictionary, Third Edition, (1983), (Oxford: Oxford University Press).

Sober, E. and Wilson, D.S. (1998), *Unto Others: The Evolution and Psychology of Unselfish Behavior* (Cambridge, MA: Harvard University Press).

Toombs, K. (1993), *The Meaning of Illness* (Dordrecht, Boston, London: Kluwer).

Wittgenstein, L. (1980), *Remarks on the Philosophy of Psychology* (Chicago: University of Chicago Press).

Iso Kern and Eduard Marbach

Understanding the Representational Mind

A Prerequisite for Intersubjectivity Proper

This paper argues that, from the perspective of phenomenological philosophy, the study of intersubjectivity is closely tied to questions of the representational mind. It focuses on developmental studies of children's understanding of the human mind, setting out some of the main findings and theoretical explanations. It then takes up Husserl's idea of looking at persons in the 'personal attitude'. Understanding motivational connections among a person's subjective experiences is an essential feature of this attitude. Proposing a unified theoretical interpretation of children's representational achievements, the paper suggests that understanding motivational connections among one's representations requires an ability for reflection that children apply in progressively more refined ways to themselves and others.

Phenomenology is a reflective analysis of conscious experiences, in which the study of intersubjectivity is closely tied to questions of the representational mind. Perhaps the central task of the study of intersubjectivity consists in elucidating how one creature as a conscious subject of representations is able to experience another creature as a conscious representational subject in her own right, in her own situation, or as another point of view. Accounting for how intersubjective relations are possible at all is a task for phenomenological philosophy, but tracing the actual course of development of these relations is a matter of empirical investigation.

In the last two decades, developmental psychologists have intensely studied the development of children's understanding of the human mind and have produced a wealth of findings and theoretical interpretations that are philosophically, and especially phenomenologically, relevant to clarifying the origins and early development of properly intersubjective relations.

In the present paper, we look at this literature from the point of view of phenomenology. We begin by simply recalling some well-established evidence that is indicative of a major shift in children's understanding of the representational mind. Then we discuss some psychological explanations of this significant turning point in children's development. In this context, we examine the fundamental concept of representation itself, arguing that it is amenable to a complex analysis involving distinctly different

Journal of Consciousness Studies, **8**, No. 5–7, 2001, pp. 69–82

conscious mental activities. Following Husserl's lead, we finally introduce the idea of looking at persons as subjects of experiences from the so-called 'personal attitude' or 'attitude focusing on mind'. Understanding motivational connections among a person's subjective experiences is an essential feature of this attitude. We try to show that forming such a personal understanding has much in common with the crucial shift pointed out by psychologists studying the development of children's understanding of the representational mind. In our discussion, Husserl's notion of motivation, itself linked to the notion of rationality, plays a prominent role in developing a unified theoretical interpretation of children's representational achievements. We suggest that understanding motivational connections among one's representations requires an ability for reflection that children apply in progressively more refined ways to themselves and others.

I: Evidence for an Important Shift in Children's Understanding of the Mind

In the last two decades, psychologists studying children's developing understanding of the human mind (so-called 'theory of mind' development) discovered that it underwent an important transformation at around four years of age.[1] Psychologists such as M.J. Chandler and M. Boyes, J.H. Flavell, H.M. Wellman, H. Wimmer, J. Perner, A. Gopnik and others have emphasized that the progress in question is not simply a gradual or cumulative extension of children's cognitive faculties due to an increase in memory and central processing capacity; nor is it due to children's acquisition of new theoretical rules about the human mind. Rather, it is viewed as a matter of developing 'a novel cognitive skill' (Wimmer and Perner, 1983, p. 126), or 'some underlying new ability', which itself involves 'a deep-seated and profound conceptual difference' (Astington and Gopnik, 1988, pp. 202, 204), another 'metacognitive domain' or 'level' (Flavell, 1988, p. 244, 257), a 'deeper conceptual-theoretical change' (Perner, 1991, p. 154), or a 'theory transition in the child's understanding of mind' (Bartsch and Wellman, 1995, ch. 6, pp. 161ff; see also Wellman, 1990; 1993).

   According to this psychological literature, this novel ability manifests itself first and foremost in the following achievements: understanding that other persons may have a *false belief* on the basis of their information or lack of information about a current situation known to the understanding subject. Experimental studies by Heinz Wimmer and Josef Perner are frequently cited in this regard. Very briefly, in their standard enacted story of 'Maxi and the chocolate', children are shown small dolls symbolizing Maxi and his mother, and a cardboard stage symbolizing their kitchen, with three different-coloured boxes on the wall as cupboards (A, B, C). In one of its versions, the children see Maxi helping his mother unpack the shopping bag and put the chocolate in one of the cupboards (A). After Maxi has left for the playground, his mother puts the chocolate in another cupboard (B) before the very eyes of the

---

[1] More recently, using clever experimental modifications of some of the standard tasks (modifications such as deceptive games, trickery, fairy-tales, reduced information processing tasks, modality changes), researchers have shown that children may undergo this transformation even several months earlier. See, e.g., Rice *et al.* (1997); Surian and Leslie (1999) and the research mainly from the 1990s referred to in these papers. Importantly, however, the basic trend in this developmental trajectory has not been disputed — see J. Perner (1999), referring to Wellman *et al.*'s (1999) paper. As Bartsch and Wellman note, in this kind of research 'specific ages are not the issue but rather sequences and concurrences' (Bartsch and Wellman, 1995, p. 199).

onlooking children. The mother thereupon leaves the kitchen and Maxi returns from the playground, hungry, wanting his chocolate. Only at about the age of four do children generally understand that Maxi will look for the chocolate in cupboard A since he *falsely believes* that it is there, and not in cupboard B where the children themselves know the chocolate to be (Wimmer and Perner, 1983).

'False appearance' tests have been carried out with similar results. For example, in one standard task, children are shown a familiar tube of smarties. On the basis of its external appearance, the children first believe that the tube contains sweets, only discovering after opening it that it has been filled with pencils. The tube is closed up again, and they are asked what other children will think is inside. Children under the age of four have trouble understanding that children who have not yet seen inside the tube will think (like they first did) that there are smarties, and not pencils, inside (Hogrefe *et al.*, 1986; Perner *et al.*, 1987).

Simultaneously with the understanding that beliefs can differ between themselves and other people, there emerges in children at this critical time an ability to manipulate an other person's beliefs, that is, an ability to deceive others intentionally and so deliberately lie to them (cf. Perner, 1991, ch. 8, pp. 189ff). At this age children also begin to appreciate that other people cannot come to know certain things because they lack the necessary information. Up to the age of four, the question why someone knows or does not know something is incomprehensible to children. But after that age they themselves start asking how or why someone knows something. They also begin to distinguish between a lucky guess and real knowledge (cf. Perner, 1991, ch. 7).

A further ability that contemporaneously manifests itself involves the 'aspectuality of knowledge', that is, an ability for 'perceptual and conceptual perspective taking' (cf. Perner 1991, p. 160; Flavell, 1988, pp. 250–3). For example, at this age children begin to appreciate that someone who is blindfolded and merely touches a ball is able to tell whether it is soft or hard, but cannot know what colour it is; or that another child sitting across from them and looking at a turtle depicted on a sheet is seeing it upside down even though they themselves are seeing the turtle right side up; or that someone else, looking at a large picture of an elephant through a hole in a cardboard cover, is not seeing the elephant in its entirety but only a grey spot. Children at this age also begin to distinguish between *reality* and *appearance*, understanding, for instance, that a piece of soft sponge that *looks* just like a rock will be perceived as a rock by someone else as long as she has merely *seen* it but not touched or squeezed it with her hands (e.g., Flavell *et al.*, 1983).

All of these achievements hint at the development of a special kind of understanding of the human mind. Moreover, given their simultaneous emergence, it seems that there must be *one* fundamental skill or capacity that underlies them all. The theoretical challenge has been to give a successful unifying account of this skill or capacity that goes beyond noting its representational character.

II: Various Accounts of the Underlying Skill in Recent Developmental Psychology

Developmental psychologists have made a number of rival proposals in relation to these findings. However, resolving these into a theoretical account of a unifying skill or capacity that underlies the children's achievements is no easy matter. In their accounts, the authors seem partly in agreement with each other, but they always also

advance objections, some of them justified, against each other's theories. One is left
with the impression that there is as yet no unanimity among psychologists and no
truly satisfying unified account in sight.

In the following summary of four theoretical accounts we draw attention to a
common difficulty, that of properly understanding the *representational* features of
the human mind. We think a right understanding can be acquired from the point of
view of phenomenology, into which we lead at the end of this section.

1. Representational difference (Flavell, 1988)

J.H. Flavell's bid for a unified account takes the form of a generalization of his earlier
theory, which made a distinction between Level 1 and Level 2 knowledge in relation
to visual perception (1988, p. 244; Flavell, 1977). According to this earlier formulation, the young child 'thinks about viewing objects . . . but not yet about views of
objects' (Flavell, 1977, p. 126). This is Level 1. The generalized theory interprets the
child's novel understanding as a transition between Levels 1 and 2. At Level 1 the
conception of the mental or of internal experiences (such as seeing objects, wanting
them, and so on) is merely a cognitive connection to external objects and events. At
Level 2 there is a realization that these cognitive connections engender inner, mental
representations of their external objects, and that 'the *same* object can be represented
in *different, seemingly contradictory* ways' (1988, p. 247, our emphasis). What, for
Flavell, is fundamental in respect of Level 2 in the elaborated sense is the realization
that *the same object* is able to appear *subjectively differently*, to be perceived differently, to be conceived differently, in short to be represented *differently, contradicto-
rily*. He quotes as very similar the view of, e.g., Chandler and Boyes (1982, p. 393).
According to them, there occurs a shift from an object-centred or copy theory of knowledge to a subject-oriented or constructivist epistemology (Flavell, 1988, p. 246).

2. Dual model theory (Wimmer and Perner, 1983)

In a similar way, H. Wimmer and J. Perner (1983) viewed the abilities, acquired at
around four to six years of age, to understand *false beliefs*, to construct a deceitful or
truthful utterance relative to a person's wrong beliefs, etc., as 'the ability to represent
the relationship between two or more persons' epistemic states' (p. 126). Or, as the
authors put it with regard to the understanding of false beliefs, representing wrong
beliefs requires 'the construction of two different models of the world' and the
explicit representation of the falseness relation between propositions in one model
and the corresponding propositions in the other model (p. 123). So, in this interpretation, too, the novel ability of the 4- to 6-year old children seems to consist in their
ability to understand the complexity of several *different*, contradictory beliefs or representations in relation to the *same* object or the *same* state of affairs.

Later, however, both Wimmer and Perner modified their theoretical understanding
of the ability in question. Wimmer *et al.* (1988) refer critically to Wimmer and Perner
(1983). They point out that the interpretation of young children's difficulty with false
beliefs, given in the 1983 paper, located the problem in the contradiction between the
other's belief (e.g., the chocolate is in the green cupboard) and the actual state of
affairs (e.g., the chocolate is in the red cupboard). A profound analysis of representational requirements posed by pretend play, as discussed in the work of Alan Leslie
(1987; 1988) convinced them, however, that their first account couldn't be correct.

The problem is that according to their first account, pretence poses the same representational problem as false belief. Pretence, however, is already acquired in the child's second year of life, while false belief attribution is mastered only in the fifth (pp.184–5).

Exactly the same criticism is put forward by Wimmer *et al.* (1988) with regard to Flavell's theory of a first and second *level* in understanding the mind, a theory that is centred on children's difficulty with the *appearance–reality distinction*. The authors explain that according to Flavell's analysis the difficulty arises because the appearance–reality distinction requires that two contradictory representations are set up and maintained for one and the same object. In essence, then, according to Wimmer *et al.* (1988), Flavell proposes a representational complexity account (a 'dual coding' theory) of children's difficulty with the appearance–reality distinction. And this account, they observe, turns out to be quite similar to Wimmer and Perner's (1983) original representational complexity explanation of children's difficulty with false belief understanding. Again it is noted that this version of the representational complexity account is at odds with the very early emergence of pretence, which also requires two contradictory representations of one and the same fact to be set up and maintained (p. 188).

3. Informational origins (Wimmer et al., 1988)

The new theory that Wimmer *et al.* (1988) now present holds that children in the second stage, beginning in the fourth and fifth years, grasp sources of information like perceiving and communication as causes of knowledge and belief. As they explain, in this second stage children relate such informational conditions as seeing or hearing in an explicit way to their already existing conceptions of knowledge and belief, and thus 'they become aware of the informational conditions *as causal origins* of knowledge and belief' (p. 174, our emphasis). In the same way, Wimmer *et al.* also explain the ability to distinguish between appearance and reality that emerges at the second stage. For the important point of the appearance–reality distinction is that mental representations are marked according to where they come from, that is, 'according to their informational origins' (p. 188).

Josef Perner (1991), in turn, has objected to this theoretical explanation. He refers to tests by Alison Gopnik and Janet Astington from 1988. These show that younger children prior to that second stage have as much trouble *remembering* their *own* false beliefs, that they in the meantime had given up, as they have understanding the false beliefs of *others*. According to Perner, this finding speaks decisively against Wimmer's theory. Perner makes clear that if changes in their own beliefs are as difficult for children to understand as beliefs in others, then understanding the causal origin of belief cannot be the critical factor. After all, children can internally experience their own beliefs without having to understand how they are formed (p. 186). Perner's argument would seem to be this: In the case of their *own* past false beliefs, unlike what obtains with the tests about the understanding of false beliefs in others, children do *not* have *causally to infer* these beliefs on the basis of informational conditions; they have direct access to them as their *own* mental states instead. If they still do not recall them, this is according to Perner's new theory because they cannot understand their false beliefs as *representations* which as such can also *misrepresent*. As Perner has it: 'they cannot *represent* that something is a *representation*' (p. 186) or, put another way, they do not yet have *metarepresentation*.

4. *Metarepresentation (Perner, 1991)*

According to Perner (1991), this is the decisive point at the new stage of understanding the human mind that children reach at about the age of four years: the *understanding* of the *representational relation*, i.e. *metarepresentation*. And this does not only apply to mental representations but to *all* representations — to pictures, models, and sentences, as well. In Perner's view, a representation is any medium that represents something (the referent) as *being in a certain way* (i.e., the *sense* of the representation), and so can also misrepresent the referent (1991, ch. 2). According to Perner (1991), 2- to 3-year-old children can already use and distinguish a variety of representations. So they have perceptual representations; they represent past situations in their memories; they represent imaginary situations in *pretend play*; they understand what it is in a picture or in a sentence that is represented in a particular way. What they do not yet understand is the representational relation and, therefore, they cannot understand *false* representations (*false beliefs*) either, nor can they understand that *the same thing* can *appear differently* or can be conceived in several different ways depending on the informational conditions. For such an understanding, in Perner's view, meta-representation (representation of representation) is necessary, which is supposed to arise only at about four years of age (1991, chapters. 7 and 8).

Bartsch and Wellman (1995) have, in turn, criticized this view of Perner's. According to them, already 3-year-olds understand that 'people have representational mental states including representational beliefs' (p. 195). What is new — and according to Bartsch and Wellman arises only at around four years of age — is the understanding that the entire desiring and behaving of human beings is *necessarily determined* by their mental representations of the world. As the authors emphasize, older preschool children, beginning at age four or so, not only recognize the existence of representational entities such as thoughts and beliefs, but also 'begin to appreciate something of the ever-present processes of representation that characterize human life' (p. 199). Or, as Wellman (1993) expressed it, by the age of four, children 'see people as living their lives within a world of mental content that determines how they behave in the world of real objects and acts', they are 'construing people's real-world actions as *inevitably* filtered through representations of the world rather than linked to the world directly' (pp. 31–2). Bartsch and Wellman (1995) criticize Perner's theory in particular with regard to the fact that it postulates a *synchronous* arising of the understanding of *all sorts* of representations. More precisely, they point out that, according to Perner, '*mental* representation is understood by children because they are achieving a *larger* understanding of representation *itself*'. In their view, it remains critical to Perner's account that children fail to understand beliefs and false beliefs until age four or later. They observe that Perner argues for 'a concurrence between children's understanding of *mental* representation and their understanding of *other* representations such as pictures or drawings', pointing out that, for Perner, age four is a watershed for understanding 'all sorts of representational devices and systems', because, for him, what children acquire at about this time is 'a general conception of representation'. By contrast, Bartsch and Wellman believe that it is 'more likely that children come to understand representation within specific domains more independently' (p. 199).

From the point of view of a phenomenological philosophy, this criticism of Perner by Bartsch and Wellman, made in an empirical developmental perspective, has much plausibility. For, methodologically speaking, phenomenology reflectively analyses different modes of consciousness as having a noetic (act) and a noematic (intentional content) structure and, from this perspective, it makes very good sense to differentiate the concept of representation itself according to distinctly different modes of representing something. Thus, for example, to understand or appreciate that an externally perceived picture or model as a simple object *represents* (darstellt) something in a certain way, and to understand that another person as another subject *represents* something in a certain way, namely by mentally *figuring or representing something to herself* (sich etwas vorstellen), would seem to be rather different modes of consciousness. In German, different terms are used for the intentional (noematic) correlates of these modes of consciousness: A model or a picture *stellt etwas dar* (represents something out there); by contrast, a person or a subject stellt *sich* etwas *vor* (represents something innerly or mentally to herself). In French, too, we have the distinction between a non-reflexive and a reflexive verb: représenter and se représenter. To understand that another person figures something mentally *to herself* (*sich* etwas vorstellt) is not to understand that this person herself *represents* (darstellt), or stands for, something else out there. Such an understanding, it is true, is also possible, e.g., at the theatre, when one understands that an actor himself represents, say, king Oedipus. But such an understanding of the representational relation is not an understanding of that which the actor thereby represents mentally to himself. The understanding of a person representing something mentally to herself essentially consists in, both, the understanding that this person as a subject presents the object in mental activities *to herself* in ways that correspond to these mental activities and that in this presenting the person is *for herself*, i.e. is in a certain way conscious of herself.

Perner (1991) is by no means blind to such considerations regarding different modes of representation. He points out, for example, that without a representational view of mind it is difficult to understand that seeing informs only about certain aspects of an object. As he explains, if seeing is treated by the young child non-epistemically, that is, if seeing is treated 'not as *a mental (intentional) activity* but more like the physical relationship of looking at', then it is difficult for the child to understand that by looking at an object a person comes to know its colour but not its weight (p. 160, our emphasis). Here, Perner himself takes the understanding of a mental representation to be an understanding of a mental (intentional) *activity*.[2] However, his general theory of metarepresentation, built on an understanding of the representational relation as it obtains with physical models or pictures (photographs, etc.) out there, seems unable to account for the special character of the understanding of mental representation as mental (intentional) activity of a subject. Incidentally, Perner (1991) is rather at a loss regarding the fact that autistic children, whom he supposes to lack insight into the representational nature of mind (p. 202), quite understand the representational relation when it comes to pictures. As he writes, '. . . as expected, only four of the sixteen autistic children gave correct answers to the belief task, but — quite surprisingly — all but one gave the correct answer in the photo task. This suggests that autism is not characterized by a general metarepresentational deficit' (p. 312). But on the basis of his theory of metarepresentation, by which he

---

[2] Most recently, Perner (1999) concluded his illuminating overview on 'Theory of Mind' research in young children with the following statement: 'The greatest prospect for theory of mind research is that it will shed light on the *development of consciousness*' (Internet manuscript, p. 19; our emphasis).

explains the understanding of beliefs, Perner is unable to explain why autistic children succeed in understanding representation in the case of photographs, but not in the case of the representational *mind*; for according to his theory it is a question of principally the same relation everywhere.

III: Philosophical Considerations Concerning the Understanding of Mental Representation

As the preceding survey clearly shows, it is not easy to grasp what in principle is at stake when children at about the age of four years or so begin to appreciate the significance of the representational character of the human mind. Attempting to simplify the theoretical understanding of what happens to children at this age, psychologists applied the paradigm of understanding *non-mental* conditions, be they pictorial or linguistic representations, or causal relations in the natural world. As we see it, this paradigm made understanding more difficult rather than less. We think what is needed above all for explaining the children's new skill at about the age of four years is a concept of understanding *subjective* representation, i.e. 'representation' not in the sense of a relation between one objective thing (e.g., a photograph, picture, model, linguistic sign) and another thing (the referent), but in the sense of a mental activity of a subject who, by this activity, represents something for herself.[3] For the elaboration of such a specific concept of understanding subjective (as distinct from objective) representation, we would here like to introduce some ideas from the phenomenological philosopher Edmund Husserl (1859–1938). We thereby hope to shed new light on the philosophically highly relevant developmental literature discussed so far.

Under the title of personal attitude ('personale Einstellung') or attitude focusing on mind ('Geisteseinstellung' — as opposed to the attitude focusing on Nature, 'naturale Einstellung'), Husserl offers an account of what is characteristic of the understanding of persons as subjects of experiences ('Erlebnisse') that are intentionally related to the surrounding world. He characterizes this personal understanding in a way that comes very close to the 'novel cognitive skill' of the 4-year-olds' 'theory of mind'. According to Husserl (1989), when we adopt the attitude *focusing on mind* (or the standpoint of mind), we posit other subjects (and ourselves by reflection) in a theoretical way, by taking them and ourselves exclusively as subjects of experiences that are states of our subjectivity or theirs and as subjects having experiences of surrounding things and persons. Accordingly, these things and persons are taken here exactly in the way they present themselves to the subject, i.e., precisely as an experienced environment for the subject. As such, these things and persons are taken as *correlates* of the subject's respective experiences. This is to say, they are taken not as things in themselves, but as the things that we or others see, grasp, touch, etc., and this in *just the way in which* we or others see them, grasp them, etc. If others see such things differently, then, in the personal attitude or standpoint of mind, the differently seen things are, *as seen by them*, just *their* correlate-things. If, for example, those things are ghosts *for them*, then, they just are *their* ghosts, i.e. things that, for us, are non-existing (pp. 300–1).

---

[3] For a detailed analysis of the concept of mental representation as an activity of a subject in contrast to objective (pictorial, etc.) representation, see Marbach (1993).

In connection with the distinction between these two attitudes, Husserl (1989, §§54ff) introduces the concept of *motivation*. He views motivation to be the 'fundamental law' of the mental or intentional life as understood in the personal attitude. Note that, for Husserl, the fundamental phenomenological concept of motivation is an extension of that concept of motivation that occurs when we say, e.g., that the willing of the *end* motivates the willing of the *means*. But not all motivations are motivations on the basis of willing some end. Rather, for Husserl, all connections among temporally succeeding experiences are motivational connections. Thus, he speaks of motivations of reason with regard to the way judgments are motivated by perceptions or by other judgments, or he speaks of associative motivations with regard to passive connections of consciousness, such as when a thought reminds a person of other thoughts and calls back into her memory a past experience. The decisive point is that with motivations it is a matter of dependency relations that are cognizable (understandable) among *experiences themselves* (acts and contents of conscious experiences) *without* having to have recourse to physical and physiological processes (subject to causality in the natural world) for such cognition.

Correspondingly, motivation is conceived by Husserl 'in contrast to the concept of *causality*'.[4] Usually, Husserl speaks of causality in relation to matters of fact in the world of nature. According to Husserl, on the one hand, it is also possible to view the sphere of the psyche, at all levels, including the mental and cultural, as a mere matter of fact of nature, following causal laws of nature. It is possible to treat the connections between mind and nature, as well as connections between one mental fact and another mental fact, in analogy to mere mechanical connections. These would be mindless connections that constitute the field of psychophysics in the broadest sense of the term.

On the other hand, however, and this is crucial for our present purpose, Husserl holds that in the mental sphere there are specifically mental connections, connections that can certainly be understood or made intelligible.[5] This leaves it open, however, whether all of the mental can be *explained* by natural science, because for him 'making intelligible' is not equivalent to explaining.[6] So what does understanding here mean? Essentially, in Husserl's view, to make mental connections understandable is a matter of entering into the motivational connections. Importantly, as Husserl also puts it, 'motivation is something individual'.[7] When contrasting causality in nature

---

[4] See, e.g., Husserl (1982), § 47, note on p. 107. For an extensive study of Husserl's views about 'causality and motivation', see B. Rang (1973). When Husserl discusses the relation between motivation on the one hand and causality in the natural world on the other, he emphasizes that the 'because–therefore' ('weil–so') of motivation has a totally different sense from causality in the sense of nature. The point is of course not merely terminological; for Husserl (1989) also freely speaks of 'relations of subjective–objective "causality"' which he explains as a causality that is not a natural, physical causality but rather an intentional or psychic causality, calling it even 'motivational causality'('Motivationskausalität') (p. 227). Or he speaks of all mental modes of behaviour as 'causally' linked together through relations of motivation (p. 241). It may be appropriate to remind the reader that the same problems with which Husserl was confronted have, in recent analytic philosophy, been addressed in discussions of the relationship between 'reasons' and 'causes' (e.g., G. von Wright, D. Davidson, F. Dretske, etc.).

[5] See, e.g., Ms. M III 3 VIII, probably from 1918: 'in der Geistessphäre gibt es spezifisch geistige Zusammenhänge, Zusammenhänge der Verständlichkeit' (p. 6).

[6] Compare Ms. M III 3 VIII: 'Ich lasse es hier dahingestellt, ob alles Geistige naturwissenschaftlich zu erklären ist, sicher ist jetzt nur dies, dass Geistiges verständlich zu machen ist und dass Verständlichmachen nicht Erklären ist' (p. 9)

[7] See, e.g., Ms. E III 2, probably from 1915: 'Motivation ist etwas Individuelles' (p. 53).

with motivation, as briefly discussed above, Husserl (1989) stresses that the unity of motivation is 'a nexus founded in the relevant acts themselves' and that when we inquire into the 'because' ('weil'), into the reason ('Grund') of a personal behaviour, we seek to know nothing but precisely this nexus (p. 241).

To illustrate, suppose a subject knows that a decision results from motivating premises. The subject does not explain the sequence 'motivation–decision' as a mere individual case of a law (or an inductive rule) that regulates the temporal course of consciousness according to its succession. A clear case of a motivational sequence is *intelligible in itself* ('in sich verständlich'); it does not require any recourse to a general law in order to become understandable, i.e. intelligible (see Ms. E III 2, pp. 53f.). After giving a number of concrete examples of what constitutes obeying the 'motivational because', Husserl (1989) writes that all these 'causalities' can be exhibited fully *intuitively* (as opposed to a theoretical construction by means of functional laws), since they are precisely motivations (p. 230). Of course if we consider the mind together with the body as a natural object, the mind is intertwined with the causality of nature. Husserl argues, however, that the physiological processes in the sense organs, neurones etc. '*do not motivate me*' when they psychophysically condition the appearance of sense data, apprehensions, psychic experiences in my consciousness. As Husserl has it: 'What I do not "know", what in my experiencing, my representing, thinking, acting is not facing me *as represented*, as perceived, remembered, thought about etc., does not "determine" ("bestimmt") me mentally. And what is not intentionally implied in my experiences, be it even unattended or implicit, does not motivate me, not even in an unconscious way' (p. 231, our emphasis).

Quite generally, then, in understanding mental life from the personal attitude or attitude of mind, it is a question of how, for example, perceptions and other cognitive acts motivate judgments, how judgments become warranted and rectified through further experience, how a person's acts of judging are motivated in her reasoning by other acts of judging. In a different way, it is also a question of how judgments are motivated by affects and affects by judgments, how suppositions or questions, how feelings, desires, volitions, etc., are motivated.

So, what Husserl calls 'personal attitude' or 'attitude focusing on mind' is characterized by the understanding that a person as a subject experiences the world in a *way* peculiar to her, that this peculiar way of experiencing the world is determined by the course of her various intentional experiences of perceiving, conceiving, remembering, being affected, willing, etc., and that these experiences stand in motivational connections among each other. It can also very well be said in a Husserlian perspective that it is a question of *understanding that a person represents* the world in a certain way, namely, that she mentally figures *to herself* ('*sich* vorstellt') the world. However, the representation here to be understood is *not a general, abstract representational relationship*. Rather, it is a matter of understanding the *motivational connections among intentional experiences* taking their course *through time*, in which a person *as a subject* perceives objects of the world, conceives of them, and posits them as real ('believes' in them) or abandons them as merely apparent, or unreal — in short, has her own views of the world.

Importantly, such an understanding does not only concern *other* persons, but equally one's *own* person. We have seen above (p. 73) that children prior to the age of four years or so show just as much, if not more (cf. Astington and Gopnik, 1988,

p. 201), trouble remembering their *own* former *false beliefs*, that they have given up in the meantime, as they show understanding *false beliefs* in others. In our view, this is a plausible finding, precisely because in neither case do children yet reflect upon and understand this salient fact: the objects that count for a person at a given time are the objects as they are conceived by this person at this time solely on the basis of the preceding history of her subjective experiences.

What is it that underlies such an understanding? Above all it is a kind of *reflection* upon these experiences and their connections and upon the *way* that objects of the world are made to appear to a certain subject and brought to bear *in and through* these connections. In Husserl's terminology, it is at the same time a noetic (subjectively-oriented) and a noematic (objectively-oriented) reflection, that is, a reflection upon the intentional experiences or acts of perceiving, imagining, remembering, thinking, etc., and a reflection upon the objects intended in these acts, *just as* they are intended therein. In short, it is a reflection upon the intentional experiences and their objects in their *correlation*.

A completely uncompromising reflection of this sort, one suspending all other interests or attitudes (in particular, the attitude focusing on Nature that is interested in causal relations among spatial-physical things), is, according to Husserl, the phenomenological reflection. But already the personal attitude that, in Husserl's view, is adopted in understanding persons as subjects in everyday life, reflects this correlation between subjective experiencing and the How of objective givenness. For Husserl, this attitude focusing on the person is a precursor in everyday life of the methodically elaborated philosophical-phenomenological reflection on the mind. We suggest that it may be the *reflection* upon this correlation or this connection of which children from about four years or so become progressively capable in ever more refined ways.

To be sure, reflection comes in many forms and degrees. Clearly, we do not claim that children at the age of four or so engage in a properly phenomenological reflection upon structures or forms of conscious experiences as such and of their correlates! Children in everyday life, just like the rest of us, perform — or are first of all pre-reflectively engaged in — a variety of intentional conscious experiences, and thereby they are interested in, or directed toward, the things and persons out there in the surrounding world. For example, in perceiving (seeing, hearing, touching, etc.) children and adults alike perceive things and persons in their behaviour; they hear a bell ringing or someone singing a melody, they see the blackbird flying up into the sky, they touch the warm sand on the beach, etc. Thereby, things and persons appear in appearances that most of the time are continually changing; they appear in looks and perspectives that also have parallels in the acoustic field, in various light intensities and shades etc. However, it is *not these appearances* that we *at first* and *in general* perceive, but rather that which appears in them — the appearing things and persons, which in their properties and ways of behaving, in which we are interested, are not affected by the changing appearances. Even in our cooperation with other people we are at first not attentive to their subjective appearances and conceptions of the things and persons that are common to all of us in our perceiving and acting upon them; instead, we are interested in these objective things and persons themselves. In order to become attentive to the appearances as such, a special interest and, with it, a specific reflection is required. So, for example, visual appearances, as they are prominently at stake in many tests submitted to young children (see above), are first of all and *quite naturally* not heeded to as such, but need precisely to be *reflected upon* at some point in order to bring it about that a child begins to understand the relativity and subjectivity of her own visual perception of the thing. Such a reflection turns itself upon something that was previously *unattended* in the child's mental activity, something that could not even be attended without reflection but was nevertheless at stake while performing the perception. It would seem plausible that essentially second-order objects, namely, objects of reflection such as appearances as such — but also, correlatively, such as one's own mental activities of perceiving, imagining, remembering, thinking, talking etc., when they are not simply performed but themselves turned into objects of *reflection* — do not at once begin to be relevant in the life of young children. Rather, as the many empirical studies in the field of cognitive development amply demonstrate, such alertness and awareness take time.

The reflection or attitude focusing on mind can also apply to *other* persons, to their intentional experiences and the corresponding objective ways of givenness. Thus, I can understand an action of another person, I grasp *her* goal and understand *her* choice of the means. I also understand how and what the other person values and so I understand that she desires such and such things und strives after them in her action. Or I understand her belief as motivated by certain perceptions or lack of perceptions. However, such a reflection concerning other persons is, we suppose, only possible if one's own intentional experiences with their intentional correlates can be reflected, be they past or future, immediately past or merely imagined ones, etc. It would be astonishing if a child were able to understand, say, *false beliefs in others*, but *not* her *own false beliefs*. For in the most original way a person undergoes subjective intentional experiences as different modes of consciousness of objects only by herself, in the *first* person. She has these experiences, even if she does *not* reflect upon them. However, not until a child starts reflecting upon them is she likely to become aware that *other* creatures, *too*, who behave in a certain way, have *such experiences*. Without such a reflexive relation to one's own (first) person, the intentional experiences in other persons would be mere theoretical constructs whose sense would be exclusively determined by the functional relations of regularities among external things. That this is hardly the case is already evident in that the understanding of mental representation involves insight into the *necessity* of certain relations, insight that it *cannot be otherwise*.

According to Perner (1991), children after the age four understand that 'access to sufficient and reliable information is a *necessary prerequisite*' (p. 145, our emphasis) or 'a *necessary condition* for knowing' (p. 162, our emphasis). And on Wellman's (1993) view, the fundamental theoretical shift in the understanding of the mental after the age of four consists in 'construing people's real-world actions as *inevitably* filtered through representations of the world' (p. 32, author's emphasis). Would consciousness or awareness of such *necessity* be possible if the understanding of the mental were *merely* based on conceptual constructions in view of explaining *external* causal conditions?[8] In such a way, we suspect, one could only get at conditions and

---

[8] J. Perner for one seems quite open to integrating introspective data about children's own conscious inner experiences and mental states into his theory of children's understanding of the mind. E.g. in Perner (1991, chapter 11), he evaluates alternative accounts of the origin of children's commonsense psychology. On the one hand, he refers to an account that says 'that children are familiar with mental states from their own inner experience'. Such an account is often taken to rely on a so-called Cartesian

concepts that are determined by *inductive* rules and are not supported by the insight that *it cannot be otherwise*. Only in understanding the motivational conditions of one's own intentional experiences is it possible to understand that one *cannot* know certain things if one has not seen, heard or otherwise experienced what is relevant for such knowing. Again, only then is it possible to understand that for someone to act 'inevitably', this person's own representations of the objects must be motivationally fundamental. As we discussed above (p. 78), the motivational connection is *intelligible in itself* and does not require any recourse to an inductive rule in order to be rational. In other words, in order to understand other persons as *representational* subjects, one must *oneself* enter into the motivational connections of their experiences, i.e. understand them as *subjects*, in the *first* person. Only then can *properly* intersubjective relations begin to be established, namely, relations from a person as a self-reflexive subject to other persons *as subjects* of variously motivated experiences and conceptions of the objective world, in contrast to more elementary levels of interpersonal relationships as they develop already during human infancy (see, e.g., Stern, 1985; Lock, 1978).

Thus, we suppose that the ability for such a reflective attitude with regard to one's own and the other person's subjectivity makes up the 'novel cognitive skill' that enables children at around four years of age to bring about the new achievements referred to in section I. Such a conception of the novel cognitive skill seems to us not to be subject to the shortcomings that we pointed out in other accounts (see section II). Our conception makes clear what a radically new and specific attitude emerges with children at around four, with regard to themselves and to other persons. This attitude simultaneously involves a new interest and a new insight, namely the insight that it is the motivational history of our subjective experiences that determines how, at a given time, objects are perceived and conceived by us and as what they count for us (as real or unreal). This 'reflexive' account of the new skill seems to us to be apt to integrate various ideas in the accounts discussed in section II without, as we hope, succumbing to their shortcomings; but showing in detail how this can be done has to wait for another occasion.[9]

References

Astington, J.W. and Gopnik, A. (1988), 'Knowing you've changed your mind: Children's understanding of representational change', in *Developing Theories of Mind*, ed. J.W. Astington, P.L. Harris, and D.R. Olson (Cambridge: Cambridge University Press).
Bartsch, H. and Wellman, H.M. (1995), *Children Talk About the Mind* (New York, Oxford: OUP).

---

view for which 'the mind is transparent to itself'. On the other hand, Perner refers to 'the theory view of mind', according to which 'the mind is a theoretical construction for explaining observable behavior'. This view takes the position that 'mental terms do not denote internally observable states but are *theoretical terms*, which get their meaning by being embedded in a coherent body of knowledge or theory'. Here, Perner takes himself the following position: 'I opt for a refined view that admits information about inner (privately observable) states as an integral part of the theory' (pp. 257–8). And a little later he states: 'I also think it would be a mistake to discount 'inner life' altogether as a source of useful information' (p. 264). See also, e.g., Flavell *et al.* (1995), especially section IV. Introspection Studies, pp. 52ff., and P.L. Harris' (1995) commentary 'The Rise of Introspection', pp. 97ff.

[9] We would like to thank Dr. Klaus Petrus (Bern) for his acute critical reading of our first draft and also two anonymous referees for very helpful critical comments. Time prevented all the detailed suggestions being incorporated into this paper, but they will be valuable in projected future work. For linguistic improvements in the submitted version we thank Anthony Freeman, managing editor of *JCS*.

Chandler, M. and Boyes, M. (1982), 'Social-cognitive development', in *Handbook of Developmental Psychology*, ed. B.B. Wolman (Englewood Cliffs, NJ: Prentice-Hall)

Flavell, J.H. (1977), *Cognitive Development* (Englewood Cliffs, NJ: Prentice-Hall).

Flavell, J.H. (1988), 'The development of children's knowledge about the mind: From cognitive connections to mental representations', in *Developing Theories of Mind*, ed. J.W. Astington, P.L. Harris, and D.R. Olson (Cambridge: Cambridge University Press).

Flavell, J.H., Flavell, E.R. and Green, F.L. (1983), 'Development of the appearance-reality distinction', *Cognitive Psychology*, **15**, pp. 95–120.

Flavell, J.H., Green, F.L. and Flavell, E.R. (1995), *Young Children's Knowledge About Thinking*. With Commentary by P.L. Harris, J.W. Astington. Monographs of the Society for Research in Child Development, Serial No. 243, Vol. 60, No. 1.

Harris, P.L. (1995), 'The Rise of Introspection', commentary in Flavell, J.H., Green, F.L. and Flavell, E.R. (1995) *Young children's knowledge about thinking*. Monographs of the Society for Research in Child Development, Serial No. 243, Vol. 60, No. 1.

Hogrefe, G.J., Wimmer, H. and Perner, J. (1986), 'Ignorance versus false belief: A developmental lag in attribution of epistemic states', Child Development, **57**, pp. 567–82.

Husserl, E. (1982), *Ideas Pertaining to a Pure Phenomenology and to a Phenomenological Philosophy.First Book: General Introduction to a Pure Phenomenology*. Translated by F. Kersten, Edmund Husserl, Collected Works, vol. II (The Hague: Martinus Nijhoff Publishers). (Originally published in German: Ideen zu einer reinen Phänomenologie und phänomenologischen *Philosophie. Erstes Buch: Allgemeine Einführung in die reine Phänomenologie, Husserliana* Edmund Husserl Gesammelte Werke, vol. III/1, 1976, neu herausgegeben von Karl Schuhmann (Den Haag: Martinus Nijhoff – First German edition 1913).

Husserl, E. (1989), *Ideas Pertaining to a Pure Phenomenology and to a Phenomenological Philosophy. Second Book: Studies in the Phenomenology of Constitution*. Translated by Richard Rojcewicz and André Schuwer, Edmund Husserl, Collected Works, vol. III (Dordrecht: Kluwer) (Originally published in German: *Ideen zu einer reinen Phänomenologie und phänomenologischen Philosophie. Zweites Buch: Phänomenologische Untersuchungen zur Konstitution, Husserliana* Edmund Husserl, Gesammelte Werke, vol IV, 1952, ed. M. Biemel (Haag: Martinus Nijhoff)

Leslie, A.M. (1987), 'Pretense and representation: The origins of "theory of mind"', *Psychological Review*, **94**, pp. 412–26.

Leslie, A.M. (1988), 'Some implications of pretense for mechanisms underlying the child's theory of mind', in *Developing Theories of Mind*, ed. J.W. Astington, P.L. Harris, and D.R. Olson (New York: Cambridge University Press).

Lock, A. (ed. 1978), *Before Speech: the Beginning of Interpersonal Communication*. (NY: Academic Press).

Marbach, E. (1993), *Mental Representation and Consciousness: Towards a Phenomenological Theory of Representation and Reference* (Dordrecht: Kluwer Academic Publishers).

Perner, J. (1991), *Understanding the Representational Mind* (Cambridge, MA: MIT Press).

Perner, J. (1999), 'Theory of Mind', in *Developmental Psychology: Achievements and Prospects*, ed. M. Bennett (Hove, East Sussex: Psychology Press).

Perner, J., Leekam, S.R. and Wimmer, H. (1987), 'Three-year olds' difficulty with false belief: The case for a conceptual deficit', *British Journal of Developmental Psychology*, **5**, pp. 125–37.

Rang, B. (1973), *Kausalität und Motivation. Untersuchungen zum Verhältnis von Perspektivität und Objektivität in der Phänomenologie Edmund Husserls* (Haag, Martinus Nijhoff).

Rice, C. and Koinis, D., Sullivan, K., Tager-Flusberg, H. and Wimmer, E. (1997), 'When 3-year-olds pass the appearance–reality test', *Developmental Psychology*, **33**, No. 1, pp. 54–61.

Stern, D. N. (1985). *The Interpersonal World of the Infant*. (New York: Basic Books).

Surian, L. and Leslie, A.M. (1999), 'Competence and performance in false belief understanding: A comparison of autistic and normal 3-year-old children.

Wellman, H.M. (1990), *The Child's Theory of Mind* (Cambridge, MA: Bradford Books/MIT Press).

Wellman, H.M. (1993), 'Early understanding of mind: The normal case', in *Understanding Other Minds: Perspectives From Autism*, ed. S. Baron-Cohen, H. Tager-Flusberg and D.J. Cohen (Oxford: OUP).

Wellman, H.M., Cross, D. and Watson, J.K. (1999), 'A meta-analysis of theory of mind development: The truth about false-belief'. Paper presented at the Biennial Meeting of the Society for Research in Child Development, Albuquerque, New Mexico, April 15–18, 1999.

Wimmer, H. and Perner, J. (1983), 'Beliefs about beliefs: Representation and constraining function of wrong beliefs in young children's understanding of deception', *Cognition*, **13**, pp. 103–28.

Wimmer, H., Hogrefe, J. and Sodian, B. (1988), 'A second stage in children's conception of mental life: Understanding informational accesses as origins of knowledge and belief', in *Developing Theories of Mind*, ed. J.W. Astington, P.L. Harris, and D.R. Olson (Cambridge: Cambridge University Press).

Shaun Gallagher

The Practice of Mind

Theory, Simulation or Primary Interaction?[1]

Theory of mind explanations of how we know other minds are limited in several ways. First, they construe intersubjective relations too narrowly in terms of the specialized cognitive abilities of explaining and predicting another person's mental states and behaviours. Second, they sometimes draw conclusions about second-person interaction from experiments designed to test third-person observation of another's behaviour. As a result, the larger claims that are sometimes made for theory of mind, namely that theory of mind is our primary and pervasive means for understanding other persons, go beyond both the phenomenological and the scientific evidence. I argue that the interpretation of 'primary intersubjectivity' as merely precursory to theory of mind is inadequate. Rather, primary intersubjectivity, understood as a set of embodied practices and capabilities, is not only primary in a developmental sense, but is the primary way we continue to understand others in second-person interactions.

In psychology, philosophy of mind and, more recently, in the neurosciences, studies of how one person understands and interrelates with another person have been conducted under the heading of 'theory of mind'. Discussions of theory of mind are dominated by two main approaches: theory theory and simulation theory. The major tenets of theory theory are based on well-designed scientific experiments that show that children develop an understanding of other minds around the age of four. One version of theory theory claims that this understanding is based on an innately specified, domain specific mechanism designed for 'reading' other minds (Baron-Cohen, 1995; Leslie, 1991). An alternative version claims that the child attains this ability through a course of development in which the child tests and learns from the social environment (Gopnik and Meltzoff, 1997). Common to both versions of theory theory is the idea that children attain their understanding of other minds by implicitly employing a theoretical stance. This stance involves postulating the existence of mental states in others and using such postulations to explain and predict another person's behaviour. In the earliest level of development, the four- to five-year-old child's theory of mind involves 'first-order

---

[1] My thanks to an anonymous referee for constructive remarks on a previous version of this paper. I have also benefited from discussions following presentations of this material at York University in Toronto and at the British Society for Phenomenology meeting at Oxford University.

Journal of Consciousness Studies, **8**, No. 5–7, 2001, pp. 83–108

belief attribution' in which she distinguishes her own belief from someone else's belief. The next level involves 'second-order belief attribution', the ability to 'think about another person's thoughts about a third person's thoughts about an objective event' (Baron-Cohen, 1989, p. 288). Normal children between the ages of six and seven years old are able to achieve the second level. The very few autistic children who attain the earliest level, do so late, and they fail to attain the second level.

The second approach, simulation theory, argues that one does not *theorize* about the other person but uses one's own mental experience as an internal model for the other mind (e.g. Gordon, 1986, 1995a; Goldman, 1989; and Heal 1986, 1998a,b). To understand the other person, I simulate the thoughts or feelings that I would experience *if I were in the situation of the other.* I emulate what must be going through the other person's mind; or I create in my own mind pretend beliefs, desires or strategies that I use to understand the other's behaviour. My source for these simulations is not a theory that I have. Rather, I have a real model of the mind at my immediate disposal, that is, I have *my own mind*, and I can use it to generate and run simulations. I simply run through the sequence or pattern of behaviour or decision making that I would engage in if I were faced with the situation in question. I do it 'off line', however. That is, my imaginary rehearsal does not lead to actualizing the behaviour on my part. Finally, I attribute this pattern to the other person who is actually in that situation. According to simulation theory, this process may remain non-conscious, with only an awareness of the resulting understanding or prediction. The process itself, nonetheless, is structured as an internal, representational simulation (Gordon, 1986).

Across both of these approaches in the theory of mind literature one can distinguish two specific kinds of claims. First, *developmental claims* involve the timing and order of development, the importance and balance of innate mechanisms versus experience, and so forth. The experimental and neurological evidence used to support such claims and to justify the theory or simulation interpretations is impressive. It is possible, however, to raise questions about certain background assumptions that shape the design of such experiments and the interpretation of data as supportive of certain aspects of theory of mind. Second, *pragmatic claims* concern the scope of the applicability of theory of mind.[2] Pragmatic claims may be strong or weak. Some theorists (e.g. Baron-Cohen, 1995; Tooby and Cosmides, 1995; Leslie, 2000) make a very strong pragmatic claim for theory of mind, namely that, once formed, theory of mind is our primary and pervasive means for understanding other persons. It is not clear, however, that the experimental evidence used to support the developmental claims counts as evidence to support the strong pragmatic claim. Although I will question the interpretation of the science that informs the developmental claims, in this paper my main target is the strong pragmatic claim — that ordinarily and for the most part theory of mind forms the basis for our understanding of others.

To make clear what the strong pragmatic claim entails, let me review several of its various formulations. Recently, in a long conversation with Paul Ricoeur, the neuroscientist Jean-Pierre Changeux proposed that 'one's relation to others' depends

---

[2] These specific claims aside, the distinction between developmental aspects and pragmatic aspects of theory of mind is mirrored in recent research suggesting that the development of theory of mind may depend on normal language development (Astington and Jenkins, 1999), but that near perfect performance on theory of mind tasks does not depend on normal language functioning (Varley and Siegal, 2000).

on a 'cognitive device' that allows for the representation of the other's mental states, 'their sufferings, plans of action, [and] intentions'. He specifically cites experiments that support the concept of a theory of mind, and he maintains that it is just this type of mechanism that allows humans to acquire a system of moral values and aesthetic preferences (Changeux and Ricoeur, 2000, pp. 154–7). Two important researchers of this cognitive mechanism, Tooby and Cosmides (1995), suggest that 'humans everywhere interpret the behavior of others in . . . mentalistic terms because we all come equipped with a "theory of mind" module (ToMM) that is compelled to interpret others this way, with mentalistic terms as its natural language' (p. xvii). Baron-Cohen (1995, p. 3) writes: 'it is hard for us to make sense of behavior in any other way than via the mentalistic (or "intentional") framework'. Quoting Dan Sperber he continues: ' "attribution of mental states is to humans as echolocation is to the bat." It is our natural way of understanding the social environment' (p. 4). The conclusion proposed by Uta and Christopher Frith (Frith and Frith, 1999), that mental state attribution plays a major role in all social interactions, is echoed by Alan Leslie (2000), who defines ToMM as a specialized component of social intelligence, but claims that it is necessarily involved 'whenever an agent's behavior is attended', for example, 'in conversations and other real-time social interactions' (p. 1236).[3]

I do not propose simply to criticize the approaches of theory theory and simulation theory without offering something in their place. The alternative that I will propose is that the understanding of the other person is primarily neither theoretical nor based on an internal simulation, but is a form of embodied practice. In explicating this idea I do not want to deny that we do develop capacities for both theoretical interpretation and simulation, and that in certain cases we do understand others by enacting just such theoretical attitudes or simulations. Such instances are rare, however, relative to the majority of our interactions. Theory theory and simulation theory, at best, explain a very narrow and specialized set of cognitive processes that we sometimes use to relate to others (this would constitute a weak pragmatic claim for theory of mind).[4] Neither theoretical nor simulation strategies constitute the primary way in which we relate to, interact with or understand others.

The Embodied Practice of Primary Intersubjectivity

There is good scientific evidence to support the developmental claim that around the age of four children come to recognize that others are capable of having beliefs different from their own. Prior to this, however, the basis for human interaction and for understanding others has already been laid down by certain embodied practices — practices that are emotional, sensory-motor, perceptual and nonconceptual. I want to suggest that these embodied practices constitute our primary access for understanding others, and continue to do so even after we attain theory of mind abilities. Development that is specific to theory of mind happens within a wider framework of interpersonal pragmatics which can be characterized as second-person interactions with other persons perceived as others.

---

[3] Also, Wellman (1993): children at age four begin to 'see people as living their lives within a world of mental content that determines how they behave in the world of real objects and acts', they construe 'people's real-world actions as *inevitably* filtered through representations of the world rather than linked to the world directly' (pp. 31–2).

[4] Concerning a related narrowness of theory theory, see Chandler and Carpendale (1998).

The basic claim that I will defend is that in most intersubjective situations we have a direct, pragmatic understanding of another person's intentions because their intentions are explicitly expressed in their embodied actions. For the most part this understanding does not require us to postulate some belief or desire that is hidden away in the other person's mind, since what we might reflectively or abstractly call their belief or desire is expressed directly in their behaviour. The evidence to support this claim overlaps to some extent with evidence that is sometimes cited for both theory theory and simulation theory. I will review and reinterpret this evidence first, and then go on to discuss evidence that suggests that theory theory and simulation theory are unable to capture the full range of second-person interactions.

Many of those who argue for the theory or simulation approach acknowledge that for either a theoretical stance or a simulation routine to get off the ground some understanding of the context and behaviour of the other person must be had first; otherwise I would have nothing to simulate or to theorize about. This suggests that before I can develop a theory of mind I must already have an understanding of the other and their experience — including the other as the subject of intentional action. Prior to the possibility of knowing the other's mind in either a theoretical or simulation mode, one already requires (a) an understanding of what it means to be an experiencing subject; (b) an understanding of what it means that certain kinds of entities (but not others) in the environment are indeed such subjects; and (c) an understanding that in some way these entities are similar to and in other ways different from oneself. Furthermore, to form a theory about or to simulate what another person believes or desires, we already need to have specific pre-theoretical knowledge about how people behave in particular contexts.

One way to summarize these pre-theoretical conditions is to say, following a formulation suggested by Bruner and Kalmar (1998) concerning our understanding of the self, that the understanding of others in terms of their mental states requires a 'massively hermeneutic' background. This suggests that there is much going on in our understanding of others, in excess of and prior to the acquisition of theoretical and/or simulation capabilities. How do we get this background understanding? Some theorists answer this question by pointing to capabilities in infants and young children that they consider 'precursors' of theory of mind (Baron-Cohen, 1995; Gopnik and Meltzoff, 1997; Meltzoff, 1995; Meltzoff and Prinz, 2001; Nadel and Butterworth, 1999). In contrast, I interpret these capabilities as clues for an alternative approach to the issue of how we understand other people.

Pre-theoretical (non-conceptual) capabilities for understanding others already exist in very young children. Children, prior to the age of three, already have a sense of what it means to be an experiencing subject; that certain kinds of entities (but not others) in the environment are indeed such subjects; and that in some way these entities are similar to and in other ways different from themselves. This sense of others is already implicit, at least in a primitive way, in the behaviour of the newborn. We see evidence for it in instances of neonate imitation, which depends not only on a distinction between self and non-self, and a proprioceptive sense of one's own body, but the recognition that the other is in fact of the same sort as oneself (Bermúdez, 1996; Gallagher, 1996; Gallagher and Meltzoff, 1996). Infants are able to distinguish between inanimate objects and people (agents), and can respond in a distinctive way to human faces, that is, in a way that they do not respond to other objects (see

Legerstee, 1991; Johnson, 2000; Johnson *et al.*, 1998). Experiments by Meltzoff and Moore (1977, 1994) demonstrate that from birth the action of the infant and the perceived action of the other person are coded in the same 'language', a cross-modal system that is directly attuned to the actions and gestures of other humans. In the case of imitated facial gestures, one does not require an intermediate theory or simulation to translate between one's proprioceptive experience of one's face and the visual perception of the other's face. The translation is already accomplished at the level of an innate body schema that integrates sensory and motor systems (Gallagher and Meltzoff, 1996). There is, in this case, a common bodily intentionality that is shared across the perceiving subject and the perceived other. As Gopnik and Meltzoff indicate, 'we innately map the visually perceived motions of others onto our own kinesthetic sensations' (1997, p. 129).

Should we interpret this intermodal and intersubjective mapping as a primitive form of theorizing or 'an initial theory of action'? Gopnik and Meltzoff (1997) think so. They suggest that infants form a 'plan', an internal representation of what they will do, and then they 'recognize the relationship between their plan to produce the action and the action they perceive in others' (p. 130). On this view, this is the beginning of an inference-like operation that is eventually promoted into a theoretical attitude. But is the motor plan equivalent to a mental state? They suggest it is, although not a very sophisticated mental state. But if, in this case, we ask what a mental state is, it seems to be nothing other than a certain disposition of the body to act intentionally, plus the phenomenal sense of what it is like to do the action. Certainly it does not have the status of an ideational event that intervenes to mediate vision and proprioception. Intermodal experience is characterized as phenomenologically transparent. That is, the sensory-motor process does not require an internal copy that the infant consults in order to know what to do. Although neonates do in fact perfect their imitative actions (improving the match between their gesture and the perceived gesture — therefore indicating that they register the difference between themselves and the other), they need no internal plan to consult since they have a visual model right in front of them, namely the face of the other, as well as a proprioceptive model, namely the gesture that is taking shape on their own face. Even in those cases where the infant has cause to remember the presented gesture in order to imitate it after a delay (see Meltzoff and Moore, 1994), it is difficult to construe a sensory-motor memory as a theory of action.

Accordingly, the body schema does not function as an 'abstract representation' (Gopnik and Meltzoff, 1997, p. 133). If, as Meltzoff himself proposes, the body schema is an innate system designed for motor control, it seems more appropriate to understand it as a set of pragmatic (action oriented) capabilities embodied in the developing nervous system (see Gallagher *et al.*, 1998). In the human infant this system accounts for the possibility of recognizing and imitating other humans.

To the capabilities implicit in neonate imitation we need to add a number of other early interactive capabilities that constitute what Trevarthen (1979) has called 'primary intersubjectivity'. Although these aspects of behaviour are sometimes enlisted in the cause of theory theory (see Baron-Cohen, 1995, p. 55; Gopnik and Meltzoff, 1997, p. 131), it is quite possible to understand them as supporting a more immediate, less theoretical (non-mentalistic) mode of interaction. Baron-Cohen (1995), for example, proposes two mechanisms as necessary, but not sufficient, components of a theory of mind mechanism. The first he terms the 'intentionality detector' (ID). He considers this to be an innate capability that allows the infant to read 'mental states in behaviour' (p. 32). The ID allows the infant to interpret (notably without the intervention of theory or simulation) bodily movement as goal-directed intentional movement. In effect, the infant is capable of perceiving other persons as agents. On the one hand, this mechanism may not be specific enough to limit the attribution of agency to just humans (see Scholl and Tremoulet, 2000). On the other hand, combined with other capabilities, such as imitation of human gestures and eye-tracking (see below), ID is quickly honed to serve intersubjective interpretation. The interpretation fostered by ID, however, does not require advanced cognitive abilities. It is perceptual and, as Scholl and Tremoulet suggest, 'fast, automatic, irresistible and highly stimulus-driven' (p. 299).

Evidence for early, non-mentalistic interpretation of the intentional actions of others can be found in numerous studies. Baldwin and colleagues have shown that infants at ten to eleven months are able to parse some kinds of continuous action according to intentional boundaries (Baldwin and Baird, 2001; Baldwin *et al.*, in press). Eighteen-month-old children can comprehend what another person intends to do. They are able to re-enact to completion the goal-directed behaviour that an observed subject does not complete (Meltzoff, 1995; Meltzoff and Brooks, in press). Quite obviously ID provides an understanding of what an intentional state is; in the first place, another's intentional state is simply the other's action or the state of a perceived body. This understanding is non-mentalistic in the same sense that our understanding of our own intentional actions is non-mentalistic. To be precise, we do not interpret our own action on either an abstract, physiological level ('I am activating a certain group of muscles'), or in terms of a mentalistic performance ('I believe P, so I will do X'). Rather, quite naturally, we understand our own actions on the highest pragmatic level possible (see e.g. Jeannerod, 1997; Gallagher and Marcel, 1999). For example, if, as I reach for a cup, someone asks me what I am doing, I do not say, ordinarily, 'I am reaching for a cup'; rather I say, 'I'm taking a drink'. I tend to understand my actions just at that pragmatic, intentional (goal-oriented) level, ignoring possible sub-personal or lower-level descriptions, and also ignoring ideational or mentalistic interpretations, e.g. 'What are you doing?' 'I'm acting on a belief (desire) that I am thirsty'. Likewise, the interpretation of the actions of others occurs at that same pragmatic (intentional) level. We interpret their actions in terms of their goals and intentions set in contextualized situations, rather than abstractly in terms of either their muscular performance or their beliefs.[5]

---

[5] Do our interpretations of such actions depend on inference? Baldwin and Baird (2001) argue that inference is required to sort out which one of many possible interpretations is correct. They cite Searle's example.

If I am going for a walk to Hyde Park, there are any number of things that are happening in the course of my walk, but their descriptions do not describe my intentional actions, because in acting what I am doing depends in large part on what I think I am doing. So for example, I am also moving in the general direction of Patagonia, shaking the hair on my head up and down, wearing out my shoes and moving a lot of air molecules. However, none of these other descriptions seems to get at what is essential about this action, as the action it is. (Searle, 1984, p. 58)

According to Baldwin and Baird, to work out the right interpretation of Searle's action we need much more information about him and human behaviour, and on that basis we proceed to make an inferential judgment about his intentions. But clearly, given the situation, Patagonia, bouncing hair

The second mechanism proposed by Baron-Cohen is what he terms the 'eye-direction detector' (EDD). EDD allows the infant to recognize where another person is looking. Obviously, this mechanism is more specific than ID since it is linked to the perception of eyes and faces. It allows the infant to see (1) that the other person is looking in a certain direction and (2) that the other person sees what she is looking at. Does EDD involve an inference in moving from step (1) to step (2)? Baron-Cohen suggests that an inference is necessary to understand that the other person actually sees what she is looking at. Specifically, he points out that the infant experiences its own vision as contingent on opening versus closing its eyes. His suggestion is more in line with simulation theory: 'from very early on, infants presumably distinguish seeing from not-seeing . . . Although this knowledge is initially based on the infant's own experience, it could be generalized to an Agent by analogy with the Self' (Baron-Cohen, 1995, p. 43). But, one could ask, how does seeing differ from looking? Of course *by virtue of experience* we may come to discover that someone can be looking in a certain direction and not seeing something that is located in that direction. But that would seem to be something that we learn rather than a default mode of EDD. *On the face of it*, that is, at a primary (default) level of experience, there does not seem to be an extra step between looking at something and seeing it.[6]

Baron-Cohen makes it clear that ID and EDD separately or together are sufficient to enable the child to recognize dyadic relations between the other and the self, or between the other and the world. The child can understand that the other person *wants* food or *intends* to open the door, that the other can *see* him (the child) or is *looking at* the door. These are basic intentional relations. Of course children do not simply observe others, they interact with others, and in doing so they develop a further capability which Baron-Cohen terms the 'shared attention mechanism' (SAM). Behaviour representative of joint attention begins to develop around nine to fourteen months. The child alternates between monitoring the gaze of the other and what the other is gazing at, checking to verify that they are continuing to look at the same thing. The child also learns to point at around this same time. Phillips, Baron-Cohen and Rutter (1992) show that infants between nine and eighteen months look to the eyes of the other person to help interpret the meaning of an ambiguous event. In such interactions, well before the development of a theory of mind mechanism, the child looks to the body and the expressive movement of the other to discern the intention of the person or to find the meaning of some object. In this kind of second-person interaction two-year-olds are even capable of recognizing pretend behaviour, for example the mother pretending the banana is a telephone (Leslie, 1994).

---

and shoe-wear as such, and molecular movement, simply do not enter into my interpretation, unless I start making abstract, theoretical inferences. Rather, if I see John Searle walking toward Hyde Park, I'm likely to say, 'There's John Searle out for a walk.' Or, 'That guy is heading for the park.' The other interpretations simply do not come up, unless I start making large and abstract inferences. Since I don't see John Searle every day, I may in fact start to wonder what his further intentions are — is he going to philosophize in the park? But if I were to seriously pursue this question I would have to take action — follow him, stop and ask him, ask someone else who might know, etc. Without such action my inferences would be blind.

[6] See Leslie and Frith (1988). Their discussion of seeing and not seeing in terms of a geometrical-causal line of sight suggests that the default does not involve a distinction between seeing and looking. Baron-Cohen (1995), who carefully provides evidence for the other aspects of EDD, does not provide evidence for there being an inference between looking and seeing.

There are many more intention-signalling behaviours that infants and young children are capable of perceiving. In addition to the eyes, it is likely that various movements of the head, the mouth, the hands, and more general body movements are perceived as meaningful or goal-directed. Such perceptions are important for a non-mentalistic (pre-theoretical) understanding of the intentions and dispositions of other persons as well as for social reinforcement (see review by Allison, Puce and McCarthy, 2000), and they are operative by the end of the first year (Baldwin, 1993; Johnson, 2000; Johnson et al., 1998). In effect, this kind of perception-based understanding is a form of body-reading rather than mind-reading. In seeing the actions and expressive movements of the other person one already sees their meaning; no inference to a hidden set of mental states (beliefs, desires, etc.) is necessary.

There is also evidence for affective and temporal coordination between the gestures and expressions of the infant and those of the other persons with whom they interact. Infants 'vocalize and gesture in a way that seems "tuned" [affectively and temporally] to the vocalizations and gestures of the other person' (Gopnik and Meltzoff, 1997, p. 131). At five to seven months infants are able to detect correspondences between visual and auditory information that specify the expression of emotions (Walker, 1982). Importantly, the perception of emotion in the movement of others is a perception of an embodied comportment, rather than a theory or simulation of an emotional state. Moore, Hobson and Lee (1997) have demonstrated the emotional nature of human movement using actors with point-lights attached to various body joints.[7] Non-autistic subjects view the abstractly outlined but clearly embodied movement of the actors in a darkened room and are able to identify the emotion that is being represented. The emotional states of others are not, in primary experience, mental attributes that we have to infer. One perceives the emotion in the movement and expression of the other's body.[8]

Given the capabilities that are available under the title of primary intersubjectivity, I propose what in relation to theory theory or simulation theory is a revised, and in some sense enhanced or extended *developmental claim*. Before we are in a position to form a theory about or to simulate what the other person believes or desires, we already have specific pre-theoretical knowledge about how people behave in particular contexts. We are able to get this kind of knowledge precisely through the various capabilities that characterize primary intersubjectivity, including imitation, intentionality detection, eye-tracking, the perception of intentional or goal-related movements, and the perception of meaning and emotion in movement and posture. This kind of knowledge, which is the 'massively hermeneutic' background required for the more conceptual accomplishments of mentalistic interpretation, derives from embodied practices in second-person interactions with others. As a result, before we are in a position to theorize, simulate, explain or predict mental states in others, we

[7] As early as five months of age infants show preferential attentiveness to human shape and movement in such displays (Bertenthal, Proffitt and Cutting, 1984). The subjects in Moore, Hobson and Lee (1997) were older children classified as normal, autistic and non-autistic mentally retarded. The results demonstrated that the autistic children had relatively more difficulty in recognizing (or simply failed to recognize) emotional attitudes.

[8] Hobson (1993) provides a strong argument along this line. He cites Merleau-Ponty (1994) who notes the 'simple fact that I live in the facial expressions of the other, as I feel him living in mine' (p. 146). Also see Cole (1998, 1999) on the importance of the face in such contexts.

are already in a position to interact with and to understand others in terms of their gestures, intentions and emotions, and in terms of what they see, what they do or pretend to do with objects, and how they act toward ourselves and others.

I also want to argue for the following *pragmatic claim*. Primary, embodied intersubjectivity is not primary simply in developmental terms. Rather it remains primary across all face-to-face intersubjective experiences, and it subtends the occasional and secondary intersubjective practices of explaining or predicting what other people believe, desire or intend in the practice of their own minds.

What Can Phenomenology Show?

There are significant differences between theory theorists and simulation theorists, as well as between nativist and non-nativist accounts of theory theory. There are also disagreements among both simulationists and theory theorists on the question of implicit versus explicit processes. I do not mean to simply brush over these differences. They will motivate a variety of qualifications on the points that I will outline here. The main qualification is that all of the following critical points do not apply to every representative of these richly diverse positions. Notwithstanding this qualification, the following points do apply to a large part of the literature on theory of mind.

A common and basic assumption implicit to theory of mind accounts is that to know another person is to know that person's mind, and this means to know their beliefs, desires or intentional states. I will refer to this as the *mentalistic supposition*. Furthermore, theory of mind suggests that we use our knowledge of another person's mind to explain or predict the other person's behaviour. Since we have no direct access to another person's intentional states, we either postulate what their beliefs or desires are on the basis of a set of causal-explanatory laws (theory theory) or we project the results of certain simulation routines. There is no requirement that such theorizing or simulating be conscious or explicit. We may learn to engage in such interpretation to the point that it becomes habitual and transparent.

The mentalistic supposition implies that an explicit recognition of another person's beliefs, desires or intentional states is clearly conceptual; and that an implicit recognition is informed by such conceptual knowledge. One requires a concept of belief or desire before one can attribute such things to another person. This conceptual recognition involves an element of abstractness. To discover a belief as an intentional state even in myself requires that I take up a second-order reflective stance and recognize that my cognitive action can be classified as a belief. Indeed, to explicitly recognize that I myself 'have a mind' is already something of a theoretical postulate. This is not to deny that I might have something like a direct access to my own experience, or that this experience can be characterized as self-conscious. I can easily say, for example, 'I feel very good about planning my trip.' But to say that this experience of feeling good is in fact a *feeling*, and that this feeling depends on a *belief* that I will actually take the trip, requires something like a reflective detachment from my phenomenal experience, and the positing of a feeling (or belief) as a feeling (as a belief). It would involve a further postulation that such feelings and beliefs are in some fashion part of what it means to have a mind. This kind of metacognitive theorizing is always possible for the adult human, but for the most part I would suggest that, in practice, this is

not the way we think of ourselves — unless we are practising philosophical meditations of the sort Descartes practised.

Perhaps the fact that we have something like a direct access to our own experience
does not require that to know our own mind we take a conceptual, abstract, theoretical
attitude toward our own experience. Rather, for theory theory, the idea (the pragmatic
claim) is that to understand the other person, to whom we have no direct access, we take
just such a theoretical attitude. In order to understand that the other person feels very
good about planning her trip, I can only hypothesize that she has a certain set of feelings
and beliefs that normally go along with a situation like that. One's theory depends upon
and is complicated, however, by what one knows of such situations. Some people do
not have good feelings about planning trips; they actually get stressed out. Sometimes
they may even say 'I don't believe that I am actually going!' Clearly if I am to take a
theoretical stance toward what the other person is experiencing, I need to interpret her
behaviour on the basis of what I see and hear, and on the basis of what I know of such
things. What I know of such things, however, is not easily summarized. Part of what I
know includes the kind of pre-theoretical knowledge that I get through capacities that
belong to primary intersubjectivity, as described above. If I were to formalize a rule that
guided my theoretical stance, it would probably include aspects of pre-theoretical
knowledge. Consider the following formulation. 'When someone is planning a trip and
she says something like "I don't believe that I am actually going," with intonations that
signal exasperation, she really means that she does believe that she is going and she is
not enjoying the planning process.' An exasperated intonation, however, is something
that I learn about at the level of primary intersubjectivity.

Do we react to the exasperation in a person's voice by appealing (implicitly or
explicitly) to a theory? It seems possible to describe it in this way in cases where the
situation is not typical, or when, perhaps, the behaviour of the other person is out of
character or out of context, or when we don't know the person, or in cases where we
are talking with someone else about a third person. When we do not know the person
we may need to run through certain possibilities and perhaps engage in a process of
interpretation from a distance, much as a historian might attempt to understand a historical figure — forming a hypothesis on the basis of evidence.[9] Even in cases where
we know (or think we know) a person very well, we may express puzzlement about
their behaviour. In discussing a friend's behaviour with someone who doesn't know
her as well, we may come to devise a theory about why she is acting in a certain way.
It seems very possible to describe such cases in terms of a theory of mind. Is this a
good description of our ordinary interactions with others?

Simulation theory claims that it is not. It is not clear that we represent, explicitly or
implicitly, the sorts of rules (causal–explanatory laws) that would summarize what
we know of human situations and that would operate as the bases for a theoretical
understanding of the other person. Indeed, we find it difficult even to formulate such
rules, and this seems odd if we actually use them all the time (Goldman, 1989). Furthermore, at least on the developmental version of theory theory, there is no way to
account for the fact that children as young as three or four years putatively develop

---

[9] Davies and Stone (1998) consider certain limitations of historical analysis based on simulation, citing
     Collingwood's claim that historical understanding can be achieved by the re-enactment of the histori-
     cal character's thought.

the very same theory (a common folk psychology), when theory formation in general usually leads to a diversification of theory (Carruthers, 1996; Goldman, 1989).

Do we, then, simulate the other person's belief? Again, this process itself may remain implicit, with only an awareness of the resulting prediction. The process itself, nonetheless, is structured as an internal, representational simulation (Gordon, 1986). The simulation model is closer than theory theory to what I described above as an embodied practice of primary intersubjectivity. It involves something more like a practiced skill than a theoretical stance. Indeed, there is some suggestion that the result of simulation is not so much a mental model of the other's mind, but a motor adjustment in my own system that allows me insight into the other person's behaviour (Gordon, unpublished MS, cited in Stich and Nichols, 1992; Grezes and Decety, 2001). On the other hand, various descriptions of simulation invoke the idea of predicting behaviour on the basis of hypothetical beliefs and desires that are fed into a cognitive decision-making system (see Carruthers (1996) for a description of an approach that combines theory and simulation along this line). The result of this process is to project or attribute relevant intentional states to the mind of the other person. Like theory theory, simulation theory understands the other person as a collection of such mental states, and often understands the simulation itself as a mental state.

In the situation of talking with someone else about a third person, it seems possible to describe our attitude toward the person under discussion as theoretical or as involving a simulation of the other person's mental states. But does the same description capture the dynamics of our interaction with our interlocutor? That is, in a second-person conversational situation, although we may indeed tacitly follow certain rules of conversation, our process of interpretation does not seem to involve a detached or abstract, third-person quest for causal explanation. Nor does it seem to be a theory-driven interpretation that takes the other person's words as evidence for a mental state standing behind what he has just said. Even if we are trying to read between the lines and we reach the conclusion that the person we are conversing with believes the wrong thing concerning the other person, our understanding of this is poorly described as resulting from formulating a theoretical hypothesis or running a simulation routine about what he believes. We do not posit a theoretical entity called a belief and attribute it to him. We do not interact with him by conceiving of his mind as a set of *cogitationes* closed up in immanence (Merleau-Ponty, 1962, p. 353).

Both theory theory and simulation theory conceive of communicative interaction between two people as a process that takes place between two Cartesian minds. It assumes that one's understanding involves a retreat into a realm of *theoria* or *simulacra*, into a set of internal mental operations that come to be expressed (externalized) in speech, gesture or interaction. If, in contrast, we think of communicative interaction as being accomplished in the very action of communication, in the speech, gesture and interaction itself,[10] then the idea that the understanding of another person involves an attempt to theorize about an unseen belief, or to mind-read, is problematic.

---

[10] Here I follow Merleau-Ponty (1962), who conceives of thought as being accomplished in speech. In contrast, a leading theorist of mind, Baron-Cohen (1995), endorses a traditional Augustinian view of language: 'language functions principally as a "printout" of the contents of the mind' (p. 29). It follows that 'in decoding speech we go way beyond the words we hear or read, to hypothesize about the speaker's mental states' (p. 27).

This phenomenologically based criticism is subject to an objection that is typically raised at this point. Is an appeal to phenomenology in this context justified? Theory theorists and simulation theorists often claim that the employment of a theory of mind or simulation routine is unconscious and that what we experience or seemingly experience is not a good guide for what is really going on in such cases (e.g. Goldman and Gallese, 2000). On this account we should think of the theory or simulation routine as somehow programmed into the very structure of our experience of others. If that is the case and our engagement in a theory or simulation procedure is not always explicit or conscious does this mean that our phenomenology is simply wrong? Or does it mean rather that what we capture in phenomenological reflection is something else?

In principle, phenomenology would not be able to say whether a subpersonal cognitive routine is operative; but it would be able to say whether my normal experience of the other person is best characterized as *explanation* and *prediction*, the kind of interpretations that both theory theory and simulation theory posit. I suggest that what phenomenology tells us is that explanation and prediction are specialized and relatively rare modes of understanding others, and that something like evaluative understanding about what someone means or about how I should respond in any particular situation best characterize most of our interactions. The kind of phenomenology I have in mind here is close to a Heideggerian existential phenomenology. It tells us that our primary and usual way of being in the world is pragmatic (characterized by action, involvement and interaction based on environmental and contextual factors), rather than mentalistic or conceptual (characterized as explanation or prediction based on mental contents).[11]

Both theory theory and simulation theory construe our encounter with other people in terms of explaining or predicting the other's beliefs, desires and behaviours. Phenomenology cannot tell us whether our response to the exasperation in a person's voice involves an implicit (sub-conscious) theory or pretend belief. But a careful and methodical phenomenology[12] should be able to tell us whether, when we hear the exasperated voice, our usual response involves formulating an explanation or predicting what the person will do next? Our encounters with others are in fact not normally occasions for theorizing or simulating if such nonconscious procedures are cashed out phenomenologically as explaining or predicting on the basis of postulated mental states. Rather, pragmatic interaction and evaluative understanding take up most of our effort. Only when second-person pragmatic interactions or our evaluative

---

[11] Heidegger's famous description of the carpenter's hammer is a relevant example. For the most part the carpenter's experience of the hammer is a pragmatic one. She hammers without thinking of the hammer as an object, using it rather as an extension of her body. Her relationship to it is not theoretical or conceptual, but fully caught up in a complex set of pragmatic activities. Only when something goes wrong with the hammering, or when the hammer breaks, does she regard the hammer as an object and as something to be explained. A theory of the hammer is experientially secondary to its use (Heidegger, 1968). The suggestion is not that one's relation to another person is equivalent to one's relation to equipment but that, as in the case of the hammer, one's relation to others is not primarily theoretical or conceptual, but is first of all an interactive one.

[12] In contrast to non-methodical introspection. This qualification is meant to head off the standard reply that introspective reports are notoriously suspect guides to what subjects are doing even at the conscious level, since they are infected (as it were) by what one of my referee's called 'local politics (currently popular psychological views, tried and true folk-notions, and so forth and so on)'. In the method of a phenomenological reduction of the sort practised by Husserl, care is taken to systematically eliminate such prejudices.

attempts to understand break down do we resort to the more specialized practices of third-person explanation and prediction.

The distinction between explanation and evaluation is an important one to make in this context.[13] In our everyday and ordinary encounters we rarely look for causal-mentalistic explanations for people's actions. Rather than being folk psychological, in the sense of involving a folk theory, our encounters are primarily occasions for interactions and evaluations. My action, or the action of another, may be motivated in part by the fact that the situation is just such that this is the action that is called for. In such cases, an action is not caused by a well-formed mental state, but is motivated by some aspect of the situation, as I experience and evaluate it.

One way to understand what I mean by evaluation is to reframe a distinction made by Perner (1991) in his explication of theory theory. He distinguishes between 'situation theory', employed by three-year-olds prior to attaining a theory of mind, and 'representational theory' or theory of mind. According to Perner, three-year-olds employ some aspect of the environment plus some understanding of desire, but are unable to comprehend the concept of the other's belief. One should note, however, that the environment, or the situation, is not something that the child, or the adult, objectively confronts as an outside observer. The notion of situation should be understood to include the experiencing subject (that is, oneself) and the action of that subject. Our involvement in a situation is not as a third-person observer developing a situation theory, as if we were not part of the situation ourselves. Our interaction with another human being is not equivalent to a detached observation (or explanation) of what that person is doing. The notion of evaluation signifies an embedded cognitive practice that relies on those pre-theoretical embodied capabilities that three-year-olds have already developed to understand intersubjective situations. Even to the extent that evaluation becomes reflective, it is more like an embedded reflection on possible actions (Gallagher and Marcel, 1999) than a detached consideration of mental states. Rather than drawing up a theory about a particular situation, or taking an objective, observational stance toward the other person, we have the capacity for measuring it up in pragmatic terms. This capacity does not disappear when the child reaches the age of four, but is rather enhanced by further experience.[14]

Consider the following example that Baron-Cohen (1995, p. 28) cites from Pinker (1994):

---

[13] See (Jacobson, 2000). What Jacobson says of eliminative materialism and more generally of function-alism, can equally be said of theory theory and simulation theory: 'each take the *defining role* of folk-psychological terms to be in causal discourse while it is instead in significant part in evaluative discourse'. On the relation between theory and explanation, see Schwitzgebel (1999a).

[14] Perner (1991) goes on to suggest that theory of mind doesn't actually replace situation theory. It simply amends it to cover problem cases. Even as adults 'we stay situation theorists at heart. We resort to a representational theory only when we need to.' Barresi and Moore (1996) also argue that more primary processes of social understanding are not replaced by the more mentalistic ones, but that the more primary ones continue to function. I disagree with Gordon (1995b) who, in a gloss on Perner, suggests that what passes as situation theory in adult behaviour is really a sophistication in simulating and attributing beliefs and intentions which becomes manifest only when there is a problem. The sophistication of our simulation abilities, he contends, simply makes it seem as if we are not simulating. Gordon does suggest that prior to the development of simulation abilities, the mental, in some sense, 'is already "out there" in the environment, though not yet conceptualized as mental'. My point is that a good part of the mental does not end up hidden away. It becomes embedded in our embodied and communicative practices.

Woman: I'm leaving you.

Man: Who is he?

Overhearing this bit of discussion, the task, according to Baron-Cohen, is to explain why the man utters this phrase. The explanation: 'the man must have thought [formed a belief] that the woman was leaving him for another man'. A certain thought or belief causes the man to say what he says. What causes the thought? Perhaps some cognitive schema that associates this scenario with the influence of a third party. If indeed an explanation is needed this may be a good folk-psychological one, but the question to start with is whether, upon overhearing this bit of conversation, we would be motivated *to explain it* rather than to comprehend it in an evaluative way. From our perspective, as interlopers who are listening in, the thought expressed in the man's words does not have the status of a belief in his head; the thought is already given to us in the words and we have no need to posit a belief over and above them. Would we not already have a pre-theoretical understanding of what was meant, and instead of formulating an explanation would we not be taking some stance or action — choosing up sides or perhaps moving as far away as we could to give the couple privacy? In reality, the man himself may have no such discrete belief. He may have blurted out the question as a question that had never before dawned on him, because he saw something like shame or defiance in the woman's eyes.

Theory of mind conceptualizes beliefs and other intentional states as discretely representational. There are good reasons, however, to view beliefs as dispositions that are sometimes ambiguous even from the perspective of the believer. To have a belief is not to have an all-or-nothing mental representation, but to have some more or less complete set of dispositions to act and to experience in certain ways. Dispositions are actualized, not only in overt behaviour, including verbal behaviour, but also in phenomenal experience.[15] Thus, given a particular context, one may have a disposition to feel upset or to perceive things as grating, depending on a variety of circumstances. For our understanding of other people, I am suggesting that we rarely need to go beyond contextualized overt behaviours (actions, gestures, speech-acts, etc.). We are rarely required to postulate an idealized and abstract mental belief standing behind these behaviours in order to grasp the disposition that is overtly constituted and expressed in the contextualized behaviour. In certain contextualized interaction I need go no further than the person's gestures or emotional expressions to gain my understanding of how it is with that person.

Even if explaining and predicting another person's intentional states and behaviours are structured as theories or simulations, a more basic question is whether our ordinary attempts to understand other people are best characterized as explanations and predictions. Those who defend theory of mind might reply that even if our relations with others phenomenologically *seem* to be pragmatically interactive, they are, in fact, implicitly matters of theorizing or simulating. Even if we are aware of only direct evaluative responses, such responses may be the result of busy sub-personal

---

[15] This view, a 'phenomenal, dispositional account of belief' (Schwitzgebel, in press), clearly does not involve a reductionist type of behaviourism, as one finds in the usual interpretation of Ryle (1949). Schwitzgebel's excellent account, framed in a purely analytic exposition, is quite consistent with phenomenological accounts found in theorists like Merleau-Ponty. For its implications in the developmental context see Schwitzgebel (1999b)

mechanisms that have the structure of theory or simulation. In this case, controlled experimentation (rather than phenomenology) is the only way to investigate such cognitive mechanisms. Thus, we clearly need to examine the scientific evidence in support of this claim.

The Science of Other Minds

Both theory theory and simulation theory claim the support of good science. Theory theory appeals to classic false-belief tests in developmental psychology for its justification. Simulation theory has recently received support from neuroscience. If one is going to challenge either of these approaches, it is important to consider the scientific evidence and to indicate whether the challenge puts the scientific evidence into question, or whether a new theory would be consistent with the established evidence. I can not review all of the scientific evidence for either of these approaches here, but I will look at a representative sampling and try to indicate certain limitations in the empirical data consistent with my remarks in the previous sections.

1. False-belief experiments

In the 'standard' false-belief task a subject is asked about the thoughts and actions of another person or character who lacks certain information that the subject has. For example, the subject knows that a candy box actually contains pencils. Someone else (this could be a puppet or a real person) enters the room. The question that is posed to the subject is 'What will the other person say is in the candy box?'. Four-year-olds generally answer correctly that the other person will think that there are candies in the box. Three-year-olds are unable to see that the other person may falsely believe that there are candies in the box. So three-year-olds answer that the other person will say there are pencils in the box (see e.g. Perner, Leekam and Wimmer, 1987). False belief tests can be made more or less complicated.

In a series of experiments often sited in support of theory theory, Heinz Wimmer and Josef Perner (1983) investigated a subject's competence in representing another person's belief when that belief differs from what the subject knows to be true. In four experiments children between the ages of three and nine were divided into three groups: three- to four-year olds, four- to six-year olds, and six- to nine-year olds. Each child was told stories that involved, first, a cooperative situation and then a competitive situation. For example, a kid named Maxi puts a piece of chocolate in a blue cupboard and then goes out to play. While he is gone, and without his knowledge, the chocolate is moved into a green cupboard. In the cooperative version of the story Maxi, upon returning, cooperates with another character in obtaining the chocolate. In the competitive version Maxi is in competition with an antagonist. All stories are told up to the point where the main characters look for the hidden object. At this time, each subject is asked to indicate (a) where the chocolate actually was located (the reality question), (b) where Maxi would look for the chocolate (the belief question) and (c) where Maxi would tell the other character to look.

All age groups were able to answer the reality question correctly. Answers to the other questions generally varied in relation to the age of the subjects. When asked where Maxi would look for the object (the belief question) most of the four- to five-year-olds chose the green cupboard incorrectly. However, most of the six- to nine-year-olds chose the blue cupboard, correctly, despite the fact that the object was really in the green cupboard. When asked, in the competitive version, where Maxi would say the object was hidden, most of the subjects who answered correctly on the belief question were able to create a deceitful utterance required for the competitive versions of the stories. These subjects understood that Maxi would deceive his competitor purposely. Most of the same subjects were also able to create a truthful utterance for the cooperative versions of the stories.

Why were the youngest subjects unable to correctly ascribe a wrong belief to Maxi? A second experiment was designed to answer this question. The same stories were used as in the previous experiment, but with several modifications. A memory question (Do you remember where Maxi put the chocolate?) was asked when the subject answered incorrectly to the belief question. Also, subjects were reminded of what Maxi did before he went outside before being asked the belief question. The results showed an improvement of the five- to six-year-olds in their responses to the belief question. The three- to four-year-olds were unable to correctly ascribe a wrong belief even with the modifications.

Wimmer and Perner concluded from these and several other experiments that children age six and above are able to cope with representational complexities. Four- to six-year-old children have the ability to represent wrong beliefs, but are sensitive to modifications in the task. Few in the three- to four-year-old group are able to represent wrong beliefs or another person's absence of knowledge. Most children who are able to represent wrong beliefs are also able to construct deceitful utterances. Children between the ages of four and six are able to demonstrate inferential skills.

These experiments, and many others based on the same experimental paradigm (see e.g. Baron-Cohen, Leslie and Frith, 1985) are often cited as evidence for the development of a theory of mind at around four years of age. As Stich and Nichols (1992) point out, however, theory theory, as well as simulation theory, are compatible with but do not necessarily entail the Maxi experiments (see Gordon, 1995b). So these experiments cannot be used to support one approach over another. Indeed, a number of authors argue that subjects who fail false-belief tests do not necessarily fail them because they lack a theory of mind. It may be that the intellectual processing involved in the testing is simply too complicated.[16] Furthermore, the false-belief paradigm does not capture all there is to say about children's abilities to understand others. Bloom and German (2000), who generally support a theory approach, cite various aspects of primary intersubjectivity as already providing such capabilities prior to age four. They conclude, rightly, that the false-belief test is 'an ingenious, but very difficult task that taps one aspect of people's understanding of the minds of others' (p. B30).

---

[16] Leslie and Thaiss (1992) show that when photographs are used to represent mental states four-year-olds do worse than their performance on the standard false-belief tests. If it were a matter of picturing mental states as representations, the four-year-old should do equally well on the photograph test (see Leslie, 2000). Three-year-olds fail both the photograph tests (in which false beliefs are not at stake) and the false-belief tests, suggesting not that children have problems with beliefs *per se*, but with the complexity of the problems (Bloom and German, 2000). Furthermore, Siegal and Beattie (1991) and Surian and Leslie (1999) have shown that three-year-olds are capable of passing false-belief tests if the wording of the questions is modified. This suggests that 'normally developing children's performance on false-belief problems is limited by processing resources rather than by inability to represent belief states in others' (Leslie, 2000, p. 1242). Bloom and German (2000) and Barresi and Moore (1996) present similar arguments.

The fact that these experiments are designed to test one aspect of how people understand the minds of others is both their strength and their weakness. The experiments clearly show that something new happens at age four, and that what happens is somewhat consistent with certain assumptions that are shared by both theory theory and simulation theory. The experiments are designed to test whether children at certain ages have acquired an ability to explain or predict the behaviour of others. But, as indicated above, explaining and predicting are very specialized cognitive abilities, and do not capture the fuller picture of how we understand other people.[17]

Two other important limitations of false-belief tests in relation to theory of mind should be pointed out. First, subjects are asked to predict the behaviour of others with whom they are *not* interacting. Based on a third-person observation, the child is asked to predict what the other person will do. Can the results of these experiments be used to characterize second-person ('I–you') interaction?[18] If second-person interaction is the primary and ordinary way of encountering the other person, can we be certain that results based on third-person observation can truly characterize our understanding of others? It is interesting to note that in the three-year-old subject's second-person interaction with the experimenter, the subject does not seem to have difficulty understanding the experimenter in the way that she seems to misunderstand the third person about whom she is asked. It is not at all clear that how we interact with another person directly in a second-person relationship can be captured by activities in the category of third-person observation.

Second, false-belief experiments, like the one conducted by Wimmer and Perner, are designed to test a conscious, metarepresentational process. That is, in such experiments, the subjects are not only provided with the task of explaining or predicting, but they are asked to perform these tasks consciously, and in a reflective manner. In contrast, many theorists claim that theory of mind mechanisms are sub-personal, operating below the level of consciousness. In effect, the experimental design simply does not address the issue of how theory of mind mechanisms function non-consciously.

There are thus at least three factors that limit the conclusions that can be drawn from such experiments for theory of mind, and especially for the pragmatic claim that theory of mind characterizes all of our interpersonal interactions.

(1) The experiments explicitly call for the specialized cognitive activities of explaining and predicting.

(2) The experiments involve third-person perspectives rather than second-person interactions.

(3) The experiments involve conscious processes and do not address theory of mind mechanisms that operate non-consciously.

---

[17] Stich and Nichols (1992) suggest, concerning these experiments, 'the explanation of the data offered by the experimenters is one that presupposes the correctness of the theory-theory'. One could further suggest that the kinds of questions that are asked, and the kinds of answers that are sought in these experiments, are framed by theory of mind's contention that explanation and prediction are primary ways of interpreting other's minds.

[18] For more on the concept of second-person interaction, and its irreducibility to first-person and/or third-person perspectives, see Gomez (1996) and Reddy (1996), as well as the previous section.

It might seem that the following experiment could address the second limitation. In Wimmer, Hogrefe and Sodian (1988), two children face each other and each answers questions about what they know or about what the other child knows concerning the contents of a box into which one of them has looked. Children of three and four years of age answer correctly about their own knowledge, but incorrectly about the other child's knowledge, even when they see the other child has looked into the box. Although this seems closer to second-person interaction, the children are not really interacting on the cognitive level that is being tested. That is, questions are posed by the experimenter (with whom the children are interacting), but they call for third-person explanation or prediction of the other person with whom they are not interacting.

A theory theory interpretation of this experiment is that these children use different mental processes to assess what they themselves know as opposed to what the other child knows. To answer about their own knowledge the children use an 'answer check procedure'. 'They simply check to see whether they have an answer to the embedded question in their knowledge base, and if they do they respond affirmatively' (Stich and Nichols, 1992). According to this account they do not know that they know the contents of the box until they find a belief or piece of knowledge in their own cognitive system. To say that they know what is in the box, it would not be enough to have looked inside the box; they would also have to look inside their own minds. They have to 'check' with themselves in something like a metarepresentative introspection (Leslie, 1988).

It seems more likely, and much more parsimonious, however, that their answer about what they know is based simply on looking inside the box rather than looking inside their own mind. The child looks inside the box and is then asked whether she knows what is in the box. Her positive answer is based on the fact that she just saw what was inside the box, rather than on an introspective discovery of a belief about the contents of the box (see Gordon, 1995b). Her knowledge, one might say, is already in her action. If a subject is asked 'Do you believe that p?' the subject does not start searching in her mind for the *belief that p*. Rather, she straightforwardly considers whether p is or is not the case (see Evans, 1982). In cases when the child does not know what is in the box, her failure to acknowledge that another child who has looked inside the box does know would be surprising only to someone who would expect her to think theoretically, in terms of intentional states abstracted from her own actions. What is not surprising, however, is that the subject has no problem understanding the question put to her by the experimenter with whom she is interacting. Nor is there any indication that she is surprised by the possibility that someone else may or may not have knowledge.

Children aged four to five years have progressed to the point of having the ability to tell correctly what another child who has seen the transfer of a piece of candy from one box to another knows about the contents of the second box. In this part of the experiment, however, both children (the subject and the other) have seen the transfer together. One could still say that their knowledge is in their action. But the same age group fails to understand that in certain circumstances the other child, without visual knowledge, might know the same fact by inference. Again, this would be surprising only if the subject understood the other child in terms of having abstract mental states. The same experiments show that a six-year-old child is capable of precisely this realization and has thus attained some advanced part of a theory of mind. Yet to show that a child attains a theory of mind at some specific point in development, such that they can consciously explain or predict what someone with whom they are not interacting knows, is not to demonstrate that the child's primary understanding of others is based on theory of mind capabilities. These same children, we would assume, were able to play together and communicate prior to learning that knowledge and beliefs can be caused by inference as well as by direct perceptual access.

2. *Mirror neurons*

A different sort of scientific evidence has recently been cited in support of simulation theory, namely the proposal that the specific operations of mirror neurons can contribute to a simulation model of how we understand others. Mirror neurons, located in the premotor cortex (area F5) of the macaque monkey and, as evidence suggests, in the premotor cortex and Broca's area in the human (see Fadiga *et al.*, 1995; Rizzolatti *et al.*, 1996; Grafton *et al.*, 1996), respond *both* when a particular motor action is performed by the subject *and* when the subject observes the same goal-directed action performed by another individual. Mirror neurons thus constitute an intermodal link between the visual perception of action or dynamic expression and the first-person, *intra*subjective, proprioceptive sense of one's own capabilities.

Simulation theorists suggest that mirror neurons help us to translate our visual perception of the other person's behaviour into a mental plan of that behaviour in ourselves, thus enabling an explanation or prediction of the other person's thoughts or actions. Mirror neurons facilitate the creation of pretend ('off-line') actions (motor images) that correspond to the visually perceived actions of others (Gallese and Goldman, 1998). Mirror neurons, of course, are part of the motor system, so that the 'plan' that is generated is a motoric one. This, it is argued, at least prefigures (or is a primitive kind of) mental simulation, and as such it supports simulation theory rather than theory theory. 'The point is that [mirror neuron] activity is not mere theoretical inference. It creates in the observer a state that matches that of the target [person]' (Gallese and Goldman, 1998, p. 498).

This approach addresses some of the limitations found in the false-belief experiments. First, the activation of mirror neurons can be thought to be most appropriately the result of specific second-person interactions, although they also operate in third-person perspectives on how others interact.[19] Second, studies of mirror neurons are clearly studies of non-conscious, automatic processes that may or may not be experienced at a conscious level, although they surely shape conscious behaviour. Nonetheless, the process described as prefiguring a more mature simulation routine is described in a fashion similar to the theory theory approach, as resulting in the specialized cognitive activities of explaining, predicting and 'retrodicting'. Indeed, only by describing the activity as involving a representational 'plan' (Goldman and Gallese (2000) reject the idea of a non-representational intentionality) can simulation

---

[19] In experimental situations, of course, third-person perspectives are often employed. That is, the observation of the other person is conducted in a detached rather than interactive setting. This difference is usually ignored. For example, Ruby and Decety (2001) use the term 'third-person simulation' to signify the motor simulation of another person's action (in contrast to 'first-person simulation' of one's own action), without considering whether interactive observation might be different from detached observation, or for that matter whether the simulation of another's action could itself take the form of egocentric simulation (that is, I simulate the other's action as if it were my own) or allocentric simulation (I simulate the other's action as if it were her action performed where she is).

theorists claim that mirror neuron activity prefigures the more developed representational processes involved in explaining and predicting.

The implication of this representationalist view is that the understanding of the
other's behaviour is mediated by a model of ourselves. Goldman and Gallese (2000)
suggest that mirror neurons rely on an 'internal representation of goals, emotions,
body states and the like to map the same states in other individuals' (p. 256). On the
simulation account it would not be enough to see another person's actions and for
them to register in the mirror system; the activation of the neurons must generate an
extra copy of the actions as they would be if they were the perceiver's own actions.
We then read off the meaning of the other, not from *her* actions, but from the internal
simulation of *our own* 'as if' actions. This view suggests that in this regard, the subject who understands the other person is not interacting with the other person so much
as interacting with an internally simulated model of himself pretending to be the other
person. In effect, in contrast to the eclipse of second-person interaction by third-person
observation in false-belief tests, here second-person interaction is reduced to a
first-person internal activity.

Not only is this interpretation not phenomenologically parsimonious, it is also not
clear that the neurological picture supports it. Neuronal patterns (representations)
responsible for either implicit or explicit action simulation are in large part the same
neuronal patterns that are activated in the case of observing action and in performing
action (Grezes and Decety, 2001). In an experimental situation I may be asked to execute an action, simulate an action or observe an action performed by someone else.
There is significant overlap between action execution, simulation and observation in
the supplementary motor area (SMA), the dorsal premotor cortex, the supramarginal
gyrus and the superior parietal lobe. Mental simulation is, in addition, associated with
activation in the ventral premotor cortex, which may indicate a linguistic contribution. Observation of action is associated with additional activation in the temporal
pathway, consistent with visual processing. Grezes and Decety suggest that other
non-overlapping areas may be responsible for distinguishing our own agency from
the agency of others (see Ruby and Decety, 2001). There is, however, following the
observation of another person's action, no evidence for a secondary activation of the
overlapping areas that would count as an internal copy (simulation) over and above
the original activation generated by the observation. In other words, if I observe
another person perform action X, then there is activation in the relevant brain areas
that corresponds to the observation. There is no evidence that there is something like
a second activation of those same areas that would correspond to an internal copy or
simulation of action X. The neurological underpinnings of what could count as the
simulation are part and parcel of the activation that corresponds to the original observation. In effect, perception of action is already an understanding of the action; there
is no extra step involved that could count as a simulation routine.

On this view, mirror neurons are not primarily the mediators of simulation
(although they may play an important role in simulation, which is always a possibility
for the subject), but of direct intersubjective perception and direct action. In principle
there is no reason to think that mirror neurons do not function at birth.[20] If they do,

---

[20] The fact that at birth mirror neurons may be unmyelinated would not prevent them from functioning.
The lack of myelination would simply slow their activation

they may play a role in neonate imitation. To imitate a facial gesture that it sees, however, the infant has no need to simulate the gesture internally. It is already simulating it on its own face. Its own body is already in communication with the other's body at a perceptual level.

Conclusion

Some of the empirical evidence generally cited in support of theory of mind reflects an underlying theoretical bias shared by both theory theorists and simulation theorists. Namely that a normal understanding of others amounts to the explanation and prediction of their behaviour by ascribing to them specific mental states. Given a different theoretical conception of how we understand others, that is by employing capabilities of primary intersubjectivity, new experiments may be designed and old ones may be reinterpreted in ways that would offer important qualifications to theory of mind.

In regard to the developmental claim, I have argued that the picture is more complicated than that presented in theory of mind approaches, and that an embodied practice of mind begins much earlier than the onset of theory of mind capabilities. That this is an embodied practice, and that in the capabilities that characterize primary intersubjectivity the intentions and emotions of other persons are perceptually interpreted in movements, gestures, postures, facial expressions and contextualized behaviours — such facts go directly against the mentalistic supposition that guides theory theory and simulation theory. Developing a sophisticated understanding of others depends, first and foremost, on building the capacity for the embodied practices that come to be manifested in everyday encounters. Capacities for the simulated and theoretical understanding of others (a more specialized set of cognitive abilities) depend on the development of these more basic practices.

In regard to the pragmatic claim sometimes made for theory of mind, I have argued that understanding others in everyday life does not usually involve either taking a theoretical stance or deploying a simulation routine. It depends instead on a capacity for embodied practice that begins early (and is likely to be partially innate) and continues throughout normal (non-pathological) experience. Thus, in contrast to the strong pragmatic claim for theory of mind, namely that it is our primary and pervasive means for understanding other persons, I would substitute a strong pragmatic claim for primary intersubjectivity. It is not just primary in developmental terms: it continues to characterize most of our interpersonal interactions, and it forms the basis for the more specialized mentalistic interpretations of how others perform in the practice of their own minds.

Postscript on Autism

A specific developmental delay in the theory of mind mechanism has been an important element in recent explanations of autism. Autistic children demonstrate impairment of certain social abilities. Specifically, autistic children show inadequate development in the mentalistic understanding of others. Proponents of the theory of mind approach link these social impairments to delayed development of the cognitive abilities associated with the theory of mind mechanism. Experiments in support of this view are based on the standard false-belief tasks, comparing the performance of normal and Down's Syndrome children to the performance of autistic children. In such tests, children are asked to judge or predict what other people (or puppets) in a story believe or how they will act when one of the characters has a false belief. The results are quite dramatic. Baron-Cohen (1989) shows that autistic children, more advanced in mental age than normal and Down's Syndrome children who pass the test, are unable to recognize the significance of false belief. Leslie and Frith (1988) suggest that autistic children are specifically impaired in their capacity for metarepresentation, and this in turn impedes their formulation of a theory of mind. To the extent that metarepresentation is also necessary for pretence, this view is also consistent with impairments in pretend play in autistic subjects.

Metarepresentation involves taking a view on oneself as if upon another person, and on some accounts it develops only as an internalization of an already established social interaction. On this view, however, with respect to autism, the etiological order is not clear. Rather than understanding a deficit in metarepresentation as the cause of problems in social interaction, it seems just as feasible to understand a deficit in metarepresentation as the result of more primary problems in social interaction. Furthermore, there is good evidence to suggest that in autism the deficiency in social interaction is not confined to cognitive dimensions. In some limited respects the autistic's cognitive understanding of others can be at age level. For example, the autistic child may be able to say correctly that the other person does not know that a sought-for object is in a particular location. In spite of that understanding, the same child will predict that the person in question will look for it there — an incorrect response to the false-belief task. Leslie and Frith (1988) explain this as based on an independence between understanding that the other has limited knowledge and the understanding of false belief — in effect, a difference between knowing two different cognitive states. Might it not also be explained as a difference between knowing that the other person has limited knowledge (a cognitive state) and knowing how the other person will act? The action will require a certain kind of movement of the other's body and it may be just that which confuses the prediction.

There is evidence to suggest that across emotional and perceptual dimensions the autistic child does not understand the embodied behaviour of the other person in the same way that a normal child would. Autistic children, for example, have difficulties in perceiving the bodily expression of emotion in others (Moore, Hobson and Lee, 1997) and in imitating certain stylistic aspects of actions performed by others, especially those stylistic aspects indicative of emotional state. They also have problems in understanding the other person as a self-oriented agent (Hobson and Lee, 1999). Some autistic children attempt to perform the imitative action on the experimenter's body rather than on their own, and thus demonstrate a sensory-motor confusion between egocentric and allocentric spatial frameworks.[21]

---

[21] This is a tentative conclusion based on reviewing videotape of the Hobson and Lee experiments. The autistic child does not represent his own body in the action of the other. This would also interfere with any attempt at simulation. In such cases it is as if the autistic child's mirror neurons are not working properly (see Gallagher, 2001). Also, Ohta (1987) notes a pattern of 'partial imitation' of manual gestures in a significant proportion of autistic subjects. For example, subjects positioned face-to-face with the model produced gestures that reversed the orientation of the hands. Barresi and Moore (1996) suggest that such problems can be caused by a failure of intermodal integration of first-person (proprioceptive) information and third-person (visual) information. In the failed imitation, third-person, visual information, predominates. As a result the autistic person fails to attain the capacity for shared intentional experience normally evident in infants at the end of their first year.

Rutter and Bailey (1993) object to theory of mind explanations based on the fact that autism appears at the end of the first year of life, that is, prior to the normal developmental timeframe for theory of mind. Baron-Cohen's (2000) response to this objection, whilst admitting that the pre-theory of mind aspects of primary intersubjectivity are already amiss in autistic children, interprets such primary intersubjective practices as 'infancy precursors to theory of mind' (p. 1251). If we view embodied practices of primary intersubjectivity as necessary conditions rather than as precursors to theory of mind, then the objections of Rutter and Bailey remain cogent. Autistic problems involving various aspects of social interaction, including emotional and motor-sensory aspects, as well as the developmentally later cognitive aspects, are likely to be the result of earlier disruptions in primary intersubjectivity.

References

Allison, T., Puce, Q. and McCarthy, G. (2000), 'Social perception from visual cues: Role of the STS region', *Trends in Cognitive Science*, **4** (7), pp. 267–78.

Astington, J.W. and Jenkins, J.M. (1999), 'A longitudinal study of the relation between language and theory-of-mind development', *Developmental Psychology*, **35**, pp. 1311–20.

Baldwin, D.A. (1993), 'Infants' ability to consult the speaker for clues to word reference', *Journal of Child Language*, **20**, pp. 395–418.

Baldwin, D.A. and Baird, J.A. (2001), 'Discerning intentions in dynamic human action', *Trends in Cognitive Science*, **5** (4), pp. 171–8.

Baldwin, D.A. *et al.* (in press), 'Infants parse dynamic action', *Child Development*.

Baron-Cohen, S. (1989), 'The autistic child's theory of mind: A case of specific developmental delay', *Journal of Child Psychology and Psychiatry*, **30**, pp. 285–98.

Baron-Cohen, S. (1995), *Mindblindness: An Essay on Autism and Theory of Mind* (Cambridge, MA: MIT Press).

Baron-Cohen, S. (2000), 'The cognitive neuroscience of autism: Evolutionary approaches', in *The New Cognitive Neurosciences* (2nd edn.), ed. M.S. Gazzaniga (Cambridge, MA: MIT Press), pp. 1249–57.

Baron-Cohen, S., Leslie, A. and Frith, U. (1985), 'Does the autistic child have a theory of mind?', *Cognition*, **21**, pp. 37–46.

Barresi, J. and Moore, C. (1996), 'Intentional relations and social understanding', *Behavioral and Brain Sciences*, **19** (1), pp. 107–54.

Bermúdez, J. (1996), 'The moral significance of birth', *Ethics*, **106**, pp. 378–403.

Bertenthal, B.I., Proffitt, D.R. and Cutting, J.E. (1984), 'Infant sensitivity to figural coherence in biomechanical motions', *Journal of Experimental Child Psychology*, **37**, pp. 213–30.

Bloom, P. and German, T.P. (2000), 'Two reasons to abandon the false belief task as a test of theory of mind', *Cognition*, **77**, pp. B25–B31.

Bruner, J. and Kalmar, D.A. (1998), 'Narrative and metanarrative in the construction of self', in *Self-Awareness: Its Nature and Development*, ed. M. Ferrari and R.J. Sternberg (New York: Guilford Press), pp. 308–31.

Carruthers, P. (1996), 'Simulation and self-knowledge: A defence of theory-theory', in *Theories of Theories of Mind*, ed. P. Carruthers and P.K. Smith (Cambridge: Cambridge University Press), pp. 22–38.

Chandler, M.J. and Carpendale, J.I.M. (1998), 'Inching toward a mature theory of mind', in *Self-Awareness: Its Nature and Development*, ed. M. Ferrari and R.J. Sternberg (New York: The Guilford Press), pp. 148–90.

Changeux, P. and Ricoeur, P. (2000), *What Makes Us Think?*, tr. M.B. DeBevoise (Princeton, NJ: Princeton University Press).

Cole, J. (1998), *About Face* (Cambridge, MA: MIT Press).

Cole, J. (1999), 'On "being faceless": Selfhood and facial embodiment', in *Models of the Self*, ed. S. Gallagher and J. Shear (Exeter: Imprint Academic), pp. 301–18.

Davies, M. and Stone, T. (ed. 1995a), *Folk Psychology: The Theory of Mind Debate* (Oxford: Blackwell Publishers).

Davies, M. and Stone, T. (ed. 1995b), *Mental Simulation: Evaluations and Applications* (Oxford: Blackwell Publishers).

Davies, M. and Stone, T. (1998), 'Folk psychology and mental simulation', in *Contemporary Issues in the Philosophy of Mind*, ed. A. O'Hear, Royal Institute of Philosophy, Supplement 42 (Cambridge: Cambridge University Press).

Evans, G. (1982), *The Varieties of Reference*, ed. J. McDowell (Oxford: Oxford University Press).

Fadiga, L. *et al.* (1995), 'Motor facilitation during action observation: A magnetic stimulation study', *Journal of Neurophysiology*, **73**, pp. 2608–11.

Frith, C.D. and Frith, U. (1999), 'Interacting minds — A biological basis', *Science*, **286**, pp. 1692–5.

Gallagher, S. (1996), 'The moral significance of primitive self-consciousness', *Ethics*, **107**, pp. 129–40.

Gallagher, S. (2001), 'Emotion and intersubjective perception: A speculative account', in *Emotions, Qualia and Consciousness*, ed. A. Kazniak (Cambridge, MA: MIT Press and Naples: Instituto Italiano per gli Studi Filosofici), pp. 95–100.

Gallagher, S., Butterworth, G., Lew, A. and Cole, J. (1998), 'Hand–mouth coordination, congenital absence of limb, and evidence for innate body schemas', *Brain and Cognition*, **38**, pp. 53–65.

Gallagher, S. and Marcel, A.J. (1999), 'The self in contextualized action', *Journal of Consciousness Studies*, **6** (4), pp. 4–30.

Gallagher, S. and Meltzoff, A.N. (1996), 'The earliest sense of self and others: Merleau-Ponty and recent developmental studies', *Philosophical Psychology*, **9**, pp. 213–36.

Gallese, V. and Goldman, A.I. (1998), 'Mirror neurons and the simulation theory of mind reading', *Trends in Cognitive Science*, **2**, pp. 493–501.

Goldman, A.I. (1989), 'Interpretation psychologized', *Mind and Language*, **4**, pp. 161–85; reprinted in *Folk Psychology: The Theory of Mind Debate*, ed. M. Davies and T. Stone (Oxford: Blackwell Publishers, 1995).

Goldman, A.I. and Gallese, V. (2000), 'Reply to Schulkin', *Trends in Cognitive Science*, **4** (7), pp. 255–6.

Gomez, J.C. (1996), 'Second person intentional relations and the evolution of social understanding', *Behavioral and Brain Studies*, **19** (1), pp. 129–30.

Gopnik, A. and Meltzoff, A.N. (1997), *Words, Thoughts, and Theories* (Cambridge, MA: MIT Press).

Gordon, R.M. (1986), 'Folk psychology as simulation', *Mind and Language*, **1**, pp. 158–71; reprinted in *Folk Psychology: The Theory of Mind Debate*, ed. M. Davies and T. Stone (Oxford: Blackwell Publishers, 1995).

Gordon, R.M. (1995a), 'Simulation without introspection or inference from Me to You', in *Mental Simulation: Evaluations and Applications*, ed. M. Davies and T. Stone (Oxford: Blackwell Publishers, 1995).

Gordon, R.M. (1995b), 'Developing commonsense psychology: Experimental data and philosophical data', APA Eastern Division Symposium on Children's Theory of Mind, 27 December 1995 (http://www.umsl.edu/~philo/Mind_Seminar/New%20Pages/papers/Gordon/apakids9.htm).

Grafton, S.T. *et al.* (1996), 'Localization of grasp representations in humans by PET: II: Observations compared with imagination', *Experimental Brain Research*, **112**, pp. 103–11.

Grezes, J. and Decety, J. (2001), 'Functional anatomy of execution, mental simulation, observation, and verb generation of actions: A meta-analysis', *Human Brain Mapping*, **12**, pp. 1–19.

Heal, J. (1986), 'Replication and functionalism', in *Language, Mind, and Logic*, ed. J. Butterfield (Cambridge: Cambridge University Press); reprinted in *Folk Psychology: The Theory of Mind Debate*, ed. M. Davies and T. Stone (Oxford: Blackwell Publishers, 1995).

Heal, J. (1998a), 'Co-cognition and off-line simulation: Two ways of understanding the simulation approach', *Mind and Language*, **13**, pp. 477–98.

Heal, J. (1998b), 'Understanding other minds from the inside', in *Current Issues in Philosophy of Mind*, ed. A. O'Hear (Cambridge: Cambridge University Press).

Heidegger, M. (1968), *Being and Time*, trans. J. Macquarrie and E. Robinson (New York: Harper and Row).

Hobson, P. (1993), 'The emotional origins of social understanding', *Philosophical Psychology*, **6**, pp. 227–49.

Hobson, P. and Lee, A. (1999), 'Imitation and identification in autism', *Journal of Child Psychology and Psychiatry*, **40**, pp. 649–59.

Jacobson, A. (2000), 'The soul unto itself: Self-knowledge and a science of the mind', *Arobase: Journal des lettres et sciences humaines*, **4** (1–2), pp. 100–24.

Jeannerod, M. (1997), *The Cognitive Neuroscience of Action* (Oxford: Blackwell Publishers).

Johnson, S.C. (2000), 'The recognition of mentalistic agents in infancy', *Trends in Cognitive Science*, **4**, pp. 22–8.

Johnson, S. *et al.* (1998), 'Whose gaze will infants follow? The elicitation of gaze-following in 12-month-old infants', *Developmental Science*, **1**, pp. 233–8.

Legerstee, M. (1991), 'The role of person and object in eliciting early imitation', *Journal of Experimental Child Psychology*, **51**, pp. 423–33.

Leslie, A. (1988), 'Some implications of pretense for mechanisms underlying the child's theory of mind', in *Developing Theories of Mind*, ed. J. Astington, P. Harris and D. Olson (Cambridge: CUP).

Leslie, A. (1991), 'The theory of mind impairment in autism: Evidence for a modular mechanism of development?', in *Natural Theories of Mind: Evolution, Development and Simulation of Everyday Mindreading*, ed. A. Whiten (Oxford: Blackwell).

Leslie, A. (1994), 'ToMM, ToBy, and Agency: Core architecture and domain specificity', in *Mapping the Mind: Domain Specificity in Cognition and Culture*, ed. L. Hirschfeld and S. Gelman (Cambridge: Cambridge University Press).

Leslie, A. (2000), ' "Theory of mind" as a mechanism of selective attention', in *The New Cognitive Neurosciences*, ed. M. Gazzaniga (Cambridge, MA: MIT Press), pp. 1235–47.

Leslie, A. and Frith, U. (1988), 'Autistic children's understanding of seeing, knowing and believing', *British Journal of Developmental Psychology*, **6**, pp. 315–24.

Leslie, A. and Thaiss, L. (1992), 'Domain specificity in conceptual development: Neuropsychological evidence from autism', *Cognition*, **43**, pp. 225–51.

Meltzoff, A.N. (1995), 'Understanding the intentions of others: Re-enactment of intended acts by 18-month-old children', *Developmental Psychology*, **31**, pp. 838–50.

Meltzoff, A.N. and Brooks, R. (In press), ' "Like me" as a building block for understanding other minds: Bodily acts, attention, and intention', in *Intentions and Intentionality: Foundations of Social Cognition*, ed. B.F. Malle *et al.* (Cambridge, MA: MIT Press).

Meltzoff, A. and Moore, M.K. (1977), 'Imitation of facial and manual gestures by human neonates', *Science*, **198**, pp. 75–8.

Meltzoff, A. and Moore, M.K. (1994), 'Imitation, memory, and the representation of persons', *Infant Behavior and Development*, **17**, pp. 83–99.

Meltzoff, A.N. and Prinz, W. (2001), *The Imitative Mind; Development, Evolution, and Brain Bases* (Cambridge: Cambridge University Press).

Merleau-Ponty, M. (1962), *Phenomenology of Perception*, trans. C. Smith (London: Routledge and Kegan Paul).

Merleau-Ponty, M. (1964), *The Primacy of Perception*, trans. W. Cobb (Evanston, IL: Northwestern University Press).

Moore, D.G., Hobson, R.P. and Lee, A. (1997), 'Components of person perception: An investigation with autistic, non-autistic retarded and typically developing children and adolescents', *British Journal of Developmental Psychology*, **15**, pp. 401–23.

Nadel, J. and Butterworth, G. (1999), *Imitation in Infancy* (Cambridge: Cambridge University Press).

Ohta, M. (1987), 'Cognitive disorders of infantile autism: A study employing the WISC, spatial relationship conceptualization, and gesture imitation', *Journal of Autism and Developmental Disorders*, **17**, pp. 45–62.

Perner, J. (1991), *Understanding the Representational Mind* (Cambridge, MA: MIT Press).

Perner, J., Leekam, S.R. and Wimmer, H. (1987), 'Three-year olds' difficulty with false belief: The case for a conceptual deficit', *British Journal of Developmental Psychology*, **5**, pp. 125–37.

Phillips, W., Baron-Cohen, S. and Rutter, M. (1992), 'The role of eye-contact in the detection of goals: Evidence from normal toddlers, and children with autism or mental handicap', *Development and Psychopathology*, **4**, pp. 375–83.

Pinker, S. (1994), *The Language Instinct* (Baltimore: Penguin).

Reddy, V. (1996), 'Omitting the second person in social understanding', *Behavioral and Brain Sciences*, **19** (1), pp. 140–1.

Rizzolatti, G. *et al.* (1996), 'Localization of grasp representations in humans by PET: I. Observation versus execution', *Experimental Brain Research*, **111**, pp. 246–52.

Ruby, P. and Decety, J. (2001), 'Effect of subjective perspective taking during simulation of action: A PET investigation of agency', *Nature Neuroscience*, **4** (5), pp. 546–50.

Rutter, M. and Bailey, A. (1993), 'Thinking and relationships: Mind and brain', in *Understanding Other Minds: Perspectives from Autism*, ed. S. Baron-Cohen and H. Tager-Flusberg (Oxford: Oxford University Press).

Ryle, G. (1949), *The Concept of Mind* (New York: Barnes and Noble).

Scholl, B.J. and Tremoulet, P.D. (2000), 'Perceptual causality and animacy', *Trends in Cognitive Science*, **4** (8), pp. 299–309.

Schwitzgebel, E. (1999a), 'Children's theories and the drive to explain', *Science and Education*, **8**, pp. 457–88.

Schwitzgebel, E. (1999b), 'Gradual belief change in children', *Human Development*, **42**, pp. 283–96.

Schwitzgebel, E. (in press), 'A phenomenal, dispositional account of belief', *Nous*.

Searle, J.R. (1984), *Minds, Brains, and Science* (Cambridge, MA: Harvard University Press).

Siegal, M. and Beattie, K. (1991), 'Where to look for children's knowledge of false beliefs', *Cognition*, **38**, pp. 1–12.

Stich, S. and Nichols, S. (1992), 'Folk psychology: Simulation or tacit theory?', *Mind and Language*, **7**, pp. 35–71

Surian, L. and Leslie, A. (1999), 'Competence and performance in false belief understanding: A comparison of autistic and three-year-old children', *British Journal of Developmental Psychology*, **17**, pp. 141–55.

Tooby, J. and Cosmides, L. (1995), 'Foreword' to S. Baron-Cohen, *Mindblindness: An Essay on Autism and Theory of Mind* (Cambridge, MA: MIT Press), pp. xi–xviii.

Trevarthen, C. (1979), 'Communication and cooperation in early infancy: A description of primary intersubjectivity', in *Before Speech*, ed. M. Bullowa (Cambridge: Cambridge University Press).

Varley, R. and Siegal, M. (2000), 'Evidence for cognition without grammar from causal reasoning and "theory of mind" in an agrammatic aphasic patient', *Current Biology*, **10**, pp. 723–6.

Walker, A.S. (1982), 'Intermodal perception of expressive behaviors by human infants', *Journal of Experimental Child Psychology*, **33**, pp. 514–35.

Wellman, H.M. (1993), 'Early understanding of mind: The normal case', in *Understanding Other Minds: Perspectives from Autism*, ed. S. Baron-Cohen, H. Tager-Flusberg and D.J. Cohen (Oxford: Oxford University Press).

Wimmer, H. and Perner, J. (1983), 'Beliefs about beliefs: Representation and constraining function of wrong beliefs in young children's understanding of deception', *Cognition*, **13**, pp. 103–28.

Wimmer, H., Hogrefe, J. and Sodian, B. (1988), 'A second stage in children's conception of mental life: Understanding informational access as origins of knowledge and belief', in *Developing Theories of Mind*, ed. J. Astington, P. Harris and D. Olson (Cambridge: Cambridge University Press), pp. 173–92.

Victoria McGeer

Psycho-practice, Psycho-theory and the Contrastive Case of Autism

How practices of mind become second-nature[1]

Eleanor: *You must know Henry isn't through with John. He'll keep the Vexin till the moon grows blue from cold and as for Richard's wedding day, we'll see the second coming first; the needlework alone can last for years.*

Geoffrey: *I know. You know I know. I know you know I know, and we know that Henry knows and Henry knows we know it. We're a knowledgable family. Do you want my services or don't you?*

— James Goldman, Act I, scene iii, *The Lion in Winter*

The Lion in Winter is a masterful comedy of plot and counterplot, of alliances made and broken, of deceitful strategies pursued in earnest and earnest strategies pursued in deceit. It is the family Christmas from hell, as King Henry the Second of England holds Court at his palace in Chinon attended by his estranged wife, Eleanor of Aquitaine, their adult sons Richard, Geoffrey and John, each vying for the throne, Eleanor's once adopted daughter, the French princess Alais, now mistress to Henry and promised bride to whichever son inherits Henry's kingdom, and, last but not least, cousin Philip, King of France, one time lover of Richard now turned potential aggressor against England. The ostensive purpose of this gathering is to celebrate the holiday and make peace; but in reality it is to continue the family practice of everyone scheming against everyone else for power, position and the sheer perverse pleasure of it. The audience watches in fascination as each character tries to gain some advantage over every other by disguising what they know, or by playing on the others' sentiments, or by goading them into some ill-judged betrayal of themselves or someone else. Moreover, since the characters all know that they are playing a complicated game of bluff and double-bluff, no one is above suspicion. The challenge for each of them is to see beyond the surface of what's being said, and assumed to be said deceptively, in order to know what everyone else is really wanting, thinking, plotting.

Now what about the audience? The playwright aims not to deceive us, of course, but to show us a family of characters helplessly tangled up in their own schemes. For this, the characters need to be revealed to us in their multiple acts of deceiving one another. Hence, the players' lines are not just rife with subtext; they are also all about

[1]   I am greatly indebted to Philip Pettit for helpful discussion during the drafting of this paper. I also gratefully acknowledge the support of the McDonnell foundation through a grant received from the McDonnell Project for Philosophy and the Neurosciences.

Journal of Consciousness Studies, **8**, No. 5–7, 2001, pp. 109–32

it. Our challenge, then, is to read between the lines of the characters' reading between their lines. Yet despite these layers of meaning within meanings, the play is perfectly coherent. We know what is going on, and we know this even without knowing exactly what all the characters know or think they know at any given time. We are able to follow the twists and turns of plot as each family member tries to out-guess all the others, and so orchestrate the next move and counter-move to their own duplicitous ends.

None of these moves and counter-moves come off as planned, of course; but what does happen is perfectly explicable in terms of the family's constant manoeuvrings and what they know and don't know in consequence. In fact, the play is an ingenious combination of comedy and drama, deftly exploiting our own capacity, as well as the capacity of the characters in the play, to pass what psychologists call first-, second- and even third-order false belief tasks. We are indeed a 'knowledgable' species — knowledgeable in the ways human beings act, and can be expected to act, in light of the complex mental states we are able to attribute to them, sometimes on the basis of the most subtle cues imaginable — a shrug of the shoulders, a sideways glance, a barely perceptible start, a too-ready laugh. How on earth do we do it? What kind of knowledge is it that we deploy, occasionally with effort and uncertainty, but often with such ease that we are barely aware we are making inferences about other minds at all? How is this knowledge acquired? Does it help that we become psychologically complex creatures ourselves? If so, how does it help?

Naturally enough, this has been a controversial area of research and debate in both philosophy and psychology. In philosophy, the last thirty years or so has seen a split between 'simulation theorists' and 'theory-theorists',[2] with a number of variations on each side. In general, simulation theorists favour the idea that our knowledge of others is based on using ourselves as a working model of what complex psychological creatures are like. Theory-theorists claim that our knowledge of complex psychological creatures, including ourselves, is theoretical in character and so more like our knowledge of the world in general. There are many nuances to the arguments and counter-arguments both sides have made. While theory-theorists have tended to dominate the field in both philosophy and psychology, there is growing consensus that some sort of 'hybrid position' is called for since neither approach seems entirely adequate on its own (Stone and Davies, 1996).

Here I will argue for a third approach that aims to combine the insights of both these views without embracing the central tenets of either. I will use the dominant theory-theory approach as the argumentative backdrop to developing what I call a 'know-how' approach to normal psychological knowing, allowing differences to emerge with the simulation view along the way. (A full discussion of the simulation view must wait for another time.) As its label suggests, the 'know-how' approach distinguishes the practical knowledge involved in normal psychological knowing from theoretical knowledge proper, even if such knowledge is necessarily belief-involving.[3]

---

[2] I will use the term 'theory-theory' and 'theory of mind' approach to refer indifferently to nativist and constructivist versions of this overall position. Nevertheless, it should be noted that there are deep differences between these views that I do not mean to discount by this terminological decision of convenience.

[3] I do not say that what we know in the manner of practical knowledge isn't open to theoretical regimentation. But theoretical regimentation has its limits in capturing the dynamic aspects of know-how, since knowing how often involves modifying what one is doing (in new, but knowing ways) in the process of acting according to one's current know-how. Of course, theoretical regimentation may have its uses in this process as well. It makes explicit the guiding norms of current practices and hence can be

Theoretical knowledge simply involves coming to know about how other things are, or what other things do. Practical know-how, by contrast, consists in the development of a skill — the 'internalization' of methods for doing something *oneself* which are normatively guided by considerations of what constitutes doing it well.

Consider, for instance, what goes into being a good chess-player, or an Olympic diver, or a savvy experimental scientist. All of these activities involve methods that are developed and honed by individuals in the context of trying to do the activities themselves, and which reflect their growing sense of what it is to do the activity well or badly. The ability to do something thus involves developing a sensibility that is richly attuned to the shape of the practice in which one is engaged, as well as to the demands it makes on any of its practitioners. Skilled practitioners become attuned, for instance, to the kinds of mistakes anyone engaged in the practice is prone to make, the kinds of conditions which affect how things go and to which practitioners must therefore pay some mind, the kinds of corrections practitioners can make if things do begin to go awry, the kinds of innovations practitioners can institute, and finally the kinds of limits practitioners must be prepared to face, whether these involve their own capacities or are simply inherent in the nature of the activity itself. Such practical ability therefore involves not just the ability to do something; it also involves the ability to follow the ins and outs of others who are engaged in the same activity. Indeed, this ability to follow others in an activity by its nature outstrips the ability to engage in the activity oneself (Ryle, 1949, Chapter II). Participants in a practice are thus always potentially poised to learn about their own practices from those around them.

According to the position I will defend in this paper, our ways of knowing others involves this kind of practical expertise. It involves our becoming, therefore, psychologically able creatures *ourselves*; it involves the internalization of normatively guided practices of mind. These are methods of mind we are trained to take on as our own, though they are nevertheless the methods of a shared practice. Philosophers have generally come to call this practical capacity 'folk-psychology', though, from my perspective, a more fitting term would be 'psycho-practical know-how' or 'psycho-practical expertise'. I further distinguish the *study* of such expertise, whether this is conducted by philosophers or by psychologists, from the practical skill itself. 'Psycho-theory', on my account, is the study of the shape of certain normatively guided human practices and of how we in turn become shaped by them, thereby acquiring the capacity to know creatures like ourselves inside and out.

The body of this paper is divided into three parts. In Part I, I introduce the 'contrastive case' of autism. Autism is a developmental disorder that has recently become the focus of sustained philosophical and psychological attention because of the selective way in which it affects individuals' social capacities. Theory-theorists argue that autistic children's unique profile of assets and deficits is most fruitfully explained by their inability to develop and deploy a theory of mind. After considering the strengths of this hypothesis, I claim theory-theorists face two unresolved difficulties: (1) explaining why high-functioning autistics who develop some theory of mind capacities still fail to engage in normal psychological knowing; and (2) explaining why autistics are generally as unknowable to us in the privileged sense of normal psychological knowing as we are to them. In Part II, I provide the theoretical framework

useful for review, negotiation, instruction and a host of other meta-level practices we engage in as part and parcel of knowing how (Pettit, 1998).

for addressing these challenges by developing an account of normal psychological knowing as psycho-practical expertise. In Part III, I return to the problem of autism, showing how this psycho-practical approach to normal psychological knowing may further suggest how to encompass various aspects of the disorder that tend to be ignored under the prevailing theory-theory approach.

I: Normal Psychological Knowing and the Contrastive Case of Autism

Normal psychological knowing is distinctive in two broad respects. It is distinctive in how we know about human behaviour, and it is distinctive in what we know about it. Simulation theorists have tended to focus on the first of these qualities: they have insisted, and rightly so, that understanding the nuances of human behaviour well enough to follow a play like *The Lion in Winter* or negotiate the myriad forms of complex social interaction that structure our everyday life is deeply unlike our theory-guided understanding of objects and events in the world. These are things we know only from the 'third-person point of view'. But our knowledge of others seems at once too intimate, too resonant, too marked by a sense of 'getting' what it's like to be minded, to pass as theoretical in the standard sense. I will return to this point below. For now I want to focus on the second distinctive quality of normal psychological knowing, agreeing with theory-theorists that our judgments about human behaviour reflect a fairly sophisticated conceptual grasp of the causes and consequences of mental states and processes. Numerous empirical studies have traced the development of this understanding, and it seems clear that our success as social beings is tied to a growing facility with the abstract concept of mental representation. Theory-theorists may quibble about whether this facility matures in keeping with an innate program or is acquired somehow in development; but either way they have amassed an impressive body of evidence detailing the widespread transformations in children's social behaviour that march in step with their unfolding understanding of the representational nature of mind.

One body of evidence now claimed to provide considerable support for this view comes from studies in autism. Autistic subjects show wide-ranging abnormalities that vary considerably with age and individual ability. Nevertheless, they share a diagnostic triad of impairments in social, communicative and imaginative capacities (the latter demonstrated by the absence of pretend play in childhood and restricted interests and activities that persist throughout life) (Rutter and Schopler, 1987; Wing and Gould, 1978; 1979). Although seventy-five per cent of diagnosed autistics are mentally handicapped in a general way (as reflected in low IQ scores), the remaining twenty-five per cent have normal to high IQs and often perform well, sometimes better than average, on reasoning tasks that don't require any understanding of the mental life of agents. By contrast, on so-called 'theory of mind' tests, these 'high-functioning' autistic children are significantly impaired when compared with normal children and even those with Downs Syndrome who are matched with them for mental age (for a review of research see Baron-Cohen, 2000). For instance, on first-order false-belief tasks, which require subjects to predict another's behaviour on the basis of attributing to them a false belief, children will normally pass by a mental age of four years (Wimmer & Perner, 1983).[4] Autistic subjects, if they pass at all, only do so when they are considerably older: on average, at a verbal mental age of nine (Happe, 1995).

A prime example of this dissociation between social and non-social reasoning skills, involves the Zaitchik 'false-photograph' task, which is modelled on the standard false-belief task except insofar as it tests children's ability to reason about physical (photographic) representation instead of mental representation (Zaitchik, 1990). In one version of this task, children are shown how a Polaroid camera works. Then a picture is taken of a play scene in which a toy cat is sitting on a chair. The photograph is taken from the camera and put face down on a table. As the photograph develops the experimenter changes the play scene by moving the cat from the chair to a nearby bed. Then, before turning the picture face up, the experimenter asks the children: 'in the photo, where is the cat sitting?'. High-functioning autistics who fail the false-belief task have no trouble answering this question correctly. They understand that the photograph will show the cat sitting on the chair and not on the bed (Leslie and Thaiss, 1992). This pattern of failing false-belief while passing false-photograph tasks does not occur in normal four-year olds. Although some studies indicate normal children may show dissociation in the opposite direction (passing false-belief and failing false-photograph) (Leslie and Thaiss, 1992; Zaitchik, 1990), more recent studies suggest this may be an artifact of experimental design. Normal four-year olds do equally well on both tasks once incidental conversational and linguistic differences between them have been eliminated. Autistic subjects, on the other hand, continue to show the dramatic physical–mental dissociation seen in earlier studies (Peterson and Siegal, 1998; Slaughter and Mealey, 1998).

Results like these strongly suggest a specific inability in autistic individuals to reason about, and perhaps even conceptualize, mental states and processes. Theory-theorists claim that this is indeed the core deficit in autism, explaining the triad of abnormalities in social, communicative and imaginative capacities.[5] For instance, characteristic social abnormalities might easily be connected with an inability to attribute mental states to others, especially if these abnormalities reflect an apparent indifference or insensitivity to what others are thinking and feeling. Thus, autistic children show no interest in, and even a positive aversion to, meeting another's eyes. They show no tendency to engage in social referencing behaviours, i.e. directing another's attention towards an object in order to share their interest in it or gather information about it. They show little understanding of how their actions affect others or how others' actions are meant to affect them. They may often be confused by what other people do, but show little capacity to be hurt by intentionally malicious behaviour, or touched by intentionally kind behaviour whether or not the behaviour is experienced as beneficial. They may be amused by other people's physical 'antics', even when those antics betray extreme distress or pain. They understand sabotage, but are blind to deceit and other forms of slyness. Jokes, as opposed to pratfalls, are impossible to 'get'.

---

[4]   There are a number of variations of this task, but one simple version that has been used on autistic populations is the so-called 'Sally-Ann' task (Baron-Cohen et al., 1985; cf. Wimmer and Perner, 1983): Children are shown two dolls, 'Sally' and 'Ann'. Sally has a basket in which she places a marble. Then she goes away leaving her basket behind. Ann takes Sally's marble out of the basket and puts it in a box. Sally returns and the children are asked: 'where will Sally look for her marble?' To pass, children must correctly predict that Sally will look in the basket where *she* believes her marble to be, as opposed to the box where they know the marble is themselves.

[5]   For a defence of this perspective and for details of autistic abnormalities from which the following limited summary is culled, see the collected papers in Baron-Cohen *et al.* (2000). See also Frith (1989); Happe (1994a).

Communicative abnormalities may also be rooted in this mentalizing deficit. Language skills vary widely across the autistic population. But even amongst those who develop fair linguistic capacity, typical problems remain. These are connected in particular with communicative and pragmatic aspects of language use that depend on the speaker's awareness of the conversational situation, including especially the listener's point of view: abnormal prosody (rhythm, stress, tone), abnormal shifts in topic, inability to give and receive conversational cues, abnormal accompanying gestures and facial expressions, pronoun reversals ('I' for 'you'), idiosyncratic use of words, abrupt interruptions and terminations of conversation, insensitivity to taboos on personal topics, and so forth. Autistic individuals also tend towards extreme literal-mindedness — showing an insensitivity to metaphor, irony, sarcasm, even idioms *as* idioms: to autistic individuals, 'he went the whole nine yards' means, literally, 'he went nine whole yards'. There is little or no understanding that others may intend to convey by their words something more or other than just what their words mean.

Some of these communicative abnormalities are closely related to the final element in this triad of deficits: autistic lack of imagination. From early childhood, autistics show a notable absence of spontaneous pretend play, as if it never occurs to them to think about things (represent them) other than as they are. Instead, autistics will engage in repetitive, stereotyped activities such as sorting objects or lining them up in rows. They also tend to show limited or absent interest in the larger meaning of things (function, associations, symbolic properties) but focus instead on superficial details, with obsessive interests that are circumscribed accordingly. It may be memorizing bus routes, timetables, birthdates, or even door colours. Many autistics are notable for their rote memory skills, even though they show little concern with focusing on what's worth remembering for other cognitive purposes. Perhaps this is because they have a limited capacity for imagining what those purposes might be, hence a limited capacity for opportunistic planning (for a discussion of planning deficits as connected with theory of mind capacities, see Currie, 1996; for an alternative perspective, see Russell, 1997).

Some more than others of these characteristic abnormalities may be more plausibly connected with an inability to conceptualize and attribute mental states. But there are in addition other kinds of autistic abnormalities that seem to have little to do with 'theory of mind' capacities, at least *prima facie*. These include sensory-motor problems: e.g. extreme and unusual physical sensitivities and insensitivities; slowed orienting of attention; oddities of posture and gait; tics, twitches and unusual mannerisms; stereotypes such as rocking, hand-flapping, spinning, thumb-twiddling and echolalia. They also include abnormalities in perceptual processing, leading to a characteristic autistic profile of assets and deficits on various perceptual tasks: e.g. insusceptibility to certain perceptual illusions, superior performance on finding embedded figures within a larger design, superior visual memory and capacity for rendering scenes in precise detail, perfect pitch, difficulties with 'gestalt' perception — seeing whole figures or scenes as opposed to their parts, absence of perceptual 'switching' with ambiguous figures such as the duck–rabbit, and so on.

Some theorists have argued that accounting for these abnormalities in conjunction with autistic mentalizing difficulties points not to a specific theory of mind deficit, but to a more global kind of cognitive disorder with a variety of effects across different domains (see, for instance Russell, 1997, on 'executive dysfunction'; Frith, 1989, on 'weak central coherence'). I will not discuss the pros and cons of these alternative views here. Suffice to say that any account which purports to explain autistic mentalizing difficulties must also confront a potentially confounding fact that has emerged from studies in autism. This concerns a small, but significant proportion of high-functioning autistics who are categorized as having Asperger Syndrome in light of their superior linguistic and social abilities, as compared with the majority of autistic individuals. Interestingly, Asperger individuals do eventually acquire something like a representational theory of mind, allowing them to pass first- and sometimes even second-order false belief tasks, albeit well beyond the normal mental age at which non-autistic subjects pass.[6] Nevertheless, these individuals are still notably autistic in a number of respects: they suffer the same kinds of sensory-motor problems as other autistics, though these may become more controllable over time; they have the same autistic abnormalities in perceptual processing; finally, and most importantly, they continue to show characteristic disturbances in social, communicative and imaginative capacities despite the fact that they develop sufficient skills to function (abnormally) in relation to other people. In other words, Asperger individuals' learned capacity to explain and predict behaviour by means of attributing representational mental states ameliorates, but in no sense obliterates, the characteristic difficulties they experience in understanding and relating to others in day-to-day interactions. Indeed, the most striking fact about these autistic subjects is that their way of knowing others seems *more* theory-like than does our method of normal psychological knowing. That is, they seem to explain and predict others' behaviour in much the same way they would explain and predict the behaviour of other complex things in their environment, slowly and with effortful calculation based on a vast repertoire of (third-person) observations. Consequently, from the autistic point of view, there is a sense in which other people do not become easier to understand at all: they do not become 'familiar'. Rather, the strange behaviour of so-called 'normals' simply becomes easier to negotiate as a consequence of acquiring better tools for seeing predictable patterns in it. Undoubtedly this improves autistic 'social functioning'. But in the words of one such high-functioning autistic, Temple Grandin, she continues to feel 'like an anthropologist on Mars' (Sacks, 1995, p. 259) (cf. Grandin, 1995; O'Neill, 1999; Schneider, 1999; Willey, 1999).

What conclusions might we draw from the fact that Asperger autistics continue to experience such difficulties with others? For those that equate normal psychological knowing with developing and applying a representational theory of mind, there are two possibilities. First, it may be that because Asperger Syndrome autistics do not acquire a theory of mind in the same way as non-autistics, their use of it may be less expert than the use of non-autistics for whom it is 'second-nature'; alternatively, because of the way it is learned, the theory itself may be less fully elaborated than it is for non-autistics (Frith and Happe, 1999, pp. 6–7). A second possibility is that Asperger autistics do not really develop a *theory* of mind at all: that is, they may have

---

[6] To pass second-order false-belief tasks, children are required to predict what someone else will do based on attributing to them a false belief about *someone else's* belief (e.g. predicting where *Sally* will say Ann will look for her marble based on Sally's (false) belief about where Ann believes her marble is located). Children normally pass such second-order false belief tasks around six years of age. More complex tasks involving bluffs and double-bluffs are normally passed by children around eight years of age (Baron-Cohen, 1989; Happe, 1994b).

a hard-won body of empirical knowledge which is loosely organized into generalizations and paradigm cases, but which fundamentally lacks a set of governing (e.g. causal) principles that gives genuine theories their coherent structure and generative predictive/explanatory power (Gopnik *et al.*, 2000). Thus, even though their activities of explanation and prediction may look theory-like, they are not really theory-governed in the proper sense of the word.

Both of these options have some initial plausibility, but they both suffer from a crucial difficulty that goes right to the heart of the theory-theory view. They both assume that because expertise in the manner of theoretical knowing might account in principle for the *ease* with which we normally understand one another, such expertise must thereby account in principle for the sense of attunement we normally experience in understanding one another and which Asperger autistics notably lack — namely, the sense we develop of ourselves as one kind of creature, experiencing a common way of being in the world. But theoretical expertise in other domains does not generally produce such feelings of attunement between the knower and the objects known, even when the objects known are (in some sense) ourselves (cf. The consequences of becoming neuroscientific theories of cognitive functioning). Of course, becoming expert in various theories may well alter our perceptual experiences, as many philosophers and psychologists have justly observed. Thus, experts within the requisite domains may come just to *see* cancer in an ultrasound image, or the threatening economic recession in stock-market fluctuations, or a poor vintage in water-bloated grapes. But this is not the same as seeing in other people *our own ways of being*, and vice versa. What then could account for this difference?

In what follows I will be arguing that theoretical expertise, no matter how well-developed, remains third-person expertise: it is the expertise of an outside observer looking on. Folk-psychological expertise, by contrast, is insider expertise: it is the first-person expertise, not of a neutral 'inside observer' (whatever Cartesian fantasies that might conjure up), but of a normatively invested skilled participant who is attuned to others because she knows the nuances of minded behaviour in two distinct but deeply related ways: she knows how to read the thoughts and actions of others by understanding these in accord with shared folk-psychological norms; and she knows how to make her own thoughts and actions meaningful to others by operating in accord with those same norms.

This is what autistic individuals lack. That is, they do not just lack what is, by their own lights, a *sense* of attunement with 'normals', a sense that they are in the world in a way that differs from us. More significantly, they *are* out of tune with 'normals'; they are out of tune with us; and being out of tune with us, they are as strangely unknowable to us as we are to them. Their minded ways of being do not conform to ours; and, hence, in a thousand different ways, *we* do not 'get' the nuances of their behaviour any more than they get the nuances of ours. We may develop theories, of course — (third-person) theories of what it is like to be autistic. But we must be wary about how such theories get constructed. From our point of view, the most salient feature of autistic existence is their inability to engage in normal social interactions. This points, we think, to some lack of interpretive capacity in them that accounts for their inability to understand us. But we must be sure that however we specify what is lacking in autistic individuals, it explains our inability to get them as much as it explains their inability to get us. This means that, as theorists, we need to focus on how autistics do not become good psychological objects for us by acting in accord with shared norms, as much as it means focusing on how they do not become adept at understanding us in light of those same norms.

II: The Normative and Regulative Dimensions of Psycho-practical Expertise

It is time now to introduce an alternative approach to the analysis of normal psychological knowing which can address these outstanding issues in a fruitful way. The approach that I espouse involves two crucial elements. The first involves a fundamental shift away from thinking of psycho-practical expertise in terms of acquiring and deploying an empirical theory of how human beings generally behave towards thinking of such knowledge in terms of our investing in a normative stance. The second element, to which I will shortly turn, involves analysing what regulative impact this investment has on our own behaviour.

With regard to the first element, as many philosophers have noted, understanding one another involves not just explaining and predicting what we do; it involves *making sense* of what we do, and this means bringing norms to bear in our judgments of one another's thoughts and actions (Blackburn, 1991; Davidson, 1984; Dennett, 1978;1987; McDowell, 1981). We do, of course, have views about what human beings generally do under various circumstances. But our views about what they generally do, what they can be *expected* to do, are heavily influenced by our views about what they *ought* to do, what it makes sense to do, in the circumstances.

This shift to a normative perspective invites two further questions. First, where do our views about what people ought to do under various circumstances come from? Second, how do we explain why people generally do what they ought to do, so that making normative judgments about them works pretty well as a technique for explaining and predicting their behaviour? In philosophical discussions of these questions, much emphasis is placed on human rationality as the decisive explanatory feature in successful psychological knowing. Firstly, our views about what people ought to do in various circumstances stem from our capacity to determine the rational thing to do in the circumstances; and, secondly, people generally do what they ought to do in various circumstances because they too have a capacity to determine the rational thing to do, and generally do what they think it is rational to do in the circumstances. Of course, this is a very general constraint on behaviour and interpretation, and there are things to be said in its favour. But without discounting the rationality of many of our social practices, it seems by far too minimalistic to account for the myriad norm-governed expectations we develop around social behaviour, and the myriad norm-governed ways we learn to act so as to meet and break those expectations in sense-making ways. Is it *rational* to dress in a particular way when we appear before others in some authoritative role? In one sense, no. But it is a matter of social usage; so not dressing appropriately sends a message whether we intend it to or not. So it goes for countless other details relating to our daily interactions. Our ways of organizing our environment, our ways of conducting ourselves in spatial orientation to one another, our ways of using voice and body, our ways of dressing, all come to be normatively guided, conveying our thoughts and feelings to one another as much as our explicit communicative acts (Garfinkel, 1967; Gergen, 1982; Goffman, 1959).

Skilled psycho-practitioners are aware of these nuances of minded behaviour and conduct themselves accordingly, observing or transgressing social norms and routines as suits their current purposes. On the one hand, many of our day-to-day transactions are made meaningful just by our conforming to such norms and routines. On the other hand, we often draw attention to ourselves by saying or doing things that are unexpected in context, creating 'surplus meanings' that others will respond to with interpretive efforts (Bruner, 1990; Grice, 1989). Depending on what we say and do we may also direct these interpretive efforts in particular ways. Of course, as with any skilled activity, degrees of proficiency may vary widely, and in varying respects. Some people may be acutely aware of these various dimensions of social-communicative life, but little able to manipulate the interpretations others make. Others may be less aware of these dimensions in some articulable sense, yet highly competent in conveying meanings that suit them best, including sincere assertions of what they take to be the case. What kind of awareness, then, is required to make us skilful in producing meaningful acts that are readable by one another? Again, as with any skilled activity, the link between the ways we deport ourselves as minded beings and our conscious appreciation of that deportment is rarely direct, even though con-scious appreciation can play an important role in mediating change or development. That is, we can pay greater attention both to the norms that structure our meaningful activities and to those activities themselves, becoming aware in new ways of how our doings affect our interactions with others. We may even guide and monitor what we are doing, shaping our behaviour in this way and that. But until such actions become second nature, sinking below the level of regulation by conscious awareness into a kind of practical awareness-in-action and -reaction, our performances will seem awk-ward and artificial, not just to ourselves but to others who are remarkably adept at detecting the fluidity and grace of someone at home in their practices. In many cases, however, we don't pass through any consciously mediated phase of change or devel-opment. Self-regulation in terms of norms often occurs without deliberate attention or effort, occasionally even to our surprise or embarrassment as we become suddenly self-conscious of mimicking those around us in gesture, word or deed.

These observations highlight the second element of normal psychological knowing I mentioned above: skilled psycho-practitioners are not just able to read other people in accord with shared norms; they also work to make themselves readable in accord with those same norms. This aspect of psycho-practical understanding is often ignored, perhaps for reasons that are not altogether surprising. Philosophers and psy-chologists tend to inscribe their own project of inquiry into our ordinary methods of understanding one another, so that in the context of everyday life we too are presented as navigating in our social world primarily by observing, hypothesizing, predicting how creatures like us operate. We may be supposed to do so by using ourselves as a working model, or by developing and testing progressively more sophisticated theo-ries which we apply indifferently to ourselves and everyone else. But in either case there is an implicit distinction made between our behaviour insofar as we are objects of folk-psychological theoretical attention and our behaviour insofar as we are folk-psychological theorists. The latter is supposed to revolve around explanation and prediction; the former around what calls for explanation and prediction. Of course everyone agrees that the more able we are as folk-psychologists, the more sophisti-cated our interactions will be. But the explanation for this generally emphasizes how the increasing theoretical knowledge we develop as folk-psychologists makes us more adept at anticipating the thoughts and actions of the creatures we have under study. It does not much focus on how we, as 'objects' of such theoretical attention, become shaped and shape ourselves in this process of development. But surely this half of the equation is just as vital for understanding the ease with which we ordinarily make reliable, yet fairly complex inferences about one another's thoughts and actions. As Goffman reminds us: 'Of course, others also live by inference in their dealings with the physical world, but it is only in the world of social interaction that the objects about which they make inferences will purposefully facilitate and hinder the inferential process' (Goffman, 1959, p. 3).

In terms of understanding our psycho-practical expertise, there are in fact four specific advantages to focusing theoretical attention on our aptitude for making ourselves understandable to one another, as much as on our aptitude for understanding one another. These four points build on each other according to the order in which I discuss them. The first two suggest a shift in the way theorists model individual folk-psychological capacities in order to account for the ease with which we understand one another as mature human beings; the third discusses how this kind of account connects naturally with an explanation of the phenomenological distinctiveness of normal psychological knowing; and the fourth explores the developmental implications of this shift as a way of setting the stage for some concluding reflections on how we conceptualize the disabilities involved in autism.

1. If we learn to govern our behaviour in ways that make us more readable to others, then their work as interpretive agents is greatly reduced. The same is true for us, if they learn to govern themselves likewise. This banal observation challenges an all too common assumption that understanding must require remarkable interpretive skills on the part of each individual if we are too explain the ease with which we ordinarily interact with one another. But just as one person's weight-lifting skills are not so remarkable if they lift a weight with others, so too a person's individual 'interpretive capacities' are not so remarkable if the burden of understanding is normally distributed between them and the person they come to understand (cf. Millikan, 1993). We can, of course, show considerable interpretive ingenuity when called upon to do so; and this may require drawing upon fairly generalized knowledge about the psychological springs of human behaviour in addition to whatever particular knowledge we may have of individual peculiarities. However, what is exceptional about these moments is not just their relative infrequency, but also the difficulty and uncertainty with which such interpretive efforts proceed. Moreover, if these moments become too frequent, we abandon our interpretive efforts altogether, adopting an 'objective' stance towards those who seem generally unresponsive to psycho-practical norms. We judge such individuals to be: 'eccentric', 'irrational', 'disordered', 'mad', 'compelled', 'discursively unreachable'. At the extreme, such individuals fall outside the realm of subjects we can interact with as free and responsible agents, able to make commitments to us or to understand the commitments we make to them (Bilgrami, 1998; Dennett, 1987; Pettit, 1993a; Strawson, 1982).

2. If we make ourselves more readable to one another by conforming to shared norms of readability, it follows that much of the work of understanding one another in day-to-day interactions is not really done by us at all, explicitly or implicitly. The work is done already and carried by the world, embedded in the norms and routines that structure such interactions. Hence, it is not just that we often behave in ways that make sense from a psycho-practical point of view; it is that many of our sense-making

ways of behaving already have their significance built into them. Indeed, this foundation of pre-determined meaning dramatically expands our resources for what we can make meaningful, not just by ordinary recursive methods, but, as already noted, by creative transgression. That is, in breaking with norms and routines, we expect our actions to signal the need for special interpretation. But, equally, we generally only succeed in conveying what we mean when such interpretations can be reasonably guided by the meaning of whatever norms and routines are transgressed (metaphors, for instance, only work if the literal meaning of the words used serve as a plausible guide to what the speaker means). When we develop as psycho-practitioners, we no doubt hone our interpretive skills; but, more importantly, we come to live in a world where the kind of interpretive work we need to do is enormously enhanced by how much meaning our interactions already carry for us and carry because of the way we habitually conform to norms that invest our actions with common meaning. Becoming a good psycho-practitioner is, in this sense, no different from becoming a native speaker within a linguistic community. The ease with which we speak comprehensibly and understand others is based on the practices we share. Of course, the relationship between conforming to psycho-practical norms and conforming to linguistic norms is closer than mere analogy: in becoming proficient speakers of our native tongue, we become able psycho-practitioners, *and* vice versa. These two skills are importantly intertwined, since so many of our methods of being comprehensibly minded are embedded in the semantics and pragmatics of our language.

3. I claimed earlier that psycho-practical expertise is *insider* expertise, the 'first-person' expertise of someone who is skilled at reading others in accord with shared norms because she is skilled at living herself in accord with those norms, and vice versa. As with the insider expertise of linguistic fluency, these two capacities come together. Indeed, it would be more accurate to say they are one and the same capacity exercised in two different respects: *speaking*, on the one hand, and *listening*, on the other — or, more generally, *expressing* and *attending to what is being expressed*. These are two sides of exercising a skill or competency; they are the two sides of what Gilbert Ryle called 'knowing how':

> If understanding does not consist in inferring, or guessing, the alleged inner-life precursors of overt actions, what is it? If it does not require mastery of psychological theory together with the ability to apply it, what knowledge does it require? We saw that a spectator who cannot play chess also cannot follow the play of others; a person who cannot read or speak Swedish cannot understand what is written or spoken in Swedish; and a person whose reasoning powers are weak is bad at following and retaining the arguments of others. Understanding is part of knowing *how*. The knowledge that is required for understanding intelligent performances of a specific kind is some degree of competence in performances of that kind. The competent critic of prose-style, experimental technique, or embroidery, must at least know how to write, experiment or sew. Whether or not he has also learned some psychology matters about as much as whether he has learned any chemistry, neurology or economics. These studies may in certain circumstances assist his appreciation of what he is criticising; but the one necessary condition is that he has some mastery of the art or procedure, examples of which he is to appraise. For one person to see the jokes that another makes, the one thing he must have is a sense of humour and even that special brand of sense of humour of which those jokes are exercises (Ryle, 1949, p. 54).

Analysing normal psychological knowing in terms of psycho-practical know-how makes its phenomenological distinctiveness quite unmysterious. The way we 'get' what another person is up to is by knowing what it's like to be the kind of person whose sayings and doings are expressive of ways of being minded according to the norms we share. This attunement does not depend on putting ourselves in others' shoes. We are already in their shoes, as they are in ours. This doesn't mean that we can always express our psycho-practical know-how as others do. Hence their thoughts and actions may be surprising, intriguing, innovative, instructive from our own point of view. Nevertheless, they make sense to us because we have some competence in being a person *like that*: our understanding is schooled in precisely the way our own expressive performances are schooled, so we feel in our bones what it's like — what it *would* be like — to express ourselves in word or deed as they have done. Of course, others can sometimes act in ways that make no sense to us; but, then, so too can *we* sometimes act in ways that make no sense to us either. In both cases, our performances have failed to live up to norms that transform mere doings into actions that have meaning for us. In both cases our relation to the 'other' changes, from being someone on the inside familiar with the sense of agency expressed by our performances, to being on the outside where that sense of familiar agency fails. Needless to say, such failures are more disconcerting in our own case. But this is not because we have failed to *perceive* something that should be obvious to us from our first person point of view — viz. the causal springs of our own behaviour. It is because those ways of behaving, which we know to come from us, are not second-nature to us *as ways of being minded.* Our ordinary competence for acting in comprehensibly self-regulated ways has somehow failed and we have limited resources for making sense of such failures except as departures from what we ought to do, and can work to try to do better in keeping with the normative dictates of our psycho-practical know-how (cf. McGeer, 1996; McGeer and Pettit, 2001).

4. Even supposing this skill-based account of psycho-practical expertise is on the right track, there remains the developmental question of how the norms which govern our shared ways of being minded become habitual for us, i.e. how they become '- second-nature'. Must we begin life with some innate sense of the special qualities of human behaviour in order to become conversant in the norms which govern our daily interactions? Or do we develop this sense as a consequence of becoming conversant in the norms? Here, too, a satisfying answer to such questions depends on keeping all parties involved in the process of normal psychological knowing clearly in view — namely, the child as developing psycho-practitioner and other people as the objects of her developing psycho-practical knowledge. For, as in the non-developmental context, there is work that must be done on each side in order for this kind of knowing to succeed, although the work that's done will naturally be of a somewhat different kind reflecting the peculiarities of the developmental situation.

To begin with the child as a developing psycho-practitioner, a number of empirical studies provide substantial evidence of an innate human disposition to respond differentially to social stimuli. From birth, infants will orient preferentially towards the human face and voice, seeming to know that such stimuli are particularly meaningful for them. Moreover, they register this connection actively, imitating a variety of facial gestures that are presented to them — tongue protrusions, lip pursings, mouth openings. They will even try to match gestures with which they have some difficulty, experimenting with their own faces until they succeed. When they do succeed, they show pleasure by a brightening of their eyes; when they fail, they show distress. In other words, they not only have an innate capacity for matching their own kinaesthetically experienced bodily movements with those of others that are visually perceived; they have an innate drive to do so. That is, they seem to have an innate drive to imitate others who they judge to be 'like me' (Meltzoff and Gopnik, 1993; Meltzoff and Moore, 1977; 1983; 1994; 1997). Within a few months, infants will use this awareness of their essential link with others in yet more elaborate ways, imitating simple actions others perform on objects by nine months and more elaborate goal-directed activities by eighteen months. Moreover, studies indicate that by eighteen months babies are not just imitating what others actually do; they are performing their actions based on their understanding of what others mean to do. That is, they read through others' 'failures', improving on their actions in order to accomplish unmet, but apparently intended, goals (Meltzoff and Moore, 1995). (For a more elaborate summary of this progression, see Gopnik *et al.*, 2000.) By this age, babies also show clear signs of using others' emotional responses to the world as a guide for their own behaviour, avoiding things that elicit fear, disgust or anger in others and approaching those in which others manifest interest or delight (Campos and Sternberg, 1981; Repacholi, 1998). They engage in 'joint attention' behaviours, following another's gaze or point to an object outside their visual field, and use pointing gestures themselves to direct another's attention in similar fashion. While some of these pointing gestures are 'instrumental', aimed at getting the object indicated, others seem clearly intended to do nothing more than elicit the other's response to something shared (Bates *et al.*, 1975). In these ways and many others, even very young children show a basic readiness to learn from others' expressions and actions, interpreted therefore as having particular import for themselves. As Bruner says, 'we come initially equipped, if not with a "theory" of mind, then surely with a set of predispositions to construe the social world in a particular way and to act upon our construals. This amounts to saying we come into the world already equipped with a primitive form of folk-psychology' (Bruner, 1990, p. 73).

Now what about the objects of this primitive form of 'folk-psychology'? Though infants clearly respond differentially to social stimuli, it is crucial to keep in mind that they are helped along at every stage of this developmental trajectory by those who provide such stimuli. Human infants do not confront a world of 'unstructured experience', and not just because they have innate mechanisms for ordering whatever experience is given to them. Their own ordering capacities are given a significant boost, not just once but again and again over the course of development, by parents who shape their children's experience by involving them in structured interactions governed by the sense-making norms of psycho-practical knowledge. That is to say, parents treat their children as intentional participants in practices that initially extend beyond their intentional competence, leaving the parents to maintain, and even exaggerate, the formal structure and affective import of such interactions for both. In fact, parents will often treat their children as initiating just such interactions, elaborating on what they do in ways that direct and enrich their children's initial intentions. Jerome Bruner has called this sense-making structuring of activity, 'parental scaffolding' (Bruner, 1983). It begins in early infancy, when child and parent engage in 'conversational dances', trading vocalizations, gestures and expressions that the parent ensures are made 'conversationally relevant' to one another, not just by rhythm and affective tone, but often through responsive imitation (Brazleton and Tronick,

1980; Kaye, 1982; Trevarthen, 1979). These mutual imitation games, delighted in by child and parent alike, are the primary means by which the child identifies him- or herself as like another and so, eventually, as a person whose thoughts and actions belong to the kind that persons produce (Meltzoff and Gopnik, 1993). They are also the primary means by which the parent moulds the child to react, think and feel about things as persons do. As Meltzoff and Gopnik remark:

> . . . mutual imitation games are a unique and important constituent of early interpersonal growth. Adults are both selective and interpretive in the behaviour they reflect back to the child. They provide interpretive imitations to their infants, reflections that capture aspects of the infant's activity, but then go beyond it to read in intentions and goals to that behaviour . . . This, in turn, leads the infant beyond his or her initial starting point. Likewise, selected actions, especially those that are potentially meaningful in the culture, will be reflected back [to the infant] more often than others . . . (Meltzoff & Gopnik, 1993, p. 349).

Thanks to these kinds of structured and progressively more sophisticated interactions with others, the experiences children have and the responses they are called to give shape their own sense of agency, both viscerally and conceptually. In the course of normal development, children are thus bootstrapped into regulating their own experiences, feelings, thoughts and actions, not just in concert with others, but in accord with the intersubjective norms of a shared psychological practice. In a word, they become comprehensible agents, i.e. good psycho-practical objects; but the manner in which they become such agents, no less than what they become, accounts in important ways for their capacity to understand others 'like them', i.e. others in whose image they have been substantially made.[7]

---

[7] To emphasize the role of others in the development of agents whose dispositions are regulated in accord with shared norms of mindedness is not to deny the need for innate machinery. However, it does suggest modifications in the way theorists conceptualize the nature of what is innate and the role it plays in this same process. There is considerable dispute about this even amongst those who favour a theory of mind approach to explaining our psycho-practical talents. Some argue the theory is innate, consisting in a dedicated 'theory of mind' mechanism (ToM) for generating representation of mental representations. This mechanism is considered to be 'hardwired' and simply triggered by appropriate experience (e.g. Baron-Cohen, 1994; Leslie, 1987). Others claim the theory is more genuinely like a theory insofar as it consists in a causally-governed set of abstract entities posited to account for a variety of observed events, in this case human activities. Theory of mind is therefore domain specific, but the innate structures that support its construction *qua* theory are domain general: powerful inferential mechanisms that allow human beings to move from their observations of events to substantive hypotheses about the underlying causal structure of the world. On this view, the child's 'experience' is not just a trigger, but constitutes data in the full scientific sense of that word (e.g. Gopnik & Meltzoff, 1996; Wellman, 1990).

A number of considerations have been raised to adjudicate this dispute, prominently the rapid development of a highly sophisticated facility in social reasoning on the basis of relatively limited experience. For 'ToM' proponents such experience is not just limited, but 'impoverished'— and impoverished largely because they have lurking in the background a picture of the child's transactions with others as consisting in the passive presentation of stimuli to a cognitive system that must extrapolate indifferently from what's given. Constructivist theory-theorists improve on this picture, contesting both aspects: On their conception, the presentation of social stimuli is not seen as passive; nor is the child pictured as extrapolating indifferently from what's given. The kind of feedback adults give to their children is carefully geared to their current stage of development, going some way beyond their capacity to respond as self-standing participants in these interactions, but not so far that they lose all sense of being involved in a mutually responsive *inter*action. In this way the child's extrapolations are directed towards elaborating on the special properties of agentive behaviour. Nevertheless, on this approach, the child is still conceptualized as engaged in what seems to be primarily a cognitive enterprise aimed at developing a more comprehensive understanding of the world. The regulative dimension of these interactions are not especially highlighted, with critical consequences for research in autism. I return to this point in the following section.

III: Some Concluding Notes on Autism

This paper began with a challenge: to account for our capacity to follow the ins and outs of other people's actions in a way that does justice to its various distinctive features. I have argued that our ability to follow such ins and outs hinges on our becoming psychologically complex creatures ourselves, in the manner of those we follow. However, this is not to agree with standard simulation accounts that we use ourselves as a *model* for understanding others except *per accidens*. It is rather to say we come to develop, through our regulative interactions with others, an intersubjectively shared psycho-practical know-how. As with any know-how, psycho-practical expertise involves the practical application of norms in what we do and in what we interpret others as doing, so that we become at once comprehensible to one another and comprehending of one another. Acquiring psycho-practical expertise is thus like becoming expert in our native tongue: we become adept both at speaking and understanding others who speak the language we share.

Where does this leave the autistic child? I ended Section I with the observation that, however we characterize what is lacking in autistic individuals it must account for our inability to understand them, as much as it accounts for their inability to understand us, in the privileged insider sense of normal psychological knowing. On the present proposal, this amounts to saying we must account for their inability to become structured as normally minded persons, who regulate themselves and understand others to be regulated in terms of the myriad norms and routines of an intersubjectively shared folk-psychology. Thus, I agree with Hobson that autism is '. . . best viewed as an interpersonal impairment, an impairment in what can and cannot transpire *between* the young autistic child and others' (Hobson, 1992, p. 164). This is not, as Hobson adds, to take the focus away from abnormalities present in the autistic child. But it does suggest that we be cautious of any account, including Hobson's, that conceptualizes these abnormalities in unilaterally recognitional terms — that is, which emphasizes how the autistic child cannot see *us* a certain way because she lacks a theory of mind, or because she lacks even more basic 'perceptual-affective' capacities geared to 'directly perceiving and empathetically responding to the bodily expressed attitudes of other people' (Hobson, 1993b).

This recognitional paradigm can seem particularly compelling from our standpoint. For whatever else may be amiss with autistic children, their most salient abnormality to us is unquestionably their lack of normal social engagement. Almost all descriptions begin with this (diagnostic) aspect of the disorder. Hobson himself provides a representative example. In order to describe what autistic children are like, he writes: '. . . one needs to convey what it is like to relate to an autistic individual, how it feels to communicate or otherwise become engaged with the child. In such a situation, it is not uncommon to feel that one is faced with a strangeling who moves on some other plane of existence, a person with whom one cannot "connect". The experience of being with an autistic child seems to correspond with something essential that is lacking in the child's own experience of other people.' (Hobson, 1993a, p. 2)

It is fascinating to compare this kind of report of what it feels like to be with autistic children with another kind of report stemming from verbally able high-functioning autistics themselves: reports of what it is like *to be* autistic. For, in contrast to what *we* see as the most salient feature of autistic experience — their lack of awareness of us

— what emerges as particularly salient for *them* seems to be the intensity of their sensory engagement with a vibrantly noisy, often terribly distracting and occasionally terrifying world. In many cases, this sensory intensity seems to be coupled with a remarkable capacity to become detached from their own bodily sensations, so that sensory stimuli are perceived without being experienced, in any *mattering* kind of way, as happening to them. Indeed, this capacity to detach from sensations often seems to serve as a means of coping with the overwhelming sensory stream and the powerful affective reactions thereby induced. Yet it also seems to generate for some autistics a pathological experience of self-identity fractured by a sense of disembodied embodiment. It is hard to convey the depth of these abnormalities with a few quotations, but the following representative excerpts give a taste of the autistic sensory world.

> I had — and always had had, as long as I could remember — a great fear of jewellery. That terror also included hairclips and metal buttons. I thought they were frightening, detestable, revolting. If I was made to touch jewellery, I felt a sharp whistling metallic noise in my ears, and my stomach turned over. Like a note falsely electrified, that sound would creep from the base of my spine upwards until it rang in my ears, tumbled down into my throat and settled like nausea into my stomach . . .
> My insensitivity to pain was now as good as total . . . nothing hurt at all. And yet I felt — my actual feelings were not shut off — because when I was aware that I had injured myself somewhere, I could sense something, a non-pain, which branched out into my body from the place where the injury was. But the fact was, it didn't hurt (Gerland, 1997, p. 54, p. 157).

> I could hear but had no need to listen and appeared to be deaf . . . In response to sudden loud noises there was no response, not because I was deaf, for I could certainly hear sound and perhaps even more sound and more clearly than most people, but because I had no capacity to process sound, to interpret it and make the normally instinctual physical connections to respond to it.
> I could feel but had no need of touch and appeared to be unable to feel pain. I could feel physical sensations but they were slow to register and were floaty and without distinct location or meaning or even a developed sense of whether they were internal or external to me. There was no response because the information, though perceived, remained unprocessed and uninterpreted.
> I was somewhere between three and five when my body called to me . . . [I]t started to make its presence felt as though nagging me to listen to it and respond to it. At first, I tuned out this foreign invasion as was natural and instinctive to do with things that gave the feel of robbing one of control. Later, I tried to escape the sensed entrapment of physical connectedness, first spiritually by getting out of it and later physically by trying to pull it off from its suffocation of the me inside, slapping at it, punching it and later trying — physically — to run from it but the damn thing just came after me. As far as I was concerned, my body was welcome as a sensory tool, but as a body with something of a competing will of its own, it was like a leech that happened to be there by coincidence but wouldn't take the hint and couldn't be got rid of. It was my first known enemy (Williams, 1999, p. 53).

> When I was little loud noises were also a problem, often feeling like a dentist's drill hitting a nerve. They actually caused pain. I was scared to death of balloons popping, because the sound was like an explosion in my ear. Minor noises that most people can tune out drove me to distraction. When I was in college, my roommate's hair dryer sounded like a jet plane taking off. Some of the sounds that are most disturbing to autistic children are high-pitched, shrill noises made by electric drills, blenders, saws and vacuum cleaners. Echoes in school gymnasiums and bathrooms are difficult for people with autism to tolerate. The kinds of sounds that are disturbing vary from person to person. A

sound that caused me pain may be pleasurable to another child. One autistic child may love the vacuum cleaner, and another will fear it. Some are attracted to the sound of flowing, splashing water and will spend hours flushing the toilet, while others wet their pants in panic because the flushing sounds like the roar of Niagara Falls.

Children with autism often appear to be deaf. They respond to some sounds and not to others . . . I still have problems with losing my train of thought when distracting noises occur. If a pager goes off while I am giving a lecture, it fully captures my attention and I completely forget what I was talking about . . . (Grandin, 1995, p. 67).

Many a time, my actions brought my parents and me to the hospital. I loved to chew crunchy things, even if they were poisonous. When I was finished with my little tin foil table settings, I used to chew them until they crackled their way into a tight, neat ball. I shaved the sand from Emory boards with my front teeth. I took great delight in grinding the striking strip of a match book between my back teeth. I chewed sugar packets whole, loving the way the grainy sweet sugar overcame the bitter paper packet. I ate school paste and play dough and paraffin . . .

As much as I loved to chew scratchy and gritty textures, I often found it impossible even to touch some objects. I hated stiff things, satiny things, scratchy things, things that fit me too tightly. Thinking about them, imagining them, visualizing them . . . any time my thoughts found them, goose bumps and chills and a general sense of unease would follow. I routinely stripped off everything I had on even if we were in a public place. I constantly threw my shoes away, often as we were driving in the car. I guess I thought I would get rid of the nasty things forever! . . .

I also found many noises and bright lights nearly impossible to bear. High frequencies and brassy, tin sounds clawed my nerves . . . Bright lights, mid-day sun, reflected lights, strobe lights, flickering lights, fluorescent lights; each seemed to sear my eyes. Together, the sharp sounds and bright lights were more than enough to overload my senses. My head would feel tight, my stomach would churn, and my pulse would run my heart ragged until I found a safety zone.

I found solace underwater. I loved the sensation that came from floating with the water. I was liquid, tranquil, smooth; I was hushed. The water was solid and strong. It held me safe in its black, awesome darkness and it offered me quiet — pure and effortless quiet (Willey, 1999, pp. 25–6).

I wanted to feel the good of being hugged, but when people hugged me the stimuli washed over me like a tidal wave. When I was 5 years old, I used to daydream about a mechanical device I could get into that would apply comforting pressure. Being able to control the device was very important. I had to stop the stimulation when it became too intense. When people hugged me, I stiffened and pulled away to avoid the all-engulfing tidal wave of stimulation. The stiffening up and flinching was like a wild animal pulling away (Grandin, 1992, p. 108).

When I was very young I can remember that speech seemed to be of no more significance than any other sound . . . I began to understand a few single words by their appearance on paper.

It was ages before I realized that people speaking might be demanding my attention. But I sometimes got annoyed once I realized that I was expected to attend to what other people were saying because my quietness was being disturbed (Jolliffe *et al.*, 1992, p. 13).

There is no question that other people figure rather oddly in these autobiographical accounts. Significantly, they are not presented as other centres of meaningful action, thought or even sensation; they do not appear as a resource for empathetic contact or comfort. Instead, they tend to be presented as constituting additional sources of sensory stimulation that may be more or less confusing, dangerous or upsetting. This implies something like a recognitional deficit, to be sure; but it is so dramatically subsumed under the scope of autistic sensory disturbances that it is hard to see this as a deficit relating specifically to other people, except insofar as they are a particularly interactive and, hence, intrusive features of the autistic's environment.

Still, how dependable are these autobiographical accounts as a guide to theorizing about the underlying source of autistic social and communicative abnormalities? On the one hand, it is not surprising that the scope and importance of autistic sensory disturbances might be underestimated from the (non-autistic) third-person point of view. We, after all, do not live in that kind of sensory world. On the other hand, it is not surprising that autistic individuals would themselves be blind to the centrality of their social handicaps. They, after all, do not live in the kind of social world where other people figure so significantly for one another. Hence, we could easily be misled by the autistics' slanted perspective into misidentifying the actual source of their difficulties.[8] As Happe cautions:

> Abstracting the content from these accounts, without considering style or possible limitations in the writer's insight, not only discards valuable data, but must lead to questionable conclusions. What are we to make, for example, of an autistic person's comment that his mental processes or sensations are radically different from other people's when he is likely to have severely impaired insight into other minds? Is it not probable too, that an autistic child will have peculiarly unreliable memories from a childhood without self-awareness? While these remain open questions, we must be careful in how we use the contents of autistic autobiographies (Happe, 1991, pp. 222–3).

Unfortunately, this observation cuts both ways. As theorists, we too must be careful about how we use the contents of autistic autobiographies. For it may be tempting simply to minimize or sideline possibly central features of reported autistic experience that do not fit easily into our preferred theories, especially as these theories reflect the preoccupations of our own slanted perspective.[9] Our own theories are geared after all to the pivotal role others play in shaping the warp and weft of normal human subjectivity. This makes it more difficult for us to see how abnormalities apparently unrelated to us could play any role in autistic 'mindblindness'. Some methodological humility is therefore in order.

Perhaps the most neutral way to proceed is by what Dennett calls, in another context, the method of *heterophenomenology* (Dennett, 1991): we take subjects' at their word, letting their descriptions of what it's like to be them stand as an authoritative account of their 'heterophenomenological' world — the world of their own experiences, including, of course, the world as they experience it. Our task as theorists is then to develop a scientific explanation of this heterophenomenological world *in all its details*, reconciling it with what we observe to be true of their capacities from a third-person point of view. It may be that our best explanations of why their

---

[8] Another problem with using these autobiographical accounts as representative of autistic experience is that such high-functioning autistics only comprise about twenty-five per cent of the autistic population. Clearly, any suggestions for further research based on phenomena reported in these accounts must find third-person means of corroborating the existence of such phenomena more generally within the autistic population.

[9] One minor way this bias may show up is in the simple reporting of these features, as when Happe asks what we are to make of 'an autistic person's comment that his mental states or processes *are radically different from other people's*'. In fact, autistic observations seem to be focused on what it's like to be them, without particular regard for how their experiences compare with others'. Indeed, their writing often evinces little sense of how odd their claims might seem to us, as Happe herself elsewhere notes. Of course, the implications are certainly everywhere that their experiences are different from ours, but the *judgment* that they are so comes mainly from us who are struck by the abnormality of their reports.

experiences seem to them a certain way do not gibe with their own understanding of these experiences, but we shouldn't prejudge this question by beginning — in this case unnecessarily — with theories developed purely on the basis of third-person observations of their abilities and disabilities.

What kind of theory could reconcile the data provided by first-person autistic accounts of their unusual sensory experience with the non-autistic 'interactional' appearance of their suffering a specific impairment relating to the recognition of other people? A first step towards sketching such a theory is to focus on what normal infants get in the kinds of reciprocal, affectively patterned relations they normally have with others. On the view I've been developing in this paper, infants are not just learning about others and the world through these interactions; they are themselves becoming well-regulated by them. As I argued in Part II, this is not to deny the need for 'innate machinery' supporting the infant's capacity to engage with others. But it does suggest that an infant's innate proclivity for imitating others may be driven as much by machinery dedicated to serving a self-regulative goal as it is to machinery dedicated to the epistemic goal of understanding self and others.

This fits with a theme emphasized by Hobson and other theorists that what matters to a child's normal social cognitive development is the *affective quality* of her intersubjective experience (Hobson, 1991; 1993b; Stern, 1985; Trevarthen, 1979; Trevarthen and Hubley, 1978). That is to say, the initial innate bridge between self and other is not just sustained by the cognitive satisfaction of finding and imitating something 'like me'; it is sustained by perceiving and reproducing the bodily expressed *feelings* of others: smile for smile, frown for frown, fearful look for fearful look (Hobson, 1991; 1993b; cf. Stern, 1985; Trevarthen, 1979; Trevarthen and Hubley, 1978). This makes others potentially significant for the infant in two respects at once: not only do they provide information about the world and human experience; they also serve as a critical source of sensory-affective regulation. Thus, for instance, a mother may comfort a distressed child by, first, adopting in face and voice expressions that are recognizable to the child as mirroring its own distress, then modulating these in a way that expresses the easing of distress. The child, carried along by its innate proclivities for imitation, will often follow the direction of the mother's expressive modulation, experiencing the easing of its own distress in consequence (Gergely, 1995). Indeed, the regulative benefits of imitation may be so critical to an infant's well-being that it is they, rather than any direct epistemic rewards, which drive the infant's interactions with responsive others. For in learning how to be like others, the infant is learning how to be itself in tolerable contact with the world. Of course, these structured interactions, first with others then later with objects and situations via the mediation of others, become enormously rewarding on the epistemic front as well. For they allow the growing child to metabolize its experiences in ways that are conducive to developing a picture of the world as a stable, predictable place. The normal child who becomes well-regulated in the manner of other people thus derives a double epistemic benefit from this process: the world, including the progressively more complex and differentiated behaviour of other people, is made open to manageable exploration, while at the same time other people become known to the child inside and out in a way that precedes more elaborate theories about them.

If this is a reasonable sketch of what happens in normal development, it suggests a clear connection between autistic sensory disturbances and their failure to engage with others in the preferential ways children normally evince. Autistic individuals need not lack a basic capacity, or even drive, to imitate others — indeed, some autistics show extraordinary if oddly selective parroting tendencies. But this innate capacity for imitation would hardly be evoked in a sustained and potentially regulatory manner were autistic children to find their contact with others, on the whole, far too stimulating to be tolerated. Indeed, in an effort to manage their sensory experiences, autistics might need to shut other people out in a fairly pointed way. But so far from indicating that they lack any specialized machinery for attending to others, this may well show that they *have* such machinery with the consequence that others constitute a disproportionately powerful source of stimuli that quickly become overwhelming for them. In any case, the devastating effects of finding in others an abnormal source of sensory disregulation rather than a normal source of helpful regulation are twofold. (1) Autistic individuals would be cast back on their own resources for managing their sensory experiences perhaps by reducing, repeating or drowning out incoming sensory stimuli in ways they can control. This could explain a number of characteristic autistic behaviours that range from being seemingly dull and repetitive to bizarrely self-stimulatory and even self-abusive: lining up blocks, counting and calculating, repetitively flushing toilets, examining grains of sand, chewing things regardless of taste or danger, spinning, hand-flapping, rocking, echolalia, head-banging, biting and slapping oneself, and so forth. (2) Being excluded from the regulative influences of other people, autistics will not develop habits of agency that conform to shared norms of what it is to experience, think and act in recognizably normal ways. Hence they will be deprived of the very kinds of interactions that give rise to ordinary psycho-practical know-how, a disability reflected in the perplexing nature of their own behaviour as well as in their own perplexity at the behaviour of others.

If these speculations are on the right track, it suggests that becoming minded as others are minded, and sharing thereby in the advantages of normal psychological knowing, may finally depend on something as basic as having sensory access to others in a way that makes possible their regulative influence on us as developing children. In general, philosophers and cognitive psychologists have paid scant attention to the possible link between autistic sensory disturbances and autistic 'mindblindness', despite the suggestive label. In part, this may be due to a tendency in cognitive science to look for dedicated systems underlying higher-order cognitive functions. In part, it may be due to the conceptual gulf that seems to separate such higher-order functions from lower-order sensory processes. In this paper, I have tried to bring these two features of our embodied nature together, suggesting along the way that higher order cognitive functions are as much dedicated to regulating our sensory experiences as they are to using our sensory experiences as an informational conduit to aspects of the world.

In support of this general approach, I have one final observation to make: if autistic sensory disturbances do indeed lie at the developmental core of these other diagnostic abnormalities, then it would seem that other clinical populations with sensory problems ought to show similar kinds of higher-order abnormalities — and indeed this is the case. Although I have not been able to discuss such research in this paper, deaf children of hearing parents as well as congenitally blind children suffer autistic-like deficits in social, communicative and imaginative skills, as well as selective incapacity to pass reasoning tasks with a mentalistic component (Brown *et al.*, 1997;

Hobson, 1993b; Peterson *et al.*, 2000; Peterson and Siegal, 1998; 1999).[10] Indeed, the parallels among these populations are so stunning as to call for a unifying explanation. Generalizing, then, from the conclusion I reach about the source of autistic social and communicative disabilities above, I suggest that any child will be unable to develop the skills of a normal psycho-practitioner so long as it is sensorially impossible for her to make good regulative use of other people. This may stem from having a missing sensory avenue to others, as much as it may stem from having one's sensory avenues to others overwhelmed by the over-stimulation involved in sustained exposure to them. This apparent connection between autistic, deaf and blind populations makes Donna Williams' first-person reflections on her own autistic difficulties singularly apt. I therefore conclude with her words, as a fitting spur to further research on the centrality of autistic sensory-motor abnormalities to the consequent development of their alternative practices of mind:

> Mine was not a situation unlike that of the deaf-blind. Unable to filter information and being flooded with information at a rate I could not process in the context in which it happened, I was left meaning deaf and meaning blind as well as context deaf and context blind. Sometimes a sensory experience had no interpretation at all, leaving me in the sensory, struggling for the literal. At others it had a literal meaning but had no significance.
>
> I perceived sound and visual information directly and consciously only at the cost of its cohesion. I could interpret the part but lost the whole. I saw the nose but lost the face, saw the hand but continued to see the body but would not know what it was except piece by piece. I'd get the intonation but lose the meaning of the words or get the meaning of the words but only at the cost of tuning out the intonation, as though independent of the words.
>
> The conscious mind, however, is not the only way of taking things in. The preconscious state takes things in, not directly, but indirectly. Using peripheral perception, we accumulate all the knowing we aren't always aware we are taking in. Taking things in indirectly, peripherally, the fragmentation didn't happen; things were more cohesive, they retained context. Yet the mind-jolting senses of direct vision and direct hearing could not be consistently relied upon as meaningful primary senses. In spite of this, I didn't remain under-developed, so much as I became differently developed. Like the deaf-blind, I used other systems more fully than most would ever develop them (Williams, 1999, pp. 62–3).

References

Baron-Cohen, S. (1989), 'The autistic child's theory of mind: a case of specific developmental delay', *Journal of Child Psychology and Psychiatry*, **30**, pp. 285–98.
Baron-Cohen, S. (1994), 'How to build a baby that can read minds: cognitive mechanisms in mind reading', *Cahiers de Psychologie Cognitive*, **13**, pp. 513–52.

---

[10] It is interesting to compare these various clinical populations with Downs Syndrome children who do pass false-belief tasks at the same mental age as normal children. Hence, Downs Syndrome children are developmentally retarded, but they seem to follow a normal developmental trajectory (see, for instance Baron-Cohen *et al.*, 1985). By contrast, congenitally blind children and deaf children of hearing parents follow the same abnormal developmental trajectory as autistic children: they are unusually delayed in passing theory of mind tasks compared with non-social reasoning tasks. They also show autistic-like abnormalities in social, communicative and imaginative abilities; but, as is not the case with autistic children, these abnormalities tend to disappear as they become more able to relate to others through developing skills that overcome their handicaps in a context of able and responsive others (Brown *et al.*, 1997; Peterson and Siegal, 1998). It is also notable that deaf children whose parents are native signers, and who therefore have rich proto-conversational and conversational interactions with others from an early age, do not show any 'autistic' social or cognitive abnormalities in the nature of their conversational behaviour (Meadow *et al.*, 1981). In particular, they do not have any difficulty passing 'theory of mind' reasoning tasks. These comparative results are discussed in Peterson and Siegal (1999).

Baron-Cohen, S., Leslie, A.M. and Frith, U. (1985), 'Does the autistic child have a theory of mind?', *Cognition*, **21**, pp. 37–46.

Baron-Cohen, S., Tager-Flusberg, H. and Cohen, D.J. (ed. 2000), *Understanding Other Minds: Perspectives from Developmental Cognitive Neuroscience* (Oxford: Oxford University Press).

Bates, E., Camaioni, L. and Volterra, V. (1975), 'The acquisition of preformatives prior to speech', *Merrill-Palmer Quarterly*, **21**, pp. 205–26.

Bilgrami, A. (1998), 'Self-knowledge and resentment', in *Knowing Our Own Minds*, ed. C. Wright, B. Smith and C. Macdonald (Oxford: Oxford University Press).

Blackburn, S. (1991), 'Losing your mind', in *The Future of Folk Psychology*, ed. J. Greenwood (New York: Cambridge University Press).

Brazleton, T.B. and Tronick, E. (1980), 'Preverbal communication between mothers and infants', in *The Social Foundations of Language and Thought*, ed. D.R. Olson ((New York: Norton).

Brown, R., Hobson, R.P. and Lee, A. (1997), 'Are there "autistic-like" features in congenitally blind children?', *Journal of Child Psychology and Psychiatry*, **38** (6), pp. 693–703.

Bruner, J. (1983), *Child's Talk: Learning to Use Language* (New York: Norton).

Bruner, J. (1990), *Acts of Meaning* (Boston, MA: Harvard University Press).

Campos, J.J. and Sternberg, C.R. (1981), 'Perception appraisal and emotion: the onset of social referencing', in M.E. Lamb and L.R. Sherrod (eds.), *Infant Social Cognition* (Hillsdale, NJ: Erlbaum).

Currie, G. (1996), 'Simulation theory, theory-theory and the evidence from autism', in *Theories of Theories of Mind*, ed. P. Carruthers and P. Smith (Cambridge: Cambridge University Press).

Davidson, D. (1984), *Inquiries into Truth and Interpretation* (Oxford: Oxford University Press).

Davies, M. (1994), 'The mental simulation debate', in *Objectivity, Simulation and the Unity of Consciousness*, ed. C. Peacocke (Oxford: Oxford University Press).

Dennett, D. (1978), *Brainstorms* (Montgomery, VT: Bradford Press).

Dennett, D. (1987), *The Intentional Stance* (Cambridge, MA: MIT Press).

Dennett, D. (1991), *Consciousness Explained* (Boston, MA: Little, Brown and Company).

Frith, U. (1989), *Autism: Explaining the Enigma* (Oxford: Blackwell).

Frith, U. and Happe, F. (1999), 'Theory of mind and self-consciousness: what it is like to be autistic?', *Mind and Language*, **14** (1), pp. 1–22.

Garfinkel, H. (1967), *Studies in Ethnomethodology* (Englewood Cliffs, NJ: Prentice Hall).

Gergely, G. (1995), 'The role of parental mirroring of affects in early psychic structuration', *IPA's 5th Conference on Psychoanalytic Research*.

Gergen, K.J. (1982), *Toward Transformation in Social Knowledge* (New York: Springer-Verlag).

Gerland, G. (1997), *A Real Person: Life on the Outside* (trans. J. Tate) (London: Souvenir Press).

Goffman, E. (1959), *The Presentation of Self in Everyday Life* (New York: Anchor Books).

Gopnik, A., Capps, L. and Meltzoff, A. (2000), 'Early theories of mind: what the theory theory can tell us about autism', in Baron-Cohen *et al.* (2000).

Gopnik, A. and Meltzoff, A. (1996), *Words, Thoughts and Theories* (Boston, MA: Bradford/ MIT Press).

Grandin, T. (1992), 'An inside view of autism', in *High-Functioning Individuals with Autism*, ed. E. Schopler and G.B. Mesibov (New York: Plenum Press).

Grandin, T. (1995), *Thinking in Pictures: And Other Reports from my Life with Autism* (NY: Doubleday).

Grice, H.P. (1989), *Studies in the Way of Words* (Cambridge, MA: Harvard University Press).

Happe, F. (1991), 'The autobiographical writings of three Asperger syndrome adults: problems of interpretation and implications for theory', in *Autism and Asperger Syndrome*, ed. U. Frith (Cambridge: CUP).

Happe, F. (1994a), *Autism: An Introduction to Psychological Theory* (Cambridge, MA: Harvard UP).

Happe, F.G. (1994b), 'An advanced test of theory of mind: understanding of story characters' thoughts and feelings by able autistic, mentally handicapped and normal children and adults', *Journal of Autism and Developmental Disorders*, **24**, pp. 129–54.

Happe, F. (1995), 'The role of age and verbal ability in the Theory of Mind task performance of subjects with autism', *Child Development*, **66**, pp. 843–55.

Hobson, R.P. (1991), 'Through feeling and sight to self and symbol', in *Ecological and Interpersonal Knowledge of the Self*, ed. U. Neisser (New York: Cambridge University Press).

Hobson, R.P. (1992), 'Social perception in high-level autism', in *High-Functioning Individuals with Autism*, ed. E. Schopler and G. Mesibov (New York: Plenum Press).

Hobson, R.P. (1993a), *Autism and the Development of Mind* (East Sussex: Lawrence Erlbaum Assoc.).

Hobson, R.P. (1993b), 'Understanding persons: the role of affect', in S. Baron-Cohen, H. Tager-Flusberg and D.J. Cohen (eds.), *Understanding Other Minds: Perspectives from Autism* (Oxford: OUP).

Jolliffe, T., Lansdown, R. and Robinson, C. (1992), 'Autism: a personal account', *Communication*, **26** (3), pp. 12–19.

Kaye, K. (1982), *The Mental and Social Life of Babies* (Chicago: University of Chicago Press).

Leslie, A. (1987), 'Pretence and representation: the origins of "Theory of Mind" ', *Psychological Review*, **94**, pp. 412–26.

Leslie, A. and Thaiss, L. (1992), 'Domain specificity in conceptual development: evidence from autism', *Cognition*, **43**, pp. 225–51.

McDowell, J. (1981), 'Anti-realism and the epistemology of understanding', in Parret and J. Bouveresse (eds.), *Meaning and Understanding* (Berlin: de Gruyter).

McGeer, V. (1996), 'Is "self-knowledge" an empirical problem? Renegotiating the space of philosophical explanation', *Journal of Philosophy*, **93**, pp. 483–515.

McGeer, V. and Pettit, P. (2001), 'The self-regulating mind', *Language and Communication*, forthcoming.

Meadow, K.P., Greenberg, M.T., Erting, C. and Carmichael, H. (1981), 'Interactions of deaf mothers and deaf preschool children: comparison with three other groups of deaf and hearing dyads', *American Annals of the Deaf*, **126**, pp. 454–68.

Meltzoff, A. and Gopnik, A. (1993), 'The role of imitation in understanding persons and developing a theory of mind', in S. Baron-Cohen, H. Tager-Flusberg and D.J. Cohen (eds.), *Understanding Other Minds: Perspectives from Autism* (Oxford: Oxford University Press).

Meltzoff, A.N. and Moore, M.K. (1977), 'Imitation of facial and manual gestures by human neonates', *Science*, **198**, pp. 75–8.

Meltzoff, A.N. and Moore, M.K. (1983), 'Newborn infants imitate adult facial gestures', *Child Development*, **54** (3), pp. 702–9.

Meltzoff, A.N. and Moore, M.K. (1994), 'Imitation, memory and the representation of persons', *Infant Behaviour and Development*, **17** (1), pp. 83–99.

Meltzoff, A.N. and Moore, M.K. (1995), 'Infants' understanding of people and things: from body imitation to folk-psychology', in *The Body and the Self*, ed. J. Bermudez *et al.* (Cambridge, MA: MIT Press).

Meltzoff, A.N. and Moore, M.K. (1997), 'Explaining facial imitation: a theoretical model', *Early Development and Parenting*, **6**, pp. 179–92.

Millikan, R.G. (1993), *White Queen Psychology and Other Essays for Alice* (Cambridge, MA: MIT Press).

O'Neill, J.L. (1999), *Through the Eyes of Aliens: A Book About Autistic People* (London: Jessica Kingsley).

Peterson, C.C., Peterson, J.C. and Webb, J. (2000), 'Factors influencing the development of a theory of mind in blind children', *The British Psychological Society*, **18**.

Peterson, C.C. and Siegal, M. (1998), 'Changing focus on the representational mind: concepts of false photos, false drawings and false beliefs in deaf, autistic and normal children', *British Journal of Developmental Psychology*, **16**, pp. 301–20.

Peterson, C.C. and Siegal, M. (1999), 'Insights into theory of mind from deafness and autism', *Mind and Language*, **15** (1), pp. 77–99.

Pettit, P. (1993a), *The Common Mind: An Essay on Psychology, Society and Politics* (New York: OUP).

Pettit, P. (1998), 'Practical belief and philosophical theory', *Australasian Journal of Philosophy*, **76**.

Repacholi, B.M. (1998), 'Infants' use of attentional cues to identify the referent of another person's emotional expression', *Developmental Psychology*, **34**, pp. 1017–25.

Russell, J. (ed. 1997), *Autism as an Executive Disorder* (Oxford: Oxford University Press).

Rutter, M. and Schopler, E. (1987), 'Autism and pervasive developmental disorders: conceptual and diagnostic issues', *Journal of Autism and Developmental Disorders*, **17**, pp. 159–86.

Ryle, G. (1949), *The Concept of Mind* (Chicago: University of Chicago Press).

Sacks, O. (1995), *An Anthropologist on Mars* (New York: Vintage Books).

Schneider, E. (1999), *Discovering My Autism: Apologia Pro Vita Sua* (London: Jessica Kingsley).

Slaughter, V. and Mealey, L. (1998), 'Seeing is not (necessarily) believing', *Behavioral and Brain Sciences*, **25**, p. 130.

Stern, D. (1985), *The Interpersonal World of the Infant* (New York: Basic Books).

Stone, T. and Davis, M. (1996), 'The mental simulation debate: A progress report', in *Theories of Theories of Mind*, ed. P. Carruthers and P. Smith (Cambridge: Cambridge University Press).

Strawson, P. (1982), ''Freedom and resentment', in *Free Will*, ed. G. Watson (Oxford: OUP).

Trevarthen, C. (1979), 'Communication and cooperation in early infancy: a description of primary intersubjectivity', in *Before Speech*, ed. M. Bullowa (New York: Cambridge University Press).

Trevarthen, C. and Hubley, P. (1978), 'Secondary intersubjectivity: confidence, confiding and acts of meaning in the first year', in *Action, Gesture and Symbol*, ed. A. Lock (London: Academic Press).

Wellman, H. (1990), *The Child's Theory of Mind* (Boston, MA: Bradford/MIT Press).

Willey, L.H. (1999), *Pretending to Be Normal: Living with Asperger Syndrome* (London: Jessica Kingsley).

Williams, D. (1999), *Autism and Sensing: The Unlost Instinct* (London: Jessica Kingsley Publishers).

Wimmer, H. and Perner, J. (1983), 'Beliefs about beliefs: representation and the constraining function of wrong beliefs in young children's understanding of deception', *Cognition*, **13**, pp. 103–28.

Wing, L. and Gould, J. (1978), 'Systematic recording of behaviours and skills of retarded and psychotic children', *Journal of Autism and Childhood Schizophrenia*, **8**, pp. 79–97.

Wing, L. and Gould, J. (1979), 'Severe impairments of social interactions and associated abnormalities in children: epidemiology and classification', *Journal of Autism and Developmental Disorders*, **9**, pp. 11–29.

Zaitchik, D. (1990), 'When representations conflict with reality: the preschooler's problem with false belief and "false" photographs', *Cognition*, **35**, pp. 41–68.

J. Allan Cheyne

The Ominous Numinous

Sensed Presence and 'Other' Hallucinations

A 'sensed presence' often accompanies hypnagogic and hypnopompic hallucinations associated with sleep paralysis. Qualitative descriptions of the sensed presence during sleep paralysis are consistent with the experience of a monitoring, stalking predator. It is argued that the sensed presence during sleep paralysis arises because of REM-related endogenous activation of a hypervigilant and biased attentive state, the normal function of which is to resolve ambiguities inherent in biologically relevant threat cues. Given the lack of disambiguating environmental cues, however, the feeling of presence persists as a protracted experience that is both numinous and ominous. This experience, in turn, shapes the elaboration and integration of the concurrent hallucinations that often take on supernatural and daemonic qualities. The sense of presence considered here is an 'other' that is radically different from, and hence more than a mere projection of, the self. Such a numinous sense of otherness may constitute a primordial core consciousness of the animate and sentient in the world around us.

It is as if there were in the human consciousness *a sense of reality, a feeling of objective presence, a perception* of what we may call '*something there*', more deep and more general than any of the more special and particular 'senses' (James, 1958, p. 61).

Virtually everyone has had, at some time, the experience of feeling that he or she was not alone, despite otherwise confident knowledge that there really was no other person nearby. This feeling may range from a vague almost embarrassingly unwarranted suspicion to a feeling of absolute certainty. We commonly associate such feelings with darkness, strange surroundings and, of course, being isolated from our fellows (James, 1958; Suedfeld, 1987; Zusne and Jones, 1982). We may experience such a sensed presence when walking alone on a dark street, or through a wood lot, or even at home alone, especially if it is a 'dark and stormy night' filled with vague rustlings, howling winds and distant animal sounds. Specific locales may become, through tradition, well-known sites for such experiences (Reed, 1988; Suedfeld, 1987; Suedfeld and Mocellin, 1987).

The sensed presence consists of a feeling of raw otherness present-at-hand, its only quale an ineffable sense of 'thereness'. Guy de Maupassant, in a short story in which

Journal of Consciousness Studies, **8**, No. 5–7, 2001, pp. 133–50

an ineffable and frightening presence plays a central role, coined an intriguing name for the presence, the 'Horla'. There has been considerable speculation about the manner in which Maupassant came up with that particular name (e.g. Cogny, 1970). Perhaps the most obvious is simply that it is *le hors-là* — the outside-there — a sort of everted and perverse *Dasein* of utter otherness. There is, throughout Maupassant's account of the *Horla*, a strong element of dreadful foreboding, underscoring the threatening and alien nature of the presence. One knows, often with a dreadful certainty that transcends mere evidential support, that something is out there, sentient and, in particular, aware of us. Indeed, this presence seems expressly to have come to find us, for it now watches us — often with a malevolent aura of evil.

In recent work quantitative analyses have provided evidence that the sensed presence is a common concomitant of sleep paralysis that is particularly associated with visual, auditory and tactile hallucinations, as well as intense fear (Cheyne, Rueffer and Newby-Clark 1999). Sleep paralysis itself is a conscious state of involuntary immobility occurring prior to falling asleep or immediately upon wakening. An episode may last from a few seconds to several minutes. Although individuals in this state are unable to make gross bodily movements, they are able to open their eyes and to perceive and subsequently report on external events (Hishikawa, 1976; Hishikawa and Shimizu, 1995). Recent surveys suggest that approximately 30% of young adults report some experience of sleep paralysis (Cheyne, Newby-Clark and Rueffer, 1999; Fukuda *et al.*, 1998; Spanos *et al.*, 1995). Out of combinations of particular sensory experiences grow elaborate and complex scenarios that have been identified as experiential sources of accounts of incubus attacks, daemonic possession, old hag attacks and, more recently, alien abductions (Baker, 1990; 1992; Cheyne, Rueffer and Newby-Clark, 1999; Firestone, 1985; Hufford, 1982; Ness, 1978; Spanos *et al.*, 1993). These experiences are typically quite frightening and are the original referents for the term 'nightmare' (Liddon, 1967; Hufford, 1982).

Sleep paralysis experiences are referred to as hypnagogic (sleep-onset) or hypnopompic (sleep-offset) *hallucinations*. The term hallucination is appropriate because the experiences occur while one is awake and aware of the immediate surroundings. These hallucinations are also, however, a form of dreaming inasmuch as they are associated with sleep-onset REM states (Hishikawa and Shimizu, 1995). Sleep paralysis hallucinations are, in effect, the superpositioning of dream imagery and affect on waking consciousness. Indeed, the various experiential features of these hallucinations are readily mapped onto known neurophysiology of REM (Cheyne, Rueffer and Newby-Clark, 1999). Of particular relevance to the present argument are recent neuroimaging studies of REM-related activation of subcortical and cortical *limbic* centres including the extended amygdala, nucleus basalis of Meynert in the substantia innominata, and anterior cingulate cortex (see Hobson *et al.*, 1998 for a review of this work). As Hobson *et al.* note, these studies reveal 'an unexpectedly prominent role of the limbic system in the selection and elaboration of dream plots' (*ibid.*, p. R1).

The sensed presence during sleep paralysis is often experienced as ominous or threatening. This is quite consistent with the involvement of the limbic structures associated with REM. Whalen (1998) suggests that there is a 'vigilance system' associated with the extended amygdala and related structures such as the nucleus basalis of Meynert. The vigilance system is normally activated by an initial detection of possible danger. The vigilance system initiates procedures that monitor the environment for further cues to corroborate or disconfirm the existence of an emergency. In a similar vein, but with specific reference to consciousness, Ellis (1999) speaks of these processes as *motivated* interpretive activities and further notes that sensory processing remains unconscious until affective midbrain and cortical structures such as the anterior cingulate highlight particular features of the sensorium. The specific nature of those features is specified by biases, or perhaps more accurately, *interests* induced by the vigilance system. Evolution has selected certain environmental features as cues that warn us of things in the immediate environment that constitute a potential threat to the organism. These cues are, individually, inherently ambiguous in the absence of further corroborating evidence. Indeed, Whalen suggests that the function of the vigilance system is the disambiguation of prior warning cues. The immediate task under such conditions is to 'flesh-out' what is merely implied by biologically prepared cues. The resultant state of vigilance entails lowered and biased sensory thresholds for further threat cues and may set the stage for false alarms. These temporary biases are adaptive because the initial cues for danger change the *a priori* probabilities of immediate danger (LeDoux, 1994; 1996). The chain of events (threat cue — ambiguity — search — disambiguation) is normally accomplished quite rapidly. That is, environmental cues ordinarily quickly corroborate or disconfirm the existence of threat.

Cheyne, Rueffer and Newby-Clark (1999) argue that feelings of presence such as emerge during sleep paralysis arise from the same limbic neurophysiology underlying threat detection. I suggest further that the sensed presence represents the experiential component of the resulting ambiguity. During sleep paralysis endogenous REM-based activation of the vigilance system produces, in the absence of external threat, an irresolvable ambiguity. This radical ambiguity is experienced as a protracted threatening, though insubstantial, sense of presence. The sensed presence, on this view, constitutes a liminal *feeling* on the edge of what Damasio (1999) has called core consciousness. It is important to note that, although external cues are absent, there is a concurrent quasi-random endogenous activation of affective, sensory and motor areas. These normally constitute the source of REM dream-imagery (Hobson and McCarley, 1977). During sleep-onset REM, the sensed presence may serve to bind and shape concurrent visual and auditory hallucinations according to the adaptive biases of the vigilance system. James (1958) explicitly treated feelings of a presence as 'imperfectly developed' hallucinations (p. 62). I argue further that the sensed presence may be viewed not only as the most elementary form of hallucination but also as a neuropsychological context that motivates, initiates and shapes more elaborate hallucinoid experiences. On this view, the affective qualities of the sensed presence are critical in determining the nature of the associated hallucinations.

A critical claim of the argument of this paper is that the inherent ambiguity of the threat detection mechanism is, under the conditions just described, experienced as at least one aspect of what has been referred to as the *numinous* (Otto, 1923). Otto coined the term 'numinous' (numen praesens) to designate the ineffable sense of a sacred or daemonic presence. It is, for Otto, critical to a full understanding of the nature of the 'Holy'. Although there are clearly positive beatific aspects to the numinous, Otto frequently stresses the 'awfulness' and the 'dreadful' aspects of the numinous experience. These aspects are captured in the term 'mysterium tremendum', the mystery before which we shudder and tremble. Otto speaks of the *mysterium tremendum* as 'overpowering', 'dreadful', 'grisly' and 'horrible'. Otto took 'daemonic dread' to be that 'religious moment which would appear to have been in every case the first to be aroused in the human mind' (Otto, 1923, p. 132). Moreover, the experience of the numinous is one of 'terror fraught with an inward shuddering such as not even the most menacing and overpowering created thing can instill' (*ibid.*, p. 14). As may be inferred from the preceding quotation Otto clearly regarded such experiences as genuinely transcendent and supernatural. The present argument, however, is that the ineffable experience of the numinous may be given a straightforward naturalistic interpretation, one that provides an evolutionary basis for at least the more terrifying and daemonic aspects of religious experience. Otto, of course, would not have been satisfied to see his argument reduced to a naturalistic one. The sensed presence is, on the view offered here, the numinous in its purest form. Moreover, the subsequent hallucinations arising from the quasi-random REM-related imagery provide, at best, only a partial and incoherent resolution of the ambiguity and hence retain some of the numinous qualities of the sensed presence throughout the episode.

The Experiential Structure of Hypnagogic and Hypnopompic Hallucinations

The qualitative accounts that follow were provided by respondents to the Waterloo Unusual Sleep Experiences Survey. This instrument includes a number of items assessing features of sleep paralysis and associated hallucinoid experiences (see Table 1). The items are based on a taxonomy that has been developed through a

	Source:	Psychology Undergraduates (N = 771)	WWW Survey I (N = 1120)	WWW Survey II (N = 811)	WWW Survey III (N = 857)	WWW Survey IV (N = 2690)
HHEs:						
Intruder						
Presence		.57	.74	.67	.63	.78
Visual		.47	.50	.64	.62	.57
Sounds		.58	.61	.65	.64	.61
Touch		–[1]	–	–	.50	.51
Fear		.78	.97	.96	.96	.95
Incubus						
Pressure		.63	.66	.70	.70	.63
Breathing		–	.58	.60	.63	.59
Choking		.34	–	.21	.21	.21
Pain		.51	.31	.32	.34	.27
Death Thoughts		.49	.66	.65	.64	.64

[1] Not assessed

Table 1   Hypnagogic and Hypnopompic Hallucinations: Proportion of cases reporting each type of hallucination during sleep paralysis

combination of quantitative and qualitative analyses of the cumulative written records provided by respondents. Each item in the survey calls for a frequency and an intensity response and provides ample space after each item for a written description of the experience in the respondents' own words.

The groupings of hallucinoid experiences in Table 1 correspond to three factors extracted in quantitative analyses utilizing exploratory and confirmatory factor analysis (Cheyne, Rueffer and Newby-Clark, 1999). The first factor (Intruder) consists of sensed presence and fear, as well as visual, auditory and tactile hallucinations. This factor has been named 'Intruder' because the experiences are consistent with, and often interpreted as, the presence of an intruder in (usually) one's bedroom. The second factor (Incubus) consists of pressure (most frequently on the chest), breathing difficulties (including feelings of suffocation and choking), pain and thoughts of death. This factor was named 'Incubus' after the traditional account of a creature that sits on the chest of a tormented sleeper. The components of this factor are consistent with, and often interpreted as, physical assault. A third factor (Illusory Movement Experiences) consists of sensations of floating, flying, falling, out-of-body experiences and other sensations of movement. This factor is somewhat less related to the other two factors and hence is not systematically considered here. Numerous quantitative analyses have provided evidence of a replicable, stable and coherent factor structure. These previous analyses fail, however, to convey a qualitative sense of the phenomenology of the experiences.

The present qualitative analysis is based on approximately 7,000 pages of text provided by respondents. The organization of the discussion of the qualitative analysis in the present paper follows closely the factor structure discussed above and outlined in Table 1. In some cases, the sample accounts provided in the text have been subject to minor editing of spelling and grammar. These textual materials have been collected over a period of four years from two sources. The survey was administered to 2,715 introductory psychology students over four consecutive academic terms, yielding 771 sleep paralysis cases (502 females, 269 males) with a mean age of 19.13 (SD = 6.12). In addition, a series of electronic versions have been placed on the World Wide Web from August 1997 to the present (Cheyne, 1997–2001), yielding 7,478 responses (4,943 females, 2,565 males) with a mean age of 29.67 (SD = 10.56). The sex ratio of women to men, of approximately 2:1, is consistent with several broad surveys of hallucinoid experiences in the general population (Bentall, 2000).

Feelings of presence
Mere presence: 'There is always a presence sensed during sleep paralysis and sometimes you don't see the presence but you know it's there.' In less than a quarter of the cases, the presence is described as a neutral, or slightly apprehensive, impression of something externally present but with no corroborating sensory experiences. 'One "feels" something, never seeing it.' 'I've never seen it but there is definitely something there.' The presence is sometimes explicitly described as being just out of sight, behind one's back or just off to one side. 'There was a black object on the corner of my bed, but I couldn't move my head to see it, I could only view it from the corner of my eye.' The conviction seems to be that if only one could turn around 'it' would prove to be quite visible. There is clearly a conviction that the entity is external and that its

existence is independent of the experient (i.e. this is unquestionably the way things *seem* to the experient).

Although sometimes the presence is sensed as just being there, people will sometimes report that they sense its movement or approach; 'coming up the stairs', 'entering the room', 'approaching the bed' and 'climbing up on the bed'. Feeling the mattress being pressed down as the presence climbs on is commonly reported.

In almost half the cases, the presence is watching or monitoring the subject. It is 'as if someone that I couldn't see was there, watching.' Respondents are frequently puzzled that they are unable to specify how they know this. 'You feel that someone is looking at you and you don't know where they specifically are.' Aside from being very disconcerting, this indefiniteness must contribute to the otherworldliness of the presence. In slightly stronger terms, other respondents describe the presence as 'staring', rather than merely 'watching'.

A threatening and evil presence: One of the stronger and more consistent associations is between the sensed presence and fear. Most respondents appear to have an immediate intuition that the presence is someone or something dangerous. Over 60% of respondents indicated that the presence itself is perceived as threatening, often extremely so. More explicitly, the presence is commonly interpreted as possessed of a malevolent, evil intent. Many descriptions focus on a sense of impending doom provoked by this evil presence. 'It felt like something threatening was standing beside me.' A feeling of urgency may accompany the feelings of fear. 'I always feel like I am in grave danger if I don't wake myself up as soon as I can.'

A major difference between sleep paralysis hallucinations and dreams is the relatively high rate of reported fear during the former. Typically, slightly less than one-third of dream reports are accompanied by anxiety, fear or other negative emotions (Merritt *et al.*, 1994; Schredl and Doll, 1998; Strauch and Meier, 1996). In contrast, we have consistently found that between 78% and 98% of respondents report explicit fear (Table 1).

Given the prevalence of interpretations of threat and evil associated with the presence it is scarcely surprising that the predominant emotion is that of fear or rather, in the words of one respondent, 'absolute cold terror'. Respondents are often most emphatic about the extreme nature of their fear. 'I can't imagine anything in reality that could cause greater fear than these episodes.' Many respond to our query about 'fear' with unabashed contempt for the inadequacy of the term to describe their emotion.

Fear is not a strong enough word!

The word 'fear' doesn't even come close. Panic is more like it!

There are not words strong enough to describe the horrific fear I felt.

How about 'overwhelming terror'? These attacks leave me shuddering and crying.

These experiences of dread and terror associated with the presence may also be clearly differentiated from the fear associated with paralysis, death or suffocation (Rueffer, 2000). Thus, although fear may sometimes be ascribed to the possibility of physical harm, most acknowledge that there is something uncanny about the sense of terror. It is 'more a feeling of dread, like something terrible was about to happen'.

The terror transcends mere bodily concerns. 'I literally fear for my soul.' Although the presence may sometimes be personified as death, 'I've also felt a presence but never see it. [It was] like Death was breathing down my back', more common is simply an intense feeling of indescribable evil. 'The most disturbing thing surrounding these episodes of paralysis is the intense feelings of evil surrounding me.' Supernatural and daemonic[1] agencies are thought to be threatening to rob the sleeper of her soul or, alternatively, to enter her body.

> I also feel a presence in my mind (like something sinister or evil) that is trying to draw me into an extremely deep, permanent sleep. I feel that if I succumb, I will never wake up.

> It wants to take my soul or mind or remove me from my body.

> The presence was of a demonic nature, purest evil, out to possess my soul . . . The presence was ALWAYS evil, and I could always feel it trying to enter my body . . . I find this utterly terrifying, beyond anything I can imagine experiencing in the real world because it is so contrary to 'reality', and yet feels entirely authentic . . . Not so much 'die', more like losing possession of my soul.

Occasionally the 'soul-extraction' may be quite violent. 'Something evil is trying to rip my soul out of my body.' Such descriptions of forcible soul extraction are remarkably common. The sense of evil is often made concrete by the experience of the presence as a devil, demon or other inhuman, even unnatural, creature.

Visual hallucinations

Visual hallucinations are quite variable and range from vivid and detailed imagery to something close to a pseudo-hallucination. Pseudo-hallucinations lack the substantiality of externally perceived stimuli, are known to be nonveridical, or appear in inner subjective space rather than externally (Bentall, 1990; Reed, 1988). The visual hallucinations are clearly external although they often have an 'as if' quality, as though the strong feeling of presence were verging on becoming a visual hallucination. Approximately one-third of the respondents noted that the images are quite vague and undefined. 'Once or twice I have thought I even saw something . . . human silhouettes, but the image could have been "my imagination".' As in the case of the sensed presence, the visual images are almost out of sight, on the periphery of vision or obscured by ambient shadows. 'It was a small ugly creature behind me, that I could only see from the corner of my eyes.' 'It was a dark figure, either completely black or obliterated by shadows.' The images may also be associated with implicit threats. 'Until lately, all my sleep paralysis [episodes] involved a visible black shaped "presence" in my room, meaning to do me harm.'

The following examples illustrate visual hallucinations of varying degrees of concreteness, though few of them really achieve a definite character.

> Usually, there seems to be a kind of tangible shadow wrapped around my back, sides, and shoulders. Once, I saw a black triangle darting around in the air around me.

---

[1] I follow the convention that the spelling 'daemon(ic)' is used to refer to the more general term for spirit or genius (OED: sense 1), whereas the spelling 'demon' is used specifically to refer to an *evil* spirit (OED: sense 2). I take Otto to use daemonic (and that is how it is spelled in the English translation) in the first sense, and I use that when speaking more abstractly of a numinous spirit. Thus, when referring to the concrete experiences reported by the respondents (i.e. Being attacked by the devil or a *demon*), I use the second spelling — as do the respondents.

Another time, I saw two white fingerlike projections unfurl from behind me and extend over my arm.

I saw a black humanoid shadow move over the ceiling above my head, and then it seemed to glide down on top of me.

In less frightening episodes the figures may be of friends, parents or partners, and even, on occasion, household pets that might well be expected to enter the bedroom at night. A minority of respondents report that they see fairly detailed visual images of both objects and beings. The more concrete threatening figures typically come in the form of stereotypic demons, death's heads, skeletons, ferocious phantom dogs and, not infrequently, as the 'grim reaper'.

In the past, it has always been some indistinct, evil presence — a shadowy demon, a cowled figure. The first time I experienced this, I saw a shadow of a moving figure, arms outstretched, and I was absolutely sure it was supernatural and evil.

Sometimes an otherwise benign figure may be endowed with a sense of evil. 'At first there was nobody, then one night there was this presence, a little girl I could not see but I could feel. She was an absolutely evil presence.' The fantasy images sometimes take the character of readily available cultural images. 'I can distinctly remember seeing three dark figures standing at the end of my bed — Darth Vadar-like.' A Native American woman explicitly drew upon her heritage to identify an image. 'Spider woman came from the ceiling and wrapped me up and sang songs to me. I was 10 and later the deerwoman would come and stand at the foot of my bed.' (She explained that the spider woman and deer woman were well known figures from childhood stories.) Another experient made a somewhat more idiosyncratic association. 'The first shape I saw was a cloth-like triangle hanging or balanced in mid air and appeared to be a crude form with a hat. Funnily enough it reminded me of the Sandeman logo.'

Slightly more than one-third of the cases involve some sort of human or humanoid identity. Both male and female figures are typically dressed in black or, occasionally, white, and are described as having strikingly white faces, sometimes described as death's heads. Given the threatening nature of the sensed presence and the resulting visual images it is not surprising that the visual hallucinations may also be interpreted as conventional intruders. 'Actually, I awoke to see a figure of a man, all in black, standing at the foot of my bed. I tried to scream very loud, but all I could do was go "ah ah ah" very ineffectually.' There is also evidence of considerable within-person variability in the interpretation of visual hallucinations. 'I have imagined burglars, rapists, terrorists, monsters, demons, and the devil all in my room. Sometimes they just stare or laugh at me while I lie helpless and other times they try to attack me.'

Auditory hallucinations

Auditory hallucinations during sleep paralysis are extremely diverse. One quality does seem to pervade all of this diversity, however. The sounds are very distinctly experienced as being external to the hearer rather than 'in the head' (see below).

Many of the sounds are very elementary. Often the auditory experiences are described as 'buzzing', 'grinding', 'humming', 'hissing', 'ringing', 'roaring', 'rushing', 'screeching', 'squeaking', 'vibrating', 'whirring' and 'whistling' sounds. These sounds are often described as being very loud and 'mechanical'. For this first category there is little or no interpretative elaboration. Sounds are described in the most basic sensory terms. Other sorts of descriptions are very much like those for the elementary sounds except that they are identified with machines or materials that produce such sounds. Ringing telephones are reported, as are sirens, vacuum cleaners, power tools, electric motors, slamming doors and breaking glass. Difficult-to-identify music is also reported, sometimes described as being like the sound of a poorly tuned radio receiving several stations at once. Alternatively, the sounds may be attributed, perhaps by the less technologically minded, to natural causes. One-quarter of the participants report general environmental sounds: the 'sound of wind' or 'a rushing/roaring like waves in a sea shell' and 'sand rushing past my ears'.

The quality of the sounds may be interpretively modified only slightly when a ringing sound is attributed to a telephone, for example. Other sounds suggest more complex interpretations and narrative elaborations. 'There was a sound rather like a cardboard box of some weight being dragged across a dusty wooden floor.' One of the most commonly reported movement sounds is that of footsteps.

> I heard footsteps in my room, walking around my bed and then back out.

> I heard a door shut and footsteps coming closer. (Although the door was double locked and nobody had the key anyway.) When the footsteps entered the bedroom, I felt a presence standing over me and a warm hot tingly breath/air down my whole body.

Diverse animal sounds, described as growling, snarling, howling, screeching or barking, are commonly mentioned. Among the more human sounds, laughing and crying are mentioned. 'Sometimes I hear laughing of an old man or an old lady. Sometimes I hear a baby crying.' More often, the sounds are somewhat more sinister. 'I hear moans and voices of people whispering things in my ear and often mumbling.'

Voices: Symons (1995), following Seligman and Yellen (1987), distinguishes between hallucinatory and non-hallucinatory ('conjured') auditory imagery. Symons argues that, in dreams, voices are seldom heard as external sounds. Rather, conversations are experienced 'in the head' as internal dialogue. Thus, it is the sense and meaning of conversations that are experienced in dreams, not the concrete utterances. Bergson (1958) discusses essentially the same idea. 'Most of us at one time or another . . . have dreamed about speaking to someone or being engaged in a lengthy conversation only to have forced on us the singular realization that we are not speaking and had not spoken, and that our interlocutor had not uttered a single word. We had exchanged our thoughts and carried on an unequivocal conversation, yet we had heard nothing' (pp. 27–8). In contrast to these observations on dream voices, sleep paralysis voices are experienced as externally produced sounds but of indefinite or nonsensical meaning. Indeed, human voices are the most common auditory hallucination associated with sleep paralysis (36% of respondents). The voices may be experienced as loud shouting or soft whispering but, in either case, the sense of what is being said is often elusive. The voices are described as 'gibberish', 'garbled' or 'foreign-sounding'.

> One time I awoke to find half snake/half human thing shouting gibberish in my ears.

> An evil-sounding female voice was whispering in my ear. The words were incomprehensible, but I couldn't say whether it was a different language or not.'

In cases in which the voices are comprehensible their messages are typically simple and direct. The voices may simply call out the sleeper's name, but more often, they utter a threat, warning, command or a cry for help.

The first few times this happened I thought I heard someone crying for help and it was quite intense.

When I awoke to the women's voice telling me I was going to die if I didn't wake up.

The first time, when I was on my side, I heard heavy breathing. The second time, when I was lying on my back, I heard an evil voice saying, "I'm going to get you now, you can't get away from me." It kept repeating. Some of the things I couldn't make out.

Once I heard a man's voice in my right ear say 'This is your subconscious speaking to you.'

But as I listened I could sense this 'thing' hover over my head — very close directly over my ear. It said '[Name]!' . . . The voice continued 'I've got work for you to do!'

I heard a voice telling me I was playing the game wrong and I had to play it right or quit. It was a woman's voice and she sounded as though she was in a lot of pain and very far away, then she said, 'he's coming' and left.

In one case, a respondent heard the voice of someone who had actually threatened her in the recent past. 'At first I thought — just my roomie — but I recognized the voice as a mystery caller who has harassed me twice.' We may see here an example of someone explicitly considering alternative interpretations and settling on perhaps the most plausible given the context of sensed presence, fear and a recent threatening experience.

Tactile hallucinations

Although we have only recently begun probing for tactile experiences they appear to be a common hallucinatory experience associated with the Intruder cluster. Consistent with this association, tactile experiences are typically associated with a sense of external agency in 34% of cases. Being grabbed by the hands and wrists is particularly common. In some of the examples that follow reference is sometimes also made to Incubus hallucinations (see below). 'I had the sensation of an ugly creature touching me.' 'I did feel a "male's" hands wrapped around my arms!' 'Once the presence was a dark shadowy evil figure and once a white mist, which called my name and touched my shoulder.' 'Occasionally I feel as though someone is grabbing hold of my hand or sitting on my back and or chest.' 'I once woke up to what I thought was a man leaning over me in bed who had my right arm in a tight grip, holding me down on the bed. The man just had me "pinned" by the wrist and I was frozen for what seemed like forever staring up into his face (probably lasted less than a minute).'

The Incubus

Assault scenarios are common (see Table 1) and often involve, as a central component, being held down. Assault by supernatural beings appears extensively in the folklore tradition, as part, for example, of the 'Old Hag' experience (i.e. being assaulted by an old crone — Hufford, 1982).

I tend to feel more like I am being held down than that I cannot move, even though I can't see anybody . . . No matter what position I'm in it feels as though someone is sitting on my upper body and holding my arms in place — I consciously try to fight whatever it is that's holding me.

Breathing difficulties: People frequently report breathing difficulties during sleep paralysis (see Table 1). These tend to be associated with feelings of pressure on the chest, tightness around the neck, and feelings of suffocation or smothering.

Perceptions of breathing difficulty probably arise as a direct consequence of the paralysis of the voluntary muscles (Cheyne, Rueffer and Newby-Clark, 1999). The following remark is consistent with insight into this effect. 'My body breathes for itself. I have no control over set patterns.' Although automatic shallow breathing continues, when the sleeper attempts, unsuccessfully, to breathe voluntarily this may lead to panic over possible suffocation. The feelings of suffocation may also be induced by REM-related hypoxia and hypercapnia (Douglas, 1994). This inability to 'get one's breath' often leads to panicky feelings and to references to the possibility of dying from suffocation. Respondents frequently imagine that a pillow is being pressed against their faces. 'I have felt that I was being suffocated because I had the sensation that I was lying face down on my pillow, when in reality [I] was sleeping on my side or back.' The attacks may also be directly associated with the sensed presence.

> [There was] a sensation of something in the room watching me or sometimes even smothering me.

> Sometimes it begins when I fall asleep and (seem to) immediately wake up. My eyes pop open and I sense something ominous. Then something comes over me and smothers me, as if with a pillow, I fight but I can't move. I try to scream. I wake up gasping for air.

Pressure: The difficulty breathing is sometimes experienced either along with, or perhaps as, a severe pressure on the chest. 'I feel like I can't breathe, and I'm being crushed.' This pressure appears to be interpreted as pressing or pushing air out of the lungs. Although the classic incubus hallucination is of a crushing weight on the chest, the pressure may also be felt on the back or side of the torso. Sometimes the intensity is sufficiently intense that the language becomes somewhat stronger, referring to 'crushing sensations'. Pain is also typically localized in the torso, and most often in the chest. The pressure or pushing on the body may be so intense that the person feels as though s/he is being pushed or pulled into the bed. 'I saw a black something. I cannot explain what it was. It came into my bedroom and lay down on the bed next to me. I could feel the bed move and I felt a heavy pressure on my chest. I felt as though my body were being pushed into the bed.' The source of the feelings of pressure are often attributed to an external agent and associated with descriptions of bodily assault. In a classic 'Old Hag' account one respondent described an episode in which 'this old lady, that was sitting on top my chest beating the living daylights out my head'. The interpretation may include hallucinations of strangulation. 'I would feel like someone was sitting on my chest, trying to choke me.' The possibility that hallucinations might be associated with apnoea during sleep paralysis is consistent with the finding of Hobson, Goldfrank and Snyder (1965) of a correlation between respiratory apnea and a dream about being choked.

Whereas the feeling of presence is often associated with a nameless terror, when associated with sensations of pressure and difficulty breathing it may be more explicitly associated with thoughts of impending death. 'I feel a very strong force pushing down on my chest, and pulling me down towards the floor. I also feel a presence in my mind (like something sinister or evil) that is trying to draw me into an extremely deep, permanent sleep. I feel that if I succumb, I will never wake up.' Sometimes when difficulty in breathing is associated with the presence it is interpreted as a full-blown attack by the presence.

During my first experiences I believed a ghost was sitting on my back, pressing me down!

Commonly I will wake from a dream and sense its thick presence. Then it will rush at me, climb on my back and pin me to the bed.

Although it wasn't a pressure on my chest but the hallucination of 'someone' holding my head down with a pillow.

I thought it was some unspeakable evil trying to get hold of my throat.

I have had a woman holding me down at the shoulders and trying to suck out what I thought was my soul through my abdominal area while yelling at me in strange tongues.

Occasionally, these struggles will have a frankly sexual component, usually associated with sexual assault or rape.

I believed that the devil or an evil spirit had me pinned down and was fondling me. The time that it felt like I was being raped by the devil or an evil spirit . . . strong sexual feelings were automatic along with fear.

Discussion

I have argued that, during sleep paralysis, the sensed presence is the experiential component of a threat detection mechanism that gives rise to interpretive efforts to find, identify and elaborate sources of threat. Material for these interpretive efforts is provided by REM-related sensory imagery. The nature of the resulting interpretations betrays a potential link to mechanisms underlying initial responses to threat of predation. The sensed presence is typically described as a monitoring one, akin to a predator stalking its prey. A threatening, malignant or evil intent is frequently ascribed to the presence. Respondents are often at pains to express the intensity and depth of the accompanying terror. In addition, bodily sensations of crushing and painful pressure on the chest, back, side and neck may be interpreted as a full-fledged and potentially mortal attack by the presence. These experiences mimic responses to predation, particularly those associated with tonic immobility (Ratner, 1975). Tonic immobility refers to a state of paralysis of the major muscles with accompanying physiological responses consistent with fear and hypervigilance and that appears to engage the same fundamental neurophysiology as sleep paralysis (Gallup and Maser, 1977). The working hypothesis underlying our research is that the sensed presence and related hallucinations arise from extreme hypervigilant defensive states occasioned by paroxysmal activation of various centres in the limbic system, notably the amygdala, periaquaductal gray, anterior cingulate, and nucleus basalis of Meynert in the substantia innominata. In such states organisms are extraordinarily alert to environmental events potentially associated with danger. These states normally engage diverse bodily responses, including motor and sympathetic activity, as well as numerous sensory and motor regions of the cortex. In the case of endogenous activation, because the sense of threat is not immediately corroborated, the fear itself has a numinous quality. Many respondents explicitly claim that the fear is quite unlike any real-world fear that they have ever known. It is likely that such experiences may also be evoked by unusual or extreme environmental conditions involving threat or danger or those mimicking such conditions: sensory deprivation, isolation of the sort explorers sometimes experience, and life-threatening conditions — including near-death experiences (Saver and Rabin, 1997; Suedfeld, 1987; Zusne and Jones, 1982).

One of the more striking features of many of the visual hallucinations of sleep paralysis is that they range from vague and indistinct impressions to quite specific images. Visual hallucinations thus appear to represent attempts of the threat detection mechanisms to flesh out the sensed presence in consciousness. The more concrete images are often of quite conventional beastly and demonic figures of doom: devils, demons, witches, aliens and even cinematic villains such as Darth Vader and Freddy Kruger.

The descriptions of the most basic auditory hallucinations are quite consistent with a quasi-random activation of auditory centres and may be seen as analogous to vague and indistinct visual images. It is easy to imagine how readily meaningless white-noise-like bursts may be translated into vague environmental sounds, background whispers and unintelligible gibberish. The sudden hallucinated exclamations, including threats and warnings quite directly associated with the feelings of an alien presence, are reminiscent of classic schizophrenic hallucinations. It is commonly argued that schizophrenic auditory hallucinations are largely a matter of the transformation of one's own 'thoughts' into other's 'voices' (Bentall, 2000). There are at least two dimensions to this transformation; one from wordless thought to audible voices and another from self- to other-generated words or thoughts. Woody and Bowers (1994) stress this latter dimension and speculate on its relation to frontal lobe functioning. They argue that auditory hallucinations may be of two distinct types. One form of hallucination is the loss of the sense of agency in one's inner speech. Such are likely to be described as thought control, thought insertion and the like. The sense of thinking, or of internal conversation, is maintained. Meaning is also retained, although given the general deterioration of coherence associated with other aspects of schizophrenia, that meaning may be rather fragmented and disjointed. The second form of hallucination is that of explicit audible voices (and other sometimes difficult-to-specify sounds). It is conjectured that these are either of more peripheral origin and associated with spurious activation within the inner ear, thalamus or primary sensory cortical areas or, alternatively, with nonspecific environmental ambient noises that are misinterpreted. The auditory hallucinations during sleep paralysis thus appear to share some features of schizophrenic auditory hallucinations, namely concreteness and loss of sense of self-generation.

Curiously the voice hallucinations seem more sensual than those of dreams, at least as has been claimed by Symons (1995). Symons argues that it is essential that dreams should not have too much realism because the imagery of our dreams must not be phenomenally conflated with sensory input. If this were to happen, either external auditory signs of danger would not wake us or, conversely, we would be continually wakened by our dream imagery. Symons is particularly emphatic that auditory dream imagery must be distinct from auditory input because audition is a particularly important modality for detecting danger in the dark of night. Symons' (1995) argument makes the assumption that, to use Flanagan's (1992) terms, experiential sensitivity equals informational sensitivity. Flanagan argues against the validity of such equivalence, however. Appropriately enough for the present argument, one source of evidence he provides is based on the apparent contradiction between the phenomenological vividness of dreams and their subsequent poor recall. In addition, in spite of the compelling phenomenology of hypnagogic hallucinations, people may be easily aroused from the state of sleep paralysis by external tactile and auditory input (Hishikawa, 1976). This constitutes further support for the dissociation of phenomenological and informational sensitivity. In the case of sleep paralysis at least, the phenomenological vividness of internally generated hallucinations need not interfere with the informativeness and effectiveness of external inputs.

We have only recently begun to examine tactile sensations in the context of sleep paralysis and found them to be clearly associated with the Intruder factor. Consistent with this association, the tactile sensations are almost exclusively taken to be active touching, grabbing or embracing by the hands and arms of an animate, albeit indefinite, embodiment of the presence. Such interpretations of the tactile experiences fit well with the larger narrative of threat and assault. Indeed, the tactile sensations appear to be something of a bridge between the hallucinations of threat and those of assault. Consistent with this interpretation, tactile hallucinations are more strongly correlated with the Incubus factor than are other Intruder hallucinations. Experiences of oppression and suffocation also combine with the sense of threatening presence and with auditory and visual hallucinations to contribute to the construction of elaborate hallucinations of attacking intruders. These are interpreted as painful physical and sexual assaults by devils, demons and hags. One respondent spoke of 'wrestling with the devil, turning over and over in the air', reminiscent of Jacob's struggle with the stranger (*Genesis*, 32.24–32). Armstrong (1993) provides an account of a mystical experience of the prophet Muhammad that will sound quite familiar at this point. Muhammad awoke from sleep one night and felt enveloped by an overwhelming divine presence. An angel appeared to him and commanded him to 'Recite!' (*Iqra!*). Intimidated by the implications of this command Muhammad refused. The angel, however, enveloped him in an overpowering embrace, so he felt as if all the breath were being squeezed from his body. Just as he felt he could resist no longer, the angel released him and commanded him once again to 'Recite!'. Again Muhammad refused and again the angel embraced him until he finally relented. The Arab world of the time had many disreputable *kahins* possessed of jinni. Muhammad himself must have had qualms about becoming one of these. Ultimately the intensity of the experience appears to have won him over, however. In the account of Muhammad's struggle the features of the waking nightmare are quite evident, including awakening to a presence, hearing a brief audible command and being held in a crushing embrace.

Non-Delusional Character of the Hallucinations

Many respondents are quite emphatic that the hallucinations are entirely compelling but are able nonetheless to maintain a critical stance. Their rationality triumphs, as it were, over the evidence of their senses. One respondent, for example, who provided a vivid and detailed account of an alien abduction experience was most emphatic that, although his experiences were utterly compelling, he considered himself a hard-headed and sensible person and did not believe any of it for a minute. His experience was one of abduction but this did not make it true, even for him. Such scepticism does not appear, on the other hand, to detract from the impact of the hallucinations. '[It is] like the devil had me and I don't even believe in the devil.' Another said, 'if I were a religious man, I would certainly describe my experience as a contact with a god or devil'. This contrast between what is experienced and what is acceptable is often puzzling to the experient. 'The strange thing is how VIVID the experience is. It is real even in the face of a "conscious" effort to convince myself that it is not.' Some do, of course, accept the possibility that the presence was truly otherworldly and daemonic. A number of respondents, for example, were currently, or had been formerly, members of fundamentalist sects and, as such, readily felt a deeper spiritual meaning in their experiences and accepted the experience as truly a struggle with Satan. 'Before I knew what sleep paralysis was (I had it probably 2–3 years before I knew what it was) and I had been raised in a religion considered a cult, which I had left years before, I would wake up unable to move, feeling like I was being held down in bed, and thought it was the demons from the church doing this to me.' In some cases this sort of interpretation was that of the experient and in some cases it was the judgment of another member, or pastor, of their church. Two respondents reported undergoing formal (and unsuccessful) exorcisms.

I suggest that there are two levels of interpretation operating in these situations. The first-level interpretations are on-line, situationally embedded, automatic, intuitive and obligate. One might describe this level of consciousness as 'the way things *seem*'. There is, however, a second level of interpretation that is more explicit, critical and verbal. This level of interpretation is an off-line or 'action-neutral' (Clark, 1997) decision about the first-level experiences and may be described in everyday terms as 'the way things "really" (or probably) are'. As the parenthetical 'probably' implies these higher-order interpretations are often circumspect and tentative. The two levels of interpretation also bear some resemblance to pervasive distinctions that have been made between narrative and paradigmatic modes of thought (Bruner, 1986), experiential and rational perspectives (Epstein, 1994) and embedded and abstract self-awareness (Gallagher and Marcel, 1999). Given the general features of the REM state, namely the activation of limbic centres discussed earlier, along with the relative deactivation of executive and association cortex such as the dorsolateral prefrontal cortex (Hobson *et al.*, 1998), it is not surprising that the more critical stance is rather compromised at the time the hallucinations are actually experienced. In any case, rational analysis can hardly reduce our terror in such cases because the fear is as much a cause of the hallucinations as it is a consequence. That is, it is not simply that the hallucinations are terrifying; rather, the hallucinations are the way they are because we are already terrified. As Hobson and his colleagues put it, emotion may best be viewed 'as a primary shaper of [dream] plots rather than as a reaction to them' (Hobson *et al.*, 1998, p. R2). Of course, when one is 'successful' at creating truly frightening images, thereby corroborating the sense of threat, fear will be sustained or even increased. Thus the vigilance system hypothesis clearly suggests reciprocal feedback between affect and imagery. Beyond simply enhancing or dampening the intensity of fear the hallucinoid imagery may also change the quality of the emotional experience. Terror may yield to feelings of excitement, exhilaration, enthrallment, rapture or ecstasy. A small number of respondents, while acknowledging some fear, especially during their initial episodes, come to enjoy the experience. This seems most common among individuals who practice meditation. In some cases, they even report that they are able to experience a feeling of transcendence that eluded them during mediation.

Concluding Remarks

The other enters into discussions of consciousness rather infrequently and then usu-ally as an interlocutor: a mirror for, or a scaffold of, the self (Baldwin, 1897; Cooley, 1902; Mead, 1934). In such cases, the role and character of the other is often por-trayed as a cooperative and rather benign partner, or even a benevolent helper. Even for those, such as Heidegger, Sartre or Bakhtin, who sometimes consider otherness in less sanguine terms, the other often plays a significant and ultimately productive role in the completion or construction of the self (Cheyne and Tarulli, 1999). Even the sensed presence has been viewed as a right-hemisphere analogue of the left-hemisphere sense of self (Persinger, 1993). Considerations raised here point to a more sinister and primordial other of concern to us at the most fundamental biological roots of our being. This other is one that is radically different from the self, indeed capable of annihilating the self, and hence of instantly dominating our consciousness above all other considerations, however rarely and briefly. This other is probably more than a mere projection of, or analogue to, the self. Such an other constitutes a part of the *Umwelt*, a part that encompasses a way of understanding the animate and sentient in the world around us. Moreover, such an other opens up in a most direct and terrifying way our vulnerability, finitude and personal helplessness, supine and trembling before the carnivorous and pitiless predator.

There is indeed, Otto suggested, a daemonic aspect to the numinous. The fear of ghosts, Otto took to be but a degraded version of the daemonic experience. He appears to suggest that, as imagery becomes more specific and the experience less numinous, the religious element is somehow debased. Perhaps this is why traditional routes to purely religious and spiritual experiences have been through techniques, prayer, meditation, drugs, etc. that sustain numinosity and modulate affect. On this view, holy individuals are masters of the numinous who can sustain the ineffable and simultaneously control affect so that the experience seldom degenerates into crassly specific images.

The ominous numinous brings forth not simply thoughts of death but, more essen-tially, a sense of foreboding. Interestingly, in spite of the overwhelmingly threatening and terrifying aspects of the sensed presence and its elaborations, thoughts of death are most strongly associated not with the sensed presence, or other intruder hallucina-tions, but with incubus experiences of pressure on the chest, breathing difficulties and choking sensations. These latter experiences are all signs of assault and, hence, of a more immediate possibility of physical demise. The fear and terror associated with the feeling of presence and other intruder hallucinations is not so much a fear of death but rather an unspeakable dread of an *unknown* power. Although there is, of course, more to human spirituality than dread, the terrible and most awesome aspect of the spiritual arises in its most primordial and gripping form, I suggest, in situations that mimic basic biological challenges and threats. Spirituality, on this view, has its roots not in our most cerebral intellectual functions (though it may reach its 'highest expression' through these) but in the frailty and precariousness of our bodily selves.

References

Armstrong, K. (1993), *A History of God: The 4000-Year Quest of Judaism, Christianity, and Islam* (New York: Knopf).

Baker, R.A. (1990), *They Call it Hypnosis* (Buffalo, Prometheus).

Baker, R.A. (1992), 'Alien abductions or alien production? Some not so unusual personal experiences', Lexington, KY: October http://www.ufobbs.com/txt4/3057.ufo

Baldwin, J.M. (1897), *Social and Ethical Interpretations in Mental Development: A Study in Social Psychology* (New York, MacMillan).

Bentall, R.P. (1990), 'The illusion of reality: A review and integration of psychological research on hallucinations', *Psychological Bulletin*, **107**, pp. 82–95.

Bentall, R.P. (2000), 'Hallucinatory experiences', in *Varieties of Anomalous Experience*, ed. E. Cardeña, S.J. Lynn and S. Krippner (Washington: APA), pp. 85–120.

Bergson, H. (1958), *The World of Dreams*, trans. W. Baskin (New York: Philosophical Library; original published in 1901).

Bruner, J. (1986), *Actual Minds, Possible Worlds* (Cambridge, MA: Harvard University Press).

Cheyne, J.A. (1997–2001), 'Sleep paralysis and associated hypnagogic and hypnopompic hallucinations', http://watarts.uwaterloo.ca/~acheyne/S_P.html.

Cheyne, J.A., Newby-Clark, I.R. and Rueffer, S.D. (1999), 'Sleep paralysis and associated hypnagogic and hypnopompic experiences', *Journal of Sleep Research*, **8**, pp. 313–17.

Cheyne, J.A., Rueffer, S.D. and Newby-Clark, I.R. (1999), 'Hypnagogic and hypnopompic hallucinations during sleep paralysis: Neurological and cultural construction of the nightmare', *Consciousness and Cognition*, **8**, pp. 319–37.

Cheyne, J.A. and Tarulli, D. (1999), 'Dialogue, difference, and voice in the Zone of Proximal Development', *Theory and Psychology*, **9**, pp. 5–28.

Clark, A. (1997), *Being There: Putting Brain, Body, and World Together Again* (Cambridge, MA: MIT Press).

Cogny, P. (1970), 'Introduction', in *le Maupassant du 'Horla'* (Paris: Minard).

Cooley, C.H. (1902), *Human Nature and the Social Order* (New York, Scribner).

Damasio, A.R. (1999), *The Feeling of What Happens: Body and Emotion in the Making of Consciousness* (New York: Harcourt, Brace and Company).

Douglas, N.J. (1994), 'Breathing during sleep in normal subjects', in *Sleep*, ed. R. Cooper (London: Chapman), pp. 76–95.

Ellis, R.D. (1999), 'Dynamical systems as an approach to consciousness: Emotion, self-organization, and the mind–body problem', *New Ideas in Psychology*, **17**, pp. 237–50.

Epstein, S. (1994), 'Integration of the cognitive and psychodynamic unconscious', *American Psychologist*, **49**, pp. 709–24.

Firestone, M. (1985), 'The "old hag" sleep paralysis in Newfoundland', *Journal of Psychoanalytic Anthropology*, **8**, pp. 47–66.

Flanagan, O. (1992), *Consciousness Reconsidered* (Cambridge, MA: MIT Press).

Fukuda, K., Ogilvie, R.D., Chilcott, L., Vendittelli, A.M. and Takeuchi, T. (1998), 'The prevalence of sleep paralysis among Canadian and Japanese college students', *Dreaming*, **8**, pp. 59–66.

Gallagher, S. and Marcel, A.J. (1999), 'The self in contextualized action', *Journal of Consciousness Studies*, **6** (4), pp. 4–30.

Gallup, G.G., Jr. and Maser, J.D. (1977), 'Catatonia: Tonic immobility: Evolutionary underpinnings of human catalepsy and catatonia', in *Psychopathology: Experimental Models*, ed. J.D. Maser and M.E.P. Seligman (San Francisco, CA: W.H. Freeman), pp. 334–57.

Hishikawa, Y. (1976), 'Sleep paralysis', in *Narcolepsy: Advances in Sleep Research*, Vol. 3, ed. C. Guilleminault, W.C. Dement and P. Passouant (New York: Spectrum), pp. 97–124.

Hishikawa, Y. and Shimizu, T. (1995), 'Physiology of REM sleep, cataplexy, and sleep paralysis', *Advances in Neurology*, **67**, pp. 245–71.

Hobson, J.A., Goldfrank, F. and Snyder, F. (1965), 'Respiration and mental activity in sleep', *Journal of Psychiatric Research*, **3**, pp. 79–90.

Hobson, J.A. and McCarley, R.W. (1977), 'The brain as a dream state generator: An activation-synthesis of dream processes', *American Journal of Psychiatry*, **134**, pp. 1335–48.

Hobson, J.A., Stickgold, R. and Pace-Schott, E.F. (1998), 'The neurophysiology of REM sleep dreaming', *Neuroreport*, **9**, R1–R14.

Hufford, D.J. (1982), *The Terror that Comes in the Night: An Experience-Centered Study of Supernatural Assault Traditions* (Philadelphia: University of Pennsylvania Press).

James, W. (1958), *The Varieties of Religious Experience: A Study in Human Nature* (New York: New American Library; original published in 1902).

LeDoux, J. (1994), 'Emotion, memory, and the brain', *Scientific American*, **270**, pp. 32–9.

LeDoux, J. (1996), *The Emotional Brain* (New York: Simon and Schuster).

Liddon, S.C. (1967), 'Sleep paralysis and hypnagogic hallucinations: Their relationship to the nightmare', *Archives of General Psychiatry*, **17**, pp. 88–96.

Mead, G.H. (1934), *Mind, Self, and Society: From the Standpoint of a Social Behaviorist*, ed. C.W. Morris (Chicago, University of Chicago Press).

Merritt, J.M., Stickgold, R., Pace-Schott, E., Williams, J. and Hobson, J.A. (1994), 'Emotion profiles in the dreams of men and women', *Consciousness and Cognition*, **3**, pp. 46–60.

Ness, R. (1978), 'The old hag phenomenon as sleep paralysis: A biocultural interpretation', *Culture, Medicine, and Psychiatry*, **2**, pp. 15–39.

Otto, R. (1923), *The Idea of the Holy*, trans. John W. Harvey (Oxford: Oxford University Press).

Persinger, M.A. (1993), 'Vectorial cerebral hemisphericity as differential sources for the sensed presence, mystical experiences and religious conversions', *Perceptual and Motor Skills*, **76**, pp. 915–30.

Ratner, R.C. (1975), 'Animal's defenses: Fighting in predator–prey relations', in *Advances in the Study of Communication and Affect, Vol. 2: Nonverbal Communication of Aggression*, ed. P. Pliner, L. Krames and T. Alloway (New York, NY: Plenum).

Reed, G. (1988), *The Psychology of Anomalous Experience: A Cognitive Approach*, revised edn. (Buffalo, NY: Prometheus).

Rueffer, S.D. (2000). An in-depth examination of the construction of hallucinatory experiences associated with sleep paralysis. Unpublished master's thesis, University of Waterloo, Waterloo, Ontario, Canada.

Saver, J.L. and Rabin, J. (1997), 'The neural substrates of religious experience', *Journal of Neuropsychiatry and Clinical Neurosciences*, **9**, pp. 498–510.

Schredl, M. and Doll, E. (1998), 'Emotions in diary dreams', *Consciousness and Cognition*, **7**, pp. 634–46.

Seligman, M.E.P. and Yellen, A. (1987), 'What is a dream?', *Behavior Research and Therapy*, **25**, pp. 1–24.

Spanos, N.P., Cross, P.A., Dickson, K. and Dubreuil, S.C. (1993), 'Close encounters: An examination of UFO experiences', *Journal of Abnormal Psychology*, **102**, pp. 624–32.

Spanos, N.P., McNulty, S.A., DuBreuil, S.C., Pires, M. and Burgess, M.F. (1995), 'The frequency and correlates of sleep paralysis in a university sample', *Journal of Research in Personality*, **29**, pp. 285–305.

Strauch, I. and Meier, B. (1996), *In Search of Dreams: Results of Experimental Dream Research* (Albany, NY: State University of New York Press).

Suedfeld, P. (1987), 'Extreme and unusual environments', in *Handbook of Environmental Psychology*, ed. I. Altman and D. Stokols (New York: John Wiley).

Suedfeld, P. and Mocellin, J.S.P. (1987), 'The "sensed presence" in unusual environments', *Environment and Behavior*, **19**, pp. 33–52.

Symons, D. (1995), 'The stuff the dreams aren't made of: wake-state and dream-state sensory experiences differ', *Cognition*, **47**, pp. 181–217.

Whalen, P.J. (1998), 'Fear, vigilance, and ambiguity: Initial neuroimaging studies of the human amygdala', *Current Directions in Psychological Science*, **7**, pp. 177–88.

Woody, E.Z. and Bowers, K.S. (1994), 'A frontal assault on dissociated control', in *Dissociation: Clinical and Theoretical Perspectives*, ed. S.J. Lynn and J.W. Rhue (New York: Guilford), pp. 52–79.

Zusne, L. and Jones, W.H. (1982), *Anomalistic Psychology: A Study of Extraordinary Phenomena of Behavior and Experience* (Hillsdale: NJ: Lawrence Erlbaum).

Dan Zahavi

Beyond Empathy

Phenomenological Approaches to Intersubjectivity

Drawing on the work of Scheler, Heidegger, Merleau-Ponty, Husserl and Sartre, this article presents an overview of some of the diverse approaches to intersubjectivity that can be found in the phenomenological tradition. Starting with a brief description of Scheler's criticism of the argument from analogy, the article continues by showing that the phenomenological analyses of intersubjectivity involve much more than a 'solution' to the 'traditional' problem of other minds. Intersubjectivity doesn't merely concern concrete face-to-face encounters between individuals. It is also something that is at play in simple perception, in tool-use, in emotions, drives and different types of self-awareness. Ultimately, the phenomenologists would argue that a treatment of intersubjectivity requires a simultaneous analysis of the relationship between subjectivity and world. It is not possible simply to insert intersubjectivity somewhere within an already established ontology; rather, the three regions 'self', 'others', and 'world' belong together; they reciprocally illuminate one another, and can only be understood in their interconnection.

I: Empathy and the Problem of Other Minds

The argument from analogy is a classical attempt to come to grips with the problem of intersubjectivity. One version of the argument runs as follows: The only mind I have direct access to is my own. My access to the mind of another is always mediated by his bodily behaviour. But how can the perception of another person's body provide me with information about his mind? Starting from my own mind and linking it to the way in which my body is given to me, I then pass to the other's body and by noticing the analogy that exists between this body and my own body, I *infer* that the foreign body is probably also linked in a similar manner to a foreign mind. In my own case, screaming is often associated with pain; when I observe others screaming, I infer that it is likely that they are also feeling pain. Although this inference doesn't provide me with indubitable knowledge about others, and although it doesn't allow me to actually experience other minds, at least it gives me more reason to believe in their existence, than for denying it.[1]

---

[1] For a classical and slightly different formulation of the argument, cf. Mill (1867, pp. 237–8).

Journal of Consciousness Studies, **8**, No. 5–7, 2001, pp. 151–67

This account has been met with much criticism, not only from Wittgenstein, but also from the phenomenologists. To take one example, in Max Scheler's work *Wesen und Formen der Sympathie* (originally published in 1912) we find a whole list of counter-arguments (Scheler, 1973, pp. 232–4):

1. To assume that our belief in the existence of other minds is inferential in nature is to opt for a far too complex cognitive account. After all, both animals and infants seem to share this belief, but in their case it is hardly the result of a process of inference.

2. In order for the argument to work, there has to be a similarity between the way in which my own body is given to me, and the way in which the body of the other is given to me. But my own body as it is felt proprioceptively for me does not at all resemble the other's body as it is perceived visually by me.

3. How can the argument from analogy explain that we can empathize with creatures whose bodies in no way resemble our own, say a suffering bird or fish?

4. Even if all of these problems could be overcome, the argument from analogy would still be formally invalid. Noticing the connection between my own mind and my bodily behaviour, and the analogy between my own bodily behaviour and the behaviour of a foreign body, all that I am entitled to infer is that the foreign body is probably also linked with *my own* mind.

After this criticism, Scheler goes on to examine two of the crucial presuppositions in the argument from analogy. First, the argument assumes that my point of departure is my own consciousness. This is what is at first given to me in a quite direct and unmediated fashion, and it is this purely mental self-experience which is taken to precede and make possible the recognition of others. Second, the argument assumes that we never have direct access to another person's consciousness. We can never *experience* their thoughts or feelings. We can only infer that they must exist on the basis of that which is actually given to us, namely their bodily appearance. Although both of these two assumptions might seem perfectly obvious, Scheler rejects both. He denies that our initial self-acquaintance is of a purely mental nature, and that it takes place in isolation from others. As he puts it, the argument from analogy underestimates the difficulties involved in self-experience and overestimates the difficulties involved in the experience of others (Scheler, 1973, pp. 244–6). But Scheler also denies that we only perceive the physical appearance of the other, and that we then, in a subsequent move, have to infer the existence of a foreign subjectivity. As he writes:

> For we certainly believe ourselves to be directly acquainted with another person's joy in his laughter, with his sorrow and pain in his tears, with his shame in his blushing, with his entreaty in his outstretched hands, with his love in his look of affection, with his rage in the gnashing of his teeth, with his threats in the clenching of his fist, and with the tenor of his thoughts in the sound of his words. If anyone tells me that this is not 'perception', for it cannot be so, in view of the fact that a perception is simply a 'complex of physical sensations', and that there is certainly no sensation of another person's mind nor any stimulus from such a source, I would beg him to turn aside from such questionable theories and address himself to the phenomenological facts (Scheler, 1973, p. 254).

On the basis of considerations like these, it has been argued that we, in the face-to-face encounter, are neither confronted with a mere body, nor with a hidden psyche, but with a unified whole. Thus, a solution to the problem of other minds must start with a correct understanding of the relation between mind and body. In some sense, experiences are not internal, they are not hidden in the head, but rather expressed in bodily gestures and actions. When I see a foreign face, I *see* it as friendly or angry, etc.; that is, the very face expresses these emotions, I don't have to infer their existence. Moreover, bodily behaviour is meaningful, it is intentional, and as such it is neither internal nor external, but rather beyond this artificial distinction. For the very same reason we should realize that the body of the other differs radically from inanimate objects, and that our perception of this body is quite unlike our ordinary perception of objects.

That I have an actual experience of the other, and do not have to do with a mere inference, does not imply, however, that I can experience the other in the same way as she herself does, nor that the other's consciousness is accessible to me in the same way as my own is. But this is not a problem. On the contrary, it is only because of this difference that foreign subjectivity is at all experienced as foreign. As Husserl wrote, had one had the same access to the other's consciousness as to one's own, the other would have ceased being an other, and would instead have become a part of oneself (Husserl, 1973a, p. 139). To put it another way, the self-givenness of the other is inaccessible and transcendent to me, but it is exactly this inaccessibility, this limit, which I can experience (cf. Husserl, 1973a, p. 144). And when I do have an authentic experience of another subject, I am exactly experiencing that the other eludes me. Thus, the givenness of the other is of a most peculiar kind. As Levinas puts it, 'the absence of the other is exactly his presence as other'(Levinas, 1979, p. 89). The otherness of the other is exactly *manifest* in his elusiveness and inaccessibility. To demand more, to claim that I would only have a real experience of the other if I experienced her feelings or thoughts in the same way as she herself does, is nonsensical. It would imply that I would only experience an other if I experienced her in the same way that I experience myself; i.e., it would lead to an abolition of the difference between self and other, to a negation of the alterity of the other, of that which makes the other other.

There is much of value in this criticism of the argument from analogy, and it can serve well as exemplification of a certain type of approach to intersubjectivity, an approach which I will call the model of *empathy* or the *empathic* approach. This approach rejects the idea that the relation between self and other is established by way of analogical inference, and instead argues for the existence of a specific mode of consciousness, called empathy, which is taken to allow us to experience and understand the feelings, desires, and beliefs of others in a more-or-less direct manner. To be more specific, empathy is typically taken to constitute a unique and irreducible form of intentionality, and one of the traditional tasks of this approach has consequently been to spell out the difference between empathy and other forms of intentionality, such as perception, imagination and recollection. This descriptive enterprise has often been associated with the phenomenological tradition, in fact the empathic approach has occasionally been taken to constitute *the* phenomenological approach to intersubjectivity. It is exactly this claim which I wish to contest in the following. In my view, some of the most interesting and far-reaching phenomenological analyses of intersubjectivity are all characterized by going *beyond empathy*. Not because they deny the existence of empathy or the validity of the criticism of the argument from analogy, but because empathy understood as a *thematic encounter with a concrete other* is either taken to be a derived rather than a fundamental form of intersubjectivity — because it is taken to disclose rather than establish intersubjectivity — or because there are aspects of the problem of intersubjectivity which simply cannot be addressed as long as one remains narrowly focussed on empathy.

II: *A Priori* Intersubjectivity

Let me start with Heidegger, whose treatment of intersubjectivity is to be found in the context of his analysis of our being-in-the-world. More specifically, it is in connection with an analysis of our practical engagement in the surrounding world that Heidegger addresses the issue of others, for as he points out, the world we are engaged in is not a private world, but a public and communal one (Heidegger, 1979, p. 255). According to Heidegger, the type of entities we first and foremost encounter in our daily life are not natural objects such as oaks and cod, but artefacts or pieces of equipment, such as chairs, forks, shirts, soap, protractors, etc. And it is a fundamental feature of these entities that they all contain references to other persons. Be it because they are produced by others, or because the work we are trying to accomplish with them is destined for others. In short, in our daily life of care and concern we are constantly making use of entities which refer to others, and as Heidegger points out, this reference is frequently a reference to *indeterminate* others (Heidegger, 1979, pp. 260–61). In fact, in utilizing tools or equipment *Dasein* (Heidegger's technical term for the human being or human existence) is *being-with* (*mitsein*) others, regardless of whether or not other persons are actually present (Heidegger, 1989, p. 414). That is, *Dasein* does not initially exist alone, and does not first acquire its being-with the moment another turns up. On the contrary, qua its engaged being-in-the-world, *Dasein* is essentially social from the very start. If concrete and determinate others are absent, this according to Heidegger simply means that *Dasein*'s constitution as being-with does not attain its factual fulfilment. That is to say, one can ultimately only speak of others as 'lacking' precisely because *Dasein* is fundamentally characterized by its being-with. Thus, Heidegger ultimately claims that *Dasein*'s being-with, its fundamental social nature, is the formal condition of possibility for any concrete experience of and encounter with others (Heidegger, 1986, pp. 120–5).

According to Heidegger, *Dasein* and world are internally related, and since the structure of the world contains essential references to others, *Dasein* cannot be understood except as inhabiting a world which it necessarily shares with others (Heidegger, 1986, p. 116). But in this case, the problem of other minds — how can one (isolated) subject encounter and understand another (isolated) subject — turns out to be an illusory problem. As the influential phenomenological psychiatrist Ludwig Binswanger put it:

> By presenting this ontological connection, Heidegger has banished entire libraries on the problem of empathy, the problem of perceiving the foreign as such, the problem of the 'constitution of the foreign I', and so on, to the realm of history, for what the latter want to furnish proof of and explain is always already presupposed in the proof and the explanations; the presupposition itself can neither be explained nor proven, but rather only ontologically–phenomenologically 'disclosed'(Binswanger, 1953, p. 66).

The problem of other minds is exactly the kind of problem that Wittgenstein would later characterize as one of those pseudo problems which for far too long has spellbound philosophers. For the very same reason, the empathic approach loses some of its attraction. Even if it does not commit the same mistakes as the argument from analogy, it does misconstrue the nature of intersubjectivity, since it takes it to be first and foremost a thematic exchange between two individuals, where one is trying to grasp the emotions or experiences of the other (this connotation is particularly clear in the German word for empathy: *Einfühlung*). In contrast, as Heidegger points out, the very attempt to thematically grasp the experiences of others is the exception rather than the rule. Under normal circumstances we understand each other well enough through our shared engagement in the common world, and it is only if this understanding for some reason breaks down, that something like empathy becomes relevant. But if this is so, an investigation of intersubjectivity that takes empathy as its point of departure and constant point of reference is bound to lead us astray.

Heidegger is by no means the only phenomenologist to advocate this kind of approach to intersubjectivity. One finds related arguments in both Husserl and Merleau-Ponty as well. Both of these authors fully recognize that we are embedded in a living tradition and that the notion of empathy cannot account for the kind of intersubjectivity which is at play there. As Husserl put it, one has been together with others for as long as one can remember, and one's understanding and interpretation are therefore structured in accordance with the intersubjectively handed-down forms of apperception (Husserl, 1973d, p. 136). I live in a world which is permeated by references to others, and which others have already furnished with meaning, and I typically understand the world (and myself) through a traditional linguistic conventionality. Thus, already prior to Heidegger's analysis in *Being and Time*, Husserl pointed to the fact that there, next to the tendencies originating from other persons, also exist indeterminate general demands made by custom and tradition: 'One' judges thus, 'one' holds the fork in such and such a way, etc. (Husserl 1952, p. 269). I learn what counts as normal from others — and indeed, initially and for the most part from those closest to me, hence from those I grow up with, those who teach me, and those belonging to the most intimate sphere of my life (Husserl, 1973d, pp. 428–9, 569), and I thereby participate in a communal tradition, which through a chain of generations stretches back into a dim past.

> What I generate from out of myself (primally instituting) is mine. But I am a 'child of the times'; I am a member of a we-community in the broadest sense — a community that has its tradition and that for its part is connected in a novel manner with the generative subjects, the closest and the most distant ancestors. And these have 'influenced' me: I am what I am as an heir (Husserl, 1973c, p. 223).

At the same time, however, both Husserl and Merleau-Ponty also argue for a place for intersubjectivity in the very intentional relation to the world. But instead of anchoring it exclusively in the social character of tool-use, as Heidegger tends to do, they also focus on the public nature of perceptual objects. As they put it, the subject is intentionally directed toward objects whose horizontal givenness bears witness to their openness for other subjects. My perceptual objects are not exhausted in their appearance for me; rather, each object always possesses a horizon of coexisting profiles, which although being momentarily inaccessible to me — I cannot see the front and the back of a chair simultaneously — could very well be perceived by other subjects. Since the perceptual object is always there for others too, whether or not such other subjects do in fact appear on the scene, the object refers to those other subjects, and is for that very reason intrinsically intersubjective.[2] It does not merely exist for me, but refers to intersubjectivity — and so do my intentionality whenever I am directed at intersubjectively accessible objects (Merleau-Ponty, 1960, pp. 23, 215; Husserl, 1962a, p. 468).[3] As Husserl writes:

> My experience as mundane experience (that is already each of my perceptions) does not only entail others as mundane objects, but also and constantly in existential co-validity as co-subjects, as co-constituting, and both are inseparably intertwined (Ms. C 17 36a).[4]

As a consequence, already prior to my concrete *perceptual* encounter with another subject, intersubjectivity is present as co-subjectivity. This is what Husserl is referring to when he, in the still unpublished manuscript C 17, writes: 'When empathy occurs, is perhaps community, intersubjectivity, likewise already there, and does empathy then merely accomplish the disclosure of it?'(Ms. C 17 84b).[5] A question he then goes on to answer in the affirmative.[6]

III: The Transcendence of the Other

So far we have encountered arguments to the effect that there are other types of intersubjectivity than the one addressed by the model of empathy. Intersubjectivity cannot be reduced to the concrete encounter with another subject. However, Heidegger's account in particular also seems to suggest that the concrete encounter with another simply unfolds or articulates what was already there from the very start *a priori*, rather than adding anything new. But is this really satisfactory? According to Sartre, the answer is no.

In his discussion of intersubjectivity in *Being and Nothingness*, Sartre at first seems to accept Heidegger's observations concerning the social character of the

---

[2] In *Being and Nothingness*, Sartre nicely sums up Husserl's position in the following manner: 'Thus, each object, far from being constituted as for Kant, by a simple relation to the *subject*, appears in my concrete experience as polyvalent; it is given originally as possessing systems of reference to an indefinite plurality of consciousnesses; it is on the table, on the wall that the Other is revealed to me as that to which the object under consideration is perpetually referred — as well as on the occasion of the concrete appearances of Pierre or Paul'(Sartre, 1943, p. 278).

[3] For a more extensive presentation of this line of argumentation cf. Zahavi (1997; 2001).

[4] I am grateful to the Director of the Husserl Archives in Leuven, Belgium, Prof. Rudolf Bernet, for permitting me to consult Husserl's unpublished manuscripts. Following the standard practice, I will append the original German text in those cases where I quote from the manuscripts (the translations are my own): 'Meine Erfahrung als Welterfahrung (also jede meiner Wahrnehmungen schon) schließt nicht nur Andere als Weltobjekte ein, sondern beständig in seinsmäßiger Mitgeltung als Mitsubjekte, als Mitkonstituierende, und beides ist untrennbar verflochten.'(Ms. C 17 36a).

[5] 'Wenn Einfühlung eintritt — ist etwa auch schon die Gemeinschaft, die Intersubjektivität da und Einfühlung dann bloß enthüllendes Leisten?'(Ms. C 17 84b).

[6] Husserl's discussion of intersubjectivity is very comprehensive and contains quite a number of different suggestions. Let me just mention one more, which incidentally illustrates an aspect of Husserl's thought which is still virtually unknown outside the narrow circles of Husserl-scholars: 'Here I can only briefly point out that it is not only through social acts that such connectedness can be brought about. Just as individual subjects develop their activity on the basis of an obscure, blind passivity, so the same also holds of social activity. But passivity, the instinctual life of drives, can already bring about intersubjective connection. Thus at the lowest level, a sexual community is already established through the instinctual sexual life, even though it may only disclose its essential intersubjectivity when the instinct is fulfilled'(Husserl, 1962b, p. 514).

equipment, for as he writes (with an emphasis that at the same time indicates a characteristic lacuna in Heidegger's own account), it is undeniable that tools and artefacts
contain references to a plurality of *embodied* others (Sartre, 1943, pp. 278, 389, 391).
Just as Heidegger, Sartre consequently argues that our daily activities are intrinsically
social and reveal our participation in a community of subjects, even in the absence of
an encounter with concrete others.

> To live in a world haunted by my fellow men is not only to be able to encounter the Other
> at every turn of the road, it is also to find myself engaged in a world in which instrumen-
> tal-complexes can have a meaning which my free project has not first given to them
> (Sartre, 1943, p. 567).

But despite this congruence, Sartre nevertheless ends up directing a pointed critique
at Heidegger. According to Sartre, Heidegger's concept of being-with completely
fails to capture our original and fundamental relation to others.

There are several different steps to Sartre's criticism. At first he simply points out
that it would never occur to me to distinguish between a manufactured piece of equipment and a natural object unless I already had a prior experience of an other. It is
exactly in and through my interaction with others that I learn to handle an object as a
manufactured tool, as something that is designed for a specific purpose, as something
that *one* uses in a particular manner. For this very reason, the reference to others contained in tool-use is a *derived* reference. More generally, being-with understood as a
'lateral' relation to others is not the most fundamental type of intersubjectivity; on the
contrary it presupposes a more original and quite concrete encounter with others
(Sartre, 1943, pp. 478–9). As Sartre writes: 'The "we" is a certain particular experience which is produced in special cases on the foundation of being-for-others in
general. The being-for-others precedes and founds the *being-with-others*'(Sartre,
1943, p. 465). Thus, in Sartre's view, Heidegger made the mistake of interpreting our
original relation to others as an oblique interdependence rather than as a frontal
confrontation.

> The empirical image which may best symbolize Heidegger's intuition is not that of a con-
> flict but rather a *crew*. The original relation of the Other and my consciousness is not the
> *you* and *me*; it is the *we*. Heidegger's being-with is not the clear and distinct position of an
> individual confronting another individual; it is not *knowledge*. It is the mute existence in
> common of one member of the crew with his fellows, that existence which the rhythm of
> the oars or the regular movement of the coxswain will render sensible to the rowers and
> which *will be made manifest* to them by the common goal to be attained, the boat or the
> yacht to be overtaken, and the entire world (spectators, performance, etc.) which is pro-
> filed on the horizon (Sartre, 1943, p. 292).

In contrast, as we will see in a moment, Sartre himself takes intersubjectivity to be
first and foremost a question of conflict and confrontation rather than of peaceful
co-existence (Sartre, 1943, p. 481).

In the second step of his criticism, Sartre takes issue with Heidegger's attempt to
understand being-with as an essential, intrinsic, and *a priori* determination of *Dasein*,
rather than as a contingent and factual feature that only shows up in and through concrete encounters with others. According to Sartre, such a conception ignores what is
most crucial in intersubjectivity, the relation to radical *otherness*. As Sartre points
out, any 'theory of intersubjectivity' which attempts to bridge the gap between the
self and the other by emphasizing their similarity, undifferentiatedness, and *a priori*

interconnectedness is not only in constant danger of relapsing into a monism that in the end would be indistinguishable from solipsism, it is also losing sight of the real issue: our concrete encounter with this or that *transcendent* other. Sartre consequently argues that if solipsism is truly to be overcome, it will not do to neutralize the otherness of the other by positing intersubjectivity as an *a priori* feature of our being. On the contrary, our being-for-others must be understood as an existential dimension which only arises in and through the concrete encounter with factual others (Sartre, 1943, pp. 293–5, 412).[7]

Sartre's criticism of Heidegger, and his emphasis on the importance of understanding intersubjectivity on the basis of a concrete and thematic relation between embodied subjects does not imply, however, that Sartre's approach to intersubjectivity is simply a return to the model of empathy. As we have already seen, the empathic approach is characterized by its attempt to specify the particular intentional structure of empathy, and to distinguish it from other intentional acts such as perception, recollection, and imagination. But whereas the pertinent question for this approach has been how it is possible to experience the other in a way that preserves her subjectivity and otherness, Sartre takes this line to be misguided, and instead suggests the following reversal of the traditional direction of inquiry. According to Sartre, it is crucial to distinguish between the other, which I perceive, and the other, which perceives me; that is, it is crucial to distinguish between the other as object, and the other as subject. And what is truly peculiar and exceptional about the other is not that I am experiencing a *cogitatum cogitans*, but that I am encountering somebody who is able to perceive and objectify me. The other is exactly the being for whom I can appear as an object. Thus, rather than focussing upon the other as a specific object of empathy, Sartre argues that foreign subjectivity is revealed to me through my awareness of myself qua being-an-object for another. It is when I experience my own objectivity (for and before a foreign subject), that I have experiential evidence for the presence of an other-as-subject (Sartre, 1943, p. 302–3, 317).

This line of thought is forcefully displayed in Sartre's renowned analysis of *shame*. According to Sartre, shame is not a feeling which I could elicit on my own. It presupposes the intervention of the other, and not merely because the other is the one before whom I feel ashamed, but also and more significantly because the other is the one that constitutes that of which I am ashamed. I am ashamed not of myself qua being-for-itself, but of myself as I appear to the other. I am existing not only for myself but also for others, and this is exactly what shame undeniably reveals to me (Sartre, 1943, p. 266).

Compared to Heidegger's account, Sartre's treatment of intersubjectivity emphasizes the transcendent, ineffable and elusive character of the other, and rejects any attempt to bridge or downplay the difference between self and other. Sartre, however, is not the only phenomenologist who has stressed the importance of recognizing the transcendence of the other. In both Levinas and Husserl we find related considerations.

---

[7]   As a curiosity it can be mentioned that Heidegger in a letter to Sartre of October 28, 1945, wrote as follows: 'I am in agrrement with your critique of "being-with" and with your insistence on being-for-others, as well as in partial agreement with your critique of my explication of death' (Towarnicki, 1993, p. 84).

Just like Sartre, Levinas also takes the problem of intersubjectivity to be first and foremost a problem of radical otherness, and he explicitly denies that any form of intentionality (including empathy) will ever permit us to understand this encounter. Intentionality is a process of objectivation, and it only lets us meet the other by reducing the other to something it is not, namely an object. To put it differently, although intentionality does relate me to that which is foreign, it is, in Levinas' words, a non-reciprocal relationship. It never makes me leave home. On the contrary, the knowing subject acts like the famous stone of the alchemists, it transmutes everything it touches. It absorbs the foreign and different, annuls its alterity, and transforms it into the familiar and same (Levinas 1982, pp. 212–3). In contrast, foreign subjectivity is exactly that which cannot be conceptualized or categorized: 'If one could possess, grasp, and know the other, it would not be other'(Levinas, 1979, p. 83). My encounter with foreign subjectivity is consequently an encounter with an ineffable and radical exteriority. It is not conditioned by anything in my power, but has the character of a visitation, an epiphany, a revelation. One of the characteristic moves of Levinas is, then, that he takes the problem of justice and injustice to provide us with an original, non-reductionistic approach to the other. The authentic encounter with the other is not perceptual or epistemic, but *ethical* in nature. It is in the ethical situation where the other questions me and makes ethical demands of me, i.e., when I have to assume responsibility for the other, that he is present as other (Levinas, 1961, p. 33).

Husserl has also repeatedly focussed on the transcendence of the other, but for quite different (transcendental–philosophical) reasons than both Sartre and Levinas. As we have already seen, Husserl argues that my perceptual experience is an experience of intersubjectively accessible being; that is, being which does not exist for me alone, but for everybody. I *experience* objects, events and actions as public, not as private. It is against this background that Husserl introduces the concept of *transcendental intersubjectivity* (Husserl, 1973d, p. 110). By this, Husserl means that the objectivity of the world is constituted intersubjectively and that a clarification of this constitution calls for an examination of my experience of other subjects. Husserl's thesis is that my experience of objective validity is mediated and made possible by my encounter with a transcendent other, and that this transcendence, which Husserl designates as the first real otherness and as the source of all kinds of real transcendence, endows the world with objective validity.

> *Here we have the only transcendence which is really worth its name*, and anything else that is also called transcendent, such as the objective world, *depends* upon the transcendence of foreign subjectivity (Husserl 1959, p. 495).
>
> All Objectivity, in this sense, is related back constitutionally to what does not belong to the Ego proper, to the other-than-my-Ego's-own in the form, 'someone else' — that is to say: the non-Ego in the form, 'another Ego' (Husserl, 1974, p. 248).

But why is it that the other is a necessary condition of possibility for my experience of an objective world? Why is foreign subjectivity so central a condition of possibility for the constitution of objectivity? The explanation offered by Husserl is that objects cannot be reduced to being merely my intentional correlates if they are experienced by others. When I discover that the object I am currently experiencing is also perceived by an other, my relationship to the object is changed. Only insofar as I experience that others experience the same objects as myself, do I really experience these objects as objective and real. The intersubjective experienceability of the object testifies to its real transcendence — or to rephrase the point negatively: That which in principle is incapable of being experienced by others cannot be ascribed transcendence and objectivity — and my experience (constitution) of this transcendence is consequently mediated by my experience of its givenness for another transcendent subject; that is, by my encounter with a foreign world-directed subject.[8] It is exactly for that reason that the other's transcendence is so vital. If the other were only an intentional modification or an imaginative variation of myself, the fact that he experienced the same as me would be just as conclusive, to use an example of Wittgenstein's, as if one found the same report in several copies of the same newspaper.

Husserl continues his analyses by describing a special kind of experience of the other, namely those situations where I experience the other as experiencing myself. This kind of 'original reciprocal co-existence' where I take over the other's objectifying apprehension of myself; that is, where my self-apprehension is mediated by the other, and where I experience myself as other; is also construed to be of decisive importance for the constitution of an objective world. When I realize that I can be an *alter ego* for the other just as he can be it for me, a marked change in my own constitutive significance takes place. The absolute difference between self and other disappears. The other conceives of me as an other, just as I conceive of him as a self (Husserl, 1973b, pp. 243–4). As a consequence, I come to the realization that I am only one among many and that my perspective on the world is by no means privileged (Husserl, 1973d, p. 645).

In short, Husserl readily acknowledges that my experiences are changed when I experience that others experience the same as I, and when I experience that I myself am experienced by others. My differentiation between the merely subjective (the hallucinatory) and the objective is made possible by *concrete* intersubjectivity, by my *factual* encounter with the other. In fact, the categories *transcendence*, *objectivity* and *reality* as well as the categories *immanence*, *subjectivity* and *appearance* are all constituted intersubjectively. Thus, it only makes sense to speak and designate something as a mere appearance, as merely subjective, when I have encountered other subjects and thereby acquired the concept of intersubjective validity (Husserl, 1973b, pp. 382, 388–9).

IV: Alterity in Self

Whereas Sartre and Levinas chose to view the problem of intersubjectivity as a problem concerning the encounter with a radical otherness, and whereas they both argued that this encounter is so overwhelming that it is something the subject is absolutely unprepared for and has no chance of anticipating, we find the exact opposite approach in Merleau-Ponty and Husserl. Both of them are concerned with an analysis of the condition of possibility for intersubjectivity; that is, with an investigation into the question of how a relationship between subjects is at all possible. Both of them argue that my encounter with the other, my ability to interact with and recognize another embodied subject as a foreign subjectivity, is preempted by and made possible through the very structure of my own subjectivity. Both consequently refuse to take

---

[8]   Whereas the guaranty in every single case is fallible — what I took to be a valid experience of another could turn out to be a hallucination — this is not the case when it comes to the fundamental connection between intersubjective experiencability and objectivity.

the encounter with the concrete other as a basic and unanalyzable fact (something that Husserl, incidentally, also accuses Scheler of doing (Husserl, 1973c, p. 335)). On the contrary, the genesis and specific presuppositions of this encounter have to be clarified. We need to investigate its conditions of possibility, particularly those which concern the nature of the experiencing subject.

If we start with Husserl, one of the issues explicitly emphasized by Husserl in his phenomenological account of the body is its peculiar two-sidedness. My body is given to me as an interiority, as a volitional structure, and as a dimension of sensing, but it is also given as a visually and tactually appearing exteriority. But what is the relation between that which Husserl calls the *'Innen-'* and the *'Aussenleiblichkeit'*, i.e., what is the relation between the lived bodily inwardness on the one hand, and the externality of the lived body on the other? (Husserl, 1973c, p. 337). In both cases I am confronted with my own body. But why is the visually and tactually appearing body at all experienced as the exteriority of *my* body? When I touch my own hand, the touched hand is not given as a mere object, since it feels the touch itself. (Had the touched hand lacked this experience, it would no longer be felt as *my* hand. Anybody who has tried to fall asleep with his arm as a pillow will know how strange it is to wake up with an insensible arm. When it is touched, it doesn't respond in the appropriate way and feels most of all like the arm of another.) The decisive difference between touching one's own body and everything else, be it inanimate objects or the body of others, is consequently that it implies a *double-sensation*. It presents us with an ambiguous setting in which the hand alternates between two roles, that of touching and that of being touched. It provides us with an experience of the dual nature of the body, since it is the very same hand which can appear in two different fashions, as alternately touched and touching. This relation between the touching and the touched is reversible, since the touching is touched, and the touched is touching, and it is exactly this reversibility that testifies that the interiority and the exteriority are different manifestations of the same (Husserl, 1973b, p. 263; 1973c, p. 75). To put it differently, my bodily self-exploration permits me to confront *my own* exteriority, and according to Husserl this experience is a crucial precondition for empathy (Husserl, 1973d, p. 652). It is exactly the unique subject–object status of the body, the remarkable interplay between *ipseity* and *alterity* characterizing body-awareness that provides me with the means of recognizing other embodied subjects (Husserl, 1959, p. 62; 1973c, p. 457; 1973b, p. 263). When my left hand touches my right, or when I perceive another part of my body, I am experiencing myself in a manner that anticipates both the way in which an other would experience me and the way in which I would experience an other. This might be what Husserl is referring to when he writes that the possibility of sociality presupposes a certain intersubjectivity of the body (Husserl, 1952, p. 297).

The contrast to Sartre is striking. Sartre explicitly denies that my body-awareness contains a dimension of exteriority from the very start. In his view, it is the other who teaches me to adopt an alienating attitude toward my own body. Thus, Sartre claims that the appearance of one's own body as an object is a relatively late occurrence. It presupposes a pre-reflective acquaintance with one's lived body, a consciousness of the world as a complex of instrumentality, and most significantly a perception of the body of the other. The child has used her body to explore the world and examine the other before she starts looking at her body, and discovers its exteriority (Sartre, 1943, pp. 385–6, 408–9).

For the same reason, Sartre attempts to belittle the significance of the touching–touched reversibility. As he writes, it is a matter of empirical contingency that I can perceive and touch myself and thereby adopt the other's point of view on my own body; i.e., make my own body appear to me as the body of an other. It is an anatomical peculiarity, and is neither something that can be deduced from the fact that consciousness is necessarily embodied, nor something that can serve as the basis for a general theory of the body (Sartre, 1943, pp. 351, 408). The body's being-for-itself and the body's being-for-others are two radically distinct and incommunicable ontological dimensions of the body.

> To touch and to be touched, to feel that one is touching and to feel that one is touched — these are two species of phenomena which it is useless to try to reunite by the term 'double sensation'. In fact, they are radically distinct, and they exist on two incommunicable levels (Sartre, 1943, p. 351).

This claim must be questioned, however, not only because it seems to replace an unbridgeable dualism between mind and body with an equally unbridgeable dualism between lived body and perceived body. Rather than dealing with different dimensions or manifestations of the same body, we seem to be left with distinct bodies. And this conclusion is unacceptable, not the least because Sartre's position also makes it incomprehensible how we should ever be able to recognize other embodied subjects in the first place.

Exactly this criticism is voiced by Merleau-Ponty, whose own position can be seen as a continuation and radicalization of Husserl's view. As he asks at one point in *Phénoménologie de la Perception*:

> How can the word 'I' be put into plural, how can a general idea of the *I* be formed, how can I speak of an *I* other than my own, how can I know that there are other *I*'s, how can consciousness which, by its nature, and as self-knowledge, is in the mode of the *I*, be grasped in the mode of Thou, and through this, in the world of the 'One'? (Merleau-Ponty, 1945, pp. 400–01).

Merleau-Ponty's answer to this question is quite unequivocal. He claims that the self-experience of subjectivity *must* contain a dimension of otherness. Otherwise, intersubjectivity would be impossible. Thus, in a rather Wittgensteinian move Merleau-Ponty takes self-coincidence and the relation with an other to be mutually incompatible determinations. Or to rephrase his point in a more familiar terminology: Had subjectivity been an exclusive first-person phenomenon, were it only present in the form of an immediate and unique inwardness, I would only know one case of it — my own — and would never get to know any other. Not only would I lack the means of ever recognizing other bodies as embodied subjects, I would also lack the ability to recognize myself in the mirror, and more generally be unable to grasp a certain intersubjectively describable body as myself.

> If the sole experience of the subject is the one which I gain by coinciding with it, if the mind, by definition, eludes 'the outside spectator' and can be recognized only from within, my *cogito* is necessarily unique, and cannot be 'shared in' by another. Perhaps we can say that it is 'transferable' to others. But then how could such a transfer ever be brought about? What spectacle can ever validly induce me to posit outside myself that mode of existence the whole significance of which demands that it be grasped from within? Unless I learn within myself to recognize the junction of the *for itself* and the *in*

itself, none of those mechanisms called other bodies will ever be able to come to life; unless I have an exterior others have no interior. The plurality of consciousness is impossible if I have an absolute consciousness of myself (Merleau-Ponty, 1945, pp. 427–8).

But as Merleau-Ponty points out, subjectivity is not a 'motionless identity with itself'; rather, it is essential to subjectivity to open itself to an other and 'to go forth from itself'(Merleau-Ponty, 1945, p. 487). As he tells us, it is precisely my own experience as such that makes me open for what I am not, be it the world or the other (Merleau-Ponty, 1966, pp. 164–5). Subjectivity is not hermetically sealed up within itself, remote from the world and inaccessible to the other. Rather, it is above all a relation to the world, and Merleau-Ponty accordingly writes that an openness toward others is secured the moment that I define both myself and the other as co-existing relations to the world (Merleau-Ponty, 1964, p. 114).

For Merleau-Ponty, subjectivity is essentially incarnated. To exist embodied is, however, neither to exist as pure subject nor as pure object, but to exist in a way that transcends both possibilities. It does not entail losing self-awareness; on the contrary, self-awareness is intrinsically embodied self-awareness, but it does entail a loss or perhaps rather a release from transparency and purity, thereby permitting intersubjectivity.

> The other can be evident to me because I am not transparent for myself, and because my subjectivity draws its body in its wake (Merleau-Ponty, 1945, p. 405).

Since intersubjectivity is in fact possible, there must exist a bridge between my self-acquaintance and my acquaintance with others; my experience of my own subjectivity must contain an anticipation of the other, must contain the seeds of alterity (Merleau-Ponty, 1945, pp. 400–01, 405, 511). If I am to recognize other bodies as embodied foreign subjects, I have to be in possession of something that will allow me to do so. When I experience myself and when I experience an other, there is in fact a common denominator. In both cases I am dealing with *incarnation*, and one of the features of my embodied subjectivity is that it per definition comprises an *exteriority*. To repeat: when my left hand touches my right, or when I gaze at my left foot, I am experiencing myself, but in a way that anticipates the manner in which I would experience an other, and an other would experience me. Thus, Merleau-Ponty can describe embodied self-awareness as a presentiment of the other — the other appears on the horizon of this self-experience — and the experience of the other as an echo of one's own bodily constitution. The reason why I can experience others is because I am never so close to myself that the other is completely and radically foreign and inaccessible. I am always already a stranger to myself and therefore open to others. Or to put it differently, it is because I am not a pure disembodied interiority, but an incarnated being that lives outside itself, that transcends itself, that I am capable of encountering and understanding others who exist in the same way (Merleau-Ponty, 1964, p. 74; 1960, p. 215).

In *Phénoménologie de la Perception*, Merleau-Ponty calls attention to the fact that an infant will open its mouth if I take one of its fingers between my teeth and pretend to bite it. But why does it do that? It might never have seen its own face in the mirror, and there is no immediate resemblance between its own felt, but unseen mouth, and the seen but unfelt mouth of the adult. But Merleau-Ponty suggests that the infant is able to cross the gap between the visual appearance of the other's body and the proprioceptive appearance of its own body exactly because its lived body has an outside and contains an anticipation of the other. The infant does not need to carry out any process of inference. Its body schema is characterized by a transmodal openness that immediately allows it to understand and imitate others (Merleau-Ponty, 1945, pp. 165, 404–05; 1960, pp. 213, 221).

Merleau-Ponty's observation has recently been substantiated by a number of empirical studies concerned with infant imitation. A series of experiments conducted by Meltzoff and Moore demonstrated successful facial imitation in newborn babies (the youngest being forty-two minutes, the oldest seventy-two hours).[9] But one of the crucial questions about this imitation is, how 'do babies "know" that they have a face or facial features? How do they "know" that the face they see is anything like the face they have? How do they "know" that specific configurations of that other face, as only seen, correspond to the same specific configurations in their own face as only felt, proprioceptively, and never seen?' (Stern, 1985, p. 51). Meltzoff and Moore suggest that the infant has a primitive body schema that allows it to unify the visual and proprioceptive information into one common 'supramodal', 'cross-modal' or 'amodal' framework; i.e., that babies have an innate capacity to translate information received in one sensory modality into another sensory modality,[10] and against this background they reach a conclusion very similar to Merleau-Ponty's:

> One interesting consequence of this notion of supramodality is that there is a primordial connection between self and other. The actions of other humans are seen as like the acts that can be done at birth. This innate capacity has implications for understanding people, since it suggests an intrinsic relatedness between the seen bodily acts of others and the internal states of oneself (the sensing and representation of one's own movements). A second implication of young infants' possessing a representation of their own bodies is that it provides a starting point for developing objectivity about themselves. This primitive self-representation of the body may be the earliest progenitor of being able to take perspective on oneself, to treat oneself as an object of thought (Meltzoff and Moore, 1995, pp. 53–4).

In short, if the infant is to experience an other it has to be in possession of a type of bodily self-awareness that permits it to bridge the gap between interiority and exteriority.

V: Conclusion

I have only presented a few facets from a wide-ranging and ongoing discussion, but it should by now have become clear that the phenomenological tradition, far from presenting us with one single approach, contains rich but quite diverse and even competing accounts of intersubjectivity. In fact, four different phenomenological takes on the problem of intersubjectivity have crystallized in the course of this presentation:

---

[9] Meltzoff and Moore (1995). However, the timetable has changed drastically. Merleau-Ponty was referring to a fifteen-month-old child, and following Wallon he believed that the child lacked the neurological capacity to perceive external objects until after the process of myelinization had occurred between the third and sixth month of life (Merleau-Ponty, 1988, p. 313). For a discussion of these issues see also Gallagher and Meltzoff (1996).

[10] For a series of examples of amodal perception in children, cf. Stern (1985, pp. 47–53). As Merleau-Ponty points out, the connection between the visual and tactile experience of the body is not forged gradually. I do not translate the 'data of touch' into the language of 'seeing' or vice-versa. There is an immediate awareness of the correspondence (1945, pp.175–7, 262, 265). In Straus' formulation: 'the manyness of the modalities is controlled by the oneness of sensory experiencing' (Straus, 1958, p. 155).

- As we have seen, one possibility is to focus on the face-to-face encounter, and to try to account for it in terms of a specific mode of consciousness called empathy. The task then basically consists in analysing its precise structure and to spell out the difference between it and other forms of intentionality, such as perception, imagination and recollection. There is much of value in this approach as long as it does, in fact, involve a resolute showdown with the argument from analogy — i.e., as long as it does not contain any reminiscences of the idea that an understanding of the other is based on projection or introjection, and as long as it does not take over any unfortunate dichotomy between mind and body. It must be emphasized, however, that this line of investigation is only able to account for one of the aspects of intersubjectivity, and that it is debatable whether this aspect is the most crucial one. In short, it remains questionable whether a theory of empathy can constitute the base and centre of a theory of intersubjectivity.

- Another very promising approach is to start out by acknowledging the existence of empathy, but to insist that our ability to encounter others cannot simply be taken as a brute fact, but that it is, on the contrary, conditioned by a form of alterity internal to the embodied self, for which reason the bodily interlacement of selfhood and otherness must be investigated. Insofar as the possibility of intersubjectivity is taken to be rooted in the bodily constitution of the self, we can already at this stage witness a certain reluctance to simply equating intersubjectivity with the factual and concrete face-to-face encounter.

- The third option goes one step further since it quite explicitly denies that intersubjectivity can be reduced to a factual encounter between two individuals. On the contrary, such a concrete encounter is taken to presuppose the existence of another more fundamental form of intersubjectivity that is rooted *a priori* in the very relation between subjectivity and world. By managing to disclose entirely new intersubjective dimensions — dimensions which a narrow focus on empathy is bound to overlook — this line of investigation has its own strength. Its main weakness is that it tends to belittle the relevance of the concrete face-to-face encounter, but thereby it also ignores the constitutive or transcendental significance of the transcendence of the other. And that is unsatisfactory.

- It is this failure which the fourth approach seeks to overcome. It rightly emphasizes that the confrontation with radical otherness is a crucial and non-negligible aspect of what intersubjectivity is all about. As might be expected, however, the difficulty with this view is that it often starts emphasizing the transcendence and elusiveness of the other to such an extent that it not only denies the existence of a functioning co-subjectivity, but also the *a priori* status of intersubjectivity. Moreover, in order to emphasize the absolute and radical alterity of the other, this approach has often denied that the encounter with the other is in some way prepared and conditioned by an alterity internal to the self, but as a result the encounter with the other is turned into a mystery (cf. Zahavi, 2000).

This listing obviously does involve a certain amount of idealization. Nevertheless, most (but not all) phenomenologists have mainly focussed on one or two of the approaches at the expense of the others. This is particularly clear in the case of such authors as Scheler, Heidegger, Sartre, and Levinas. In my own view, however, taken in isolation none of these approaches are sufficient, and a systematic synthesis of the different accounts is therefore called for. To what extent do they actually exclude each other, to what extent do they merely complement each other. Ultimately, a convincing theory of intersubjectivity must necessarily be multi-dimensional and draw on considerations taken from all of the four approaches.

However, despite this diversity it is still possible to uncover certain significant and quite distinctive features that are more or less common to all of the different approaches. Let me end this contribution by briefly pointing to some of these:

- Without ever denying the eminently intersubjective character of *language* the phenomenologists have often endeavoured to unearth pre- or extra-linguistic forms of intersubjectivity, be it in simple perception or in tool-use, in emotions, drives, or body-awareness. This emphasis constitutes one of the decisive differences between the phenomenological approach to intersubjectivity, and the approach that we find in, for instance, Habermas, who famously argues that language is the foundation of intersubjectivity (Habermas, 1973, p. 198. Cf. Zahavi, 2001).
- The phenomenologists never conceive of intersubjectivity as an objectively existing structure in the world which can be described and analysed from a third-person perspective. On the contrary, intersubjectivity is a relation between subjects which must be analysed from a first-person and a second-person perspective. This is why the phenomenological point of departure is the investigation of a subject that is related to the world and to others. It is precisely such an analysis that will reveal the fundamental significance of intersubjectivity. Far from being competing alternatives, subjectivity and intersubjectivity are in fact complementing and mutually interdependent notions. Thus, the introduction of intersubjectivity should by no means be taken to imply a refutation of the philosophy of subjectivity. On the contrary, it makes a genuine understanding of such a philosophy possible for the first time.
- One of the quite crucial insights that we find in phenomenology is the idea that a treatment of intersubjectivity simultaneously requires an analysis of the relationship between subjectivity and world. That is, it is not possible simply to insert intersubjectivity somewhere within an already established ontology; rather, the three regions 'self', 'others', and 'world' belong together; they reciprocally illuminate one another, and can only be understood in their interconnection. Thus, it doesn't matter which of the three one takes as a starting point, for one will still inevitably be led to the other two: the subjectivity that is related to the world only gains its full relation to itself, and to the world, in relation to the other; i.e., in intersubjectivity; intersubjectivity only exists and develops in the mutual interrelationship between subjects that are related to the world; and the world is only brought to articulation in the relation between subjects. As Merleau-Ponty would write: the subject must be seen as a worldly incarnate existence, and the world must be seen as a common field of experience, if intersubjectivity is at all to be possible.

Much of what the phenomenologists have had to say on the issue of intersubjectivity is of obvious relevance not only for related discussions in analytical philosophy of mind, but also for empirical disciplines such as developmental psychology and psychiatry. A further exploration of this interdisciplinary crossover would be of great value.[11]

References

Binswanger, L. (1953), *Grundformen und Erkenntnis menschlichen Daseins* (Zürich: M. Niehans).

Gallagher, S. and Meltzoff, A.N. (1996), 'The recent sense of self and others: Merleau-Ponty and recent developmental studies', *Philosophical Studies*, **9/2**, pp. 211–33.

Habermas, J. (1973), *Erkenntnis und Interesse* (Frankfurt am Main: Suhrkamp).

Heidegger, M. (1979), *Prolegomena zur Geschichte des Zeitbegriffs*, GA 20 (Frankfurt am Main: Vittorio Klostermann).

Heidegger, M. (1986), *Sein und Zeit* (Tübingen: Max Niemeyer).

Heidegger, M. (1989), *Die Grundprobleme der Phänomenologie* (Frankfurt am Main: Vittorio Klostermann).

Husserl, E. (1952), *Ideen zu einer reinen Phänomenologie und phänomenologischen Philosophie II*, Husserliana IV (Den Haag: M. Nijhoff).

Husserl, E. (1959), *Erste Philosophie II (1923–24)*, Husserliana VIII (Den Haag: M. Nijhoff).

Husserl, E. (1962a), *Die Krisis der europäischen Wissenschaften und die transzendentale Phänomenologie*, Husserliana VI (Den Haag: M. Nijhoff).

Husserl, E. (1962b) *Phänomenologische Psychologie*, Husserliana IX (Den Haag: M. Nijhoff).

Husserl, E. (1973a), *Cartesianische Meditationen und Pariser Vorträge*, Husserliana I (Den Haag: M. Nijhoff).

Husserl, E. (1973b), *Zur Phänomenologie der Intersubjektivität I*, Husserliana XIII (Den Haag: M. Nijhoff).

Husserl, E. (1973c), *Zur Phänomenologie der Intersubjektivität II*, Husserliana XIV (Den Haag: M. Nijhoff).

Husserl, E. (1973d), *Zur Phänomenologie der Intersubjektivität III*, Husserliana XV (Den Haag: M. Nijhoff).

Husserl, E. (1974), *Formale und Transzendentale Logik*, Husserliana XVII (Den Haag: M. Nijhoff).

Lévinas, E. (1961/1990), *Totalité et Infini* (Dordrecht: Kluwer Academic Publishers).

Lévinas, E. (1979), *Le Temps et L'Autre* (Paris: Fata Morgana).

Lévinas, E. (1982/1992), *De Dieu qui Vient à L'Idée* (Paris: Vrin).

Meltzoff, A.N. and Moore, M.K. (1995), 'Infants' understanding of people and things: From body imitation to folk psychology', in *The Body and the Self*, ed. J.L. Bermúdez, A. Marcel and N. Eilan (Cambridge, MA: MIT Press), pp.43–69.

Merleau-Ponty, M. (1945), *Phénoménologie de la Perception* (Paris: Éditions Gallimard).

Merleau-Ponty, M. (1960), *Signes* (Paris: Éditions Gallimard).

Merleau-Ponty, M. (1964), *Le Visible et L'Invisible* (Paris: Tel Gallimard).

Merleau-Ponty, M. (1966), *Sens et Non-Sens* (Paris: Les Éditions Nagel).

Merleau-Ponty, M. (1988), *Merleau-Ponty a la Sorbonne* (Cynara).

Mill, J.S. (1867), *An Examination of Sir William Hamilton's Philosophy*, 3rd ed. (London: Longmans).

Sartre, J-P. (1943/1976), *L'Être et le Néant* (Paris: Tel Gallimard).

Scheler, M. (1973), *Wesen und Formen der Sympathie* (Bern/München: Francke Verlag).

Stern, D.N. (1985), *The Interpersonal World of the Infant* (New York: Basic Books).

Straus, E. (1958), 'Aesthesiology and hallucinations,' in *Existence. A New Dimension in Psychiatry and Psychology*, ed. R. May *et al.* (New York: Basic Books), pp.139–69.

Zahavi, D. (1997), 'Horizontal intentionality and transcendental intersubjectivity', *Tijdschrift voor Filosofie*, **59/2**, pp.304–21.

Zahavi, D. (1999), *Self-awareness and Alterity. A Phenomenological Investigation* (Evanston: Northwestern University Press).

Zahavi, D. (2000), 'Alterity in self,' *Arob@se: Journal des lettres & sciences humaines*, **4/1–2**, pp. 125–42.

Zahavi, D. (2001), *Husserl and Transcendental Intersubjectivity. A Response to the Linguistic-Pragmatic Critique* (Athens: Ohio University Press).

---

[11] For one attempt cf. Zahavi, 1999.

Natalie Depraz

The Husserlian Theory of Intersubjectivity as Alterology

Emergent Theories and Wisdom Traditions
In the Light of Genetic Phenomenology

In this paper, I have a twofold aim: First I wish to show to what extent the Husserlian Theory of Intersubjectivity can be relevant for contemporary empirical research and for ancestral wisdom traditions, both in their experiences and in their conceptual tools; and secondly I intend to rely on some empirical results and experiential mystical/practical reports in order to bring about some more refined phenomenological descriptions first provided by Husserl. The first aim will be the main concern here, while the second will only be broached by way of initial steps towards further development.

I will proceed in two stages: in the first place I will give some evidence for Husserl's relevance by giving an account of his original conceptions of (a) egoic subjectivity, (b) genetic phenomenology, and (c) lived empathy. In the second place, my purpose is to indicate how much Husserl's view on infants/children, animals/ beasts, mad people/the insane and aliens/foreigners/strangers may be of some interest for scientific empirical conceptions and for practical paths of spiritual self-development. In so doing, I hope to be able (1) to confirm the accuracy of Husserl's own intuitions and analysis, and (2) to suggest some refinements in the way Husserl described such experiences.

Throughout this paper I will focus on two main Husserlian discoveries: (1) subjectivity is from the very start *intersubjectivity*; (2) infants, animals, the insane and aliens are subjects in a full sense, precisely because they are from the very beginning *always already* intersubjective subjects; besides, they are limit-subjectivities, who compel me in a kind of feedback to enlarge and to deepen my own subjectivity.

Just a quick comment about methodology: I won't try here to bridge any gap between transcendental lived experiences in the first person and empirical experiments in the third person, nor with the praxis of spiritual self-development. In my view, starting from and staying within genetic phenomenology is *the* way to show that no gap has to be bridged because the different approaches to the same phenomena are in fact highly convergent. As I was trained in phenomenology, I will remain in my

Journal of Consciousness Studies, **8**, No. 5–7, 2001, pp. 169–78

native field but keep an eye on the others. So my phenomenological perspective will naturally be permeated, modified and renewed by the empirical/scientific and the spiritual/practical ones.

I: The Relevance of the Husserlian Intersubjectivity

In the first part I will deal with the three following original themes: egoic subjectivity, genetic phenomenology and lived empathy.

1. Intentional subjectivity as a primal self-altered egoic subjectivity

I will focus here on three main concepts: intentionality; self-alterity; self-alteration. The first one is strictly Husserlian; the two others belong to the interpretation of Husserl's intersubjectivity I have laid out in earlier work (Depraz, 1995).

(a) Intentionality

Husserl's first main discovery amounts to the suggestion of a new understanding of consciousness. Its features are no longer Cartesian; that is, inner, closed, substantial and solipsistic. Consciousness is for Husserl intentional, which does not mean first and foremost deliberate or wilful, but sheerly a *directedness* towards the external object and an *openness* to the world. In that respect, intentionality can be active or passive, voluntary or driven, attentional or affective, cognitive or emotional, static or genetic, and open directedness indicates a strong relativization of the subject–object polarity. Heidegger's original contribution to this new concept of consciousness will consist in making such a relativization still more radical by deepening intentionality into a *self-transcendence* of Dasein, the latter being sheer openness to the *world*, without any residue of a subject; as for Merleau-Ponty, his emphasis on the *lived-body* led him to a pre-conscious, anonymous, and strictly functional *immanent-embodied* intentionality.[1]

(b) Self-alterity

On the basis of such a renewed understanding of consciousness through intentionality, self-alterity suggests both a deepening and a change of emphasis: whereas Husserlian intentionality and, *a fortiori*, Heideggerian self-transcendence or Merleau-Pontian world-immanence are external openings of our consciousness to objects and to the world, self-alterity consists in an *inner opening* of our egoic subjectivity. The latter is no longer a substantial unity, but appears to be frequently inwardly self-altered. My lived-experiences, which are intentional experiences (such as remembering, imagining, reflecting or feeling) entail the meeting of an object or the encounter with the world. In most of these instances I discover that this 'I' (which I had thought of as a unity) has been different from my 'present I' as a 'past I'; could be a different 'I' from my 'effective I' as an imagined one; is not the same from my 'reflected I' as a reflecting one; and is not as a 'felt I' similar to my 'feeling I'.

---

[1]   There are broadly parallel steps in science and mysticism: (1) the questioning of the subject/object opposition in Contemporary Physics (Heisenberg, Einstein) and of subject/world duality in Gestalt Psychology/Auto-poietic Biology, and the stress laid on the embodied dynamical relationships between both; (2) the challenging of duality between subject and object and of the substantiality of subjectivity brought about by the impermanent non-duality of subject and object in Buddhism and the self-transcendent self-abnegation of one's own subjectivity in the union with God in mystical Christianity.

The primal self-alterity of ego is based on intentional/transcendent/embodied consciousness as its experiential condition but discloses the egoic subject itself as being innerly inhabited by many such egoic splittings. Moreover, self-alterity is not a unified concept. It would be contradictory to its very meaning: it corresponds to such multifarious experiences of the I that its very significance lies in its non-unifiability. However, there is no complete bursting of ego in self-alterity. The latter remains itself *as self-altered*.

Self-alterity brings about a fine tool to understand better that there is no exclusive alternative between ego and non-ego. The truth lies in a middle path, which can be called a self-altered ego. In that respect, alterology, being the science of such a self-altered-subjectivity, constitutes an inner alternative to egology.[2]

(c) Self-alteration

Still, self-alterity remains static. It needs to be complemented by the dynamics that underlies it; namely, self-alteration. After having remembered, imagined, reflected, felt, I may become conscious of these inner alterations of myself. Such a consciousness of having been altered develops only retrospectively, but I may also become aware of self-alterations of myself at the very moment when they are occurring. In that case, I am able to attend their very birth in me, and then their genesis in me. I may then be able to observe the passive, associative, affective, habitual emergence of my lived embodied consciousness. Husserl calls such a genesis of egoic subjectivity a hyletic (or material) genesis. Hyle is synonymous with passive, associative, affective, driven and habitual, and is frequently defined as *das Ichfremde*, namely what is foreign to the I but deeply inhabits me: in short, the alien within myself and inherent in me.[3]

2. Genetic phenomenology as a method

Needless to say, genetic phenomenology provides a quite helpful, rigorous, conceptual and experiential method of investigation. I will now set out its three main features: immanent genesis; transcendental genesis; transcendental empiricism. The first two are Husserl's own emphasis; through the third one, as I thematize it in a forthcoming book on lucid embodiment (Depraz, 2001), I endeavour to pave the way for a fruitful circulation between empirical and transcendental experiences.

(a) Immanent genesis and scientific emergence

The immanent genesis of egoic subjectivity is a concrete passive process, the birth of which lies in our habitual and postural body, what Merleau-Ponty called after Head (1920) our body schema, what Husserl elicits still earlier (1908) as our kinesthetic passive *I can*: my *Leib*, and later on (1918–26) as a *Triebhabitualität* (Husserl, 1966, p. 418). Even though such unconscious events are not strictly speaking sheer physiological or neural processes, they indicate an emergent dynamics of our lived consciousness that is quite near to the emergence of global consciousness proceeding from local neural properties. Such a functional (*fungierend*) habitual intentionality

---

[2] Such a view converges on the subject side mostly with the Eckhartian soul-castle and with the Buddhist egolessness, but also corresponds on the object side to Bachelard's early criticism of *chosisme*.

[3] As a genetic phenomenological process of becoming aware, self-alteration meets (1) the dynamics of the emergence of consciousness starting from the sub-personal non-conscious level, (2) the subtle impermanence of ourself in Buddhism.

includes a part of automaticity, what Husserl calls individual *Habitualität* and collective *Sedimentierung*; but unlike what happens at the neurocomputational level, where neural properties are to be found, I have the ability to *reactivate*, as Husserl says, such an unconscious functionality so as to become aware of it.

Furthermore, I quite deliberately avoided the adjectives pre-conscious, pre-personal and pre-noetic,and *a fortiori* pre-reflective, because I doubt such a passive process is *prior* to consciousness. This linear-time view results from a too heavy reliance on a single model of empirical ontogenetic (in the case of infants) or phylogenetic (in the case of animals) genesis of consciousness. On the contrary, I would claim a temporal non-linear circularity between both levels.

(b) Transcendental genesis and metaphysics
Still, immanent genesis needs to be complemented by a transcendental genesis, which insists mainly on the fact that embodied consciousness is irreducible both to the sheer bodily functioning and to the abstract reflective awareness. Subjectivity is truly embodied if it is inhabited by a self-transcending movement, a process through which consciousness exceeds itself. Now, self-transcending one's ego is precisely what is at stake in the path of experience mystics and practitioners of wisdom traditions follow.

(c) Searching for a transcendental empiricism
On the basis of both complementary processes — immanent emergence and transcendental self-excess — I suggest genetic phenomenology be called a *transcendental empiricism*. Through such a denomination, which was first introduced by Landgrebe in the forties in quite an illuminating work entitled *Faktizität und Individuation* (Landgrebe, 1982), and then claimed by Derrida in the sixties (Derrida, 1997), I wish to intensify the dynamical circulation between empirical science and transcendental phenomenology, so as to stress how they may mutually benefit from each other.

3. Lived empathy
Such a methodological background furnishes us with a more detailed understanding of the key experience of Husserlian intersubjectivity, namely, empathy.

I will examine four different and complementary stages of empathy, by underlining the first two and summing up the third and the fourth ones.

1. A passive association of my lived body with your lived body

2. An imaginative self-transposal in your psychic states

3. An interpretative understanding of yourself as being an alien to me

4. An ethical responsibility toward yourself as a person (enjoying and suffering)

(a) Paarung
Empathy is not first and foremost conditioned by my visual perception of the body of the other, which would mean that we mostly have to do with the meeting of two perceptual and reflecting body images. Empathy is grounded in a much more passive and primal experience lying in both our lived bodies (in our body schemas).

Husserl has a name for such a hyletic underground: he speaks of *Paarung* (coupling). Coupling is an associative process through which my lived-body and your lived-body experience a similar functioning of our tactile, auditory, visual, proprioceptive body-style, of our embodied behaviour in the world and of our affective and active kinaesthetic habits and acts. Coupling is a holistic experience of lived bodily resemblance.

It is the grounding process of empathy, without which no further intersubjective experience is possible, be it the experience of dissimilarity (pathological or not), or of focussing on one aspect of the body (face-to-face or shaking-hands experiences).[4]

(b) Sich Hineinphantasieren

Having experienced such a global resemblance of our body-style, I quite spontaneously transpose myself imaginatively into yourself. You are assaulted by unpleasant rememberings, pleased with some daydreamings, worried about some dark feelings. You tell me about such psychic states and I immediately transpose them as being possibly mine. I recall similar experiences where I had such mental states and I am then able to feel empathy. *Imaginative self-transposal* deals with the *cooperative encounter* of our embodied psychic states, as Spiegelberg named this second stage of empathy after Husserl (Spiegelberg, 1971; 1995).

Again, Husserl has a name for such a second stage. He calls it *sich Hineinphantasieren*. I am here and I imagine I am going there to the place where you are just now; conversely, you are here (the *there* where I am going to) and you imagine you are going there, to the place where I am (my *here*). Literally, we are exchanging places at the same time: through imagined kinaesthetic bodily exchanging we are able to exchange our psychic states. Such a second stage is highly embodied, because it relies upon a concretely dynamical spatializing of imagining.[5]

The two further steps: (3) understanding and communication, and (4) ethical responsibility can be summarized as follows: the third step of empathy involves expression (verbal or not) and interpretation, which lead to the possibility of understanding (and misunderstandings of course): it is a cognitive step; the fourth step deals with ethics, affection and considering the other as having emotions: suffering, enjoying. In that respect, Scheler in *Nature and Forms of Sympathy* is far more helpful than Husserl with his multifarious descriptions of sympathy.[6]

These four stages are not chronological, but they correspond to what Gendlin called a *logic of experiencing* (Gendlin, 1962). They occur together in our intersubjective experience, which is at each step structured by what Husserl calls a lived analogizing (*Analogisierung*): at the very moment where the other experiences and constitutes me as a body similar to his/her own body, I experience and constitute him/her as a body in this very same way similar to mine (external similarity); but, while constituting me as a body, the other discloses to me my body as an object, which I inhabited as a habitual und unreflexive lived body; while constituting the body of the other as a habitual and unreflexive lived body, I disclose to the other his/her body as a subject, which he tended to objectify (inner similarity).

---

[4] In that respect, the similarities and differences between *Paarung* and *acoplamiento* (auto-poiesis) have to be developed further.

[5] In that respect, the part played by imagination in empathy both in Husserl and in Mahayana buddhism (Atisha and Shantideva) should be investigated further, namely the *tonglen* experience of equalizing self and other and exchanging places with each other.

[6] Davidson's conception of the attribution of mental states to others as well as his principle of charity, sympathy and compassion in Buddhism are crucial leading-clues that form an underlying horizon of such stages, to be developed as such.

Intersubjectivity appears to be this *mutual discovery*: through the other's own embodiment, I become fully embodied and become aware of the constitutive efface-ment and forgetfulness of my own functioning lived-body at the very moment where the other acquires such a self-awareness (Depraz, 1995).

II: Liminal Subjects Help Me to Disclose My Own Subjectivity as a Self-Altered One[7]

In late manuscripts, Husserl mentions together very often infants/children, animals/ beasts, mad people/the insane, foreigners/aliens/strangers, as opposed to what he calls a normal subjectivity (adult, human, sane/rational and belonging to a familiar modern environment). These abnormal subjects, however, are by no means impaired ones. Husserl's theory of normality/abnormality is not a normative one, which would produce a hierarchy of values. As Steinbock quite rightly points out:

> The terms Husserl uses as contrasts to the expressions *normal* and *Normalität* are the adjectival forms of *anomal* and the substantive *Anomalität*. It is fairly well known that the terms *anomal*, and in English anomalous, have been incorrectly traced to the negation of the Greek *nomos* and the Latin *norma* (meaning rule or law). Instead, *anomal* is a con-struction of the Greek *an-omalous* (meaning literally unevenness, not level, not smooth). Contemporary usage notwithstanding, anomaly (from *anomalia*) was merely a descrip-tive term and did not express the normative negation of normal, namely abnormal.
>
> (Steinbock, 1995, p. 132; Canguilhelm, 1966, p. 81)

Not being deficient subjects who would be missing something, infants, animals, the insane and aliens are generative subjects, enabling and compelling us to learn and to become familiar with unknown dimensions of ourself and with new horizons of our world. They enrich our self and enlarge our world. As generative subjects, they gener-ate new views in us; as liminal subjects, as I call them after Husserl (*Limes-Subjekte*), they pave the way for an unlimiting of my own egoic subjectivity.

I am going to concentrate on these four types of liminal–generative subjects. Still, I will keep in mind other subjects which could be added and described in a similar per-spective: the sleeping, dreaming subjects; the ill, sick, diseased, tired, weary, exhausted subjects; but also the beloved, passionate, enjoying subjects. All these sub-jects provide examples of the way our subjectivity is able at any moment to become innerly transformed, de-centred, in other words, self-altered.

1. Infants

For this presentation I rely mainly on a manuscript by Husserl entitled *Das Kind. Die erste Einfühlung* (Husserl, 1966, pp. 604–8). In these four pages, the infant is said to have *always already* the horizon of a world. From the very start, the infant is affected by hyletic data and has a driven habituality. He/she is not the undifferentiated solipsistic primordial and chaotic realm Merleau-Ponty and Wallon thought he/she was. In order to lay emphasis on the very early differentiations infants are able to make, Husserl speaks of *Urkind* (primal infant). But *Urkind* is not a speculative word, since the manuscript then makes pregnant distinctions between *das mutterleibliche Kind* (the child still in the womb of the mother), who has already kinaesthetic

---

[7] For a more detailed analysis, see my *Lucidité du corps, op. cit.,* fourth Part: 'L'animal, l'enfant, l'aliéné, l'étranger: Quelle altérologie ?'

sensations, *das Wickelkind* (the wrapped up child), and *das Neugeborene* (the new-born), who has already motor habits traced back from the time of the pregnancy; world-perceptions from the very beginning. So the newborn has a very complex affective and kinaesthetic consciousness, but Husserl denies that he/she may dispose of a developed temporality (neither remembering nor retention) nor of reflection.

As far as empathy is concerned, the mother plays a major part: she is for the infant very early on a visual and tactile unity, although the infant experiences her as a lived-body and not as an object-body. So empathy between infant and mother starts quite early (the child is still wrapped up) during the first months, but such an empathy is not grounded on an objectifying intentionality : it is a passive, latent, driven, affective and blind intentionality, as Husserl calls it. It does not mean that there is no differentiation between mother and infant, but the difference between the infant's self and the mother's self is not an objective one. Furthermore, such empathy is mostly affective. Indeed, the primal genesis of a kinaesthetic and affective world-consciousness and the early passive, driven affective empathy are two features that converge quite precisely with Stern's analysis of the emergent self and his affect-attunement (Stern, 1985).

Although Husserl does not give many details about the way the infant empathizes, he insists, at least at one moment, on the importance of imitation:

> In der Vergemeinschaftung, die schon ganz ursprünglich und in jedem *von der Kindlichkeit an* menschliches Leben ausmacht, *spielt die Nachahmung eine ständige grosse Rolle.* [. . .] *Die menschlichen Kinder wachsen und werden zur Reife hin durch Nachahmung* und durch Belehrung [. . .].[8]

By relying on Meltzoff's abundant material on infants' invisible imitation (Meltzoff and Moore, 1995), we have here a very helpful starting point for more detailed experiential analysis of the infant's originally imitative empathy.

2. Animals

In late manuscripts from the thirties, Husserl gave many scattered indications about animals. In order to sketch the different features of his conception, I will start with three short quotations:

> Auch das Tier hat so etwas wie eine *Ichstruktur.* [. . .] Tiere, animalische Wesen, sind wie wir Subjekt eines Bewußtseinslebens, in dem ihnen in gewisser Weise auch 'Umwelt' als die ihre in Seinsgewißheit gegeben ist.[9]

> Die Tiere finden wir in unserer Welt vor durch eine Einfühlung, die eine assimilierende Abwandlung der mitmenschlichen Einfühlung ist.[10]

> Wir verstehen aber Tiere auf dem Umweg über das Menschenverstehen.[11]

---

[8]   Husserl, 1966, pp. 630–1: 'Funktion der Nachahmung': 'In the becoming communal that makes the very beginning for everybody from infancy onwards, imitation plays an important and constant part. Human infants grow and become mature human beings through imitation and education.' (My translation.)

[9]   Husserl, 1966, p. 177: 'Even the animal has something like an egoic structure [. . .] Animals, beasts are subjects of a conscious life like us. Through such a conscious life they have in a certain way also a "life-world" as their own one.'

[10] Ms. C 11 III, pp. 15–16: 'We meet animals in our life-world through an empathy which is a resembling modification of an inter-human empathy.'

[11] Ms. K III 18, p. 39: 'But we understand animals through our understanding of human beings.'

> Schon bei Tieren: sich wechselseitig verstehen und als 'Ich' die Wünsche, die Wollungen des anderen Ich verstehen, die auf 'mein' Ichverhalten gehen—so wechselseitig, und das im aufeinander Gerichtetsein und schon bewußt auf mitteilenden Ausdruck für den Anderen gerichtetsein. Wie die Köhlerschen Affen im Miteinander, in ihren höflichen Begrüssungen, in ihren Spielen als miteinander spielen.[12]

(1) Animals are egoic subjects in the full sense of the word: it means for Husserl that they have lived experiences, intentional consciousness and world-consciousness.

(2) As human beings, we have an experience of animals through empathy. We feel empathy towards them, which also means that they empathize. We therefore attribute them psychic states, cognitive or affective.

(3) But animals also experience multifarious forms of inter-empathy. Husserl mentions here polite greetings and playing together, which are telling for their mutual understanding. In that respect, it is worth quoting Merleau-Ponty: 'Ce qui existe, ce ne sont pas des animaux séparés, mais une inter-animalité' (1995, p. 247).

Unlike Gallup (1982), Husserl's contention is not that animals have an ability of self-awareness, although he attributes them an ego and an intentional world-consciousness; but unlike Povinelli (1998) and like Gallup, such a non-reflective consciousness is sufficient for him to provide them with empathy, be it empathy with human beings or inter-empathy. Finally, like de Waal (1996), Husserl is quite sensitive to the differentiated and multiple forms of empathy between animals.

Besides infants and animals, Husserl also accounts for two other generative and limit-subjectivities: the insane and alien subjects. Infants and animals give evidence for a hyletic and kinaesthetic — that is, immanent — non-reflexive but highly affective consciousness and for early differentiated forms of empathy: in that respect, they are passive and habitual self-altered subjects, who give rise to forms of intersubjectivity as *inter-affections*. On the contrary, the insane and aliens present us with a hyper-reflective self-altered ego, and consequently, with more-or-less impaired forms of empathy.

3. The insane

As before, I will start with two quotations from Husserl:

> Jeder kann verrückt werden, und ich selbst kann mein Verrücktwerden vorstellen, wenn ich schon Andere in einstimmiger Erfahrung habe und mir entsprechend denke, daß meine Erfahrungseinheiten sich auflösen, daß wieder sich solche bilden [. . .].[13]

> Können nicht alle verrückt werden, und wäre es nicht möglich, daß überhaupt viele reine Subjekte für sich sind, aber in einem weltlosen Leben, somit ohne alle Gemeinschaft, die offenbar eine gemeinsam konstituierte Welt voraussetzt? [. . .] Dann wäre [. . .] eine Vielheit von solipsistischen *egos* [. . .].[14]

---

[12] Husserl, 1966, p. 478: 'Animals undestand each other mutually and understand mutually as I the wishes, the wills of the other through consciously directed expressions. Like Köhler's apes when they are together, when they are greeting each other politely, when they are playing together.'

[13] Husserl, 1966, p. 32: 'Everybody may become insane, and I have my own representation of my becoming insane if I experience others in a concordant way and feel conversely that my experiential unities are bursting out, that they are then unified again.'

[14] Husserl, 1966, p. 32: 'Isn't it possible that we all become insane and that many subjects live without relying on a life-world, without any communal experience? We would have to do then with a plurality of solipsistic subjects.'

For Husserl, the insane (and in a paradigmatic way, but not exclusively, schizophrenic people) experience a very often highly conscious splitting-up of their unitary egoic consciousness. In that respect, they are exemplary self-altered subjects. However, such a self-alterity is not passive and habitual, as in the case of infants and animals: it is highly reflexive in the sense that they are frequently quite self-aware of when it happens to them, although they are unable to avoid the psychotic delirium or demented fit by anticipating it.

Husserl's contention is that (1) such a splitting of their ego is not irreversible, (2) everybody may experience such a splitting within his/her consciousness. So madness is not an experience that necessarily keeps me in isolation from the others. (1) I may recover a sane mind; (2) the other may experience it as I am experiencing it.

Contrary to the traditional contention that insists on the seclusion of psychotic people, Husserl invites us to take serious account of least two different forms of intersubjectivity which are at work (1) between the insane, (2) between sane and insane people.

As they experience a radical self-splitting (*Ichspaltung*), insane schizophrenic people consequently tend to withdraw into themselves. Unlike *normal* self-splittings (remembering, imagining, reflexion) that provide a valuable self-resource in order to encounter others, schizophrenic self-alteration produces first a paradoxical closing-up effect, as a kind of radicalized solipsism. As Husserl notices it, intersubjectivity between the insane, therefore, is a true co-solipsism. Every insane person lives in his/her own monadic world with similar impairments but unable to communicate it.

But psychosis is not only a secluding experience. Recent psychiatric works (Blankenburg, 1971; Kimura, 1992; Grivois, 1992) stress the empathetic intersubjectivity at work between the sane and insane; that is, between the psychiatrist and his/her patient. As Husserl already contended: everybody may become insane. In a genetic perspective this time, he underlines the process of becoming insane that is, conversely, the possible recovering. Because I may at any time experience such a radical self-alteration of myself, and because I daily experience more relative altering self-splittings while imagining and reflecting, I have the ability to feel deep empathy towards the insane. Such a possible emergent genesis of madness in me constitutes the experiential condition of my empathy with insane people.

4. Aliens

As a conclusion and in order to give a complete account of the scope of Husserl's theory of intersubjectivity, I would like to provide some rapid indications about the kind of intersubjectivity that is to be found when we bring to the fore the experience of foreigners, strangers or aliens.

Whereas infants and animals mainly correspond to the first stage of empathy I sketched (that is, *Paarung*, coupling as an embodied passive association) and psychotic schizophrenic people to the second stage (that is, *sich Hineinphantasieren*, imaginative self-transposal), aliens disclose the realm of both personal communication and emotional ethics. Like infants, animals, and the insane, aliens contribute to enlarging my own subjectivity. Unlike them, aliens are *always already* embodied in a communal, cultural and historical sedimented world-horizon.

As a subject, I am not only reactivating through empathy with infants or with animals my own affective kinaesthetic or habitual primitive (both ontogenetic or phylogenetic consciousness), or opening myself up to possible imaginative realms of madness, but a complex cultural, historical and communal world is given to me. In that respect, Husserl provides quite rich descriptions of *Heimwelten* and *Fremdwelten*. The alien consciousness is a deep communal and historical consciousness, as I am myself a subject of a certain historically sedimented community.

So intersubjective empathy is in that case a trans-individual one, which trespasses the face-to-face relationships and compels me to broach the communal experiences as such. With regard to ancestors and followers, as Schütz (1964) pointed out very early, I experience both a self-acknowledgement of myself and a self-trespassing of myself. So self-alteration means a generative self-transcendence of my limited self as belonging to an unlimited chain of generations.

In conclusion, through infants, animals, the insane and aliens, I have stressed the different stages of empathy: (1) passive association as a hyletic–kinaesthetic empathy in the case of the first two; (2) spatialized imaginative empathy in the third case; (3) personal, communal, historical, ethical empathy in the last case. Focussing on one stage or another of such a multilayered Husserlian empathy allows a feedback to my own subjectivity, which benefits a great deal from these multifarious altering experiences, as it becomes self-altered in these different ways; that is, through hyletic kinaesthesis, remembering/imagining or communal historicity.

References

Blankenburg, W. (1971), *Der Verlust der natürlichen Selbstverständlichkeit, Ein Beitrag zur Psychopathologie Symptomarmer Schizophrenien* (Stuttgart: Ferdinand Enke).
Canguilhelm, G. (1966), *Le Normal et le Pathologique* (Paris: PUF.).
Depraz, N. (1995), *Transcendance et incarnation. Le statut de l'intersubjectivité comme altérité à soi* (Paris: Vrin).
Depraz, N. (2001), *Lucidité du corps. De l'empirisme transcendantal en phénoménologie* (Dordrecht: Kluwer).
Derrida, J. (1997), *Le problème de la genèse dans la philosophie de Husserl* (Paris: PUF).
Gallup Jr, G. (1982), 'Self-awareness and the emergence of mind in primates', *American Journal of Primatology*, **2**, pp. 237–48.
Gendlin, E. (1962), *Experiencing and the Creation of Meaning : A Philosophical and Psychological Approach to the Subjective* (Glencoe: Free Press, reissued by Evanston: Northwestern UP, 1997).
Grivois, H. (1992), *Naître à la folie* (Paris: Les empêcheurs de tourner en rond).
Husserl, E. (1966), *Analysen zur passiven Synthesis*, Hua XI (The Hague: Martinus Nijhoff) p. 418.
Kimura, B. (1992), *Ecrits de Psychopathologie Phénoménologique* (Paris: PUF).
Landgrebe, L. (1982), *Faktizität und Individuation* (Hamburg, F. Meiner).
Meltzoff, A.N. and Moore, M.K. (1995), 'Infants' understanding of people and things: From body imitation to folk psychology', in *The Body and the Self*, ed. J. Bermudez, A. Marcel and N. Eilan (Cambridge, MA: MIT Press).
Merleau-Ponty, M. (1995), *La Nature* (Paris: Seuil).
Povinelli, D.J. (1998), 'Can animals empathize? Maybe not', *Scientific American*, **9**, pp. 67–75.
Schütz, A. (1964), *Collected Papers* II (The Hague: Martinus Nijhoff).
Spiegelberg, H. (1971), *Doing Phenomenology* 4. Phenomenology through vicarious experiences (p. 35–54, notamment p. 47).
Spiegelberg, H. (1995), 'Towards a phenomenology of imaginative understanding of others', in *Proceedings of the 11th International Congress of Philosophy*, Brussels, **VII**, p. 232–9).
Steinbock, A. (1995), *Home and Beyond. Generative Phenomenology after Husserl*, (Northwestern UP).
Stern, W. (1985), *The Interpersonal World of the Infant* (New York: Basic Books).
de Waal, F. (1996), *Good Natured. The Origins of Right and Wrong in Human and other Animals* (Cambridge, MA: Harvard University Press).

Anthony J. Steinbock

Interpersonal Attention Through Exemplarity

In *this article, I discuss the constellation of issues that concern the interpersonal nexus of attention. I do so by (1) drawing a distinction between presentation and revelation as modes of givenness, (2) characterizing the emotional life as peculiar to person, and describing person as essentially interpersonal, (3) articulating the phenomenon of exemplarity (a) in distinction to leadership, (b) in terms of its efficacy, (c) with respect to the types of exemplars, and (d) with a view to how they are related to one another. I conclude by (4) delineating the distinctions between perceptual and epistemic attention and interpersonal attention, and rooting the former in the latter.*

Introduction

Someone on the street is lonely or frightened: One person keeps his mind on business affairs, another approaches to talk. Two people are watching images of war on the local news: One is troubled about how it will affect tomorrow's stock market, another is overjoyed with patriotism. Someone tells a joke: One person titters out of embarrassment, another laughs explosively with a resounding contentment that seems to exceed the matter of the joke. In a waiting room, someone utters a cry of emotional distress: One patiently listens, another continues reading, and still another is preoccupied with payment.

The situations described here are unique, not merely because they involve turning toward others in a particular manner, but because in each instance they embody certain values that guide the very way in which we approach others. They occupy what I call the sphere of interpersonal attention.

Inquiries into the phenomenon of attention have generally taken their point of departure from the nature of consciousness in its relation to things in the world. This basic approach is shared by both empirical–psychological and philosophical–phenomenological approaches. In the former instance, attention is regarded as a mental response to a stimulus on the part of an object that in turn illuminates a thematic field (Fechner, 1860; James, 1890; Lipps, 1883; Wundt, 1896; Stumpf, 1907). In the latter instance, attention is described as a lived-through process that is not caused, but rather 'motivated' by the affective force of objects exerting an allure on us, issuing in a symbiotic relation between the foreground and background *vis-à-vis* an incarnate perceiver (Gurwitsch, 1964; 1966; Husserl, 2001; Merleau-Ponty, 1945).

Such analyses make contributions to the phenomenon of attention by showing how we turn our attention to something, how the world can lure us in this direction or that, how some things can modify our perceptual or epistemic orientation, how objects of thought can be provoked and become explicit themes for adjudication, how perceptual objects can come into focus while others recede into the background, how several things or aspects of things can rival to be present, and how others can coalesce to form a prominent image.

Rather than focussing in this essay on how things affect us and move us this way and that, I am interested in how we are able to speak of one person being drawn to another or to things the other likes; how a person can get or hold our attention in explicit and implicit ways; how someone can incite our actions or behaviour; how someone can stir our personal growth and transformation, or inspire our life's vocation. These issues belong primordially not to the perceptual and epistemic life, but to the emotional sphere of experience, which in their turn even structure the way in which things (perceptual and epistemic) are attractive and repulsive, and hence guide what becomes affectively significant for these other modes of attention. Accordingly, not only is the field of interpersonal attention different from perceptual and epistemic attention, but the former founds the latter and ultimately influences what becomes perceptually and epistemically significant.

I: Presentation and Revelation

Whether it concerns things in the world, beings other than human, or persons, the issue of attention has traditionally been dominated by a particular mode of givenness; namely, what I call here 'presentation'. Presentation is the way in which objects or aspects of objects are provoked into appearance as they come into appearance in relation to a perceiver or a knower. As they are given, they come into an affective relief against a background and their meanings are determined only within a 'context'. The context is precisely the interplay of perceivers and explicitly or implicitly perceived objects. Since the modes of givenness of objects, or senses, are determined according to the interplay of appearing and concealment, the objects becoming prominent as others simultaneously retreat into the horizon have the structure of 'depth'.[1] Here, things are subject to interpretation to acquire the meaning they have explicitly.

Moreover, objects that are 'presented' are given through functions and acts peculiar to this very order of givenness; namely, through perception, moving, thinking, believing, remembering, anticipating, etc. In each instance the object is presented in conjunction with the perceiver or thinker who orchestrates a schema of possible presentations that are, in turn, concordant with those aspects or those objects already presented. When they are concordant, we have the experience of the same thing being given and confirmed as such over time; we have a 'normal' perception; when they are discordant, they are abnormal where the constitution of sense is concerned (Steinbock, 1995, pp. 241–60). The object's identical sense here can be understood in

----

[1] Merleau-Ponty writes in the *Phénoménologie de la perception* that depth is the most existential dimension (p. 296), and suggests in the *Le visible et l'invisible* that depth is the very structure of Being (p. 272).

terms of its genetic style of presentation as it remains identical in and through varia-tions of perspective. This is not a one-sided operation, as we know, since the objects themselves function as allures and affectively motivate my turning towards them so that they can be ushered into appearance. In fact, in order for something to come into being as prominent it must be affectively significant and exercise an affective pull on the perceiver or thinker, whether or not it actually comes into being as an explicit theme (Husserl, 2001, esp. Part 2, Division 3). This salience and turning toward can be more or less gradual or sudden.

It is not necessary to describe this structure any further here, since it is quite well known — at the very least — through Husserl's genetic phenomenological investiga-tions, Heidegger's descriptions of *Dasein* and the structure of *aletheia*, the early writ-ings of gestalt psychologists, and Merleau-Ponty's phenomenology of perception. As far as this order of givenness is concerned, it is legitimate in its own right.

The difficulty has been and continues to be that 'presentation' is assumed to be the only mode of givenness. This has two regrettable consequences. First, if one were not attentive to any difference in the way matters give themselves, he or she could attempt to apply presentation to anything that has the potential of being given. Thus, for example, animals other than human, the other person, God, etc., would be described as being able to be presented, believed in, and subject to an interpretative nexus to gain their meanings; they would be understood as being susceptible to the same kind of intention or fulfilment, verification and disappointment that we find in the case of perceptual objects.

Second, if one were attentive to a difference in givenness, one could conclude that there are 'matters' that do not conform to this kind of givenness in principle or that there are matters that are in principle not accessible to perception or thought (e.g., the psy-che of an ape, another person, God). In this instance, they would be described as being accessible, but in the mode of inaccessibility, given as not being able to be given, experienced as not being able to be experienced; hence, they would be characterized as on the 'limit' of phenomenal givenness (Steinbock, 1998, pp. 275–96). And if one still wanted to speak of these matters, he or she would be accused of 'speculation', or 'theology', or 'dogmatic metaphysics', or 'essentialist thought', or 'foundationalism', or 'metaphysics of presence', or a nostalgia for a 'philosophy of origins', etc.

Although the dominance of presentation and the effacement of other modes of givenness is evident in the vast majority of work from classical phenomenology to postmodern philosophy, the adherence to a monolithic order of givenness — which either covers everything or defines *via negativa* what cannot count as givenness — has been called into question in contemporary thought.

The most inchoate attempts can be seen in the struggle to broaden the sphere of evi-dence to include moral and religious experience — though the presupposition is that one expand the field of presentation to cover now religious or moral themes, and only then possibly brush up against various limits to such an approach. Exemplary of this approach is Adolf Reinach who writes that 'religious experiences, especially sudden ones, cannot be "understood". They are not "motivated".' For this reason he calls for us above all to respect the sense that religious experiences have of their own accord, 'even if [their sense] leads to enigmas' (Reinach, 1989, p. 593). Under this general style, we also find Jean Hering's phenomenological study of the unique nature of reli-gious consciousness (Hering, 1926, pp. 87–140), and Kurt Stavenhagen's research into the possibility of an absolute personal comportment *vis-à-vis* an absolute sphere (Stavenhagen, 1925).[2]

These should be distinguished from other attempts that merely describe empirically the variety of religions and religious experiences — whether to catalogue their types or advance a philosophy of religion — because they not only presuppose attributes of the Divine, they fail to ask how the Holy or the other person can be given. This is the case despite the fact that even these approaches can provide a genuine starting point if they yield (or were to yield) an inquiry into modes of givenness. As examples of this kind we would include the likes of William James (1999) and G. van der Leeuw, *Phänomenologie der Religion* (1933).

Ultimately both kinds of attempts are unsatisfactory, because of their implicit and explicit adherence to presentation even when they are trying to challenge its bounds.

There are, however, other figures who have been able to mount the challenge to the dominance of presentation in a more forceful and explicit manner. Most notably are the writings of thinkers who distinguish between givenness as revelation and givenness as manifestation or disclosure: for example, Michel Henry's monumental work, *L'essence de la manifestation*, which criticizes as 'ontological monism' this kind of limitation of givenness (= monism) to one kind of being, and which understands the very essence of manifestation to be revelation (Henry, 1990; 1996; Steinbock, 1999). I also have in mind Emmanuel Levinas' work, *Totalité et infini*, which, despite the fact that it seems to qualify the Other as what is not able to be given, makes a clear distinction between givenness as disclosure and absolute givenness or givenness as revelation, and thus describes the Other positively as 'teacher'.[3] Following in this tradition is also Jean-Luc Marion, who draws a similar distinction between manifestation and revelation in his work *Dieu sans l'être*.

But by far the most forceful exposition of this problem has been provided by the phenomenologist Max Scheler, already in his writings spanning the first two decades of the twentieth century (Scheler, 1966; 1973; 1954). For Scheler, the differences between revelation and manifestation are culled from his notion of person who is qualified as such most profoundly through loving as an act of the emotional life (I take up his notion of person in the next section). Despite the fact that his writing style and terminology might be less familiar to us today, he expounds upon these issues in such a profound and consistent manner that it is worth our while to sort through this material, and in the face of our present postmodern (and even post-postmodern) sensibilities, for us to bear the burden of his articulation of the problem.

II: The Emotional Life and Loving — Calling Person to Person

Scheler addresses the distinctiveness of a different mode of givenness by appealing to the *emotional life* (not the cognitive or perceptual one) as constitutive of person; he does this further by understanding loving as the most profound and concrete act of the emotional life, namely as a movement in which the person is qualified and revealed as absolute; and he contributes to the problem of attention (although he would not call it

---

[2] Gründler's work is a good example of the problematic attempt in early phenomenology simply to apply a phenomenology of presentation to 'religious' phenomena. See Gründler (1922).

[3] Levinas (1961). After all, it is Levinas himself who writes that not every transcendent intention has the noesis–noema structure (xvii)! See also xvi. See Steinbock (forthcoming).

that), by describing the interpersonal dynamic of exemplarity, which is ultimately rooted in loving.

We would be lost under the sway of ancient prejudices to hold that the human spirit is exhausted by the contraposition between reason and sensibility, or that everything must be subordinated to either one or the other; it is just as harmful to maintain that the emotional life be equated with sensibility, and further, that meaning and evidence are the province of the rational life, and finally, that anything belonging to the emotional life — however conceived — is simply 'other' to it, i.e., as irrational, confused, unclear, blind, 'subjective', without sense or direction.

In contrast to this, and appropriating an insight from Pascal, Scheler contends that there is a distinctive 'order of the heart', an *ordo amoris* that is peculiar to the givenness of person, one that will have its own style of evidence, illusion, deception, fulfilment, powers of discernment, 'clarity', murkiness, etc. It concerns not functions and acts of perception and judgment, which have an integrity of their own, but those of the emotional life, like sympathy, co-feeling, loving, hating, etc. It is simply an act of unequalled arbitrariness, to summarize Scheler, to carry out philosophical investigations only in the case of thinking and to hand over to psychology the remaining part of spirit (Scheler, 1957, pp. 362–5 [1973, pp. 118–22]; see also Scheler, 1966, pp. 82–4 [1973, pp. 63–5]).

Of the many acts and functions belonging to the emotional life, like pity, benevolence, co-feeling, sympathy, etc., it is loving that is most profound because it is in and through loving that person is revealed as such. By loving, Scheler does not mean a sentimentality, an aimless gushing, something that happens to us passively, like 'falling in love'. Rather, loving is what he calls an 'act' as distinct from a 'function' because it is a *movement* peculiar to the level of spirit; it is oriented, expressive, 'spontaneous' and initiatory, not in the sense of being in control, exercising freedom of choice, or exerting power over another, but in the sense of being creative, of being improvisational, as it were, and not being subject to the normativity of rational laws.

As being given fully but not exhaustively in acts of the emotional life, person is never an object, but rather, a dynamic orientation who lives in and through acts and develops creatively and historically as an intrinsic coherence (Luther, 1972). Because the whole person is and lives fully in each act without exhausting him- or herself in one act or the sum of these acts, there is no act whose performance does not enhance or diminish the content of the person's being (Scheler, 1966, pp. 525–6; 1973, p. 537). Further, just because the person is not susceptible to givenness on the order of objects does not mean that person cannot be given; it does mean, however, that the person cannot be given in the mode of presentation, like a watch, a backside of a chair, a past event, a number, a geometrical figure, etc., and that as long as we attempt to 'objectify' someone, his or her person will continue to elude our grasp. (Hence, we have in the moral sphere what Levinas called the impossibility of committing murder.) The person as such is only given in the mode of revelation whereby the absoluteness (which is intrinsically dynamic) or again the uniqueness of the person ('*individuum ineffabile*' as Scheler writes) — which cannot be described in concepts — is only revealed fully in loving (Scheler, 1973, p. 163 [1970, p. 160]).

Person is revealed in loving in a twofold sense. There is, strictly speaking, no 'lover' or 'beloved' prior to the act of loving. This is the sense in which the person is revealed in loving and loving can be said to be 'creative': It qualifies the lover and beloved as such in and through loving. Second, the beloved cannot be provoked as a lover, that is, to self-givenness, charity, etc., like an object can be provoked into appearance, say, when I turn on a light and call a friend's attention to an ashtray. It is possible, however, for one to evoke the givenness of the other as person, but then this has the sense of an invitation on the order of the moral or religious sphere of experience. The evidence, disappointment, illusion, etc., of revelation is internal to the experience of the emotional life itself and the kind of givenness it is (for example, absolute as opposed to relative, immediate as opposed to mediate). This is why giving reasons (or excuses) for why one loves another or does not love another always comes after the experience of loving, not loving, hating, and so forth. It is impossible to get outside of acts in which someone is revealed in order then to justify that givenness from the order of presentation. Finally, to say that the person is absolute and given in the mode of revelation is to say that the person as absolute is not open to debate, to historical interpretation, to hermeneutics. (This is not to say that we cannot describe the structure of personhood.) To assert the possibility of the hermeneutics of the person qua singular person, however, would make the absoluteness of the person if not arbitrary, then relative; relative to a context in which things appear and become meaningful, relative to me and to my control, be it in the guise of nourishments or tools. Levinas captures this insight by saying that the face attends its own manifestation (or rather, revelation), whereas things or texts do not and cannot: The face 'teaches'; an object can be interpreted but cannot teach.

Loving, as a movement and oriented act, can of course be directed toward anything. Thus, one can love ideas, knowledge, beauty; one can love honour and nobility; one can love animals (for example, our pet hamster), trees (for example, old forests), even cars, and utensils (for example, my favourite fountain pen). This, as we will see, is essential for understanding the role of exemplarity. In each case, loving is a dynamic orientation toward this 'other' such that its intrinsic value is not exhausted in the loving; rather, as allowing it to unfold of itself, it is open toward infinity such that this 'other' realizes the highest possible value peculiar to its own being. But it does so precisely where the quality of this 'higher value' is not and cannot yet be 'given'. (Scheler, 1973, pp. 164, 191 [1970, pp. 165, 192]). The higher value can in no way be 'given' in advance because it is only revealed in and through the *movement of loving*. We love the other in the fullness of what the thing is or who the person is, which is simultaneously an opening of possibilities and an invitation 'to become'. Accordingly, loving is not an occasion for the promotion of higher values in the other (which would be correctly sensed as patronizing or controlling), and it does not 'create' higher values in the other (Scheler, 1973, pp. 151, 161 [1970, pp. 148, 158ff.]).[4]

Although loving can be directed toward any thing, the highest form of loving relates to that which bears the intrinsic value of the Holy. And this is peculiar to the sphere of *person*.

---

[4] For Levinas, of course, it would be absurd to speak of animals or things having a 'face' [*visage*] since they only have a 'side' [*face*]. But this points to a limitation in Levinas's analysis, or at least to a restriction of his purposes. In my terms, we would have to reserve the expression 'revelation' for the person-to-person givenness, which is strictly *moral*, and describe different modes of givenness, namely, what I call 'disclosure' and 'manifestation' for the unique modes of givenness respectively of animals and earthly elements, and cultural things in order to understand the movement of infinity peculiar to loving other than the person or 'face' of the Other. This is something I develop in my current work, *Verticality and Idolatry*.

Person is given immediately as interpersonal. We customarily take such a state-ment to mean something like people are always with one another socially, that we are inherently dependent upon others, that 'no man is an island', etc. *Phenomenologically*, however, this statement expresses a primordial interpersonal relation, namely, that we, as finite persons, are given to ourselves, and in this self-givenness, are immedi-ately in a relation (an absolute relation) to infinite person or the Holy. Accordingly, self-discovery is always already interpersonal, and it is impossible in this regard to start off with an isolated individual. The primordial interpersonal relation is founda-tional for individual self-awareness, which originally can be understood as 'voca-tion', as the 'good-in-itself-for-me'. It is precisely this original interpersonal relationship that is the primordial instance of interpersonal 'attention' and 'affective force' that now has to be understood most profoundly in terms of loving, which is generative, and the evocation of love as a moral invitational force.

That this relation is essentially interpersonal is attested to by unique acts peculiar to the emotional life that bear the stamp of interpersonality. As generative, loving is a movement that extends beyond what is presently given such that — on the side of the beloved — even what was experienced as 'highest' or most fulfilling or 'saturated' up until now can be overcome in the direction of what is still higher, now as 'highest', most fulfilling, saturated, and so on, without any precise limits. This is the way, for example, the mystics experience the 'presence' or givenness of God. St. Teresa of Avila, more specifically, compares the experience to a surfeit of water or intensity of flames that leads the individual in the direction of a 'perfection' peculiar to that unique person beyond all boundaries. One develops in depth as person correlative to the intensity of the experienced personal presence (Scheler, 1957, pp. 358–9 [1973, pp. 112–3]; 1976).

This relation to the Holy through which I am given to myself places me in this immediate relation as me, uniquely, in terms of an 'ought' which comes to me and to me alone; it is a 'call', a 'vocation', that as experienced is experienced in reference to me as a good-in-itself-*for-me* (Scheler, 1966, p. 482 [1973, p. 490]). This intimate, unique relation is expressed, for example, in the *Shir HaShirim* where we read Solomon/Israel saying to his God, Hashem: 'My beloved is mine, and I am His' (*Song of Songs*, 2.16), or alternately, 'I am for you, and you are for me'. The relation is abso-lute since it is not confined to past or present, or a certain period of time, but uncondi-tionally, for all time. Only loving is commensurate to this unconditionality. Hence, we can characterize this movement as an absolute relation to an absolute where this absoluteness is susceptible neither to numerical singularity nor plurality — a relation *each* person as person has precisely because of its uniqueness, not because of its uni-versality. This is the sphere of interpersonal solidarity.

This 'call' becomes 'ideal' for me, in Scheler's terms, because it lies not only in the direction of the love of the Divine, but also in the direction of this divine givenness *to me*; as a consequence, this places me in a unique (again, not numerically particular) position in the moral cosmos and obliges me with respect to actions, deeds, and works (Scheler, 1966, pp. 482, 483 fn. [1973, pp. 490, 491 fn.]). The degree to which human beings are persons, i.e., absolute, unique, is the degree to which finite persons are different. In terms of this unique personal 'ideal' each person comports him- or herself as ethically different and different in person from every other person under otherwise similar circumstances. The development of this given solidarity takes place in and through the essential diversity and absolute distinctiveness of vocations. And it is precisely this spiritual or personal diversity that demands a true democracy as providing the material conditions for the realization of each vocation in acts. In this way, the unique personal absolute differences will not be forced to be concealed by relative and finite goods (Scheler, 1966, pp. 499–500 [1973, pp. 509–10]; 1973, p. 136 [1970, p. 129]).

Moreover, this uniqueness is not merely given as a point in time or as a simple origin, since through my acts and personal life, I continue 'to accomplish' this individuation historically. And for this reason: it is not the body, sensuous nature, the spatio-temporal order, etc., that individualizes, but rather, 'spirit' as the *personal* orientation that has generative density. Because the absolute relation mentioned above springs from the emotional life as loving, and because it is the emotional life and, most profoundly, loving, that qualifies the human being as person, this relation is qualified not as intercorporeal or even intersubjective, but precisely as interpersonal (and, hence, as foundationally religious and moral).

I cannot, on the one hand, 'grasp' the sense of the loving act and, on the other, merely comport myself as if it were not experienced. I must somehow affirm or deny any reply to the felt love. While I experience the act of kindness, for example, I simultaneously co-experience a requirement for some kind of reply of love that belongs to the nature of this act (Scheler, 1966, pp. 524–5 [1973, p. 536]). But this does not mean that in loving there is an intention toward a counter love, for it belongs to the nature of loving that it cannot be commanded; and if this *intention* were present, it would destroy the very invitational 'demand' of reply, and what we would be talking about would no longer be loving. Likewise, an automatic reply to the loving would be completely inadequate, since loving is 'initiatory' and not ruled by compulsion from without.

In the case of this founding interpersonal relation, exemplified by the mystics, our personal comportment would be to love as the Godhead loves, not only in the direction of the love for the Godhead, but simultaneously in the direction of the divine givenness, which includes love of other persons and an authentic love of self such that in one's own act of love, he or she would experience the intersection of the divine and finite person's love (Scheler, 1957, p. 347 [1973, p. 99]). This loving is elicited from the other person's presence and not, for example, from me wanting to do something nice. As such it instores or expresses the moral sphere of experience and founds acts that are likewise personal, be they social, political, economic, or sexual.

This entire dynamic that belongs to the interpersonal sphere of experience, which is coloured both religiously and morally, could not be an issue if the interconnection just described were a monistic or a pantheistic one, and this for these reasons.

First, the generative character of loving does not entail God thinking, willing, loving, etc., in the human being, just as the volitional act of the human being is not the mere obedience to divine imperatives and commandments. Hence, loving God as infinite Person who in generative loving gives us to ourselves cannot fuse with us. And it is only because of this that there can be a moral sphere of experience and moral activity.

Second, persons as such are absolute, which is to say, one cannot posit God as somehow absolute and human beings qua persons as relative. The relation is absolute to absolute (person to person), not absolute to relative. Thus, as opposed to Michel Henry, the distinction *cannot* be between an absolute Life as self-affection that gives the ego to itself, and a relative self-affection which is *only* the self-affection absolute Life (Henry, 1996, pp. 212–15); rather it would have to be expressed as a relation between an absolute self-affection that is infinite, and an absolute self-affection that is finite.

Third, because the individuating principle is spirit qua the emotional life, not sensuous nature or the spatio-temporal order, we can speak meaningfully of both individual and collective persons.

The person-to-person relation as I have described it here enables us now to address the phenomenon of attention in an interpersonal framework, and not to confine it to a mode of presentation peculiar to perception or intellection, merely. I say merely, for ultimately even perceptual and epistemic attention will be coloured by interpersonal experience, infinite–finite and finite–finite: Interpersonal attention is foundational for perceptual attention. The task of section III will be to show how this is the case by treating the phenomenon of exemplarity.

III: Exemplarity

We love or hate what the exemplar loves or hates, in the manner of loving or hating along with the exemplar. What is significant to us, even what startles us and turns our head can be discerned by the styles of our loving and hating. This is the reason Scheler writes that whoever has the *ordo amoris* of a person has the person him- or herself. 'Nothing in nature which is independent of man can confront him and have an effect on him even as a stimulus, of whatever kind or degree, without the cooperation of his *ordo amoris*.' (Scheler, 1957, p. 348 [1973, p. 100].)

We read in our exemplars our *ordo amoris*. Exemplars are not norms, but 'personal models' on the basis of the value seen in the content of the exemplar. Exemplars, however, are given prejudicatively and prior to the sphere of choice, and express a particular value-dimension (for example, the Holy, spirit, the vital, use, the agreeable), and how those values are ordered.

Because exemplarity is fundamental for understanding the phenomenon of interpersonal attention, I develop the phenomenon of the exemplar in several stages. First, I show the uniqueness of exemplarity by contrasting it with the phenomenon of leadership (another mode of interpersonal attention, but which is ultimately rooted in exemplarity); second, I specify the efficacy of the exemplar; third, I describe the order and rank of exemplars; and, finally, I address the relation between different modes of exemplarity.

1. Exemplarity and leadership: The meaning of exemplarity

Reflecting on the problem of the leader nearly two decades before the explicit rise of National Socialism in Germany, Scheler saw the importance of clarifying the phenomenon of leadership for all domains of life, not just with respect to the political state, but to religion, economy, ethics, aesthetics, civic life, etc. His analyses of the relation of leaders and followers not only foreshadowed many insights won by the Frankfurt School in their momentous work on the leader–follower relation, but simultaneously pointed to another form of 'power' and efficacy peculiar to the life of the individual and community that is much more fundamental than that of leadership. This other form of power is exemplarity (Scheler, 1957, pp. 255–344). In relation to the problem of leadership, exemplarity is more fundamental because the exemplar determines the very leaders we choose. I will not enter into the detail of Scheler's analyses of leadership, even though leadership is a mode of interpersonal attention, but only mention some basic characteristics in order to distinguish exemplarity sufficiently from it, and to show how leadership is itself rooted in exemplarity.

1. Whereas the relation of leadership is reciprocal, the relationship of exemplarity is asymmetrical. The relation of leadership is reciprocated by followers, through knowledge and through volition. The leader must have followers, and the followers must consent to follow, even implicitly, if the leader is to be leader. This is the case even though quite often the leader will try to dissimulate the reciprocity of the relation (we only need think here of the logic of Totalitarianism and its politics of dissimulation) (Steinbock, 1989, esp. pp. 621–30). Thus, leaders can only be leaders if there are simultaneously followers who willingly consent to follow.

In order for a leader to be a leader, he or she must know him- or herself as a leader. Without this self-recognition, the leader cannot function as such. Moreover, there must be some type of recognition on the part of the followers that the leader is the leader, even if they do not like this particular figure or figures, do not agree with what they stand for, do not like the life they lived, etc. Thus, a sergeant can 'lead' a platoon, and still be despised by his followers.

Finally, leaders must want to lead. This does not mean that the leader set out explicitly to be a leader; he or she may have been or may even now be reluctant to be 'in the spotlight,' but as leader, he or she must take up this role, and in this sense leadership is volitional.

In contrast to leadership, exemplarity is not reciprocal; exemplars do not have 'followers,' but 'emulators' in a relationship of emulation [*Gefolgshaft*]. The difference between followers and emulators will be discussed below. Let me state here that whereas the leader must know that he or she is a leader, the exemplar does not have to be cognizant of this fact, and most often is not; in any case, knowing or not knowing does not constitute the relation of exemplarity. The fact that this is not a relation grounded in knowledge functions both ways. First, the exemplar does not need to know that he or she is an exemplar in order to function as one. One person can hold someone else as an exemplar without the exemplar knowing it. Second, someone can emulate an exemplar without him- or herself being conscious that this person or figure is functioning as exemplary. This is in part why Scheler writes that the relationship of exemplarity is much more mysterious than that of leadership. In fact, writes Scheler, we seldom recognize the exemplar as a positive idea that we could clearly describe; and the less we recognize it, the more powerful is the efficacy of the exemplar on our lives (Scheler, 1957, p. 267).

2. Whereas leadership is a real, sociological relation, the relationship of exemplarity is, in Scheler's words, an 'ideal' one. In order to function as leader, the leader must be a real person, and the leader must be present here and now. Pope John Paul II may function as a leader, but as a leader, he must exist and be present to his followers even though the 'here' in which he exerts his leadership may extend far beyond the Vatican.

Unlike the leader, however, the exemplar can function as such independently of spatio-temporal conditions. For example, someone can be an exemplar who lived years before us: Caesar, Socrates, Jesus, Buddha, Gandhi, or at present, a parent, a boss, even Bill Gates or Michael Jordan. Moreover, an exemplar need not be an actual historical person; an exemplar could be a literary figure who reveals or expresses a particular value modality, like Goethe's Faust, Shakespeare's Hamlet, Dante's Beatrice, Dostoevsky's Aloysha Karamazov, Toni Morrison's Sula, Andrei

Tarkowski's Andrei Rubelov, not to mention Star Trek's 'Captain Kirk' or Sylvester Stallone's 'Rocky Balboa'.

3. Whereas the leader is a value-free concept, exemplarity is value laden. For example, the leader can be either a saviour or an unconscionable demagogue; he or she can be the leader of a group of virtuous people or of mercenaries; a leader can lead in a positive manner and have a 'positive' value, or can be a seducer, a '*Ver-führer*', one who leads astray. In any case, in this 'sociological' sense, he or she is a leader.

But some kind of love and some kind of positive comportment with respect to value binds the person with his or her exemplar. Forming the personal centre before one wants this or that, it is *ultimately* through a loving that our willing and our actions are determined (Scheler, 1957, pp. 267–8). Insofar as someone emulates his or her exemplar, he or she regards the exemplar as good. Whereas one can despise a leader even though he leads, one cannot despise one's exemplar. Of course, exemplars can, 'objectively speaking', be good or bad, and a counter-exemplar can emerge that is in direct opposition to a prevailing exemplar. But it is only through a kind of disorder of the heart or deception where the order of values are concerned that one can prefer bad models. In either case, however, the orientation toward the exemplar is always one with a positive, ardent relation (Scheler, 1966, pp. 584–5, 561 [1973, pp. 583–4, 575–6]).

4. Whereas a leader affects followers on the level of behaviour, the exemplar summons a shape of 'person'.[5] The leader calls for action, accomplishments, behaviour or directs action, either good or bad. The point for the leader is not to get the followers to change their lives, etc., but to perform certain things: for example, acts or things that will be beneficial to the environment or on the contrary that will reap as much profit as possible without getting caught by environmental controllers; to work for a better life of grape farmers and immigrants, or to exact the highest level of production from workers regardless of their health or general spiritual well-being. In any case, the leader is directed toward altering actions and getting certain results.

Whereas a leader calls for a display of action, the exemplar is effective on the person as person, i.e., as revelatory. The exemplar solicits the transformation of person; it is on the basis of this transformation that particular acts of volition, behaviour or accomplishments will follow (Scheler, 1957, p. 263). Since the power of the exemplar functions guidingly, implicitly or explicitly, for the choices and commitments we make, the power of the leader is founded in that of the exemplar.

5. Finally, whereas followers stand in a relation of imitation or copying to leaders through acts of striving and willing, emulators live in a manner of emulation to the exemplar, which is founded in love for the exemplar. This characterization bears on the *mode of givenness* of the leader and the exemplar.

Where the leader is concerned, one copies what the leader does or what the leader wants; and the relation of imitation concerns the manifestation of external actions and results. Here the followers can act 'like' the leader, can do 'like' the leader does, etc. Whereas willing and choosing are directed toward obedience or copying, in the case of the exemplar, one 'freely' devotes oneself to the content of personal value, which must be seen for the person him- or herself. Thus, there is nothing of psychic contagion, identification, obedience, etc., where the exemplar is concerned. The emulator lives as or becomes *in manner of* the exemplar in the direction or orientation of the life lived,

[5]   Or what Scheler in his terminology calls a shape of 'being'.

emulating the *sense* of the life, keeping the exemplar's spiritual or personal 'shape' at the centre of his or her person (Scheler, 1957, p. 273). Rather than being rooted in educational directives, commands, advice, the modification of the person's orientation and sense, the formation of the person's moral tenor, or the transformation of the moral tenor of the individual (what we would call 'conversion', positive or negative) are only consequences of the growing adaptation of the person to the exemplar.[6]

In short, we will as the exemplar wills, not what he or she wills; we become as the exemplar, not what the exemplar is. Creatively or inventively appropriating the respective sense of the exemplar, perhaps with entirely different 'external' works and actions, within different milieus and historical situations, with different talents, duties, etc., the emulator him- or herself becomes a revelation of the way or manner of the exemplar. However, emulation does not amount to doing just anything one likes, if this means disregarding the sense or way of the exemplar's sense; it is not liberated from historical actions in the sense that revelatory emulation must get 'said.' But it does mean that the relation of exemplarity is liberated from copying just these particular actions in the sense that there are innumerable ways in which the revelatory core can get 'said'. Whereas the 'as' or 'way' of exemplarity is open, the 'like' of leadership has restricted venues.

2. Efficacy of the exemplar

By virtue of its very givenness, the exemplar is experienced as an 'ought-to-be,' as an invitation or a draw, or pull, or 'enticement' [*Lockung*] that originates *in the exemplar*. One does not actively move toward exemplars, rather, the exemplars draw persons toward them. The exemplar is not a goal after which one strives, rather, the exemplar functions as goal determining. The invitational quality of exemplarity at the core of personal becoming corresponds to the temporal dimension of the future and the experience of hope. This enticement, however, is not like in leadership compulsive or gained by suggestive powers, but functions by letting one see for him- or herself through the exemplar. Otherwise, the efficacy of exemplarity is destroyed (Scheler, 1966, p. 564 [1973, pp. 578–9]).

Even though the exemplar is experienced as a kind ought or invitation, the personal exemplar, who is absolute and unique, cannot be equated with a norm, which is universal by virtue of its validity and content. All norms as universal, according to Scheler, have their foundation in the value of person as absolute value. By this he means that there can be no norm of duty without a person who posits it, no rightness of a norm of duty without the essential goodness of the person who posits it. There can be no norm of duty without the person for whom this norm should be valid, and if he or she lacks the insight to see *by him- or herself* what is good. There can be no 'reverence' for a norm or moral law that is not founded in love for the person who functions as an exemplar. Rather than being efficacious on the level of normative actions, the efficacy of the exemplar pertains to the being (or to-be) of a person; to the extent that the emulator experiences the invitation or requirement on the basis of the value

---

[6] Scheler, 1966, p. 566 [1973, pp. 580–1]. In this way, leadership is founded in the relationship of exemplarity. For loving the exemplar may lead to acts of striving and willing, and only in this instance may we 'follow' the exemplar whom we love, or even a leader who embodies those values (constituting the leader in this case an exemplar). But simply following a leader through acts of striving and willing is not sufficient to qualify this individual as an exemplar worthy of love.

seen as exemplified in the exemplar, the emulator tends to become in the manner of the exemplar by loving along with the exemplar. And this is done and must be done without the intention of 'education' in the sense of 'improving' another (Scheler, 1966, pp. 558–60 [1973, pp. 572–4]).

Despite the fact that the emulator is guided by the exemplary person and 'required-to-be' in a certain way, his or her autonomy is preserved because unlike the relation of leadership, it is based on an autonomy of insight. Moreover, through an alternation in the direction of loving, exemplarity is the primary vehicle for the transformations pertaining to the person, be they moral, religious, and otherwise. As such, it is the foundation for the phenomenon and experience of conversion.

3. Types and order of exemplars

Exemplars embody the entire range of value spheres, covering the saint (the value modality of Holy), the genius (the value modality of spirit), the hero (the value modality of the vital), the leading spirit (the value modality of the useful), and the connoisseur (the value modality of the agreeable) (Scheler, 1957, see esp. pp. 269, 274ff.; 1966, pp. 493–4 [1973, p. 502]). Not only are there different types of exemplarity, but they exist in orders of foundation in relation to each other. The deepest mode of exemplarity is the saintly one, and all the others are dependent directly or indirectly upon the governing religious exemplars. The reason for this can be summarized as follows. While all exemplars have the same 'form' (see all the qualities of exemplarity mentioned above in distinction to leadership and concerning the efficacy of exemplarity), only the saintly exemplars have the form as the 'content' of their movement. 'Form' and 'content' coincide, as it were. The other types of exemplarity can be understood in terms of degrees of 'slippage' or 'abstraction' from the dimension of saintly exemplarity. Before elaborating upon this point, let me now describe the respective characteristics of this range of exemplarity.

(a) Saintly exemplar and the modality of the holy. Within the sphere of the saintly exemplar Scheler distinguishes between the so-called original saint who becomes the personal original image for the respective religion or 'founder', and the saint or holy person who both emulates the 'original' saint and who can function in his or her own right as exemplar.[7] Like all the exemplars, the saintly exemplar has an orientation of loving. In the case of the saintly person, the original orientation is toward the Holy in loving, which is to say, toward persons. In this case, the loving orientation toward the Holy disposes this person to a new revelation and to an 'expansion' of the nature of the Godhead from the perspective of finite persons.

The saintly exemplar is not given as one among others (as in the case of the genius), but as *unique* precisely through that special relation with the Holy, and as exemplary of that relation understood either in terms of grace, wisdom, enlightenment, etc. For this level of exemplarity, there is no universal measure for the person of the saint, no norms with respect to his or her actions and efficacy. These are only established after the fact and on the basis of a 'faith' in relation to them. Virtue, actions, works, deeds, are only expressions of the being and holiness of the person. Likewise, the things that he or she does are not proofs, but witnesses to his or her uniqueness. What one 'obeys'

---

[7] See the discussion in Scheler, 1957, pp. 278–87.

is the style of life, the shape of the person, not rules or laws; or rather, one only 'obeys' the latter insofar as they are ways of achieving free loving devotion of oneself.

Further, because saintly exemplars directly and indirectly encompass and 'inspire' all other exemplars, and the norms and laws that arise (i.e., as 'religious' ones) do so on the basis of this creative personal movement, they found cultural life and are not confined or reducible to it.

The saintly exemplar works on those who emulate the saint not through his or her works (like the genius who is present in them) or deeds (like the hero whose deeds have to be related), but through his or her personhood as being present with his or her emulators. Or rather, the shape of the person, his or her works and deeds, all coincide in the personality of the saintly person. For the 'material' of the saintly exemplar is the *person* of the human being him- or herself; this is why the saintly exemplar is present as embodied in those who come after in the *personal shape* of the persons now living. The saintly person can only exist in actual persons; he or she is only given secondarily through authority or tradition, which is tied to the person's historical appearance in the past. This relation is realized not by copying the saint, but by living along with the exemplar in the same orientation, etc. This is how the saintly exemplar can evoke a *Liebesgemeinschaft* (or a loving community) for all persons.

(b) The genius and the modality of spirit. The directedness of loving for the genius is *not immediately* oriented toward the Holy like the saint, but *directly* toward the being and *logos* of the world.[8] Because he or she has a spiritual loving comportment toward the world, the genius does not have the freedom either to create or not to create; the philosopher is 'compelled' by the love of wisdom, the artist, by the love of bringing a world into being, etc. Through the genius' creative love of the world, we experience an opening up of things, an inexhaustible process of allowing newer and newer values to flash forth that are peculiar to this sphere. He or she brings about the realization of spiritual goods of culture in an indispensable and irreplaceable way, and does so without conscious rules and methods.

The world as a whole is given through each work (the single work of art, the single philosophical book, the parts of a system of right, etc.), and in this sense is itself a microcosm. Thus, whatever the genius loves becomes something through which the world as a whole can be embraced in a loving manner. But whereas the saint is given as 'unique' in the sense specified above, the genius is given as 'individual' in the peculiarity of his or her way of seeing. As individual, the artist, philosopher, lawgiver, etc., can stand as one among others as given in the work.

But as individual, the efficacy of the genius is more restricted than that of the saint whose content spans the spatio-temporal world and the 'eternal' and 'infinite'. The genius is limited to unending time and space, and in this sense is cosmopolitan; the genius is directed not toward a possible personal *Liebesgemeinschaft*, but to the realm of spiritual persons insofar as they appear in the unity of the world.

Finally, whereas the 'material' of the saintly exemplar is the shape of the person which as absolute is not open to interpretation (there is, strictly speaking, no hermeneutics of the person as such), the material of the genius is the work which as a whole precisely demands interpretation to let the work speak its meaning. The task of the one interpreting the work is to carry out a re-seeing and a co-seeing of the 'spirit' of

---

[8]   See especially Scheler, 1957, pp. 290–7, 307–8, 324–6.

the work in order to rediscover, in a creative and personal manner, the meaning(s) of the work. As such, it is open to an endless historical hermeneutics.

(c) The hero and the modality of the noble. Whereas the saintly exemplar's orientation of loving is the Holy, and thus the person, and whereas the genius exemplar is oriented toward a love of the world as spiritual culture, the heroic exemplar's loving and responsibility is directed toward the life and being of his or her people, and the enhancement of its environing world [*Umwelt*] (Scheler, 1957, pp. 306–7, 311–13, 340; 1966, pp. 568–9 [1973, pp. 585–6]). According to Scheler, the hero is given in two possible modalities, in terms of the noble, and thus life-enhancing development, and in terms of welfare, and thus oriented toward technical values or maintenance.

Here we do not have an overflowing of spiritual acts as an opening to grace, not an overabundance of spiritual thinking and seeing beyond merely vital needs, but we do have the exuberance of spiritual willing over the drive of life. The hero is the person of volition and power.

(d) Leading spirit of civilization and the modality of the vital. The leading spirit also has a loving orientation, but now the loving is directed toward 'humanity' or human society. Here we see the figures of the technician, the researcher, the scientist, or the doctor (Scheler, 1957, pp. 314–16). It is not the shape of the being of the person that is significant here, i.e., what is taken as exemplary, but his or her actions and accomplishments. It is on this level of exemplarity that we can actually first speak of 'progress'. There is no progress in works peculiar to the genius, but there is progress for the technician or the scientist.

Moreover, although one can be oriented toward the person as holy or as spiritual when one functions, for example, as a medical doctor or technician, the approach is indirect, since the direct orientation is the vital well-being of the individual as a societal being. This is why the FDA (Food and Drug Administration) can see itself as making progress in formulating and distributing vaccinations and setting immunization policies that in instances are deleterious for some, but 'as a whole' seem to eradicate certain illnesses (like polio), and thus advance the 'health' of human beings as a societal whole. This is also why one can assess and take what are deemed 'necessary risks' as a medical doctor, whereas no parent who sees his or her child *as a unique person* (and not just as a member of society) could come to the same conclusions.

(e) The connoisseur and the modality of the agreeable. The connoisseur is the one who loves the agreeable such that enjoyment can become a supremely good art (Scheler, 1957, pp. 317–18). He or she is not oriented toward the fulfilment of needs, since needs arise only where something agreeable was initially given in enjoyment. Thus, overabundance or luxury precedes need. In the connoisseur's love of the agreeable he or she expands and discovers new values of the agreeable over the disagreeable.

4. The relation between the types of exemplars

As I noted above, the difference between these levels of exemplarity is expressed in a kind of slippage between form and content where the person as such is concerned. All of the exemplar types just discussed have a loving orientation, which is constitutive of person, and qua exemplar, exercises a transformation on the emulator in terms of his or her personal shape, etc. In terms of what we might call the 'form' of exemplarity, outlined above in distinction to leadership, all persons who function as exemplars bear on the core of the person or function 'personally' as unique, absolute, and so forth. But when we move from level to level the transformations that take place are fundamentally different depending on the rank of the value of the exemplar.

So, in the case of the saint, there is a *personal* loving directly oriented toward *person* as Holy in which the exemplar is given as 'unique', witnessed in terms of the being of the person; in case of the genius, there is a *personal* loving directly oriented toward the *world* in which the exemplar is given as 'individual', witnessed in terms of works, deeds, and actions; in the case of the hero, there is a *personal* loving directly oriented toward the *environing* world in which the individual is given as relative to a historical situation, in terms of will, power, and welfare, and so forth. For this reason we can see a saintly life of service come into conflict with the life of a connoisseur. Saint Teresa of Avila writes: 'On another day the Lord told me this: "Do you think, daughter, that merit lies in enjoyment? No, rather it lies in working and suffering and loving"' (Scheler, 1975, p. 336).

However — and this is an important qualification — even though we witness something like a slippage from level to level, and even though these levels are essentially distinct, we are still *indirectly* oriented in a loving manner toward person as Holy in any modality of exemplarity. The mode expressed by the exemplar becomes the way that we participate in the movement of the Holy. Depending upon the level of exemplarity concerned, we say, 'I love *this*', 'this is not what I love'. This is why Scheler can write that the *givenness* of the exemplar is experienced in various levels as a 'delimitation', as a specific way or directedness (that is more or less encompassing) into the generative movement of the Holy as a whole (Scheler, 1966, pp. 564–5 [1973, p. 579]). Thus, we participate in the movement of the Holy *as* vitally concerned, as an immunologist, etc. And this means that the delimitation that is a specification of the way of loving is thereby a *de-limitation* as an openness to the Holy.

The Holy as generative is infinite and encompasses or 'founds' all other spheres of value experience. Accordingly, the saint is not the most general form of exemplarity, but is the most profound 'way'. The saintly exemplar founds all other modes of exemplarity, all other 'vocations', while remaining irreducible to them, because its way of pointing 'reveals' the Infinite most deeply; this style of exemplarity most dramatically emulates in a way that implicitly includes the other levels of exemplarity. From its perspective, the other modes of exemplarity 'reveal' to greater or lesser degrees: as hero, connoisseur, etc., but 'reveal' nonetheless.

The problem arises when we restrict the participation just mentioned by confining, say, the technical sphere *to the technical sphere merely*, and not allowing it to point beyond itself, as it does, in the direction of the Holy. The problem arises when the delimitation of a way is not simultaneously realized as a de-limitation. Thus, for example, the ecological movement is (or should be) ultimately oriented toward the love of the Holy, but precisely *as* or *in and through* the love of, say, the rainforests. Otherwise it becomes mere 'environmentalism'.

IV: Exemplarity and Attention

I began this paper with various examples of interpersonal attention, and noted that the problem with most analyses of attention is that they focus exclusively on the perceptual or epistemic presentation of objects, and only obliquely address the interpersonal field of experience. In order to understand the interpersonal field of experience as it pertains to the phenomenon of attention, it was necessary to draw the distinction between presentation and revelation, and to describe the structure of exemplarity: in relation to leadership, exemplarity's efficacy, its types and orders, and the relation between levels of exemplarity.

In these final pages, I delineate the major features of interpersonal attention that can be gleaned from this description of exemplarity; to bring out its distinctiveness, I contrast it with the structure of perceptual attention:

- Whereas things and ideas are given in the mode of *presentation*, persons are given in the mode of *revelation*.
- Whereas the import of attention as it relates to presentation is *perceptual and epistemic*, the interpersonal dimension peculiar to revelation introduces both a *religious and a moral* tenor to the problem of attention, and as consequence a perceptual and epistemic one.
- Whereas it is peculiar to objects or things that are object-like to be presented *thematically* against a background and to be given with inner or outer spatio-temporal horizons such that what is implicit can in principle become explicit or present, persons live *fully but not exhaustively* in acts peculiar to spirit, as a movement which is most profoundly generative.
- Whereas perceptual and epistemic attention can admit of a *gradation or degrees* of attention and prominence, where interpersonal attention is concerned there are no degrees; rather, one is *struck 'in one stroke'*, as it were, by the person.
- Whereas the passage of appearances in the economy of *appearing and concealing* presents the sense of the objects that can be read off from its genetic concordance or *Einstimmigkeit*, person as a generative movement is a dynamic orientation, given absolutely but in an unfinished manner through its intrinsic coherence or *Einsinnigkeit*. But it is given in a *self-revealing* manner, and not by virtue of the interplay of appearing and concealing.
- Whereas the thematic presentation of objects emerges as *affectively* significant, the self-revelation of persons is *emotionally* significant.
- Whereas particular perceptual and epistemic objects are *relative* to a universal and to a *context*, and derive their meanings precisely within a hermeneutic field, persons are revealed as *absolutely unique* such that their meaning and value cannot be determined as presentation in a context (there is no hermeneutics of the person as such), but rather in interpersonal *solidarity*.
- Whereas the thematicity of objects or aspects of objects emerges in the mode of affective *prominence* against a background, the fullness of a person's presence is given as absolutely unique in the mode of *annunciation* peculiar to the emotional life, and most profoundly, loving.
- Whereas the affective prominence of objects exercises an *allure* on the perceiver or thinker, the annunciation of persons in their exemplary value modalities functions as an *invitational or evocative 'ought to be'*.
- Whereas an allure can '*motivate*' a perception or a thought, an annunciation '*requires*' a loving or hating, or a mode of personal comportment grounded in loving or hating.
- Whereas an object is the *end* to be seen through its affective force, an exemplar through its 'tug' is the *way* to see as an invitational force.
- Whereas I can *prompt or motivate* (though not 'cause') something into presentational appearance, I can never force or prompt or motivate the revelation of another person. The revelation of a person is a freely *self-giving movement* that is at most *inspired or aroused* through acts of loving.
- Whereas in the perceptual field we *turn toward* something, passively or actively, either continuing or instigating a new flow of appearances or actions, in the interpersonal sphere the shape of our person is transformed. And rather than speaking of turning toward, we speak here of a *turning around*, literally a *conversion* or *revolution* of the 'heart' through a co-loving or co-hating.

By way of conclusion, let me note that these two modes of attention — the perceptual/epistemic and the personal — are not merely two different modes of attention. Exemplarity as a mode of interpersonal attention is foundational for perceptual attention, and sketches the basic contours behind each instance of willing and doing, of perceptual and epistemic attraction and repulsion. For, ultimately, things only emerge as affectively prominent through the ordering of what we love and hate, since the latter opens the space for such a prominence in the first place; and this bears on the emotional sphere of experience as personal. Something can exercise an affective allure on us and motivate our turning toward it in this particular way 'because' we have already turned around in this way rather than that.

References

Fechner, G.T. (1860/1889), *Elemente der Psychophysik* (Leipzig: Breitkopf & Härtel).
Gründler, O. (1922), *Elemente zu einer Religionsphilosophie auf phänomenologischer Grundlage* (Munich: Kösel & Pustet).
Gurwitsch, A. (1964), *The Field of Consciousness* (Pittsburgh: Duquesne University Press).
Gurwitsch, A. (1966), *Studies in Phenomenology and Psychology* (Evanston: Northwestern University Press).
Henry, M. (1990), *L'essence de la manifestation*. Second Edition (Paris: PUF).
Henry, M. (1996), *C'est moi la vérité: pour une philosophie du Christianisme* (Paris: Seuil).
Henry, M. (1999), 'The problem of forgetfulness in the phenomenology of life', in *Continental Philosophy Review, The Philosophy of Michel Henry*, ed. Anthony J. Steinbock, Vol. 32, No. 3, pp. 271–302.
Hering, J. (1926), *Phénoménologie et philosophie religieuse* (Paris, Felix Alcan).
Husserl, E. (2001), *Analyses Concerning Passive and Active Synthesis: Lectures on Transcendental Logic*, trans. Anthony J. Steinbock (Dordrecht: Kluwer).
James, W. (1890/1981), *The Principles of Psychology*. Vol. 1. (Cambridge, MA: Harvard University Press).
James, W. (1999), *The Variety of Religious Experience: A Study of Human Nature* (New York: Random House).
Levinas, E. (1961), *Totalité et infini* (The Hague: Martinus Nijhoff).
Lipps, T. (1883), *Grundtatsachen des Seelenlebens* (Bonn: M. Cohen).
Luther, R. (1972), *Persons in Love* (The Hague: Martinus Nijhoff).
Merleau-Ponty, M. (1945), *Phénoménologie de la perception* (Paris: Gallimard).
Merleau-Ponty, M. (1964), *Le visible et l'invisible* (Paris: Gallimard)
Reinach, A. (1989), *Sämtliche Werke*, ed., Karl Schuhmann and Barry Smith (Munich: Philosophia).
Scheler, M. (1954), *Vom Ewigen im Menschen*, ed., Maria Scheler (Bern: Francke).
Scheler, M. (1957), 'Ordo amoris', in *Schriften aus dem Nachlaß*, Vol 1, [Gesammelte Werke, Vol. 10] ed. Maria Scheler (Bern: Francke). [English translation (1973), 'Ordo amoris', in *Selected Philosophical Essays*, trans. David R. Lachterman (Evanston: Northwestern University Press)].
Scheler, M. (1966), *Formalismus in der Ethik und die Materiale Wertethik*, [Gesammelte Werke Vol. 2], ed. Maria Scheler (Bern: Francke). [English translation (1973), *Formalism in Ethics and Non-Formal Ethics of Value*, trans. Manfred S. Frings and Roger L. Funk (Evanston: Northwestern University Press)].
Scheler, M. (1973), *Wesen und Formen der Sympathie* [Gesammelte Werke, Vol. 7], ed. Manfred Frings (Bern: Francke). [English translation (1970), *The Nature of Sympathy*, trans. Peter Heath (Hamden, CT: Archon Books)].
Scheler, M. (1976), *The Collected Works of St Teresa of Avila*. Volume One, trans. Kieran Kavanaugh OCD and Otilio Rodriguez OCD (Washington DC: ICS Publications).
Stavenhagen, K. (1925), *Absolute Stellungnahmen: eine ontologische Untersuchung über das Wesen der Religion* (Erlangen: Philosophischen Akademie).
Steinbock, A.J. (1989), 'Totalitarianism, homogeneity of power, depth', in *Tijdschrft voor Filosophie* Vol. 51, No. 4.
Steinbock, A.J. (1995), 'The Phenomenological concepts of normality and abnormality', *Man and World*, **28**.
Steinbock, A.J. (1998), 'Limit-phenomena and the liminality of experience', *Alter: Revue de Phénoménologie*, Vol. 6.
Steinbock, A.J. (forthcoming) 'Face and revelation: Teaching as wayfaring', in *Addressing Levinas*, ed. Eric Nelson (Evanston: Northwestern University Press).
Stumpf, C. (1907), *Erscheinungen und Psychische Funktionen* (Berlin: Königli. Akademie der Wissenschaften).
Wundt, W. (1896), *Grundriß der Psychologie* (Leipzig: Wilhelm Engelmann).

Yoko Arisaka

The Ontological Co-Emergence
of 'Self and Other' in
Japanese Philosophy

I: Introduction — Is there a 'Problem' of Intersubjectivity?

The coupling of the 'self and other', and their dialectic relation, has come to be one of
the essential features of the twentieth-century post-Hegelian European thought. The
related problem of 'intersubjectivity', in this context, was to make sense of how it is
that each self, possessing a realm of its own distinctive consciousness, can nevertheless 'commune' with other such consciousness. If one begins from the Cartesian
solipsistic consciousness (a *cogito*), this is indeed a problem, for there seems to be no
adequate way of explaining how such private minds can share a world and themselves. However, there have also been numerous criticisms of the Cartesian formulation in order to highlight the fact that the very 'problem' of intersubjectivity depended
upon particular ontological formulations of self and consciousness to begin with.

For instance, Merleau-Ponty claimed that the problem stemmed from a mistaken
ascription of the self as pure, disembodied subjectivity on its own. The self is rather
an embodied, perceptually 'thick' and fluid existence to begin with, *already* open to
others as well as to the natural world.[1] This line of argument, that the Cartesian *cogito*
is not a starting point but an abstraction from this fundamental reality, was prevalent
in existential phenomenology. Eve Browning Cole (1993) has argued against Descartes from a feminist perspective of a 'relational self', that our relationship to others
are not an accidental addition of an isolated individual, but it is a metaphysically primordial fact about our very existence.[2] In a similar vein, in explaining the Confucian

---

[1] For an account of his critique of Cartesian *Cogito* and his own theory of embodied and already social
self and others, see Merleau-Ponty (1962), pp. 346–65. For example, he asserts: 'The central phenomenon, at the root of both my subjectivity and my transcendence towards others, consists in my being
given to myself. *I am given,* that is, I find myself already situated and involved in a physical and social
world — *I am given to myself,* which means that this situation is never hidden from me, it is never round
about me as an alien necessity, and I am never in effect enclosed in it like an object in a box' (p. 360;
emphasis by M-P). For further references, see Dillon (1988), Chapter 7, 'Intersubjectivity'. Dan
Zahavi (1999) has also noted recently that 'for both Husserl and Sartre, mundane self-awareness
entails a self-apprehension from the perspective of the Other, and it therefore has the encounter with
the Other and the Other's intervention as its condition of possibility' (p. 164).

[2] See in particular Chapter 3 of her book. For a general feminist 'ethics of care' which relies on the notion
of the 'relational self', see Noddings (1984).

Journal of Consciousness Studies, **8**, No. 5–7, 2001, pp. 197–208

notion of selfhood, Chenyang Li (1999) observes that the Confucian self is a 'process for relatedness', that it is 'not an independent agent who happens to be in certain social relationships', but it is 'constituted of, and situated in social relationships' (p. 94). Without interpersonal social relations that assign roles and functions, one cannot 'be' a self in the full sense. Intersubjectivity, in this light, is not a problem, but a foundational or constitutive aspect of our selfhood. The problem is generated out of an ontological confusion that prioritizes pure subjectivity as the self's primary constituent.

The coupling of 'self and other' as well as the issues regarding intersubjectivity have also been central topics in modern Japanese philosophy. The dominant views can also be seen as critical of the Cartesian formulation, but the Japanese philosophers drew their conclusions also based on their own insights into Japanese culture and language. In this paper I would like to explore this theme in two of the leading modern Japanese philosophers — Kitaro Nishida (1870–1945) and Tetsuro Watsuji (1889–1960). I do not make a causal claim that Japanese culture or language was responsible for these thinkers' philosophy, although without a doubt they were strong influences. The point rather is to show an interesting convergence of concerns regarding the fundamental nature of the relation between the self and others across different cultures and intellectual traditions, and to clarify further the ontological structure of the self–other relation. After the examination, the thesis I would like to defend here is the following: Intersubjectivity is indeed a condition, rather than an accident, of the structure of lived experiences as such (not 'consciousness') but this relation also requires at the same time the recognition that the Other must remain a true negation-in-relation to the self. Let me first turn to Watsuji, although chronologically he was 20 years junior and was a student of Nishida, since Watsuji's phenomenology deals more directly with the topic of intersubjectivity. I will then turn to Nishida's broader ontological considerations.

II: Watsuji's Theory of 'Being-Between'

Watsuji was one of the major figures in modern Japanese philosophy and cultural studies in the first half of the twentieth century.[3] After studying with Heidegger in Berlin in 1927, he was also one of the most influential Japanese thinkers who grappled with Heideggerian thought. Following Heidegger's notion of *Mitsein* (Being-with), during the 1930s and 1940s he developed his own theory of an ethic based on the notion of 'in-between-ness' (*aidagara*). Etymologically, the term '*aidagara*' consists of two Chinese characters. '*Aida*' refers to the notion of 'between' or 'in-between', in both spatial and temporal terms. '*Gara*' refers to 'the quality of', or 'state of'; here, for lack of a better expression, I will translate '*aidagara*' as 'Being-between'.[4] Literally as the state of 'Being-between' *aidagara* describes the interpersonal dynamic which exists among individuals and which essentially constitutes the fundamental nature of what it means for one to be a 'self'.

---

[3] Watsuji was a younger colleague and friend of Kitaro Nishida and associate of other well-known writers and thinkers such as Soseki Natsume, Junichiro Tanizaki and Shuzo Kuki. His wide interests and scholarship encompass not only European and Asian philosophy but also Japanese, Indian, and European history, religion, and aesthetics. He is also credited for introducing Kierkegaard's thought to Japan. For more on Watsuji's life and works in English, see Sakai (1993), Bellah (1965), Dilworth (1974), LaFleur (1990), and Furukawa (1961).

[4] Other possible translations include 'interpresence' (Dilworth 1974), 'intersubjectivity', or 'subject-position' (Sakai, 1993).

The notion of Being-between evolved out of Watsuji's critique of Heidegger's conception of the spatiality of our existence with others.[5] In the Preface of *Fudo* (*Milieu*, Watsuji, 1935, 1961) he claims:

> The limitation [of Heidegger's approach] is due to the fact that Heidegger's '*Dasein*' is ultimately an 'individual'. He grasped human existence as the existence of a self. But this is merely an abstract aspect within the double structure of our individual-qua-social existence. When we grasp this double structure of human existence concretely, temporality and spatiality are coextensive. We can then show the truth of historicality, which Heidegger fails to develop fully and concretely (p. 4).[6]

Watsuji is not entirely fair to Heidegger in his criticism, since, although it could have been more developed, Heidegger did include the notion of *Mitsein* which explains the essential mode of being-with-others.[7] Nevertheless, it is true that the implications of the theory of *Mitsein* are far from adequately developed and Watsuji considers this a major problem.[8]

Perhaps Watsuji noticed the individuality of *Dasein* more acutely because he contrasted it with a sense of self that was familiar to him — the highly socially-mediated notion of the self in Japanese language and culture. For instance, in contemporary Japanese, there are more than fifteen ways to say 'I', depending upon one's gender, age, social status, situation, levels of formality, or a combination of any of these.[9] In any given social situation (private, informal or official) one must know the appropriate term by which to refer to oneself, *given* the situation one finds oneself in. Unlike English, in which 'I' has a fixed referent (the speaker), the Japanese 'I' points not to the person *per se* but rather indicates a social position in the context of a given situation. One's self-identity necessarily is highly context-dependent, and one tends to perceive oneself always *in relation to* those around her and the social situation which would define her 'place' in the overall transaction. It is linguistically transparent that the self is always a self-in-a-situation and a self-with-another in speaking Japanese.[10]

---

[5] It is interesting to note that quite independently, Watsuji's critique is comparable to Merleau-Ponty's critique of Heidegger developed some 20 years later, who especially remarked on Heidegger's lack of conception of corporeality. See Merleau-Ponty (1962; 1964).

[6] All of Watsuji's quotes are translated from Japanese by Yoko Arisaka. References to Watsuji's works in the 1930s and 40s indicate the original publication dates. His works are later compiled into *Watsuji Tetsuro Zenshu, vol 1-20* (here referred to as *WTZ*), published from 1961–1963. Watsuji (1961) refers to the English translation of his first major book *Fudo* (*Milieu*) and Watsuji (1996) refers to the translation of *Ethics*.

[7] Heidegger claims that '*Being-with* and *Dasein-with* [*Mitsein* und *Mitdasein*]' are 'equiprimordial with Being-in-the-world' (Heidegger, 1962, p.149), and that 'the world is always the one that I share with Others' (Heidegger, 1962, p.155).

[8] Frederick Olafson (1998) has recently developed an 'ethic of *Mitsein*' that is based on Heidegger but carries it beyond the Heideggerian framework.

[9] Here are some of the examples: 'Watakushi' (formal, gender-neutral); 'watashi' (standard, gender-neutral); 'atashi' (colloquial, female); 'atai' (vulgar, female); 'boku' (colloquial, male); 'ore' (colloquial/vulgar, male); 'washi' (old person or dialect, usually male); 'kochira' (literally 'this direction', usually used in business, gender-neutral); 'uchi' (literally 'home', used when speaking of family matters, gender-neutral); 'jibun' (unusual, usually male); 'wagahai' (historical, male).

[10] In addition to the linguistic features, a Japanese psychiatrist Bin Kimura — who in fact appeals to Watsuji's theory — observes that a certain cluster of phobias, which are common among Japanese patients but rarely found among non-Japanese patients, are better explained by appealing to the highly other-oriented sense of self found among the Japanese, rather than to standard explanations offered by Western psychiatry. These phobias fall under the general category of the 'fear of facing others' [*taijin kyofu-sho*] and it includes a fear of one's own face being red or extremely ugly, a fear that one's body

In this context, what is primary in human relation is not the atomically separate 'individuals', but rather what is generated 'in-between' such individuals as a result of interaction. The very dynamic of such interaction defines the way in which the self *is* for others. For instance, the way I *am* as an instructor is essentially related to the way in which students participate in an interpersonal dynamic with me. The lived experiences of *being* an instructor is devoid of content except through my relations to those who make that very idea intelligible in the first place, the students' participation. In this way what I *am* throughout my life cannot be understood in isolation from my various interactive relations to those who I care for (or have a negative relation with), and I am shaped by the contributions that the others necessarily make in this process.

Moreover, structurally speaking, the very notion of individuality presupposes at least one relation to other(s), since this is what allows one to distinguish oneself from others. Even the notion of the radically unique sense of my 'ownmost possibilities' and 'my own project' presupposes a contrast, i.e., other people's possibilities which are *not* mine. In this way, the sense of self necessarily depends upon its inherent relation to others, but what is operative is the state of what is 'in-between' which defines the qualitative terms of the relation itself through which one knows oneself to be distinct.[11]

The theory of Being-between also adds a dimension to the general theory of intentionality. According to Watsuji, it is impossible for one's consciousness and its intentional acts to be independent of others. He states,

> My being conscious of you is intertwined with your being conscious of me. I call this characteristic 'Being-between' in order to distinguish it from the general intentionality of our consciousness. Our conscious acts are not determined by ourselves alone, but they are also determined by others. This does not mean that there is an 'exchange' of otherwise one-directional intentional acts back and forth between people. Rather, there is only one 'connection' that is determined by both participants. Thus in the relation of Being-between, the consciousness of the participants are mutually permeated through one another's. When you are angry, my consciousness is colored by that anger, and when you are grieving, my consciousness is influenced by it (Watsuji, 1934, *Ethics* p. 73).

Watsuji admits that intentionality has a radically individual aspect. However, this aspect is by no means the dominant aspect, but rather a lack, or a retreat, from Being-between. The prior condition of Being-between would determine the way in which I would retreat to my 'ownness'; this cannot just appear out of nowhere, but what conditions it is no other than Being-between which constantly structures our existence. Intentionality is thus not strictly limited to that individualistic aspect. To further illustrate the communal nature of Being-between, Watsuji offers the example of a conversation:

> In an intimate relation of Being-between you and I, suppose we have a conversation on an important topic. When I hear the series of words, I do not experience them as a string of sounds, as a series of 'nows'. Rather I grasp the development of Being-between as you speak. *What* you say shows your concern for me, and it draws out my reaction. Thus if you should stop talking in the middle of an important topic, I do not experience a 'discontinuation of sound', but I experience 'intense tension', that is, 'abnormal continuation' to the next word. Or if you say something which shocks me, then your words might go on

---

exudes offensive odors, a fear of being looked at, or a fear that one's eye-contact is offensive to others (Kimura, 1972, 1993, p.186). The chief characteristic of these phobias is that 'rather than the patient evaluating the self from the standpoint of the self, the patient wholly evaluates himself externally (and negatively) from the standpoint of others' (Kimura 187). These pathological cases, according to Kimura, are quite unique to the Japanese and they testify to the tendency of the Japanese to regard the self always in relation to others.

[11] Zahavi (1999) discusses a similar reading of Husserl (p. 161).

but I may dwell on a single thought. The continuation stops here. In this way, what I hear is not simply a string of sounds, but rather it is the 'event' of expressing the Being-between of you and I. Even if it is the case that you utter the words, the 'event' itself is maintained communally between you and I. (Watsuji, 1934, *Ethics*, pp. 81–2)

The notion of Being-between is a part of a broader definition of another term, '*ningen*' ('human being'). This is an ordinary Japanese term, but Watsuji gives it a philosophical twist and uses it as a technical term. The word consists of two characters, '*nin*' (person) and '*gen*' ('between' — although pronounced differently, the character is the same as '*aida*' of '*aidagara*'). Paying close attention to the original meanings of characters (conscious of course of Heidegger's reflections on the Greek terms), Watsuji claims that 'what is meant by 'human being' (*ningen*) is not simply 'man' (*anthropos, homo, homme, Mensch*). It includes society as the coexistence or unity of a people. This is the fundamental double structure' (Watsuji, 1935, *Milieu*, p.18). Again the emphasis is on the second character, 'between'. A human being is a sort of being whose existence includes the characteristic of this 'between-ness' among others. Etymologically, '*ningen*' goes back to a Buddhist term which denoted 'the world in which human beings dwell' as opposed to the world of animals and the enlightened ones (Yuasa, 1981, p. 268). Originally it meant something closer to 'the affairs of the society' rather than a human being, and Watsuji is trying to evoke this aspect of our existence.

Finally, Watsuji adds that this double structure of human-qua-social being is 'no other than the actualization of the activity of negation' (Watsuji, 1935, *Milieu*, p.18). Yuasa (1981) explains this 'negation' using the analogy of a 'school' (p. 269). The school is the 'whole' which signifies Being-between by which individual roles such as 'instructor' and 'student' have meaning. As such, it exists prior to the individuals who fulfill these roles. However, the school cannot exist without individuals actually becoming instructors, administrators, and students. In this sense, it could be said that individuals exist prior to Being-between. These relations mutually negate one another depending upon what is being focused upon. When the school as a whole is at issue the distinctions among individuals who belong to Being-between are negated. On the other hand, from the standpoint of the individuals, the Being-between (the school as a whole) recedes to the background, as in a dispute among several students *within* the school system. In any individual/Being-between relation, the individual exists both as *defined by* Being-between *and* necessarily in a negative relation to it and vice versa.[12]

Although Watsuji developed the notion of negation to some extent, ultimately his emphasis favoured the 'whole' generated from Being-between over the significance of the individual. The structural significance of negation (as an essential component of relation) is much more robustly developed by his mentor, Nishida.

III: Nishida's Theory of 'Co-Determination in Negation'

Kitaro Nishida, considered the father of modern Japanese philosophy, had several major theoretical works from the1910s to 1940s. The earliest of which was his theory of 'pure experience', developed in his maiden work *An Inquiry into the Good* (1911/1987a) under the influence of William James. During the 1920s and 1930s, he developed his signature metaphysical theory, the logic of 'place' (*basho*). Toward the end

---

[12] Watsuji develops the notion of negation further in Chapter 6, 'The Negative Structure of a Human Being', in *Ethics* (Watsuji, 1996, pp. 101–42).

of his career in the late 1930s to 1940s, the logic of place gained a historical and polit-ical flavour.[13] I will discuss some aspects of the theory of pure experience and then his later theory of 'action-intuition', as these are the most relevant for the topic of intersubjectivity.

A. The theory of pure experience

First, however, let me turn briefly to James' theory of pure experience in order to pro-vide a theoretical background.[14] Toward the end of his career, parting from his earlier theory of psychology James developed a quasi-metaphysical theory of pure experi-ence in his *Essays in Radical Empiricism* (1912). According to James, 'pure experi-ence' is not a subjective experience, but a 'simple *that*', an immediate *thisness* of experience, which can be taken as subjective or objective states.[15] He claims that when one reflects on the activity of knowing, experience splits into two terms, one of which becomes the knowing subject and the other the object known (James, 1967, p. 4).[16] Thus, prior to the retrospective experience which divides it into subjectivity and objectivity, pure experience is itself a unity which is neither subject nor object but potentially both. If neither subject nor object, pure experience is also neither material nor psychical; pure experience can be both a thought and a thing at the same time:

> Just so, I maintain, does a given undivided portion of experience, taken in one context of associates, play the part of a knower, of a state of mind, of 'consciousness'; while in a dif-ferent context the same undivided bit of experience plays the part of a thing known, an objective 'content'. In a word, in one group it figures as a thought, in another group as a thing. And, since it can figure in both groups simultaneously we have every right to speak of it as subjective and objective both at once (James, 1967, pp. 9–10).

James notes that just as a point at the intersection of two lines can belong to either line, pure experience can be 'counted twice over, as belonging to either group, and spoken of loosely as existing in two places, although it would remain all the time a numerically single thing' (James, 1967, p.12). In short, there is no dualism of consciousness vs. the thing, reality, matter; they are two ways of 'taking' the same reality.[17]

---

[13] Nishida's works are collected as *Nishida Kitaro Zenshu vol. 1-19* (*Collected Works of Nishida*), hereafter Nishida (1987, *NKZ*). All the quoted passages are translated by Yoko Arisaka. Nishida's philosophy throughout was also influenced by Zen Buddhism, as he was a practitioner, but references to Zen do not appear explicitly in his writings. He became a politically controversial figure, as his followers, the 'Kyoto School' (to which also Watsuji belonged), became involved in Japanese nationalism during the Pacific War. For more on the political aspects of his thought, see Arisaka (1996; 1997); Heisig & Maraldo (1994).

[14] Nishida's first book is translated as Nishida (1987a). For a more detailed comparison of James and Nishida, see Feenberg and Arisaka (1990). For a helpful clarification of Nishida's notion of experi-ence, see Feenberg (1999). For a comparison between Nishida and phenomenology, see Noe (1994). Other sources on Nishida in English include Abe (1988; 1992).

[15] In his words, 'the instant field of the present is always experience in its "pure" state, plain unqualified actuality, a simple *that*, as yet undifferentiated into thing and thought' (James, 1967, p. 74).

[16] Further, as 'subjective' we say that the experience represents; as 'objective' it is represented. What represents and what is represented is here numerically the same; but we must remember that no dual-ism of being represented and representing resides in the experience *per se*. In its pure state, or when iso-lated, there is no self-splitting of it into consciousness and what the consciousness is 'of'. Its subjectiv-ity and objectivity are functional attributes solely, realized only when the experience is 'taken', i.e., talked-of, twice, considered along with its two differing contexts respectively, by a new retrospective experience, of which that whole past complication now forms the fresh content (James, 1967, p. 23).

[17] As is well known, James' theory influenced the development of Husserl's early theory of 'horizon', but some have also argued that James had much influence on Husserl's development of the notion of intentionality (Edie, 1987, pp. 24–32).

But what is pure experience, this 'stuff' that is both mind and thing? Bertrand Russell once called this theory 'neutral monism', but James explicitly rejects such a conception. In his theory of radical empiricism, James goes on to claim that consciousness is a not a thing, a mental substance, but it is a *function* of knowing (James, 1967, pp. 3–4). Just as a 'program' is not a thing but an operation that is 'realized' as the functionalists would point out, consciousness is an operation that is realized as language-use, memory, or behaviour and desire patterns. But unlike the functionalists who would explain the function in objective, behavioural-causal terms, James, as well as the phenomenologists who later followed his insights in the theories of intentionality, tried to retain the robust 'first-person' content of experience which is a necessary component of pure experience.

Nishida accepts from James the rejection of ontologizing the mind, but like James he calls pure experience the only reality that is both subjective and objective. As with James, Nishida also defines pure experience as immediate or prereflective experience prior to conceptual categorization. He agrees that pure experience is 'as yet neither subject nor object', and that 'knowledge and its object are one' (Nishida, 1987, *NKZ 1*, p. 9). The distinction of subject and object, according to Nishida, 'occurs as an opposition when the unity of experience is lost' (p. 42). It is not that the subject 'has' the pure experience 'of' the object to begin with; rather, these distinctions come to be differentiated within pure experience itself. Thus in a surprising reversal Nishida claims: 'Individual experience is no more than a particular, limited area within experience', and that 'it is not that there is the individual and thus the experience, but rather, there is the experience and thus the individual' (p. 28).

This kind of 'primordial unity' with the object of experience is also expressed by Merleau-Ponty (1962) in his notion of perception as a 'non-thetic, pre-objective and pre-conscious experience' (p. 242):

> In perception we do not think the object and we do not think ourselves thinking it, we are given over to the object and we merge into this body which is better informed than we are about the world, and about the motives we have and the means at our disposal for synthesizing it. In its primary layer of sense experience which is discovered only provided that we really coincide with the act of perception and break with the critical attitude, I have the living experience of the unity of the subject and the intersensory unity of the thing, and do not conceive them after the fashion of analytical reflection and science (p. 239).

In his later works, this line of thought is more fully developed in his notion of 'chiasm'.

The consequence of the theory of pure experience that is relevant to our discussion of intersubjectivity is the following: Once pure experience — immediacy — is defined as the prereflective 'simple *that*' prior to subject and object, then subjectivity is not a fundamental fact but derived from pure experience. But if so, as the prereflective 'simple *that*', pure experience is potentially many subjects and objects. The difference between 'my' flow and 'your' flow is not a fundamental fact, but it is a result of the different ways in which the same pure experience is abstracted, or 'taken', to use James' phrase. Following this logic to its conclusion, Nishida claims that as pure experience 'one is unable to make absolute distinctions between oneself and another' (Nishida, 1987, *NKZ 1*, p. 55).

For Nishida, then, selfhood or the individuality of experience is derived from pure experience-qua-event, which in itself is not individuated; 'pure experience transcends the individual' (Nishida, 1987, *NKZ 1*, p. 28). Consistent with this idea is Nishida's claim that even emotions and will, which we normally attribute to individual selfhood, are part of the 'totality' of pure experience: 'In pure experience, there are not yet distinctions among thought, emotion, and will. There is only a unified activity, and thus, not yet the opposition of subject and object' (p. 59). Emotions are not psychological states belonging to a presupposed self, but an aspect of the pure experience/event itself. For example, experientially, when we encounter something frightening, we often attribute the quality to the event itself even though it is I who is experiencing the fright, if there are others present, we treat the phenomenon as if it is the general feature of the event itself that is inherently shared from the beginning.

Using this line of thought, Nishida argues that we can recognize 'different consciousnesses' only on the basis of a fundamental unity of consciousness which would make that distinction intelligible. As Nishida puts it, 'even if there were a world which is governed by a wholly different unity of consciousness, such a world would be utterly unrelated to ours. The world which we can comprehend must be governed under the same unifying principle — i.e., ours' (Nishida, 1987, *NKZ 1,* p. 76). Insofar as we can comprehend each other's 'worlds' — which we can, for instance by sharing a language or using logic, according to Nishida — there must be a single unifying principle. So the very notion of 'different individual consciousnesses' presupposes an underlying singular unity, which is pure experience.

But there is obviously a problem that must be explained. Nishida has so far presumably explained the logical necessity of the unity of pure experience among different individuals, but he hasn't given an account of how this pure experience, which in itself is 'singular', generates different indexical reference points which would establish different individual experiences. How do different subjectivities arise out of pure experience? Nishida argues that these different 'subjectivities' must now be accounted for in terms of the configurations of pure experience-qua-event and not in terms of different individuals. As Nishida states, arguing indirectly against Kant, 'the notion that consciousness must belong to someone merely means that consciousness must be unified in some way. It does not mean that there must be an owner; such a thought is plainly dogma' (Nishida, 1987, *NKZ 1*, p. 55). The 'unity' of consciousness, i.e., the fact that the succession of experience is not merely chaotic but forms a meaningful totality *from a point of view*, must therefore be functionally explained by Nishida in terms of the characteristics of pure experience itself and not reduced to mere 'ownership' by a subject. Ontologically speaking, the Kantian 'transcendental apperception' is already committed to an individuated 'I', but Nishida wants such a principle of unity to be embedded in the experiential content itself so that it would serve as the condition for the emergence of the 'I' as well as different 'selves'.

Nishida's task then is to find a structural order in experience itself which would generate a self, rather than making experience an event that already belongs to a self. If he could establish such a principle, then this 'primordial experience' would indeed be fundamentally intersubjective in the sense that it could belong to or be shared by any number of selves. In fact, it would be the condition under which different 'personal experiences' become intelligible.

However, instead of rigorously pursuing a structural analysis of experience in phenomenological terms, Nishida's theory of pure experience at this point takes a metaphysical turn and begins to resemble German Idealists such as Schelling.[18] Pure experience is objectified and ontologized as the self-creative reality/existence which operates by a unifying force: 'An event of pure experience is the universal realizing

---

[18] Nishida borrows the notion of 'intellectual intuition' in German Idealism; the 'I' is not a presupposition, but rather, reflection *produces* its object, the I.

itself' (Nishida, 1987, *NKZ 1*, p. 25). Individuals are parts of this reality, reflecting the unifying force of the 'whole'—pure experience-qua-the totality of events, i.e., the universe, even God. Thus, despite its experiential starting point, the theory unfortunately appears to regress to a version of Idealist metaphysics. The first-person perspective is lost, and the traditional metaphysical framework returns, with a God's eye perspective from which to view the unfolding reality, but this is hardly a solution to founding intersubjectivity as an experientially salient event.

B. The theory of 'action-intuition'

Nishida ultimately abandons the theory of pure experience, both for the term's inherent subjectivist connotation as well as its theoretical limitations such as above. But he did not abandon the basic insight, that somehow an explanation of reality must be based on concrete experience, and this reality, experienced directly, is fundamentally not encapsulated in pre-existing individuals. The identities of different selves should be accounted for in terms of its underlying principles based concretely in experience and not vice versa. But so long as these principles are attributed to some 'features of reality', he is back to old style metaphysics — looking at reality from a third-person God's eye view — a standpoint which he rejected. So the principles must be found in concrete experience itself, that is, without leaving the first-person point of view.

The main problem which generated the difficulty of the earlier theory was the fact that experience was still implicitly taken as consciousness. Nishida examined this issue at length and came to the conclusion that the objects of our concrete experience are objects of action, not objects of consciousness. The 'I', as a concrete unity of experience, is immediately grasped as an individual thing in real contact with other individual things, and the access is not conceptual mediation or even intentionality, but an *embodied act* grasped as immediate involvement, much in the way Heidegger's notion of *ready-to-hand* deals with the self's concrete actions. The 'world' is first and foremost not a world of abstraction and representation; rather it is a lived world of acting and its objects.

Although this new theory of embodiment may appear to contradict the earlier theory of pure experience, in that it appears to assert the individual (body) prior to experience, in my view a phenomenological reconstruction of what is new in Nishida's theory is the following: The 'body' as lived experience is not a given, but it emerges out of the concrete ways in which the experiential interactive world is already organized and 'enacted'. It is this concrete network of action-mediated reality which gives rise to 'different selves' which presumably have 'different personal experiences', but these are based on a more basic fact of concrete events that unfold. If Nishida could give an account of this action-mediated reality, then that would be an account of an inherently shared world which would found intersubjectivity.

The new embodied theory is not a complete rejection of the theory of pure experience, in that originally, pure experience was conceived as prior to subject and object but potentially both, but the error was made because it was analyzed primarily from the subjective side of the coin. But from the beginning it had a robustly concrete, objective side, that pure experience was also real events in the world. Nishida's term for this 'concretized' notion of pure experience is 'action-intuition' (*koi-teki-chokkan*).[19]

---

[19] Other possible translations include 'active intuition' or 'act intuition'. German translations include 'Tat-Anschauung', 'tathandelnde Anschauung', or 'handelnde Anschauung'. The concept becomes one of the central ideas in Nishida's philosophy after 1932. He wrote two essays which focused explicitly

Nishida elaborates: 'In our standpoint of action, what is outside is inside and vice versa . . .we "see" things by acting, and things determine us and at the same time we determine things. This is action-intuition. We say that experience is the foundation of knowledge, but this is because experience is understood as action-intuition in this sense' (Nishida, 1987, *NKZ 8*, p. 131). Action-intuition is this mutual process in which we physically determine our environment and are determined by it, and this process occurs *equiprimordially* with respect to the self and the world.[20] Our existence is more than contemplation and representation; we are material beings, consuming, creating, and transforming, and in this process, our 'selves' emerge as the subjective 'pole' of the events themselves.

The difficult idea here is to make sense of how the self is individualized in dealing with concrete objects and others in the world according to this theory, especially since this theory does not claim to presuppose pre-existing individuals. Nishida did not explicitly address the problem in these terms, but here is my own attempt: First, all concrete objects in the world are bare individual entities (in that there is no such thing as a 'general' thing), the self which deals with such concrete entities cannot be a 'general' self; it must be a concrete acting self in relating to concrete entities in unique spatio-temporal situations. Second, such concrete entities are always given 'perspectivally', in that they 'indicate' a potentially infinite number of 'point of view' from which the thing can be handled, by the particular spatio-temporal position that they occupy, by being concretely 'located' in such and such a way.[21] So it is this perspectivalness of *things* which simultaneously generates different 'selves' which could potentially be many. Since the perspectival thing and the self arise equiprimordially, the 'individuals' are not presupposed but the very constitutive content which co-arise as the corresponding perspectival correlates of action, of the concrete givenness of objects. In this way, intersubjectivity is already embedded in the concrete things themselves in the world by the way they are concretely and perspectivally given.

C. Co-determination in negation

Nishida elaborates a few further points. Experientially, to the extent that these 'objects of action' that generate different 'selves' are *concrete*, the ways in which the objects 'indicate' have social and historical content; they are not simply 'objects' but objects of a such and such kind that emerged out of a long series of transactions and emplacements. This is a field of social and historical actions and things in which they are constantly co-emerging. Moreover, in such a field, the so-emerged 'selves' interact amongst themselves as well. In this process the field as a whole is also determined as objective social reality, which in turn determines the actions of the selves. However,

---

on the concept, 'The Standpoint of Action-Intuition' (1935) (*NKZ 8*, pp. 107–218) and 'Action-Intuition' (pp. 541–71), but the concept is discussed extensively in almost all his work after 1932.

[20] Instead of the emphasis on consciousness, in the theory of action-intuition our 'living body' (*shintai*) becomes the central notion of the self. But by 'body', Nishida does not mean a biological entity nor a mechanistic physical entity. The body which relates to the world through action-intuition may be thought of as a *historically embodied* intentionality with a creative force. Action-intuition grasps the concrete individual entity in 'dealing' with it and in this action it determines itself vis-a-vis the other. As Ohashi puts it, 'In phenomenological terms, the notion combines "cognitive subjectivity" and "lived body"' (Ohashi, 1995, p.63). For further discussions on the connection between Nishida and phenomenology, see also Nitta *et al* (1978), Ogawa (1978), Feenberg & Arisaka (1990), Feenberg (1999). Noe (1994) draws a parallel between Nishida's notion of action-intuition and the later Husserl and Merleau-Ponty.

[21] See also Husserl's numerous discussions (for instance in *Ideas*, 1962) on the perspectival givenness of a thing, though his analysis focused more on intentionality rather than actions.

in this process, to the extent that the 'acting selves' that emerge in this process must truly function as 'agents' (to be a 'self') rather than the simple correlates within the dynamic process, such a self would also have to possess freedom to negate others from its own agency. Therefore, co-determination inherently contains moments of 'negation' by others and vice versa as well. In Ohashi's words, 'an individual is not a mere part of some universal, but must possess freedom of inverse determination, that is, it must be able conversely to determine itself and the universal' (Ohashi, 1995, p. 61). It is 'dialectical' in the sense that the very existence of the self depends on 'negating' itself *vis-à-vis* others and others *vis-à-vis* itself. In other words, paradoxically all individuals in the dialectical universal must be 'absolutely' independent from one another, each opposing the other, even though they share the underlying unity that defines them in the first place. For the self and others to exist *as* self *and* others, the Other cannot simply a part of the self; the Other must be transcendent to the self.[22]

'Opposition' here does not have a negative connotation as in 'confrontational'; it simply means that the other must be truly an independent interlocutor. My interlocutor cannot be reduced to a part of myself, either as an object of consciousness or action, but it must *recognize* me as her other, a true Thou. But it is in this very opposition and essential independence that the individuals maintain fundamental relation to one another; they are co-dependent through opposition, as in a match of tennis. As Feenberg puts it, 'each gesture of combat is part of a pair, the other part of which must be and can be supplied only by the adversary. Every move in the game is in some deeper sense an element of a larger pattern produced through the collaborative competition of the players' (Feenberg, 1995, p. 217). This 'field of action' is what Nishida calls the 'place of dialectical universal'. In Nishida's words, 'The individuals oppose one another and mutually negate each other, and this is the self-negation of the place, but this very negation is itself the self-affirmation, the inverse-correspondence of the individuals. This is the self-formation of the place, from "the making" to "the made"' (1987, *KNZ 19*, p. 379). The concrete place is this field of interaction-in-opposition.

Strictly speaking, in Nishida's mature theory there is no 'intersubjectivity', because the notion of 'subjectivity' is thoroughly replaced by the notion of embodied active selves that emerge from the field of concrete experience-qua-reality. But this 'reality' is thoroughly shared to begin with, through their perspectivally concrete organization that could simultaneously indicate numerous acting selves. However the fundamental relation between the selves, the 'inter' part of 'intersubjectivty', is concretely retained in his field theory as well as his notion of co-determination in negation.

IV: Summary

We have here two models of intersubjectivity from Japanese thought. On the one hand is Watsuji's phenomenological account which articulated the quality of 'Being-between' various selves, which are fundamental to the very constitution of the self. However, this account lacked a robust theory of how it is that different selves came to be differentiated vis-à-vis one another. This difference-in-relation is better explained by Nishida's dialectical theory, because it contains a theory of negation which is a constitutive aspect of selfhood, through which the 'self and other' are distinguished in their relation. But since this relation must be founded upon the underlying 'field' which would make it concretely intelligible in the first place, this field is the 'intersubjective' basis that is defined in terms of action and embodiment. From

---

[22] See Zahavi (1999), p. 167, for his discussion of Sartre on this point.

the beginning, both thinkers reject the Cartesian *cogito*, that being a self is not a question of having private experiences. This rejection is especially evident in Nishida's later theory of the lived body and action. Japanese language and culture may be mentioned as contributing factors for prioritizing intersubjectivity and inter-relations among people, but philosophically the theories stand on their own right as presenting distinct theories of the self–other relation.

References

Abe, M. (1988), 'Nishida's philosophy of "place",' *International Philosophical Quarterly,* **28** (4), pp. 355–71.

Abe, M. (1992), '"Inverse correspondence"" in the philosophy of Nishida: The emergence of the notion', *International Philosophical Quarterly,* **32** (3), pp.325–44.

Arisaka, Y. (1996), 'The Nishida enigma: 'The principle of the New World Order',' *Monumenta Nipponica,* **51** (1), pp. 81–105.

Arisaka, Y. (1997), 'Beyond East and West: Nishida's universalism and postcolonial critique', *The Review of Politics,* **59** (3), pp. 541–60.

Bellah, R. (1965), 'Some reflections on the work of Watsuji Tetsuro', *Jnl Asian Studies* **24** (4), pp. 573–94.

Cole, E.B. (1993), *Philosophy and Feminist Criticism: An Introduction* (New York: Paragon House).

Dillon, M.C. (1988), *Merleau-Ponty's Ontology* (Evanston: Northwestern University Press)

Dilworth, D. (1974), 'Watsuji Tetsuro: Cultural phenomenologist and ethician', *Philosophy East and West,* **24** (1), pp. 3–22

Edie, J. (1987) *William James and Phenomenology* (Bloomington: Indiana University Press).

Feenberg, A. (1995), *Alternative Modernity* (Berkeley: University of California Press)

Feenberg, A. (1999), 'Experience and culture: Nishida's Path 'To the things themselves',' *Philosophy East and West* **49** (1), pp. 28–44.

Feenberg, A. and Arisaka, Y (1990), 'Experiential ontology: The origins of the Nishida philosophy in the doctrine of pure experience', *International Philosophical Quarterly* **30** (2), pp.173–205.

Furukawa, T. (1961), 'Watsuji Tetsuro, the man and his work', in *A Climate*, ed. Watsuji Tetsuro, tr. G. Bownas (Tokyo: Japanese National Commission for Unesco and Printing Bureau, Japanese Govt.).

Heidegger, M. (1962), *Being and Time*, ed. E. Robinson and J. Macquarrie (New York: Harper).

Heisig, J. and Maraldo, J. (1994), *Rude Awakenings* (Honolulu: University of Hawaii Press)

Husserl, E. (1962) *Ideas: General Introduction to Pure Phenomenology*, tr. W. Gibson (NY: Collier Books).

James, W. (1967), *Essays in Radical Empiricism and a Pluralistic Universe* (New York: Peter Smith)

Kimura, Bin (1972/1993), *Hito to Hito to no Aida: Seishinbyorigaku-teki Nihon-ron* (Tokyo: Kobundo)

LaFleur, W. (1990), 'A turning in Taisho: Asia and Europe in the early writings of Watsuji Tetsuro', in *Culture and Identity*, ed. J. Thomas Rimer (Princeton: Princeton University Press).

Li, Chenyang (1999), *The Tao Encounters the West* (Albany: SUNY Press).

Merleau-Ponty, M. (1962/1986), *Phenomenology of Perception*, tr. C. Smith (London: Routledge and KP).

Merleau-Ponty, M. (1964), *The Primacy of Perception* (Evanston: Northwestern University Press).

Nishida, K. (1987/1989), *Nishida Kitaro Zenshu (Collected Works) 1-19* (Tokyo: Iwanami Shoten).

Nishida, K. (1987a) *An Inquiry into the Good*, tr. M. Abe and C. Ives (New Haven: Yale University Press).

Nitta, Y, Tatematsu, H. and Shimomisse. E. (1978), 'Phenomenology and philosophy in Japan', in *Annalecta Husserliana 8*, ed. Y. Nitta and H. Tatematsu (Dordrecht: D. Reidel Publisher).

Noddings, N. (1984) *Caring: A Feminine Approcach to Ethics and Moral Education* (Berkeley: UC Press)

Noe, K. (1994), '"The non-Cartesian subject" in Japanese philosophy: The case of Nishida Kitaro', *Social Discourse* **6** (1–2), pp. 79–87.

Ogawa, Tadashi (1978) 'The Kyoto School of philosophy and phenomenology', in *Annalecta Husserliana 8*, ed. Y. Nitta and H. Tatematsu ((Dordrecht: D. Reidel Publisher)

Ohashi, R. (1995), 'Gunron-teki Sekai: Nishida Tetsugaku to "Sekai"Gainen', in *Shiso* **857**, pp. 56–70.

Olafson, F. (1998), *Heidegger and the Ground of Ethics: A Study of Mitsein* (Cambridge & New York: CUP)

Sakai, Naoki (1993), 'Return to the West/ Return to the East: Watsuji Teturo's anthropology and discussions of authenticity', in *Japan in the World*, ed. M. Miyoshi and H. Harootunian (Durham: Duke UP).

Watsuji, T. (1935/1979/1991) *Fudo: Ningengaku teki Kosatsu* (Tokyo: Iwanami Bunko)

Watsuji, T. (1934/1951/1971/1993) *Ningen no Gaku to shite no Rinri-gaku* (Tokyo: Iwanami Shoten)

Watsuji, T. (1961–1963), *Watsuji Tetsuro Zenshu* (Tokyo: Iwanami Shoten)

Watsuji, T. (1996), *Watsuji Tetsuro's Rinrigaku: Ethics in Japan*, tr. Yamamoto & Carter (SUNY Press).

Yuasa, Yasuo (1981), *Watsuji Tetsuro: Kindai Nihon Tetsugaku no Unmei* (Kyoto: Minerva Shobo).

Zahavi, Dan (1999), *Self-Awareness and Alterity* (Evanston: Northwestern University Press).

B. Alan Wallace

Intersubjectivity in Indo-Tibetan Buddhism

This essay focuses on the theme of intersubjectivity, which is central to the entire Indo-Tibetan Buddhist tradition. It addresses the following five themes pertaining to Buddhist concepts of intersubjectivity: (1) the Buddhist practice of the cultivation of meditative quiescence challenges the hypothesis that individual human consciousness emerges solely from the dynamic interrelation of self and other; (2) the central Buddhist insight practice of the four applications of mindfulness is a means for gaining insight into the nature of oneself, others and the relation between oneself and the rest of the world, which provides a basis for cultivating a deep sense of empathy; (3) the Buddhist cultivation of the four immeasurables is expressly designed to arouse a rich sense of empathy with others; (4) the meditative practice of dream yoga, which illuminates the dream-like nature of waking reality is shown to have deep implications regarding the nature of intersubjectivity; (5) the theory and practice of Dzogchen, the 'great perfection' system of meditation, challenges the assertion of the existence of an inherently real, localized, ego-centred mind, as well as the dichotomy of objective space as opposed to perceptual space.

Introduction

The theme of intersubjectivity lies at the very core of the Indo-Tibetan Buddhist way of viewing the world and seeking spiritual awakening. According to this worldview, each person does exist as an individual, but the self, or personal identity, does not exist as an independent ego that is somehow in control of the body and mind. Rather, the individual is understood as a matrix of dependently related events, all of them in a state of flux. There are three aspects of this dependence. (1) The self arises in dependence upon prior contributing causes and conditions, such as one's parents and all others who contribute to one's survival, education and so on. In this way, our existence is invariably intersubjective, for we exist in a causal nexus in which we are constantly influenced by, and exert influence upon, the world around us, including other people. (2) The individual self does not exist independently of the body and mind, but rather exists in reliance upon a myriad of physical and mental processes that are constantly changing. (3) How does this self come into existence, if it is not inherently present either in any single psycho-physiological process or in all of them combined?

According to the Madhyamaka, or 'Middle Way', view, of Indo-Tibetan Buddhism, which seeks to avoid the two extremes of substantialism and nihilism, the self is brought into existence by the power of conceptual imputation. That is, on the basis of either some aspect of the body (e.g. I am tall) or some mental process (e.g. I am content), the self is conceptually imputed *upon something which it is not*. Thus, even though I am not the height of my body, nor am I the affective state of being content, within the conceptual framework in which I think of myself and others think of me, it is conventionally valid to assert that I am tall and content.

Moreover, Buddhism maintains that conceptual frameworks are not private. They are public and consensual. So the ways in which I perceive and conceive of myself and others are inextricably related to the community of language-users and thinkers with whom I share a common conceptual framework. We view ourselves, others and the world around us by way of shared ideas, without which the world as we perceive it and conceive of it would not exist. Thus, our very existence as individuals, whether living in a community or in solitude, is intersubjective to the core.

What are the ramifications of this way of viewing reality? In this essay I shall focus on the following five questions, all pertaining closely to the idea of intersubjectivity. (1) Does individual human consciousness emerge solely from the dynamic interrelation of self and other, making it therefore inherently intersubjective? I shall address this topic within the framework of the Buddhist practice of the cultivation of *meditative quiescence*, in which the conceptual mind is stilled and the attention is withdrawn away from the physical senses and purely into the realm of mental consciousness. (2) In what ways does Buddhist meditation cultivate a sense of empathy as an indispensable means for gaining insight into the nature of oneself, others and the relation between oneself and the rest of the world? This theme will be presented in accordance with the central Buddhist insight practice of the *four applications of mindfulness*, in which one attends to the nature of the body, feelings, mental states and mental objects. (3) How does the theme of intersubjectivity pertain to Buddhist practices designed to induce greater empathy with others? In response to this question, I shall explain the Buddhist cultivation of the *four immeasurables*, namely, loving kindness, compassion, empathetic joy and equanimity. (4) What significance does the Buddhist emphasis on the dream-like nature of waking reality have on the issue of intersubjectivity? Here I will focus on the meditative practice of *dream yoga*, which begins with training to induce lucid dreaming, or apprehending the dream-state for what it is while dreaming. (5) Finally, how does Buddhism challenge the assertion of the existence of an inherently real, localized, ego-centred mind, and in what ways does it challenge the dichotomy of objective space as opposed to perceptual space? This theme will be addressed by explaining some of the essentials of the theory and practice of *Dzogchen*, the 'Great Perfection', system of meditation aimed at fathoming the essential nature of awareness.

Meditative Quiescence

The Buddhist cultivation of meditative quiescence is regarded as an indispensable prerequisite for the cultivation of contemplative insight. The fundamental distinction between the two disciplines is that in the practice of quiescence, one refines the attention by means of enhancing attentional stability and vividness and counteracting the mind's habitual tendencies toward alternating attentional excitation and laxity. The cultivation of contemplative insight, on the other hand, entails the precise examination and investigation of various facets of reality, using as one's instrument one's previously refined attentional abilities. Thus, the training in quiescence may be regarded as a kind of contemplative technology, aimed at developing the one tool by means of which mental phenomena can be directly explored. The training in insight, on the other hand, may be viewed as a kind of contemplative science, aimed at acquiring experiential knowledge of the mind, the phenomena that are apprehended by the mind, and the relation between the two.[1]

Buddhism asserts that human beings with unimpaired sense faculties have six modes of perception. Five of those modes are by way of the five physical senses, and the sixth is mental perception, that faculty by means of which we perceive mental phenomena, such as thoughts, mental imagery, dreams and emotions. Mental perception is viewed as being quite distinct from our capacity to think, remember and imagine, all of which are conceptual faculties. Among the six modes of perception, the five physical senses can, at least in principle, be corrected, enhanced and extended by external, technological means. Common examples in the modern world (though not in classical India or Tibet) are the use of eyeglasses to correct vision and the use of telescopes and microscopes to enhance and extend our visual capacities.

If one's eyesight or hearing is defective, there is little if anything one can do by means of meditative or any other cognitive training to help matters. Mental perception, on the other hand, is not so easily amenable to technological enhancement, but among the six senses it is, according to Buddhism, the one that can be the most refined and extended. To start with, the normal untrained mind, which is so prone to alternating bouts of compulsive excitation and laxity, is regarded as 'dysfunctional'. So the bad news is that most of us are 'attentionally challenged', regardless of whether we suffer from attention deficit (laxity) and hyperactivity (excitation) disorders. But the good news is that this mental disability can be successfully treated with rigorous, sustained training.

Traditionally, Buddhists who are dedicated to exploring the extent to which attentional stability and vividness can be enhanced are advised to disengage temporarily from a socially active way of life. Withdrawing for a period of weeks, months, or even years, into solitude, they radically simplify their lifestyle and devote themselves single-pointedly to training the attention, while remaining as free as possible from all distracting influences. As long as one is actively engaged in society, one's very sense of personal identity is strongly reinforced by one's intersubjective relations with others. But now, as one withdraws into outer and inner solitude, one's identity is significantly decontextualized. Externally, by disengaging from social interactions, one's sense of self as holding a position in society is eroded. Internally, by disengaging from ideation — such as conceptually dwelling on events from one's personal history, thinking about oneself in the present, and anticipating what one will do in the future — one's sense of self as occupying a real place in nature is eroded. To be decontextualized is to be deconstructed. Surely this is why in traditional societies

---

[1] For a more elaborate discussion of meditative quiescence and its relation to contemplative insight see Wallace (1998 and 1999a), and for the relation between such contemplative modes of inquiry and modern science see Wallace (2000).

being sent into exile was regarded as one of the most severe forms of punishment, almost as drastic as capital punishment itself. In the penal systems of modern society one of the most severe forms of punishment is solitary confinement. Such isolation from society may be experienced as a terrible loss of personal freedom or as a marvellous opportunity for personal liberation. In both these ways it is like death itself.

This existential shift is not undertaken casually or without suitable preparation. To illustrate this point, the Buddha gave the analogy of a great elephant that enters a shallow pond in order to enjoy the pleasures of drinking and bathing (*Anguttara Nikaya*, V, 201 ff.). Due to its great size, the elephant finds a footing in the deep water and enjoys itself thoroughly. But when a cat seeks to emulate the elephant by jumping into the pond, it finds no footing, and either sinks or thrashes around on the surface. Here is the meaning of this parable. If one is inadequately prepared for the simplicity of the reclusive life, while dwelling for a sustained period in solitude the mind either sinks, by way of laxity, into dullness, boredom and depression, or else rises, by way of excitation, into compulsive ideation and sensory distractions. The critical issue here is whether one has cultivated sufficient emotional stability and balance to be able to live happily without reliance upon pleasurable sensual, intellectual, aesthetic and interpersonal stimuli. The single most powerful practice for achieving such emotional health is the cultivation of a sense of connectedness with others. This is done by empathetically reflecting again and again on others as subjects, like oneself, with their hopes and fears, joys and sorrows, successes and failures. In this way, whether alone or with others, one overcomes the sense of loneliness and isolation.

Among the many techniques taught in Buddhism for training the attention, the most widely practised method entails cultivating mindfulness of the breathing.[2] In this practice one begins by focusing the attention on the tactile sensations where one experiences the breath at the apertures of the nostrils. As one progresses in this training, the body comes to feel light and the respiration becomes more and more subtle. Eventually, while focusing the attention on the point of contact of the breath, right there a mental image spontaneously arises, on which one then sustains the attention. The type of image that arises varies from one person to the next, but may appear, for example, like a star, a round ruby or a pearl (Vajirañana, 1975, p. 249). This mental object remains the focus of one's attention until eventually it is replaced by a far more subtle 'after-image', which also may arise in a variety of forms.

At this point, one's attention is so concentrated in the field of mental perception that the mind is free of all physical sense impressions, including the presence of one's own body. If one then disengages the attention from the after-image, without relinquishing the heightened sense of attentional stability and vividness, in this absence of appearances one experiences a primal state of contentless awareness, known in Sanskrit as the *bhavanga*, or 'ground of becoming', from which all active mental processes arise (Harvey, 1995, p. 160). This mode of awareness is said to shine in its own radiance, which is obscured only due to external stimuli; and it is experienced as being primordially pure, regardless of whether it is temporarily obscured by adventitious defilements (see Vajirañana, 1975, pp. 151, 327–8; Kalupahana, 1987, pp. 112–15; *Anguttara Nikaya*, A.I.9–10, A.I.61). Remarkably, Buddhist contemplatives have also concluded that the nature of this ground of becoming is loving

---

[2]   This practice is explained in detail in the opening chapters of Wallace (1999b).

kindness, and it is regarded as the source of people's incentive to meditatively develop their minds in the pursuit of spiritual liberation (*Anguttara Nikaya*, A.I.10–11).

The experience of such a state of contentless mental awareness is common to various schools of Indian and Tibetan Buddhist meditation, as well as other non-Buddhist contemplative traditions.[3] So there seem to be good grounds for concluding that this is not simply a matter of speculation, but rather an element of experience for contemplatives trained in a variety of techniques and adhering to a wide range of philosophical beliefs. If this is indeed the case, the possibility of such experience has profound implications for questions concerning the intersubjective nature of consciousness. Is consciousness essentially intersubjective in the sense that the very nature of consciousness, with its own innate luminosity, is constituted by the relation of the self to others? The observation that the *bhavanga* is of the nature of love would imply that empathy is innate to consciousness and exists prior to the emergence of all active mental processes. One might infer from this that empathy on the part of researchers must be a prerequisite for any genuine science of consciousness. On the other hand, the assertion that this state of awareness is free of all sensory and mental appearances implies a certain degree of autonomy from language, conceptual frameworks and active engagement with others. This could suggest that consciousness is not really *constituted* by the relation of the self to others, but rather that it is intersubjective in the weaker sense of simply being inherently open to, and connected with, others. We shall return to this important theme later in this essay.

The Four Applications of Mindfulness

The cultivation of compassion is like a silken thread that runs through and connects all the pearls of Buddhist meditative practices. Compassion is based upon empathy, but in a very deep sense insight into the nature of oneself, others and the relation between oneself and the rest of the world is also based upon empathy. Moreover, a common Buddhist adage states that compassion without wisdom is bondage, and wisdom without compassion is just another form of bondage. Thus, wisdom and compassion must be cultivated together, and empathy is a common root of both.

The classic Buddhist matrix of meditative practices known as the four applications of mindfulness is based on the *Satipatthanasutta*, the most revered of all Buddhist discourses in the Theravada Buddhist tradition.[4] This practice entails the careful observation and consideration of the body, feelings, mental states and mental objects of oneself and of others. A common theme to each of these four applications of mindfulness is first considering these elements of one's own being, then attending to these same phenomena in others, and finally shifting one's attention back and forth between self and others. Especially in this final phase of practice, one engages in what has recently been called *reiterated empathy*, in which one imaginatively views one's own psychophysical processes from a 'second-person' perspective. That is, I view my body and mind from what I imagine to be your perspective, so that I begin to sense my own presence not only 'from within' but 'from without'. Such practice leads to

---

[3] See the section 'Quiescence According to Mahamudra and Atiyoga', in Wallace (1998); Woods (1983); and Forman (1990).

[4] For a translation of this discourse, together with a modern commentary see Nyanaponika Thera (1973).

the insight that the second-person perspective on one's own being is just as 'real' as the first-person perspective; and neither exists independently of the other.

Another of the central aims of these four applications of mindfulness is to distinguish between the phenomena that are presented to our six modes of perception and the conceptual superimpositions that we often unconsciously and involuntarily impute upon those phenomena, including labels, categories and thoughts aroused by our emotional reactions. The Buddha summed up this theme when he declared: 'In what is seen there should be only the seen; in what is heard, only the heard; in what is sensed, only the sensed; in what is perceived mentally, only the mentally perceived' (*Udana*, I, 10).

The first subject for the close application of mindfulness is the body, for this is our physical basis in reality, on which we most readily identify our own whereabouts and distinguish ourselves from others. The Buddha quintessentially describes this practice as follows: 'One dwells observing the body as the body internally, or one dwells observing the body as the body externally, or one dwells observing the body as the body both internally and externally.' (*Satipatthanasutta*, 5). In Pali (the language in which the Buddha's teachings were first recorded) the term translated here as 'observing' (*anupassati*) has the various meanings of observe, contemplate and consider, which override any strict demarcation between pure perception versus conceptual reflection. It means taking in the observed phenomena as fully as possible, both perceptually and conceptually, while still being sensitive to practical distinctions between what is presented to the senses and what is superimposed upon them. Such practice is done not only while sitting quietly in meditation, but while engaging in the various postures of walking, standing, sitting and lying down, as well as the activities of looking, bending, stretching, dressing, eating, drinking, excreting, speaking, keeping silent, staying awake and falling asleep.[5]

As one first attends to one's own body, one observes, among other things, the various events or factors that give rise to the emergence and dissolution of one's own experiences of and in the body. By *observing* one's own body, rather than simply *identifying* with it, one cultivates a kind of self-alterity, by experiencing one's own body simply as a matrix of phenomena, rather than as a self. Then on the basis of the experiential insights gained in this way, one perceptually observes the body of another, experiencing that also as a matrix of phenomena. Finally, one alternates between observing both one's own and another's body, perceiving qualities that are unique to each one, as well as discerning common characteristics, which might include events that lead to the emergence and dissolution of body-events from moment to moment.

The most important common characteristic between one's own and others' bodies is that none of them either is or contains a self, or personal identity. They are simply phenomena, arising in dependence upon prior causes and conditions. In this way one begins to break down the reified sense of the locality of one's own presence as being solely within the confines of one's own body. As William James reminds us, phenomenologically speaking, '*For the moment, what we attend to is reality . . .*' (James, 1890/1950, p. 322). By habitually failing to attend either to one's own body

---

[5] For a discussion of observing the four subjects of mindfulness inwardly, outwardly and both inwardly and outwardly see Nyanaponika Thera (1973), pp. 58–60.

or those of others, the bodies that we disregard are eventually not counted as existents at all. As James comments, 'they are not even treated as appearances; they are treated as if they were mere waste, equivalent to nothing at all' (*ibid.*, pp. 290–1). Moreover, by attending internally, externally, and finally internally and externally in immediate succession, one balances out any biases of attention one may have as a result of one's own introverted or extraverted disposition. In addition, in this final phase of alternating the attention between self and others, one is in a position to observe relationships between self and others that may not be apparent as long as one is focused on one to the exclusion of others. As James cogently argues, very much in accordance with Buddhist principles, '*the relations that connect experiences must themselves be experienced relations, and any kind of relation experienced must be accounted as "real" as anything else in the system*' (James, 1912/1977, in McDermott, 1977, p. 195).

In the traditional practice of applying mindfulness to feelings, one observes the arising and dissolution of the three basic kinds of feelings of physical and mental pleasure, pain and indifference in oneself, others, and alternately between oneself and others. Other more complex affective states are left to the next practice, but special attention is given to pleasant and unpleasant feelings because these have such an enormous effect on the kinds of choices we make and the ways we conduct ourselves. According to Buddhism, for all sentient beings the most fundamental drive is to experience pleasure and joy and to avoid pain and suffering. Buddhist literature far more often makes references to 'all sentient beings', who share this common desire than it does to 'all human beings' alone. This is an indication that Buddhism is rightly characterized as more biocentric than anthropocentric.

While classical cognitive science has been 'cognocentric', in the sense of maintaining that humans are cognizers first and foremost, recent advances in affective neuroscience suggest that emotions are primary, and cognition has a secondary role as its organizing influence. According to Buddhism, neither cognition nor emotion is primary; rather, they are co-emergent, neither one capable of existing without the other. It is important to bear in mind, however, that the feeling of indifference, which some might regard as being an *absence* of feeling, is regarded in Buddhism as also being an affective state.

When observing the arising, presence and dissolution of feelings firsthand, one recognizes that they are not experienced by any means solely in the head, but rather in various regions throughout the body. Some do not appear to have any identifiable location at all. When it comes to empathetically attending to others' joys and sorrows, pleasures and pains, one can legitimately ask: Are such 'observations' of others' internal affective states strictly inferential? That is, are these observations really conceptual conclusions based upon perceived outward signs of affective states? Or might this type of empathetic awareness be more direct, more akin to perception? I am not aware that either Buddhism or modern science has reached a consensus regarding these questions, but I believe they are worthy of careful consideration.

In the cultivation of mindfulness of mental states, one follows the threefold sequence as above, while observing the mind as it is affected by different affective and cognitive states, such as craving, hatred, delusion, anxiety, elation, concentration and agitation. The aim of this practice is explicitly therapeutic in nature. Some affective and cognitive states are conducive to one's own and other's wellbeing, while others are harmful. By attending closely to the factors that give rise to a wide range of mental processes and by observing the effects they have on oneself and others, one begins to recognize through experience those processes that are conducive to one's own and others' wellbeing and those that are destructive. In this way one identifies the distinctions between wholesome and unwholesome mental states. In particular, like a physician diagnosing an illness, one pays special attention to what Buddhism calls 'mental afflictions', which can be identified by the criterion that they disrupt the balance and equilibrium of the mind. While some wholesome mental processes, such as compassion, may indeed disturb the calm of the mind, this disruption is not deep, and its long-term effects on one's mental states and behaviour are healthy. Other mental processes, however, such as resentment, have a deep and harmful impact on one's cognitive and affective health, as well as one's subsequent behaviour, so they are deemed mental afflictions.

As in the previous practices of attending mindfully to the body and feelings, in this phase of the practice one observes one's own and others' mental processes simply as impersonal phenomena, arising in dependence upon prior causes and conditions. In particular, one pays special attention to the duration of these mental states: how long does each one last, and for as long as it lasts does it exist as a stable entity persisting through time, or as a sequence of momentary events? When one observes a process in one's own mental continuum, is it affected by the sheer fact of being observed? Is it possible to observe one mental state with an awareness that is not itself in that same state? For example, is it possible to observe anger with an unangry mind? Does one observe an intentional mental process *while* it is occurring, or is such mindfulness always retrospective? It is important to bear in mind that the Pali term commonly translated as 'mindfulness' (*sati*) also has the connotation of 'recollection', implying that many, if not all, acts of mindfulness may actually be modes of short-term recall. The issue of observer-participancy is obviously crucial to the first-person examination of mental states, and it should by no means disqualify such introspective inquiry any more than the fact of observer-participancy has disqualified exploration in the field of quantum mechanics.

The fourth phase of this practice is the cultivation of mindfulness of mental objects, which include all non-intentional mental processes as well as all other kinds of phenomena that can be apprehended with the mind. Thus, this category is all-inclusive. At the same time, there is a special emphasis in this phase of practice on observing in oneself, others, and both oneself and others the contents of the mind affiliated with wholesome and unwholesome mental states, as well as the conditions leading to their emergence and dissolution. In addition, one mindfully observes all the phenomena of one's environment, from one's own perspective by means of direct perception and from the perspective of others by means of imagination. The over-arching theme of all these practices is the cultivation of a multi-perspectival view of oneself, others and the intersubjective relations between oneself and all other sentient beings. These techniques are explicitly designed to yield insights into these facets of the lived world, but they all have a strong bearing on the cultivation of compassion and other wholesome affective states, without which the cultivation of wisdom alone is said to be one more form of bondage.

The Four Immeasurables

Just as the qualities of cognizance and loving kindness are co-existent in the ground state of awareness known as the *bhavanga*, so too in the course of spiritual maturation must the light of insight and the warmth of a loving heart be cultivated together. In Buddhism the matrix of practices that traditionally complements the four applications of mindfulness is the cultivation of the four immeasurables, namely loving kindness, compassion, empathetic joy and equanimity.[6]

Each of these affective states can easily be conflated with other emotions that are fundamentally dissimilar. To help distinguish between the affective states to be cultivated and their counterfeits it may be helpful to draw on different types of relations as proposed by Martin Buber in his classic work *I and Thou* (Buber, 1937/1996). We can begin with what Buber calls an 'I–it' relationship, in which one engages with another sentient being simply as an object, to be manipulated in accordance with one's own desires. In such a relationship the other's existence as a subject, fundamentally like oneself, is ignored or minimalized. One views this person only in terms of how he or she (really 'it') may either be of aid in the pursuit of one's own goals, be an obstacle in that pursuit, or be irrelevant. On that basis this individual comes to be regarded as a friend, enemy or as someone of no consequence. In an 'I–it' relationship there is effectively only one subject, oneself, but in explicitly dehumanizing the other, one is implicitly dehumanizing oneself as well.

An 'I–you' relationship, on the other hand, is essentially dialogical in the sense of one subject truly engaging with the subjective reality of another person. While an 'I–it' relationship is fundamentally manipulative, an 'I–you' relationship is truly intersubjective and therefore based upon a sense of empathy. According to Buber, in the midst of an 'I–you' relationship, one may transcend the polarity of self and other and engage with a sphere of between-ness of self and other, in which both subjects access the 'eternal thou' that transcends individuality. This eternal thou cannot be accessed unless *both* subjects are involved in an I–you relationship. It is at heart a participatory experience that cannot be accessed on one's own.

While Western thought, inspired by the Judeo-Christian and Greco-Roman traditions, is largely anthropocentric when it comes to intersubjective relationships, Buddhism, as mentioned before, may be deemed biocentric, for its central emphasis is on *all* sentient beings, and not on human beings alone. The aim here is to cultivate loving kindness and the other wholesome affective states in this tetrad to a degree that transcends all boundaries and demarcations.

The first of the four states to be cultivated is loving kindness, which is understood as the heartfelt yearning for the wellbeing of others. Although it is very tempting to translate the corresponding Sanskrit term (*maitri*) simply as 'love', the reason this is not commonly done is that in English this term is often used in ways that conflate an 'I–you' relationship with an 'I–it' relationship. The loving kindness cultivated in Buddhist practice emphatically entails an 'I–you' relationship, for one is vividly aware of the other person's joys and sorrows, hopes and fears. But in English the word 'love' is also used in cases of sexual infatuation, personal attachment, and even strong attraction to inanimate objects and events, all of which involve 'I–it' relationships. In

[6] For a detailed explanation of all these practices see Wallace (1999b). One of the most authoritative traditional accounts of these practices is found in the fifth-century classic by Buddhaghosa (1979), I: IX.

Buddhism an entirely different term (*raga*) is generally used to denote such kinds of attraction, and it is variously translated as 'attachment', 'craving' or 'obsession'.

According to Buddhism, attachment is an attraction for an object on which one conceptually superimposes or exaggerates desirable qualities, while filtering out undesirable qualities. In cases of strong attachment, one transfers the very possibility of one's own happiness onto the object on which one's mind is bent, thereby disempowering oneself and empowering the object of one's fancy. Even when such attachment is directed toward another person, it entails more of an 'intrasubjective' than an intersubjective relationship, for one is engaging more poignantly with one's own conceptual superimpositions than with the other person as a genuine subject. When the reality of one's idealized object of attachment — with all his or her faults and limitations — breaks through one's fantasies, disillusionment may ensue. That in turn may lead to hostility and aversion, in which one now superimposes negative qualities upon the person whom one previously held dear. Thus, according to Buddhism, loving kindness does not readily turn into aversion, but attachment does. While loving kindness is a wholesome affective state that is conducive to one's own and others' wellbeing, attachment is a major source of anxiety, distress and interpersonal conflict. It is therefore very important not to conflate them, but in most close human relations, such as between parents and children, spouses and friends, they are normally mixed. In these complex human relationships the Buddhist ideal is to attenuate the mental affliction of attachment and cultivate the wholesome affective state of loving kindness.

In what may appear at first glance to be paradoxical, in traditional Buddhist practice one first cultivates loving kindness for oneself, then proceeds to extend this affectionate concern to others. The rationale for this is based on a fundamental premise expressed by the Buddha: 'Whoever loves himself will never harm another.' (*Udana*, 47). This strategy seems especially appropriate in the modern West, where feelings of self-contempt, low self-esteem, guilt, and a sense of being unworthy of happiness appear to have reached epidemic proportions.[7] In the meditative practice itself, one first attends to one's own longing for happiness and wish to be free of suffering, and one generates the loving wish: 'May I be free of animosity, affliction and anxiety, and live happily.' In a way, this practice, like the preceding practices of mindfulness, entails a kind of self-alterity, in the sense that one is objectifying oneself and yearning for the person whom one has brought to mind: 'May you be well and happy.' Thus, one has entered into an 'I–you' relationship with oneself!

In the next phase of this practice one brings to mind someone else whom one loves and respects. Recalling this person's acts of kindness and virtues, one brings forth the heartfelt wish: 'May this good person, like myself, be well and happy.' Continuing in this practice, one similarly brings to mind in sequence a dearly loved friend, then a person toward whom one has been indifferent, and finally a person for whom one has felt aversion. The aim of the practice is to gradually experience the same degree of loving kindness for the dear friend as for oneself, for the neutral person as for the dear friend, and finally for the enemy as for the neutral person. In this way, the artificial

---

[7] For a fascinating account of a cross-cultural dialogue with the Dalai Lama on this theme, see Goleman (1997), pp. 189–207.

'I–it' barriers demarcating friend, stranger and foe are broken down, and immeasurable, unconditional loving kindness may be experienced.

As stated previously, the counterfeit of loving kindness is attachment. According to Buddhism, the opposite of loving kindness is not indifference, but hatred. While indifference may be viewed as being turned 90 degrees away from loving kindness, hatred is turned 180 degrees away, for when the mind is dominated by hatred one actually feels *unhappy* at the prospect of another's wellbeing. The proximate cause of loving kindness is seeing loveable qualities within others, not merely their outer, surface attractions. One is successful in this practice when it causes animosity to subside, and one fails when the practice leads only to selfish affection, or attachment, for this implies that one is still stuck in an 'I–it' mentality.

The second of the four immeasurables is compassion, which is inextricably linked with loving kindness. With loving kindness one yearns that others may find genuine happiness and the causes of happiness, and with compassion one yearns that they may be free of suffering and its causes. These are really two sides of the same coin. While attachment is frequently confused with loving kindness (especially when they are both called by the same name — 'love'), righteous indignation for others can easily be confused with compassion. If one's 'compassion' extends only to the victims of the world, and not to the victimizers, this is likely to be one more case of attachment to the downtrodden, combined with aversion for the oppressors. In other words, one is still trapped in an 'I–it' mentality. The compassion cultivated in Buddhist practice is focused not only on those who are experiencing suffering and pain but on those who are sowing the seeds of further suffering and pain, namely those who harm others. According to Buddhism, all the evil perpetrated in the world stems from attachment, aversion, and the ignorance and delusion that underlie both. These destructive tendencies are regarded as mental afflictions, very much like physical afflictions, and those who are dominated by them are even more deserving of compassion than those afflicted with physical diseases. But to feel compassion for evil-doers is not to condone the evil they commit. It is to yearn that they be free of the impulses that compel them to behave in such harmful ways, and thereby to be free of the causes of suffering.

In the meditative practice of cultivating compassion, one attends first to someone who is wretched and miserable, wishing 'If only this person could be freed from such suffering!' As one progresses in this practice, one then sequentially focuses on an evil-doer (regardless of whether he or she seems happy at present), on a dear person, a neutral person, and finally on someone for whom one has felt aversion. The goal of the practice is like that for the cultivation of loving kindness, namely, to break down the barriers separating these different types of individuals until one's compassion extends equally to all beings.

The counterfeit of compassion is grief. In English, compassion is often verbally expressed with a comment such as 'I feel so sorry for that person', but according to Buddhism merely feeling sorry for someone does not necessarily entail compassion. When one empathetically attends to another person who is unhappy, one naturally experiences sadness oneself. But such a feeling may actually lead instead to righteous indignation and the vengeful wish to exact retribution on the one who has made the other person unhappy. On the other hand, in the cultivation of compassion, empathetic sadness or grief acts instead as fuel for the warmth of compassion. One does not simply remain in a state of sadness or despair, but rises from this with the wish: 'May you be free of this suffering and its causes!' One moves from the reality of the present suffering to the possibility of freedom from that suffering. Thus, empathetic sadness may act as a catalyst for compassion, but it is not compassion itself.

The opposite of compassion is not indifference, but cruelty. When this mental affliction dominates the mind, one does insidiously acknowledge the subjective reality of the other, and one consciously wishes for that person to experience misery. This is widely regarded as the greatest evil to which the mind can succumb. The proximate cause of compassion is seeing the helplessness in those overwhelmed by suffering and its causes. One succeeds in this practice when one's own proneness to cruelty subsides, and one fails when the practice produces only sorrow. It is important to emphasize that the Buddhist meditative cultivation of loving kindness and compassion was never intended as a *substitute* for active service to others. Rather, it is a *mental preparation* for such altruistic service that raises the likelihood of such outer behaviour being truly an expression of an inner, benevolent concern for others' wellbeing.

The cultivation of the final two immeasurables is virtually effortless if one has fared well in the cultivation of the first two. If one feels loving kindness and compassion for others, then when they experience joy the spontaneous response is empathetically to take delight in their happiness. But such empathetic joy can also be cultivated as a practice in its own right. In the Buddhist meditative technique, one focuses first on a very dear companion who is constantly of good cheer, then on a neutral person, and finally on a hostile person. In each case, one imaginatively enters into the joy of the other and experiences it as if it were one's own. On the other hand, one may take pleasure merely in the superficial appearances of others' wellbeing, which is the counterfeit of empathetic joy. The opposite of this wholesome affective state is envy, its proximate cause is the awareness of others' happiness and success, and one fails in this practice when it yields a merely frivolous state of mind.

Equanimity, the fourth of the immeasurables, actually suffuses the other three, as one breaks down the self-centred divisions that are superimposed on other people. With equanimity, one's loving and compassionate concern for others extends out evenly, with no bias toward friends or against enemies. Such equanimity is based upon empathy, recognizing that all sentient beings, like oneself, are equally worthy of happiness. This meditative practice begins by focusing on a neutral person, then a dear person, and finally a hostile person, in each case resting in a state of equanimity free of attachment and aversion. The counterfeit of the equanimity to be cultivated here is stupid indifference, with which one simply does not care about the wellbeing of others, whoever they are. The opposite of equanimity is attachment for one's loved ones and aversion for one's enemies, and its proximate cause is said to be taking responsibility for one's own conduct. One succeeds in this practice when one experiences equanimity that is a fertile, level ground for the growth of loving kindness and compassion; and one fails when it produces mere indifference.

In the Indo-Tibetan Buddhist tradition, the cultivation of loving kindness and compassion is combined in a classic practice known in Tibetan as *tonglen*, meaning 'giving and taking'.[8] Here the enactment of loving kindness is the 'giving' component of

---

[8] A more complete presentation of this practice can be found in Wallace (2001), which is a commentary on the eleventh-century *Seven-Point Mind-Training* inspired by the Indian scholar contemplative Atisha, which is a primary source for the practice of *tonglen*.

the practice of giving and taking, and the enactment of compassion is the 'taking' component. The taking component begins by bringing vividly to mind a loved one or a community of people or other sentient beings who is either suffering or sowing the seeds of suffering by means of harmful conduct. One begins by empathetically entering into the suffering and the sources of suffering of this person, then one generates the wish 'May you be relieved of this burden and may this adversity ripen upon me.' Whatever the affliction or adversity, physical or mental, one imagines taking it upon oneself in the form of a black cloud being removed from the other's body and mind and being drawn into one's heart. As one does so, one imagines that the other person is gradually relieved of this burden. As soon as this dark cloud enters one's heart, one imagines that it meets with one's own sense of self-centredness, visualized as an orb of darkness. In an instant both that cloud of misery and the darkness of one's self-centredness mutually extinguish each other, leaving not a trace of either behind.

In the 'giving' component of this practice, one imagines all the prosperity, happiness, and goodness in one's life as a powerful wellspring of brilliant white light emanating from one's heart in the reverse direction. One imagines these powerful rays of light reaching out and suffusing the person with the wish, 'All that is good in my life, my possessions, my happiness, my good health, my virtues, I offer to you. May you be well and happy.' As one does so, one imagines the light of this virtue and happiness suffusing the person who has been brought to mind, and one imagines his or her most meaningful desires and aspirations being fulfilled. Yet as this light from one's heart flows forth unimpededly, it is not depleted, for it is imagined as arising from an inexhaustible source.

As one becomes familiar with this meditative practice, one may expand the scope of one's awareness finally to include all sentient beings, taking in all suffering and mental afflictions and sending forth all one's virtue and goodness. This practice may then be conjoined with the breath: During each inhalation, one imagines taking in the burden of suffering and the sources of suffering, and with each exhalation one imagines rays of white light emerging from one's heart, bringing happiness and the causes of happiness to all the world.

The eighth-century Indian Buddhist saint Shantideva, on whose writings this practice is based, sums up the rationale behind this meditation: 'I should eliminate the suffering of others because it is suffering, just like my own suffering. I should take care of others because they are sentient beings, just as I am a sentient being.' (Shantideva, 1997, VIII: 94). This is a pure expression of an 'I–you' relation with all sentient beings. The 'I–thou' relationship as it is cultivated in Buddhist practice will be discussed in the next section.

Dream Yoga

The word 'buddha' means 'one who is awake', and the implication is that everyone who is not a buddha is asleep, most of us leading lives very much akin to a non-lucid dream. According to the Madhyamaka view, mentioned at the beginning of this essay, waking experience has a dream-like quality because of the disparity between the way things appear and the way they exist. All phenomena — oneself, others and everything else in the experienced environment — *appear* as if they bear their own inherent existence, independently of the conceptual frameworks within which they are apprehended. But in terms of the way they *exist*, all conditioned phenomena are dependent upon (1) the causes and conditions that gave rise to them, (2) their own parts and attributes, and (3) the conceptual designations by which they are demarcated from other phenomena and *bear* their own components and qualities. In short, oneself, other sentient beings, and all other phenomena appear to exist in-and-of-themselves, but nothing has such an independent existence. According to the Madhyamaka view, that very absence of an inherent identity of any phenomenon is called *emptiness*.[9]

The fourteenth-century, Tibetan Madhyamaka philosopher Tsongkhapa asserts in this regard: 'Although the objects of perception have forever utterly lacked a final self-nature or objective existence, nonetheless they indisputably appear with the nature of having real, inherent existence . . . These things function conventionally on the basis of the laws of interdependence and causality.' (Mullin, 1996, p. 174). According to this view, the objects of perception — colours, sounds, smells and so forth — do not exist in the objective world, independently of the sense modalities by which they are perceived. But, for example, do trees exist apart from our perception of them? The Madhyamaka answer is that trees and the many other objects in the natural world do indeed exist independently of our perceptions. Flowers continue to grow and bloom when no one is looking, and trees fall to the forest floor, sending out ripples in the atmosphere and over the ground, and then begin to decay, whether or not anyone is there to witness these events.

One may then ask: 'Do flowers, trees and other natural phenomena exist independently of any conceptual designations of them?' To this the answer is that the words 'flowers', 'trees' and so on have no meaning apart from their definitions which we have attributed to them. Thus, the question has no meaning. But we may then push this point and ask: 'Does *anything* exist independently of human language and thought?' This question implies that the word 'exist' is somehow self-defining, that it stands on its own, independent of any consensually accepted definition. But all terms such as *subject, object, existence, reference, meaning, reason, knowledge, observation* and *experience* have a multitude of different uses, and none has a single absolute meaning to which priority must be granted. Since these terms are not self-defining, we employ their definitions according to the conceptual schemes of our choice. That is, we choose our definitions; they are not determined by objective reality. So, once again, proponents of the Madhyamaka view conclude that the question is meaningless: if the word 'exist' has no meaning independently of all conceptual frameworks, then it makes no sense to ask whether anything exists independently of all conceptual frameworks.

For this reason the Madhyamaka view rejects metaphysical realism, which has been defined as the view that (1) the world consists of mind-independent objects, (2) there is exactly one true and complete description of the way the world is, and (3) truth involves some sort of correspondence between an independently existent world and a description of it.[10] In this regard, Nagarjuna, the second-century Indian philosopher who initially systematized the Madhyamaka philosophy, would concur with the

---

[9] The primary treatise expounding the Madhyamaka view is Nagarjuna's *Mulamadhyamakakarika*, translated by Garfield (1995).

[10] This definition is taken from Putnam (1990), p. 30.

statement by the twentieth-century physicist Werner Heisenberg: 'What we observe is not nature in itself but nature exposed to our method of questioning.' (Heisenberg, 1962, p. 58). Scientists question nature with the types of measuring devices created in collaboration with engineers. But the data collected by such a device arise in dependence upon both the objective phenomenon being studied and the measuring device itself. The data are thus produced as dependently related events, much as we hear sounds that are produced through the interaction of vibrations in some objective medium and our auditory faculties. But the *sounds we hear* do not exist independently in the objective world, nor do any of the other data collected by the instruments of technology.

Proponents of metaphysical realism might well grant this point but then counter that the conceptual world of physics exists, based upon objective magnitudes, and corresponds to the real, objective world, existing independently of language and thought. But to this point Einstein raises the concern, '. . . on principle, it is quite wrong to try founding a theory on observable magnitudes alone. In reality the very opposite happens. It is the theory which decides what we can observe.' (Cited in Heisenberg, 1971, p. 63). As scientists interpret the data gathered from their measuring devices, they must distinguish between significant data and 'noise'. The theory they are using plays an instrumental role in making such choices, just as it does in determining what types of measuring devices to create, and how to interpret the data gathered from them. What is finally 'observed' is deeply theory-laden.

Thus, not only do the perceptual objects detected with the senses or with the instruments of technology not exist independently of those modes of detection, they do not exist independently of the conceptual frameworks through which such measurements are filtered. Moreover, the theoretical entities conceived by physicists arise as related events arising in dependence upon both observational data and the conceptual faculties of the scientists who interpret and make sense of those data. This implies the intersubjective nature of both perceptual as well as conceptual experience, especially when we consider the consensual nature of conceptual frameworks.

While the Madhyamaka view finds certain similarities with the thought of some of the founders of quantum theory, among contemporary philosophies it is perhaps most akin to the pragmatic realism of Hilary Putnam. In a statement closely in accord with the writings of Nagarjuna, Putnam declares, 'elements of what we call "language" or "mind" *penetrate so deeply into what we call "reality" that the very project of representing ourselves as being "mappers" of something "language-independent" is fatally compromised from the very start*' (Putnam, 1990, p. 28). If there were no language users, there would not be anything true or anything with sense or reference. Thus the rich and ever-growing collection of truths about the world is the product of the experienced world intertwined with language-users, who play a creative role in producing our knowledge of the world.

According to the views of both Madhyamaka and pragmatic realism, once we have chosen a conceptual scheme there are facts to be discovered and not merely legislated by our language or concepts. Our conceptual scheme restricts the range of descriptions available to us, but it does not predetermine the answers to our questions. In accordance with the Madhyamaka view, Putnam writes, '. . . the stars are indeed independent of our minds in the sense of being causally independent; we did not make the stars ... The fact that there is no one metaphysically privileged description of the universe does not mean that the universe depends on our minds.'[11]

While the Madhyamaka view rejects the philosophical extreme of metaphysical realism, it equally rejects the cultural relativist or post-modernist view that no truth-claims can be made about anything independently of the culture in which they are imbedded. For example, the assertion that all phenomena are empty of inherent existence is regarded as a universal truth, not contingent upon the beliefs of any one person or society. The Madhyamaka view also rejects materialism as well as philosophical idealism as two more philosophical extremes, each one reifying the phenomenon of its choice — matter or mind — as being inherently real, independent of conceptual designation.

The Madhyamaka view provides the philosophical framework for the contemplative practice of dream yoga. In a non-lucid dream — that is, one in which there is no recognition that one is dreaming — all objective phenomena seem to exist in-and-of-themselves. They, like one's own persona in the dream, seem to be real. But upon waking, one recognizes that neither one's own mind in the dream, nor any person or situation encountered in the dream, had any such independent existence. This is equally true during the waking state and in the daytime practice of dream yoga, one maintains this awareness as constantly as possible. Everything one experiences throughout the day — contrary to appearances — arises in relation to one's own perceptions and conceptions. Every person one encounters is perceived and conceived in relation to one's own sensory and conceptual faculties. Never does one encounter the radically and absolutely 'other', for one's apprehension of the other is always dependent upon one's own subjective input. Thus, upon fathoming the emptiness of inherent existence of all waking phenomena, one maintains throughout the day a sense of the dream-like nature of all events, recognizing the profoundly intersubjective nature of all human relationships.[12]

As in modern techniques for inducing lucid dreaming, the daytime practice of dream yoga is complemented with night-time practices.[13] Although many specific techniques are taught, one practice common to the modern techniques and to dream yoga is to fall asleep with the strong resolution to apprehend the dream-state as such when one is actually dreaming. While it can be difficult to recognize the dream for what it is and difficult to maintain that awareness without either waking up immediately or fading back into a non-lucid dream, when success in this practice is achieved it often comes with a sense of great freedom and exhilaration. One now knows that one's own body and everything else in the dream is an expression of one's own psyche, and even though one has no sensory experience of one's body lying in bed, one knows it is there, outside the context of the dream. In a non-lucid dream one has a very definite sense of one's own locality in the dream: other people in the dream are apprehended as being really 'over there'. But in a lucid dream, one is aware that everyone in the dream is an individual expression of some facet of the dreamer's mind.

---

[11] Putnam (1991), p. 407. I have discussed this point at greater length in the chapter 'The World of Human Experience', in Wallace (2000).

[12] Traditional Tibetan Buddhist accounts of the practice of dream yoga can be found in Padmasambhava (1998), Part II, ch. 4, and Mullin (1996), pp. 172–84.

[13] For a clear, modern account of the theory and practice of lucid dreaming see LaBerge and Rheingold (1990).

To clarify this point: other people in my dream are not manifestations of my mind as one more character in the dream, but they, like myself in the dream, are manifestations of the dreamer, who is asleep *outside* the dream. The dreamed person's mind still seems to be local, but in a lucid dream one is aware that the dreamer's mind pervades all people , things and events in the dream. So the lucid dreamer is, so to speak, localized as the dreamed persona, but non-localized in the knowledge of oneself as being the dreamer. Another way of saying this is that as a dreamed persona one engages in *intersubjective* relations with others in the dream, but with the recognition of oneself as the dreamer one knows all these encounters with others to be *intrasubjective*. As a lucid dreamer, one is aware of both these perspectives, and in the awareness that transcends the duality of oneself and others in the dream, one enters into an 'I–thou' relationship with the other who is none other than oneself.

This insight into nonduality enables one to see the fallacy of viewing others in the dream as being independently worthy either of hatred or attachment. If someone else in the dream has done something reprehensible, the agent of that act is not really different from oneself and has no independent existence whatsoever. Likewise, if there is someone very attractive in the dream, out of habit one may still experience desire, but one knows that the object of one's craving is none other than a creation of one's own mind. To overcome that habitual craving, one must thoroughly familiarize oneself with the insight that the object of one's craving has no independent, objective existence.[14] When this insight penetrates one's waking experience as well, this opens up the possibility of cultivating an 'I–thou' relationship with others throughout the course of one's life.

Particularly in a lucid dream one has the sense of perceiving events in the 'private theatre' of one's mind, but Indo-Tibetan Buddhism nevertheless maintains that this theatre is pervious to external, spatially and temporally non-local influences. For example, this tradition accepts the possibility of precognition and remote viewing occurring in a dream, as well as during the waking state. Given the possibility of outside influences impinging upon one's dream, the dreamscape may be likened to an open-air theatre, in which one may perceive not only what is taking place on stage, but also hear crickets from the surrounding fields and jets flying overhead. Likewise, during the waking state, the field of one's mental perception — that domain in which one experiences mental imagery while awake and dreams while asleep — is equally open to outside influences. This raises the fascinating question as to the whereabouts of the borders of the mind and how porous those borders are, if any can be found.

In the practice of dream yoga there are further techniques to be applied after one has apprehended the dream-state for what it is, but for the present purposes I shall focus on the practice of cultivating lucid dreamless sleep. The eighth-century Indian Buddhist contemplative Padmasambhava writes of this practice, 'When you are fast asleep, if the vivid, indivisibly clear and empty light of deep sleep is recognized, the clear light is apprehended. One who remains without losing the experience of meditation all the time while asleep, without the advent of dreams or latent predispositions, is one who dwells in the nature of the clear light of sleep.' (Padmasambhava, 1998, p. 164). What he is describing here is the nature of awareness when it is perceived

---

[14] This same point is made regarding one's realization of emptiness during the waking state in Shantideva (1997), IX, 30–2.

nakedly, devoid of content and conceptual structuring. This is called the 'clear light' nature of awareness, about which Padmasambhava writes: 'The nature of the clear light, even after the stream of thoughts has ceased and you have gone asleep, is a clear and empty phenomenon of the dream-state, which is like the center of limpid space, remaining nakedly, without an object' (*Ibid.*, p. 168).

This description of the clear-light nature of the mind sounds remarkably similar to the earlier account of the *bhavanga*, a primordially pure state of awareness that is said to shine in its own radiance and which is obscured only due to external stimuli. While the cultivation of meditative quiescence alone may withdraw one's mind into this ground state of awareness, that does not ensure that one will actually *ascertain* the clear, empty, luminous nature of the mind. That is one of the goals of dream yoga, which is practised while sleeping, and it is also the goal of Dzogchen, or the 'Great Perfection', which is primarily practised while in the waking state.

Dzogchen

The theory and practice of Dzogchen is based upon and is perfectly compatible with the Madhyamaka view discussed earlier. Dzogchen is considered by many Tibetans as the pinnacle of Buddhist insight, and it challenges the view that the human mind exists as an entity independently of how we constitute it as an object of knowledge within a given conceptual framework. Cutting to the core of our very identity, Dzogchen practice probes into the deeply held assumption that there is such a thing as an inherently real, localized, ego-centred mind.

The classic strategy for investigating the ontological status of the mind according to this tradition is to examine firsthand the mode of origination, the location, and the mode of dissolution of mental events, including awareness itself.[15] A primary challenge in this practice is to distinguish, by means of close mindfulness, between what is perceptually given and what is conceptually superimposed upon perceptual experience when examining the nature of these mental events. For example, most cognitive scientists believe that all mental events originate from the brain, and indeed they are in the process of discovering an ever-growing range of correlates for specific mental and neural processes. But there is also growing evidence to suggest that not only are mental events conditioned by brain events, some brain events are conditioned by mental events. The existence of close mind/brain correlations is uncontested, even in traditional Buddhist accounts. What is open to question is the exact nature of those correlations.

In this mode of contemplative inquiry, one focuses entirely on the *phenomena* of mental events, attending closely to the precise manner in which they arise in the field of one's mental perception. This contemplative inquiry is guided by such questions as, 'Do they arise all at once or gradually? Can their place of origin be identified? What is the nature of that out of which these mental events arise?' In English, as in Sanskrit and Tibetan, it is often said that thoughts and emotions emerge from, or are produced by, the mind. One now seeks out the referent of 'the mind', from which mental events allegedly arise.

---

[15] Detailed, traditional presentations of this mode of investigation are found in the 'Insight' chapter in Padmasambhava (1998), and the 'Insight' chapter of the seventeenth-century classic by Karma Chagmé (1998).

In the second phase of this investigation one attends closely to the location of mental events. Once again one seeks to let *experience* answer this question, as opposed to one's preconceptions. For example, many neuroscientists claim that all mental events are located in the brain, and the basis for their assertion is, once again, the wide range of mind/brain correlates that they have ingeniously discovered. But the fact that two events, A and B, are temporally or causally correlated does not logically or empirically require that B is located in A, or that A is located in B. Thus, the close correlations between mental and neural events no more requires that the mental events are located in the neural events than it does that the neural events are located in the mental events. The temporal or causal correlation of the two certainly does not necessitate the conclusion that they are equivalent! Another recent scientific hypothesis is that mental processes are embodied in the sensorimotor activity of the organism and are embedded in the environment. In this contemplative practice one puts all such speculations to the experiential test by closely examining the location of mental events firsthand. This inquiry is led by questions such as, 'Are mental events located in the body? If so, in exactly which part of the body are they experienced as being present? If they are found to exist outside the body, where in the environment are they specifically located? Does the awareness of mental events have the same location as those objects of awareness?' Mental events are commonly said to exist 'in the mind', so in this practice one examines with great precision the nature of the perceptual space in which these events purportedly take place. It is worth noting that such contemplative inquiry is commonly practised while sitting motionless, so one's sensorimotor activity is held to a minimum. This has been found to facilitate attentional stability, but it certainly does not, by itself, decrease the amount of one's mental activity, which would be surprising if such activity were actually located in sensorimotor processes.

Finally, in this sequence of investigations, one examines how mental events disappear, whether gradually or suddenly, and one inspects that into which they disappear. Some Buddhist writings suggest that they disappear back into a subconscious realm of the mind, where they are stored as propensities, or latent impulses. In this practice one seeks to identify how and where mental events disappear into, once again seeking out the real referent of the word 'mind'.

The core of the Dzogchen practice of investigating the nature of the mind is stated succinctly by Padmasambhava, who took an instrumental role in introducing this practice in Tibet in the eighth century:

> While steadily maintaining the gaze, place the awareness unwaveringly, steadily, clearly, nakedly and fixedly without having anything on which to meditate in the sphere of space. When stability increases, examine the consciousness that is stable. Then gently release and relax. Again place it steadily and steadfastly observe the consciousness of that moment. What is the nature of that mind? Let it steadfastly observe itself. Is it something clear and steady or is it an emptiness that is nothing? Is there something there to recognize? Look again and report your experience to me! (Padmasambhava, 1998, p. 116).

By means of such inquiry, generations of Buddhist contemplatives have come to the conclusion that the mind and awareness itself are not intrinsically identifiable. When sought out as inherently existing things or events, they are not to be found. This is equally true of all other perceptual and conceptual objects of awareness. The mind, like all other phenomena, is discovered to be empty, but it is not a mere vacuity. Rather, it is luminous, cognizant and empty, like boundless space, with no centre or periphery, suffused with transparent light. Out of this luminous space of non-local awareness all phenomena arise in relation to the conceptual frameworks within which they are designated. But neither the objects of awareness nor awareness itself can be said to exist independently of their conceptual designations. Recognition of this fundamental nature of the world of experience yields a dream-like quality to life as a whole, in which all reified distinctions between subject and object, self and other, have vanished.

Once one has recognized the lack of inherent existence of the mind and all mental objects, one is ready to be introduced to the primordial nature of awareness that transcends all conceptual constructs, including the notions of existence and non-existence. This is the central theme of Dzogchen practice and is considered the deepest of all insights. Padmasambhava points out the fundamental nature of awareness as follows:

> To introduce this by pointing it out directly, past consciousness has disappeared without a trace. Moreover, future realization is unarisen, and in the freshness of its own present, unfabricated way of being, there is the ordinary consciousness of the present. When it peers into itself, with this observation there is a vividness in which nothing is seen. This awareness is direct, naked, vivid, unestablished, empty, limpid luminosity, unique, non-dual clarity and emptiness. It is not permanent, but unestablished. It is not nihilistic, but radiantly vivid. It is not one, but is manifoldly aware and clear. It is not manifold, but is indivisibly of one taste. It is none other than this very self-awareness. This is an authentic introduction to the primordial nature of being (Padmasambhava, 1998, p. 108).

In this intimate exchange between contemplative mentor and student, the mentor ideally speaks directly out of his or her immediate experience of pure awareness, and by receiving this introduction the student's own pure awareness is aroused and identified firsthand. Unlike conventional modes of cognition, here that which is apprehended and that which apprehends are identical. Such a mentor–student encounter is a paradigmatic 'I–thou' relationship, in which both realize a non-local reality that transcends the individuation of both subjects. But the realization of the primordial nature of awareness can also occur without engaging with another person. It does not arise from the interaction of two subjects, but rather transcends the distinctions among all subjects and objects.

In Dzogchen practice, close attention is paid to the spaces in which physical and mental phenomena appear to originate, abide and disappear. At the outset there seem to be two distinct kinds of space: external space, in which one experiences the environment, other people, and even one's own body, and internal space, in which one experiences one's own private mental processes, such as thoughts, emotions, mental imagery and dreams. According to Buddhist theory as a whole, all outer, public events and all inner, private events are equally 'natural', in the sense of arising in dependence upon prior causes and conditions. The notion that only matter and its properties are 'natural', while anything immaterial is 'unnatural' or 'supernatural' is utterly alien to the Buddhist understanding of the world. According to Buddhism, the natural world is filled with a myriad of phenomena, many of which are composed of atoms and their emergent properties, but also many of which are not. Contemporary examples of such immaterial phenomena would include not only consciousness and other mental events, but such phenomena as justice, information, numbers, geometrical forms, the mathematical laws of nature, space and time. Buddhism does not endorse materialism, but nor does it embrace Cartesian dualism. It is rather pluralistic, recognizing that the natural world is far too rich to be categorized as being of only one or two types of substance.

On investigating the nature of external and internal space by means of Dzogchen practice, one discovers that these two spaces are also empty of any inherent nature. They are fabricated by conceptual imputations, and the boundary between them is unreal. This realization enables one to identify what is called the 'mysterious space', which is the nonduality of external and internal space. A central aim of Dzogchen practice is to maintain one's recognition of this nondual space of pure awareness not only while in meditation but while actively engaging with the environment and other sentient beings. Dwelling in such a realization has been found to open up the reservoir of all-embracing, unconditional loving kindness and compassion that is innate to the true ground state of awareness. The distinction between wisdom and compassion has now vanished and there is no bondage anywhere in sight.

All the previous practices of meditative quiescence, the four applications of mindfulness, the four immeasurables and dream yoga are said to culminate in this one realization. Primordial awareness is the ground of all such practice. Its gradual realization is the essence of the entire sequence of practices, and its perfect actualization is the final fruition of the practice. The immensely rich world of diverse natural phenomena, all arising as dependently related events, is seen as the play of this non-local awareness, which is fully present in each individual. Thus, according to this contemplative tradition, to know oneself is to know others. To know oneself is to know the whole of reality as an expression of the nondual wisdom and compassion of the clear light of awareness.

References

Buber, Martin (1937/1996), *I and Thou*, trans. Walter Kaufmann (New York: Touchstone).

Buddhaghosa (1979), *The Path of Purification*, trans. Bhikkhu Ñanamoli (Kandy: Buddhist Publication Society).

Forman, Robert K.C. (ed. 1990), *The Problem of Pure Consciousness: Mysticism and Philosophy* (New York: Oxford University Press).

Garfield, Jay L. (trans. 1995), *The Fundamental Wisdom of the Middle Way: Nagarjuna's Mulamadhyamakakarika* (New York: Oxford University Press).

Goleman, Daniel (ed. 1997), *Healing Emotions: Conversations with the Dalai Lama on Mindfulness, Emotions, and Health* (Boston: Shambhala).

Harvey, Peter (1995), *The Selfless Mind: Personality, Consciousness and Nirvana in Early Buddhism* (Surrey: Curzon Press).

Heisenberg, Werner (1962), *Physics and Philosophy: The Revolution in Modern Science* (New York: Harper and Row).

Heisenberg, Werner (1971), *Physics and Beyond: Encounters and Conversations* (New York: Harper and Row).

James, William (1890/1950), *The Principles of Psychology* (New York: Dover Publications).

James, William (1912/1977), 'A world of pure experience', in John J. McDermott (1977).

Kalupahana, David J. (1987), *The Principles of Buddhist Psychology* (Albany, NY: State University of New York Press).

Karma Chagmé (1998), *A Spacious Path to Freedom: Practical Instructions on the Union of Mahamudra and Atiyoga*, comm. Gyatrul Rinpoche, trans. B. Alan Wallace (Ithaca: Snow Lion).

LaBerge, Stephen and Rheingold, Howard (1990), *Exploring the World of Lucid Dreaming* (New York: Ballantine).

McDermott, John J. (ed. 1977), *The Writings of William James: A Comprehensive Edition* (Chicago: University of Chicago Press).

Mullin, Glenn H. (trans. 1996), *Tsongkhapa's Six Yogas of Naropa* (Ithaca, NY: Snow Lion).

Nyanaponika Thera (1973), *The Heart of Buddhist Meditation* (New York: Samuel Weiser).
Padmasambhava (1998), *Natural Liberation: Padmasambhava's Teachings on the Six Bardos*, comm. Gyatrul Rinpoche, trans. B. Alan Wallace (Boston, MA: Wisdom).
Putnam, Hilary (1990), *Realism with a Human Face*, ed. James Conant (Cambridge, MA: Harvard University Press).
Putnam, Hilary (1991), 'Replies and comments', *Erkenntnis*, **34** (3).
Shantideva (1997), *A Guide to the Bodhisattva Way of Life*, trans. Vesna A. Wallace and B. Alan Wallace (Ithaca, NY: Snow Lion).
Vajirañana, Paravahera (1975), *Buddhist Meditation in Theory and Practice* (Kuala Lumpur, Malaysia: Buddhist Missionary Society).
Wallace, B. Alan (1998), *The Bridge of Quiescence: Experiencing Tibetan Buddhist Meditation* (Chicago, IL: Open Court).
Wallace, B. Alan (1999a), 'The Buddhist tradition of *Samatha*: methods for refining and examining consciousness', *Journal of Consciousness Studies*, **6** (2–3), pp. 175–87.
Wallace, B. Alan (1999b), *Boundless Heart: The Four Immeasurables* (Ithaca, NY: Snow Lion).
Wallace, B. Alan (2000), *The Taboo of Subjectivity: Toward a New Science of Consciousness* (New York: Oxford University Press).
Wallace, B. Alan (2001), *Buddhism with an Attitude: The Tibetan Seven-Point Mind-Training* (Ithaca, NY: Snow Lion).
Woods, James Haughton (1983), *The Yoga System of Patañjali* (Delhi: Motilal Banarsidass, reprint).

Annabella Pitkin

Scandalous Ethics

Infinite Presence with Suffering

I: Introduction

The ethical problem of how we respond to someone suffering is intimately related to the question of what our relation to other people in fact is. As Elaine Scarry (among others) has pointed out, suffering acts as a crucible for empathy and for intersubjective notions of the self (Scarry, 1985). The way we understand language as working, the way we investigate experience and analyse the sources of wisdom which guide us; all these are called to account when we confront another being's need for relief. For certain thinkers, responding ethically and understanding intersubjectivity correctly are actually part of a single human effort — the ultimate effort, as expressed in religious language, to find redemption, or liberation from suffering.

Certain religious statements[1] about suffering treat it as a kind of scandal within human existence — as something that cries out irresistibly for resolution. At the same time, these religious responses to suffering are themselves scandalous, as I shall explain; deliberately so.

Of course, scandal in its conventional sense is generally a negative thing. It may be crazy or wicked and is certainly always disruptive. It is not generally heralded as a moral force. (Indeed, to draw an example from a tradition I do not discuss here, when the Paul of the New Testament calls the crucified Jesus 'a stumbling block [*skandalon*] to the Jews and foolishness to the Greeks' [*I Corinthians* 1.23], he means among other things that the crucifixion and resurrection of Jesus is shocking, and shatters the ways people had previously understood reality.[2])

---

[1] I hope readers will allow me to group these responses as 'religious' despite the host of problems with that word. I distinguish religious language in this article in order to indicate language that communicates about issues of ultimate concern, including ultimate responses to suffering. (I suspect that the word 'philosophy' might act to domesticate the scandalous quality of the formulations I describe here.) I assume readers already understand the word 'religious' in a conventional way, and that such conventional understandings will be adequate for the purposes of this article. I am not offering to generalize from my use of the word 'religious' here to any other contexts.

[2] Indeed, from the Christian point of view, Paul's statement demonstrates how the scandal of the crucified and risen Christ would function by subverting precisely the accepted patterns of meaning in each community mentioned. Thus, his statement might be read as pointing to a 'religious' scandal for Jews and a 'philosophical' scandal for Greeks. (I am indebted to Anthony Freeman for this observation.)

Journal of Consciousness Studies, **8**, No. 5–7, 2001, pp. 231–46

I want to argue here that certain Buddhist and Jewish thinkers say scandalous things on purpose. More scandalously still, I suggest that these statements are infused with deeply transformative ethical power, intended specifically as a way of relating to the dreadful fact of suffering. As scandals, these special responses to suffering intentionally rupture normal semantic patterns and sequences of thought, often through statements or actions which appear paradoxical. These scandalous statements are, in fact, always communicative in function, structure, and intent, but they are designed to create a kind of 'cognitive dissonance'.[3] The thinkers I consider here say scandalous things in order to cause a breaking-open in the consciousness of the hearer and practitioner, which produces compassion, transformation, and liberation. Counterintuitively, this rupture highlights intersubjectivity and language.

In thus talking about scandal and about ethical responses to suffering, this essay brings into dialogue ideas from two very different source traditions (admittedly a project which is fraught with some methodological risks). I engage Mahayana Buddhist ideas (of the Prasangika-Madhyamika variety)[4] in conversation with the modern Jewish philosopher Emmanuel Levinas.[5]

On the face of it, these two frames of reference are incommensurable; unlikely to resonate together. The two appear to conflict directly on numerous points: Buddhism can be described as non-theistic, since Buddhists do not find the idea of a universal creator deity ultimately meaningful, whereas Jewish religious thought is by definition concerned with God and God's relation to human beings (although Levinas specifically may not understand the word God to mean the same thing as it does for his more traditional predecessors).

Mahayana Buddhist thought encourages practitioners to develop toward the goal of Buddhahood for themselves and others; Jewish thinkers, and Levinas in particular, are, as we will see, generally quite uncomfortable with any suggestion of union between human beings and God, and even with union as a category. Mahayana Buddhists, and Prasangikas in particular, emphatically reject the idea of an inherently existing fixed self in the human consciousness. Jewish thinkers like Levinas, on the other hand, employ categories such as judgement and mercy to describe the human relationship to God, all of which appear to presuppose some sort of self.

However, I want to suggest that within two these dissimilar frameworks, there are crucial elements which make it fruitful to consider them together. First, both

---

[3] I draw this idea from Robert Thurman's work on the Prasangika thinker Jey Tsong Khapa. See Thurman (1984).

[4] Prasangika-Madhyamika is a philosophical approach within Mahayana Buddhism which developed in India around the ideas of the great philosophers Nagarjuna (circa second century CE), and Aryadeva (circa third century CE) as interpreted by Buddhapalita (circa 470–550 CE) and Candrakirti (during the latter part of the sixth century CE). These ideas remain extremely influential in present-day Tibetan Buddhism, (especially in the Gelug-pa (Gelugs-pa) school, which may be best known in the West as the school of His Holiness the Dalai Lama). Tibetan Buddhist thinkers have analyzed these ideas in great detail, perhaps the most notable example being the extraordinary thinker Jey Tsong Kha-pa (1357–1419), founder of the Gelug-pa order. In this article, while I will periodically generalize about Prasangika philosophy as a whole, I will primarily draw on the formulations of Nagarjuna and Jey Tsong Khapa (as his name is generally written).

[5] Emmanuel Levinas (1906–1995) was, in fact, born in Kovno, Lithuania, though he became a French citizen and played an significant role in postwar French intellectual developments. The tension between his Jewish identity and his identity as a European philosopher, and his experiences while interned in a camp for French army officers during the Second World War provide important friction in his philosophical work, as I will note.

approaches give top priority to a particular quartet of problems with regard to human suffering, as I describe below.[6] This follows directly from the fact that, as noted, suffering is a topic of paramount importance for both the Prasangikas and for Levinas, and gives both ethical and intellectual urgency to analytical and exegetical projects. Second, both Prasangika thinkers and Levinas (like Jewish thinkers in general), give practices of interpretation a central role in addressing suffering. Finally, both frameworks respond to suffering as a scandal, in languages that are scandalous. Both deploy the shock of scandal in various ways in order to respond to suffering.

The 'quartet of problems' which both philosophies confront are four cognitive and moral pitfalls that seem to loom whenever human beings think about suffering. These four are all intimately related and all urgent for both Levinas and the Prasangikas.

The initial problem is the egocentric self. From this flow the intertwined philosophical and moral errors of absolutism, nihilism, and the desire to escape suffering — to run away and be somewhere else. All of these, unchecked, obstruct compassion and ethics, and lead to further suffering.

Levinas and Prasangika thinkers address their attention (and their most scandalous statements) directly at these problems. And yet, as one might suspect from the dramatic differences in their philosophical universes and languages noted already, the results are quite distinct.[7]

On the one hand, Prasangikas develop their ideas about compassion and liberation explicitly around a notion of the *non-duality* of self and others. At the level of ethical practice, this non-duality expresses itself in the idea that all beings fundamentally want the same things — to be truly happy, and free of suffering. This is extended in many practical techniques for cultivating love and compassion toward other beings, including, for example, the practice of considering all beings as one's beloved mother.[8]

For Prasangikas and Buddhists in general, suffering is rooted in the misknowledge that causes attachment to the egocentric self. It is precisely this misknowledge that their scandalous statements confront. As I will describe, it is the realization of non-duality which liberates the practitioner from the egocentric trap, with its attendant sufferings and unethical tendencies. For Prasangikas, liberation from the egocentric self, from all absolutisms, and from the desire to escape, lies in the wisdom of non-dual understanding, in which the pivotal scandal is the emptiness of phenomena.

On the other hand, Levinas is urgently concerned with the *alterity* of the other person. My infinite ethical responsibility for the other explicitly occurs in the context of recognizing the other's difference from me: 'The *for-the-other* responsive to the neighbour . . . is a responsibility that signifies — or commands — precisely the face in its alterity. . . .' (Levinas, 1987, p. 106). For Levinas, the fundamental ethical

[6] These problems are both philosophical challenges, and obstacles to ethical engagement. Indeed, arguably a crucial point of contact between Levinas and the Prasangikas is a refusal to separate 'philosophy' from ethical practice.

[7] I would like to thank all those who read and made suggestions about this essay, especially for urging me to expand my discussions of the differences between the two approaches.

[8] This great compassion (*maha karuna*) is described as rooted in equanimity, in that there is no element of grasping toward some beings, and rejecting others. This equanimity should not, however, be confused with indifference, as it sometimes is in Western translations. Indifference is a form of ignorance, and as one of the three root poisons (together with grasping and aversion), it must be overcome in the development of the limitless compassion needed for Mahayana Buddhahood. (I thank Geshe Lobsang Tsetan for clarifying this point.)

relationship is one of 'proximity'. Proximity is the opposite of any union that would collapse self and other into a totality, in which Levinas fears the other would be over-whelmed (destroyed, subjugated, assimilated by violence).

In ethical proximity, the other, precisely as 'stranger', is my neighbour.[9] The other is the one to whom I am infinitely obligated, or for whom I am infinitely responsible, but whom I never possess, and never assimilate into myself (Levinas, 1987, p. 94). For Levinas, preserving alterity with distance is crucial to the ethical relation. The alterity of the other (and the infinitude this evokes), offer a scandalous corrective to the reification of absolutes into totality and is the heart of ethical engagement.

There is thus a profound distinction in approach between Levinas and the Prasangikas. One might say that Levinas emphasizes difference as a hallmark of his ethics, while Prasangikas stress non-difference. To go even further, one could say that there is, in fact, something scandalous for Levinas about the Prasangika approach, and vice versa. They seem not simply different, but opposed to each other. Each approach could be caricatured using the terms of the other, as precisely that which should be rejected.

Perhaps, therefore, there is an underlying scandal in this very project of comparison. I hope to evoke a certain fruitful cognitive dissonance, by presenting together two analyses of suffering that not only employ scandalous elements internally, but that seem to collide together. Yet I suggest that a relationship-in-difference will emerge between the two when brought together, via the notion of scandal. In what follows, I will trace the scandal of emptiness and the scandal of alterity by describing how each system approaches the four pitfalls.

II: Egocentrism

The egocentric problem is posed by the grasping self, the self which, focussed upon itself, experiences lack, and which tries to satisfy itself by consuming something, lit-erally or figuratively. Both the Prasangikas and Levinas pose this as in some sense *the* fundamental issue facing consciousness, though with a crucial difference. Since the critique of the egocentric self is such a fundamental for both frameworks, let us look at it in some detail, as an entry point for mapping out key elements of each approach.

For Prasangikas, as for Buddhists in general, the egocentric problem stems from a fundamental misunderstanding. People (and non-enlightened beings in general) mis-takenly believe that the reality they experience through their senses, (i.e., the external world, the self which they understand themselves to have), all have some sort of 'in-trinsic' self-adhering and permanent identity, apart from the way they exist conven-tionally or are talked of in conventional language.[10] This view has the quality of being profoundly egocentric.

In misperceiving the 'self' as a permanent, absolutely real entity that exists inde-pendently of other phenomena —'from its own side', as it were — human conscious-ness is capable of vast attachment to this self. This attachment yields an enormous

---

[9] Levinas explicitly evokes the biblical formula of the 'stranger, widow, and orphan' for whom Jewish
      tradition insists the individual is responsible. He often plays with the tension between the alienness of
      the other-as-stranger — the I's resistance to alterity — and the other-as-neighbour; that is, as the one
      right in front of me, whose face commands inexorably.

[10] In Buddhist analysis, this basis of clinging is the fundamental 'wrong understanding' — ignorance, or
      misknowledge (*avidya*, in Sanskrit).

desire, either to consume or to utterly exclude all other phenomena, an attitude which is profoundly unethical (as expressed in the Kantian idea of instrumental relationships with others). This grasping attitude toward the misperceived self and toward others is, for Buddhists of all orientations, the true source of all suffering.

The misunderstanding of a supposed intrinsically, absolutely existing self as independent of all other phenomena causes beings to see all things as separate from each other and from the self. Because of this perceived separation, the reality of change and impermanence is experienced as agonizing. If self and phenomena are separate and private in this way, change seems unbearable; an absolute experience of loss. When people long for things they feel they don't have, or feel aversion to experiences they do have (two sides of the same coin), they are trying to assuage their distress by additional grasping. It is a sort of addiction: The human consciousness is addicted to clinging, and to the perception that there are selves and objects to which clinging is possible.[11]

For the Prasangikas in particular, this problem of the egocentric self — of the misknowledge that causes it, and the suffering to which it gives rise — links the 'philosophical' or 'cognitive' issue of understanding reality with the idea of compassion and of ethical responses to suffering. Misknowledge and the egocentric self do not simply offer an intellectual challenge — for example, a problem of epistemology, or an ontological problem (although many Buddhists, depending on orientation, have confronted this misknowledge with epistemological or ontological tools).

The misknowledge of the egocentric self is also understood as the profound basis, together with the desire from which it is inextricable, of the 'three poisons': the hatred, greed, and ignorance that are the source of all suffering in 'moral' or relational terms. By the same token, the crux of liberation from suffering lies precisely in curing the misknowledge of that egocentric self. In this cure lies the sweetness of relief from the addictions of desire, aversion, and fear of life's impermanent nature. At the same time, it turns out that the freeing of the egocentric self from its burden of ignorance liberates a limitless outpouring of compassion for others — the possibility of the ethical. As we will see below, such liberation from the egocentric position is accomplished by Prasangika thinkers (such as Nagarjuna) through understanding that the egocentric self is empty of the inherent existence it is mistakenly believed to have.

Levinas's presentation of the egocentric problem (my term, not his) is surprisingly complementary. Levinas does not employ a Nagarjunian kind of critique of the intrinsic existence of a self — that belongs to a different frame of reference. However, in a parallel kind of philosophical move, he devotes himself to refuting what he describes as the 'ontologically constructed' notion of the self.

In the context of what Levinas calls the 'ontological adventure' (Levinas, 1988, p. 84), the self's primary concern is with its own being, and it approaches all others from the perspective of making them the same as itself, or of using them to satisfy its needs — to digest them, as it were. This self is fundamentally non-ethical, even 'allergic' to ethics, since it at its base does violence to the other. As Levinas puts it, the problem is an unwillingness to 'leave the other in its otherness'; the desire to

---

[11] More accurately, the consciousness of unenlightened beings is addicted to clinging, and the misperception of self and others. For Buddhists, this category includes sentient beings in all six realms of existence, including animals and beings like ghosts and gods. Buddhist ethics extends to this entire range of consciousness. Interestingly, while Levinas primarily talks of the other *person*, he does consider ethics concerning animals. See Llewelyn (1991).

'include [the other] in the whole. . . . From this stems the inability to recognize the other person as other person, as outside all calculation, as neighbour . . . .' (Levinas, 1994, p. 35).

In contrast to this self-absorbed stance, Levinas is concerned to think Western philosophy 'otherwise': in terms of an ethically understood self which is ultimately responsible for the other person in the face-to-face encounter with them. The ethical, 'non-egocentric' self exists in the 'relationship with another' (a relationship that 'puts me into question, empties me of myself', toward an 'insatiable compassion'). (Levinas, 1963, p. 351)[12]

As a number of scholars have discussed (see, for example, Gibbs, 1992), Levinas develops these ideas around an opposition between his own 'radically transcendent' (Gibbs, 1992, p. 23) understanding of ethics and what he views as the privileging of ontology throughout the dominant paradigm of Western philosophy, inherited from the Greek. For Levinas, transcendence is 'the welcoming of the other by the same, of the Other by me', it is the 'ethics that accomplishes the critical essence of knowledge', and 'call[s] into question' the 'egoist spontaneity of the same'. (Levinas, 1969, p. 43) (It is also, as I will discuss in a moment, a locus of scandal.) Levinas's interest in transcendence, like his interest in infinity, is part of a consistent concern with what ruptures totality, and goes 'beyond being'. By contrast, ontology 'reduces the other to the same', and in so doing it closes off movement toward the Other and toward the infinite, in favour of an 'infinite regression': the same returning always to itself (Levinas, 1969).

Levinas maps these concerns onto the dual philosophical and linguistic categories of the 'Hebrew' and the 'Greek'.[13] In this mapping, the 'Hebrew' tradition maintains the insistence on the primacy of the ethical, and indeed offers the paradigm for it — the paradigm of the non-egocentric self, which is endlessly opened, called out of itself by its responsiveness and responsibility for the other. The 'Greek', by contrast, represents the ontologically oriented aspect of the European phenomenological tradition.

In Levinas' work, this is portrayed most vividly in the contrast between the Biblical story of Abraham, and the Greek narrative of Odysseus.[14] Abraham leaves home, at

---

[12] As John Wild says in his introduction to Levinas's *Totality and Infinity*, for Levinas, in 'the world as I originally experience it . . . [m]y primary experience is definitely biased and egocentric . . . I take precedence over the various objects I find around me, and . . . learn to manipulate . . . them to my advantage'. This 'primordial experience of enjoyment' and its capacity for violence toward the other is not addressed by Heideggerian ontology. The needs of the other are only recognized second to the ontological understanding of the self. Against this, Levinas offers 'the phenomenology of the other', wherein ethics — the moment where I heed the other's call — comes first. (Levinas, 1969, p. 13)

[13] As Gibbs has described, the Hebrew and Greek mutually correct each other (Gibbs, 1992). The Hebrew corrective to the Greek (probably more urgently articulated in Levinas's writings) supplies the crucial ethical understanding which egocentric ontology lacks. The Greek offers universal, abstract and political ideas, and allows the particularity of the ethical vision to encounter categories like justice, involving general principles. However, these universal-tending categories from the Greek remain troubling for Levinas. Approaching the universal from another route, Levinas also reads Talmudic statements as teaching a vision of universality, but a universality without abstraction (See Aronowicz's Introduction to Levinas (1994), also Gibbs's discussion of Levinas's project as 'translation').

[14] For example, Levinas, 1969, p. 271; See also Levinas, 1994, p. 34, on the 'temptation' in philosophy for the ego to return to itself.

God's command, never to return to that home, and never to arrive in the Promised Land. This is the Hebrew ethical: the orientation infinitely commanded by the Other, which yields up the egocentric position to embrace a homelessness of being-for-the-Other, and of being infinitely responsible for the other person. For Levinas, the face of another person, like God, is the transcendent which ruptures the totalised self with its command, orienting it infinitely toward a future it does not arrive at, and so can never grasp, reify, or consume.[15]

In the story of Odysseus, on the other hand, Levinas sees the egocentric self of a phenomenological paradigm which over-privileges ontology. Odysseus leaves his home to wander, but his wandering is cyclical. The closed circle of his wandering revolves around the self; metaphorically speaking, it returns him home, to himself. For Levinas, the story of Odysseus is one of motion that does not ever move outside the totality of its pre-given conclusion, and which thus assimilates all experiences and others encountered, causing them in a sense to disappear.

At its darkest extreme, the closed circle of the egocentric self, which Levinas discusses as 'totality'[16] can lead to the actually totalitarian — to the anti-ethical. Levinas's particular concern in the realm of the non-ethical, self-centred self is the assimilationist attitude which this ontologically understood self maintains towards the Other. The ontologically constituted idea of the self always tries to make the other a part of it, to make the Other into the same. This is fundamentally a move of violence against the Other, a move which aims to destroy the Other's Otherness.[17] It is the impulse to devour.[18]

III: Absolutism, Nihilism, and the Role of Language

Prasangika thinkers and Levinas thus offer distinct but mutually resonant analyses of the ethical and cognitive disasters that result from the egocentric self. Both insist instead on a radical rethinking of the nature of the self and its relation to others, directed toward some opening out toward the other — words like homelessness and giving oneself away come to mind.

---

[15] This command is often visual in Levinas' thinking (involving the sight of the other's face) as well as oral, (hearing God's command) as is usual in Judaism. In deploying these categories, Levinas reveals the influence of the German-Jewish thinkers Franz Rosenzweig and Hermann Cohen.

[16] Wild glosses totality as the attempt to 'gain an all-inclusive, panoramic view of all things, including the other, in a neutral impersonal light like the Hegelian *Geist* or the Heideggerian Being.... It puts itself forth as the only rational answer to anarchy. To be free is to be rational, and to be rational is to give oneself over to the total system that is developing in world history.... All otherness will be absorbed in this total system of harmony and order' (Levinas, 1969, p.15).

[17] See, for example, 'Metaphysics and Transcendence', *Ibid.*

[18] More than 'mere' philosophizing, the moral and personal stakes are real for Levinas. During the Second World War, Levinas was interned in a special camp for Jewish French officers (though his adopted French citizenship and officer status prevented his being sent to a concentration camp). While he survived the war, his Lithuanian relatives did not. Moreover, as someone who had played a key role in introducing Heidegger's ideas to French intellectuals, he was deeply affected by Heidegger's involvement in National Socialism, and by the failure of Heidegger's philosophical understanding to prevent this involvement. One has a sense reading Levinas that he demands why Heideggerian phenomenology failed during those years. Levinas hints that the Heideggerian approach lacked the ethical corrective of the Hebrew. Locked into ontology as first philosophy, it could not hear the command of the other.

In rethinking the egocentric self, Levinas and Prasangikas like Nagarjuna and Tsong Khapa also emphatically reject the twin philosophical errors that haunt the egocentric self: absolutism and nihilism. Prasangikas do this by showing the fallacies of the two extremes; in a sense 'dissolving' them with the notion of emptiness. Levinas for his part understands absolutism and nihilism as resulting from the over-reification of immanence or transcendence. He critiques both, disrupting understandings inherited from the 'Greek' via the explosive idea of alterity. He sometimes also employs a process of linguistic slippage — 'unsaying the said'— which plays with linguistic possibilities such that his own ideas resist reification.

In their rejection of absolutism and nihilism, both Levinas and the Prasangikas insist upon the adequacy and importance of language and communication. Both approaches forcefully refute, as mystifying and authoritarian, claims about the failure of language to confront issues of ethical ultimacy. Both Levinas and the Prasangikas also make use of scandalous language, which by its nature explodes or dissolves the extremes, but I argue that they do this with deeply communicative, rather than mystifying, intent.

Robert Thurman, in the context of explicating the Prasangika point of view, points out the direct relationship between an egocentric philosophical position and the absolutizing pitfall, using Wittgensteinian terms. 'The outlook of philosophical egocentrism is characterized by an avid grasp of the "given", a sort of "private object", self-evident and indubitable, the substance of all order . . . used to justify materialism, sceptical nihilism . . . or any other form of ancient or modern absolutism' (Thurman, 1984, p. 95).

As Thurman says, 'logical privacy' (which is the same thing as 'an absolutely private, not a conventionally private language' and thus is a privacy from which communication is not possible) is 'the inevitable absurd consequence forced upon the philosophical egocentrist, as he tries to give an account of his "absolute", "given", . . . that is the prime element constitutive . . . of his world' (Thurman, 1984). In the entombment of the egocentric self in this silent privacy, we see the Prasangika argument that grasping after absolutes leads to a breakdown of conventional language and communicability.

The absolutizing tendency of the egocentric position is a disaster for empathy, compassion, and ethics. In logical privacy, without the communicability that only conventional language can provide, the self is locked away from others. Belief in a private, intrinsically identifiable object is the building block of a philosophical approach which makes intersubjectivity impossible, giving rise to coldness, distance, or manipulation (see Loizzo, 1997).

The problem of nihilism is in a sense simply absolutism of another variety: it is the opposite extreme. To assert that nothing exists in the conventional sense is a dreadful pitfall for Prasangikas — it is the reification of the idea of emptiness, the idea that there is some absolute emptiness 'out there' that really exists.[19] As Nagarjuna says of this, 'Emptiness misperceived is like a snake incorrectly handled or a miscast spell' (Garfield, 1995, p. 68). This is especially serious for the Prasangikas, because when emptiness is understood correctly, it is precisely the scandal that liberates us from suffering and opens us to compassion. (I discuss this in more detail in the next section.)

---

[19] As Thurman points out, nihilism is a charge often levelled in error by a distressed egocentrist (Thurman, 1984, p. 95). This accusation has often been made against Prasangikas.

For Levinas, as noted, the absolutizing position appears as the assimilation of the other into the same in a totalising union. Such assimilation occurs in 'knowing onto-logically'. To know in this sense 'amounts to grasping being, . . . removing from it its alterity' (Levinas, 1969, p. 44). Removal of alterity collapses the distance between the self and other: 'It is not a relation with the other as such but the reduction of the other to the same' (Levinas, 1969, p. 46). Levinas at one point refers to this as 'a philosophy of immanence in which we would truly come into possession of being when every "other" [cause for war], encompassed by the same, would vanish at the end of history'.[20]

On the other hand, for Levinas the reverse is not preferable. For him, what I have called the nihilist extreme corresponds to the over-reification of the other's transcen-dence (such that same and other still collapse, albeit in the opposite direction). Levinas says of this 'philosophy of transcendence' that it 'situates elsewhere the true life to which man, escaping from here, would gain access in the privileged moments of liturgical, mystical elevation, or in dying'.[21] Therefore, although Levinas is some-times read as developing a philosophy of transcendence, he nevertheless resists the possibility of reifying this extreme. One might say that Levinas is interested in theo-rizing 'beyond the possible', and about the 'height' of the other,[22] but that he is not interested in simply getting beyond the possible and staying there, or in 'getting high' in the intoxicated sense of the term. Transcendence and height are *relations* for Levinas, always involving tension between proximity and otherness. They are not to be made into totalities.

In locating totality or absolutism in both the reified immanent and transcendent, Levinas shows from a different perspective how language can stop working as com-munication. When the other's alterity is eliminated, there is no space in which to speak, or to relate. Discourse, by contrast, requires profound attentiveness to the other person (Levinas repeatedly speaks of being commanded by the other person's face and eyes). Yet discourse also requires the respectful separation that is the antithesis of devouring. It requires proximity.

Levinas thus counters the two silenced and totalised extremes with his model of relationship which preserves difference; a relationship 'that does not result in a divine or human totality, that is not a totalisation of history but the idea of infinity' (Levinas, 1969, p. 52). Infinity here is the ethical relationship of conversation with an Other whom we do not assimilate. Levinas movingly discusses what it means to approach the Other 'in conversation', with 'generosity, incapable of approaching the Other with empty hands'. He calls this conversation 'a non-allergic relation, an ethical rela-tion' (Levinas, 1969, pp. 50–51).

In the moment of conversation, the other's face 'breaks through' into the self; 'I' am, as said above, called out of myself; commanded by the other, I overflow the

---

[20] *Ibid*, p. 52. Here, the Hegelian echoes have an almost National Socialist quality to them.

[21] *Ibid*, p. 52. Levinas' critical use of the term 'mystical' is provocative here. Like Rosenzweig, Levinas refers to 'mysticism' in negative terms. Levinas understands mysticism as over-reification of transcen-dence; the situating 'elsewhere' of the true life of human beings (precisely the sort of 'bad' escape con-sidered in the next section).

[22] 'Height' for Levinas structures the ethical relation. The face of the other commands me; I am infinitely responsible for the other's need, but the other does not beseech from below. The other is my master, and commands me from a height. (Note the structural parallel between this notion of height and bibli-cal ideas about God's elevation.)

bounds of my being: 'To hear a voice speaking to you is *ipso facto* to accept obligation toward the one speaking. . . . Consciousness is the urgency of a destination leading to the other person, and not an eternal return to self.'[23]

Of course, the idea that we are commanded in an infinite way by the face of the
other, to 'leave home' toward an infinity we cannot grasp — this is a deeply scandalous notion. Perhaps unsurprisingly, the most scandalous statements of this occur in
the midst of Levinas's overtly Jewish Talmudic writings — correcting by their explo-
siveness, as it were, the absolutizing tendency of 'Greek' ontology.

IV: The Desire to Escape

The desire to escape is the most subtle barrier to ethics. In Buddhist terms, beings erro-
neously believe it is possible to avoid change and therefore pain — beings 'think there
is somewhere to go' where they can keep their private personal selves from suffering.
Even at moments where human beings act to address suffering, there is a subtle impulse
to slip away from its difficulty, from the blow suffering deals to the illusion of permanent selves. This impulse to get away can manifest in many ways — in the desire for
gratitude, or the desire to control outcomes; in a tendency to reify a helper role or a vic-
tim role. People simply do not like to pay attention to what is actually going on moment
by moment if it is uncomfortable. Because of this, arguably the first layer of scandal in
talking about suffering is the mere fact of forcing it upon the attention at all.

Levinas bluntly acknowledges the desire to escape, noting as well that the vision of
human freedom and responsibility which he offers is difficult (this even forms the title
of one of his books, *Difficile Liberté*). In Levinasian terms, this desire for escape is a
desire to mitigate the shocking otherness — the scandal — of the encounter with suffering, to assimilate the experience and make it one with the self in some way (something
we have already seen him critique as totality). This is, of course, an act of violence
toward the sufferer, the exact reverse of what is required. Levinas, in keeping with the
Jewish tradition on which he draws, insists instead on a sort of ethical hermeneutics —
a special sort of attentiveness to the other.

For Prasangikas, the confrontation with this desire to flee is, in fact, the rejection of
absolutism and nihilism. In emotional terms, there is no place to go; there is no reified
separate Nirvana of blissfulness which does not relate to samsara. Liberation, in fact,
lies in a different understanding of the relation between the absolute level of liberation and its relation to the conventional samsaric realm. That is to say, for the
Prasangikas as for Levinas, correct hermeneutic practice is inextricable from developing an ethical relationship to suffering.[24]

The desire to escape from suffering, intimately entwined with both the egocentric
self and the temptation to absolutism and nihilism, is the ultimate target of scandalous

---

[23] Levinas, 1994, p. 48. Levinas builds on Rosenzweig in this idea of relation in difference — what
Rosenzweig calls 'correlation'.

[24] Prasangikas (and Mahayanists in general) confront a logical problem in discussing enlightenment
related to this: From the non-enlightened point of view, I suffer in samsara, and aspire to nirvana. And
indeed, from the point of view of a Buddha's Form Body (the *Rupakaya*), a Buddha emenates infinitely
to liberate beings. Yet at the level of the Buddha's Body of Truth (the *Dharmakaya*), there is in a sense
no samsara, nor was there ever any. There is nothing excluded from the reality of enlightenment.
Mahayanists must, therefore, strive to avoid reifying one side or the other.

statements, both by the Prasangikas and by Levinas. In each case, the pivotal scandalous rupture applies in the context of a hermeneutical practice of self (and world) transformation.

No escape: The Prasangika scandal

Because the source of suffering is a fundamental misapprehension of reality, it makes sense for Prasangikas to talk about solving the problem of suffering via interpretation of reality. This involves developing a hermeneutic that is explicitly valid for interpreting texts and teachings as well. Parallelling Levinas, this hermeneutic provides a way of relating to what is scandalous without domesticating the paradoxical truth into one of the tidy extremes of absolutism or nihilism.

The Prasangika hermeneutic revolves around the notion that there are Two Truths. Nagarjuna says: 'The Buddha's teaching of the Dharma / Is based on two truths:/ A truth of worldly convention / And an ultimate truth' (Garfield, 1995, p. 68). The purpose of this distinction is clear understanding, not complication, since ultimately this hermeneutic is aimed at liberation from suffering. 'Without a foundation in the conventional truth / The significance of the ultimate cannot be taught. / Without understanding the significance of the ultimate, / Liberation is not achieved.' (Garfield, 1995, p. 68)

The Prasangika interpretation of the Two Truths of the absolute and relative, as noted, means that there is actually nothing to reify. A correct understanding of the Two Truths eliminates both absolutist and nihilist errors, and dissolves the egocentric position. Even more than that, correct understanding develops one's willingness to relate with the hugeness of samsaric suffering, without running away from it. How this works in language is intimately tied to the Prasangika statements which seem most scandalous — the statements concerning emptiness.

Nagarjuna's *Mulamadhyamika-karika* is the path-breaking text on emptiness *par excellence*. Unsurprisingly, it is full of scandalous statements. These statements, in fact, make utterly lucid sense when approached via the Two Truths hermeneutic above, but they are deliberately framed to shock away the traces of clinging to one or the other of the absolutist positions.

For example, Nagarjuna's most famous line: 'There is not the slightest difference between cyclic existence (samsara) and Nirvana. / There is not the slightest difference between Nirvana and cyclic existence (samsara)' (Garfield, 1995, p. 75) has the shock value of a thunderclap within the tradition. So also does Nagarjuna's statement that 'No Dharma was taught by the Buddha / At any time, in any place, to any person' (Garfield, 1995, p. 76). Yet both these statements make perfect sense, indeed are inescapably true, once one absorbs Nagarjuna's point that since all phenomena are dependently originated, all are empty of inherent existence.

Both of the scandalous statements just cited are easily misunderstood from the absolutist or nihilist position. Indeed, perhaps it is helpful to acknowledge again here the conventional meaning of 'scandal' with its negative connotation of 'shockingly outrageous' and 'terrible'. If the above two scandalous statements are misunderstood, they appear crazy, or even wickedly nihilist (and so they have at times been perceived). This points to the very serious philosophical and psychological dangers involved in talking about emptiness, in the event that one misunderstands. These are dangers which inhere in scandalous language in general. As Nagarjuna says himself, (as quoted above) 'By a misperception of emptiness / A person of little intelligence is destroyed. / Like a snake incorrectly seized/ Or like a spell incorrectly cast' (Garfield, 1995, p. 68).

Just as there is a risk of mystifying emptiness, of claiming that language fails in the face of true realization, there is the risk of mystifying the notion of scandal as well. Then we would be left with a language- and reason-destroying fantasy of a philosophy whose unintelligible statements reveal its 'depth'.

It is, therefore, important to be clear about what it means to use scandal as a way to describe Prasangika language. Prasangikas, like Nagarjuna in the Prasangika reading of him, make 'scandalous' statements to shatter the misconceptions and complacency of the egocentric position in its nihilist and absolutist forms. Scandal is not a tool of mystification here; it is not designed to close off language with mystified authority (the 'I understand, but what I say is too deep for you to follow, so you must do as I say' approach). Rather, these apparent paradoxes make lucid and logical sense — yet in order to see that, the conversation must shift to a new level.

It is, in fact, crucial for Nagarjuna to make the two scandalous statements cited above. If he did not insist, radically, that samsara and Nirvana, because of emptiness, are not different from each other, it would be possible to reify them as separate from each other, as self-existing entities, one at each extreme. It is only in understanding these categories as empty of such inherent existence that we become free, and free specifically to experience our liberation.

Moreover, Nagarjuna explicitly connects the understanding of emptiness with compassion and the end of suffering: 'If suffering had an essence,/ Its cessation would not exist. . . . If the path had an essence, / Cultivation would not be appropriate. . . . If it (the world) were not empty, / Then action would be without profit. The act of ending suffering and / abandoning misery and defilement would not exist' (Garfield, 1995, p. 72). That is, the emptiness of phenomena is precisely their capacity to change — emptiness makes the space for liberation.

In Mahayana Buddhism, practitioners carry the mental model of the bodhisattva, who vows to remain in samsaric existence until every single other sentient being that exists is completely liberated from all suffering. This radical vow is the ultimate expression of the rejection of escape. Precisely in the great commitment to be always in the middle of suffering of every kind (so as to alleviate it) lies the bodhisattva's extraordinary capacity for ultimate liberation, and, in fact, Buddhahood.[25] Mahayana Buddhists insist that with this orientation, Buddhahood is an attainable goal; without the compassion to remain with all suffering beings infinitely, such attainment is impossible.

I suspect that even the vastness of this goal functions as a liberating sort of scandal: since the goal of liberating all sentient beings is infinite, and the resources are also infinite (since the capabilities of a Buddha are infinite), success is both truly possible, and utterly divorced from the egocentric idea of the self. In the face of an infinite task, with an infinite possibility for success, there is no room for clinging to results. This ensures the purity of the response to the suffering beings.

---

[25] Probably the best loved statements about this are from Shantideva's *A Guide to the Bodhisattva's Way of Life* (*Bodhisattvacharyavatara*). For example, 'May I be a protector for those without one. . . . And until they pass away from pain / May I also be the source of life / For all the realms of varied beings that reach into the realms of space'(Batchelor, 1993, p. 25).

The Heart Sutra[26] insists that there is no old age and death and no end to old age and death; no attainment and nothing to attain. There is no escape from the suffering of samsara, no place of absolute and reified Nirvana to get away to or its opposite. And yet, the sutra simultaneously reveals that this is no problem: precisely there, in the no-escape, is liberation.

> In emptiness there [is] . . . no ignorance or elimination of ignorance, and so forth up to no old age and death, or elimination of old age and death; there are [none of the Four Noble Truths]: no suffering, origination of suffering, cessation of suffering, or path to the cessation of suffering; there is no knowledge, no attainment, no non-attainment . . . because of non-attainment, a bodhisattva relies on the Perfection of Wisdom and stays free of mental hindrances. And because of this freedom from mental hindrances he is unafraid. . . . [27]

Again we see the scandal of emptiness. The Four Noble Truths, the heart of the Buddha's teaching, are said not to exist 'in emptiness'. The ignorance with which Buddhist analysis begins does not exist, and neither does its cessation, and so forth, up to the ambiguous promise that neither the final, inescapable sufferings of old age and death exist, nor does their cessation. Not even the Buddhist path itself exists. There is nowhere to get to. And precisely in knowing this emptiness, in this 'non-attainment', is the liberation. Knowledge of emptiness is the reliance upon Transcendent Wisdom (who is both a concept, and the Goddess *Prajna-Paramita*, the recipient of devotion as the Womb of the Buddhas). This reliance, this correct understanding of emptiness, is the freedom that releases from fear.

The message is that liberation is not elsewhere. This is a teaching about what the contemporary Tibetan nun Pema Chodron (1991) calls 'the wisdom of no escape'. Realization of this makes possible the extraordinary ethical stance of the bodhisattva vow.[28]

No escape: Levinas' scandal

On the other hand, the central scandal toward which Levinas directs us in his Talmudic writings is, as noted, precisely the alterity of God and other people. God's shocking, commanding, infinite alterity is the meaning of holiness in the Jewish context. According to Annette Aronowicz, 'The term "God", Levinas reminds us, is always referred to in the Talmud as The Holy One, Blessed be He: Holiness in rabbinic thought evokes most of all separation. . . . This term therefore names . . . a mode of being or a beyond being rather than an essence' (Levinas, 1994, p. xxvi, Aronowicz's Translator's Introduction).

---

[26] The Heart Sutra is a distillation of the vast *Prajna-Paramita* — 'Transcendent Wisdom'— sutras (which Nagarjuna is traditionally credited with bringing to practitioners). It is widely beloved and recited throughout Mahayana Buddhist communities.

[27] Edward Conze, Trans. *Thirty Years of Buddhist Studies* (London: Bruno Cassirer, 1967) pp. 148–67, cited in Strong (1995) pp. 141–2.

[28] The bodhisattva ideal resonates with Levinas's vision of infinite responsibility, and prophetic Judaism's emphasis on relating ethically with other people. (For example, Micah 6.8, on 'doing justice and loving mercy'.) On the other hand, Buddhists often emphasize a reclusive life; Shantideva himself does so in his eighth chapter. There are parallels for this in Jewish tradition, like Isaiah 33.15, which talks of the righteous person 'shutt[ing] his eyes from looking upon evil'. Perhaps in both Judaism and Buddhism, there is a tension between ethical engagement and self perfection, which Levinas might find troubling. (I thank Lewis Warshauer for the biblical citations, and an anonymous reviewer for highlighting Shantideva's eighth chapter.)

God in God's Otherness breaks in upon the I and ruptures the totality of the self. Levinas describes the Holy Scriptures as doing the same thing, as signifying precisely through their rupturing effects: '[The Holy Scriptures] command all the gravity of the ruptures where in our being the good conscience of its being-there is put into question. Therein resides their very holiness. . . . ' (Levinas, 1985, p. 117).

This rupturing is scandalous, in the level of shock it delivers to the ontologically constituted self. Yet the rupture of God's Otherness and the otherness of the holy texts delivers the ultimate ethical charge, intimately related to acknowledging other beings. Levinas says that 'The Holy Scriptures do not signify through the dogmatic tale of their supernatural or sacred origin, but through the expression of the face of the other man, before he gives himself . . . a pose'.[29]

The scandalous quality of God's Otherness and the otherness of the scriptures is deeply disruptive to the self (rendering it 'homeless', as with Abraham), and yet is deeply ethical. God in God's Otherness cannot be appropriated into a theodicy which justifies suffering (that would be a different sort of scandal, of a deeply non-liberating kind), but always commands with the ultimate ethical call, in the same way that we are commanded by the sight of another person's face.

Poignantly, Levinas describes God by saying 'God is perhaps nothing but [the] permanent refusal of a history which would come to terms with our private tears' (Levinas, 1994, p. 20). This is not a functionalist reduction of religious categories to moral rules — such reduction would be an act of interpretive violence, an abrogation of the holy otherness of the religious texts, which Levinas's Talmudic hermeneutic abjures. On the contrary, Levinas insists that 'The ethical is not merely the corollary of the religious but is, in itself, the element in which religious transcendence receives its original sense' (Levinas, 1982, p. 146).

Just as the Otherness of God and of other people cannot be overcome without profound ethical violation, so, too, the hermeneutical practice of interpreting the holy texts must never impose an order or sameness upon them. Hermeneutics itself must always be ethical; it must never be a totalising project.

Therefore, hermeneutics, like being commanded by God or interacting with other people, is not entirely comfortable. Since Levinas's hermeneutic models the ethical relationship (Levinas, 1994, p. xv of Aronowicz's Introduction), its practice cannot make the disturbing or disruptive elements in the text go away. Instead, Levinas's ethical hermeneutic must engage with the hard and painful parts of the text, even at cost to the interpreter, with the same exigency that one would engage a suffering or difficult person.[30]

In the most direct sense, the Talmudic approach, by its very difficulty and struggle with the text, is the counter to all totalising ideology. Levinas says,

---

[29] *Ibid*, p. 117. This resonance between God's command, and the command issued by the face of the other person is a scandal from the Jewish point of view, in light of the Jewish prohibition on imaging God or anthropomorphizing God. Here, Levinas again echoes Rosenzweig.

[30] Unfortunately, Levinas is unwilling to act on this intention regarding gender. Levinas uses the 'feminine' as the category of alterity *par excellence*, analysing responsibility and infinity via the tropes of (heterosexual) eros and fecundity. He attempts to think sexual difference 'otherwise', but ultimately reinscribes many categories of the feminine that he sets out to undo. An ethical hermeneutic must thus grapple with painful parts of Levinas's own text. Important treatments of this topic include De Beauvoir (1989), Shapiro (2000), Irigaray (1991).

The great power of Talmudic casuistry is to be the special discipline which seeks in the particular the precise moment in which the general principle runs the risk of becoming its own opposite, which watches over the general from the basis of the particular. This preserves us from ideology. Ideology is the generosity and clarity of a principle which did not take into account the inversion stalking this generous principle when it is applied. . . . The Talmud is the struggle with the Angel (Levinas, 1982, pp. 98–9).

In practising this hermeneutic, Levinas attempts to model the rejection of the desire to escape from suffering. (This approach to hermeneutics is, in fact, a deeply Jewish one.) Only by remaining with what is disruptive can we be in a relationship that does not overwhelm our precious separation from the other. Only by allowing ourselves to be disturbed, made homeless, can we acknowledge the alterity that makes communication possible.

Conclusion

Reification of inherent identity functions for Nagarjuna to close off change, liberation, and conventional language — very much as the idea of totality does for Levinas. Nagarjuna's presentation of emptiness, like Levinas's insistence upon maintaining the space of alterity, appears scandalous and paradoxical. Yet, in each case it turns out that beings can only hope to have relationships, or respond to suffering, by tolerating the 'cognitive dissonance' of a scandal which resists absolutism.

While involving radically different categories, Nagarjuna's deployment of emptiness thus potentially speaks to Levinas's concerns about totality. If the Prasangika notion of non-duality is understood on its own terms, it is a powerful solvent of all absolutisms — of the very desire to reify categories. Prasangikas address concerns about reification which occupy Levinas as well. Levinas' emphasis on infinite obligation to the other seems potentially resonant at a profound level with the Bodhisvata Vow

On the other hand, Levinas might interpret Prasangika ideas as a form of quietistic nihilism. Thus (mis)understood, Prasangikas would appear to earn Levinas's condemnation on the grounds of over-reifying transcendence. Additionally, Levinas would be uncomfortable with Prasangika statements about the sameness of beings, *qua* their emptiness. He might also resist the idea, found in some Mahayana contexts, that all beings share in the same Buddha nature (*tathagata-garbha*). For Levinas, ethics involves facing the uniqueness of each being. He is deeply wary of abrogating that uniqueness, as he is of notions of union.

Prasangikas, by contrast, might see alterity as the reification of an (illusory) intrinsically existing other, produced by misknowledge and dangerously linked to an egocentric position. Levinas's emphasis on distance and separation could then look like a reinscription of that error. Moreover, the Jewish emphasis on holiness as radically other appears to be dramatically incommensurable with Nagaruna's 'samsara is not separate from nirvana' statement.

Levinas and the Prasangika thinkers thus do not say the same things. Ultimately, they do not describe liberation in the same language. To blur the distinctions between them would be an act of violence — a totalising interpretation! Yet they complement each other in important ways, and placing them alongside one another yields crucial philosophical tools for understanding suffering.

The point of engagement between the two lies in the parallel (though nearly opposite) structure of their scandalous statements. Both emptiness and alterity rupture escapist absolutisms. Perhaps one could say that the scandal of alterity *explodes* absolutism, where absolutism is viewed as totality. Emptiness, on the other hand, acts as a *solvent*, dissolving grasping and grasper (i.e, absolutism-as-reification). In a sense, both scandals lead to a 'middle way' of relational opportunity, which ultimately reifies neither immanence nor transcendence.

In so doing, the scandal of alterity and the scandal of emptiness accomplish similar philosophical work. Both cut away complacency and force us to confront a contradiction to the self-absorbed self. Both block our ability to slip away from confrontation with what is hardest. Most of all, each kind of scandal refuses to look away, ever, from the suffering of living beings.

'Sentient beings are numberless, I vow to save them', says the Bodhisattva Vow. 'My neighbour, my master', says Levinas. Either way, there is the transformative and liberating opportunity for the 'I' to offer itself to your need, infinitely.

References

Batchelor, S. (1993), *A Guide to the Bodhisattva's Way of Life* (Dharamsala: Library of Tibetan Works and Archives).
Chodron, Pema (1991), *The Wisdom of No Escape and the Path of Loving-kindness* (Boston: Shambhala).
De Beauvoir, S. (1989), *The Second Sex*. Trans. H.M. Parshley (New York: Vintage Books).
Garfield, J.L. (1995), *The Fundamental Wisdom of the Middle Way: Nagarjuna's Mulamadhyamikakarika* (New York: Oxford University Press).
Gibbs, R. (1992), *Correlations in Rosenzweig and Levinas* (Princeton, NJ: Princeton University Press).
Hopkins, J. (1996), *Meditation on Emptiness* (Boston, MA: Wisdom Publications).
Irigaray, L. (1991), 'Questions to Emmanuel Levinas: On the divinity of love', in *Re-Reading Levinas*, ed. R. Bernasconi & S. Critchely (Bloomington: Indiana University Press).
Levinas, E. (1963), 'La Trace de L'Autre,' trans. A. Lingis, *Tijdschrift voor Philosophie* (September) pp. 605–23.
Levinas, E. (1969), *Totality and Infinity: An Essay on Exteriority*. trans. A. Lingis (Pittsburgh, PA: Duquesne University Press).
Levinas, E. (1982), *L'Au-Dela du Verset: Lectures et Discours Talmudiques* (Paris: Les Editions de Minuit).
Levinas, E. (1985), *Ethics and Infinity*, trans. R.A. Cohen (Pittsburgh, PA: Duquesne University Press).
Levinas, E. (1987), *Time and the Other*. trans. Richard A. Cohen, (Pittsburgh, PA: Duquesne University Press).
Levinas, E. (1988), *Existence and Existents*. trans. A. Lingis (Dordrecht: Kluwer Academic).
Levinas, E. (1994), *Nine Talmudic Readings*. trans. A. Aronowicz (Bloomington: Indiana University Press).
Llewellyn, J. (1991), 'Am I obsessed by Bobby? (Humanism of the other animal)', in *Re-Reading Levinas*, ed. R. Bernasconi & S. Critchely (Bloomington: Indiana University Press).
Loizzo, J. (1997), 'Intersubjectivity in Wittgenstein and Freud', *Theoretical Medicine* (18), pp. 379–400.
Scarry, E. (1985), *The Body In Pain* (New York: Oxford University Press).
Shapiro, S. (2000), 'On Thinking Identity Otherwise', in *Mapping Jewish Identities*, ed. L.J. Silberstein (New York: New York University Press).
Strong, J.S. (ed). (1995), *The Experience of Buddhism: Sources and Interpretations* (Belmont, CA: Wadsworth Publishing Company).
Thurman, R.A.F. (1984), *The Central Philosophy of Tibet: A Study and Translation of Jey Tsong Khapa's Essence of True Eloquence* (Princeton, NJ: Princeton University Press).

S. Kay Toombs

The Role of Empathy in Clinical Practice

In this essay I discuss Edith Stein's (1989) analysis of empathy and note its application in the field of clinical medicine. In identifying empathy as the basic mode of cognition in which one grasps the experiences of others, Stein notes, 'I grasp the Other as a living body and not merely as a physical body'. The living body is given in terms of five distinctive characteristics — characteristics that disclose important facets of the illness experience. Empathy plays an important role in clinical practice in aiding physicians to grasp the content of first-person reports of bodily disorder, and to comprehend the meaning of illness-as-lived. I suggest that an important task for medical education should be that of developing students' capacity for empathic understanding and I note several ways in which this task might be accomplished.

My interest in phenomenology and human intersubjectivity began with a puzzling phenomenon in my own life. This puzzle related to my experience as a multiple sclerosis patient and my difficulty communicating with my physicians. In discussing my illness with doctors, it often seemed to me that we were somehow talking at cross-purposes, never quite reaching one another. In thinking about this difficulty, it became clear to me that it was not simply a matter of doctors and patients having different levels of knowledge, or of one party being inattentive to the other, but that doctor and patient view illness from profoundly different perspectives: the one (biomedical) concerned primarily with the pathophysiology of a particular disease process and the impact of disease on the physical body; the other overwhelmingly preoccupied with the existential impact of illness — the disruption of the life that is lived in and through this particular body and in the context of a particular lifeworld. These two perspectives exemplify the fundamental distinction between immediate experience and scientific explanation. The question then, for me, was how does one elaborate the patient's perspective in a rigorous way, and how does one bridge the gap between science and human experience in the context of the doctor–patient relationship.

In pondering these questions I turned to the phenomenological analysis of the body provided by Edmund Husserl (1989), Jean-Paul Sartre (1956), and Maurice Merleau-Ponty (1962). In explicating what it means to be an embodied human being, they note that there is an important distinction between the *lived body* and the objective body.

Journal of Consciousness Studies, **8**, No. 5–7, 2001, pp. 247–58

The lived body is the body as we immediately experience it in a non-reflective or pre-reflective manner; the objective body is the body observed as an object and, furthermore, as an object that can be scientifically investigated.

To illustrate this distinction: In the normal course of events I am not explicitly conscious of my body as an object among other objects in the world, nor am I aware of it as a purely biological organism. Rather, my attention is directed outwards towards my involvements in the world and the body is largely unnoticed and taken for granted. As you read these words, for example, your attention is focussed on the meaning of the text. You are not aware of the positioning of your limbs as you sit in your chair, or the manner in which your eyes function as you scan the sentences. Paying explicit attention to your own body at this moment would require a shift in focus — a redirecting of your attention away from what you are reading towards your body as the primary object of concern. And if you tried to apprehend your body 'sitting here' as a purely biological organism (in terms of, say, what is occurring at this moment at the level of brain physiology), this would involve another shift in focus not just to your body as an object 'sitting here' but to the body as a particular kind of object. For the most part, however, this shift in consciousness does not occur. In the midst of everyday activities the lived body remains unnoticed — the background, rather than the foreground of attention.

In revealing a fundamental distinction between the lived body and the objective or physiological body, phenomenology provides important insights into the differing perspectives of doctor and patient. In particular, one notes the difference between the body construed as a material, scientific object to be investigated in order to uncover the pathophysiology of a particular disease process, and the body-as-lived in the context of everyday life.

Tolstoy (1978, pp. 520–21) has captured this difference in perspectives in the following lines from *The Death of Ivan Ilych*:

> To Ivan Ilych only one question was important: Was his case serious or not? But the doctor ignored that inappropriate question. From his point of view it was not the one under consideration, the real question was to decide between a floating kidney, chronic catarrh or appendicitis. . . . All the way home (Ilych) was going over what the doctor had said, trying to translate those complicated, obscure, scientific phrases into plain language and find in them the answer to the question: 'Is my condition bad? Is it very bad or is there as yet nothing wrong?'

In its immediacy, illness is experienced not simply as a disorder of the biological body in terms of a particular disease process but, rather, as a disruption of the lived body — a disruption that includes bodily alienation, an altered experience of space and time, the frustration of bodily intentionality, loss of corporeal identity, changes in self image related to social interaction, and a challenge to self-identity and integrity. Each of these changes can be explicated with respect to the fundamental structures of the lived body and, although the meaning of change to a particular person depends upon the context of his or her particular lifeworld, the changes themselves represent typical characteristics of the illness experience.

In thinking about the differing perspectives of doctor and patient, I want to begin by suggesting that the universal experience of empathy provides a direct basis for grasping the experience of illness-as-lived. I shall then consider the role of empathy in clinical practice and ways in which it might be possible to enhance empathic understanding in the training of physicians.

In her book, *On the Problem of Empathy*, Edith Stein (1989, pp. 3–11) notes that there is a distinction between empathy and sense perception. Whereas in sense perception one is aware of objects, in empathy one grasps experiences other than one's own. In particular, in empathy I have a direct awareness of the Other as an embodied individual *like me* (as a *living body* in contrast to a purely physical body). The living body (in contrast with the physical body) is grasped in terms of five important characteristics: I recognize it as animated by its own fields of sensations, as another centre of orientation of the spatial world, as capable of voluntary movement, as animated by general feelings of life, and as expressive of experience (Stein, 1989, p. 57). These five characteristics disclose important facets of the illness experience.

The first characteristic of the living body is that of sentience. For example, when my friend sits across from me in an easy chair, with his arm resting on the armrest, I do not perceive his arm to be an inanimate object like the coffee cup on the table beside him. Rather, I recognize the limb to be 'animated by sensations' — to be 'pressing against' the armrest more or less strongly; to be lying there limpid or stretched. The very meaning of his limb, as a living human arm, is that it is enlivened by sensations of pressure and tension. Furthermore, if my friend lifts his arm up and moves it forward to reach for the cup, I empathically grasp the fact that this action involves the sensory (as well as motor) capacities of the living body: that his tactile and visual senses coordinate to provide him with accurate information with respect to his bodily movements, his body's location in space, the distance between his arm and the cup, and so forth. I also recognize the intentional nature of his action — he moves his arm 'in order to' raise the cup to his lips and have a drink. Since my friend's body is of a similar type to mine, should he try to initiate the movement in his arm — and then grimace with exertion and alarm when his arm remained still or flopped to his side — I would immediately apprehend the frustrated effort, sense the inertness of the limb, and empathically grasp his dismay.

With respect to its sensory characteristics, the lived body is distinct from all other physical objects in that one has limited access to one's body from *within*. Kinaesthetic sensation and proprioception give one a sense of where one's body is in space, as well as an immediate sense of connectedness to the body. If I move my leg, I am conscious of the changing position of the limb (I 'know' where the limb is in space), and I am also aware that it is 'my' leg, and not another's, that moves. So certain is this experience that I do not have to look to see where my leg is when I climb the stairs. Nor do I have to look at the steps in order to prevent myself from stumbling. Merleau-Ponty (1962, p.132) has argued that my ability to get around the world in this manner demonstrates a primary 'knowing' that is a 'knowing' through the body — what he has called 'physiognomic perception'. The meaning afforded by sensorimotor experience is a direct response to the world and is prior to any act of reflection or categorization. Limbs which are numb or those which will not move in accord with one's wishes disrupt physiognomic perception, drawing attention not only to the body's inability to engage the world in the most mundane ways but to a change in the body's cohesiveness.

Sensory disturbances also disrupt the sense of 'ownedness' of the lived body. One has only to think of the mundane experience of waking in the night and discovering that one's arm has 'gone to sleep'. In those instances, one's arm is experienced as profoundly other, as 'deadened' — an object that seems no longer a part of one's body. In becoming desensitized, the limb is also dislocated spatially. If my friend has lost the feeling in his arm, he must look at the limb to find out where it is *in* space.

Illness necessarily destroys the taken-for-grantedness of bodily being. Changes in function, sensation or appearance cause one to shift one's focus away from worldly involvement towards the body as the primary object of concern. The body suddenly becomes the foreground, rather than the background, of attention. This experience of bodily awareness draws attention to the material nature of the body. When the body malfunctions, one is exquisitely conscious that it is a neurophysiological organism with its own nature, essentially beyond the control of the self.

In encountering the Other as an embodied individual (as a living body), I grasp the loss of bodily taken-for-grantedness in illness. I immediately sense my friend's unusual preoccupation with the functioning of his limb. Indeed, like him, I am drawn to shift *my* attention away from worldly involvement and towards *his* body as the primary object of concern. For instance, rather than simply losing myself in our conversation, I find myself focussed on the manner in which his body (or limb) moves abnormally, and (like him) I am unusually aware that his body is a physical organism.

In grasping the Other's living body as 'animated by fields of sensation', I grasp the ongoing coordination between the various senses — a coordination that makes possible the seamless interaction with the world. In reaching for the cup, my friend responds to visual as well as tactile clues. In drinking coffee, he is aware of the taste, the smell, the temperature, the colour, and so forth. Should bodily disorder disrupt one or other of the sensory modalities, not only does worldly involvement become problematic but the body's cohesiveness is fractured. Stein (1989, p. 62) points out that if I encounter the Other as lacking one of the senses — say, a person without sight or without hearing — although I cannot empathize with his viewpoint on the basis of my own, I immediately recognize a lack of sensory awareness.

The second characteristic of the lived body is its spatial orientation. I empathically grasp the Other as occupying his own egocentric space, as having his own perspective on the world. Since the Other's body is a living body, like mine, I know without thinking about it that he and I experience the 'same' object differently in that each of us perceives the object according to our particular spatial location and bodily placement. For instance, in sitting across the room from me, my friend necessarily sees one side of the coffee cup, whereas (given my location across from him) I see an opposite side. I also recognize that just as the dimensions of surrounding space (such as near, far, low, high) are, for me, experienced according to my bodily placement, so these dimensions are experienced differently for him given his placement in the world and his spatial relationships to the rest of the spatial world. The coffee table may be near to my friend, but a distance away from me. These spatial dimensions are not only dependent on bodily placement, however. They are also intimately related to bodily capacity. Should my friend suddenly find it difficult to move his arm, the cup which had hitherto appeared to him to be situated 'within easy reach' would now be experienced as 'far' away. Should he be seated in a wheelchair and attempt to switch off the light, the wall switch would be 'high', whereas its distance from his hand would be negligible, if he were standing upright.

In grasping the Other's lived body as animated by fields of sensation and as another centre of orientation of the spatial world, I concurrently grasp it in terms of the third characteristic: voluntary movement. Voluntary movement discloses the lived body as belonging to an experiencing subject and as the instrument of the I's will. Voluntary movement has the character of 'I' will, 'I' move. Disruption in voluntary movement thus challenges the sense of bodily control, as well as the 'I's' perception of bodily identity. When limbs will not move voluntarily, the sense of 'ownedness' of the body is disrupted precipitating a sense of bodily alienation. One encounters the parts of the body as no longer responsive to the *I* move, *I* can. As a multiple sclerosis patient I can no longer lift my legs — although I retain sensation in them. If I sit in a chair and 'will' my legs to move in certain ways, they remain obdurately still and unresponsive. In refusing my command, the limbs appear to have a will of their own. I note to myself that 'the' legs, rather than 'my' legs remain still.

The disruption of voluntary movement also affects the self in that it affects the range of existential possibilities. As Husserl (1989, p. 271) notes, from the very outset the character of subjective movement, the 'I move', is apprehended as something practically possible. It is here that the 'I can' and 'I will' emerges.

In grasping these aspects of voluntary movement, I recognize the lived body to be not only orientational, but also intentional locus in the world. Not only does the Other perceive the world from a particular perspective, but she continually moves towards the world and organizes it in terms of her projects. As the locus of intentionality, the lived body has a fundamental value sense (Straus, 1966; Zaner, 1981, pp. 60–63) as that which enables one to carry out one's projects in the world. Parts of the living body are also imbued with this fundamental value sense. As Sartre (1956) notes, my leg is more than a mechanical limb. It is the possibility which I *am* of running, of walking down the lane with my child, or of dancing the night away with my beloved. It is also the possibility that I might *become* of learning to mountain climb, or engaging in a particular kind of career.

Changes in body necessarily disrupt bodily intentionality. Under normal circumstances the world and the objects within it are experienced as invitations to the body's possible actions according to one's particular aims and projects. Contained in the action of reaching for the pen is the intention to use it for some purpose. One reaches for the pen *in order to* write with it. Moreover, this intention is determined by personal goals. I reach for the pen in order to write a letter to my spouse or, perhaps, to complete an overdue report required by my employer. In illness this taken-for-granted interaction with the world becomes problematic. Objects which were formerly used unthinkingly now present themselves as problems to the body. For my friend with the problematic arm, the coffee cup represents a concrete difficulty to overcome — how to get the cup to his lips without spilling the contents; for the man with angina, stairs are not simply there 'to be climbed' but a threatening obstacle to be avoided. In thwarting the 'I's' ability to carry out personal projects, bodily change threatens the integrity of self.

Stein (1989, p. 68) notes that just as fields of sensation and voluntary movement are co-seen at the living body, so it is possible empathically to grasp 'feelings'. By the Other's walk, posture, and his every movement, we 'see' how he feels, his 'vigour, sluggishness, etc.'. In this connection, bodily comportment not only expresses 'feelings of life' but also identifies the lived body as belonging to a particular individual.

Distinct bodily patterns (gestures, ways of moving, facial expression, tone of voice, and so on) express a unique corporeal style. Not only is it the case that I 'see' my friend's *fatigue* in his stooped shoulders and dragging steps but I am struck by his unfamiliar way of moving and holding himself upright. Corporeal style is intimately related to the sense of personal identity. When I catch sight of my bodily reflection as I move past a store window, I immediately recognize not only 'a' physical body, or even 'my' physical body, but I see an embodied being who is ME and nobody else.

Changes in body style engender a loss of corporeal identity, alienating one from the lived body. For example, as a multiple sclerosis patient, my patterns of movement have altered in a variety of ways. In every instance of change, I have had difficulty recognizing the altered movements as my own. In catching sight of myself in a mirror, my increasingly peculiar way of moving engenders a sense of puzzlement. I catch myself thinking 'Is that person in the mirror really ME?' At the same time, when I watch home movies that show me walking, I find it hard to remember what it was like to move in that way, or even to *be* that person. People who know me well share this sense of puzzlement. On seeing an old photograph that depicted me standing up, my husband remarked in a tone of astonishment, 'Weren't you tall?'

The lived body is also expressive of affective experience. In observing the Other's facial expressions and bodily demeanor, I empathically grasp his experience of joy, anger, despair. Emotions are not simply 'in one's head', they are concretely embodied. Redness in the face is not just an expression of anger, it IS anger. Psychical qualities are ways in which the body is lived. 'The voices of aggressive people are hard, their muscles are bunched, their blood pulses more fiercely through their vessels.' (Van den Berg, 1955). Fear manifests itself as a constriction in the throat, a pounding of the heart, and a trembling of the knees. In neurological disorder, shame is experienced as an increase in the severity of physical symptoms. In the experience of being looked at, an already existing tremor invariably intensifies, spastic limbs become more rigid, difficulty controlling movement is more pronounced.

Stein (1989, p. 85) makes the important point that, in the case of 'equivocal' expressions, when I empathize the emotion of another, I can pay attention to the context in which the emotion occurs.

> Whether a blush means shame, anger, or is a result of physical exertion is actually decided by the other circumstances leading me to empathize the one or the other. If this person has just made a stupid remark, the empathized motivational context is given to me immediately as follows; insight into his folly, shame, blushing. If he clenches his fist or utters an oath as he blushes, I see that he is angry. If he has just stooped or walked quickly, I empathize a causal context instead of a motivational one.

In emotional experiences one is aware of oneself. One experiences emotions as coming from the 'depth' of the 'I' (Stein, 1989, p. 98). Furthermore, in feelings, 'we experience ourselves as not only present but also as constituted in such and such a way. They announce personal attributes to us' (Stein, 1989. p. 99).

When emotions are disrupted in illness, this disruption is perceived as directly impinging upon the sense of self. For example, Keith Mano (1999, p. 61) describes how changes in his emotional state affected his deeply rooted sense of personality. He found himself bewildered when Parkinson's disease turned up his 'emotional thermostat', causing him to cry a lot. As he puts it, 'for someone deep into machismo, such changes can be disconcerting'.

It is also the case that affective experience discloses the intimate relation between self and other. Not only is it the case that, when I see the Other blush with shame, I feel *his* embarrassment but — in my own case — *my* feelings of shame are elicited by my awareness of the Other. I feel shame in the 'gaze' of the Other. When I see (or imagine) him looking at me, I see myself through his eyes and I constitute myself, in Sartre's terms, as a 'being-for-the-Other'.

Stein analyses this interaction with the Other in terms of reiterated empathy. In reiterated empathy, I see myself from the viewpoint of another and thus grasp myself as an individual in an intersubjective world. In this experience I recognize the ambiguity of the lived body. While the lived body is that which is most intimately me or mine (the 'own' body which I am), it is — at one and the same time — an object for the Other, being both the 'expression' and the 'expressed' of my existence (Merleau-Ponty, 1962, pp. 194–5).

The experience of 'being-for-the Other' is particularly acute in the clinical encounter. In the 'gaze' of the physician, the patient experiences the lived body as an object — as a neurophysiological organism, in some way separated from the self. Furthermore, in illness and disability, the felt dimension of interaction with Others may exacerbate the loss of self-esteem. In the case of disability, one sees one's disordered body through the eyes of the Other and thus constitutes it in a negative fashion. This is not a culture which celebrates physical difference or dependence. People who stagger, use crutches, sit in wheelchairs, lack limbs, shake with tics or tremors, are far from the ideal. In directly experiencing the Other's responses (facial expressions, gestures, averted eyes) the person with a disordered body feels herself concretely diminished, devalued.

Affective experiences also bind one to the Other in another way. My relationship with another person is coloured by my feelings towards him. Such feelings can enhance, or hinder, our interaction. If I have particularly 'warm' feelings towards an acquaintance, I will — in all likelihood — act differently towards him than if my feelings for him are 'cold' or disinterested.

I would now like to turn from the characteristics of lived body and illness to a discussion of the role of empathy in clinical practice and, particularly, the question of how one might enhance the physician's capacity for empathic understanding.

First, I should make the point that people often ask me if it is indeed possible to develop empathic understanding — the assumption being that empathy is a kind of personality trait — an all-or-none phenomenon. Either a physician IS empathically inclined, or he is not. Stein's analysis, however, indicates that empathy is a given — that it is the basic mode of cognition in which we understand the experiences of others. The lack of empathic understanding in the clinical encounter amounts to a loss (or de-emphasizing) of this basic mode of cognition.

Dr. Richard Baron (1981) notes that traditional medical views of illness which stress objective pathophysiology have resulted in the exclusion of what he calls 'intuitive knowledge'. Intuitive understanding, he says, is 'a comprehension of the world as one's own'. It is 'something the physician already knows as experience that belongs to his own self. It is an understanding of illness-as-lived.' Baron goes on to say that the exclusion of 'intuitive knowledge' has resulted in a 'humanly ungrounded medicine'.

Dr. Carl Rudebeck (1998) similarly notes that, when faced with a patient's symptoms, the physician displays the 'biomedical reflex' in which his awareness of possible disease is more immediate than the awareness of the person sitting opposite him. 'The living, bodily presence of the patient may even become a disturbing element. "I can't hear you while I'm listening" the irritated doctor bursts out, while the patient under the stethoscope keeps talking.' Medical training, he says, is at the same time 'acquiring knowledge and skills related to disease and *unlearning about bodily normality*'. This is despite the fact that the first step in medical diagnosis is to grasp the experience presented by the patient prior to interpreting that experience within the biomedical framework.

Baron and Rudebeck make the point that empathic understanding plays two important roles in the clinical context: First, it aids the clinician in grasping what the patient is experiencing in terms of bodily disorder; second, through empathy, the clinician grasps the lived experience of illness — the meaning of lived body disruption in the context of this particular patient's life situation.

If medicine is to be 'humanly grounded', an important task for medical education is to educate students not only about disease but also to provide skills that enhance understanding of illness-as-lived. Such empathic understanding amounts to a learning, or 're-learning', about bodily normality and a renewed emphasis on the intuitive knowledge that we already possess by virtue of our humanity.

Empathic understanding of the Other's experience of embodiment is intimately connected to the lived experience of one's own body. An important component of empathy involves the effort to move into the Other's experience, to grasp it in its particularity, 'as if' one were in the Other's place. In this way I clarify for myself the content of his experience. That I am able to do this with some success is due to the fact that his body is of a type similar to mine, that he is 'like me'. In other words, my ability to move fully into his bodily experience is predicated on my own experience of the lived body.

One of the barriers to grasping the content of another's bodily experience is a lack of experiential awareness of one's own body. It is not just that medical training results in the 'unlearning of bodily normality', but that, for the most part, we remain remarkably unattuned to our bodies. In the normal course of events, the body is experientially absent, escaping conscious experience (Gallagher, 1986). Furthermore, it is often the case that I become aware of bodily experience only when the body malfunctions — an inability to breathe suddenly draws attention to my breathing. So while I have a vivid awareness of breathlessness, I have (paradoxically) minimal awareness of the lived experience of normal breathing.

One way to enhance experiential consciousness of bodily normality is by engaging in embodied practices such as mindfulness meditation. Mindfulness meditation brings the lived body into conscious awareness. The practitioner is directed to turn her attention to the immediate experience of the body by focussing on the breath — concentrating on the movement of the belly as it expands and contracts with each inhalation and exhalation, or the feeling of the breath as it flows past the nostrils. Each time the mind wanders off the breath, one notes that a thought has occurred, one observes the content of the thought and the activity of the mind in judging and evaluating one's experience, and then one gently redirects one's attention back to the breath. At times in the meditation one may widen the focus of attention around the breath to include an awareness of the body as a whole, sitting or lying (Kabat-Zinn, 1990, p. 29).

Another mindfulness practice is the body scan. This involves directing one's attention to different regions of the body. The idea is actually to feel each region, to linger 'in' it or 'on' it, to note differing sensations in as much detail as possible, and then to 'let go' of that region and move to another. Having 'scanned' the different regions, one then focusses on the body as a whole and then on a more encompassing awareness that dissolves the boundaries between body, world, and self.

Several aspects of mindfulness meditation practice seem particularly valuable to the process of 'relearning about bodily normality'. Focussing on the breath moving in and out of the body causes one to shift one's attention explicitly to the experience of embodiment. This shift in attention re-establishes a fundamental sense of connectedness with the body. One becomes acutely aware of processes such as breathing, the beating of one's heart, the sensations involved in sitting or lying. One can also widen the attention to focus on particular senses such as hearing, smelling, touching, tasting, and seeing. Learning to move one's attention around the body allows one to develop an experiential awareness of specific regions of the body, as well as to develop a sense of bodily cohesiveness.

Embodied practice also illuminates the affective dimension of the lived body. Paying close attention to what is occurring in the body puts one concretely in touch with the embodied expression of one's emotions. For instance, anger that may be hidden from the thinking mind reveals itself as the tightening of the jaw and the tightness in the shoulders. Furthermore, in disclosing the constant activity of the judging mind, mindfulness demonstrates the manner in which bodily sensations such as pain may be exacerbated through personal evaluations, assessments, emotions, and so forth. Pain in a particular part of the body is experienced not simply in terms of its sensory characteristics but, accompanying the pain are thoughts such as 'If this continues I won't be able to stand it', 'This pain is tearing me apart', and so forth. Comprehending the affective and evaluative aspects of body/mind is crucial to the understanding of illness-as-lived.

Embodied practices such as mindfulness training could be very helpful in the task of re-learning about bodily normality. However, while knowledge of one's own body is the starting point for grasping the Other's bodily experience, the ability to 'move in' to the Other's situation (and grasp the meaning of illness-as-lived) requires two additional skills: (1) what I call 'empathic listening', and (2) the exercise of imagination.

Empathic listening requires that one give one's full attention to the Other's story. In the clinical encounter this act of attentiveness includes close observation of the patient's embodied presence (demeanor, gestures, facial expressions, tone of voice, and so forth) — an observation that is informed by the doctor's knowledge of the lived body — but it also requires that the physician focus directly on the clinical narrative (the story of the illness as told by the patient). The clinical narrative is to be distinguished from the medical history. The medical history details the impact of disease on the body; the clinical narrative conveys the impact of illness on the person.

Empathic listening achieves two important goals: (1) it enables the doctor to grasp what the illness is like *for this particular patient*. No two patients will experience an illness in exactly the same way. Since illness represents a disruption of the lived body and not just the biological body, the meaning of the patient's experience is determined by her unique biographical situation and the values inherent in that situation. In this respect, it is vital to pay attention to the contextual nature of meaning. A symptom, such as stiffness in the joints, might be of minor significance to one person, yet represent a catastrophic change to another (say, a concert pianist for whom flexibility in the fingers is not only essential for optimum performance but for the continuation of a career that deeply defines his sense of self.); (2) clinical narratives deepen the physician's understanding of the lived experience of specific diseases. For example, a patient's description of what it is like to have multiple sclerosis immeasurably broadens one's understanding of that particular neurological disorder. While one can, of course, limit one's knowledge of MS to its manifestation in terms of the effects of demyelination on the central nervous system, such knowledge captures nothing of the lived experience of the disease.

In the context of medical education the skill of empathic listening could be developed by insuring that the clinical narrative is afforded equal status with the medical history. This might mean, for example, requiring that when students study Parkinson's disease they read works such as Oliver Sacks, *Awakenings* (1983) along with their standard neurology texts; when they study the causes of blindness, they read personal accounts such as John Hull's (1990) *Touching the Rock.*

Cultivating empathic listening would also mean introducing students to patients early in their training, requiring that they record, and listen carefully to, illness narratives. In this respect, it is vital that medical educators take seriously the significance of the patient's story. Unless educators give as much credence to the clinical narrative as they do to the clinical data, students will 'get the message' that patients' stories are relatively unimportant and will relegate this information to a footnote on the patient's chart.

Clinical narratives are also necessary to supplement the intuitive knowledge we possess of our own bodies. Stein (1989, p. 62) notes that there are occasions when I am unable empathically to project myself into the Other's living body. For example, as a sighted person, I cannot intuitively grasp the experience of blindness.

> A person without eyes fails to have the entire optical givenness of the world. Doubtless, a world image suiting his orientation exists. But if I ascribe it to him, I am under a gross empathic deception. . . . This is so because of my 'actual, lifelong habits of intuiting and thinking'. All that is given to me is the 'lack of intuitive fulfilment'.

If I am to understand more of the blind person's experience than 'a lack of intuitive fulfilment', I must refer to something other than my own bodily being. I can, for instance, 'delve into' the Other's world image by asking 'What is it like for you?' So, for example, Hull's (1990, p. 81) narrative of blindness conveys how a person without sight is oriented to the world acoustically rather than visually. In describing an experience of sitting in the park, he notes:

> I heard the footsteps of passers by, many different kinds of footsteps. There was the flip-flop of sandals and the sharper, more delicate sound of high-heeled shoes. There were groups of people walking together with different strides, creating a sort of patter, being overtaken now by one, firm, long stride, or by the rapid pad of a jogger. There were children, running along in little bursts, and stopping to get on or off squeaky tricycles or scooters. . . . From the next bench, there was the rustle of a newspaper and the murmur of conversation. Further out, to the right and behind me, there was the car park. Cars were

stopping and starting, arriving and departing, doors were being slammed. Far over to the left, there was the main road. I heard the steady, deep roar of the through traffic, the buses and the trucks. In front of me was the lake. . . . The ducks were quacking, the geese honking, and other birds which I could not identify were calling and cranking.

From Hull's account, the sighted person learns that, unlike visual space, acoustic space is necessarily filled with action. Where nothing is happening, there is silence, and that part of the world disappears. When Hull's children call to him from a passing paddleboat, they are momentarily in front of him. However, he has no awareness of the children until they call and, once their voices cease, their bodily presence is no longer apparent to him. The world of the blind is 'not a world of being; it is a world of becoming'. (Hull, 1990, p. 82) Since, without vision, the surrounding landscape and architecture does not necessarily impinge upon the senses, only the world of 'happenings, movement and conflict' is there.

In the case of many disorders, such as Parkinson's disease, it may likewise be impossible to empathically grasp the Other's experience (except in a vague way) given that the bodily experience is so far removed from normal everyday functioning. Nevertheless, a patient's description of what it is like to have a disease can broaden one's understanding immeasurably. In his book, *Awakenings*, Sacks (1983) reports how he asked his Parkinsonian patients to explain what life was like for them. In their stories they tell of profound disruptions of time and space — descriptions that can be found in no textbook of disease.

For instance one patient, Rose R — initially diagnosed as catatonic — appeared to onlookers to be in a trance, 'absorbed and preoccupied in some unimaginable state'. Sacks reports that she sat upright and motionless in her wheelchair, with little or no spontaneous movement for hours on end. After treatment with L-Dopa she was able to describe what this experience was like for her (Sacks, 1983, p. 69):

What are you thinking about Rosie?
Nothing, just nothing.
But how can you possibly be thinking of nothing?
It's dead easy once you know how.
One way is to think about the same thing again and again. Like 2=2=2; or I am what I am what I am. . . . It's the same thing with my posture. My posture continually leads to itself. Whatever I do or whatever I think leads deeper and deeper into itself. . . . And then there are maps. I think of a map; then a map of that map; then a map of that map of that map, and each map perfect, though smaller and smaller. . . . Worlds within worlds within worlds within worlds. Once I get going I can't possibly stop. It's like being caught between mirrors, or echoes, or something. Or being caught on a merry-go-round which won't come to a stop.

It is clear that if one is to attempt to grasp experiences so unlike one's own, one must have the capacity to *imagine* what it might be like. And, indeed, *imagination* is integral to the task of understanding the meaning of illness-as-lived. If one is to come to some understanding of the patient's meanings, interpretations, values, and so forth, it is essential to grasp (as nearly as possible) what it is like for the other person to be in this particular situation. This task entails what Herbert Spiegelberg (1974) has referred to as 'imaginative self-transposal'. Thus, simply listening to the other's story is not enough. To get to the heart of things, one must imaginatively project oneself into the other person's situation, and attempt *to see the world through the eyes of the other*. This endeavour is not the same as 'putting oneself in the other person's shoes'.

Seeing the other's situation 'through one's own eyes' from within the context of one's own value system is more likely to hinder empathic understanding.

It seems clear that if one has not cultivated one's imagination, one is less likely to be able to engage in 'imaginative self-transposal'. Thus, to the extent that medical training underemphasizes, or even discourages, the development of imaginative faculties, to that extent such training makes it difficult for physicians to grasp the moral dilemmas and existential crises that arise in the clinical situation. An important goal for medical education should be the cultivation of the imagination and I would think that this means placing vigorous emphasis on involvement in the creative arts as a crucial component of the training of healthcare professionals.

In sum, then, I want to suggest that empathy plays an important role in the clinical encounter in aiding physicians both to grasp the content of first-person reports of bodily disorder (patients' descriptions of what they are experiencing in terms of alien sensations, changes in physical or mental functioning, and so forth), and to comprehend the meaning of illness-as-lived (the disruption of the lived body in the context of a particular individual's life circumstances). An important task for medical education should be the task of developing students' capacity for empathic understanding. In demonstrating that empathy is a given — the basic mode of cognition which enables us to comprehend the lived experience of others — phenomenology reminds us that this task is one of re-awakening, or cultivating, the students' intuitive understanding of the lived body. Such comprehension is necessary for a humanly grounded medicine that is concerned not only with the biomedical aspects of disease but with the patient's actual lived experience of illness.

References

Baron, R. (1981), 'Bridging clinical distance: An empathic rediscovery of the known', *Journal of Medicine and Philosophy,* **6** (1), pp. 5–23.
Gallagher, S. (1986), 'Lived body and environment', *Research in Phenomenology,* **16**, pp. 139–70.
Hull, J. (1990), *Touching the Rock: An Experience of Blindness* (New York: Pantheon Books).
Husserl, E. (1989), *Ideas Pertaining to a Pure Phenomenology and to a Phenomenological Philosophy: Second Book: Studies in the Phenomenology of Constitution.* Tr. R. Rojcewicz and A. Schuwer (Dordrecht, The Netherlands: Kluwer Academic Publishers).
Kabat-Zinn, J. (1990), *Full Catastrophe Living: Using the Wisdom of Your Body and Mind to Face Stress, Pain and Illness* (New York: Dell Publishing).
Mano, D.K. (1999), 'Bert and me', *Modern Maturity,* **March–April**, pp. 59–61.
Merleau-Ponty, M. (1962), *Phenomenology of Perception,* tr. C. Smith (London: Routledge and Kegan Paul).
Rudebeck, C.E. (1998), 'The doctor, the patient and the body', Paper given at the 11th International Balint Congress, Oxford.
Sacks, O. (1983), *Awakenings* (New York: Harper Collins).
Sartre, J-P. (1956), *Being and Nothingness: A Phenomenological Essay on Ontology.* Tr. H.E. Barnes (New York: Pocket Books).
Spiegelberg, H. (1974), 'Ethics for fellows in the fate of existence', in *Mid-Twentieth Century American Philosophy.* Ed. P. Bertocci (New York: Humanities Press).
Stein, E. (1989), *On The Problem of Empathy.* Tr. W. Stein (Washington, DC: ICS Publications).
Straus, E.W. (1966), *Phenomenological Psychology. Selected Papers.* Tr. E. Eng (New York: Basic Books).
Tolstoy, L. (1978), 'The death of Ivan Ilych', in *Story and Structure,* ed. L. Perrine (New York: Harcourt Brace Jovanovich).
Toombs, S.K. (1992), *The Meaning of Illness: A Phenomenological Account of the Different Perspectives of Physician and Patient* (Norwell, MA: Kluwer Academic Publishers).
Van den Berg, J.H. (1955), *The Phenomenological Approach to Psychiatry* (Springfield, IL: Charles C. Thomas).
Zaner, R. (1981), *The Context of Self: A Phenomenological Inquiry Using Medicine as a Clue* (Ohio: Ohio University Press).

Francisco J. Varela

Intimate Distances

Fragments for a Phenomenology of Organ Transplantation

L'intrus n'est pas un autre que moi-même et l'homme lui-même. Pas un autre que le même qui n'en finit pas de s'altérer, à la fois aiguisé et epuisé, dénudé et suréquipé, intrus dans le monde aussi bien qu'en soi-même, inquiétante poussée de l'etrange, *conatus* d'une infinté excroissante.

J.L. Nancy, L'intrus[1]

I: 5.00 pm, Day 5

The scene is viewed from the side. The patient is lying on his half-raised hospital bed. Tubes, sutures and drains cover his body from nose to abdomen. On the other side of the bed, two masked men in surgical outfits look at the screen of a portable scanner. The senior doctor explains and demonstrates rapidly to his apprentice, the probe searching around the right side under the ribs and over the stomach, in sweeping motions. The intern listens raptly, nodding repeatedly. The screen is turned so that the patient can also see it. It is J+5.

I emerged from surgery with the liver of an unknown five days ago. My attention now shifts to the two men as they speak, I follow their conversation and wait expectantly for words directed to me. It is a crucial moment: if the veins and arteries have not taken to their new place, my whole adventure comes to a halt. The graft, from their point of view, represents hardly anything more than a successful fixture. I am short of breath as I pick up the doctor's overheard telegraphic comments: Good portal circulation, no inflammation. . . . Abruptly he smiles to me and says : 'Tout va bien!'

I am now my prostrate body that feels broken up, in bits and pieces, aching from a visible incision that goes from right to left in an arching path, and suddenly bifurcates over the chest right to my sternum, almost immobile from the multiple intubations and perfusions. His reassuring statement oddly makes me feel my liver as a small sphere, as if I am carrying an infant (I remember the pictures of my last son's beating heart in his mother's belly); it is tinged with a light pain, it is definitely present. In the

---

[1] Jean-Luc Nancy (2000), p. 45. This brief but profound text is, I believe, the only extant attempt to grapple head-on philosophically with transplantation from a lived perspective. The impact of Nancy's work is present throughout my own exploration here.

Journal of Consciousness Studies, **8**, No. 5–7, 2001, pp. 259–71

background, the brokenness of my body beckons me with an infinite fatigue, and a primordial desire to close my eyes and rest for eternity. Yet the screen is a few centimeters away and a simultaneous curiosity perks up unflinchingly. I can see my new liver, inside me. I follow the details: the anastomoses of the cava and the porta veins, the two large hepatic arteries, the II then the III lobule squished one into the other. I travel within, gliding inside and out of the liver capsule, like an animation. I listen with unabashed interest to the explanations to the intern ('Here, look at how best to catch the flow with the Doppler'; it goes swishhh, swishhh now, as histograms display the parameters in charts and line drawings; 'Here is the best way not to miss the hepatic peduncle'; this time the object is lost to me in a sea of grey).

We are looking at the scene from the side, you and I. And yet for me alone is echoed in multiple mirrors of shifting centres each of which I call 'I', each one a subject which feels and suffers, which expects a word, which is redoubled in a scanner's image, a concrete fragment that seems to partake with me of a mixture of intimacy and foreignness.

II: Contingency, Obsolescence

So there it is: some two years ago I received the liver of another human being. An organ came tumbling down a complex social network from a recently dead body to land into my insides in that fateful evening of June 1. My sick liver was cut from its circulatory roots, and the new one snugly fitted in, replacing the vital circulation by laborious suture of veins and arteries. I can thus pronounce a unique statement (with a few hundred people around the world) with all the sense of truth that is given to humans: I have received someone else's organ!

Such an assertion has no echo in the past; human history remains mute. Ten years ago I would have died rapidly from my complications of Hepatitis C, transformed into cirrhosis, then rampantly turned into liver cancer. The surgical procedure is not what creates the novelty of a successful transplant. It is the multiple immuno-suppressor drugs that prevent the inevitable rejection. (A code word for a phenomenon specious in itself; we will return to it.) Had it happened in ten more years it would have been a different procedure and my post-transplant life entirely different. I would surely have been another kind of survivor. In the thousands of years of human history, my experience is a speck, a small window of technical contingency in the privileged life of upper-class Europeans.

From this narrow window I must (we must) reflect on and consider an unprecedented event, that no accumulated human reflection and wisdom has ventured into. I take tentative steps, consider everything as only a tentative understanding, a lost cartographer with no maps. Fragments, no systematic analysis. We are left to invent a new way of being human where bodily parts go into each other's bodies, redesigning the landscape of boundaries in the habit of what we are so definitively used to call distinct bodies. Opening up the landscape where we can borrow a piece from another, and soon enough, order it to size by genetically modified animals. One day it will be said: I have a pig's heart. Or from stem cells they will graft a new liver or kidney and preselect the cells that will colonize what was missing in us, in a sort of permanent completion that can be extrapolated beyond imagination, into the obscene. This is the challenge that is offered to us to reflect on through and through, to live up to the challenge, to give us the insight and the lucidity to enter fully into this historical shift.

My life in its contingency mirrors the history of techniques, the growing know-how about human bodies, which knows nothing about the lived-bodies that can and will come from it. Technology, as always, stands as the mediation that reveals the interelatedness of our lives. Contingencies of life that accumulate in the history of body-technologies, from antibiotics, to tailor-made drugs, to genetic engineering. All the more so now that the contingency of life, always at the doorstep of reflection on human destiny, acquires a speed that impinges even on our ability to conceive, to assimilate, to work through the ramifications.

In ten years, these reflections will probably be obsolete, the entire reality of transplantation having changed the scenario from top to bottom; all the work I must do is for a little window of history before it snaps out of focus and we are to re-start anew.

III: Frame, Paradox

As I peer inside me (but which me?) at the other's liver, the medical gesture explodes into a hall of mirrors. These are the points where the transplantation situation can be carried to the sentimental extremes of either having being touched by 'a gift' (from somewhere, from 'life' or 'god'), or else the simplicity of the doctors who remain set at the level of their technical prowess. In between lies the lived phenomenon, that must be drawn out otherwise, in other parameters.

Transplantation creates and happens in a mixed or hybrid space. There are several subjects that are decentred by exchanging body parts; or decentred as the 'team' that makes the technical gesture, or even further, as the distributed network of the National Graft Centre who that fateful day decided it was my turn. At the same time this is an embodied space, where my body (and his/her now dead) are placemarkers, experiencing the bodily indicators of pain and expectation. As if the centre of gravity of the process oscillates between an intimate inside and a dispersed outside of donor, receiver and the 'team'.

We can start with the embodied sentience of the organism, the 'natural' basis for the study of lived events. Sentience, in this sense, has a double value or valence: natural and phenomenal. Natural because sentience stands for the organism and its structural coupling with the environment, manifest in a detailed and empirical sense. It thus includes, without remainder, the biological details of the constitution and explanation of function, an inescapable narrative. Phenomenal, because sentience has as its flip side the immanence of the world of experience and experiencing; it has an inescapably lived dimension that the word organism connotes already. Moreover, that the organism is a sentient and cognitive agent is possible only because we are already conscious, and have an intrinsic intuition of life and its manifestations. It is in this sense that 'life can only be known by life' (Jonas, 1966, p. 91). This intertwining can be grounded on the very origin of life and its world of meaning by the self-producing nature of the living. Given that the scientific tradition has construed the natural as the objective, and thus has made it impossible to see the seamless unity between the natural and the phenomenal by making sure they are kept apart, no 'bridging' or 'putting together' would do the work. The only way is to mobilize here a re-examination of the very basis of modern science. But this gets, all of a sudden, too ambitious.

Exploring the phenomenal side of the organism requires a gesture, a procedure, a phenomenological method, contra the current prejudice that we are all experts on our own experience. Little can be said about this lived dimension without the work that it requires for its deployment. (In a basic sense, this is also close to the recent interest in 'first-person' methods in cognitive science.) And therein resides its paradoxical constitution: our nature is such that this gesture needs cultivation and is not spontaneously forthcoming. This is why it is appropriate to reserve the name of feeling of existence (*sentiment d'existence*, a term I borrow from Maine de Biran) as the core phenomenon here, the true flip side of sentience.

The feeling of existence, in itself, can be characterized as having a double valence too. This is expressed as a tension between two simultaneous dimensions: embodied and decentred. Embodied: on the one hand examining experience always takes us a step closer to what seems more intimate, more pertinent, or more existentially close. There is here a link between the felt quality or the possible depth of experience, and the fact that in order to manifest such depth it must be addressed with a method in a sustained exploration. It is this methodological gesture which gives the impression of turning 'inwards' or 'excavating'. What it does, instead, is to bring to the fore the organism's embodiment, the inseparable doublet quality of the body as lived and as functional (natural/phenomenal; Leib/Körper). In other words, it is this double aspect that is the source of depth (the roots of embodiment go through the entire body and extend out into the large environment), as well as its intimacy (we are situated thanks to the feeling-tone and affect that places us where we are and of which the body is the place marker).

Decentred: on the other hand, experience is also and at the same time permeated with alterity, with a transcendental side, that is, always and already decentred in relation to the individuality of the organism. This defies the habitual move to see mind and consciousness as inside the head/brain, instead of inseparably enfolded with the experience of others, as if the experience of a liver transplant was a private matter. This inescapable intersubjectivity (the 'team') of mental life shapes us through childhood and social life, and in the transplantation experience takes a tangible form as well. But it is also true in the organism's very embodiment, appearing as the depth of space, of the intrinsically extensible nature of its sentience, especially in exploring the lived body.

These parallel themes serve as the hidden scaffolding for the analysis here. First, the lived body as focus: the intrusion, the alien as flesh, and the always already mobile subject of enunciation and hence the mobility of the lived body's identity. Second, the networks of dissemination playing in unison: the social network of the gift, and the imaginary circles of the images that give this inside a metaphorical concreteness.

IV: Rejection, Temporality.

I've got a foreign liver inside me. Again the question: Which me? Foreign to what? We change all the cells and molecules of a liver every few weeks. It is new again, but not foreign. The foreignness is the unsettledness of the belonging with other organs in the ongoing definition that is an organism.

In that sense my old liver was already foreign; it was gradually becoming alien as it ceased to function, corroded by cirrhosis, with no other than a suspended irrigation of islands of cells, which are then left to decay and wither away. Years before the transplant, during a biopsy the surgeon came to see me: 'I saw your liver, it looks very sick, you must do something about it.' The statement made this silent organ suddenly un-me, threatening and already designated to be put at a distance in the economy of the body's self. Seeing from outside had penetrated me as a blade of alterity, altering my habitual body for ever.

'Self' is just the word used by immunologists to designate the landscape of macromolecular profiles that sit on the cell surfaces and announce the specificity of a tissue during development. Each one of us has a particular signature, an ecology of somatic markers. Within that landscape, the lymphocytes, the active cells of the immune system, constantly touch and bind to each other and to the tissue markers, in a tight network of two-way interaction. This ongoing mutual definition between the immune network and the tissues is the nature of this bodily self and defines its borders. Not the skin, a mere thin veil, but the self-defining network of molecular profiles. The boundaries of my body are invisible, a floating shield of self-production, unaware of space, concerned only with permanent bonding and unbonding (Varela & Cohen, 1989; Varela & Coutinho, 1991).

The self is also an ongoing process every time new food is ingested, new air is breathed in, or the tissues change with growth and age. The boundaries of the self undulate, extend and contract, and reach sometimes far into the environment, into the presence of multiple others, sharing a self-defining boundary with bacteria and parasites. Such fluid boundaries are a constitutive habit we share with all forms of life: microorganisms exchange body parts so often and so fast that trying to establish body boundaries is not only absurd, but runs counter to the very phenomenon of that form of life.

Is a graft as foreign as the rigid boundaries of a skin-enclosed boundary suggest? Conversely, what is this me that is being intruded? The intrusion is always already happening, the constant intrusion and extrusion dancing at the edge of a tenuous, fragile identity (my self, then), with no boundary defined except as a fleeting pattern. But the boundary is reinforced and sharply marked nonetheless, and easily irritated when the alteration is imposed too fast, too soon, too much. As when a new microorganism penetrates the mucosa, and the organism mounts an intense reaction (inflammation, fever, allergy). It is too much of a change, too quickly.

Rejection, they say. ('There's a rejection!' The intensive care doctor bursting into my room at J+7, just as I was recovering from the trial of massive surgery, patiently recovering a sense of this placemarker called my body. I was abruptly thrown off balance. Yet, I knew about the stages of the transplantation adventure: the recovery from traumatic surgery is almost always followed by rejection, where the true danger zone begins. But in the joy of feeling more recovered, those words opened an abyss into which no sensation pointed, which showed no signs or indices, silent and imaginary in the suddenness of its irruption.) My process-identity of making a somatic home I call self was being thrown out, new mechanisms acquired in the Ur-ancestry of my molecular cellular environment were awakened. A whole new organ is way too much, too quickly. The ex-trusion is initiated by massive tagging of the cells marked as foreign, the cells destroyed by T lymphocytes, the new organ slowly but surely dissolved into biochemical air.

Intrusion is thus temporality itself, the timing of the approach, the slow motion of that which approaches from a distance and closes in, by stages. Intrusion is inseparable from welcoming: both are linked by their intrinsic temporality which the medical gesture violates at the root. It is not the liver, but the 'team's' strategy, that constitutes the intrusion, for the body-technologies are out of synchronization with the temporality of the welcoming that is our basic condition. The paradox of alterity is a paradox of the timing of hospitality.

The body-technologies to address rejection are absurdly simple: disable the ongoing process of identity, weaken the links between the components of the organism. Immunosuppression is, to date, the inescapable lot of transplantation. One starts by special suppressive drugs and massive doses of corticoid (leaving the mind disjointed, hallucinating, and with an obsessive compulsion to repeat certain inner discourses; nights spent in the corticoid desert are certainly a form of hell). As the rejection does not yield, the treatment mounts one step, I am treated with the 'heavy' means as the doctor says. As in napalm warfare, the entire repertoire of immune cells is massively eliminated by a slow injection. (As I felt the effect coming in a few minutes, my whole body was swept by uncontrollable shaking, like an alien possession that left the me [who?] in a limbo of non-existence; looking steadily into my wife's face the only reference point in a disappearing quagmire.)

Complete immunosupression does stop the rejection, but now simply being in the world is a potential intrusion, as the temporality of my somatic identity has been erased for a few days. A new lifestyle of masks, careful watching for the slightest sign of fever, and concern about opening windows, makes the body into a life of withdrawal, its proud movement and agency shrivelled down. In time, the body is allowed to reconstitute; I recover my assurance of my daily embodiment, as the immunosupression is milder. This becomes a life condition. Weakening the links that are the backbone of the temporality of the lived-body, this alteration is experienced as a newly acquired attention to symptoms, as a travelling to destinations of unknown hygiene. Immunosuppression is a walking stick; I feel the world as through an extension.

V: Touching the Lived Viscera

According to my doctors I cannot feel my liver. There is no innervation for the organ, and the connective capsule surrounding it is left with the old, cirrhotic one. *Eppure* . . . I do feel my organ right here, under my ribs, slightly eccentric. It beckons my attention, like a fist that presses my side from the inside, just enough to let me know it is there. Sometimes it stretches and speaks with a tension, which is not quite pain, but makes me move for relief. It is so tangible, stuck like an envelope of the hidden organ. (Interesting: browsing through the internet, I stumbled into a web page addressed to transplantees, displaying a chat room where a dozen people gave the same account: we feel our livers, doctors say we shouldn't.)

Such is the presence of the unfeeling liver. Maybe a dis-membered proprioception from the terminals left behind in the hole of my previous liver. And when the new one comes to lodge, as a newcomer lays down to sleep in a warm bed, I imagine those connective tissue membranes that were left there, dangling like the veils of a mummy, senseless, sentient-less. In time (I imagine) they will find their way into the new nooks and crannies of those new cells. They will have become entrapped into new fascia fibres that pull them, carrying them along as lost relatives.

Thus between this me (which one?) that imagines and thinks, and the other I blended into the lost tissue fibres — driven as one by this bottomless desire for integration — we have reached a balance, almost a cooperative agreement. They provide me the basis to dress the fantasies with flesh, and we give him the credit to manifest in this lived body.

In phenomenology, the lived body (*corps propre*) is the hallmark of intimacy wherein I am, wherein I can be. It is not mine, but it is indissociable from me in this single centre of orientation. The intimacy is multiple. It constantly reappears as the lived body disappears into the background, into a transparent mode while I am immersed in the world. And then a pain, an emotional upsetness, a sudden breakdown brings this absent body back to its deeply present presence (Leder, 1991). There is also the touching that brings it out, the feeling of one's own surfaces. In the classical example, one of my hands touching the other is the very paradigm of the self-based experience of intimacy. It is the 'solipsistic' level of the lived body that Husserl finely describes (Husserl, 1952, §43–47).

The touch afforded by the extended surface of one hand over the other, or over other sensitive skin, leads us directly to the experience of the darkened side of the *corps propre*, the innards, the viscera. Husserl proposes an analysis of 'I feel my heart' (*ibid.*, p. 165). To do so I stretch my palm over the heart region, and press gently. The inner sensation surges up and I close the link between the self that touches itself in the mediation of the distance, the space of the body itself. I touch through a surface. Likewise I can press through, and my fingers can awake in my right side the liver and its boundaries, which show up clearly. I can feel the boundaries up into the ribs and down into the abdomen. The organ responds with a heightened sensation, and in fact with a tinge of pain as if inflamed. (The persistent Hepatitis C virus surely creates a degree of inflammation; I imagine this heightened sensation as also the mediation of those invisible dots of molecular agency which co-exist with my new liver.) All of this is 'given to myself as interdependencies in co-presence' (*ibid.*, p. 166: *fur mich selbst in Kompräsenz zusammengehörig gegeben*).

But, as Derrida remarks incisively, even in the ideal case of hand-to-hand touching this intervening space is already, and constitutively, the presence of the foreign, the other, the distance (Derrida, 2000, Tangent II, pp.183–208). No exploration of the lived body, even in the 'pure' case of two hands touching, can be conceived as pure self-affection, as an internal feeling that rests on itself alone. There is a hetero-affection that slips in place precisely because of the intervening space:

> cette expérience est deja hantée, au moins, mais constitutivement hantée, par quelque hétéro-affection liée à l'espacement, puis à la spatialité visible: par ou l'intrus, l'hôte, un hôte desiré ou indesiré, un autre de secours ou un parasite à rejeter . . . (*ibid.*, p. 205).

The received notion of the solipsistic lived body appears incomplete in this light: it leaves aside the irrepressible presence of the alien. All sensing is an admixture of auto-hetero-affection, which makes the intimacy of the body possible, and visible even when the distance between the touching hand and the viscera is 'mere' skin and bone. But the constitution of the lived body presupposes in its heart the passage through the other as an outside and the Other as horizon. A horizon is not itself an appearance, but is always pre-given — that is, it mediates the relation between what is given and the anticipations of what is possible. This Other lodges the openness to a multiplicity: the image of a scanner of its 'inside', the mounting infection, the gentle touch of friendship, but also the needful absence. It can also be the passage through which the body-technology forces open a wider space by an imposed shift to the body as subject of technique, as Körper, forcing a temporality of foreignness.

Tentative conclusion: it is not the body-technology that introduces the alterity in my lived body as a radical innovation. That technology widens and slips into what is always already there. The alien and the foreign of the transplantation gesture is not a sharp boundary marker for how my body holds its place as the locus of intimacy. Can I then say that the transplant makes me different? As if the *propre* of my *corps* was settled and pure? The appropriation of intimacy as interminable, as at the same time possible and impossible.

VI: Transference, Metaphor

An organ is transferred. If we listen to the Greek roots, we can say it was *metaphoros* from somewhere into me. The exchange has the logic of a metaphor, of something standing in for something else, a limp piece of tissue packed in ice standing in for a gift of life, it is said. At some point the abstract idea of the transplant becomes specific as the transfer is decided and the metaphor on its way. A new something is standing in, marking the place. One can say that the whole is so impossible to enunciate in its totality that we can grapple with it only as a metaphor, as that which speaks the unsayable and the apophatic.

As I arrived in the hospital after the crucial phone call stating that a donor had been found for me (paradoxical myself, altered as I was by the nearness to death, by a cancer eating up my cells, with a finite horizon for the disappearance of identity), the nurses at the reception, professional and kind, let out: 'It's coming from Marseille, it's an organ in excellent condition.' This mere suggestion is like the skeleton onto which the imagination unleashes the full contents of the transfer-metaphors. (I see a young motorcyclist sprawled next to the autoroute, his brains spread over the tarmac, and the paramedics frantically calling the family to get their authorization for taking the organs. One of a thousand scenarios that go through my mind. I will never know.)

That is, then, the beginning of the relation with my donor, the source of the *don*. I was not alone any more in my spontaneous representation of myself: there was the donor, that other X whose path had ended one afternoon somewhere in Marseille. Saying that there was a *don*, also says that there was a gift, according to a received, canonical interpretation. Since Marcel Mauss, a gift is an event-action that belongs to the symbolic order. The key of the gift is its reciprocity: what is given is returned, sealing a pact. The Maussian account of the *don* has been both refined and contested (Godelier, 1996, Part I). In spite of ever-present refinements, the gift remains a key for the understanding of early human societies. Since then, our modern life has evolved to constitute other social norms, and the gift has become strict exchange or commerce. Gifts exist now in the personal sphere, within our immediate circle, and have lost the power to be the ground of social links.

Was X in Marseille a donor? The core of giving is that one is personally addressed. Once a donation is made *in absentia*, to a general population, like the philanthropist to a common cause, its nature is profoundly different. The personal touch is lost, replaced by a quality of possibility lacking a direct address. Yet by law the donor is to remain forever anonymous. In its place there is a mediation between the family who authorizes, a complex arrangement put in place over many years by the National Graft Centre for centralization and re-distribution. It so happens that the Graft Centre is located not a block away from my apartment in Paris. During the interminable wait, I used to take walks in front of it, and ponder the almost tangible contingency of my life (if I survived) within this arrangement. Being inscribed on the waiting list is already a matter of decision, done locally by the 'team' to which I was never privy. I trusted my surgeon who seemed to have taken a liking to me (but what is this feeling in the riddle of the acceptance of a life-death?). The local list somewhere reaches a central list, at the Centre where I went for my reflective walks. After months I was requested to carry on me at all times a dedicated portable phone, and to never be far from the hospital. At some point I am told (in confidence, as an aside) that I am on top of the list, but this still depends on the city and blood group, and whether other patients are or are not put ahead, their conditions being more threatening. Weeks without end; every minute the pressure of my portable phone as witness awakening me to the immense fragility of my life and the tenousness of my identity in this tangle of deferred causalities. And then, as the decision is made (will I ever know who or how?), the phone call, the hurried trip to the hospital, the assembling of the medical team, at the end of the day, tired technicians coming after dinner for all-night surgery around that emblematic figure, the chief surgeon.

And in his position as middle man, the surgeon is the only one who knows both the donor's and the recipient's identities. He thus represents a unique link between us, a meta-instance who holds the key to a riddle that must be kept secret by an unbreakable ethical code. This triangle is emblematic of the strength of the imaginary social link that makes the transference possible, and at the same time binds the entire network from donor to recipient in a single stroke, as if joining a total stranger in too short a time to make acquaintance, to welcome, and thus to arrive without clash. In my experience, surgeons are entirely oblivious of their place and role as transferential passageway; it was up to me to deal with the enormous alterity in which I found myself. His business centred on the *techné*, he has little time to listen to the relentless production of imaginary contents, even after the first weeks and months of the transplant. At best he receives with a nod what the patient says as personal thanks.

In the early temporality of the experience, I said, the social imaginary link is intense and gripping. And the longing to find the source of this *don* of life is clearly present; it feels as ancestral and ancient as the compulsion to bury our dead; it surges forth from roots too old to be conscious. It is here that there is a more appropriate use of the term 'gift' in the anthropological sense. Even as modern Western subjects, we experience, as if in a distant echo, the marks of our ancestors. I found myself spontaneously desiring a reciprocity, to seal a pact with the anonymous donor. In fact, in anthropological studies one constant is the stable nature of the rights of the giver over the gift. This translates on the imaginary level to the presence of the donor in the gift itself, attached to it, and following its transferences. Since gifts are never detached, the links established are of a personal nature, between individuals that engage with one another, and the gift is the representation of their obligations (*ibid.*, pp. 76, 94).

I have another in me, I am partly another, it is commonly said. Some report having acquired new dispositions (to eat meat, to like animals) as a direct manifestation of this spirit that came with the gift. Transplant patients routinely find personal ways to deal with the impasse of the search for the unfindable donor. They go to a cemetery and offer flowers to an unknown grave. Or to a wood and make an offering to the spirit of the deceased donor. It is clear that only a strict regulation of anonymity stops this strong urge from becoming a delicate dealing with the misplaced forms of gratitude-driven obligations.

As the days went on, the fantasies began to fade and to lose sense. Having the gift in me did not make me become another in any way that experience could attest with any stability. On the contrary, it was the work (again) of temporality that became central: the welcoming, the acceptance of this new form of alterity in spite of immuno-suppression, the imaginary elaboration of this intrusion that was willed and wished, regaining the equilibrium from the brutalness of the technology. The images began to disappear, the sudden emotions for the dead giver gave way to a decentring into a larger field of intersubjectivty.

VII: Offering, Giving

Pointing to the field of intersubjectivity here is also a way of pointing to a shift in our understanding of the gesture of organ donation (so-called). In the statement: I give to you, one follows the long trail of the recognition proper to the gift, which 'primitive' societies manifest so clearly. But here, in the gesture of organ donation, what we are concerned with is more an *offering*, a passing without exchange or with the hope of receiving back. The offering is not mine — that would bring it into the realm of com-merce — but just 'taken' from an open field, from whom or how I do not know.

The offer proposes to us that we keep it. In the world of gifts, what is kept and not given, is just as much the key as the exchange. And what is kept is what is sacred, making the gift possible (Weiner, 1992). What I keep as an offering is special; it is to be kept safe. It's yours for keeps. It's to be kept close to you, in the greatest intimacy. We must thus distinguish the gift from the offer, or better the offer within the gift. A gift is an offering when there is, at the heart of the gift, the withdrawal of the gift, the disappearance of its ways of being present (Derrida, 2000, p. 112).

The liver I have, then, is not a gift but an offer, a gift which has been 'withdrawn' as such by death, by the law, by the social mediation. It comes to me from nowhere, there is no presence of the donor in it. It arrived for keeps, if only I could keep it. Donors should be called *offerers*. In the temporality that is proper to accepting and keeping an offer, the imaginary exchanges, which seemed so present in the gift, disappear, are transmuted as part of the constant alterity, the ongoing alterations that are the very nature of this me-ness.

VIII: The Image, the Touch

Modern medical imaging accomplishes what began in the eighteenth century as a desire and a search for illuminating every dark corner, especially for seeing the insides of the human body. Modern man has since been rendered somatically transpar-ent, in gestures that extend into putting into full view not only the hidden but the ulti-mate microscopical, the DNA fingerprinting, the biochemical profiles, the immune cellular probes and markers. Our times have renewed the visible and the explicit as a preeminent presence, compared with times in which only the rarefied world of pure ideas and Logos was supreme and the image mere appearance (Stafford, 1993).

Increasingly we communicate with images of people, with virtual persons existing as bytes in optical fibre ready for multiple displays. The radiologist looks at his echography machine, not at me. The image becomes the inevitable mediator between my lived intimacy and the dispersed network of the expert medical team for which the images are destined, the larger medical world. I am disseminated in image fragments that count more as the relevant interface than this presence (my lived body then, but again the question of which one?). The image holds the bond at just the right distance: sufficiently close in liking to be a habitual part of my intimacy, sufficiently detachable to introduce a wide space wherein the intrusion of otherness arrives massively every time I go back to the stretcher and raise my shirt, and the probe glides over my abdomen (in these situations, habit has transformed them almost into a self-touching — a tribute to the force of the image: I can feel those black and white patterns on the screen).

Occasionally in one of the check-up visits the clinician asks me to lie down, and he touches my liver region. I experience it as a relief, as return to an embodied presence. The touch reestablishes an older intimacy through his touching hand, touching/being-touched the paradigm of oneness, me-ness. These gestures are always considered supplementary: only the images and the charts speak the reliable truth, having captured the essence of the story. These body-techniques seem to stand for all that was haptic, tangible and ready-to-hand, now transformed into weightless apparitions. The new body is constantly on the verge of losing its seemingly invincible spatial and temporal structure.

It would be idle to set up an opposition of correct/incorrect between these pervasive images and the contrasting sense of touch, anchored in the lived body. Even in touching, the alterity is constitutive, the image rides on this doubling as a thorough mediation. We witness a push and counterpull between depth and imaginary surfaces that become a new identity in post-transplantation life.

IX: Intimate Distance

From the place where I now write, the old new alterity of the distributed selves has re-acquired its own temporality. But there was, there has been, the encounter with the radical alteration of death, which approached closely over the years, and then finally made its irruption in all the brutality of a night when my chest and abdomen were laid open. It was done; I was not there, drowned in anaesthetics (which I? certainly there was presence, I suffered).

The descent was slow. First, waiting in a room; then getting undressed and covered with a hospital gown; then naked under a sheet so that the nurse could shave me entirely in a form of nudity that seemed to reach me under the skin. Then transferred to a wheeling stretcher, parked in the surgical room, shaking from cold and fear as nurses made conversation. The anaesthetist comes, takes the perfusion tube and perfunctorily injects the first wave of anaesthetic. I have a minute or so to let anything that was left of me go as if in an involuntary flight. Never had I felt more acutely my fragile ontology, the impossibility of grasping onto anything, a living dot suspended in a space that goes so beyond anything representable. The utter loneliness for which there is no utterance. Deprived of any intimacy, nothing left but gaping gap for intrusion.

Then they opened me up, cut the circulation, replaced it by machines, took the organ from an ice pack, and proceeded to rebuild me again back into a normal body. Or that is what they say. Awakening into my new state, I see that the night when death travelled through my open body is to remain indelibly. It is there each time somebody looks at my torso, and I see their eyes darting quickly down to check the trace that crosses from side to side and up the chest with suture point (with big stitches, like a sack of merchandise). It's death's trace, which never lets me slip by this memory that is not a memory, but rather a feeling of recognition of its presence, of an inevitable guest whose movements are way beyond anything within my reach. From then on the trace of death has set its own agenda, its own rhythm to my life. I have, in fact, become another never entirely re-done after being so meticulously undone.

X: Which Life?

The life retaken, is taken differently, forever changed (but to whom shall we attribute this change?) by a triple movement: the one that led to being on the waiting list; the one that led to an organ to be transferred; and the one that leads me into my present condition. *This* is the living reality of transplantation, my entire identity grazed profoundly by the opening to death, sutured back and left to function in the world with a 'new' life.

Soon the traces of the last movement began to enter my life as multiple foreignness. There is first and foremost the drug treatments, which are prescribed in quantities and taken by grammes per day, and that mark the temporality of the day, of travel always present in its medicine bags, bulky and obtrusive. Then the drugs themselves. The cortisone and immunosuppressors, which induce a diabetes needing careful checking three or four times a day. The effect on the stomach, producing sometimes uncontrollable diarrhoea that in all its undignified presence overtakes my life. And of course the repetitive medical controls, the enzyme levels to keep track of, the overload of the kidneys to verify. The virus is, we all knew it, still with me, and we know it to be back in full action, the most mysterious of my foreignness, degrading the new liver. It must also be suppressed and controlled. It is an imaginary circle: I am back from where I started from, intertwined with these amazing dots whose molecular structures I sometimes contemplate in awe of their twisted proteins and minute RNA. But the only known antiviral treatment is inteferon, an immunitary stimulant, which produces a permanent feeling of fatigue as if one has a budding cold. In fact, for effectiveness it must be a bi-therapy with ribavirine, which leads to anaemia. Oddly, the immunosupression to avoid rejection is exactly a counter move to interferon, so that the body is pushed on opposite sides at the same time. (A constant paradox: immunosuppressed to avoid rejection; immunostimulated to avoid the virus. A telling metonymy of my condition). There is also the return to the hospital for a sudden explosion of viral activity, for the accumulation of liquid around the liver that needs extensive examinations. Changing symptoms that emerge and subside. . . . Echographies; weight control; blood samples so often my veins seem to expect the needles.

Thus the foreignness of the grafted liver is less and less focused. The body itself has become a constant, ongoing source of foreignness altering itself as in echo, touching every sphere of my waking life. This is the life that I have survived for, not a coming back to where I was (but I was already alienated by the disease for long years, and before seems distant and abstract). A life with its own temporality to put together and live with the multiple manipulation that technology demands (once again the historical contingency of the body-technologies: in ten years more I would have been some other kind of survivor). Compensation to the decompensations that multiply in a hall of mirrors. The suffering varies from one person to the next in its extremes. The phenomenon rests: transplantation has made the body a fertile ground of opposed, coincidental intrusions.

Transplantation is never in the past, then. It produces an inflexion in life that keeps an open reminder from the trace of the scar altering my settledness, bringing up death's trace. It is my horizon, an existential space where I adapt slowly, this time as the guest of that which I did not arrange, like a guest of nobody's creation. This time, the foreign has made me the guest, the alteration has given me back a belonging I did not remember. The transplant ex-poses me, ex-ports me in a new totality. The expression of it all, I know, eludes me, makes me face a twilight language. Nancy goes further:

> Je le sens bien, c'est beacoup plus fort que'une sensation: jamais l'etrangeté de ma propre identité, qui me fut pourtant si vive, ne m'a touché avec cette acuité. 'Je' est devenu clairement l'index formel d'un enchaînement invérifiable et impalpable. Entre moi et moi, il y eut toujours de l'espace-temps: mais à présent il y a l'ouverture d'une incision, et l'irréconciliable d'une immunité contrarié (Nancy, 2000, p. 36).

XI: Inconclusion

Old themes from phenomenology have reappeared throughout this analysis: the lived body and its exploration, the unalienable alterity of our lives, the key ground of temporality, body-technologies and ethics. Yet these classical themes re-appear under a new light, perhaps even pushed to an extreme that both sharpens them and moves beyond their initial scope. The radical novelty pushes our analysis into new steps.

Perhaps we are all (the growing numbers that have entered into the sphere of this transference) 'les commencements d'une mutation' (Nancy, 2000, p. 43). I can see it: all of us in a near future being described as the early stages of a mankind where alterity and intimacy have been expanded to the point of recursive interpenetration. Where the body *techné* will and can redesign the boundaries ever more rapidly, for a human being which will be 'intrus dans le monde aussi bien que dans soi-même' as the epigraph says; we would do well to consider every sentence of it. It is this urgency that drives this examination of the ancient ethos of the human will to power re-expressed as transplantation. Even if my own window is narrow in time and fragmented in understanding. Somewhere we need to give death back its rights.

References

Derrida, Jacques (2000), *Le toucher, Jean-Luc Nancy* (Paris: Galilee).
Godelier, Maurice (1996), *L'Enigme du don* (Paris: Fayard).
Husserl, Edmund (1952), *Ideen zu einer reinen Phänomenologie und phänomenologischen Philosophie. Zweites Buch: Phänomenologische Untersuchungen zur Konstitution*, ed. W. Biemel, Husserliana Vol. III (The Hague: Martinus Nijhoff).
Jonas, H. (1966), *The Phenomenon of Life* (Chicago: University of Chicago Press).
Leder, Drew (1991), *The Absent Body* (Chicago: University of Chicago Press).
Nancy, Jean-Luc (2000), *L'Intrus* (Paris: Galilée).
Stafford, Barbara (1993), *Body Criticism: Imagining the Unseen in Enlightenment Art and Medicine* (Cambridge, MA: The MIT Press).
Varela, F and Cohen, A. (1989), 'Le corps evocateur: une relecture de l'immunité', *Nouvelle Revue de Psychanalyse*, **40**, Automne, pp. 193–213.
Varela, F. and Coutinho, A. (1991), 'Second generation immune networks,' *Immunology Today*, **12**, pp. 159–67.
Weiner, A. (1992), *Inalienable Possesions: The Paradox of Keeping-While-Giving* (Berkeley: University of California Press).

Editor's Addendum

On May 28, 2001, Francisco J. Varela passed away at his home in Paris.
He died calm and at peace, in the loving embrace of his family.

Sue Savage-Rumbaugh,
William M. Fields & Jared P. Taglialatela

Language, Speech, Tools and Writing

A Cultural Imperative

Ape Brains versus Human Brains: The Language Rubicon

Psychology traditionally held that the proper investigation of basic learning processes would lead to the explanation of all behavioural phenomena (Mackintosh, 1994). It also maintained that learning processes were the same for all species and that just as one can learn about basic biological phenomena by studying cell function in the simplest of organisms, it is possible to understand much about learning, memory, perception and other cognitive skills by studying animals. Linguists (Bickerton, 1990; 2000; Pinker, 1994), on the other hand, have held that human brains differ fundamentally from those of other species in their peculiar and unique capacity for grammar. They suggest that these differences free human beings from a stimulus-response mode of interacting with the world and make possible, instead, a mental world configured by culture in an infinite variety of ways. Ethologists have also challenged the position of behavioural psychology by reporting that many animals do not have to learn complex behaviours, as they come equipped to respond in well-defined ways that appear to be neurologically predetermined (Hinde, 1970; Tinbergen, 1965; Smith, 1997, pp. 7–53).

Reports that apes could acquire human language without training (Savage-Rumbaugh *et al.*, 1994), that they could use proto-syntactical structures (Greenfield and Savage-Rumbaugh, 1991, pp. 235–58) and they could comprehend word inversion and recursion (Savage-Rumbaugh *et al.*, 1993, pp. 1–242) challenged the views of both camps. They suggested that the human capacity for language was neither unique nor dependent upon a special neurological structure absent in other species. Apes acquired language when raised as members of a human community if their parental surrogates accompanied their speech with lexical information. Even though these apes were unable to utter sounds in the human register, they understood comments addressed to them and attempted to emulate human speech (Hopkins and Savage-Rumbaugh, 1991; Savage-Rumbaugh *et al.*, 2000). These reports suggest that language is not an innate capacity unique to *Homo*. Rather, it may exist in some as yet unrecognized and ill understood form in other species. They also suggest that the ethologist's construction (Smith, 1997) of all animal communication systems as being largely innate and limited to 80 or fewer discrete signals may be incorrect. If bonobos can

Journal of Consciousness Studies, **8**, No. 5–7, 2001, pp. 273–92

understand complex human speech, simply as a function of being reared in a human environment, they may well be utilizing a similarly complex system in the feral societies.

If it can be shown that even one nonhuman species possesses a significant capacity
for language, then we must open our minds to the possibility that other species may
posses complex languages as well. It is possible that these have gone unidentified
because scientists have searched only for linguistic systems that are like our own. It has
been assumed that 'primate calls' could not become language unless the sound stream
contained consonants, vowels, morphemes and phonemes similar to those found in
human speech (Liberman, 2000). Since no nonhuman primate call system contains
these components, the conclusion that they do not have language has been accepted
without reflection or critique. In fact, the view that humanlike phoneme production is
essential for language is so pervasive that it has even been concluded that a nonliving
form of *Homo*, Neanderthal man, could not speak because of an inability to produce
modern CVCs (Liberman and Crelin, 1971). If other means of forming distinctive sound
units with combinatorial complexity exist in animals, there is no reason that other
species could not have some form of language, albeit with a syntax that differs from our
own. However, scientists have not discerned an appropriate unit of analysis upon which
such a sound system might be able to hang semantic and syntactic information. Recently,
however, some are beginning to attempt to do so (Owings and Morton, 1998).

The fact that no precursors to language have been found to exist in the 'call systems' of other primates is referred to as the 'Paradox of Continuity' (Bickerton,
1990). Evolutionary theory predicts continuity, but language seems to be an exception. Thus, some scholars have posited the existence of a sudden mutation to explain
this discrepancy (Burling, 1993; Calvin and Bickerton, 2000), while others suggest
that natural selection has acted upon an unspecified structure extant only in modern
humans (Pinker and Bloom, 1990).

What is Language?

The data from Kanzi suggest that the paradox of continuity is false and that it may
reflect little more than our inability to properly analyse and understand the vocal systems of other primates (Savage-Rumbaugh *et al.*, 1993). Nonetheless, linguists and
anthropologists have responded to reports of Kanzi's syntactical competency in apes
by maintaining that true language entails far more than the capacity to demonstrate
initial syntactical skills (Noble and Davidson, 1996). It requires proficiency with the
complete array of human syntactical forms that are manifest in speech (Bickerton,
2000; Pinker, 1994). Ignoring Kanzi's demonstrable capacity to deal with positional
inversion and relative clauses, as well as the structural rules he employed during production (and in one case invented), Bickerton (1990) concludes that apes are capable
of only a proto-syntax. By proto-syntax, he means one that is heavily dependent upon
semantic content rather than grammatical structure. Grammatical structure, for
Bickerton, is not 'just rules' but a complete (hypothetical) grammatical analyser that
permits us to form complex sentences in which individual words lack specific referents, yet the sentence is nonetheless fully comprehensible.

All human languages, for example, produce sentences such as 'What is that over
there?' The words in such a sentence have no specific semantic referent that can be
identified in a dictionary and yet speakers of the language readily understand them. It
is possible, in the above sentence, to recognize that the word 'that' is being employed

with the word 'there' to indicate an object at some spatial distance from us. The nature of the object or the exact degree of the distance does not matter. Moreover, the word 'what' requests specific semantic information about an unknown marked object. Neither semantic information nor a proto-grammar is deemed sufficient to process a sentence of this sort. Through the linguistic gymnastics that permit us to interpret such sentences, it is thought that we have achieved our ability to create everything else that makes us human (Pinker, 1994).

According to this view, apes could never make the jump into true culture as man has done, since to do so requires a freeing of the mind from the here and now, and from responding to stimuli as they impinge upon one (Donald, 1991; Terrace *et al.*, 1979). Man is said to have achieved this capacity only as he gained the ability to produce syntactically complex structures freed from specific semantic content. Proponents of this view argue that whether or not apes exhibit different cultural traditions of tool use in the wild (McGrew, 1992), they can never create the complex cultures built upon myth and ritual that characterize all human societies. These creations are thought to require sophisticated linguistic capacities far beyond anything apes might achieve (Taylor-Parker and McKinney, 1999; Noble and Davidson, 1996).

Semantics as 'The Rubicon'

Not all scholars agree with this view. Some argue that it is not syntax but semantics that is the essential Rubicon between man and ape (Deacon, 1997). They point out that referential specificity only appears to be more real for words like 'bird' and 'limb' than for words such 'here' and 'there'. 'Limb', for example, means one thing in a sentence like 'He was out on a limb'. and quite another in 'See the bird on the limb'. Whatever the neurological capacity that underlies the ability to appropriately decode the different meanings of 'limb' in these two sentences, it is arguably similar to the capacity that permits us to interpret sentences that lack terms of referential specificity. (For example, 'Put that thing over there.') And the issue goes deeper than the structural relationships between the words themselves. 'Limb' is used metaphorically in the first case, but not in the second, and there are no grammatical markers to signal the listener of the need for metaphorical decoding. Still, the metaphorical meaning is somehow detected and understood. Yet, it cannot be looked up in a book nor explained by the history of word usage because novel metaphors work as well as overused ones.

For proponents of this view, the issues are a) how one thing comes to stand for another in the first place, and b) how is it that what something 'stands for' can change quickly from one conversation to the next, yet still be understood by both parties who are engaged in a social dialogue (Taylor, 1984). Some linguists would argue that this process is basically linguistic, structural and innate (Pinker, 1994). Others scholars maintain that even though it is innate, it is not reducible to linguistic structures. Rather, it is based upon deeper cognitive schemas that affect the entirety of our world perceptions (Deacon, 1997). However we characterize the process, it is fundamentally interpersonal in nature (Trevarthan, 1977) for it requires the construction of joint social perceptions that can be shared through a learned communication system. Even more critical, though less obvious, is the fact that the construction of a system of joint social perception requires the ability to recognize that individual perceptions of reality are not the same. Consequently, they must be co-joined to permit coordinated differential social action.

Trevarthan (1977) discusses the way in which infants move from a state of partial consciousness in which 'Mommy and I are one' to full consciousness. Fully conscious infants recognize the existence of a mental separation between the mother and self. As this occurs, the infant comes to recognize that its reactions to events may not be synonymous with those of its mother. As this realization arises, it serves to motivate the infant to strive to find ways to share his/her mental world and subjective experience with the mother through self-expression. This desire leads to the development of the capacity to communicate subjective states of knowledge and feeling through the process of symbolizing. This process of mental separation is widely recognized for human children, but not for other species. It is hard to imagine that non-human primate infants would not go through a similar recognition of self-separation from other members of their species. It is assumed, however, that nonhuman species do not make such a leap. If this view is correct, it means they remain in a sort of semi-conscious state. There, they function as individual bodies, but lack the realization that their mental perceptions differ from one another. It is difficult to understand how the complex coordination of social behaviour, such as male chimpanzees positioning themselves at the bottom of different trees to block the escape route of a colobus monkey, could occur if participants did not appreciate that their perceptions differed.

Theory of Mind as 'The Rubicon'

In a recent book entitled *The Cultural Origins of Human Cognition*, Tomasello (1999) explores the question of how modern human cultures arose and whether or not our closest nonhuman relatives could generate the kind of complex societies that characterize *Homo sapiens*. He suggests that many things that seem to make us so different from apes, such as our capacity to construct buildings; our capacity for music and song, for weaving, for art, for storytelling, for mathematics, and for classification and categorization, are not unique to us. Indeed, he argues that the prerequisites of these skills might arise in apes given the right kind of early environmental exposure. The critical difference, according to Tomasello, is that these cultural skills would never be elaborated and perpetuated in *Pan* because apes do not view other apes as having minds different from their own. Thus, cultural innovations might appear, but eventually vanish as apes would not actively seek to transfer them to other generations. Consequently, the cumulative elaboration of cultural innovation, so characteristic of human culture, could not materialize among apes, regardless of the genius of any given ape.

The suggestion that only human beings possess a fully developed 'Theory of Mind' was first set forth by Premack and Woodruff (1978), Premack (1986). Premack coined the term Theory of Mind (ToM) to suggest that each human being comes to postulate that other human beings have minds that are filled with ideas, thoughts, plans, and so on that are quite different from their own. Many highly controlled experimental studies (Povinelli and Eddy, 1996) have been done with apes in an attempt to determine whether or not they are capable of demonstrating such awareness. In these studies, which employ highly artificial communication tests, researchers have concluded that apes lack the capacity to appreciate that differences in direction of gaze result in differential knowledge (Povinelli and Eddy, 1996; Call and Tomasello, 1999). Consequently, it is assumed that they cannot differentiate their own subjective world from that of their compatriots.

Although apes fail ToM tests, a multitude of observations made under natural circumstances suggest that they do not lack such capacities. Why, for example, does a chimpanzee male cover his mouth when he cannot not stop himself from uttering excited food barks — unless he does not want others to hear him (Goodall, 1986) and realize that he has found a new source? Why would such a male try to stop his own noises from reaching their ears unless he realized that their perceptions were already different from his own and that he knew something that they did not? Even more pointedly, might he have understood that his noises would communicate specific information about the kind and perhaps quality of food? And why would another chimpanzee male hide the fact that he had an erection when a more dominate male approached unless he did not want the other male to recognize his interest in a female that he knew was 'off limits' (deWaal, 1998)? And if he wanted to hide his state, he must have realized that it was possible to 'fool' another chimpanzee by creating a false belief. While these observations are not common, one should not conclude that it is rare for chimpanzees to intentionally deceive each other. It is more probable that the above examples reflect rare instances in which they failed to inhibit behaviours they would normally successfully inhibit. It is important to note that successful acts of deception will not, by definition, be detected.

Why should apes fail tests designed to reveal ToM capacities, yet seemingly exhibit these capacities under natural conditions? Are the tests inaccurate or are observers reading intentions into apes that are not warranted? The difficulty lies in the fact that the tests given to apes have been nonlinguistic, while similar ToM tests given to children are language mediated. Lacking a linguistic means of posing questions about subjective knowledge, researchers resort to a cumbersome and somewhat confusing array of people hiding things and acting in a variety of conflicting and unusual ways. These manipulations are required in order to tease apart the many variables that such inferential tests inevitably confound. These procedures can appear arbitrary and capricious to laboratory apes accustomed to caretakers who feed and clean in a routine manner. Test failure is to be expected if the intent of the experimenter–caretaker enacting the various manipulations is ambiguous.

By contrast, apes who have been reared with exposure to human cultures, and who have acquired comprehension of spoken language, readily pass linguistically mediated ToM tests (Savage-Rumbaugh, 1997; NHK, 2000). They answer questions such as 'What does X want?' even when they know that what X is trying to retrieve from a box and what is actually in the box differ. Thus, they reveal that when their state of knowledge differs from that of another party, they perceive this difference. They can symbolically characterize the intent of another party as distinct from their own. Given that they have such a capacity, they should, according to Tomasello (1999), possess the needed cognitive structures for passing culture on to future offspring. If Tomasello is correct, then the culture of language competence should transfer information to their offspring in a manner qualitatively different from that of nonlinguistically competent apes.

Why does language make it possible for these apes to demonstrate ToM? Are they truly different from other apes or does language itself permit a form of the ToM test that 'makes more sense' to the ape psyche? We suggest that language permits the construction of a joint perceptual reality. With language, one can construct common scenarios and pose questions about subjective perceptions of those scenarios. Without the ability to pose questions, nonlinguistic test manipulations reduce to a series of unconnected events. There is no reason, for example, to link walking in and out of the room to knowledge-based observation of action or to placement and removal of items from boxes. When actions carried out by experimenters standing in front of cages appear arbitrary or nonobvious, tests based on solid experimental principles can become fatally flawed. They rely, for their inferential power, upon the actions of experimenters being perceived as a series of meaningfully connected events. By contrast, linguistically posed comments and questions can serve to relate individual events into a coherent whole.

If apes reared in a human culture can acquire human language and demonstrate an understanding of ToM, what are they doing with these capacities in the wild? Some observations suggest that language capacities fall within the competencies of feral apes. Wild bonobos appear to differentially mark travel paths ostensibly to provide information to group members who will follow them at a later point in time (Savage-Rumbaugh et al., 1996, pp. 173–84). Similarly, chimpanzees have been observed to indicate travel direction by drumming (Boesch, 1991). Studies of linguistic acts in the field are difficult because of the heavy vegetation and the distances that may separate communicating parties. The conclusion that feral apes are incapable of language and/or ToM is probably premature. Such a conclusion reflects the perspective of an outside observer who lacks a common cultural bias and understanding with the subjects being observed. Were similar studies to be conducted in a human culture from the perspective of an 'outsider' who had not striven to integrate himself or herself meaningfully into the group, they would be dismissed as irrelevant.

Culture Begins in the Womb

The ease with which language appears in toddlers has startled parents and offered linguists their strongest case for the innateness view of language. Human beings are trained to read, to write, to add and subtract, but not to speak or to become cultural beings. Indeed, the process of learning one's native language and becoming a member of one's culture is seen as something magical that happens only once in life and can never repeat itself with the same degree of force and commitment. It is becoming clear that culture first exerts itself during foetal development (Blum, 1993). The foetus develops a sensitivity to, and predisposition for, the socio-environmental events that surround the mother during her pregnancy. It also develops an aversion for the events that alter the mother's affective system in a negative way during this period. These aversions and preferences can be highly specific; for example, infants prefer not only the language of their prenatal period, but the specific stories that are read to them during this time as well as the specific music that is played. Moreover, they also show a preference for the voice of the story reader. Such preferences are engraved deeply upon the neural substrate and linked affectively to the emotional arousal system. They have the capacity to affect the individual's responsiveness to stimuli for a lifetime and thus to mold the developing neural substrate.

We are now learning, for example, that the brains of identical twins are not identical (Liberman, 2000), and that connections headed toward the visual system can be rerouted to the auditory system where they become functional (von Melchner et al., 2000). In addition, foetal tissue from one animal implanted into the developing brain of another species can either follow the plan of the host brain or exert its own unique influence on the new neural substrate as well as on the peripheral structure of the host species (Deacon, 1997; Balaban, 1997). For example, vocalization-related neural tissue from a Japanese quail, when transplanted into a chick embryo, transforms the vocal repertoire of one species into that of another (Balaban, 1997). These findings reveal that species differences presumed to be genetically based can, in some cases, be attributed instead to localized changes in neuronal circuitry. The brain is neither 'prewired' nor genetically fixed, but is a highly plastic system responsive to external stimuli from the moment it blossoms from the neural tube. Species differences in complex social behaviour can be attributed to a minor change in a single gene regulating neuromodulatory action (Katz and Harris-Warrick, 1999) or to environmental variables. Neuronal circuits and even single neurons show dramatic alterations in activity with very small changes in parameters such as the density of ion channels. Minor changes in the distribution of receptors of peptide co-transmitters can result in major changes in 'species-typical' patterns (Kolb, 1999). For example, although the pattern of oxytocin and vasopressin immunoreactivity in the brains of the two species of monogamous and nonmonogamous voles is similar, the distribution of receptors for oxytocin differs. This difference alone appears to account for the species-typical mating patterns in each vole species (Young *et al.*, 1997). It has also been shown that environmental experience can increase the brain's production of neurotrophins (Schoups *et al.*, 1995). Thus, there exist

> multiple mechanisms of brain plasticity (in both the developing and the adult brain) that range from gross cortical changes such as the generation of neurons and glia, to more subtle changes such as the alteration of synapses or changes in the production of chemical messengers (Kolb, 1999, p. 32).

The brain is most plastic during foetal development. At this time, sound stimuli provide the greatest source of external events that impinge upon the developing brain. When language is spoken around the foetus, the amniotic fluid muffles the vowels and consonants, rendering the pattern of tonal resonance the salient feature of language for the baby (Mehler *et al.*, 1988). Thus, a sentence such as 'My dog Bingo ran around the world' is heard as a series of tonal resonances prior to birth rather than as a series of consonants and vowels. During foetal maturation, the developing nervous system is exposed to a large array of tonal patterns, the majority of which are produced by its mother's own voice. The developing neural system is probably capable of mapping each and every varying rhythmic tonal pattern, as cortical mechanisms are primarily concerned with recording rapidly changing input events by the processing of information in narrow slices of time (Merzenich and Jenkins, 1995, pp. 247–72). If the brain does so, when the infant emerges from the womb it will already be able to discriminate recognizable tonal resonance patterns. It would then need only to map the clear consonantal sounds onto the extant resonance patterns to begin learning the consonantal peculiarities of its particular language. Supporting this view are the observations that infants treat vocalizations of themselves and others as a kind of song (Papousek and Papousek, 1981), that babbling by eight-month-olds contains the intonational patterns of the surrounding language (de Boysson-Bardies *et al.*, 1984), and that intonation is used to segment out word boundaries within speech and thus to aid the acquisition of syntax (Sansavini, 1997).

Thus, the brain of the infant would be 'bootstrapped' into the language of its culture long before birth through listening to, and recording, the changing time-dependent resonance patterns of speech. Since sound is the most salient external stimulus regularly delivered to the developing brain, it is difficult to imagine that the brain would not record and organize such input, as well as develop differential sensitivity to it. We know that the far less plastic brains of adults have such capacities, therefore it is reasonable to suspect that the developing brain has them as well (Grafman and Christen, 1999).

By the same token, the brain of an infant ape will be exposed to the sounds around its mother. If its mother experiences, throughout her pregnancy, the close company of favoured human companions, the infant's brain will be exposed to both the rhythms of their speech and that of its mother. It will thus be bootstrapped into the vocal systems of both species. Supporting this view is the observation in our laboratory that surrounding bonobo mothers with speech during their pregnancy results in more rapid acquisition of human language skills in their offspring.

The Units of Speech: Words, Phrases or Tonal Patterns?

Studies of early infant speech perception reveal that children initially perceive language as occurring in tonal clumps, rather than as configurations of different words (Peters,1983). It is possible that the view that words and/or morphemes serve as elemental speech units may be incorrect. It has possibly derived from a focus upon written rather than spoken language. Sonographic analysis of speech shows that natural breaks occur at the end of tonal patterns rather than between words (Perkins and Kent, 1986). Given that it is tonal resonance patterns that are heard by the developing infant, rather than consonant–vowel morphemes and/or phonemes, it is reasonable that speech is initially perceived as clumps of sound.

What linguists perceive as 'words' — which they take to be the basic building blocks of language — may simply be semantic units that we have conveniently identified with certain individual written forms. Written words exist as independent classifiable and repeatable entities within a dictionary or when spoken in isolation, as in reading a list. However, the phonetic form and configuration of all words changes markedly in the context of real speech. They meld and blend with the sounds that come before and after them in a variety of patterns. In the physics of the speech stream, the only identifiable naturally occurring units are the tonal/rhythmic resonance patterns of which there could be hundreds of thousands of unique configurations. These units are separated by timing parameters rather than by consonantal or morphemic boundaries.

The work of Remez and Rubin (1984; 1990) has demonstrated that no particular elements of articulation are required for speech perception. Rather, it is the changing pattern of resonances between different formant frequencies that underlies speech perception. This is not to say that words do not exist as individually perceptible entities, they surely do. But it is to say that whatever they may represent and sound like as separate entities is dramatically different from what they become when they are incorporated into the flow of ongoing speech. The way in which our ear identifies separate words is also distinctly different from how it is that we identify words within a speech stream. Some readers may recall as toddlers, thinking that groups of words were, in fact, one big word with a rhythmic sound. The first author can remember being very surprised to learn that 'Ohsaycanyousee' was not one word but five. Once it 'broke apart' for me, I never quite appreciated the song in the same way.

The view that language may become mapped prenatally as sets of tonal/rhythmic patterns is also supported by observation of the Longondo people of the central Congo who employ whistle and drum languages, which they map isomorphically onto the tonal patterns of the spoken language (Personal observation). Since neither whistles nor drums produce consonants, it is the rhythm and tone that carry the meaning. Producers of these languages describe the drum and whistle as speaking phrases that sound like their words, and they explain that they can decode them because they map the rhythm and tone of their speech. Even children as young as two- and three-years-of-age can understand the drum and whistle communications and employ them. Whistle and drum languages are reported to be highly specific and limited to certain redundant phrases. Thus, even though listeners may be decoding the tonal pattern, it is thought that such a system still could not provide sufficient differentiation to carry the full structure of a language. However, when I asked Longondo whistlers to translate different narratives into the whistle language they were able to do so.

The perspective that basic linguistic units may be tonal and rhythmic changes in resonance patterns is supported by the work of Remez and Rubin (1984; 1990), which reveals that the linguistic encoding inherent in speech production can be carried in a single tonal sine wave. It is not necessary to actually hear the complex speech pattern with glottal and labial stops, consonants and fricatives in order to perceive their presence in the changing resonances of sine-wave speech. By converting English into sine-wave speech, Remez and Rubin (1984; 1990) have created a computer-based version of English that is tonal. When an individual first hears sentences in this signal it sounds like a whistle of varying pitch, almost songlike. Yet, when a person is informed of the speech content in the signal, their ability to hear the sound as a tonal pattern vanishes. They then process the sound stream as speech and are unable to hear it only as tones. The brain thus 'adds' to the signal something that is not there initially. One explanation for this phenomenon is that human speakers are able to mentally recreate the articulatory gestures needed to form the tonal patterns and it is from their attempts to recreate that they can fill in the missing consonants. Indeed, it has been assumed that this is the same process by which ordinary speech is interpreted since there are no definitive breaks between words and no definitive patterns for each word. However, Kanzi is not a human speaker and he does not have a human articulatory apparatus, but he can, nonetheless, interpret human speech. Consequently the 'gestural articulatory' explanation of speech comprehension would seem to be insufficient.

A related, but different, explanation is that the brain is already familiar with the tonal resonance patterns of its native language. These patterns are all that is needed for the brain to determine what is being said and to perceptually 'fill in' the missing consonantal information once the listener 'listens' for speech. The visual system is constantly accomplishing a similar sort of 'filling in' of the expected visual pattern, which is why we do not perceive ourselves to be 'blind' in the blind spot of our retina. If the young brain is processing tonal patterns and eventually learning to break these patterns down into the grammatical and phonemic expressions of its culture, then the phenomena of whistle speech, drum language, comprehension of sine-wave speech, the seeming ease with which children parse complex grammatical structures, the ease with which all speakers separate a sound stream that has no physical breaks into reliable word units, all reduce to a similar problem instead of different ones. Recent studies in the field of child language reveal that grammar and word learning are not independent of one another (Dale *et al.*, 2000), as would be expected if the basic unit is neither word, nor grammar, but tonal pattern.

Tonal Patterns as the Harbingers of Culture

These facts suggest that varying tonal resonance patterns — extant in the language as repeatedly occurring groups of words — serve as the basic input for language perception. They also support the view that language was initially a songlike phenomenon, dependent upon tonal pattern alone and lacking consonants, phonemes and morphemes (Darwin, 1872; Skoyles, 2000). These resonance patterns also carry information about the emotional state of the speaker. Thus, as the foetus is exposed to the emotions of those around him, manifest through their voice as sound waves, emotions can exert an effect upon the developing brain. In a sense, the 'tone' and emotional expressions of the culture, as embodied through speakers, affect the brain of each foetal speaker even before birth. The patterns of sound are thus carried across generation after generation as they imprint the brain and mould the neural substrate long before they are imitated, understood or produced by the speaker. Worden (2000) has proposed that language and emotion are facets of the same symbolic social intelligence faculty; a faculty that we share with other primates. He suggests that emotional reactions trigger hormonal changes that eventually manifest themselves in behaviours that affect rank and status through alteration of brain chemistry. Because the foetus is receptive to sound and because emotion is manifest in vocal sound, it is likely that this process begins even before birth. What is perceived as the 'personality' of a primate infant may not in fact be 'innate', but rather may be determined by the foetal sound-based experience during pregnancy.

Armed with a brain able to analyse and parse the tonal speech units of its language, the infant is plunged into the external culture at birth, primed to operate as a linguistic cultural entity. Because of this preparation, language acquisition is an easy task for the infant. By contrast, an adult learning a second language in school has already acquired a written language, an alphabet, and has learned to rearrange tonal speech patterns into morphemes and phonemes that can be expressed atonally or in written form. The fact that children acquire their first language very rapidly, but adults experience considerably difficulty in acquiring other languages, has been used to bolster the view that language acquisition is innate. This argument overlooks the obvious fact that the brain of the infant has been doing little but listening to linguistic input from the time of conception and all during the first year of life. Throughout this time, very few demands have been placed on the developing organism, leaving it free to devote its entire attention to auditory patterns before birth and to the auditory and visual patterns following birth.

We would predict that if adult brains were given identical input, they might acquire another language at least as readily as a child and perhaps much faster. The essential ingredients would be nine months of exposure to the tonal speech patterns of the second language, employed in a meaningful social context during both sleeping and waking states — with no speaking, work or social demands of any sort placed on the person. In addition, if the tonal speech patterns could be produced by entities to which the adult had a positive attachment, acquisition should proceed even more rapidly and the speech patterns acquired should be completely like those of the model. Following this time there would be a period of dependency (similar to that experienced after birth) in which the adult heard the language spoken around them while all their needs were cared for by others. At this point it would be important for the caretakers to utilize many opportunities to describe things that were being done or about to be done, just as mothers do with children as a matter of course. It would also be essential that the adult would speak no competing language. Only if adults could not easily acquire language under such situations would we have reason to conclude that the 'innateness' hypothesis should account for the relative ease with which children acquire their first language.

Bonobos and Speech

In our laboratory, bonobos reared in an English-speaking culture where writing and tool manufacture are regular components of daily life, like children, make spontaneous attempts to speak. Due to the biological constraints of their anatomy, however, when they attempt to produce English words, their supralarengeal apparatus modifies the sound in a manner that is not immediately recognizable by English speakers whose ears and auditory cortices are inexperienced with the bonobo's acoustic range and tonality. Listeners who *are* so experienced can detect words, while those who are not hear only tonal sounds, much as is the case with the sine-wave speech produced (Remez and Rubin, 1984; 1990). In fact, the bonobo's vocal tract tends toward the production of a much simpler and higher form of sound than does the human vocal tract. The advantage of using a pure form of high-pitched sound is that of increased distance transmission. Living in a dense forest arboreal environment, distal sound transmission assumes an importance not required by village life in cleared compound areas specific to *Homo*.

Kanzi employs vocalizations in a communicative manner not unlike his use of lexical symbols. In order to determine whether or not the acoustic structure of Kanzi's vocal utterances varied consistently with the linguistic context in which they were produced, Kanzi's vocalizations were categorized and analysed spectrographically. A video archive consisting of hundreds of hours of video footage was used as the source of behavioural data. All vocalizations were collected during linguistic interactions between Kanzi and one or more researchers and were classified according to the semantic context in which they were produced. The semantic meaning of a vocalization was determined based on behavioural correlates, rather than the acoustic properties of the calls. These behavioural correlates included lexigram use, indicative pointing, and response to queries. For example, if Kanzi vocalized while pointing to a lexigram for a particular object, the vocalization was coded with the name of that object. Only those vocalizations produced in conjunction with one or more such behavioural correlates and characterized by only a single semantic context were considered for analysis. This meant that Kanzi's behaviour defined the vocalization's referential semantic content rather than its acoustic structure or the subjective judgement of an observer. It is important to note that Kanzi vocalizes many thousands of times each day and that his sounds are completely spontaneous. They have never been trained and he does not produce them 'on command' but rather when he deems appropriate. The hypothesis that Kanzi sometimes appears to 'translate' his sound by showing us the corresponding lexigram or photo was what we sought to verify, or disprove. If Kanzi were making sounds of a consistent acoustic form for different indicated referents, it should be possible to differentiate the sounds structurally and these results should correspond appropriately to Kanzi's translations.

Once the data collection procedure was complete, each vocalization was quantified in order to compare the acoustic properties across and within semantic categories. Sound spectrograms of each vocalization were constructed using a signal analysis software program and four on-screen measurements. Twelve calculations were performed yielding 16 acoustic variables for each vocalization.

One-hundred-and-eighty-six vocalizations comprising 34 semantic contexts were collected. For the purpose of statistical reliability, only those vocal categories with ten or more exemplars were included in the analysis. The four vocalization groups were named according to the semantic context that characterized the members of that group as assigned by Kanzi. They were 'banana', 'grape', 'juice', and 'yes'. To avoid redundancy in the data, the covariance structure of the 16 acoustic variables was examined. Five acoustic variables (Peak-Endpoint, Frequency Mean, Peak-Minimum Range, Onset-Peak Range, Endpoint-Peak Range) failed the tolerance test for multi-colinearity, and were therefore excluded from subsequent analyses. A series of one-way analyses of variances were performed in order to determine, for each remaining acoustic variable, the proportion of variance accounted for by semantic context. Five of the eleven acoustic variables accounted for one or more statistical differences between semantic contexts as assigned by Kanzi.

Figure 1 [see outside back cover] characterizes the four vocalization groups according to their corresponding mean values for the acoustic variables: onset, peak, endpoint, and minimum. Figure 2 [below] depicts sound spectrograms of a single vocalization from each of the four semantic categories. Inspection of the graphs reveals that the vocalizations do indeed appear distinct from one another. This is corroborated by the results of statistical analyses. These results suggest that Kanzi is capable of selectively producing physically distinct vocalizations, which vary systematically according to their referential semantic content as assigned by Kanzi.

Bonobos and Stone Tool Manufacture

There are many similarities between the production of stone tools and the production of speech. Tools act upon the physical world to alter it in a manner desired by the organism, while utterances act upon the social world to alter it in a manner desired by the organism. The production of the tool takes place with the coordinated bimanual action of two hands, while the production of language takes place with the coordinated action of tongue, lips and the vocal tract. Further, the tongue and the mouth act as co-participants in language production, each with a distinct function employed synchronously and differentially in order to modulate the sound stream, just as the left and right hands act in a coordinated synchronous but differential manner during stone tool percussion. The lips and tongue, being of different forms, must if they are to produce a spoken tonal speech unit, operate simultaneously in different ways, upon a propelled stream of air. The two hands, being mirror images of one another are not so constrained. They can act in the same manner and they can act sequentially instead of simultaneously. The neocortical areas governing the motoric movements necessary for both complex hand action and mouth/tongue action reside in close proximity in the brain (Calvin, 1983).

In apes, hands that are employed for locomotor functions such as brachiation have developed specialized motor programs for the repetitive execution of motorically identical sequential actions. In the case of brachiation, each hand must grasp and

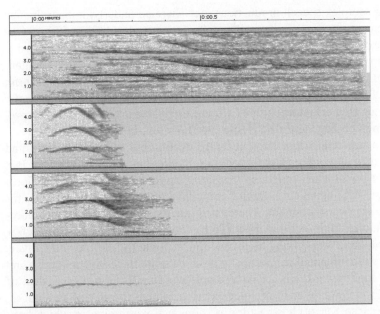

Figure 2
Sound spectro-
grams of a single
vocalization from
four different
semantic
categories.

move in sequential synchrony. Stone tool manufacture, by contrast, necessitates differential simultaneous synchronous activity, quite unlike the similar sequential synchronous activity of brachiation. This differential synchronous activity of the left and right hands during tool use is similar to the differential synchronous activity of the tongue and mouth during language production. In both cases, different bodily structures must interact at a high rate of speed in a highly coordinated manner across short bursts of time. The tongue and mouth are structurally dissimilar and yet are anatomically conjoined. Therefore, they must, when employed, engage in differential synchronous activity. However, the production of language-based sound resonance patterns requires an extraordinarily complex series of coordinated movements that are not repetitive in nature. These movements are so rapid that the neural system cannot plan and execute them as individual actions, but only as bursts of planned sequences (Calvin, 1989).

To successfully engage in stone tool production, one hand must support the weight of the core and hold it steady while the other hand strikes a glancing aimed power blow. All of the required component motor capacities for such an act — that is, grasping, holding in a supporting manner, and moving the hand and arm forward rapidly — are present within the locomotor repertoires of great apes but organized sequentially, rather than synchronously. The synchronous organization needed to flake stone requires neurological programming very different from that which propels alternate limb movement during brachiation. During stone tool manufacture, both the hands and the visual system must act jointly and intently on a common spatial coordinate for a single purpose. In addition, the action of the hands must be differentially coordinated and the blows must be rapid and well aimed. To produce such blows requires neural machinery similar to that needed for throwing and for planning complex rapid, sequential lip and tongue movements (Calvin, 1989). And like those movements, the blows must be planned in advance, for the action patterns are too rapid to permit constant adjustment once initiated (Calvin, 1989). This suggests that the two activities (rapid aimed blows and complex speech production) may share an underlying neurological machinery for generating complex planned motoric action (Calvin, 1989). If this is the case, one would expect that the first use of such neural machinery would be devoted to the processing and production of speech as the mouth and tongue come under voluntary motor control before the limbs, for the maturation pattern is cephal–caudal in form. Supporting this view is the fact that stone tool production appears ontogenetically much later than language in human cultures. (Interestingly, language is assumed to pre-cede tool production phylogenetically; Noble and Davidson, 1996).

If stone tool manufacture is a late-occurring event, both phylogenetically and ontogenetically; then what were, or are, the cultural forces that led *Homo* and not *Pan* down this unusual evolutionary trajectory? Observations of a bonobo, Kanzi, at Geor-gia State University's Language Research Center have revealed that the capacity for aimed throwing and powerful bimanual percussion are extant in *Pan* and can be boot-strapped with relatively little external input (Toth *et al.*,1993). Kanzi, after only a few demonstrations of stone tool flaking by archaeologist Nick Toth of Indiana Univer-sity, began attempting bimanual percussion to produce stone flakes to cut a string and gain access to a food reward. His initial attempts were inefficient; a great deal of power and effort were employed to produce extremely small flakes with dull edges. This occurred because Kanzi chose a form of bimanual percussion in which both hands simultaneously performed identical functions aimed toward the midplane, much like what occurs during 'clapping'. That is, Kanzi held a stone in each hand and slapped them together in the midplane of his body, much as he would do if he were clapping his hands. This resulted in the direction of insufficient force toward the edge of the stone. When great strength is directed toward the centre of the stone, the rock and the hand absorb the force. Only aimed glancing blows directed toward platforms near the edge of the stone can result in flakes.

Hand clapping was a component of Kanzi's motor repertoire and had been since infancy. He became a proficient hand clapper at 18 months of age after watching Austin and Sherman, two large male *Pan troglodytes*, use this gesture symbolically and communicatively between themselves to initiate games of chase. This gesture is interesting because no similar action of bringing the hands together in a coordinated fashion in front of the midplane of the body has been reported for any feral population of *Pan*. Even where stone tool usage is frequent — as in the culture of the chimpan-zees of the Tai forest who regularly engage in Kola nut cracking — such tool use activities *do not* entail simultaneous bimanual hand action. With a single hand, an anvil is placed on the ground, a nut is located on the anvil, and a blow is struck (Boesch and Boesch, 1989; Matsuzawa, 1994, pp. 351–70). Such a series of motor actions involve all aspects of stone tool manufacture, but in a sequential, rather than a simultaneous synchronous fashion. Clapping, by contrast, requires simultaneous coordinated bimanual motor action.

Although Kanzi was able to produce small usable stone flakes by clapping the rocks together, they were so dull that it often required several of them to complete even the simplest food extraction task. Kanzi responded to these constraints with innovation and creativity. On his own, he began to devise means to increase the power of his blows. He first attempted to do so by standing bipedally and throwing the stone against a hard substrate. A successful throw caused the stone to break into multiple large flakes, each with a cutting edge superior to that produced by bimanual clapping.

When Kanzi invented this method, he at once abandoned the method he had acquired through observation — that of bimanual stone clapping. Throwing the stone against a hard substrate was, for Kanzi, a far more efficient means of producing many usable flakes. When Kanzi threw, he stood bipedally and employed either hand. Kanzi was sufficiently proficient in this technique that he likely would have retained it had not the experimenters intervened by requiring him to produce flakes in an area lacking a hard substrate.

When the hard substrate was removed, Kanzi at once adopted a new technique — but not the bimanual percussion the experimenters had hoped would occur. Instead, he replaced the missing hard substrate by electing to throw an aimed stone at another stone on the ground. This aimed power throwing placed a new and much more exacting constraint on Kanzi. To be successful with this technique he had to make certain that his aim was accurate. If the thrown rock missed the rock on the substrate, even by a centimetre, no flakes were produced. This new constraint, a co-construction of the environmental alteration set in place by the experimenters and the behavioural innovation brought forth by Kanzi, produced immediate and definitive right-hand biases for throwing. Why? When Kanzi assumed a bipedal stance and threw with his left arm and hand, his right arm and hand inevitably engaged in an alternative movement pattern. This pattern was an overhand motion, much as might occur during an act of brachiation if one hand was preparing to grasp as the other was preparing to release. Although it could be radically subdued, this unwanted arm and hand movement appeared difficult, if not impossible, to fully eliminate during the act of aimed bipedal power throwing. This movement did not seriously affect Kanzi's ability to throw from a bipedal stance. It did, however, alter his capacity to produce a precisely aimed throw because the synchronous movement itself inevitably altered the trajectory of the aimed projectile. This was because the synchronous movement of the right arm occurred just at the moment the stone was being released on the opposite side of the body.

Thus, having settled upon the technique of aimed throwing — with the core stone 'held' by the substrate and the hammer thrown by the right hand — Kanzi became an efficient manufacturer of stone flakes without bimanual percussion, but with rapid, aimed, powerful throwing movements. At this point, the only thing that could be done to move Kanzi back toward bimanual percussion was to take away the capacity to employ the substrate to 'hold' the core. This we did by encouraging Kanzi to flake in a waist-deep pool of cool water. He happily obliged on very hot days. Once in the water, he had to hold the core or it sank to the bottom of the pool. And in a pool of water, it was useless to attempt to throw the hammer stone as the presence of the water altered and dampened the effects of throwing, rendering it a completely ineffective solution. Faced with this situation, Kanzi immediately returned to the technique of bimanual percussion, only now, because he had become skilled in the interim in the technique of aimed power throwing, he began to employ his hands simultaneously, but differentially. He no longer clapped the rocks together employing the identical motor pattern with both hands. Instead, he steadied the core with his left and engaged in a controlled aimed throw with his right, producing a precisely positioned glancing blow onto a stabilized and perfectly oriented substrate (on the edge of the stone), as do all proficient *Homo sapiens* knappers around the world.

With time, Kanzi began to rotate the core in his left hand while visually searching for the best striking platform. He also began to listen to the sound of each blow and used this information, in coordination with the visual information, to plan the location of his next blow. Kanzi realizes instantly, from the sound alone, when he has produced a usable flake. This is evidenced by the fact that often, as he has struck a successful blow, he signals the event by sound *while* the flake is separating itself from the core and *before* he has had a chance to inspect it visually. His flakes have consistently moved toward larger, sharper and more angular tools (NHK, 1993; NHK, 2000).

Bonobo Writing

As the number of artifacts increase systematically in any culture, the need to organize them, to keep track of them and to maintain them in an orderly and accessible manner across time increases as well. We must devise classification and coding systems that can be readily acquired and recognized by all members of the culture. Initially, these identification marks, which at first delineate ownership and location of derivation, serve as the cultural substrate for the eventual development of a written form of record keeping and eventually for a written representation of speech (Olson, 1995). These written markings then become ubiquitous within the environment as visual patterns. These marks are two-dimensional and quite different from the kinds of visual patterns created by natural phenomena. Once writing has emerged in a culture, all newborn infants are exposed to these two-dimensional linear markings from birth. The prevalence of such markings primes their visual system to easily recognize and then later to produce 'writing systems' in much the same way that the tonal speech units prime the auditory system prenatally.

The visual system, unlike the auditory system, does not function prenatally as a seeing device. The eyes are closed before birth and in some species for several weeks after birth. However, during the first six to eight months of human development, the infant remains in a partially quiescent state as the motor competency to actively explore the external world is not yet sufficiently matured. Nonetheless, the desire to explore the external world is strongly present and so the infant explores the world with his or her eyes. The fact that the body, hands, and mouth are not yet actively engaged in rather constant exploration is critical because this permits a high degree of visual attention during the continuing formation of the neural substrate. Thus, the developing visual system can be programmed anew each generation by the kinds of visual artefacts encountered by the newborn infants before they begin to locomote.

In our laboratory, it has proven critical to expose *Pan* infants to the lexical symbols from birth (Savage-Rumbaugh *et al.*, 1994). When passive exposure to lexical stimuli is present from birth, there is no need to teach lexical pattern discrimination. The lexigrams are impressed upon the neural substrate as they are flashed on television screens at night, hung around cribs and painted on the walls of nurseries. Lacking this early exposure, training in visual discrimination of lexical patterns becomes necessary. This training is tedious, time consuming and effective only with great effort on the part of both subject and experimenter (Savage-Rumbaugh, 1986). By contrast, early passive exposure leads automatically to the emergence of lexical discrimination, followed by lexical comprehension, then lexical production through the keyboard and finally writing (Savage-Rumbaugh *et al.*1985; NHK, 2000).

It is writing that ultimately frees language from the auditory phenomenon on which it is originally based and pushes communication toward an emotionally independent system. Writing separates tonal resonance patterns into arbitrary word units and visually locates them on a substrate, thereby providing a form of nontemporality to the message (Olson, 1995). Writing can thus depersonalize language and permit the emergence of a reflective editorial and evaluative process that is not possible with realtime utterances.

Additionally, it permits the construction of a record of the spoken exchanges that can be utilized for future reference. Perhaps this is its most valuable function. In any case, it was with the second author's initiation of a chalk-based written record of the bonobos' utterances that Panbanisha began to write as well. Like stone tool knapping, this event appeared after the second author produced only a few demonstrations of chalk record-keeping on the substrate of the bonobos' living enclosure. Panbanisha observed this activity and began to attempt to produce written lexigrams for communicative purposes. Figure 3 provides a few examples that represent the very complex lexigrams that Panbanisha has been observed to write.

Other examples of lexigrams much easier for apes and humans to write are 'raisin' (a straight vertical line), 'go' (an extended horizontal line) and the iconic symbol 'A-frame'. These are frequently used in Panbanisha's written expressions and are easily recognizable. In the instance below (Figure 4), Panbanisha was writing on the floor and the second author was busy with Nyota and Kanzi. Panbanisha waited patiently, but when her work continued to go unnoticed she used the voice-activated keyboard to utter six spoken 'A-frames' in a row to direct the second author's attention to her floor writing. Her 18-month-old son then selected a piece of chalk and wrote the 'A-frame' symbol as well. Kanzi followed with his own cursive expression of six written 'A-frames'.

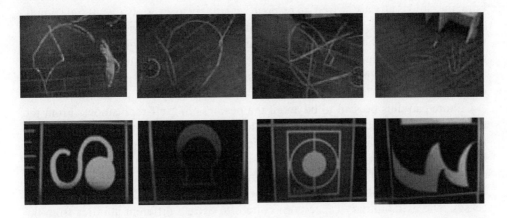

Figure 3
Panbanisha's renditions, from left to right, of 'gorilla', 'mushroom trail', 'apple', and 'marshmallow'. These drawings were not selected to 'match' the lexigrams. Rather they were made by Panbanisha as unique communications. These writing reflect moments of intense concentration on her part and were spontaneous. They were motivated by her desire to communicate about going outdoors for these specific reasons. When asked to write in settings other than communicating her desires about where she would like to go outdoors, she is hesitant and her writing is often not clear.

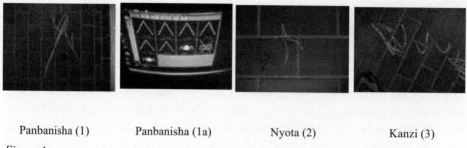

| Panbanisha (1) | Panbanisha (1a) | Nyota (2) | Kanzi (3) |

Figure 4

Above are 3 spontaneous requests to go to the A-frame. The first was produced by Panbanisha, the second by Nyota and the third by Kanzi, all within a 15 minute time span.

Summary

The *Pan/Homo* culture that has emerged at the Language Research Center has in one generation created the following components of human culture in bonobos:

(a) Comprehension of spoken English semantics and syntax.
(b) The production of English-based speech sounds through the bonobo vocal tract.
(c) Stone tool manufacture.
(d) Writing of lexical symbols.

Philip Liberman has called the effect of environment on the development and structuring of the neuronal system 'soft inheritance' and suggested that it smacks of Lamarckian overtones. However, a more apt analogy is with DNA itself. DNA recreates itself by unravelling the helical strands and creating a new symmetrical strand. From that newly composed DNA, cells begin to divide in a manner that will lead to a human form. During the construction of that form, the hand of culture impresses itself, shaping the biological form in ways that match its extant patterns. Upon being born, the child is already 'wired' to respond sensitively to a variety of cultural stimuli. Throughout the relatively quiescent stage of infancy, this process increases in degree and specificity. By the time the child becomes an active self-willed member of the community, culture has already molded the perceptual characteristics of the child's auditory, visual and kinaesthetic system to such a degree that the child is 'mapped' to continue the trajectories set by its culture.

Culture can thus be said to be about the business of 'self-replication'. From the moment of conception, it impresses its patterns and rhythms on the developing, infinitely plastic neuronal substrate of the foetal organism. It shapes this substrate to become preferentially sensitive to its patterns and thus to seek to replicate them as an adult. This process of neural shaping continues throughout life as the capacity of the brain to reorganize itself according to the uses to which it addresses itself never ceases. The extraordinary capacity of culture to extract different abilities from the biological form is clearly manifest in the lexical, vocal, tool manufacture, and writing capabilities emerging in bonobos raised in a *Pan/Homo* culture. These findings render moot old questions regarding the innate limits of the ape brain. They raise instead far more productive questions about the form and function of the perpetual dance that is constantly taking place between plastic neuronal systems and their external culturally devised ways of being.

References

Balaban, E. (1997), 'Changes in multiple brain regions underlie species differences in a complex congenital behavior', *Proceedings of the National Academy of Science*, **94**, pp. 2001–6.

Bickerton, D. (1990), *Language and Species*. (Chicago: University of Chicago Press).

Bickerton, D. (2000), 'Foraging versus social intelligence in the evolution of language', paper presented
at The Evolution of Language 3rd International Conference, Paris, April 3–6, 2000.

Blum, T. (1993), *Prenatal Perception, Learning and Bonding*. (Berlin: Leonardo).

Boesch, C. (1991), 'Symbolic communication in wild chimpanzees', *Human Evolution*, **6**, pp. 81–90.

Boesch, C. and Boesch, H. (1989), 'Hunting behavior of wild chimpanzees in the Tai Forest National
Park', *American Journal of Physical Anthropology*, **78**, pp. 547–73.

Burling, R. (1993), 'Primate calls, human language and nonverbal communication', *Current Anthropology*, **34**, pp. 1–37.

Calvin, W.H. (1983), *The Throwing Madonna*. (New York: McGraw-Hill).

Calvin, W.H. (1989), *The Cerebral Symphony: Seashore Reflections on the Structure of Consciousness*.
(New York: Bantam Books).

Calvin, W.H. and Bickerton, D. (2000), *Lingua ex Machina: Reconciling Darwin and Chomsky with the
Human Brain*. (Cambridge, MA: MIT Press).

Dale, P.S., Dionne, G., Eley, T.C. and Plomin, R. (2000), 'Lexical and grammatical development: a
behavioral genetic perspective', *J. of Child Language*, **27**, pp. 619–42.

Darwin, C. (1872), *The Origin of the Species by Means of Natural Selection*. 6th ed. (London: Murray).

de Boysson-Bardies, B., Sagart, L. and Durand, C. (1984), 'Discernible differences in the babbling of
infants according to target language', *Journal of Child Language*, **11**, pp. 1–15.

de Waal, F. (1998), *Chimpanzee Politics: Power and Sex among Apes*. (Baltimore: Johns Hopkins University Press.)

Deacon, T.W. (1997), *The Symbolic Species: The Coevolution of Language and Brain*. (London: Penguin).

Donald, M. (1991), *Origins of the Modern Mind: Three Stages in the Evolution of Culture and Cognition*.
(Cambridge: Harvard University Press).

Goodall, J. (1986), *The Chimpanzees of Gombe*. (Cambridge MA: Harvard University Press).

Grafman, J. and Christen, Y. (eds.) (1999), *Neuronal Plasticity: Building a Bridge from the Laboratory to
the Clinic*. (Berlin: Springer).

Greenfield, P.M. and Savage-Rumbaugh, E.S. (1991), 'Imitation, grammatical development, and the
invention of proto-grammar by an ape', in *Biological and Behavioral Determinants of Language
Development*, ed. D. M. R. R. L. S. M. S.-K. Norman and A. Krasnegor (Hillsdale, NJ: Lawrence Erlbaum).

Grieser, D.L. and Kuhl, P.K. (1988), 'Maternal speech directed to infants in a tonal language: Support for
universal prosodic features in motherese', *Developmental Psychology*, **24**, pp. 14–20.

Hinde, R.A. (1970), *Animal Behaviour: A Synthesis of Ethology and Comparative Psychology*. (New
York: McGraw-Hill).

Hopkins, W.J. and Savage-Rumbaugh, E.S. (1991), 'Vocal communication as a function of differential
rearing experiences in Pan paniscus: A preliminary report', *International Journal of Primatology*, **12**,
pp. 559–83.

Katz, P.S. and Harris-Warrick, R.M. (1999), 'The evolution of neuronal circuits underlying species-specific behavior', *Current Opinion in Neurobiology*, **9**, pp. 628–33.

Kolb, B. (1999), 'Towards an ecology of cortical organization: Experience and changing brain', in
Neuronal Plasticity: Building a Bridge from the Laboratory to the Clinic, ed. J. Grafman and Y. Christen (Berlin: Springer).

Liberman, P. (1984), *The Biology and Evolution of Language*. (Cambridge: Harvard Univ. Press).

Liberman, P. (2000), *Human Language and our Reptilian Brain*. (Cambridge:Harvard University Press).

Liberman, P. and Crelin, E.S. (1971), 'On the speech of Neanderthal man', *Linguistic Inquiry*, **2**, pp. 203–22.

Mackintosh, N.J., (ed.) (1994), *Animal Learning and Cognition*. (San Diego: Academic Press).

Matsuzawa, T. (1994), 'Field experiments on use of stone tools in the wild', in *Chimpanzee Cultures*, ed.
R. Wrangham, W.C. McGrew, F. de Waal, P. Heltne and L.S. Marquardt (Cambridge, MA: Harvard).

McGrew, W. (1992), *Chimpanzee Material Culture*. (New York: Cambridge University Press).

Mehler, J., Jusczyk, P., Lambretz, G., Halsted, N., Bertoncini, J. and Amiel-Tison, C. (1988), 'A precursor
of language acquisition in young infants', *Cognition*, **29**, pp. 143–78.

Merzenich, M.M. and Jenkins, W.M. (1995), 'Cortical plasticity, learning and learning dysfunction', in
Maturational Widows and Adult Cortical Plasticity, ed. B. Julesz and I. Kovacs I. (Addison-Wesley).

NHK (G. Niio) (1993), Kanzi I. [Video-documentary]. (Tokyo, Japan: National Japanese Television).

NHK (G. Niio) (2000), Kanzi II. [Video-documentary]. (Tokyo, Japan: National Japanese Television).

Noble, W. and Davidson, I. (1996), *Human Evolution, Language and Mind*. (Cambridge: CUP).

Olson, D.R. (1995), *The World on Paper: The Conceptual and Cognitive Implications of Writing and
Reading*. (Cambridge UK: Cambridge University Press).

Owings, D.H. & Morton, E.S. (1998), *Animal Vocal Communication: A New Approach*. (Cambridge: CUP).

Papousek, M. and Papousek, H. (1981), 'Musical elements in the intant's vocalization', *Advances in
Infancy*. **1**, pp. 163–218.

Perkins, W.H. and Kent, R.D. (1986), *Functional Anatomy of Speech Language.* (San Diego: College-Hill).

Peters, A. (1983), *The Units of Language Acquisition.* Cambridgeshire, NY: Cambridge University Press).

Pinker, S. (1994), *The Language Instinct: How the Mind Creates Language.* (New York: William Morrow).

Pinker, S. and Bloom, P. (1990), 'Natural selection and natural language', *Behavioral and Brain Sciences,* **13**, pp. 707–84.

Povinelli, D.J. and Eddy, T.J. (1996), *What Young Chimpanzees Know about Seeing.* Vol. Series 247, vol. 612). (Chicago: University of Chicago Press).

Premack, D. (1986) *'Gavagai!', or the Future History of the Animal Language Controversy.* (Cambridge, MA: MIT Press).

Premack, D. and Woodruff, G. (1978), 'Does the chimpanzee have a theory of mind?', *Behavioral and Brain Sciences,* **4**, pp. 515–26.

Remez, R.E. and Rubin, P.E. (1984), 'On the perception of intonation from sentences', *Perception & Psychophysics,* **35**, pp. 429–40.

Remez, R.E. and Rubin, P.E. (1990). 'On the perception of speech from time-varying acoustic information: Contributions of amplitude variation', *Perception & Psychophysics,* **48**, pp. 313–25.

Sansavini, A. (1997), 'Neonatal perception of the rhythmical structure of speech', *Early Development and Parenting,* **6**, pp. 3–13.

Savage-Rumbaugh, E.S. (1986), *Ape Language: From Conditioned Response to Symbol.* (New York: Columbia University Press).

Savage-Rumbaugh, E.S., and Lewin, R. (1994), *Kanzi: The Ape at the Brink of The Human Mind.* (New York: John Wiley).

Savage-Rumbaugh, E.S., Fields, W.M. and Taglialatela, J.P. (2000), 'Language, culture and tools', paper presented at The Evolution of Language, Paris, April 3–6.

Savage-Rumbaugh, E.S., Murphy, J., Sevcik, R., Brakke, K.E., Williams, S.L. and Rumbaugh, D.M. (1993), 'Language comprehension in ape and child', *Monographs of the Society of Research in Child Development,* Serial No. 233, vol. 58, nos.3–4, pp. 1–242.

Savage-Rumbaugh, E.S., Sevcik, R., Rumbaugh, D.M. and Rubert, E. (1985), 'The capacity of animals to acquire language: do species differences have anything to say to us?', *Philosophical Transactions of the Royal Society of London,* **308**, pp. 177–85.

Savage-Rumbaugh, E.S., Williams, S.L., Furuichi, T. and Kano, T. (1996), 'Language perceived: Paniscus branches out', in *Great Apes Societies,* ed. B. Mc Grew, L. Marchant and T. Nishida (London: Cambridge University Press).

Schoups, A.A., Elliott, R.C., Friedman, W.J., Black, I.B. (1995), 'NGF and BDNF are differentially modulated by visual experience in the developing geniculocortical pathway', *Developmental Brain Research,* **86**, pp. 326–34.

Skoyles, J.R. (2000), 'The singing origin theory of speech', paper presented at The Evolution of Language, Paris, April 3–6.

Smith, W.J. (1997), 'The behavior of communicating, after twenty years', in *Communication. Perspectives in Ethology,* **12**, ed. D.H. Owings, M.D.Beecher and N.S. Thompson (New York: Plenum Press).

Taylor, T.J. (1984), 'Linguistic origins: Bruner and Condillac on learning how to talk', *Language & Communication,* **4**, pp. 209–24.

Taylor-Parker, S. and McKinney, M.L. (1999), *Origins of Intelligence: The Evolution of Cognitive Development in Monkeys, Apes and Humans.* (Baltimore: Johns Hopkins Press).

Tinbergen, N. (1965), 'On aims and methods of ethology', *Zeitschrift fur Tierpsychologies,* **20**, pp. 410–33.

Tomasello, M. (1999), *The Cultural Origins of Human Cognition.* (Cambridge, MA: Harvard UP).

Toth N., Schick, K.D., Savage-Rumbaugh, E.S. (1993), Pan the toolmaker. Investigations into the stone toolmaking and tool-using capabilities of a bonobo (Pan paniscus). *Journal of Archaeological Science,* **20**, pp. 81–91.

Trevarthan, C. (1977), 'Descriptive analyses of infant communicative behaviour', in *Studies in Mother–Infant Interaction,* ed. H.R. Schaffer (London and New York: Academic Press).

von Melchner, L., Pallas, S.L. and Mriganka Sur, (2000). 'Visual behaviour mediated by retinal projections directed to the auditory pathway', *Nature,* **404**, pp. 871–5.

Westergaard, G. and Suomi, S. (1993), 'Use of a toolset by capuchin monkeys', *Primates,* **34**(4), pp. 459–62.

Worden, R. (2000) 'The co-evolution of language and emotion', presented at the conference entitled The Evolution of Language. Paris: April 3–6.

Young, L.J., Winslow, J.T., Nilsen, R. and Insel, T.R. (1997), 'Species differences in V!a receptor gene expression in monogamous and nonmonogamous voles: Behavioral consequences', *Behavioral Neuroscience,* **111**, pp. 599–605.

Acknowledgment: Supported by NICHD 06016

Barbara Smuts

Encounters With Animal Minds

In this article I draw on personal experience to explore the kinds of relationships that can develop between human and nonhuman animals. The first part of the article describes my encounters with wild baboons, whom I studied in East Africa over the course of many years. The baboons treated me as a social being, and to gain their trust I had to learn the troop's social conventions and behave in accordance with them. This process gave me a feeling for what it means to be a baboon. Over time, I developed a sense of belonging to their community, and my subjective identity seemed to merge with theirs. This experience expanded my sense of the possible in interspecies relations. The second part of the article describes a mutual exploration of such possibilities in my relationship with my dog, Safi. I describe how Safi and I co-create systems of communication and emotional expression that permit deep 'intersubjectivity', despite our very different biological natures. In my relationships with baboons, dogs, and other animals, I have encountered the presence in another of something resembling a human 'self'. I emphasize the importance of recognizing and honoring this presence in other animals as well as in humans.

Prelude

In Praise of Ch'an Master Wang
You who Cares for the Bonnet Monkeys around his Mountain Studio

From
Tree after tree
In the undisturbed courtyard
The fruit's dropped
On the frost.

They even love
Entering the thatched hall
To listen to *Dharma*. How is it
Other species know courtesy
And limits?

Coming in each time,
They sit opposite one another
On the meditation benches.

Chi Yuan (Pine & O'Conner,nd, p. 100)

Journal of Consciousness Studies, **8**, No. 5–7, 2001, pp. 293–309

Introduction

Resting in the shade of a tree, Alex, Daphne and I lazily contemplate the landscape, dotted here and there with herds of zebra and impala. A breeze rises, fluffing up the hair on Daphne's head. I fiddle with a brightly colored stone and Alex leans over to peer at my find. Then he rests his head against the tree and dozes. I look past him at Daphne and our gazes meet. She makes a friendly face and moves a little bit closer. Daphne, too, begins to nap, and soon I'm drifting off as well, lulled to sleep by the sound of her gentle breathing and the birds flitting about in the tree above. My body relaxes completely, secure in the presence of my companions.

Many of us have shared such peaceful moments with dear friends. But my experience under the tree had an unusual twist because Alex and Daphne were baboons, members of a wild troop that for over two years daily welcomed me into their midst. Through this close association, I discerned in each baboon a distinct presence that seemed much like the kind of 'self' that dwells within me. Among scientists, applying concepts like 'self' or 'consciousness' to nonhuman animals[1] is very controversial, both because no one agrees on how to define these terms, and because however we define them, they retain a subjective dimension that makes them resistant to investigation by scientific methods. Rather than enter this treacherous territory, I will pursue two modest goals. First, I will tell some stories to give a feeling for what it is like to encounter a 'self' in wild baboons and other animals. Second, I will propose a preliminary framework for conceptualizing the ways that humans and animals can relate to one another.

Baboons

During multiple forays to Kenya and Tanzania over the past 25 years, the baboons I came to know the best belonged to Eburru Cliffs troop (EC), named after a rocky outcropping in the Great Rift Valley near Lake Naivasha. EC's 135 members moved as a cohesive unit in search of food throughout a huge area of roughly 70 km^2. For two years, I joined the baboons at dawn and travelled with them until they reached some sleeping cliffs at dusk, twelve hours later. With occasional days off, I repeated this routine seven days a week. For several months, I lived alone and went for days without seeing another human. Later, I lived with other researchers whom I saw in the evening, but I interacted with people infrequently while with the baboons.

I came to live with baboons as a result of my lifelong curiosity about animals. Although I entered their world as a scientist interested in primate social behaviour, many of the skills I used to get to know them were inherited from my ancestors rather than learned in graduate school. Until recent times, all humans possessed profound familiarity with other creatures. Paleolithic hunters learned about the giant bear the same way the bear learned about them: through the intense concentration and fully aroused senses of a wild animal whose life hangs in the balance. Our ancestors' survival depended on exquisite sensitivity to the subtle movements and nuanced communication of predators, prey, competitors, and all the animals whose keener senses of vision, smell, or hearing enhanced human apprehension of the world.

---

[1]   Hereafter, I refer to nonhuman animals simply as 'animals'.

Each of us has inherited this capacity to feel our way into the being of another, but our fast-paced, urban lifestyle rarely encourages us to do so. During my life with the baboons, I discovered that, plunged back into the wild world from which we emerged, ancient skills come alive, and once again human and animal minds meet on equal ground.

However, at the beginning of my study, the baboons and I definitely did not see eye to eye. I wanted to get as close to them as possible; they wanted to keep their distance. Convincing them that I was not a threat was the first major challenge I faced.[2]

I began with the obvious first step: In open country I approached the wary troop from a great distance and halted whenever they began to move away. The baboons gradually allowed me to inch closer, but progress was slow. Then I began to notice more subtle responses to my presence. For example, baboons, ever vigilant for predators, look around a lot while foraging, and I realized that as I drew closer, more of their looks were directed at me. A little later I noticed that even before this happened, females began to issue calls and direct stern looks at their infants to signal them to return to mom, just in case the dangerous human moved any closer. By tuning in to these more subtle signals, I was able to stop approaching *before* most of the baboons got nervous. Soon they let me get much closer, and eventually I was allowed to move among them freely.

When speaking about this process at professional gatherings, I've used the accepted scientific term, 'habituation'. The word implies that the baboons adapted to me, that they changed, while I stayed essentially the same. But in reality, the reverse is closer to the truth. The baboons remained themselves, doing what they always did in the world they had always lived in. I, on the other hand, in the process of gaining their trust, changed almost everything about me, including the way I walked and sat, the way I held my body, and the way I used my eyes and voice. I was learning a whole new way of being in the world — the way of the baboon. I was not literally moving like a baboon — my very different morphology prevented that — but rather I was responding to the cues that baboons use to indicate their emotions, motivations and intentions to one another, and I was gradually learning to send such signals back to them. As a result, instead of avoiding me when I got too close, they started giving me very deliberate dirty looks, which made me move away. This may sound like a small shift, but in fact it signalled a profound change from being treated as an *object* that elicited a unilateral response (avoidance), to being recognized as a *subject* with whom they could communicate. Over time they treated me more and more as a social being like themselves, subject to the demands and rewards of relationship. This meant that I sometimes had to be willing to give more weight to their demands (e.g., a signal to 'get lost!') than to my desire to collect data. But it also meant that I was increasingly often welcomed into their midst, not as a barely-tolerated intruder but as a casual acquaintance or even, on occasion, a familiar friend.

Being treated like a fellow baboon proved immensely useful to my research, because I experienced directly critical aspects of baboon society. For example, I soon learned that the baboons' most basic social conventions entail acknowledgement of relative status through respect for personal space. In general, each baboon has a small invisible circle around him or her that a lower-ranking animal will rarely invade

---

[2]   See Smuts 1999b for more details about adapting to baboon society.

without first signalling intent (usually by grunting) and receiving from the other an
indication that it is safe to approach (usually a reciprocal grunt and/or the 'come
hither' face).[3] If the approaching animal is dominant, he or she may or may not
respect the other's personal space; it depends on the nature of their relationship and
the current context. For example, when a higher-ranking female approaches a mother
in order to greet her young infant, she often pauses to grunt and make appealing faces
at the infant outside the boundaries of the mother's personal space. This indicates that
the female's intentions are friendly, which reduces the chances that the mother will
leave with her baby. In contrast, if a female is approaching a lower-ranking mother in
order to take over her feeding site, she'll usually enter the mother's personal space
without pausing, causing her to move away.

Once I became sensitive to the importance of personal space in baboon society, I
realized that the boundaries of personal space could shrink or grow, depending on the
individuals concerned and the situation. For example, when a male courts a female,
her personal space tends to expand, and to woo her the male needs to be very sensitive
to this shift (Smuts, 2000). In a similar vein, if a subordinate, S, has recently been
threatened or attacked by a more dominant animal, D, S's personal space in relation to
D will expand until they have reconciled (by touching or through vocal communication [Cheney et al., 1995]) or until enough time has passed to neutralize S's fear of D.
Sometimes personal space shrinks to nothing. This occurs most often among very
young animals, kin, or close friends. In such intimate relationships, no one worries
too much about being polite. Thus, the way baboons construct and relate to personal
space reflects, among other things, the intentions of each party; their age, gender, and
relative statuses; their degree of familiarity; the trust a subordinate feels toward a
dominant; recent histories of interaction; and the particular circumstances of the
moment.

Primatologists have long recognized the fundamental importance of personal space
by considering 'approach–retreat' interactions a valid measure of relative status
(Hausfater, 1975). But status is just one of many factors influencing how baboons
relate to one another. Familiarity and trust — which allow two individuals to overlap
their circles of personal space, regardless of gender, age, or relative status — are
every bit as important. In my relations with baboons, these two elements proved more
salient than status.

Every well-trained field worker knows that it is critical not to move too close to the
animals one is studying, so as to minimize one's influence on their emotions and
behaviour. But less often do field workers acknowledge the subtle and complex issues
that arise when the animals regard the scientist as a social subject. For example, as a
graduate student I was told by more experienced primatologists that I should always
ignore or slowly move away from any study animal who came near me or tried to
interact with me (in other words, any animal who entered my personal space). The
idea was that, by ignoring the animals, we would discourage them from paying attention to us. The baboons soon taught me otherwise.

One day, when I was sitting on the edge of the troop, a foraging female approached
me. When she was about two feet away (an undeniable overlap of personal space), she

---

[3]   When a baboon makes the come hither face, he or she flattens the ears back against the skull and raises
      the brows to reveal the white skin on the eyelids. This expression conveys friendly intent. See Smuts
      (1999a) for a photographic example.

grunted softly several times without looking up. I turned my head to see whom she was grunting at, and, spotting no other baboons within 15 yards, realized that she was talking to me. After that epiphany, I paid much more attention to what it meant to the baboons to ignore another's approach.

I soon learned that ignoring the proximity of another baboon is rarely a neutral act, something that should have been obvious to me from my experience among humans. Whether or not a baboon ignores another conveys a great deal about the relationship. At one end of the spectrum, as mentioned above, baboons who are closely related or good friends sometimes completely ignore each other's proximity, especially during foraging, much as we might disregard a family member who approaches while we are absorbed in a task. At the other end of the spectrum, a female with a young infant will often flee when a male new to the troop merely glances her way. Most relationships fall somewhere between these extremes, and usually when two baboons meet, they acknowledge each other's presence through conventions like grunting, the 'come hither' face, or brief greeting rituals involving body contact (Smuts and Watanabe, 1990; Watanabe and Smuts, 1999). Depending on the context and the animals involved, ignoring another can be a sign of trust (as among close kin), or an indication of great tension. For example, among adult males vying over status, the ability to ignore a rival's approach signals a refusal to submit to him and often provokes even closer proximity as the other male attempts to force the rival to lose his composure (Smuts, 1999a).

Thus, although ignoring the approach of a baboon may at first sound like a good strategy, those who advised me to do so did not take into account the baboons' insistence on regarding me as a social being. After a little while, I stopped reflexively ignoring baboons who approached me and instead varied my response depending on the baboon and the circumstances. Usually, I made brief eye contact or grunted. When I behaved in this baboon-appropriate fashion, the animals generally paid less attention to me than they did if I ignored them. It seemed that they read my signals much as they read each other's. By acknowledging a baboon's presence, I expressed respect, and by responding in ways I picked up from them, I let the baboons know that my intentions were benign and that I assumed they likewise meant me no harm. Once this was clearly communicated in both directions, we could relax in one another's company.

Ignoring an animal in a neutral or mildly friendly situation is usually a low-cost mistake, but ignoring a hostile animal can have grave consequences. I learned this lesson not from a baboon but from a brash adolescent male chimpanzee named Goblin. Shortly after I arrived at Gombe National Park in Tanzania, Goblin began to stalk me. He would materialize before me, give me a hostile look, and then disappear into the vegetation, only to re-emerge minutes or hours later to glare at me again. After a few days of this, he began to attack me. Sometimes, he would charge, slapping me as he passed by. Sometimes he would sneak up behind me, punch me in the back, and then flee. At other times he would lurk in the bushes until he saw me adopt a vulnerable position, such as squatting on the edge of an incline. Then he would throw himself through the air, land on my back, and pummel me as we tumbled down the slope together.

This went on for a couple of weeks. Goblin had not hurt me seriously, but I was bruised, and more importantly, I was a nervous wreck. I spoke to the research director about my problem, who recommended that I just ignore him, confident that he would soon tire of his games. Then I found out that another researcher who was small like me had been so tormented by Goblin that she could no longer follow chimps out of camp. I became plagued by imaginary headlines ('researcher foiled by chimpanzee stalker') and feared an ignominious end to my studies.

I tolerated a few more of Goblin's attacks. Then one day he snuck up behind me and stole my rain poncho, which I had looped around my belt. Getting hit was one thing, but losing precious and irreplaceable rain gear was too much. Without thinking, I spun around and grabbed an edge of the poncho just as Goblin twirled to run away with it. I pulled hard. Goblin stood bipedal and pulled at his end. Suddenly, he relinquished his grip, and as I leaned forward to maintain my balance, I swung a hard right. The blow, softened by the poncho covering my fist, rammed into Goblin's nose. I had acted instinctively, without thought. Indeed, had I thought about it I never would have done it, because several of Goblin's adult male allies were nearby. But I was lucky. After I punched him, Goblin crumpled into a whimpering child and went to Figan, the alpha male, for reassurance. Without glancing up, Figan reached out and patted Goblin several times on the top of the head.

I later realized that Goblin had been treating me just as he was treating some of the adult female chimpanzees. He was at the age when a young male chimp climbs up the female hierarchy as a prelude to taking on adult males. Goblin apparently viewed me (and the other chimp-sized woman he had so badly intimidated) as another female to dominate. He had already subdued every chimp female except Figan's sister, Fifi, and the biggest and toughest female, Gigi. One day when Goblin was harassing Gigi, much as he'd harassed me, she turned and smacked him hard and I realized that my instincts had been on target. A female chimpanzee being harassed by an adolescent male will either submit (removing the reason for his attacks) or, like Gigi, fight back. By ignoring Goblin I had failed to send a clear signal either way, and so he persisted. After the poncho episode, he did not bother me again.

The baboons never attacked me, fortunately, since the males' two-inch-long razor-sharp canines can inflict lethal wounds. People sometimes ask me, 'Weren't you scared?' In fact, while studying chimps at Gombe, I was initially terrified of the baboons who shared the park, because they were so unfamiliar to me. However, by the time I got close to Eburru Cliffs, I felt confident that, if a baboon felt like attacking me, I would know it. The degree to which they accepted me among them suggests that they felt much the same about me.

Because I wanted to minimize the ways in which my presence might change their behaviour, I did not cultivate personal relationships with the baboons or encourage them to cultivate such relationships with me. I turned away from juveniles who invited me to play, and when a baboon touched me, I waited for a moment and then slowly moved away. Over time, such overtures became less rather than more common, suggesting that my low-key responses reduced the baboon's curiosity. The mutually respectful but somewhat distant relationships we developed provided ideal circumstances for my research.

Although I didn't relate to the baboons one-on-one (aside from the nuanced responses described above), I did develop a feeling of intimacy with the troop as a whole. I spent most of my waking hours with them. I ate my own food and drank my own water, but otherwise my routine was identical to theirs. I walked wherever they did, and I rested when and where they rested. Often, during siesta time, there were only a few big trees in sight, and it seemed natural to for us to share the shade.

After doing much of what they did for some time, I felt like I was turning into a baboon. A simple example involves my reactions to the weather. On the savanna during the rainy season, we could see storms approaching from a great distance. The baboons became restless, anticipating a heavy downpour. At the same time, because they wanted to keep eating, they preferred to stay out in the open as long as possible. The baboons had perfected the art of balancing hunger with the need for shelter. Just when it seemed inevitable to me that we would all get drenched, the troop would rise as one and race for the cliffs, reaching protection exactly as big drops began to fall. For many months, I wanted to run well before they did. Then something shifted, and I knew without thinking when it was time to move. I could not attribute this awareness to anything I saw, or heard or smelled; I just knew. Surely it was the same for the baboons. To me, this was a small but significant triumph. I had gone from thinking about the world analytically to experiencing the world directly and intuitively. It was then that something long slumbering awoke inside me, a yearning to be in the world as my ancestors had done, as all creatures were designed to do by aeons of evolution. Lucky me. I was surrounded by experts who could show the way.

Learning to be more of an animal came easily as I let go of layers of thinking and doing that sometimes served me back home but were only hindrances here. All I had to do was stick with the baboons and attend to what they did and notice how they responded. After a while, being with them felt more like 'the real world' than life back home.

Baboons are nothing if not highly idiosyncratic individuals, as distinct from each other as we humans are (Smuts, 1999a,b). But, they also exist as selves-in-community. This aspect of their being is particularly salient in certain contexts. For example, when baboons respond to a neighbouring troop's intrusion into their home range, they move together toward the enemy. They most vividly convey a sense of group spirit when they share a highly pleasurable experience. Once, after few days of heavy rain, we stumbled upon a plethora of newly emerged mushrooms — a baboon delicacy that normally evokes competition. This day, however, there were enough mushrooms for everyone. To my amazement, before anyone dug in, they all paused to join in a troop-wide chorus of food-grunts, their bodies literally shaking with excitement. In that moment, I realized that collective rejoicing in celebration of sustenance must have begun long ago.

The baboon's thorough acceptance of me, combined with my immersion in their daily lives, deeply affected my identity. The shift I experienced is well described by millennia of mystics but rarely acknowledged by scientists.[4] Increasingly, my subjective consciousness seemed to merge with the group-mind of the baboons. Although 'I' was still present, much of my experience overlapped with this larger feeling entity. Increasingly, the troop felt like 'us' rather than 'them'. The baboons' satisfactions became my satisfactions, their frustrations my frustrations. When I spotted a gazelle fawn in the distance, I apprehended it as prey, and if the baboons succeeded in catching one, my mouth watered while they tore flesh from the bones, even though I don't eat meat. When on the cliffs after dark, the baboons warned each other of a predator

---

[4] Some notable exceptions include Jane Goodall (1990) and Aldo Leopold (1949).

drawing near, my body tensed up as if I, too, were in danger, even though my rational mind knew that there were no predators large enough to attack me within many miles.[5]

I sensed the mood of the troop as soon as I arrived in the morning. I could usually tell whether we were going to travel a short or long distance that day. Often, I anticipated exactly where we would go, without knowing how I did it. Even though no one had yet changed direction, I knew when we were about to head for the sleeping cliffs. When we got there and the baboons lay around in soft green grass in the glow of the setting sun, I lay around with them. They had eaten their full, and I had gathered my day's observations. With nothing more to do, we shared the timeless contentment of all social animals relaxing in the company of their friends. After I left them each night, I felt strangely empty, eager to join them again the next morning.

I had never before felt a part of something larger, which is not surprising, since I had never so intensely coordinated my activities with others. With great satisfaction, I relinquished my separate self and slid into the ancient experience of belonging to a mobile community of fellow primates.

There were special occasions when the experience of community intensified. Once, when I was travelling with baboons at Gombe,[6] I lost the troop during a terrific downpour. Far from camp, I ran to the lakeshore and crawled into an abandoned fisherman's shelter for protection. The inside of the hut was pitch dark, but I soon realized I was not alone. About thirty baboons were crowded into a space the size of an average American kitchen. When I entered, some baboons must have moved slightly to make room for me, just as they would do for one of their own. But they didn't move far. Baboons surrounded me and some of them brushed against me as they shifted their positions. The rain continued. The hut filled with the clover-like smell of their breath, and our body heat transformed the hut into a sauna. I felt as if I'd been sitting this way, in the heart of a baboon circle, my whole life, and as if I could go on doing this forever. When the rain stopped, no one stirred for a little while. Maybe they felt the same contentment that I did.

Another time, when I had a bad cold, I fell asleep in the middle of the day, while baboons fed all around me. When I awoke at least an hour later, the troop had disappeared, all but one adolescent male who had decided to take a nap next to me. Plato (we gave the baboons Greek names) stirred when I sat up, and we blinked at each other in the bright light. I greeted him and asked him if he knew where the others were. He headed off in a confident manner and I walked by his side. This was the first time I had ever been alone with one of the baboons, and his comfort with my presence touched me. I felt as if we were friends, out together for an afternoon stroll. He took me right to the other baboons, over a mile away. After that, I always felt a special affinity for Plato.

One experience I especially treasure. The Gombe baboons were travelling to their sleeping trees late in the day, moving slowly down a stream with many small, still pools, a route they often traversed. Without any signal perceptible to me, each baboon sat at the edge of a pool on one of the many smooth rocks that lined the edges of the

---

[5]   At this particular field site, there were no lions or leopards, the only predators large enough to take on an adult baboon or a human.

[6]   After studying olive baboons in Kenya for several years, I returned to Gombe and studied the same species there.

stream. They sat alone or in small clusters, completely quiet, gazing at the water. Even the perpetually noisy juveniles fell into silent contemplation. I joined them. Half an hour later, again with no perceptible signal, they resumed their journey in what felt like an almost sacramental procession. I was stunned by this mysterious expression of what I have come to think of as baboon sangha. Although I've spent years with baboons, I witnessed this only twice, both times at Gombe. I have never heard another primatologist recount such an experience. I sometimes wonder if, on those two occasions, I was granted a glimpse of a dimension of baboon life they do not normally expose to people. These moments reminded me how little we really know about the 'more-than-human world' (Abram, 1996).

Animals As Individuals

Although animals had always fascinated me, my time with baboons and chimps in Africa greatly enhanced my awareness of the individuality of each animal I encounter. Before Africa, if I were walking in the woods and came across a squirrel, I would enjoy its presence, but I would experience it as a member of a class, 'squirrel'. Now, I experience every squirrel I encounter as a small, fuzzy-tailed, person-like creature. Even though I usually don't know this squirrel from another, I know that if I tried, I would, and that once I did, this squirrel would reveal itself as an utterly unique being, different in temperament and behaviour from every other squirrel in the world. In addition, I am aware that if this squirrel had a chance to get to know me, he or she might relate to me differently than to any other person in the world. My awareness of the individuality of all beings, and of the capacity of at least some beings to respond to the individuality in me, transforms the world into a universe replete with opportunities to develop personal relationships of all kinds. Such relationships can be ephemeral, like those developed with the birds in whose territories we might picnic, or life-long, like those established with cats, dogs, and human friends.

Developing relationships with birds or other animals when we enter their space is surprisingly easy, if we approach the experience with sensitivity and humility. Like the baboons, most birds, mammals, and at least some of the reptiles I've met are highly attuned to human body language and tenor of voice. By moving slowly and without jerky motions, by sitting still and quietly observing one's surroundings, by announcing benign intentions in a gentle voice and through facial expressions, gestures, and posture, it is usually possible within minutes to reassure most animals that it is safe to go about their business close by.

One of my favourite examples of the unexpected rewards of such an approach involves a notoriously shy creature. I was standing in a forest, gazing around at the trees when I noticed a movement in the vegetation on the ground in front of me. As I turned my head to look, out popped a tiny mouse. She reared up on her haunches, twitched her nose, and stared at me intently. She knew I was there because instead of freezing like a statue I gently cocked my head, gazed back at her, and whispered a greeting. I was certain she would dart away at any moment and was surprised when she instead resumed her busy foraging, about three feet away. I watched her quick, efficient movements. Then, to my utter astonishment, she curled up at my feet and closed her eyes. I held vigil over her napping body, mesmerized by the rapid rise and fall of her tiny chest. After a minute or so, she awoke, glanced at me briefly, and went about her business, soon disappearing into the undergrowth.

In this case, I was the huge and potentially dangerous animal, but in other instances, the tables turn. During a visit with Diane Fossey and the mountain gorillas she studied, I found myself alone one day with a peaceful cohort of females and young. After a while, I noticed an adolescent female staring at me. I sensed a friendly attitude and tried to convey the same back to her. Suddenly she was standing right in front of me, pressing her flat nose against mine and fogging up my glasses. I was entranced. An instant later she wrapped her arms around me and for a moment held me close. Then she moved away nonchalantly, while I sat there, stunned, feeling like I did indeed belong on this planet. Who could argue with a blessing like that?

For those of us lucky enough to know wild animals on their own turf, on their own terms, such experiences are not exceptional. Ample evidence exists that when people have extended opportunities to co-exist with wild animals, profound relationships based on mutual trust (as with the baboons), or at least mutual understanding (as with the chimpanzee Goblin) can develop. With such prolonged exposure, members of two different species can co-create shared conventions that help to regulate interspecies encounters. Elizabeth Marshall Thomas (1994) gives a fascinating example. As a young woman, she lived with Ju/wa hunter-gatherers in the Kalahari desert of southern Africa with her family, who were studying and filming the people. The Ju/wa, she writes, had a truce with the local lions, such that neither harmed the other. Her brother John filmed an illustrative encounter. Four Ju/wa hunters were tracking a wildebeest that one of them had hit with a poison arrow. When they caught up with the dying wildebeest, a pride of about thirty lions surrounded it. The men, who were unarmed and of small stature, moved slowly toward the lions and announced that the meat belonged to the people. Several lions retreated. Others held their ground for a little while, but as the men descended on the wildebeest, still speaking quietly but firmly, the rest of the lions faded into the bush. The Ju/wa, apparently unworried, killed the wildebeest and processed the carcass. Years later, when Thomas returned to the area, the situation was very different. The Ju/wa were gone, forced to move into settlements, and the new people in the area did not understand lions. An ancient interspecies tradition was broken, replaced by mutual fear and mistrust.

I suspect that reciprocal understandings of this kind between people and at least some of our nonhuman neighbors were common during our time as hunter-gatherers, which constituted 99% of our history as a species. Numerous examples of researchers and photographers who have learned to relate, directly, on foot, to potentially dangerous wild animals (such as tapirs, elephants, hyenas, lions, wolves, bears, chimpanzees and gorillas) without harming or being harmed, attests to the potential for the widespread development of such relationships. If we valued other species enough, how far might we be able to go in re-establishing peaceful understandings with them, at least in places in which the animals are fully protected from human hunting and harassment?

Safi

Because it is important not to interfere in the lives of wild animals, the personal examples I've described so far involve an important but limited degree of interspecies interaction. I turn now to an enduring relationship predicated on an ever-deepening meeting of a human and nonhuman mind. Safi is an 80-lb German shepherd-Belgian sheepdog mix who resembles a black timber wolf with oversized ears (Smuts, 1999b). I acquired her from an animal shelter when she was about eight months old, a stray of unknown background. We have lived together for ten years.

Before Safi, I shared my life with other dogs, but because Safi was post-baboon, I related to her differently. I assumed from the start that she was a sentient being with the kind of wisdom I had discovered in the wild animals I had known. As much as possible, I tried to surrender expectations about who she was or what she could or could not do based on her species identify. I communicated with her in the richest way possible, using words, nonverbal vocalizations, body language, gestures, and facial expressions. I spoke to her constantly, especially about things of mutual interest or concern. I soon discovered that I did not need to train her with commands because, from the beginning, she responded appropriately when I politely asked her to do something the way I would ask another person, using full sentences, like, 'Excuse me, would you please move out of my way?' or 'Go downstairs, get the ball, and bring it back up here so we can play.'

Safi has an inherent sense of appropriate behaviour in different circumstances, making it possible for me to take her almost anywhere off leash. When we are in the human world of the city, I make most of the decisions about where to go and what's off limits, and I protect her from cars and other human dangers. But the further we go from human habitation, the more our roles shift. When in the wilderness, Safi mostly takes the initiative because I am now in her world, and she usually knows much more than I do about what's up. She decides where to hike (usually off-trail, which is safe, because she can always find her way back to our campsite or car), and she chooses the best camping spots. These locales are always in the open, and, just like the locations of wolf dens, they usually include a small rise that she can lie on to watch over the landscape (Mech, 1970). Safi becomes exceedingly alert to any potential danger and lets me know with a single deep 'woof' when she spots a person or animal in the distance (another example of wolf-like behaviour). When travelling after sunset, she always walks ahead of me (dogs have better night vision than humans), and during the day she will not close her eyes to rest unless I sit up tall, look intently all around, and announce in a spirited voice that I'm taking over the watch for a while. Even then, she takes only brief naps and insists on resuming her vigil before long. Yet, until she spots something, there is no tension in her body, and it's clear that being lookout is a welcome job. So is collecting wood for our fire, and periodic forays to scent-mark the periphery of our campsite and sniff the air in all directions. Most fun are the daily explorations, when Safi leads me to one marvel after another. As I approach the hidden stream or beaver dam or fox den that she's found, I express my delight, and her tail never wags harder than at this moment of shared discovery. She is also exhilarated by my request, 'Safi, please find the way home,' a signal to sprint in a beeline toward what proves to be camp, running back to urge me on, and then sprinting off again, until this routine has been repeated dozens of times and we finally reach our destination.

The more freedom Safi has to express her wild self, the more I delight, and the more I delight, the more she expresses herself. As with the baboons, I get to relinquish my separate, analytic self, turning myself over to the deeper wisdom of an animal whose ancestors adapted to this North American landscape long before mine did.

Back home, our shared rituals are less dramatic but equally satisfying. When I wake up in the morning, Safi presses her forehead against mine and holds it there, another characteristically lupine behaviour (Fox, 1980). When I get out of bed and say, 'let's stretch', Safi places her front feet close together facing my hands and we synchronize yoga's 'downward dog' position (at which she naturally excels), touching our heads together briefly as we stretch forward. Then we both shift to 'upward dog', and our eyes lock as we lift our heads to face one another. Thus begins our day, synchronous movements expressing our emotional alignment, in the way of wild animals.

Safi and I have created many such rituals involving synchronous or complementary movements, but I can't explain how any of them came into being. Certainly, I did not invent them, and I don't think she did either. Rather, they developed spontaneously in the intersubjective space we inhabit together. They are part of our shared culture, a way of being-together unique to the two of us. This shared culture emerges from our deep bond, and its expression continuously deepens our relationship still further. Every vocalization by her or me that the other understands, every subtle movement that the other tunes into, every ritual we enact together, simultaneously reveals a mutual past and an ongoing commitment to a common future in which the circle of shared experience and fellow feeling grows ever larger. This is the way of female baboons living their lives together in the same troop. This is the way of wolves whose survival depends on enduring commitments to other pack members. This is also the way of humans, a way we forget all too often in this day and age. It is a language of bodies and sounds and movements that preceded the spoken word and that tends to speak the truth, where words might lie.

As Evan Thompson describes in this issue, deep intersubjectivity requires empathy. I've worked hard to empathize with Safi, so that I can meet her needs and desires as fully as possible. Safi's communication is subtle and refined, and I employ everything I learned from baboons in feeling my way into her being. When Safi wants something, she never makes a peep or nudges me but instead sits very erect and stares intently into my eyes, as if willing me to enter her mind. When this occurs, I say, 'Show me what you want!' and she will, most often by moving toward a desired goal, stopping a few feet away, and directing her long and very pointy nose right at it, like a laser beam. I think she is often better at understanding me than I am at understanding her. Once, after sharing a few cookies, I removed the bag and placed it on the other side of the room, high on a shelf. A little while later I looked up from my book to find Safi gazing at me intently, a thin thread of saliva hanging from her lips. I said to her, 'No more, the cookies are gone' (a phrase I routinely emit after I put treats away). She immediately turned her head to point directly at the treats on the shelf, and then turned back to me as if to say, 'No they're not!' I felt humbled, caught in a lie by my dog!

Safi's social skills seem to transcend species' boundaries. In addition to her many dog and human friends, she has also befriended cats, ferrets, and at least one squirrel. But her most remarkable 'interpersonal' connection involved Wister the donkey — a species her ancestors preyed upon. Wister belonged to a neighbour in a remote part of Wyoming where Safi and I lived for five months. He wandered freely through our yard and beyond. Wister's reaction to dogs suggests that he recognized them as potential predators. Whenever he saw one, he charged, braying loudly, and if he got close, he kicked at them with his sharp hooves. When he first encountered Safi, he charged her and kicked. Safi danced away and replied with a delectable play bow. Momentarily nonplussed, Wister stared at her, and then resumed his charge. Safi danced some more and again invited him to play. Wister kicked at her again. Worried for her safety, I led Safi away, but every time she met Wister, she invited him to play. Eventually he succumbed, and after about a month, they become inseparable. Each dawn, after being released from his corral, Wister would stand outside our door and bray until I let Safi out, and then they would play and wander together for hours.

Donkeys and dogs have very different ways of communicating and very different styles of play, but somehow Safi and Wister co-created a system of communication that worked for them. Safi taught Wister to jaw wrestle, like a dog, and she even convinced him to carry a stick around in his mouth, although he never seemed to have a clue what to do with it. Wister enticed Safi into high-speed chases, and they'd disappear over the horizon together, looking for all the world like a wolf hunting her prey. Occasionally, apparently accidentally, he knocked her with a hoof, and she would cry out in pain. Whenever this occurred, Wister would become completely immobile, allowing Safi to leap up and whack him several times on the snout with her head. This seemed to be Safi's way of saying 'You hurt me!' and Wister's way of saying, 'I didn't mean it.' Then they would resume playing. After they tired of racing, Safi often rolled over on her back under Wister, exposing her vulnerable belly to his lethal hooves in an astonishing display of trust. He nuzzled her tummy and used his enormous incisors to nibble her favourite scratching spot, just above the base of her tail, which made Safi close her eyes in bliss. They shared a water bowl and lay down side by side for naps. When we moved away, Wister became despondent, losing his appetite and refusing to play. Clearly he missed her, and when they met again four years later, they recognized each other instantly.

Sometimes I feel as if Safi's being and mine merge, although our bodies remain separate. Our moods often synchronize, although I cannot tell whether I'm mirroring her or she me; perhaps we're both responding to something else in our environment. After I return from several days away, I often catch Safi contemplating me from across the room, as if soaking up my presence. When I'm away from her, my hands feel restless and bereft, deprived of the feel of her thick fur.

When I'm sad, Safi always senses it and usually lies next to me with her head on my heart. She does this not just for me, but for friends when they begin to talk about something sad. She seems as calm and dignified as ever at these moments, so I do not think she offers comfort to make herself feel better but rather for the other's sake.

Safi's most extraordinary expression of empathy occurred one day when she was just over a year old, barely out of puppyhood. I was feeling very low. Unable to shake my despairing mood, I took Safi to the woods, hoping this would cheer me up. For a while, we played fetch with sticks in the river, her favourite game. Yet soon she refused to go after the stick, which was unheard of. I kept trying to entice her to play, but she just stood in the water looking at me. Finally, she moved to an island in the stream, about thirty feet from the bank where I stood, and lay down facing me. Her penetrating gaze caught my attention, and I sat down to face her. She held her body completely still and continued to hold my gaze. Looking into her eyes, my body relaxed. Her face became the world, and I seemed to fall into her being. I was vaguely aware of people in canoes passing behind her on the other side of the island, and I noticed her ears rotate to track them, but her eyes and her body remained motionless.

She held her position and my gaze for about twenty minutes and then quietly approached and lay down next to me. My dark mood had vanished.

This was my first lesson in meditation. I took it to heart and began to practise regularly, usually outside. Whenever I sat in meditation posture, Safi would move about ten feet away, lie down facing me, and gaze into my eyes. After gazing back for a brief time, I would close my eyes and surrender to the rhythm of my breath. When I opened them again, she was always in the same place and always looking at me. After about two weeks, something new occurred. Our meditation began the same way, but when I opened my eyes, Safi was sitting right next to me, facing the direction I was facing. Ever since that moment, whenever I meditate outside, I open my eyes to find her next to me. Although during meditation my senses are finely attuned, I have never once heard her approach. I don't know how she does it.

Such experiences, and many others like them, reveal Safi to be a highly aware being, more so than many dogs I know; in fact, more than some people I know! Her attunement to others probably has something to do with her genetic endowment, but I think at least as important, if not more so, is the fact that she has shared her life with another being who sees who she is. Similarly, Safi seems to sense the spirit within me, perhaps more completely than anyone else has ever done. When two beings delight in one another this much, their relationship becomes a haven for free and creative expression of being. Trust deepens, mutual attunement grows, and that elusive quality we call consciousness seems to extend beyond the boundaries of a single mind.

The Meeting and Merging of Minds

In my interactions with baboons and other animals, including Safi, I have experienced the relationship between self and other in different ways that seem to form a natural hierarchy. At the most basic level, an animal responds to me (or to any other animal)[7] in an impersonal and reflexive way, based on 'instinct' or habitual responses to similar stimuli in its past environment. An example is the baboons' flight reaction when I first appeared on the scene.

At the next level, an animal attempts to learn or detect something about me, for example, whether or not I am a threat. The baboons' reactions to me during the initial phases of 'habituation' typify this level. No longer terrified by my novelty, they remained wary but interested in me — from a safe distance.

At the third level, an animal recognizes me as an individual and begins to respond to me in ways that might differ from its response to another member of my species. After several weeks, the baboons were less nervous around me than they were around visiting friends who looked like me. Clearly, they had both identified me as a particular human and developed expectations about how I would behave.

At the fourth level, an animal recognizes that I am a social being like them, and that communication back and forth is possible. As I described above, reaching this stage represented a turning point in my relations with the baboons because it created the opportunity to 'negotiate' the terms of our relationship. When members of two different species reach this level, they face the additional challenge of learning to interpret each other's signals. The baboons and I achieved a degree of success in this regard, in

---

[7]   For the sake of convenience, I describe these relationships in terms of dyads, but the same conceptual framework can apply to multi-party relationships.

part through my attempts to 'speak' baboon and their ability to understand me despite an outrageous human accent.

A fifth level, which requires the communicative abilities of the fourth level, occurs when both parties are motivated to maintain a mutually beneficial relationship, for example, a voluntary sexual partnership, an alliance, or reciprocity of any kind.

A sixth level occurs when individuals maintain a mutually beneficial relationship for its own sake. Such relationships often begin because they allow an animal to engage in activities such as play, sex, grooming, or effective joint action (e.g., hunting) that contribute to survival, reproduction, or other utilitarian outcomes. But in humans and, I believe, many other animals, affection often develops between individuals who share such activities over time, and the bond may take on a life of its own even when the rewarding activities are no longer important (former human–dog working partners who end up 'just friends') or possible (baboon mates who remain friendly during the two-year hiatus between female estrous cycles [Smuts, 1999a]). I refer to this level of relationship as 'mutuality' (Bonder, 1998). Whether mutuality occurs within or between species, the participants typically move beyond merely understanding each other's standard signals to the development of a new language and culture that transcends the particulars of either animals' individual or species-specific repertoire. Many people experience this kind of relationship with a mate, a child, a close friend, or a companion animal.

A seventh (and final?) level develops when individuals experience such a profound degree of intimacy that their subjective identities seem to merge into a single being or a single awareness (at least some of the time). A personal example is the experience that Safi and I shared when we gazed for so long into each other's eyes. Of course, I cannot know for certain the nature of Safi's experience, but both repeated encounters of this kind with her and similarities between Safi's behaviour and that of people with whom I have shared level-seven experiences make me believe that she and I experience similar subjective states when we connect in this way.

The first three levels do not imply 'positive' motives for relating to another. For example, prey animals may very well recognize individual predators that they encounter often and learn some of their idiosyncratic habits, and a predator might do the same (level three). There is presumably no friendly motive in such relationships. Also, at any of the first three levels, there is no necessary correlation between the level achieved by one member of the relationship and the level achieved by the other. I might contemplate a beetle long enough to discern its individuality, but the beetle might never respond to me as anything other than a looming threat.

The fourth level and beyond, however, depend, at least to a degree, on both parties mutually recognizing the other as a communicative being, and they therefore also require at least a degree of cooperation. Consider, for example, Thomas's description of the relationship between the Ju/wa hunters and the lions with whom they share their habitat. Although their interests are often in conflict, both parties agreed not to fight over carcasses, and when Ju/wa and lions encountered one another in the bush, they left each other alone — a truce presumably worked out long ago and passed on as cultural traditions within and *between* members of each species. Cooperation, at levels four and five, does not imply mutual affection or altruistic motives, but simply the capacity in both individuals to recognize and communicate about what's in their best interests.

Level six is distinguished from 'lower' levels by 'pureness' of motives. I do not mean to imply that individuals receive no practical benefits from intimate friendships, but rather that the nature and persistence of these relationships transcends those benefits. They involve a kind of commitment to the relationship 'no matter what' (Nesse, 2001). Those of us who have experienced such relationships know that they are deeply rewarding. Indeed, for many people, they are the most fulfilling part of life.

Level seven relationships are paradoxical because 'relationship' implies interaction between two separate beings, and at this level, such separation dissolves (at least temporarily). How common such experiences are is hard to say, because, in our culture at least, we do not tend to talk about them, and most of us do not grow up expecting to merge with others in this way. However, many people seem to have experienced such moments with others, perhaps especially with companion animals. Published accounts of human-animal bonds support this claim (Corrigan and Hoppe, 1989; Fox, 1980; Hogan *et al.*, 1998; Rosen, 1993).

Conclusion

How does this conceptual framework relate to intersubjectivity or consciousness? 'Intersubjectivity' could be a label for interactions or relationships occurring at levels six and seven. There is an inherent paradox in intersubjectivity so defined because at both of these levels, participation in the relationship cannot be coerced but must, by definition, reflect independent agency by each animal. Yet at the same time, the relationship creates for each individual a new subjective reality — a shared language, culture, or experience — that transcends (without negating) the individuality of the participants (Wilber, 1995).

In my view, such intersubjectivity implies the presence in another of something resembling a human 'self'. This 'presence' is not exactly the same thing that scientists refer to when they speculate about 'self-awareness' or 'consciousness' in nonhuman animals. Scientists define these concepts in terms of the mechanisms that allow an animal to achieve an instrumental act, such as solving a problem 'in its head' without trial and error, or being able to attribute beliefs and knowledge to another ('theory of mind') in ways that allow an individual to find a resource or obtain some other practical objective (Heyes, 1998; Povinelli and Preuss, 1995). Even when scientists investigate 'social cognition' in other species, they are interested in how an animal might use its understanding of someone else to further its own utilitarian goals (Byrne & Whiten, 1990; Cheney & Seyfarth, 1990). In contrast, the 'presence' we recognize in another when we meet in mutuality is something we feel more than something we know, someone we taste rather than someone we use. In mutuality, we sense that inside this other body, there is 'someone home', someone so like ourselves in their essence that we can co-create a shared reality as equals.

I do not care what we call this presence. What matters is recognizing its importance and honouring it in ourselves and in others, including nonhuman animals. This presence is encountered directly through creative and caring intersubjectivity. The capacity for such intersubjectivity exists at birth in many kinds of animals. It flourishes or languishes depending on the social worlds we encounter — and deliberately create. Experience suggests that by opening more fully to the presence of 'self' in others, including animals, we further develop that presence in ourselves and thus become more fully alive and awake participants in life.

References

Abram, D. (1996), *The Spell of the Sensuous: Perception and Language in a More-than-Human World* (New York: Pantheon).

Bonder, S. (1998), *Waking Down: A Breakthrough Way of Self-Realization in the Sanctuary of Mutuality* (San Rafael, CA: Mt. Tam Awakenings).

Byrne, R.W. & Whiten, A. (1988), *Machiavellian Intelligence* (Oxford: Clarendon Press).

Cheney, D.L. and Seyfarth, R.M. (1990), *How Monkeys See the World* (Chicago, IL: University of Chicago Press).

Cheney, D.L., Seyfarth, R.M. & Silk, J.B. (1995), 'The role of grunts in reconciling opponents and facilitating interactions among adult female baboons', *Animal Behaviour*, **50**, pp. 249–57.

Corrigan, T. and Hoppe, S. (ed. 1990), *And a Deer's Ear, Eagles Song and Bear's Grace: Animals and Women* (Pittsburgh, PA: Cleis Press).

Fox, M.W. (1980), *The Soul of the Wolf: A Meditation on Wolves and Man* (New York: Lyons & Burford).

Goodall, J. (1990), *Through a Window* (Boston, MA: Houghton Mifflin).

Hausfater, G. (1975), 'Dominance and reproduction in baboons (*Papio cynocephalus*)', *Contributions to Primatology*, **7**, pp. 1–150.

Heyes, C.M. (1998). 'Theory of mind in nonhuman primates', *Behavioral and Brain Sciences*, **21**, pp. 101–14.

Hogan, L., Metzger, D. & Peterson, B. (ed. 1998), *Intimate Nature: The Bond between Women and Animals* (New York: Fawcett Books).

Leopold, A. (1949), *Sand County Almanac and Sketches Here and There* (Oxford: Oxford University Press).

Mech, L.D. (1970), *The Wolf* (Chicago, IL: The University of Chicago Press).

Nesse, R. (2001), 'Natural selection and the capacity for commitment', in *Natural Selection and the Capacity for Commitment*, ed. R. Nesse (New York: Russell Sage Press), in press.

Pine, R. & O'Conner, M. (nd), *The Clouds Should Know Me by Now: Buddhist Poet Monks of China* (Boston, MA: Wisdom Publications).

Povinelli, D.J. & Preuss, T.M. (1995), 'Theory of mind: evolutionary history of a cognitive specialization', *Trends in Neurosciences*, **18**, pp. 418–24.

Rosen, M.J. (ed. 1993), *In the Company of Animals* (New York: Doubleday).

Smuts, B.B. (1999a), *Sex and Friendship in Baboons*, 2 ed. (Cambridge, MA: Harvard University Press).

Smuts, B.B. (1999b), 'Commentary', in J.M. Coetzee, *The Lives of Animals* (Princeton, NJ: Princeton University Press).

Smuts, B.B. (2000), 'Battle of the sexes', in *The Smile of a Dolphin: Remarkable Accounts of Animal Emotion*, ed. M. Bekoff (New York: Discovery Books).

Smuts, B.B. & Watanabe, J.M. (1990), 'Social relationships and ritualized greetings in adult male baboons (*Papio cynocephalus anubis*)', *International Journal of Primatology*, **11**, pp. 147–72.

Thomas, E.M. (1994), *The Tribe of the Tiger* (New York: Simon and Schuster).

Watanabe, J.M. and Smuts, B.B. (1999), 'Explaining religion without explaining it away: Trust, truth, and the evolution of cooperation in Roy A. Rappaport's "The Obvious aspects of ritual"', *American Anthropologist*, **101**, pp. 98–112.

Wilber, K. (1995), *Sex, Ecology, Spirituality* (Boston, MA: Shambhala).

Index

Contributors

Yoko Arisaka, Philosophy Department, University of San Francisco,
  2130 Fulton St., San Francisco, CA 94117, USA
J. Allan Cheyne, Department of Psychology, University of Waterloo,
  200 University Avenue, Waterloo, Ontario N2L 3G1, Canada
Jonathan Cole, Clinical Neurophysiology, Poole Hospital, Poole, BH15 2JB, UK
Natalie Depraz, Collège International de Philosophie, University of Sorbonne,
  Paris, France
William M. Fields, Georgia State University,
  Language Research Center, 3401 Panthersville Road, Decatur, GA 30034, USA
Shaun Gallagher, Department of Philosophy, Canisius College,
  Buffalo, NY 14208, USA
Vittorio Gallese, Istituto di Fisiologia Umana, Università di Parma,
  Via Volturno 39, I-43100 Parma, Italy
Iso Kern, Institute of Philosophy, University of Bern,
  Laenggasstra. 49A, CH-3000 Bern 9, Switzerland
Eduard Marbach, Institute of Philosophy, University of Bern,
  Laenggasstra. 49A, CH-3000 Bern 9, Switzerland
Victoria McGeer, Department of Philosophy, New York University,
  503 Main Building, 100 Washington Square East, New York, NY 10003, USA
Annabella Pitkin, Barnard College, Columbia University,
  3009 Broadway, New York, NY 10027, USA
Sue Savage-Rumbaugh, Georgia State University,
  Language Research Center, 3401 Panthersville Road, Decatur, GA 30034, USA
Barbara Smuts, Department of Psychology, University of Michigan,
  525 East University, Ann Arbor, MI 48109-1109, USA
Anthony J. Steinbock, Department of Philosophy, Southern Illinois University
  Carbondale, IL 62901-4505, USA
Jared P. Taglialatela, Georgia State University,
  Language Research Center, 3401 Panthersville Road, Decatur, GA 30034, USA
Evan Thompson, Department of Philosophy, York University,
  4700 Keele Street, North York, Ontario M3J 1P3, Canada
S. Kay Toombs, Department of Philosophy, Baylor University,
  PO Box 97274, Waco, TX 76798-7274, USA
Francisco J. Varela (died 2001; former senior researcher at CNRS, Paris, France)
B. Alan Wallace, Department of Religious Studies, University of California,
  Santa Barbara, CA 93106-3130, USA
Dan Zahavi, Danish Institute for Advanced Studies in Humanities,
  Vimmelskaftet 41A, 2, DK-1161 Copenhagen K, Denmark